Global Applications of the Internet of Things in Digital Marketing

Arshi Naim
King Kalid University, Saudi Arabia

V. Ajantha Devi
AP3 Solutions, India

IGI Global
PUBLISHER of TIMELY KNOWLEDGE

A volume in the Advances in Marketing, Customer Relationship Management, and E-Services (AMCRMES) Book Series

Published in the United States of America by
IGI Global
Business Science Reference (an imprint of IGI Global)
701 E. Chocolate Avenue
Hershey PA, USA 17033
Tel: 717-533-8845
Fax: 717-533-8661
E-mail: cust@igi-global.com
Web site: http://www.igi-global.com

Library of Congress Cataloging-in-Publication Data

Names: Naim, Arshi, DATE- editor. | Vairamani, Ajantha Devi, DATE- editor.
Title: Global applications of the internet of things in digital marketing / edited by Arshi Naim, Ajantha Devi Vairamani.
Description: Hershey, PA : Business Science Reference, [2023] | Includes bibliographical references and index. | Summary: "This book will answer the questions on applications of IoT communications between marketers and consumers, how to monitor their interaction and what information should be given to the consumers. The book will provide benefits to marketers in building brand awareness to expand customer base and enter new markets, Generate leads for the business, To engage and provide valuable information, Generate sales via online or offline channels. The book links the industry with academia by providing useful insights on how to improve businesses' ability to create and customize customer value and loyalty. Covering topics including e-commerce, mobile marketing, website development, and physical customer experiences"-- Provided by publisher.
Identifiers: LCCN 2023002136 (print) | LCCN 2023002137 (ebook) | ISBN 9781668481660 (h/c) | ISBN 9781668481677 (eISBN) | ISBN 9781668481684 (s/c)
Subjects: LCSH: Internet marketing. | Internet of things--Economic aspects.
Classification: LCC HF5415.1265 .G575 2023 (print) | LCC HF5415.1265 (ebook) | DDC 658.8/72--dc23/eng/20230324
LC record available at https://lccn.loc.gov/2023002136
LC ebook record available at https://lccn.loc.gov/2023002137

This book is published in the IGI Global book series Advances in Marketing, Customer Relationship Management, and E-Services (AMCRMES) (ISSN: 2327-5502; eISSN: 2327-5529)

British Cataloguing in Publication Data
A Cataloguing in Publication record for this book is available from the British Library.

For electronic access to this publication, please contact: eresources@igi-global.com.

Advances in Marketing, Customer Relationship Management, and E-Services (AMCRMES) Book Series

Eldon Y. Li
National Chengchi University, Taiwan & California Polytechnic State University, USA

ISSN:2327-5502
EISSN:2327-5529

Mission

Business processes, services, and communications are important factors in the management of good customer relationship, which is the foundation of any well organized business. Technology continues to play a vital role in the organization and automation of business processes for marketing, sales, and customer service. These features aid in the attraction of new clients and maintaining existing relationships.

The Advances in Marketing, Customer Relationship Management, and E-Services (AMCRMES) Book Series

addresses success factors for customer relationship management, marketing, and electronic services and its performance outcomes. This collection of reference source covers aspects of consumer behavior and marketing business strategies aiming towards researchers, scholars, and practitioners in the fields of marketing management.

Coverage

- Data mining and marketing
- Mobile CRM
- Web Mining and Marketing
- E-Service Innovation
- CRM strategies
- B2B marketing
- CRM and customer trust
- Mobile Services
- Customer Retention
- Relationship Marketing

IGI Global is currently accepting manuscripts for publication within this series. To submit a proposal for a volume in this series, please contact our Acquisition Editors at Acquisitions@igi-global.com or visit: http://www.igi-global.com/publish/.

The Advances in Marketing, Customer Relationship Management, and E-Services (AMCRMES) Book Series (ISSN 2327-5502) is published by IGI Global, 701 E. Chocolate Avenue, Hershey, PA 17033-1240, USA, www.igi-global.com. This series is composed of titles available for purchase individually; each title is edited to be contextually exclusive from any other title within the series. For pricing and ordering information please visit http://www.igi-global.com/book-series/advances-marketing-customer-relationship-management/37150. Postmaster: Send all address changes to above address.

Titles in this Series

For a list of additional titles in this series, please visit: http://www.igi-global.com/book-series/advances-marketing-customer-relationship-management/37150

Big Data Marketing Strategies for Superior Customer Experience
Jose Ramon Saura (Rey Juan Carlos University, Spain)
Business Science Reference • © 2023 • 346pp • H/C (ISBN: 9781668464540) • US $240.00

Managing Festivals for Destination Marketing and Branding
Sharad Kumar Kulshreshtha (Department of Tourism and Hotel Management, North-Eastern Hill University, Shillong, India)
Business Science Reference • © 2023 • 366pp • H/C (ISBN: 9781668463567) • US $250.00

Cultural Marketing and Metaverse for Consumer Engagement
Amandeep Singh (Chitkara Business School, Chitkara University, India) Sandhir Sharma (Chitkara Business School, Chitkara University, India) Amrinder Singh (Jain University, India) Murat Unanoglu (İstanbul Aydin University, Turkey) and Sanjay Taneja (Uşak University, Turkey)
Business Science Reference • © 2023 • 335pp • H/C (ISBN: 9781668483121) • US $250.00

Handbook of Research on Consumer Behavioral Analytics in Metaverse and the Adoption of a Virtual World
Pantea Keikhosrokiani (School of Computer Sciences, Universiti Sains Malaysia, Malaysia)
Engineering Science Reference • © 2023 • 404pp • H/C (ISBN: 9781668470299) • US $325.00

Global Developments in Nation Branding and Promotion Theoretical and Practical Approaches
Andreas Masouras (Neapolis University, Cyprus) Sofia Daskou (Neapolis University, Cyprus) Victoria Pistikou (Democritus University of Thrace, Greece) Dimitrios Dimitriou (Democritus University of Thrace, Greece) and Tim Friesner (University of Winchester, UK)
Information Science Reference • © 2023 • 320pp • H/C (ISBN: 9781668459027) • US $240.00

Global Agricultural and Food Marketing in a Global Context Advancing Policy, Management, and Innovation
Aluwani Maiwashe-Tagwi (University of South Africa, South Africa) Ailweli Solomon Mawela (University of South Africa, South Africa) and Phineas Khazamula Chauke (University of South Africa, South Africa)
Business Science Reference • © 2023 • 236pp • H/C (ISBN: 9781668447802) • US $250.00

Global Perspectives on the Strategic Role of Marketing Information Systems
Jose Melchor Medina-Quintero (Tamaulipas Autonomous University, Mexico) Miguel A. Sahagun (High Point University, USA) Jorge Alfaro (Universidad Catolica del Norte, Chile) and Fernando Ortiz-Rodriguez (Tamaulipas Autonomous University, Mexico)
Business Science Reference • © 2023 • 320pp • H/C (ISBN: 9781668465912) • US $250.00

IGI Global
PUBLISHER of TIMELY KNOWLEDGE

701 East Chocolate Avenue, Hershey, PA 17033, USA
Tel: 717-533-8845 x100 • Fax: 717-533-8661
E-Mail: cust@igi-global.com • www.igi-global.com

Table of Contents

Detailed Table of Contents

interested in the field of digital marketing.

Internet of things (IoT) is one of the new technologies that is expanding exponentially and is presenting new opportunities in a variety of industries, including business, academics, healthcare, transportation, industry, environment, and making our home and cities smart, among others. The IoT system's smart gadgets will be able to perceive, gather, and transport data via the internet without the need for human interaction. Large businesses strive to include technology into their marketing or digital marketing plan that reshapes consumers' expectations, attitudes, and requirements toward businesses in addition to communication style and product promotion. Due to the utilization of several smart devices, networks, and software that are weak and susceptible to hacking, it has a number of security vulnerabilities. The study focuses on the impression of IoT in digital marketing, IoT surface attack and security flaws, technological and security issues in digital marketing, and tries to present some preventive solutions for using IoT's in digital marketing.

The field of human resource management (HRM) has been impacted by the rise of the internet of things (IoT) in recent years. IoT technology allows for the collection and analysis of data on employee behaviour, performance, and engagement. This data can be used to improve HRM processes such as recruitment, training, and retention. Additionally, IoT technology can be used to improve communication and collaboration between employees and managers. However, there are also concerns about privacy and security when using IoT technology in the workplace. Overall, HRM is becoming increasingly dependent on IoT technology to gather important data and improve processes, but it is important to consider the potential negative impacts and take steps to mitigate them. This chapter has an implication on the organisations of all sizes that may utilise the IoT and digital marketing in strengthening their HRM practices, that shall help them to attract good talent and lead to satisfaction and loyalty among employees.

This is an extended research article discussing the role and the applications of the internet of things (IoT) in industrial transformation (ITN) in general and in marketing management (MMgnt) under five research proposals. IoT has already reached its threshold of success in all the disciplines and MMgnt has also been applying it in many of its areas for optimum growth, development, and safe working. This chapter is a case-based qualitative analysis which involves the role of IoT in three fields of MMgnt, namely customer relationship management (CRM), business process models (BPM), and product life cycle (PLC). For study, many instances from the real retail firms are compared before and after the application of IoT and presented the distinguished achievement of classification of IoT. This study proposes five IoT plans for measuring the effectiveness of IoT for the above-mentioned three sections of MMgnt that depend on the collection and sharing of data from external and internal environments.

This chapter provides a practical sketch of the fundamentals of digital marketing. The framework comprises an overview of digital marketing development. This research is based on secondary data collected from social networking sites and e-commerce (E-com) sites for various firms to explain how they are using E-com business models. The research explicates the (E-com) different business models and the techniques used for the development of web presence, web search marketing that focuses on search engine optimization (SEO) and search engine marketing (SEM), e-mail marketing which offers interesting content to develop a successful newsletter, as well as social media marketing that addresses planning and the most important tools used to maximize communication through social media. The chapter presents a synopsis of digital marketing concepts and examples of some successful as well as an effective Web presence of some online firms.

This study aims to understand the relationship between the internet of things (IoT) and digital marketing (DM) by conducting a bibliometric analysis of existing literature. The analysis includes mainly the co-occurrence analysis to explore the major terms and keywords in the arena of IoT and DM. Results indicate a growing interest in the IoT and DM, with a significant increase in publications in the recent years. However, the findings reveal that very limited studies have been conducted in the intersection of IoT and digital marketing. This study thus looks at IoT and DM minutely, and attempts to identify the trends, works, and future possibilities. Thus, this study can serve as a valuable resource for researchers and practitioners in the field.

The internet of things (IoT) is a concept that connects objects via the internet. The extensive adoption of IoT technologies unleashes various capabilities of designing a broad range of high-quality consumer applications. Smart cities, smart buildings, and e-health are among various application domains which benefit from IoT technologies. However, the precise use of IoT in evaluating content digital marketing is ambiguous. This chapter identifies the content digital marketing aspect of the IoT applications as well as the technological aspects of web development through literature review. The focus in this chapter lies in how IoT can be taken as a content marketing tool in the IoT applications. IoT offers unlimited creativity for content creation as well as targeted delivery of content. This research finding further presents a design of a monitoring control system based on the IoT. These results demonstrate the significant shift in marketing strategies that need to take place as they adopt IoT and the development of web applications for effective remote monitoring in IoT devices.

Over the past few decades, curiosity and enthusiasm in science and technology have grown tremendously, to the extent that IoT is now being applied to a wide variety of sectors including business, marketing, manufacturing, sustainability, blockchain, and sports. Digital marketers are leveraging IoT technology in the current digital age to develop marketing strategies and adapt to changing industry trends. Marketers can implement new service-oriented strategies by combining IoT, Big Data, and data analytics. Among these technologies, IoT is crucial in assisting businesses in increasing utilization and manufacturing organizations. With the extensive exploration of IoT solutions, marketing practitioners and businesses can collect consumer data, store it in databases, increase sales, improve products and services, and develop revenue-boosting strategies. This chapter specifies how the consistent use of IoT technologies results in substantial organizational competitiveness and explains how IoT can be referred to as a new component of business analytics and digital marketing.

The COVID-19 issue has, albeit at varied rates, pushed digital transformation in industry and services across the majority of nations. Achieving the objectives on the path to excellence depends on the delivery of customized goods or services and changing consumer needs. Digital marketing can aid in expanding customer reach internationally and strengthening client relationships. While data-driven decision-making reduces risk, technology can help marketers deliver customers more of what they want and need. Artificial intelligence (AI), the internet of things (IoT), remote collaboration, cloud computing, blockchain, and data analytics are among the technologies that are rapidly transforming the way that digital marketers do business and develop strategies leading to global economic growth. This book chapter explores the potential of AI and IoT in digital marketing. It also provides information on the impact of new technologies on digital marketing and the top trends in this field.

The internet of things (IoT) is a network of physical objects or "things" embedded with electronics, software, sensors, and network connectivity, which enables them to collect and exchange data. These objects can include everyday devices such as smart thermostats, home security systems, wearable fitness trackers, and even vehicles. However, IoT also raises concerns about privacy, security, and reliability, as the increasing number of connected devices creates new opportunities for cyber attacks and data breaches. As such, the development and deployment of IoT technology must be done in a responsible and secure manner. Through the use of sensors, it is now possible to collect, transmit, and transform data into knowledge. The marketing and sales sectors are capable of using data gathered through IoT to interact with customers on an individual basis. Python is an object oriented, scripted and interpreted language for both learning and real-world programming. Work in this chapter first introduces Python as a language, and gives summary about data science, machine learning, and IOT.

The internet of things (IoT) and digital marketing are two rapidly growing fields that have the potential to revolutionize the way businesses operate. However, for businesses to truly take advantage of the opportunities these technologies provide, it is important to understand the critical success factors that must be in place. This paper explores the critical success factors of IoT and digital marketing, including the importance of data analytics, security, and integration with existing systems. For this purpose, bibliometric analysis has been utilized from the Scopus database. It was identified that not many studies have been conducted in this field, and hence a huge gap was explored and addressed. Through the inferences of literature and the practices in the arena of IoT and digital marketing, the critical success factors have been proposed. This chapter will provide valuable insights for organizations looking to implement IoT and digital marketing strategies, as well as for researchers studying the field.

This study is exploratory in nature and influences the behavioral change factors of online customers. This design was neglected in early studies. The main objective of this study is to empirically test the explanatory factors of the changeover behavior from online banking to mobile banking by customers, as well as to test their degree of importance. The data was collected from a sample of 430 Saudi customers. Participants were selected on the basis of convenience sampling. The results showed the advantage of using banking services, sources of enabling conditions, the influence of groups and the technology used. The financial advantage of the mobile bank is the most important factor in the influence of its influence on the attitude of the customers. Again, the conditions of the facilitating sources and the conditions of the technological sources are the two factors in the explanatory power of the perceived control of behavior.

Electronic commerce (E-com) is now adopted by most of the firms, especially after the first phase of the COVID-19 pandemic. Consumers are conscious of increasing online purchases and demand sustainable consumption friendly actions. This study aims to analyze the intellectual, conceptual, and social knowledge of consumer buying behavior in E-com research to generate new understandings for online consumer behavior. A survey on LinkedIn was conducted to measure the impact of E-com on consumer behavior and results are shown on Likert's five scale. The survey questions were closed ended and not specific to any industry or firm rather general questions to measure the impact of E-com on consumer buying behavior. The questions were based on factors of customer satisfaction, security, information quality, payment methods, shipping, time, and delivery services. Analysis shows a variation in types, factors, and method of consumer buying behavior in an online environment.

This research study is based on changing media ownership and its relationship with the audience, keeping ethics in context. Thematic review of literature was done to check the availability of information for the four objectives. The methodology adopted was case study of Network 18 and NDTV, taken over by business conglomerates Adani and Reliance. The study was also conducted by talking to senior journalists of NDTV, Network 18, Aajtak, ABP News, and News X. Ethics and connection with the audience in content by journalists was a major concern. The researcher has studied channels' ownership patterns, marketing strategies, and to established the role of ownership in media businesses.

yet that is geared toward marketing IoT. Thus, this chapter might provide a brief overview of the subject.

Preface

INTRODUCTION

In today's modern world, it is essential for businesses to remain competitive and up to date on the latest technology that can support their processes. The use of the internet of things (IoT) in marketing, particularly in digital marketing, is an evolving field that requires further study to better understand its potential. We live in a world where consumers are using multiple devices, many channels for accessing the information and they are unable to differentiate between noise and information because brands are also producing more contents than required. As marketers their task is to make sure that content creates value both for the brand as well as the consumer. This book will focus on applications of IoT in customizing contents and developing a data-based marketing framework that make marketers to create totally different experiences in bridging the digital and physical world, get closer connection with the consumers, enabling the marketers to provide highly contextual and tailored messages to consumers. IoT application will evaluate existing content strategies; introduce new objectives and new measurement, format contents of brands regardless of the devices or channels that eventually make Content marketing go beyond blog posts and social media, reaching connected devices. This book will answer the questions on applications of IoT communications between marketers and consumers, how to monitor their interaction and what information should be given to the consumers. The book will provide benefits to marketers in building brand awareness to expand customer base and enter new markets, Generate leads for the business, To engage and provide valuable information, Generate sales via online or offline channels. The book links the industry with academia by providing useful insights on how to improve businesses' ability to create and customize customer value and loyalty. Covering topics including e-commerce, mobile marketing, website development, and physical customer experiences, this book is essential for marketers, brand managers, advertisers, IT consultants and specialists, customer relations officers, managers, practitioners, business owners, marketing and business associations, students, researchers, and academicians interested in incorporating the latest technologies and marketing strategies into their businesses and studies.

The business world today is changing enormously due to many factors that affect every element of the business cycle worldwide. From globalization to recession, in addition to other environmental forces, companies today face numerous challenges that have a great impact on business. Among the factors that are affecting the current way business is conducted are the emergence of marketing tools including the internet, internet of things (IoT), virtual reality, mobile applications, social media, electronic word of mouth (eWoM), artificial intelligence, digital marketing, and more that have a great impact not only on customers but also on companies. It is imperative for businesses to embrace the utilization of these tools in order to expand their customer base and provide unique, successful consumer experiences. IoT,

Digital Transformation, and the Future of Global Marketing provide comprehensive coverage of current global marketing trends related to the use of technology.

CHAPTER DESCRIPTIONS

Chapter 1. Emerging Green Practices, Internet of Things, and Digital Marketing: A Response to Global Economic and Climate Crises

Planetary sustainability has emerged as a challenging phenomenon today. There have been various discussions and deliberations in reducing the carbon footprints and adoption of green practices, things are not really moving in the right direction. However, the emergence of many new green practices cannot be ignored at the same time. Climate change is real and possesses many unexpected disasters to happen if not addressed on time. The researchers have claimed already that this threat needs to have a collective response rather than waiting for some specific governments to act on. This chapter attempts to make an account of green practices around the globe and explores the way Internet of Things and Digital marketing is playing or can play in the propagation of the same. This study makes an account of possible best practices and the way they have been promoted in the recent past. This will have an implication on the social scientists, ecologists, digital marketers, environment activists, and government bodies.

Chapter 2. Digital Marketing Through Social Media Best Practices: A Case Study of HEIs in the GCC Region

The exponential growth of social media usage during the past few years has unfolded unprecedented opportunities. The effective utilization of relevant social media tools, which was once considered the domain of business organizations only, is gradually shifting to various kinds of organizations functioning in the society and educational institutions are no exception. The current study aims at finding out the best practices followed by the top higher education institutions in GCC region, focusing on how they are tapping the vast potential of their online presence, specifically in the social media. The researchers take into consideration the different kinds of social media used and the nature of content shared by the selected higher education institutions, to gain interesting insights through comparative analysis in order to discover the critical success factors for the desired objectives. This chapter has an implication on all the HEIs in the GCC, Education Consultancies, digital marketers, businesses, and other stakeholders who are interested in the field of Digital Marketing.

Chapter 3. Impact of IoT Applications Using Digital Marketing

Internet of Things (IoT) is one of the new technologies that is expanding exponentially and is presenting new opportunities in a variety of industries, including business, academics, healthcare, transportation, industry, environment, and making our home and cities smart, among others. The IoT system's smart gadgets will be able to perceive, gather, and transport data via the Internet without the need for human interaction. Large businesses strive to include technology into their marketing or digital marketing plan that reshapes consumers' expectations, attitudes, and requirements toward businesses in addition to communication style and product promotion. Due to the utilization of several smart devices, networks, and software that are weak and susceptible to hacking, it has a number of security vulnerabilities. The study focuses on the impression of IoT in digital marketing, IoT surface attack and security flaws, technological and security issues in digital marketing and tries to present some preventive solutions for using IoT's in digital marketing.

Chapter 4. Exploring Dependence of Human Resource Management (HRM) on Internet of Things (IoT) and Digital Marketing in the Digital Era

The field of Human Resource Management (HRM) has been impacted by the rise of the Internet of Things (IoT) in recent years. IoT technology allows for the collection and analysis of data on employee behaviour, performance, and engagement. This data can be used to improve HRM processes such as recruitment, training, and retention. Additionally, IoT technology can be used to improve communication and collaboration between employees and managers. However, there are also concerns about privacy and security when using IoT technology in the workplace. Overall, HRM is becoming increasingly dependent on IoT technology to gather important data and improve processes, but it is important to consider the potential negative impacts and take steps to mitigate them. This chapter has an implication on the organisations of all sizes that may utilise the IoT and Digital Marketing in strengthening their HRM practices, that shall help them to attract good talent and lead to satisfaction and loyalty among employees.

Chapter 5. Role of IoT in Industrial Transformation and Marketing Management

This is an extended research article discussing the role and the applications of the Internet of Things (IoT) in Industrial Transformation (ITN) in general and in Marketing Management (MMgnt) under five research proposals. IoT has already reached its threshold of success in all the disciplines and MMgnt has also been applying it in many of its areas for optimum growth, development, and safe working. This research paper is a case-based qualitative analysis which involves the role of IoT in three fields of MMgnt namely Customer Relationship Management (CRM), Business Process Models (BPM), and Product Life Cycle (PLC). For study, many instances from the real retail firms' are compared before and after the application of IoT and presented the distinguished achievement of classification of IoT. This study proposes five IoT plans for measuring the effectiveness of IoT for the above-mentioned three sections of MMgnt that depend on the collection and sharing of data from external and internal environments.

Chapter 6. Understanding Digital Marketing: An Exemplary Approach

This chapter provides a practical sketch of the fundamentals of Digital marketing. The framework comprises an overview to digital marketing development. This research is based on secondary data collected from social networking sites and E-Commerce (E-com) sites for various firms to explain how they are using E-com business models. The research explicates the (E-com) different business models and the techniques used for the development of web presence, web Search Marketing that focuses on Search Engine Optimization (SEO) and Search Engine Marketing (SEM), E-mail Marketing which offers interesting content to develop a successful newsletter, Social Media Marketing that addresses planning and the most important tools used to maximize communication through social media. The chapter presents a synopsis of digital marketing concepts and examples of some successful as well as an effective Web presence of some online firms.

Chapter 7. Understanding the Relationship Between IoT and Digital Marketing: A Bibliometric Analysis

This study aims to understand the relationship between the Internet of Things (IoT) and digital marketing (DM) by conducting a bibliometric analysis of existing literature. The analysis includes mainly the co-occurrence analysis to explore the major terms and keywords in the arena of IoT and DM. Results indicate a growing interest in the IoT and DM, with a significant increase in publications in the recent years. However, the findings reveals that very limited studies have been conducted in the intersection of IoT and digital marketing. This study thus, looks IoT and DM minutely, and attempts to identify the trends, works and future possibilities. Thus, this study can serve as a valuable resource for researchers and practitioners in the field.

Chapter 8. Use of IoT in Evaluating Content Digital Marketing and Optimization and Web Development

The Internet of Things (IoT) is a concept that connects objects via the internet. The extensive adoption of IoT technologies unleashes various capabilities of designing a broad range of high-quality consumer applications. Smart cities, smart buildings, and e-health are among various application domains which are benefited from IoT technologies. However, the precise use of IoT in evaluating content digital marketing is ambiguous. This paper identifies the content digital marketing aspect of the IoT applications as well as the technological aspects of web development through literature review. The focus in this paper lies in how IoT can be taken as a content marketing tool in the IoT applications. IoT offers unlimited creativity for content creation as well as targeted delivery of content. This research finding further presents a design of a monitoring control system based on the IoT. Our results demonstrate the significant shift in marketing strategies that need to take place as they adopt IoT and the development of web applications for effective remote monitoring in IoT devices.

Chapter 9. Applications and Impact of Internet of Things in Digital Marketing

Over the past few decades, curiosity and enthusiasm in science and technology have grown tremendously, to the extent that IoT is now being applied to a wide variety of sectors including business, marketing, manufacturing, sustainability, blockchain, and sports. Digital marketers are leveraging IoT technology in the current digital age to develop marketing strategies and adapt to changing industry trends. Marketers can implement new service-oriented strategies by combining IoT, Big Data, and data analytics. Among these technologies, IoT is crucial in assisting businesses in increasing utilization and manufacturing organizations. With the extensive exploration of IoT solutions, marketing practitioners and businesses can collect consumer data, store it in databases, increase sales, improve products and services, and develop revenue-boosting strategies. This chapter specifies how the consistent use of IoT technologies results in substantial organizational competitiveness and explains how IoT can be referred to as a new component of business analytics and digital marketing.

Chapter 10. Abridging the Digital Marketing Gap, Artificial Intelligence (AI), and Internet of Things (IoT) in Boosting the Global Economic Growth

The COVID-19 issue has, albeit at varied rates, pushed digital transformation in industry and services across the majority of nations. Achieving the objectives on the path to excellence depends on the delivery of customized goods or services and changing consumer needs. Digital marketing can aid in expanding customer reach internationally and strengthening client relationships. While data-driven decision-making reduces risk, technology can help marketers deliver customers more of what they want and need. Artificial intelligence (AI), the Internet of Things (IoT), remote collaboration, cloud computing, blockchain, and data analytics are among the technologies that are rapidly transforming the way that digital marketers do business and develop strategies leading to Global Economic Growth. This book chapter explores the potential of AI and IoT in digital marketing. It also provides information on the impact of new technologies on digital marketing and the top trends in this field.

Chapter 11. Applications of the Internet of Things and Machine Learning Using Python in Digital Marketing

The Internet of Things (IoT) is a network of physical objects or "things" embedded with electronics, software, sensors, and network connectivity, which enables them to collect and exchange data. These objects can include everyday devices such as smart thermostats, home security systems, wearable fitness trackers, and even vehicles However; IoT also raises concerns about privacy, security, and reliability, as the increasing number of connected devices creates new opportunities for cyber-attacks and data breaches. As such, the development and deployment of IoT technology must be done in a responsible and secure manner. Through the use of sensors, it is now possible to collect, transmit, and transform data into knowledge. The marketing and sales sectors are capable of using data gathered through IoT to interact with customers on an individual basis. Python is an object oriented, scripted and interpreted language for both learning and real world programming. Work in this paper first introduce Python as a language, and give summary about Data science, Machine learning and IOT.

Chapter 12. Critical Success Factors of Internet of Things and Digital Marketing

The Internet of Things (IoT) and digital marketing are two rapidly growing fields that have the potential to revolutionize the way businesses operate. However, for businesses to truly take advantage of the opportunities these technologies provide, it is important to understand the critical success factors that must be in place. This paper explores the critical success factors of IoT and digital marketing, including the importance of data analytics, security, and integration with existing systems. For this purpose, bibliometric analysis has been utilized from the Scopus database. It was identified that not much studies have been conducted in this field, and hence a huge gap was explored and addressed. Through the inferences of literature and the practices in the arena of IoT and Digital marketing, the critical success factors have been proposed. This study will provide valuable insights for organizations looking to implement IoT and digital marketing strategies, as well as for researchers studying the field.

Chapter 13. Explanatory Factors of the Behavior of Passage From Online Banking to Mobile Banking by Customers

Our study is exploratory in nature and influences the behavioral change factors of online customers. This design was neglected in the early studies. The main objective of this study is to empirically test the explanatory factors of the changeover behavior from online banking to mobile banking by customers. As well as to test their degree of importance. The data was collected from a sample of 430 Saudi customers. Participants were selected on the basis of convenience sampling. The results showed the advantage of using banking services, sources of enabling conditions, the influence of groups and the technology used. The financial advantage of the mobile bank is the most important factor in the influence of its influence on the attitude of the customers. Again, the conditions of the facilitating sources and the conditions of the technological sources are the two factors in the explanatory power of the perceived control of behavior.

Chapter 14. Impact and Assessment of Electronic Commerce on Consumer Buying Behaviour

Electronic Commerce (E-com) is now adopted by most of the firms especially post first phase of Covid 19 pandemic. Consumers are conscious of increasing online purchases and demand sustainable consumption friendly actions. This study aims to analyze the intellectual, conceptual, and social knowledge of consumer buying behavior in E-com research to generate new understandings for online consumer behavior. Survey on linkedin was conducted to measure the impact of E-com on consumer behavior and results are shown on likert's 5 scale. The survey questions were closed ended and not specific to any industry or firm rather general questions to measure the impact of E-com on consumer buying behavior. The questions were based on factors of customer satisfaction, security, information quality, payment methods, and shipping, time and delivery services. Analysis shows a variation in types, factors and method of consumer buying behavior in an online environment.

Chapter 15. Changing Trends of Media Ownership: Marketing Through Community Engagement on Hindi Television News Channels

This research study is based on changing media ownerships and its relationship with the Audience, keeping ethics in context. Thematic Review of literature was done to check the availability of information for the four objectives. The methodology adopted was case study of Network 18 and NDTV, been taken over by business conglomerates, Adani and Reliance. The study was also conducted by talking to senior journalists of NDTV, Network 18, Aajtak, ABP News and News X. Ethics and connect with the audience in content by journalists was a major concern. The researcher has studied channels' ownership pattern, marketing strategies and to establish role of ownership in media business.

Chapter 16. NFT Sports Collectibles: Characteristics and Factors of Consumer Value

This chapter examines characteristics of non-fungible tokens (NFTs) and factors of perceived consumer value that influence the intention to purchase NFT sports collectibles. It further offers recommendations through which NFT experiences can be enhanced for collectors. The role of NFT sports collectibles is introduced in the context of the internet of things and internet of value, before defining NFT characteristics and consumer value factors relevant to this study. The respective conceptual model is then analyzed and discussed. The main findings explain that NFT characteristics including scarcity, uniqueness, aesthetics, and functional utility have no direct effect on the purchase intention for NFT sports collectibles. However, they have a significant and positive influence on the purchase intention when mediated through consumer values like the enjoyment of collecting NFTs, the creativity stimulated from assembling a digital collection, and the social relationships that can be fostered with other collectors.

Chapter 17. E-Marketing, E-Commerce, E-Business, and Internet of Things: An Overview of Terms in the Context of Small and Medium Enterprises (SMEs)

Small Medium Enterprises (SMEs) are often considered as an economic engine. The Digital boom that has happened in the recent years offers variety of tools to these SMEs to reach out to their target audience in a very cost effective manner. Automation of marketing is often related with the digitization of marketing, Internet of things and related activities. This mainly harness upon the use of internet and other electronic sources to communicate with their stakeholders. The terms like E-Marketing, E-Commerce, E-Business and Internet of Things (IoT) have gained prominence in the arena of modern business management. In this chapter, an attempt has been done to connect E-Marketing, E-Commerce, E-Business and Internet of Things in context of SMEs and Marketing automation, by performing bibliometric analysis of Scopus database and review of literature. This will help in understanding the way concepts have evolved in the recent times. This chapter also attempts to differentiate the four terms in light of literature and theories.

Chapter 18. Internet of Things in Marketing: Applications and Concerns

The internet of things (IoT) has emerged as one of the most significant 21st-century technologies in recent years. People can work and live more efficiently with the aid of the internet of things. Along with offering smart home automation gadgets, the Internet of Things is essential to businesses. IoT gives businesses a real-time glimpse into how their systems actually function, offering insights into everything from machine performance to supply chain and logistics operations. The expectations, attitudes, and needs of consumers are being altered by the technology that large businesses are attempting to incorporate into their marketing strategies. The article makes an effort to explore various elements of leveraging the Internet of Things for marketing, identify some of the key issues, and propose potential solutions. The marketers can make use of IoT's enormous potential in the future. However, there isn't a lot of literature out there yet that is geared toward marketing IoT. Thus, this article might provide a brief overview of the subject.

CONCLUSION

Global Applications of the Internet of Things in Digital Marketing focuses on the applications of IoT in customizing content and developing a data-based marketing framework that helps marketers create different experiences in bridging the digital and physical world, develop a closer connection with the consumers, and provide highly contextual and tailored messages to consumers. Covering key topics such as brand image, social media, and website development, this premier reference source is ideal for business owners, managers, marketers, researchers, scholars, academicians, practitioners, instructors, and students.

1. This book answers the questions on applications of IoT communications between marketers and consumers, how to monitor their interaction and what information should be given to the consumers.
2. The book provides benefits to marketers in building brand awareness to expand customer base and enter new markets, generate leads for the business, to engage and provide valuable information, generate sales via online or offline channels.
3. The book links the industry with academia by providing useful insights on how to improve businesses' ability to create and customize customer value and loyalty. Covering topics including e-commerce, mobile marketing, website development, and physical customer experiences.

Arshi Naim
King Kalid University, Saudi Arabia

V. Ajantha Devi
AP3 Solutions, India

Chapter 1
Emerging Green Practices, Internet of Things, and Digital Marketing:
A Response to the Global Economic and Climate Crises

Shad Ahmad Khan
University of Buraimi, Oman

Ravinder Rena
Durban University of Technology, South Africa

ABSTRACT

Planetary sustainability has emerged as a challenging phenomenon today. Though there have been various discussions and deliberations in reducing carbon footprints and adapting green practices, things are not really moving in the right direction. However, the emergence of many new green practices cannot be ignored at the same time. Climate change is real and possesses many unexpected disasters to happen if not addressed on time. The researchers have claimed already that this threat needs to have a collective response rather than waiting for some specific governments to act. This chapter attempts to make an account of green practices around the globe and explores the way internet of things and digital marketing are playing or can play in the propagation of the same. This study makes an account of possible best practices and the way they have been promoted in the recent past. This will have an implication on the social scientists, ecologists, digital marketers, environment activists, and government bodies.

DOI: 10.4018/978-1-6684-8166-0.ch001

1. INTRODUCTION

The world is currently facing two major crises: the global economic crisis and the climate crisis. Both of these crises have significant impacts on businesses and consumers alike, and they are closely linked. The economic crisis has led to a decrease in consumer spending and a decrease in demand for goods and services, while the climate crisis has led to increased costs for businesses due to the need to reduce carbon emissions and adapt to the changing climate.

The global economic crisis is the result of a number of factors, including the collapse of the housing market, the failure of major financial institutions, and the decline of the global economy. This has led to a decrease in consumer spending and a decrease in demand for goods and services. Businesses have been forced to reduce costs and lay off employees in order to survive.

The climate crisis on the other hand is the result of non-sustainable practices of the humans, such as the burning of fossil fuels and deforestation. This has led to an increase in greenhouse gas emissions and a warming of the Earth's atmosphere that led to changes in weather patterns, rising sea levels, and increased frequency and intensity of natural disasters. The climate crisis also has significant impacts on businesses and consumers, as companies are forced to adapt to the changing climate and consumers are faced with higher costs for goods and services.

In response to these crises, many businesses are turning to green practices in order to reduce costs and mitigate the impacts of the climate crisis. These practices include using renewable energy sources, reducing waste, and increasing energy efficiency. For example, many companies are now using solar and wind power to generate electricity, and they are also using more energy efficient lighting and heating systems. In addition, companies are also investing in green technologies, such as electric cars and smart buildings, in order to reduce their carbon footprint and become more sustainable.

Another emerging trend that is helping businesses to adapt to the economic and climate crises is the Internet of Things (IoT). IoT refers to the growing network of connected devices, such as smartphones, smart homes, and industrial equipment, that are able to communicate with each other and with the internet. IoT is being used to increase efficiency and reduce costs by automating processes and collecting data to optimize performance. For example, companies are using IoT to monitor energy usage in buildings and to optimize the performance of industrial equipment.

Digital marketing is also playing a critical role in helping businesses to navigate the economic and climate crises. Digital marketing is the use of digital channels, such as social media, search engines, and email, to promote products and services. Digital marketing is allowing businesses to reach a wider audience, target specific demographics, and measure the effectiveness of their marketing campaigns. This is helping companies to reduce costs and increase efficiency, while also allowing them to better understand their customers' needs and preferences. This chapter takes up these two issues, and tries to draw conclusions on the based on the fact that, the global economic and climate crises are having a significant impact on businesses and consumers alike. However, by embracing green practices, IoT, and digital marketing, companies can reduce costs and mitigate the impacts of the climate crisis while also increasing efficiency and reaching a wider audience. These trends are helping businesses to adapt to the changing economic and environmental landscape and to remain competitive in the global marketplace.

2. GLOBAL ECONOMIC CRISIS: IN THE RECENT PAST

The global economic crisis is caused by various reasons. There are many governing theories that suggest what economic crisis is and how it is triggered (Mach, 2019). One of the biggest economic crises happened recently is termed as great recession, began in 2008 and has had far-reaching effects on economies worldwide (Brancaccio & Fontana, 2011; Rena & Msoni, 2014). The crisis was triggered by the collapse of the housing market in the United States, which led to the failure of several major financial institutions. The crisis then spread to other countries through the interconnectedness of the global economy (Brancaccio & Fontana, 2011; Rena & Msoni, 2014). The root cause of the crisis was the proliferation of subprime mortgages, which are loans given to borrowers with poor credit. These loans were often bundled together and sold as securities to investors, who believed they were low-risk investments. However, when housing prices began to fall, many of these borrowers defaulted on their loans, causing the value of these securities to plummet. This led to the collapse of several major banks and investment firms, including Lehman Brothers, which was one of the largest investment banks in the world.

The crisis had a severe impact on the global economy, leading to a sharp contraction in economic activity. GDP growth slowed significantly, and unemployment rates skyrocketed. In the United States, for example, GDP growth fell from 2.7% in 2007 to -2.8% in 2009, and the unemployment rate rose from 4.6% in 2007 to 10% in 2009. (Roberts, 2009; Surn & Khatiwada,2010). The crisis also had a significant impact on the financial sector, leading to a reduction in credit availability and a decline in the value of stocks and other financial assets. This led to a decrease in consumer and business spending, which further exacerbated the economic downturn (Surn & Khatiwada,2010).

In response to the crisis, governments and central banks around the world took a number of measures to stabilize the economy. Fiscal stimulus packages like cutting down of taxes, increase in government spendings along with the efficient monetary policies were announced and implemented (Siripraphanukul & Wasi, 2009). The measures taken by governments and central banks helped to stabilize the economy and prevent a complete collapse. However, the recovery has been slow, and many countries are still dealing with the aftermath of the crisis. For example, in the United States, GDP growth has been slow, and the unemployment rate remains elevated (Siripraphanukul & Wasi, 2009; Mach,2019; Brancaccio & Fontana, 2011).

The crisis also had a significant impact on businesses and the global economy. Many companies went bankrupt as a result of the crisis, while others struggled to survive. The crisis also led to a sharp decline in the value of many financial assets, including stocks and bonds. This decline in asset values led to significant losses for investors and pension funds around the world (Surn & Khatiwada,2010; Rena,2010; Chang et al., 2013; Roberts, 2009).

Despite the severity of the 2008 crisis, there are important lessons that can be learned from the events of 2008 that could help prevent similar disasters in the future. One of the most important lessons from the crisis is the need for stronger regulation of the financial industry. Prior to the crisis, there were few regulations in place to prevent banks and other financial institutions from taking on excessive risk. This lack of oversight allowed banks to engage in risky practices such as issuing subprime mortgages and packaging them into complex financial instruments known as mortgage-backed securities. These securities were then sold to investors around the world, many of whom were unaware of the risks involved. The result was a global financial system that was highly vulnerable to collapse (Chang et al., 2013; Mohan, 2009).

Another important lesson from the crisis is the importance of transparency and accountability in the financial industry. Prior to the crisis, many financial institutions were not required to disclose important information about their operations and financial condition. This lack of transparency made it difficult for investors, regulators, and other stakeholders to fully understand the risks involved in the financial system. In the aftermath of the crisis, many countries have implemented new regulations and reporting requirements to increase transparency and accountability in the financial industry (Rena,2010; Rena & Msoni, 2014; Chang et al., 2013).

The crisis also highlighted the need for greater international cooperation in dealing with financial crises (Rena & Msoni, 2014). The failure of major financial institutions in the United States quickly spread to other countries, causing a global financial crisis that required a coordinated response from governments and central banks around the world. The crisis also highlighted the importance of having an effective framework in place for resolving failed financial institutions. In addition to these lessons, the crisis also had a number of broader implications for the global economy. The crisis led to a severe recession, with many countries experiencing high levels of unemployment and low economic growth. The crisis also highlighted the need for governments to take a more active role in stabilizing the economy during times of crisis (Mach,2019; Brancaccio & Fontana, 2011).

Thus, it can be seen that the global economic crisis of 2008 was a severe and far-reaching event that had a significant impact on the global economy. However, the measures taken by governments and central banks helped to stabilize the economy and prevent a complete collapse. The recovery, however, has been slow, and many countries are still dealing with the aftermath of the crisis.

2.1. Economic Crisis During and Post- Covid 19

The global economy has been greatly impacted by the COVID-19 pandemic (Lustig & Mariscal,2020). As countries around the world have implemented lockdowns and other measures to slow the spread of the virus, businesses have been forced to close and people have lost their jobs. This has led to a significant decrease in economic activity and a rise in unemployment (Lustig & Mariscal,2020; Carletti et al., 2020; Bocar et al., 2022).

One of the most significant impacts of the pandemic on the global economy has been a decrease in consumer spending. With people losing their jobs and facing financial uncertainty, they have been less likely to spend money on non-essential items. This has led to a decrease in demand for goods and services, which has hurt businesses and led to a decrease in economic activity ((Lustig & Mariscal,2020; Carletti et al., 2020). Another major impact of the pandemic on the global economy has been a decrease in investment. With the uncertainty surrounding the pandemic, many businesses and investors have been hesitant to make new investments. This has led to a decrease in economic growth and has made it more difficult for businesses to expand and create new jobs (Lustig & Mariscal,2020; Carletti et al., 2020).

In addition to these impacts, the pandemic has also led to a rise in government debt. Governments around the world have had to spend large amounts of money on stimulus packages and other measures to support their economies. This has led to a rise in government debt and has raised concerns about the long-term sustainability of these measures (Kharroubi et al., 2021; Lustig & Mariscal,2020; Carletti et al., 2020).

Despite these challenges, there are also some signs of hope for the global economy. Many countries have begun to ease their lockdown measures and businesses are starting to reopen. This has led to an increase in economic activity and has helped to reduce unemployment. Additionally, there have been some positive developments in the development of vaccines and other treatments for COVID-19, which could help to bring the pandemic under control and boost the global economy (Maritz et al., 2020; Carletti et al., 2020).

In conclusion, the global economy has been greatly impacted by the COVID-19 pandemic. The pandemic has led to a decrease in economic activity, a rise in unemployment, and a decrease in investment. The post covid era looks to be bright, however, the brighter tomorrow would require sensible approach in terms of economy and society. One of the breakthrough incident that has happened in the times of Covid 19, was the quick spread of digitalisation and improvement in digital space (Magd & Khan,2022; Bocar et al., 2022). This has happened specially in terms of acceptance of digital technology (Khan et al., 2021; Khan & Magd,2021). This gives a rise on exploring the aspects of green and digital practices in the arena of business economy.

3. GLOBAL CLIMATE CRISIS AND PLANETARY SUSTAINABILITY

The global climate crisis is a pressing issue that affects every living being on Earth, as It talked about the sustainability of the planet (i.e., earth), many scientists refer it as planetary sustainability (Agreement,2015). The Earth's climate is changing at an unprecedented rate, and if left unchecked, it could have devastating consequences for humans, animals, and the environment. The primary cause of the climate crisis is human activity, particularly the burning of fossil fuels and deforestation (Agreement,2015; Ansu-Mensah, 2021).

One of the most significant effects of the climate crisis is the increase in global temperatures. The Earth's average temperature has risen by about 1 degree Celsius since the Industrial Revolution, and it is projected to rise by an additional 2-4 degrees Celsius by the end of the century. This warming is causing the Arctic ice to melt, sea levels to rise, and extreme weather events to occur more frequently. These changes are already affecting millions of people around the world, particularly those living in low-lying areas and on small islands (Lindsey & Dahlman, 2020).

Another major effect of the climate crisis is the increase in extreme weather events such as hurricanes, floods, and droughts. These events can have devastating effects on communities, causing loss of life, property damage, and displacement of people. The frequency and severity of these events are expected to increase as the planet continues to warm (Vanham et al., 2019).

The climate crisis is also affecting the natural world in a number of ways. Changes in temperature and rainfall patterns are causing shifts in the distribution of plants and animals, and some species are at risk of extinction. Coral reefs are also at risk as rising ocean temperatures cause coral bleaching, which can lead to the death of the coral (Lindsey & Dahlman, 2020; Vanham et al., 2019).

To address the climate crisis, there are a number of actions that need to be taken. The first step is to reduce greenhouse gas emissions, particularly carbon dioxide. This can be done by transitioning to renewable energy sources, such as solar and wind power, and by investing in energy efficiency (Kuzemko et al., 2020). Additionally, deforestation needs to be stopped and reforestation needs to be promoted. During the lockdown of Covid-19, certain interesting patterns in favour of the planetary sustainability were observed (Singh & Chauhan, 2020). The air quality, stream water quality, and other pollution levels were found to be improved (Adam et al., 2021; Singh & Chauhan, 2020).

The problem of climate change and planetary sustainability is mainly due to the unsustainable practices widely practices among the people globally (Seegebarth et al.,2016; Shittu,2020). To combat this the global community to address the climate crisis together. Climate change is a global problem that requires a global solution. This means that countries need to work together to reduce emissions, adapt to the changes that are happening, and support those who are affected by the climate crisis. Failure to take action now will have devastating consequences for future generations and the planet.

3.1. Solving Global Climate Crisis

To solve the global climate crisis and global warming, there are several steps that we can take as individuals, communities, and as a global society. Reduce Greenhouse Gas Emissions is one of the most important steps in solving the global climate crisis and global warming is to reduce our greenhouse gas emissions (Erickson, 2017; Kuzemko et al., 2020)). This can be achieved through various ways such as: Switching to renewable energy sources such as solar, wind, and geothermal power; Improving energy efficiency in buildings and vehicles; Planting trees and other vegetation to absorb carbon dioxide from the atmosphere; Using public transportation and biking or walking instead of driving; Eating a plant-based diet, as the meat and dairy industry is a significant contributor to greenhouse gas emissions (Hertwich et al., 2019; Erickson, 2017).

The next solution is to Invest in Climate Adaptation, this can be done by way of: Building infrastructure that can withstand extreme weather events such as floods and heat waves; Developing drought-resistant crops; Relocating people and wildlife from areas that are at risk of flooding or sea level rise; Improving water management to ensure that communities have access to clean water during droughts (Herman et al., 2020)

The next proposed solution is Educating and Raising Awareness. This includes, educating children and adults about the causes and effects of climate change; Encouraging people to take personal responsibility for their actions and make changes in their daily lives to reduce their carbon footprint; Encouraging people to support politicians and policies that prioritize the environment; Encouraging people to support organizations that are working to combat climate change (Reid, 2019).

Further, the world has to work like a one global family i.e., through International Cooperation, this can be done by way of: Encouraging countries to work together to reduce greenhouse gas emissions and invest in climate adaptation; Encouraging countries to support each other in their efforts to combat climate change; Encouraging countries to support organizations that are working to combat climate change (Ferrari & Pagliari, 2021)

Solving the global climate crisis and global warming requires a multifaceted approach that involves reducing greenhouse gas emissions, investing in climate adaptation, educating and raising awareness, and international cooperation (Sanson et al., 2019; Ferrari & Pagliari, 2021). It is up to all the individuals, communities, and as a global society to take action and work together to protect the planet for future generations.

4. INTERNET OF THINGS (IOT)

The Internet of Things (IoT) refers to the interconnected network of physical devices, vehicles, buildings, and other items embedded with sensors, software, and connectivity which enables these objects to collect and exchange data. The IoT allows for the seamless integration of the digital and physical worlds, resulting in increased efficiency, accuracy, and economic benefits (Kramp et al., 2013).

The IoT is made possible by a combination of technologies such as low-cost computing power, high-speed internet, and miniaturized sensors. These devices can be connected to the internet and communicate with other devices, allowing for the collection and analysis of large amounts of data. This data can be used to control and automate various processes, such as lighting and temperature control in buildings, and to make decisions based on real-time information (Schoder, 2018; Coetzee & Eksteen, 2011). Few examples of IoT applications include- Smart homes that can be controlled remotely via a smartphone app (Umair et al., 2021); Wearable devices that track fitness and health data (Huifeng et al., 2020); Industrial control systems that monitor and optimize manufacturing processes (Lu et al., 2020); Smart cities with connected infrastructure for transportation and energy management (Umair et al., 2021); Agricultural IoT that monitor and control irrigation systems and crop health (Rani et al., 2019) etc .

The IoT has the potential to revolutionize many industries and change the way we live, work, and play. However, the widespread adoption of IoT technology also raises significant security, privacy, and ethical concerns (Alwarfy et al., 2020). The future belongs to the IoT and imagining any activity without IoT would be injustice to the present time.

5. GREEN PRACTICES AND ECONOMIC CRISIS

In recent years, there has been growing concern about the potential for an economic crisis triggered by climate change and environmental degradation (Prideaux et al., 2020; Bashir et al., 2020). The effects of global warming, such as droughts, floods, and extreme weather events, have the potential to disrupt entire economies and cause widespread financial losses. However, there is a growing body of evidence that suggests that green practices can help prevent an economic crisis (Chen et al., 2020).

Green practices, or environmentally sustainable actions and policies, can play a significant role in solving economic problems. The economic benefits of green practices are numerous and can include cost savings, job creation, and increased economic growth (Afum et al., 2021; Khan & Gurung, 2019).

One-way green practices can help solve economic problems is through cost savings. Implementing energy-efficient technologies, such as solar panels and LED lighting, can significantly reduce energy costs for businesses and households. This can lead to increased profits for businesses and increased disposable income for households, which can then be used to boost the economy (Kumar & Rodrigues, 2020; Ekung et al., 2022; Khan & Gurung, 2019).

Green practices can also lead to job creation. The growth of the renewable energy industry, for example, has led to an increase in jobs related to the installation and maintenance of solar and wind energy systems. This can provide employment opportunities for individuals who may have been affected by job loss in other industries (Dantas et al., 2021).

In addition, green practices can promote economic growth. By investing in sustainable infrastructure and technologies, businesses and governments can attract more environmentally conscious consumers and investors. This can lead to increased demand for products and services, which can then drive economic growth (Khan & Gurung, 2019; Pimonenko, 2019).

Furthermore, green practices can also help to solve economic problems related to climate change. By reducing greenhouse gas emissions and implementing sustainable practices, businesses and governments can help to mitigate the negative impacts of climate change on the economy. This includes reducing the costs associated with extreme weather events and protecting industries that are vulnerable to the effects of climate change (Dantas et al., 2021; Khan & Gurung, 2019). Further the green practices can lead to establishment of green culture where a culture is developed to undertake every activity considering the Sustainable Development Goals (SDGs) leading to culture like social entrepreneurship (Khatri et al., 2022; Magd et al., 2022; Magd & Khan, 2022), green businesses (Hasan et al., 2022), Self-help groups (Gangwar & Khan, 2022); Green start-ups (Singh et al., 2020) etc.

Thus, it can be seen that green practices can have a positive impact on the economy by reducing costs, creating jobs, promoting economic growth, and mitigating the effects of climate change. By investing in sustainable practices, businesses and governments can help to solve economic problems and promote a more sustainable future.

6. GREEN PRACTICES AND DIGITAL MARKETING

Green practices, also known as sustainable or environmentally-friendly practices, refer to the actions and strategies that businesses and organizations implement in order to minimize their negative impact on the environment. These practices can include reducing energy and water usage, recycling and repurposing materials, and using renewable energy sources (Khan & Gurung, 2019; Kuzemko et al., 2020)).

One important aspect of green practices is digital marketing. Digital marketing refers to the use of various online platforms and technologies to promote products and services. This can include social media marketing, email marketing, content marketing, and search engine optimization (SEO) (Panchal et al., 2022; Saleem et al., 2022).

The role of digital marketing in promoting green practices is significant for several reasons. First, digital marketing allows businesses and organizations to reach a large audience with minimal environmental impact. For example, email marketing and social media marketing allow businesses to communicate with customers and promote their products and services without the need for paper or physical mailings (Chen et al., 2021). In addition, digital marketing can help businesses and organizations build a reputation for being environmentally-friendly. By promoting their green practices and sustainability efforts through digital channels, businesses can attract customers who are looking for environmentally-friendly products and services. This can help to increase brand loyalty and customer retention, as well as attract new customers who value sustainability (Khan et al., 2021; Gangwar & Khan, 2022). Another way digital marketing can support green practices is by promoting eco-friendly products and services. By highlighting the environmental benefits of these products, businesses can help consumers make more sustainable choices (Tariq et al., 2022).

Moreover, digital marketing can also support green practices by helping businesses to track and measure their environmental impact. For example, businesses can use digital analytics tools to track their energy and water usage, and to monitor their carbon footprint. This allows them to identify areas where they can improve their environmental performance and make more sustainable choices (Chen et al., 2021). Overall, digital marketing plays an important role in promoting green practices. By using digital channels to reach customers and promote environmentally-friendly products and services, businesses can help to minimize their environmental impact and attract customers who value sustainability.

7. EMERGING GREEN PRACTICES

Emerging green practices are innovative and sustainable ways of conducting business and living that promote environmental conservation and social well-being. These practices are designed to reduce the negative impact of human activities on the planet, while also improving the quality of life for people (Khan & Gurung, 2019).

One of the most significant emerging green practices is the use of renewable energy sources. Renewable energy sources, such as solar, wind, and hydro power, produce electricity without the use of fossil fuels, which are a major contributor to climate change. The use of renewable energy sources also reduces dependence on fossil fuels and reduces the environmental impact of energy production (Kuzemko et al., 2020).

Another important emerging green practice is the use of sustainable transportation. This includes the use of electric cars, hybrid vehicles, and public transportation, which reduces emissions and air pollution. It also promotes a more efficient use of resources and reduces the need for oil and gas (Bibri et al., 2020).

Green building practices are also becoming increasingly popular. These practices involve the use of sustainable materials, efficient energy systems, and water conservation techniques in the construction of buildings. This not only reduces the environmental impact of the building, but it also improves the health and well-being of the occupants (Bibri et al., 2020; Ebekozien et al., 2022).

Another emerging green practice is the use of sustainable agriculture. This includes the use of organic farming methods, which reduces the use of pesticides and fertilizers and promotes biodiversity. It also includes the use of water conservation techniques and the use of renewable energy sources in the production of food (Khan et al., 2020; Khan et al., 2022a; Khan et al., 2022b).

Further, the circular economy is an emerging green practice that aims to reduce waste and promote sustainability. The circular economy is a concept that involves the use of materials and resources in a closed loop, where waste is minimized and resources are reused. This reduces the need for new resources and reduces the environmental impact of production and consumption (Chen et al., 2020; Dantas et al., 2021).

The procurement and promotion of green products is another consideration. Green products and services refer to those that are environmentally friendly and sustainable. These products and services are designed to minimize their impact on the environment, reduce pollution, and promote conservation of natural resources (Khan & Gurung, 2019).

The emerging green practices are innovative and sustainable ways of conducting business and living that promote environmental conservation and social well-being. These practices include the use of renewable energy sources, sustainable transportation, green building practices, sustainable agriculture, and the circular economy. By implementing these practices, we can reduce the negative impact of human activities on the planet and improve the quality of life for people.

8. DISCUSSION AND CONCLUSION

Digital marketing is an incredibly powerful tool for reaching and engaging customers, and it can be used to promote a wide range of sustainable products and services. For example, companies can use digital marketing to promote green energy solutions, such as solar and wind power, and to promote sustainable transportation options, such as electric cars and bikes. Additionally, digital marketing can be used to educate customers about the importance of reducing their carbon footprint and to promote eco-friendly products and services.

IoT (Internet of Things) technology is also playing an increasingly important role in the global economy. IoT devices, such as smart thermostats, smart appliances, and sensor-based systems, can help reduce energy consumption, improve efficiency, and increase the overall sustainability of our economy. For example, IoT-enabled appliances can be programmed to run during off-peak hours when energy prices are lower, and smart buildings can be designed to optimize energy usage.

Green products, on the other hand, are products that are designed to be environmentally friendly and sustainable. These products can include things like organic food, eco-friendly clothing, and green cleaning products. By promoting these products and services, companies can help to reduce their environmental impact and promote sustainable consumption. Additionally, by investing in green products, consumers can help to support environmentally friendly companies, and encourage other companies to adopt sustainable practices.

The global economy is currently facing a number of challenges, including rising inequality, sluggish growth, and the ongoing threat of climate change. These issues are interconnected and require a holistic approach to solve. One such solution is to harness the power of digital marketing, IoT, and green practices to create a more sustainable and equitable economy.

Green practices are essential for creating a sustainable economy. This includes reducing energy consumption, conserving resources, and reducing waste. By adopting green practices, businesses can reduce their environmental impact and improve their bottom line. Additionally, green practices can also be used to promote a more equitable economy, by creating jobs and reducing poverty.

To address all these issues, the power of digital marketing, IoT, and green practices needs to be harnessed. By promoting sustainable products and services, collecting and analysing data, and adopting green practices, we can create a more sustainable and equitable economy for all.

9. LIMITATIONS AND DIRECTION FOR FUTURE STUDIES

The conclusions drawn in this study mainly takes an inspiration through the review of literature. The argument building lacks the actual data or empirical testing. Hence, as a guiding note from this study, the future studies should focus on identifying and developing business models that are sustainable, equitable, and profitable. This can include researching and implementing new technologies, such as IoT, to improve resource efficiency and reduce waste. Further certain studies can be done focusing on measuring the impact of digital marketing campaigns on consumer behavior and the environment. This can include analyzing data on consumer engagement, product sales, and resource consumption. The future researchers can examine the impact of green practices on the economy whereby, the impact of green practices on the economy, including job creation, poverty reduction, and GDP growth. This can include analyzing data on green business revenues, employment, and income distribution are examined taking the real data. As the field of IoT is relatively new for the green practices and digital marketing, the researches on implementing IoT technologies to improve resource efficiency, reduce waste, and promote sustainable business practices would be recommended. Last but not the least, the study on sustainable consumption, green product consumer behaviour, and resource consumption would be also advised to the future researchers.

REFERENCES

Adam, M. G., Tran, P. T., & Balasubramanian, R. (2021). Air quality changes in cities during the COVID-19 lockdown: A critical review. *Atmospheric Research, 264*, 105823. doi:10.1016/j.atmosres.2021.105823 PMID:34456403

Afum, E., Zhang, R., Agyabeng-Mensah, Y., & Sun, Z. (2021). Sustainability excellence: The interactions of lean production, internal green practices and green product innovation. *International Journal of Lean Six Sigma, 12*(6), 1089–1114. doi:10.1108/IJLSS-07-2020-0109

Paris Agreement. (2015, December). Paris agreement. In *Report of the Conference of the Parties to the United Nations Framework Convention on Climate Change (21st Session, 2015: Paris).* HeinOnline.

Alwarafy, A., Al-Thelaya, K. A., Abdallah, M., Schneider, J., & Hamdi, M. (2020). A survey on security and privacy issues in edge-computing-assisted internet of things. *IEEE Internet of Things Journal, 8*(6), 4004–4022. doi:10.1109/JIOT.2020.3015432

Ansu-Mensah, P. (2021). Green product awareness effect on green purchase intentions of university students': An emerging market's perspective. *Future Business Journal, 7*(1), 1–13. doi:10.118643093-021-00094-5

Bashir, M. F., Ma, B., & Shahzad, L. (2020). A brief review of socio-economic and environmental impact of Covid-19. *Air Quality, Atmosphere & Health, 13*(12), 1403–1409. doi:10.100711869-020-00894-8 PMID:32837620

Bibri, S. E., Krogstie, J., & Kärrholm, M. (2020). Compact city planning and development: Emerging practices and strategies for achieving the goals of sustainability. *Developments in the built environment, 4*, 100021.

Bocar, A. C., Khan, S. A., & Epoc, F. J. (2022). COVID-19 work from home stressors and the degree of its impact: Employers and employees actions. *International Journal of Technology Transfer and Commercialisation, 19*(2), 270–291. doi:10.1504/IJTTC.2022.124349

Brancaccio, E., & Fontana, G. (2011). The global economic crisis. *New perspectives on the Critique of Economic Theory and Policy.*

Carletti, E., Claessens, S., Fatás, A., & Vives, X. (2020). *Post-Covid-19 World.* Centre for Economic Policy Research.

Chang, S. S., Stuckler, D., Yip, P., & Gunnell, D. (2013). Impact of 2008 global economic crisis on suicide: Time trend study in 54 countries. *BMJ (Clinical Research Ed.), 347*(sep17 1), 347. doi:10.1136/bmj.f5239 PMID:24046155

Chen, T. L., Kim, H., Pan, S. Y., Tseng, P. C., Lin, Y. P., & Chiang, P. C. (2020). Implementation of green chemistry principles in circular economy system towards sustainable development goals: Challenges and perspectives. *The Science of the Total Environment, 716*, 136998. doi:10.1016/j.scitotenv.2020.136998 PMID:32044483

Chen, Y., Kwilinski, A., Chygryn, O., Lyulyov, O., & Pimonenko, T. (2021). The green competitiveness of enterprises: Justifying the quality criteria of digital marketing communication channels. *Sustainability*, *13*(24), 13679. doi:10.3390u132413679

Chen, Y., Kwilinski, A., Chygryn, O., Lyulyov, O., & Pimonenko, T. (2021). The green competitiveness of enterprises: Justifying the quality criteria of digital marketing communication channels. *Sustainability*, *13*(24), 13679. doi:10.3390u132413679

Coetzee, L., & Eksteen, J. (2011, May). The Internet of Things-promise for the future? An introduction. In *2011 IST-Africa Conference Proceedings* (pp. 1-9). IEEE.

Dantas, T. E. T., de-Souza, E. D., Destro, I. R., Hammes, G., Rodriguez, C. M. T., & Soares, S. R. (2021). How the combination of Circular Economy and Industry 4.0 can contribute towards achieving the Sustainable Development Goals. *Sustainable Production and Consumption*, *26*, 213–227. doi:10.1016/j.spc.2020.10.005

Ebekozien, A., Aigbavboa, C., Thwala, W. D., Amadi, G. C., Aigbedion, M., & Ogbaini, I. F. (2022). A systematic review of green building practices implementation in Africa. *Journal of Facilities Management*.

Ekung, S., Odesola, I., & Opoku, A. (2022). Demystifying cost misperception as a challenge to green building adoption in Nigeria. *Journal of Engineering. Design and Technology*, *20*(6), 1716–1737. doi:10.1108/JEDT-01-2021-0049

Erickson, L. E. (2017). Reducing greenhouse gas emissions and improving air quality: Two global challenges. *Environmental Progress & Sustainable Energy*, *36*(4), 982–988. doi:10.1002/ep.12665 PMID:29238442

Ferrari, M. M., & Pagliari, M. S. (2021). No country is an island. International cooperation and climate change. *International Cooperation and Climate Change.(June 2021). Banque de France Working Paper*, (815).

Gangwar, V. P., & Khan, S. A. (2022). Analyzing the Role of Micro-Entrepreneurship and Self-Help Groups (SHGs) in Women Empowerment and Development: A Bottom-of-Pyramid Perspective. In Driving Factors for Venture Creation and Success in Agricultural Entrepreneurship (pp. 213-226). IGI Global.

Ganichev, N. A., & Koshovets, O. B. (2021). Forcing the digital economy: How will the structure of digital markets change as a result of the COVID-19 pandemic. *Studies on Russian Economic Development*, *32*(1), 11–22. doi:10.1134/S1075700721010056 PMID:33642845

Hasan, M. M., Nekmahmud, M., Yajuan, L., & Patwary, M. A. (2019). Green business value chain: A systematic review. *Sustainable Production and Consumption*, *20*, 326–339. doi:10.1016/j.spc.2019.08.003

Herman, J. D., Quinn, J. D., Steinschneider, S., Giuliani, M., & Fletcher, S. (2020). Climate adaptation as a control problem: Review and perspectives on dynamic water resources planning under uncertainty. *Water Resources Research*, *56*(2), e24389. doi:10.1029/2019WR025502

Hertwich, E. G., Ali, S., Ciacci, L., Fishman, T., Heeren, N., Masanet, E., Asghari, F. N., Olivetti, E., Pauliuk, S., Tu, Q., & Wolfram, P. (2019). Material efficiency strategies to reducing greenhouse gas emissions associated with buildings, vehicles, and electronics—A review. *Environmental Research Letters, 14*(4), 043004. doi:10.1088/1748-9326/ab0fe3

Huifeng, W., Kadry, S. N., & Raj, E. D. (2020). Continuous health monitoring of sportsperson using IoT devices based wearable technology. *Computer Communications, 160*, 588–595. doi:10.1016/j.comcom.2020.04.025

Khan, S. A., Devi, T. P., & Sharma, P. P. (2020). Vertical farming: Why it matters for Bhutan. *Stud. Indian Place Names, 40*(1), 1323–1329.

Khan, S. A., Epoc, F., Al Shamsi, I. R., & Shamim, A. (2022). How Far Modern Vertical Farming is Appropriate for Developing Countries Like Oman?: A Review Based Analysis. *Delhi Business Review, 23*(2), 9–15. doi:10.51768/dbr.v23i2.232202202

Khan, S. A., Epoc, F., Al Shamsi, I. R., & Shamim, A. (2022a). How Far Modern Vertical Farming is Appropriate for Developing Countries Like Oman?: A Review Based Analysis. *Delhi Business Review, 23*(2), 9–15. doi:10.51768/dbr.v23i2.232202202

Khan, S. A., Epoc, F., Gangwar, V., Ligori, T. A. A., & Ansari, Z. A. (2021). Will Online Banking Sustain in Bhutan Post COVID-19? A Quantitative Analysis of The Customer E-Satisfaction and E-Loyalty in The Kingdom of Bhutan. *Transnational Marketing Journal, 9*(3), 607–624. doi:10.33182/tmj.v9i3.1288

Khan, S. A., & Gurung, M. (2019). Green public procurement through lens of practicality and policies a study on royal university of Bhutan. *Delhi Business Review, 20*(1), 23–32. doi:10.51768/dbr.v20i1.201201913

Khan, S. A., & Magd, H. (2021). Empirical examination of ms teams in conducting webinar: Evidence from international online program conducted in oman. *Journal of Content, Community and Communication*, 159-175.

Khan, S. A., Magd, H., Al Shamsi, I. R., & Masoom, K. (2022b). Social Entrepreneurship Through Innovations in Agriculture. In *International Perspectives on Value Creation and Sustainability Through Social Entrepreneurship* (pp. 209–222). IGI Global. doi:10.4018/978-1-6684-4666-9.ch010

Khan, S. A., Sharma, P. P., & Thoudam, P. (2019). Role of attitude and entrepreneurship education towards entrepreneurial orientation among business students of Bhutan. *International Journal of Recent Technology and Engineering, 8*, 335–345.

Kharroubi, S., Naja, F., Diab-El-Harake, M., & Jomaa, L. (2021). Food insecurity pre-and post the COVID-19 pandemic and economic crisis in Lebanon: Prevalence and projections. *Nutrients, 13*(9), 2976. doi:10.3390/nu13092976 PMID:34578854

Khatri, B., Arora, S., Magd, H., & Khan, S. A. K. (2022). Bibliometric Analysis of Social Entrepreneurship. In *International Perspectives on Value Creation and Sustainability Through Social Entrepreneurship* (pp. 46–60). IGI Global. doi:10.4018/978-1-6684-4666-9.ch003

Kramp, T., Van Kranenburg, R., & Lange, S. (2013). Introduction to the Internet of Things. *Enabling things to talk: Designing IoT solutions with the IoT architectural reference model*, 1-10

Kumar, M., & Rodrigues, V. S. (2020). Synergetic effect of lean and green on innovation: A resource-based perspective. *International Journal of Production Economics*, *219*, 469–479. doi:10.1016/j.ijpe.2018.04.007

Kuzemko, C., Bradshaw, M., Bridge, G., Goldthau, A., Jewell, J., Overland, I., Scholten, D., Van de Graaf, T., & Westphal, K. (2020). Covid-19 and the politics of sustainable energy transitions. *Energy Research & Social Science*, *68*, 101685. doi:10.1016/j.erss.2020.101685 PMID:32839704

Li, K., Kim, D. J., Lang, K. R., Kauffman, R. J., & Naldi, M. (2020). How should we understand the digital economy in Asia? Critical assessment and research agenda. *Electronic Commerce Research and Applications*, *44*, 101004. doi:10.1016/j.elerap.2020.101004 PMID:32922241

Lindsey, R., & Dahlman, L. (2020). Climate change: Global temperature. *Climate. gov, 16.*

Lu, Y., Xu, X., & Wang, L. (2020). Smart manufacturing process and system automation–a critical review of the standards and envisioned scenarios. *Journal of Manufacturing Systems*, *56*, 312–325. doi:10.1016/j.jmsy.2020.06.010

Lustig, N., & Mariscal, J. (2020). 20 How COVID-19 could be like the Global Financial Crisis (or worse). *Mitigating the COVID economic crisis: Act fast and do whatever*, 185.

Mach, Ł. (2019). Measuring and assessing the impact of the global economic crisis on European real property market. *Journal of Business Economics and Management*, *20*(6), 1189–1209. doi:10.3846/jbem.2019.11234

Magd, H., & Khan, S. A. (2022). Strategic Framework for Entrepreneurship Education in Promoting Social Entrepreneurship in GCC Countries During and Post COVID-19. In International Perspectives on Value Creation and Sustainability Through Social Entrepreneurship (pp. 61-75). IGI Global. doi:10.4018/978-1-6684-4666-9.ch004

Magd, H., & Khan, S. A. (2022). Strategic Framework for Entrepreneurship Education in Promoting Social Entrepreneurship in GCC Countries During and Post COVID-19. In International Perspectives on Value Creation and Sustainability Through Social Entrepreneurship (pp. 61-75). IGI Global. doi:10.4018/978-1-6684-4666-9.ch004

Magd, H., Khan, S. A. K., & Bhuyan, U. (2022). Social Entrepreneurship Intentions Among Business Students in Oman. In *International Perspectives on Value Creation and Sustainability Through Social Entrepreneurship* (pp. 76–93). IGI Global. doi:10.4018/978-1-6684-4666-9.ch005

Maritz, A., Perenyi, A., De Waal, G., & Buck, C. (2020). Entrepreneurship as the unsung hero during the current COVID-19 economic crisis: Australian perspectives. *Sustainability*, *12*(11), 4612. doi:10.3390u12114612

Mohan, R. (2009). Global financial crisis: Causes, impact, policy responses and lessons. *Reserve Bank of India Bulletin*, 879-904.

Panchal, A., Shah, A., & Kansara, K. (2021). Digital marketing-search engine optimization (SEO) and search engine marketing (SEM). *International Research Journal of Innovations in Engineering and Technology*, *5*(12), 17.

Pimonenko, T., Liuliov, O., & Us, Y. (2019). Marketing strategies of green investments: Basic concepts and specific features. *Herald of Economics*, (1 (91)), 177–185.

Prideaux, B., Thompson, M., & Pabel, A. (2020). Lessons from COVID-19 can prepare global tourism for the economic transformation needed to combat climate change. *Tourism Geographies*, *22*(3), 667–678. doi:10.1080/14616688.2020.1762117

Reid, A. (2019). Climate change education and research: Possibilities and potentials versus problems and perils? *Environmental Education Research*, *25*(6), 767–790. doi:10.1080/13504622.2019.1664075

Rena, R. (2010). The Impact of Global Economic Crisis on the Namibian Economy: Issues and Challenges. [RBTR]. *Review of Business & Technology Research*, *3*(1), 475.

Rena, R., & Msoni, M. (2014). Global financial crises and its impact on the South African economy: A further update. *Journal of Economics*, *5*(1), 17–25. doi:10.1080/09765239.2014.11884980

Roberts, B. W. (2009). The macroeconomic impacts of the 9/11 attack: Evidence from real-time forecasting. *Peace Economics, Peace. Science & Public Policy*, *15*(2), 341–367.

Roscoe, S., Subramanian, N., Jabbour, C. J., & Chong, T. (2019). Green human resource management and the enablers of green organisational culture: Enhancing a firm's environmental performance for sustainable development. *Business Strategy and the Environment*, *28*(5), 737–749. doi:10.1002/bse.2277

Saleem, M., Khan, S. A., & Magd, H. (2022). Content Marketing Framework for Building Brand Image: A Case Study of Sohar International School, Oman. In Building a Brand Image Through Electronic Customer Relationship Management (pp. 64-83). IGI Global.

Sanson, A. V., Van Hoorn, J., & Burke, S. E. (2019). Responding to the impacts of the climate crisis on children and youth. *Child Development Perspectives*, *13*(4), 201–207. doi:10.1111/cdep.12342

Schoder, D. (2018). Introduction to the Internet of Things. *Internet of things A to Z: technologies and applications*, 1-50.

Seegebarth, B., Peyer, M., Balderjahn, I., & Wiedmann, K. P. (2016). The sustainability roots of anti-consumption lifestyles and initial insights regarding their effects on consumers' well-being. *The Journal of Consumer Affairs*, *50*(1), 68–99. doi:10.1111/joca.12077

Sharma, N., Shamkuwar, M., & Singh, I. (2019). The history, present and future with IoT. In *Internet of Things and Big Data Analytics for Smart Generation* (pp. 27–51). Springer. doi:10.1007/978-3-030-04203-5_3

Shittu, O. (2020). Emerging sustainability concerns and policy implications of urban household consumption: A systematic literature review. *Journal of Cleaner Production*, *246*, 119034. doi:10.1016/j.jclepro.2019.119034

Singh, E. H., Wangda, S., Khan, S., & Khan, S. A. (2020). Exploring the obstacles for start-ups in Bhutan: From a prevented entrepreneurs perspective. *International Journal of Innovation. Creativity and Change*, *11*(4), 70–87.

Singh, R. P., & Chauhan, A. (2020). Impact of lockdown on air quality in India during COVID-19 pandemic. *Air Quality, Atmosphere & Health*, *13*(8), 921–928. doi:10.100711869-020-00863-1 PMID:32837613

Siripraphanukul, P., & Wasi, N. (2009). Fighting Unemployment during Recessions: A Review of Fiscal Policies in Theory and Practice. *TDRI Quarterly Review*, *24*(4), 14–24.

Surn, A., & Khatiwada, I. (2010). The Nation's Underemployed in the Great Recession of 2007-09. *Monthly Labor Review*, *133*, 3.

Tariq, E., Alshurideh, M., Akour, I., Al-Hawary, S., & Kurdi, B. (2022). The role of digital marketing, CSR policy and green marketing in brand development. *International Journal of Data and Network Science*, *6*(3), 995–1004. doi:10.5267/j.ijdns.2022.1.012

Umair, M., Cheema, M. A., Cheema, O., Li, H., & Lu, H. (2021). Impact of COVID-19 on IoT adoption in healthcare, smart homes, smart buildings, smart cities, transportation and industrial IoT. *Sensors (Basel)*, *21*(11), 3838. doi:10.339021113838 PMID:34206120

Vanham, D., Leip, A., Galli, A., Kastner, T., Bruckner, M., Uwizeye, A., van Dijk, K., Ercin, E., Dalin, C., Brandão, M., Bastianoni, S., Fang, K., Leach, A., Chapagain, A., Van der Velde, M., Sala, S., Pant, R., Mancini, L., Monforti-Ferrario, F., ... Hoekstra, A. Y. (2019). Environmental footprint family to address local to planetary sustainability and deliver on the SDGs. *The Science of the Total Environment*, *693*, 133642. doi:10.1016/j.scitotenv.2019.133642 PMID:31635013

Chapter 2
Digital Marketing Through Social Media Best Practices:
A Case Study of HEIs in the GCC Region

Muhammad Saleem
https://orcid.org/0000-0003-1475-3516
University of Buraimi, Oman

Shad Ahmad Khan
https://orcid.org/0000-0001-7593-3487
University of Buraimi, Oman

Ibrahim Rashid Al Shamsi
University of Buraimi, Oman

Hesham Magd
Modern College of Business and Science, Oman

ABSTRACT

The exponential growth of social media usage during the past few years has unfolded unprecedented opportunities. The effective utilization of relevant social media tools, which was once considered the domain of business organizations only, is gradually shifting to various kinds of organizations functioning in society, and educational institutions are no exception. The current study aims at finding out the best practices followed by the top higher education institutions in GCC region, focusing on how they are tapping the vast potential of their online presence, specifically in social media. The researchers take into consideration the different kinds of social media used and the nature of content shared by the selected higher education institutions to gain interesting insights through comparative analysis in order to discover the critical success factors for the desired objectives. This chapter has an implication on all the HEIs in the GCC, education consultancies, digital marketers, businesses, and other stakeholders who are interested in the field of digital marketing.

DOI: 10.4018/978-1-6684-8166-0.ch002

1. INTRODUCTION AND BACKGROUND OF THE STUDY

The shift from traditional marketing to digital marketing has unleashed unprecedented opportunities to the marketers all over the world (Langan et al., 2019; Saleem et al., 2022). It has resulted in exploring new avenues and interesting possibilities which were unheard in the past, leading to greater customization and customer satisfaction (Khan et al., 2020; Khan et al.,2021). The use of social media in particular, has grown exponentially and organizations are effectively influencing their intended audiences on a regular basis by creating relevant and useful online content (Langan et al., 2019; Hollebeek & Macky,2019). Digital marketing, which was once considered the domain of business organizations only, is gradually shifting to various kinds of organizations functioning in the society and educational institutions are no exception. It is now very common for not-for-profit organizations to have a strong online presence and effective social media presence.

Online courses offered by education Institutions along with the availability of digital textbooks provide concrete examples that educational institutions all over the world are incorporating the digital media tools effectively (Langan et al., 2019; Khan & Magd,2021; Magd & Khan,2022b) . Covid-19 in particular, created an environment where the use of digital technology in educational institutions grew at a phenomenal rate (Bocar et al., 2022; Magd & Khan,2022a). The current study aims at finding out the best practices followed by the top higher education institutions in GCC region, focusing on how they are tapping the vast potential of their online presence, through social media best practices (Magd et al.,2022; Saleem et al., 2022).

1.1. Social Media

Social media is a term used to describe the various platforms and technologies that allow individuals and organizations to share content, opinions, and information in a digital format (Kushwaha et al.,2020; Hanaysha & Momani,2021). These platforms include popular sites such as Facebook, Twitter, Instagram, and LinkedIn, as well as newer platforms like TikTok and Clubhouse (Baumann, 2022). Social media has become an integral part of our daily lives, and its impact on society and the way we communicate is undeniable (Kushwaha et al.,2020).

The origins of social media can be traced back to the early days of the internet, when online forums and discussion boards were used to connect people with similar interests (Himelein-Wachowiak et al., 2021). The first true social media platform, Six Degrees, was launched in 1997, and it allowed users to create profiles and connect with friends (Dhingra & Mudgal,2019). Since then, social media has evolved to become a powerful tool for communication and engagement, and it has changed the way we interact with each other and consume information.

One of the most significant impacts of social media is the democratization of information (Abdullah et al., 2019). It has given individuals the ability to share their thoughts and opinions with a global audience, regardless of their background or education. This has led to a more diverse and inclusive conversation, and it has given a voice to marginalized groups that were previously unheard (Abdullah et al., 2019).

Social media has also changed the way businesses and organizations interact with their customers. The platforms provide a direct line of communication between companies and their customers, which allows them to build stronger relationships and provide better customer service. Additionally, social media has become an essential tool for marketing and advertising, as businesses can reach a large and targeted audience through paid advertising and organic content (Baumann, 2022).

However, social media has also had its share of negative impacts. The constant barrage of information and opinions can lead to information overload and can be overwhelming for some users. Additionally, the anonymity of the internet has led to an increase in cyberbullying and harassment, and the spread of fake news and misinformation can be a serious concern (Talwar et al., 2019).

Another concern is the impact of social media on mental health. Studies have shown that excessive use of social media can lead to feelings of isolation and depression, and it can also contribute to the development of anxiety and other mental health issues (Meier & Reinecke, 2021). Additionally, the constant need to present a curated and perfect version of ourselves online can lead to feelings of inadequacy and low self-esteem.

Thus, it is visible that, social media has had a profound impact on our society and the way we communicate. While it has brought many benefits, such as the democratization of information and the ability to connect with others, it has also had negative consequences, such as the spread of misinformation and the impact on mental health. As social media continues to evolve, it is important to use it responsibly and to be aware of its potential harms.

1.2. Social Media in GCC and MENA region

Social media has become an integral part of daily life in the Gulf Cooperation Council (GCC) and Middle East and North Africa (MENA) region (AlSadrah, 2021; Ghorfi & Hatimi,2020). With a population of over 400 million, the region has a high penetration of social media users, with many turning to platforms such as Facebook, Twitter, Instagram, and YouTube to stay connected with friends, family, and the world at large (Jones,2022).

One of the key drivers of social media usage in the GCC and MENA region is the high number of young people in the population. According to a report by the Arab Social Media Report, over 60% of the region's population is under the age of 30, and this demographic is highly active on social media. They use social media to stay connected with friends and family, to share information and news, and to engage in online communities.

Another key driver of social media usage in the GCC and MENA region is the high levels of mobile and internet penetration in the region. According to a report by the Arab Social Media Report, mobile phone penetration in the GCC and MENA region is at over 100%, and internet penetration is at over 70% ((AlSadrah, 2021; Ghorfi & Hatimi,2020; Jones,2022). This has made it easy for people in the region to access social media platforms, and has helped to drive the high levels of engagement on these platforms.

The GCC and MENA region is also home to a number of social media influencers, who have a large following on social media (Al-Abdallah et al., 2021). These influencers use their platforms to promote products, services, and brands, and to share their personal experiences and opinions with their followers. This has helped to drive the growth of the region's e-commerce market, as many influencers use their platforms to promote products and services that can be purchased online (Al-Abdallah et al., 2021).

However, the use of social media in the GCC and MENA region is not without its challenges. One of the main challenges is the lack of regulation and oversight of social media platforms in the region (Heydemann, 2020; Al-Abdallah et al., 2021). This has led to the spread of false information and fake news, which can have a negative impact on public opinion and decision-making. Another challenge is the lack of privacy and security on social media platforms, which has led to the leaking of personal information and the spread of cybercrime.

To address these challenges, some countries in the GCC and MENA region have introduced regulations and laws to govern social media usage (Hassib & Shires, 2022; Jones,2022). For example, the United Arab Emirates has introduced a law that requires social media users to register their accounts with the government, and to comply with certain rules and regulations. In Saudi Arabia, the government has introduced a law that makes it illegal to use social media to spread false information or to incite violence (Younies & Na, 2020).

Thus, it is evident that, social media has become an integral part of daily life in the GCC and MENA region, with a high number of users turning to platforms such as Facebook, Twitter, Instagram, and YouTube to stay connected with friends, family, and the world at large (Baumann, 2022). However, the use of social media in the region is not without its challenges, and governments and other stakeholders need to work together to address these challenges and to ensure that social media is used responsibly and for the benefit of all.

1.3. Social Media and Digital Marketing

Social media and digital marketing have become integral parts of modern business strategies. With the rise of digital platforms, businesses have access to a wide range of tools and techniques to reach and engage their target audience, build brand awareness, and drive sales.

Social media platforms such as Facebook, Instagram, Twitter, and LinkedIn allow businesses to create a presence on the platforms, post content, and interact with their audience. They also offer businesses the ability to advertise and target specific demographics, increasing the chances of reaching the right audience (Baumann, 2022). Additionally, businesses can use social media to monitor and track customer feedback, providing valuable insight into how their products and services are perceived (Hollebeek & Macky, 2019).

Digital marketing, on the other hand, is a broader term that encompasses all aspects of online marketing, including social media. It includes strategies such as Search Engine Optimization (SEO), pay-per-click (PPC) advertising, email marketing, and content marketing. These strategies are designed to reach customers through various digital channels, such as search engines, websites, and social media (Hollebeek & Macky,2019).

One of the key benefits of digital marketing is the ability to track and measure performance in real-time. This allows businesses to quickly adjust their strategies and campaigns to ensure they are reaching their target audience and achieving their desired results. Additionally, businesses can target specific demographics, such as age, location, and interests, increasing the chances of reaching the right audience.

SEO is a digital marketing strategy that focuses on improving a website's visibility in Search Engine Results Pages (SERPs). This is achieved by optimizing website content, keywords, and meta tags to ensure that the website is easily discoverable by search engines. Businesses can also use PPC advertising to boost their visibility on SERPs (Matta et al., 2020). PPC ads are sponsored links that appear at the top of search results pages, increasing the chances of attracting more visitors to a website (Matta et al., 2020).

Email marketing is another digital marketing strategy that businesses use to reach and engage their target audience. Email marketing campaigns allow businesses to send targeted messages and promotions to a list of subscribers, increasing the chances of driving sales and conversions. Additionally, email marketing campaigns can be easily tracked, providing businesses with valuable insights into how their audience is engaging with their messages (Saleem et al.,2022).

Content marketing is a digital marketing strategy that focuses on creating and distributing valuable and relevant content to attract and engage a target audience. This can include blog posts, videos, infographics, and other types of content that are designed to educate and inform customers about a business's products and services. Content marketing is an effective way to build brand awareness and drive traffic to a website (Saleem et al.,2022).

Thus, it is visible, social media and digital marketing are integral parts of modern business strategies. They provide businesses with a range of tools and techniques to reach and engage their target audience, build brand awareness, and drive sales. By using digital marketing strategies such as SEO, PPC advertising, email marketing, and content marketing, businesses can reach and engage their target audience through various digital channels, ultimately driving conversions and sales (Hollebeek & Macky,2019; Matta et al., 2020; Saleem et al.,2022). Additionally, businesses can track and measure performance in real-time, allowing them to make adjustments to their strategies and campaigns to ensure they are achieving their desired results.

1.4. Digital Marketing Strategies Through Social Media Best Practices

Digital marketing through social media is a powerful tool for businesses to reach and engage their target audience. However, with so many different social media platforms available, it can be difficult to know where to start and what best practices to follow. In this chapter, we will discuss some of the best practices for digital marketing through social media (Chaffey & Ellis-Chadwick, 2020; Vásquez & Escamilla,2014).

1. ***Understand your audience:*** Before you start creating content or running campaigns on social media, it's important to understand who one's target audience is. This includes their demographics, interests, and behaviour on social media. By understanding one's audience, you can create content and campaigns that will resonate with them and increase the chances of conversions and sales.
2. ***Create a content strategy:*** Creating a content strategy is essential for digital marketing through social media. This includes identifying the type of content that will resonate with one's target audience, determining the frequency of posts, and identifying the best times to post. Additionally, it's important to create a mix of different types of content, such as videos, images, and text, to keep one's audience engaged.
3. ***Use social media advertising:*** Social media advertising is a powerful tool for reaching one's target audience. Platforms such as Facebook, Instagram, and LinkedIn offer businesses the ability to target specific demographics, increasing the chances of reaching the right audience. Additionally, social media advertising allows businesses to track and measure performance in real-time, making it easy to adjust campaigns and strategies as needed.
4. ***Monitor and track customer feedback:*** Monitoring and tracking customer feedback is essential for digital marketing through social media. This includes monitoring comments, messages, and reviews on social media platforms. By monitoring customer feedback, businesses can quickly identify any issues or concerns and take action to address them. Additionally, businesses can use customer feedback to improve their products and services.
5. ***Measure and analyse one's performance:*** Measuring and analysing one's performance on social media is essential for identifying what's working and what's not. This includes tracking metrics such as engagement rates, click-through rates, and conversions. By analysing one's performance, you can identify areas for improvement and make adjustments to one's strategies and campaigns.

Thus it can be seen that, digital marketing through social media is a powerful tool for businesses to reach and engage their target audience. By following the best practices outlined in this article, businesses can create effective strategies and campaigns that will help them achieve their desired results. Additionally, by monitoring and tracking customer feedback and measuring and analyzing performance, businesses can make adjustments to their strategies and campaigns to ensure they are achieving their desired results.

1.5. Need for Social Media and Digital Marketing in Higher Education Institutions

Social media and digital marketing have become increasingly important for higher education institutions in recent years. These tools allow universities and colleges to reach and engage with potential students, current students, and alumni, as well as build brand awareness and reputation. In this article, we will discuss the ways in which social media and digital marketing are being used in higher education institutions (Alex et al.,2012; Saleem et al., 2022; Kushwaha et al., 2020).

1. ***Recruitment and Admissions:*** One of the primary uses of social media and digital marketing in higher education institutions is for recruitment and admissions. Universities and colleges use social media platforms such as Facebook, Instagram, and LinkedIn to reach and engage with potential students. They also use digital marketing techniques such as SEO and PPC advertising to increase visibility on search engines and drive traffic to their websites. Additionally, universities and colleges can use social media to provide information about admissions and application requirements, as well as the application process itself.
2. ***Student engagement:*** social media and digital marketing can also be used to increase student engagement. Universities and colleges can use social media platforms to create communities where students can connect with each other, share information, and ask questions. Additionally, universities and colleges can use social media and digital marketing to provide information about events, clubs, and organizations, as well as academic resources and support.
3. ***Alumni engagement:*** social media and digital marketing can also be used to engage with alumni. Universities and colleges can use social media platforms to connect with alumni, provide information about events and activities, and share news and updates about the institution. Additionally, universities and colleges can use digital marketing techniques such as email marketing to send targeted messages and updates to alumni.
4. ***Brand awareness and reputation management:*** social media and digital marketing can also be used to build brand awareness and reputation management for higher education institutions. Universities and colleges can use social media and digital marketing to share information about their programs, research, and achievements, as well as the success stories of their students and alumni. Additionally, universities and colleges can use social media and digital marketing to monitor and track customer feedback, providing valuable insight into how their institution is perceived.
5. ***Data Analysis and Insights:*** social media and digital marketing platforms offer a wealth of data that universities and colleges can use to gain insights about their target audience and campaigns. This can include data on engagement rates, click-through rates, demographics, and more. Universities and colleges can use this data to adjust their strategies and campaigns to ensure they are reaching and engaging their target audience effectively.

Thus, it can be inferred that, social media and digital marketing are essential tools for higher education institutions. They allow universities and colleges to reach and engage with potential stude ts, current students, and alumni, as well as build brand awareness and reputation (Ligori et al., 2022; Saleem et al., 2022). Additionally, universities and colleges can use social media and digital marketing to provide information about admissions and application requirements, increase student engagement, engage with alumni, and monitor and track customer feedback (Kamal et al., 2022; . By using data analysis and insights, universities and colleges can adjust their strategies and campaigns to ensure they are reaching and engaging their target audience effectively.

2. METHODOLOGY

The researchers take into consideration different kinds of social media used and the nature of content shared by the selected higher education institutions in the GCC region, to gain interesting insights through comparative analysis to discover the critical success factors for the desired objectives. The research also aims to find out how these higher education institutions are positively influencing their intended online communities through creating the timely, authentic, relevant and updated content on a regular basis. The findings can be used to create an appropriate framework and a set of guidelines for other educational institutions to derive the maximum benefit by using social media for their intended audiences. The GCC region is undergoing rapid transformation during the last many years (Magd & Khan,2022a). Dubai for instance, has been attracting tourists from all over the world and Qatar on the other hand has been able to draw the world's attention for hosting the FIFA world cup.

In addition, the region is focusing on improving its higher education standards as well and trying to attract students from across the world. The GCC HEIs, like their counterparts across the world, are strengthening their online presence to cater to the needs and expectations of the global audience. The researches will be comparing their digital marketing endeavors through social media best practices undertaken by the top universities in countries constituting the GCC region including Oman, UAE, Saudi Arabia, Bahrain, Qatar and Kuwait, by referring to the academic rankings determined by international bodies on a regular basis. The researchers will particularly focus on the social media platforms including the Facebook, Instagram and Twitter to make comparative analysis to find out the best practices. Utilizing the tools and concepts from Social Media Analytics and Netnography (Ahuja & Alavi, 2018), the study aims to gain interesting insights for social media use in the higher education arena in the GCC region, which can be used to develop model guidelines for other educational institutions.

3. FINDINGS

Since its establishment more than 40 years ago, the Gulf Cooperation Council is working on several shared objectives for a better future. One of the main objectives is fostering scientific and technical progress for which the HEIs play a pivotal role in the member states. In order to do so effectively, they are using digital marketing and indulging in social media practices to interact with their intended audiences. An overview of the interesting statistics (accessed on January 24, 2023) is provided below analysing one example of a leading university from each member state of GCC:

3.1 Sultanate of Oman

As the top public university in Oman, Sultan Qaboos University is effectively engaged in digital marketing and uses multiple social media platforms to engage the intended audiences. As per the information from the university's website, www.squ.edu.om, social media platforms like Facebook, YouTube and Instagram are frequently used to achieve the desired objectives.

Created in September 2010, the university's Facebook page has 13K followers currently. The page exhibits useful information regarding the university's academic achievements and research projects in an engaging manner. The content shared uses both Arabic and English language to cater to the preferences of a wider group of people. With engaging graphics, short videos and useful content the Facebook page is able to attract the audiences in an excellent manner. Created in September 2012, The university's Twitter account, 173.6K followers currently. It is used to share information in a timely, consistent and engaging manner. Launched in 2014, the university's YouTube channel has 10.5K subscribers. with 1,476,023 views currently. It shows engaging content related to the university's ongoing academic and research endeavours. The university also has a strong presence on Instagram with 46.1 K followers.

3.2 United Arab Emirates

As the top public higher educational institution in UAE, the United Arab Emirates University makes consistent endeavours to engage in digital marketing and effective social media practices. The university's engaging website, https://uaeu.ac.ae, gives the visitors an option for a live chat which gives the visitors a welcoming feeling. Created in January 2013, the University's Facebook page currently has 10K followers with engaging content shared both in English and Arabic language in order to reach to the wider audiences. Created in February 2012, the university's Twitter account has 52.9K followers. The university also has a strong presence on LinkedIn with 125,272 followers. The university's Instagram page has 38.6K followers. One of the interesting findings was that the university has a dedicated mobile app with innovative features useful for the students, faculty and staff and Alumni.

3.3 Kingdom of Saudi Arabia

As the leading university in Saudi Arabia, King Abdul Aziz University has a strong presence in social media and uses digital marketing effectively. As per the information from the university's official website, www.kau.edu.sa, there are various social media platforms which are frequently used by the university. Launched in August 2008, the university's YouTube channel currently has 1.73K Subscribers with 366,934 views. The university's Facebook page, launched on May 2009, currently has 109K followers. The content is shared both in English and Arabic languages to get it to the wider community effectively. Created in November 2009, the university's Twitter account 1.7M followers currently which shows the university's big impact on the intended audiences. Both English and Arabic languages are used to share the content.

3.4 State of Qatar

Being a top higher educational institution, Qatar University has managed to have a strong social media presence as indicated on its official website, www.qu.edu.qa. The university is effectively using digital marketing and social media for its academic and research endeavours. The university's Facebook page has 214,138 followers. The information shred is bilingual – both in English in Arabic languages. Created in May 2007, the university's YouTube channel currently has 14.9K subscribers with 1,994,235 views. The University has a strong presence on LinkedIn with 108,861 followers, which shows the university's strength in establishing strong professional networking opportunities. The university's Twitter account has 315K Followers, sharing bilingual content in English and Arabic languages. The university also has a strong presence on Instagram with 115K followers.

3.5 Kingdom of Bahrain

As the top public university, University of Bahrain engages in digital marketing opportunities and follows social media practices to interact with its audiences. As per the information from the official website, www.uob.edu.bh, there are various social media platforms used by the university. University of Bahrain has a Facebook account which with 14,940 followers with high resolution graphics pictures, creating an engaging visual experience for viewers. Created in January 2011, the university has 38.6K followers on its Twitter account. Created in August 2012, the university's YouTube channel has 3.44K subscribers with 435,573 views currently. The university has 109K followers on Instagram. The presence on LinkedIn can definitely be improved which currently has 543 followers.

3.6 State of Kuwait

As the leading university, Kuwait University is present on various social media platforms and uses digital marketing for its academic and research endeavours. As per the university's official website, www.kuniv.edu.kw, the university is actively engaged in Twitter and Instagram. Created in January 2011, the university's Twitter account has 151.9K followers, sharing bilingual content in English and Arabic languages. The university has 127K followers on Instagram, showing a strong presence.

4. DISCUSSION AND INSIGHTS

The statistics about the digital marketing and social media usage of these HEIs provide interesting insights. They are very active on Instagram, Facebook, Twitter, YouTube and LinkedIn. Being within the GCC region, all these HEIs use bilingual content (both in English and Arabic) in their digital marketing and social media accounts.

All these platforms provide distinct benefits to the HEIs as different types of audiences might prefer to engage in a particular type of social media. Young population, for example, may have inclination to use Instagram more as compared to Facebook. Other group of audiences more interested in professional networking opportunities may prefer to interact more with LinkedIn platform. YouTube appeals to audiences interested in more engaging and detailed information though videos. Twitter on the other hand provides the micro-blogging capabilities which the audiences find easier to use because of time constraints.

Some digital marketing practices can provide distinct competitive advantage to HEIs. The use of multilingual live chat option on HEIs official websites, for example, can be very useful for the visitors - be it the students, parents, researches, staff members or even alumni. It can lead to enhanced confidence in the offerings by a particular HEI. Similarly, going for smart portions like a dedicated HEI-centered mobile app can make things much easier leading to a positive impact on all stakeholders.

Another important aspect is the nature of content shared on the social media. Again, if the audience-specific content is created, it will be more likely to have an overall positive impact on the intended audiences. Students' parents, for examples, will be really interested to watch the content related to the Graduation Ceremonies. On the other hand, researchers will be inclined to watch the HEI's endeavors in ongoing and potential research projects and consultancies. As the digital media has a global reach, the choice of words and phrases, engaging high-resolution graphics do play a critical in influencing the audiences' perception positively. Content produced with the specific intent in mind will be more impactful to the audiences, for example, focusing on the academic and research brilliance, world-class educators, exceptional campus facilities, value-added educational experience, well-rounded curriculum focusing on the desired graduate attributes, teaching and learning activities, success stories, testimonials, theme-based activities, excellent event coverage and effective collaborations with other academic and research institutions.

4.1 Academic and Research Brilliance

Social media content focused on the academic and research brilliance can have a profound impact on the audiences. The academic developments and research contributions can be effectively highlighted in the social media. HEI's enhanced global ranking, for example, can be prominently displayed and projected through the social media accounts. On the other hand, research having a profound impact on society can be highlighted accordingly, endorsing the HEI's leading role in a particular research field, for example, physical or social sciences.

4.2. Exceptional Faculty

Being the backbone of every educational institution, the educators play a pivotal role in achieving the organizational objectives. In case the HEI is able to attract globally recognized, distinguished and prize-winner faculty members, their presence can be highlighted prominently on the social media accounts. In addition to boosting the confidence of stakeholders, it will add much more value to the HEI in general.

4.3. Exceptional Campus Facilities

A University's campus is like a second home for many students. If the campus is self-contained and provides necessary facilities for the well-rounded development of students, such aspects can be effectively highlighted on the social media. Such facilities can be used as a competitive advantage as well, for example, having exceptional access to digital and physical learning resources, high-quality dining, sports and recreational facilities. Such a conducive environment plays a vital role for the continued success of a university.

4.4. Alumni's Success Stories

HEI's distinguished alumni who have been able to add value and contribute positively to the society, can be highlighted on the social media. Their detailed success stories can provide enormous amount of confidence to the existing students while attracting many potential students in future. Such alumni can be regularly invited as the guest speakers on campus so to have meaningful interaction with the students and faculty alike. On the other hand, such a content endorses the HEI's claim to develop their alumni in particular graduate attributes.

4.5. Theme-Based Activities

HEI can take a leading role in conceptualizing, organizing and implementing theme-based activities, which add value to the society. For example, blood donation campaign, cancer awareness campaign or creating awareness about the important cultural and social issues impacting the society at large, for example, cyber-bullying, which can provide useful insights to various audiences of a university. Such a content helps to strengthen the HEI's perception as a responsible organization in terms of community engagement.

4.6. University Graduate Attributes

All universities try to inculcate certain attributes in their graduates which distinguish them from others. The specific attributes may differ from one university to the other but generally they might fall in the areas of effective communication, innovation, leadership and being responsible citizens. The university can make constant endeavors to highlight its efforts in developing the graduates in the intended attributes through ongoing curricular and extra-curricular activities. It will create a positive perception about the university's graduates in the eyes of all stakeholders especially the employers and will be particularly beneficial during the job interviews or other assignments.

4.7. Effective Collaborations

All good universities strive to maintain long-term and mutually beneficial relationship with other institutions for better future. They can have MoUs focusing on particular aspects of development and go for shared resources, faculty and student exchange program, joint training and development programs. The HEI can regularly highlight its endeavors in terms of collaborations with other academic and research institutions. Such collaborations both at national and international level, can help the HEI in maintaining or even excelling in their academic or research strengths. At the same time, the HEI can learn from others in the academic and research areas where it would like to focus in future, as the other institution might have better resources to focus on such areas.

5. LIMITATIONS OF THE STUDY

The researchers have considered a leading university from each member states of GCC for the sake of analysis. In future, the number can be increased to more universities for future research, increasing the sample size and the resultant generalizability of findings. At the same time, more social media platforms, as evolved from time to time, can be added in the future studies to gain further interesting insights into the online communities' behavior. Further analysis can be done on the use of social media by keeping in mind the demographic variables. Time constrains also pose challenges for the depth of analysis which can be improved in future studies.

6. CONCLUSION AND FUTURE DIRECTIONS

The analysis shows that the chosen universities in GCC are effectively using digital marketing and engaged in social media practices. Some of them are playing innovative role by indulging in best practices which can be used as benchmark for others. A dedicated mobile app for example, or a strong presence in media for providing excellent processional networking opportunities, can be used as competitive advantage in today's dynamic environment. The study highlights the productive role played by HEIs in today's net-centric economy by finding out the best practices in their digital marketing efforts particularly in effectively managing the social media platforms. Insights from the current research can be used as impetus for further research in the MENA region and finally leading to the global stage, where the information can be obtained from other universities of repute, excelling in the use of digital marketing and social media. The insights have implication on all the HEIs in the GCC, education consultancies, digital marketers, businesses and other stakeholders who are interested in the field of Digital Marketing. For future research endeavors, efforts can be focused on exploring the current issues further and analyzing the emerging trends in the use of digital marketing and social media in more innovative ways.

REFERENCES

Abdullah, M. H. T., Jing, H. F., Ridzuan, A. R., & Zainodin, W. H. W. (2019). Blog: A platform towards democratization of information in Malaysia. *International Journal of Academic Research in Business & Social Sciences*, *9*(3), 626–640. doi:10.6007/IJARBSS/v9-i3/5731

Ahuja, V., & Alavi, S. (2018). Using Facebook as a digital tool for developing trust amongst consumers using netnography and social media analytics: A study of Jet Airways. *Journal of Relationship Marketing*, *17*(3), 171–187. doi:10.1080/15332667.2018.1440145

Al-Abdallah, G., Khair, N., & Elmarakby, R. (2021). The impact of social networking sites on luxury vehicles purchase decision process in Gulf Cooperation Council countries. *Journal of International Consumer Marketing*, *33*(5), 559–577. doi:10.1080/08961530.2020.1867023

Alexa, E. L., Alexa, M., & Stoica, C. M. (2012). The use of online marketing and social media in higher education institutions in Romania. *Journal of Marketing Research & Case Studies*, *2012*, 1–9. doi:10.5171/2012.721221

AlSadrah, S. A. (2021). Social media use for public health promotion in the Gulf Cooperation Council: An overview. *Saudi Medical Journal*, *42*(1), 9–20. doi:10.15537mj.2021.1.25470 PMID:33399166

Baumann, S. (2022). Geopolitical Overview of Social Media Platforms: From Beijing to Berlin. The SAGE Handbook of Social Media Marketing, 183.

Bocar, A. C., Khan, S. A., & Epoc, F. (2022). COVID-19 Work from Home Stressors and the Degree of its Impact: Employers and Employees Actions. *International Journal of Technology Transfer and Commercialisation. Inderscience, 19*(2), 270–291.

Chaffey, D., & Ellis-Chadwick, F. (2019). *Digital marketing.*

Dhingra, M., & Mudgal, R. K. (2019, March). Historical evolution of social media: an overview. In *International Conference on Advances in Engineering Science Management & Technology (ICAESMT),* Uttaranchal University. 10.2139srn.3395665

Ghorfi, T., & Hatimi, I. E. (2020). Impact of Social Media Usage on MENA Countries Economy. *Business and Social Media in the Middle East: Strategies, Best Practices and Perspectives*, 77-99.

Hanaysha, J. R., & Momani, A. M. (2021). An exploration of social media marketing features and brand loyalty in the fast food industry. *Journal of content community and communication, 14*(8), 81-92.

Hassib, B., & Shires, J. (2022). Cybersecurity in the GCC: From Economic Development to Geopolitical Controversy. *Middle East Policy, 29*(1), 90–103. doi:10.1111/mepo.12616

Heydemann, S. (2020). Rethinking social contracts in the MENA region: Economic governance, contingent citizenship, and state-society relations after the Arab uprisings. *World Development, 135*, 105019. doi:10.1016/j.worlddev.2020.105019

Himelein-Wachowiak, M., Giorgi, S., Devoto, A., Rahman, M., Ungar, L., Schwartz, H. A., Epstein, D. H., Leggio, L., & Curtis, B. (2021). Bots and misinformation spread on social media: Implications for COVID-19. *Journal of Medical Internet Research, 23*(5), e26933. doi:10.2196/26933 PMID:33882014

Hollebeek, L. D., & Macky, K. (2019). Digital content marketing's role in fostering consumer engagement, trust, and value: Framework, fundamental propositions, and implications. *Journal of Interactive Marketing, 45*(1), 27–41. doi:10.1016/j.intmar.2018.07.003

Jones, M. O. (2022). *Digital authoritarianism in the Middle East: Deception, disinformation and social media.* Hurst Publishers.

Kamal, S., Naim, A., Magd, H., Khan, S. A., & Khan, F. M. (2022). The Relationship Between E-Service Quality, Ease of Use, and E-CRM Performance Referred by Brand Image. In *Building a Brand Image Through Electronic Customer Relationship Management* (pp. 84–108). IGI Global. doi:10.4018/978-1-6684-5386-5.ch005

Khan, S. A., Devi, T. P., Ligori, T. A. A., & Saleem, M. (2020). Customer Satisfaction and Customer Loyalty in Online Shopping: A Study On University Students of Bhutan. *Delhi Business Review, 21*(2), 11–22. doi:10.51768/dbr.v21i2.212202002

Khan, S.A, Epoc, F., Gangwar,V.P., Ligori T.A.A, Ansari, Z.A. (2021). Will Online banking sustain in Bhutan post Covid – 19? A quantitative analysis of the customer e-satisfaction and e-loyalty in the Kingdom of Bhutan, *Transnational Marketing Journal, 9*(3), 607-624. doi:10.33182/tmj.v9i3.1288

Khan. S.A. & Magd. H. (2021). Empirical Examination of MS Teams in Conducting Webinar: Evidence from International Online Program conducted in Oman. *Journal of Content, Community and Communication, 14.* doi:10.31620/JCCC.12.21/13

Kushwaha, B. P., Singh, R. K., Varghese, N., & Singh, V. N. (2020). Integrating social media and digital media as new elements of integrated marketing communication for creating brand equity. *Journal of Content. Community & Communication, 11*(6), 52–64.

Langan, R., Cowley, S., & Nguyen, C. (2019). The state of digital marketing in academia: An examination of marketing curriculum's response to digital disruption. *Journal of Marketing Education, 41*(1), 32–46. doi:10.1177/0273475318823849

Ligori, T. A. A., Suresh, N., Khan, S. A., Rabgay, T., & Yezer, K. (2022). The mediating effect of university image on the relationship between curriculum and student satisfaction: An empirical study of the Royal University of Bhutan. *International Journal of Pluralism and Economics Education. Inderscience, 13*(2), 192–208.

Magd, H., & Khan, S. A. (2022a). Strategic Framework for Entrepreneurship Education in Promoting Social Entrepreneurship in GCC Countries During and Post COVID-19. In Magd. H., Syed, R.T., Spicer, D. (Eds). International Perspectives on Value Creation and Sustainability Through Social Entrepreneurship (pp. 61-75). IGI Global.

Magd. H., & Khan. S.A. (2022b). Effectiveness of using online teaching platforms as communication tools in higher education institutions in Oman: Stakeholders perspectives. *Journal of Content, Community and Communication, 16*. doi:10.31620/JCCC.12.22/13

Magd, H., Nzomkunda, A., Negi, S., & Ansari, M. (2022). Critical Success Factors of E-Learning Implementation in Higher Education Institutions: A Proposed Framework for Success. *Global Business and Management Research*, 14.

Matta, H., Gupta, R., & Agarwal, S. (2020, June). Search Engine optimization in digital marketing: present scenario and future scope. In *2020 International Conference on Intelligent Engineering and Management (ICIEM)* (pp. 530-534). IEEE. 10.1109/ICIEM48762.2020.9160016

Meier, A., & Reinecke, L. (2021). Computer-mediated communication, social media, and mental health: A conceptual and empirical meta-review. *Communication Research, 48*(8), 1182–1209. doi:10.1177/0093650220958224

Saleem, M., Khan, S. A., & Magd, H. (2022). Content Marketing Framework for Building Brand Image: A Case Study of Sohar International School, Oman. In Building a Brand Image Through Electronic Customer Relationship Management (pp. 64-83). IGI Global.

Talwar, S., Dhir, A., Kaur, P., Zafar, N., & Alrasheedy, M. (2019). Why do people share fake news? Associations between the dark side of social media use and fake news sharing behavior. *Journal of Retailing and Consumer Services, 51*, 72–82. doi:10.1016/j.jretconser.2019.05.026

Vásquez, G. A. N., & Escamilla, E. M. (2014). Best practice in the use of social networks marketing strategy as in SMEs. *Procedia: Social and Behavioral Sciences, 148*, 533–542. doi:10.1016/j.sbspro.2014.07.076

Younies, H., & Na, T. (2020). Effect of cybercrime laws on protecting citizens and businesses in the United Arab Emirates (UAE). *Journal of Financial Crime, 27*(4), 1089–1105. doi:10.1108/JFC-04-2020-0055

Chapter 3
Impact of IoT Applications Using Digital Marketing

Iswarya B.
https://orcid.org/0000-0002-0011-1603
SNMV College of Arts and Science, India

Saju Mathew
https://orcid.org/0000-0003-1947-6351
SNMV College of Arts and Science, India

ABSTRACT

Internet of things (IoT) is one of the new technologies that is expanding exponentially and is presenting new opportunities in a variety of industries, including business, academics, healthcare, transportation, industry, environment, and making our home and cities smart, among others. The IoT system's smart gadgets will be able to perceive, gather, and transport data via the internet without the need for human interaction. Large businesses strive to include technology into their marketing or digital marketing plan that reshapes consumers' expectations, attitudes, and requirements toward businesses in addition to communication style and product promotion. Due to the utilization of several smart devices, networks, and software that are weak and susceptible to hacking, it has a number of security vulnerabilities. The study focuses on the impression of IoT in digital marketing, IoT surface attack and security flaws, technological and security issues in digital marketing, and tries to present some preventive solutions for using IoT's in digital marketing.

INTRODUCTION

One of the recent current technological innovations with the quickest rate of development is the internet of things (IoT). IoT Analytics predicts that by 2030, there will probably be more than 30 billion linked devices worldwide. In the year 1999 Radio Frequency Identification (RFID) technology and networked computing devices, came together and gave birth to a new technology called as Internet of Things (IoT) and which can be simply defined as - a network of connected devices (Vermesan & Friess, 2014). The term "device" can be used to describe anything from computers to smartphones to vehicles to home

DOI: 10.4018/978-1-6684-8166-0.ch003

furnishings to manufacturing equipment to medical implants to entire structures, and the list goes on. Figure 1 shows the various technologies and fields where IoT is used.

Figure 1. Various technologies and fields where IoT is used

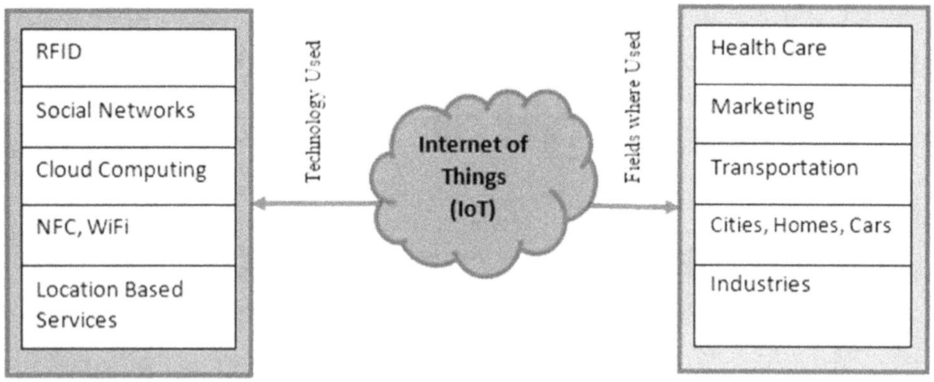

International Data Corporation (IDC) defines an IoT solution as "a network of uniquely identifiable endpoints that communicate without human interaction using IP connectivity – whether locally or globally. IoT brings meaning to the concept of ubiquitous connectivity for businesses, governments, and consumers with its innate management, monitoring and analytics".

IoT-enabled data collection, processing, and sharing provide consumers and businesses with a wide range of advantages. For instance, by implementing IoT devices, it is feasible to conduct electronic illness diagnosis, treatment, and prevention (Vermesan & Friess, 2014). Additionally, it is possible to incorporate consuming appliances into a single Internet of Things system, improving the effectiveness of power consumption (Ray, 2018). In marketing, IoT-connected smart employments can track product supply and eventually make suggestions to the owners about new purchases, deals, and fashions.

IoT defines a wide span of intercommunication among various web-oriented gadgets utilized for day-to-day needs. These gadgets will gather and perusal details, remit info by wifi and BT gesture. The marketing team can hold the info to generate effective perception, find design express to patron relationships. It will reinforce to imagine consumers priority and associate them to plan to buy.

IoT enabled devices will live with us in our daily routine as Smart Tv, Smart appliances, Smart watch and so on. It interacts with human and machine as a, IoT will assist the business doing team to enhance their business to reach an enormous growth and to achieve lot. With the help of ads played as 30 sec videos will promote their product. Apart from *traditional marketing* like TV, Radio nowadays *digital marketing* with IoT mounted sensors will promote the products and reach the customers in easy way. The public stated a query that "A sensor mounted on a device is possible to interact with human or machine to transmit an info".

In current scenario, there is a collection of gadgets that function as fragment of the Internet of Things, it includes

- Trendy devices which are attracted by all range of people is fitness gadgets to track and transmit the fitness related info.

- Traditional home appliances are rejuvenated as smart Refrigerators, washing machine, coffee maker.
- AI voice assistants such as Googles nest and Home, Amazons Alexa or Apples Siri will assist the public.

Example: While travellers moving on the road, they have to find a nearby fuel or gas stations, restaurants, malls, etc., IoT enabled devices will assist them by providing them some offers.

Comparing to offline, shopping buyers are showing interest to purchase the items in online itself because they can view multiple stores and enormous number of products and also possible to compare the price of the products. *Digital marketing* plays a major role with integrating these devices to analyse the human mind whether they have any intend to purchase a product via video clips. Today everything is in our hand at our door step itself with the help of IoT and growth of online marketing is shown in Figure 2.

Figure 2.

While the person surf anything, immediately there will be a message or video clips related to the products which is recently surfed on the browser or apps. There is a possibility to answer a query by making selection on the form or list, viewing or purchasing frequent products will track our info and create an opportunity to enhance the online marketing. This is the marketing strategy with the assistance of IoT enabled devices.

The internet of things can be used for various digital marketing activities, including

- Audience targeting
- Data collection
- Customer communication

- Product and Service promotion

In the recent times, IoT devices are considered as a crucial component of digital marketing. IoT devices, along with other cutting-edge technologies like social media, artificial intelligence, and machine learning, are used by businesses to advertise a range of goods and services (Lo & Campos, 2018). IoT devices are mostly used for marketing data collection, customer communication, and trend and performance indicator analysis. There are numerous uses for IoT in business analytics (Vermesan & Friess, 2014). The functions of IoT in business analytics and marketing is less significant due to its security and privacy issues (Vermesan & Friess, 2014; Ray, 2018; Orme, 2019). In contrast to its theoretical evolution, the practical development of the Internet of Things and digital marketing as a whole has far outpaced its theoretical foundation. Consequently, there is a greater demand for scientific investigation because it can include numerous risks and dangers. (Vermesan & Friess, 2014).

There are greater options for risk and threat removal as scientific study becomes more thorough. When talking about the Internet of Things and its prospects, one of the most frequently brought up problems and threats is its security and privacy. Three significant difficulties that must be adequately addressed by all IoT network stakeholders are consent on data transfer from users, freedom of choice, and anonymity (Vermesan & Friess, 2014. This issue is particularly significant when it comes to marketers gathering customer personal information for commercial purposes.

IoT has the potential to be a technology that will help marketing in all of its forms. Furthermore, its technical capabilities will enable marketers to develop and carry out marketing initiatives in an exclusively original manner. The most important thing, which needs to be highlighted, is the consumer convenience and their behavior (Irakli, & Marcin, 2016).

2. LITERATURE REVIEW

Murali et al. (2020) reveals about IoT applications, attack surfaces and security flaws, technological and security issues with preventative solutions, and IoT's future orientations. The IoT system's smart gadgets will be able to perceive, gather, and transport data via the internet without the need for human interaction. Due to the utilisation of several smart devices, networks, and software that are weak and susceptible to hacking, it has a number of security vulnerabilities.

Salman Zafar et al. (2022) details about impact of IoT in digital marketing, that there is a sizable group of satisfied customers and merchants. Digital marketing is well regarded by all types of business moguls due to the marketers' quick reactions and even quicker catering of services and query resolution. Everyone active in the market has become more closer to one another.

John Hughes (2020) discuss the development of digital marketing, the outlook for it, and takeaways for the future. Like all other industries, digital marketing is constantly changing as new technologies are developed. In order to stay in touch with your audience, it's important to be current. Nevertheless, in order to properly grasp contemporary approaches and ideas, it's also important to understand the field's past.

Desai et. al. (2019) objective is to describe about digital marketing, how it benefits modern businesses, and some instances presented as examples. As more and more businesses incorporate digital platforms, marketing strategies and daily lives are changing as more individuals switch to using digital gadgets Visits to physical stores are declining as more people use digital marketing tactics.

Yogesh K et. al. (2021) combines the collective wisdom of a number of top authorities on topics pertaining to social media and digital marketing. The perspectives of the experts provide a thorough narrative on the most important aspects of this subject as well as viewpoints on more specialised issues like artificial intelligence, marketing using augmented reality, digital content management, mobile marketing and advertising, B2B marketing, electronic word of mouth, and related ethical concerns. This research offers a significant and timely contribution to both researchers and practitioners in the form of challenges and opportunities where we highlight the limitations within the current research, outline the research gaps and develop the questions and propositions that can help advance knowledge within the domain of digital and social marketing.

3. LAYERED IoT ARCHITECTURE

The term "internet of things" refers to a huge network that connects various sensors, actuators, microcontrollers, and wide range of interconnected devices, including smartphones, commercial machinery, computers, automobiles, medical equipment, etc. IoT is also a relatively new design that differs from all of its predecessors, including all conventional, mobile, and sensor-based Internet networks and varieties of hybrid terminals. Since the bulk of these gadgets offer Internet connectivity, they typically support popular web technologies like HTTP, JSON, XML Wifi, etc. One of the advantage of using this technology is highly maintained well supported and highly adaptable to the different existing infrastructures. Since IoT is not standardized, there are numerous unique architectures related to it (Burhan et al., 2018). Five-layered architecture includes – Perception layer, networking layer, processing layer, application layer, and business layer.

Figure 3. Five-layered IoT architecture

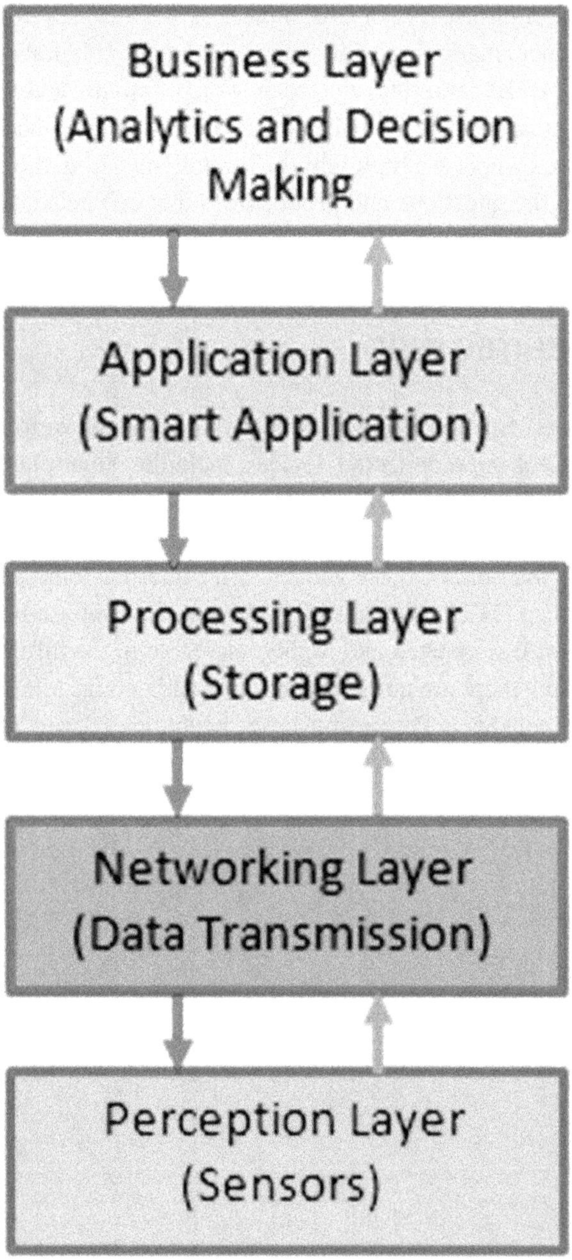

The IoT architecture can be described as,

1. **Perception Layer:** The IoT architecture's first tier is the perception layer. It comprises of sensors and actuators to measure some values like as temperature, pH, light, gas, and so on, and to detect

some functionality such as location, position and motion. It is connected to the physical world for sensing and collecting data from their environment.

2. **Networking Layer**: The second tier in the architecture is the network layer, which connects to multiple servers, gateways, and smart devices. It is in charge of sending the recorded values to other IoT network elements. These factors lead to the Internet of Things (IoT) utilizing a variety of communication standards and protocols, including 4G/5G, Wi-Fi, Bluetooth, WiMAX, and others (Atlam et al., 2018).
3. **Processing Layer**: The third tier of the IoT architecture is the processing layer, also known as the middleware layer, and which is a crucial part of an IoT system design. It often uses several linked computers at once, in the form of cloud computing, to give greater computation, storage, networking, and security performance. Processing layer is in charge of interpreting input data to produce fresh insights, useful predictions, and timely warnings. An IoT system often manages massive data volumes produced by several edge devices at numerous points on the network's edges.

The "middleware" of the processing layer prepares this data for the application layer in three steps:

a. **Data Accumulation:** Different data kinds are accurately recognized and assigned to the proper storage by middleware. Unstructured data is generally stored in data lakes because it takes up more storage space and includes things like audio and video feeds and photographs. While organized data, such as measurements, log values, and instrument readings (telemetry data), takes up less space and is kept in data warehouses.
b. **Data Abstraction:** It requires combining information from several sources and making sure that the information is transformed into a format that can be "read" by the application layer's software.
c. **Data Analysis:** It utilizes techniques for machine learning (ML) or deep learning, which are skilled at finding patterns in enormous, seemingly random data sets.
    4. **Application Layer:** It is the fourth tier of IoT architecture is which is responsible for deciphering promising patterns in IoT data and assembling them into summaries that are simple to comprehend for humans, including graphs and tables. Applications for device monitoring and control, as well as process control software, are typical examples of IoT architecture's application layer.
    5. **Business Layer:** It is the fifth tier of the IoT architecture. In this layer patterns can be decoded to further elucidate business insights, forecast future trends, and guide operational decisions that enhance productivity, security, cost-effectiveness, customer satisfaction, and other crucial business functionality factors. In fact, all of this is possible at the IoT system architecture's business layer.

4. DIGITAL MARKETING

All marketing initiatives that make use of technology or the Internet fall under the category of digital marketing. To engage with present and potential customers, businesses use digital channels including search engines, social media, email, and their websites. The terms "online marketing," "Internet marketing," and "web marketing" can also be used to describe the digital marketing. Digital marketing can be defined as utilizing a variety of digital strategies and platforms to connect with clients online for promoting their goods or services with digital technology, primarily the Internet but also incorporating mobile devices, display ads, and other digital media. A wide range of strategies fall under the category of "digital marketing," including websites, email marketing, online brochures, and other online branding assets for businesses (Desai, 2019).

Digital marketing methods such as Search Engine Optimization (SEO), Search Engine Marketing (SEM), Content Marketing, influencer marketing, content automation, campaign marketing, data-driven marketing, e-commerce marketing, social media marketing, social media optimization, e-mail direct marketing, display advertising, e–books, and optical disks and games are becoming more common in advancing technology. Digital marketing now extends to non-Internet channels that provide digital media, such as mobile phones (SMS and MMS), callback, and on-hold mobile ring tones.

With the introduction of server/client architecture and the widespread use of personal computers in 1990s, "digital marketing" was first introduced; Customer Relationship Management (CRM) software emerged as a key component of marketing technology. Vendors were compelled by fierce competition to include more services, such as apps for marketing, sales, and service, into their software. With the development of Internet technology, marketers were also able to own vast amounts of online customer data. Companies were able receive and update customer's basic data.

In the early 2000's the development in the Internet technology has helped customers to conduct product research and were able to make online decisions about their needs before consulting any sales persons. Growth in the Internet users and the introduction of the iPhone, presented a new challenge for a company's marketing department. Additionally, a survey conducted in 2000 in the United Kingdom revealed that the majority of retailers had not set up their own domain name. These issues forced marketers to look for digital means of market expansion.

The growth of digital marketing since the 1990s and 2000s has altered how companies and brands use technology for marketing. Digital marketing efforts are becoming more common and effective as more and more people use digital devices instead of going to physical stores and as digital platforms are integrated into marketing strategies and daily life.

By the year, 2010 there was a significant increase in the number of devices that could access digital media, and digital marketing grew more sophisticated and was within the reach for all the users. Recent statistics indicated that the digital marketing industry was continuing expanding. Customers developed a strong reliance on digital devices in daily life because of the rise of social media, including LinkedIn, Facebook, YouTube, and Twitter. They anticipated a seamless user experience when looking for product information through various media. The diversification of marketing technologies was improved by the shift in consumer behavior. By the year 2015, "digital marketing" has become the worldwide used term. With the introduction and incorporation of Internet of Things (IoT) in today's marketing field, the digital marketing has taken a new dimension.

To accurately gauge the performance of the business across each channel and the gadgets used, the digital marketer focuses on different key performance indicators (KPI) for each one. In small businesses, one or two marketing employees might be controlling all the digital marketing strategies. These same strategies in larger businesses employ a number of specialists, each of whom focuses on just one or two of the brand's digital platforms.

4.1 Methodologies in Digital Marketing

Figure 4. Various methodology used in the digital marketing

Following are some of the methodologies that can be used in the digital marketing.

1. **Search Engine Optimization (SEO):** It is the process of making changes to your website so that it "ranks" higher in search engine results pages, hence boosting the amount of natural (or free) traffic that your website receives. Sites like blogs, infographics, and websites all benefit from SEO.
2. **Content Marketing:** The term "content marketing" refers to the process of producing and disseminating information assets with the aim of increasing traffic, generating leads, and attracting consumers. Content marketing plan can use a variety of channels, such as blog postings, whitepapers and e-books, infographics, online brochures, and books.
3. **Social Media Marketing:** It is the technique of promoting company's name and online content to attract more customers, raise brand recognition, and improve traffic to website. You can utilise Facebook, Twitter, LinkedIn, Instagram, Snap Chat, Pinterest, and Google+ as social media marketing channels.
4. **Marketing Automation:** Software's that are used to automate routine marketing tasks is referred to as marketing automation. Numerous marketing teams can automate routine duties that would otherwise have to perform manually, including email newsletters, social media post planning, contact list maintenance, lead nurturing processes, campaign tracking, etc.
5. **Pay-per-Click (PPC):** Paying a publisher each time advertisement is clicked is one of the way to increase traffic to your website. Google Ad Words, one of the most popular PPC models, enables you to pay for prominent positions on Google's search engine results pages at a cost "per click" of the links you insert. Paid advertisements on Facebook, promoted tweets on Twitter, and sponsored messages on LinkedIn are a few additional platforms where PPC can be used.
6. **Email Marketing:** Businesses utilize email marketing to reach out to their customers. Email is the most frequently used medium to advertise events, promotions, and special material, as well as to point customers toward a company's website. Blog subscription newsletters, follow-up emails to website visitors who downloaded something, customer welcome emails, holiday promotions to loyalty program members, and tips or similar series emails for customer nurturing are some of the types of emails you might send during an email marketing campaign.
7. **Online Practices:** Online Practices is the activity of obtaining legitimate online press coverage through blogs, content-based websites, and other digital publishers. Varieties of platforms can be used to maximize online practices and they are social media outreach to journalists, engaging comments on your personal website or blog, engaging online reviews of your business, etc.
8. **Business-to-Business (B2B) Digital Marketing:** If a company is engaged in business-to-business (B2B) transactions, its digital marketing initiatives are probably focused on generating online leads with the ultimate objective of getting those leads to contact a salesperson. Marketing department's strategies will be to use the company's website and other supporting digital channels to draw in and convert the highest quality leads for your sales team. In addition to company's website, marketing department might decide to concentrate on business-focused networks like LinkedIn where targeted audience are always active online (Desai, , 2019).
    a. **Business-to-Customer (B2C) Digital Marketing:** In this type of digital marketing depending on the pricing point of the product, the major objective of the business-to-consumer (B2C) companies is to draw the attention of the visitors to the company's website and convert them into customers without ever having to engage with a salesperson. As a result the marketing department of the company does not to concentrate on "leads" in the conventional sense and more likely to concentrate on creating an accelerated buyer those who are visiting the com-

pany's website for the purchase. Channels like Instagram and Pinterest are more important for B2C businesses than business-oriented platforms like LinkedIn.

b. **Collaborative Environment:** To maximize effort, resource sharing, reusability, and communications, a collaborative environment can be established between the company, the technological service provider, and digital agencies. Customers are being invited by businesses to assist in improving their understanding of how to serve them. A large portion of data is obtained via company websites where the business invites people to offer ideas that are then assessed by other website visitors. Utilizing this technique for gathering data and creating new goods can improve an organization's interaction with its customers and generate concepts that might not otherwise be considered.

4.2 Importance of Digital Marketing

The primary benefit of digital marketing is the cost-effective and measurable way in which a specific audience can be addressed. Brand loyalty will rise, and online sales will increase, among other benefits of digital marketing. Following are the advantages of digital marketing:

a. **Worldwide Reach:** Nowadays, a large number of individuals spend most of their time in surfing Internet and search for new products. Digital marketing plays an important role if the companies make use of Internet for promoting their products electronically as a result, they can reach to appropriate targeted audience which lays a foundation stone for the digital marketing. Thus, at minimal investment, a good website may help companies to discover new customers, markets and conduct business internationally. Therefore, in order to increase audience, companies must first build a compelling online store with simple navigation. Pay-Per Click marketing, social media marketing, search engine optimization, content marketing, and other digital marketing strategies can all eventually aid in brand creation during this phase.

2. **Less Expensive:** Compared to traditional marketing strategies, a well-planned and well-targeted digital marketing campaign can reach the relevant clients for significantly less money. At the minimal cost business and brand, reputation can be built, which becomes very crucial for the digital marketing.
3. **Personalization:** With the help of Internet and digital marketing, the companies get the chance to connect to their customers. It enables companies to welcome site visitors with pertinent offers if company's customer database is connected to company's website. Companies can understand their respective consumer profile and customers behavior as a result an online analysis can be taken to provide their fulfillment and effective marketing campaigns can be achieved.
4. **Trackable and Quantifiable Results:** CRO (Conversion rate optimization) is one of the crucial segments while using the digital marketing, which has the ability to track the real-time activities in the digital marketing. The information can be used to understand the overall percentage of searches that result in leads for product purchases. By using the varieties of online marketing effort, web analytics and other metered tools we can determines the success of the online marketing done. Companies can learn in-depth details about how visitors interact with their website or react to their advertisements. Some of the popular avenues for

connecting with people and getting high conversion rates are PPC, Social media marketing, SEO services, and affiliate marketing.

5. **Community Exchange:** Using content marketing strategies and community exchange, digital marketing enables the companies to develop compelling campaigns. These can include pictures, movies, and articles, etc. that have the potential to become viral and gain community exchange.
6. **Getting an Edge on Your Rival:** When it comes to Internet business in particular, the digital industry is must be very competitive. As a result, the companies needs top reviews of their products and an extra efforts needs to be made by various digital marketing agencies to help their potential clients locate their targeted product. These steps can help companies and their client ultimately work toward the proper business objectives (Lavanya & Radhikamani, 2021).

One of the most important aspects of the digital marketing is the competitor analysis and competitor monitoring. The analysis is necessary to stay competitive, especially with rapidly expanding businesses like *Myntra, Amazon, Big Basket, Meesho, Flip cart, and Walmart.* Businesses also make an effort to push the limits of multichannel marketing, which includes PPC, SEO, social media, and numerous other platforms. These strategies will assist both small and large enterprises in achieving their unique objectives.

4.3 IoT Which Affects the Strategies of Digital Marketing

1. Incorporation
2. Drive Through
3. Promoting Opportunities
4. Survey and Acknowledgment
5. Quick-witted Platforms

4.3.1. Incorporation

Internet of Things bears the chance to unlatch consumers behaviour, it starts the process from morning alert to making coffee, cab booking for their routine service, and tracking the fitness info. These gadgets will give a reel data, it is not only vast but also deep. Eventually these data will assist marketing team to clip trusted info to give successful adventure to the consumers.

Example: A diabetes patient can be offered a membership at discount rate nearby pharmacy and online platforms.

4.3.2 Drive Through

In current scenario the universe is in need for quick contentment. Everyone in the universe expect anticipate quick services and if there is any small obstruction, they are not able to accept it and they feel it as missing their chances.

Example: Let us take an example, the smart applications will shop for you from your most likely store.

4.3.3 Promoting Opportunities

The gadgets which are transited via internet will provide a plenty of promoting chances. In future with the development IoT-enabled washing machine will promote a suitable liquid.

Figure 5. The IoT-enabled gadgets

4.3.4 Survey and Acknowledgment

Enormous amount of info created by IoT enabled devices will assist ML algorithms to enhance the abilities of critical thinking. Internet of Things can track and interact with consumers to collect info about their purchase opinions about the products.

4.3.5 Quick-Witted Platforms

A planetary volume of data will be constructed through IoT gadgets to inference its convenience. More money will have to be put into creating intelligent technology stacks that can process huge volumes of data, distribute the proper contents, and predict and benefit from outcomes.

4.4. Challenges of Digital Marketing Using IoT

As any new technical development, Internet of Things also introduces new hazards and vulnerabilities in addition to new opportunities and comfort levels. They could be loosely classified into three categories or threat levels. The first two of these are intertwined: on the one hand, there is a risk to people's health, property, and safety as a result of these attacks, and on the other hand, there are risks related to the massive amount of interconnected IoT elements (smart things, sensors), their vulnerability to physical devices (sensors and other devices can be placed in various locations, making it very difficult to ensure their protection), as well as, more importantly, cyber-attacks.

Recent studies says that new IoT device manufacturers want to hasten their introduction into use in order to take advantage of the cost-saving efficiencies that the IoT may provide due to its widespread adoption and nearly unlimited benefits. Security can, however, occasionally be neglected in the effort to make everything Internet-capable. Many people are ready to install appropriate antivirus protection software on their computers and laptops to guard against online threats. At the same time, individuals frequently disregard many linked, smart products and gadgets that are similarly vulnerable.

From the perspective of marketers, collecting consumer data is one of the most alluring aspects of IoT, but it also sparks concerns about customer security and privacy. IoT technologies can be used to retrieve data that is quite detailed and contains information that could be misused in numerous ways. It will be tough to totally eradicate all hazards and threats from the IoT network due to its size. The most interesting challenge in this process is that there are so many different sources to gather the personal information of the consumer in the IoT, including not only computers and mobile devices but also other wearables, cars, home appliances, medical implants, and other gadgets. Users' actions are monitored routinely and ubiquitously.

With respect to information flow and decision-making, traditional Internet technologies and IoT technologies are managed very differently. For instance, the active components related to data entry are users and web technologies, whereas with the Internet of Things, users are passive and the sources of data are the devices. Web technologies enable data sharing with other providers, as opposed to IoT, where data is exchanged with other devices. People act online in the digital space, whereas with the Internet of Things, users act physically. In the IoT network, devices frequently make decisions instead of their users (Weinberg et al., 2015). Apart from others, such reliance on physical devices raises the possibility of gadget malfunction, which could have a detrimental impact on people's personal lives, financial situations, or even health. Consequences can thus be gravely detrimental and occasionally even lethal. Customers that use IoT technology unwittingly put their trust in service providers, in this case marketing teams, and divulge a lot of sensitive information to them.

One of the hazards that is most commonly brought up is hacking. IoT devices provide a considerably greater risk because hackers frequently target physical things in addition to databases, which can often result dangerous to the consumer. Personal data leaks may cause harm, but they may also endanger human lives. With marketing's viewpoint, hacking a company's database that contains customers' personal information can be harmful not only for the customers who are attacked, but also for the company, which could suffer significant financial loss, reputational damage, a crisis in public relations, and even bankruptcy.

The use of IoT technologies in marketing raises further legal concerns. Customers may file a lawsuit against a firm and demand both moral and financial compensation if personal data is stolen or improperly shared to a third party. Depending on the volume, nature, and quantity of consumers involved, these situations could result in significant harm for a business. There are rule and regulations against the transmission of personal information and unauthorized access to databases, but new issues brought on by the adoption of IoT technology demand additional legislation.

One of the security attack in IoT is denial of service (DOS), which tries to block permitted access to network resources to the authenticated users and entities. It is regarded as the most common and effective attack. Attackers can typically utilize flooding attacks to deplete a system's memory, CPU, and bandwidth (Prabhakar, 2017; Hasan et al., 2018; Javed, Khan, Qahar, & Abdullah, 2017). Thus, it stops the system from offering a service. Pirates can employ a variety of techniques in this assault, including delivering erroneous packets and flooding the network with messages. Therefore, authorized users are blocked from using services. Due to this type of attack, digital marketing that is using IoT connected devices can be hacked or blocked as a result neither the companies nor the consumers can exchange their data's.

Since all the interconnected devices in the IoT are password protected, pirates have developed different methods to obtain the right password or guess the correct password, hence this type of attack is known as password guessing attack. This attack, in particular, can be carried out both online and offline. In this technique, the attacker eavesdrops on two entities' communication during the authentication step in order to obtain some relevant values. To successfully complete the authentication, an attacker must guess every likely password (Hasan et al., 2018; Sharma & Kalra, 2018).

Another technological difficulty for IoT is device compatibility and longevity because IoT systems use a variety of devices for sensing, data collection, data transfer, data analysis, and related operations. These devices all employ unique operating systems, firmware, network protocols, and APIs. Due to a lack of protocol standards, technological standards, and device standards, these devices will have interoperability problems. Durability of the devices is another issue because their lifespan is only a few years. A key issue that will hinder the IoT system's ability to grow in the future is ensuring device consistency and continuity with new devices.

In digital marketing if the IoT connected used devices used by the marketing agencies or companies are not compatible, durable and of good standards then there is high possibility that at any point of time, the devices can tear off, and the companies have to bear the consequences. Various issues that are faced in terms of IoT standards. Few of them are:

1. IoT devices do not adhere to any standards about their resources, accessibility, availability, or access control.
2. One problem with the Internet of Things is the lack of uniform communication among various networks, including wired, wireless, and satellite networks. Another technological difficulty is connecting many devices to different networks.
3. Since the Internet of Things (IoT) system involves numerous networks and devices, there is a lack of unifying software standards to access and operate the various devices.
4. Inadequate uniform storage standards for storing, accessing, and analyzing structured and unstructured data that are generated and recorded by diverse IoT system-enabled devices.
5. As an IoT system comprises numerous devices, networks, computing, and storage devices, there are no standards or operating procedures outlined for monitoring and maintaining an IoT system for a particular application area.

5. SOLUTIONS FOR IoT ISSUES AND EFFECTIVE DIGITAL MARKETING

Several points should be stressed while talking about potential hazards and solutions. Each of them should be handled independently and by various stakeholders. However, there is no absolute assurance that all potential obstacles will be removed because as technology advances, new risks and more sophisticated ways to abuse it also surface. However, the following steps can be performed to reduce damage in different directions (Irakli, & Marcin, 2016):

1. Marketing teams should inform customers that their personal data is saved and utilized for business purposes in order to prevent any confusion and hazards. Data transfer authorization must be required. Highest potential levels of transparency are required. Such a strategy will enable businesses to prevent, or at the very least, minimize, any customer unhappiness and loss. One of the

alternatives can be thought of as assembling a team of skilled specialists that will concentrate solely on safeguarding a company's digital databases. Not all businesses, however, can afford this level of security.

2. The importance of thorough scientific research cannot be overstated. Threats must be eliminated; hence, extensive research must be done. The study approach must be multidisciplinary and include not only technical considerations but also communication and marketing strategies used by businesses. Technologically oriented multinational corporations ought to take the lead in this process since they have both the financial and personnel resources necessary to perform extensive scientific research. Businesses should take into account this process as part of their social responsibility strategy rather than just as a foundation for their future commercial success.
3. Governments play a crucial role in the process of developing legal foundations. Strict laws against the misuse of personal data will greatly reduce the likelihood of thieves and hackers doing so. However, the level of proficiency of the governments of various nations in this area varies greatly. However, the use of the internet and IoT devices is growing globally. As a result, the level of security may not be the same across nations. Various worldwide conferences and seminars should be held on both a governmental and non-governmental level in order to increase awareness and competency.

Following are the solution for some of the basic security issues that IoT faces:

1. **Confidentiality:** The capacity and ability to prevent an unauthorized user from accessing sensitive data can be termed as confidentiality and can be applied at the perception layer of IoT. Therefore, it guarantees that only authorized parties will access, modify, or erase personal information. Confidentiality is one of the key security services, especially in the IoT network. However, the most frequently attacked service is confidentiality (Panchiwala & Shah, 2020). Trojans, spyware, and viruses are a few examples of malware programs that aim to compromise the privacy of a user's personal information. They can interact with the system as scripts or executable codes in order to gain illegal access.

With respect to IoT setting, encryption techniques and cryptographic methods can be used to guarantee and ensure the confidentiality of personal information acquired by sensors and prevent it from being found by a third party (Sharma & Kalra, 2018). As a result, any data sent between two devices needs to be encrypted. So that, only the legitimate entities may understand the transferred message.

2. **Availability:** It means that the tools and data must be readily available to authorized users whenever they need them regardless of their location and time of existence. Since different data transmission networks, channels, and protocols are used, it may cause some resources to become unavailable (Kumar et al., 2019). On the other hand, attackers may employ one of three harmful attacks—a denial of service (DOS), a flooding, or a black hole attack—to harm the availability. It is usually practiced in the availability condition for the first one. Pirates can deploy distributed denial of service (DDOS) attacks or basic denial of service (DOS) attacks, both of which require cooperation from a number of resources.

To ensure the availability of suitable resources, we can choose a distributed approach for running the system and employ a variety of platforms that make it easier to integrate diverse systems remotely" (Somasundaram & Selvam, 2018). The security to availability can placed at the perception and the networking layer of IoT.

3. **Authentication:** One of the toughest part in the IoT network is the authentication service, which can be imposed at the basic IoT layers such as perception, networking and application that incorporates identity verification. The devices must be able to verify the authenticity and validity of remotely using the public network during the authentication process. However, authentication stops when an unauthorized individual joins in a private, secure connection (Panchiwala & Shah, 2020). Previous authentication methods relied just on a single factor, which was a straightforward password. These approaches must deal with a number of password-related problems. Users can quickly forget their password and in addition to it, people might utilize weak passwords. Finally, either by a dictionary attack or an extensive research effort, the attackers are successful in guessing the right password. In the IoT settings one-time password (OTP), sometimes known as a dynamic password can be used as one of the good measures for the authentication. Certificate based authorization, Blockchain mechanisms can also be used for authentication purpose.
4. **Authorization:** Authorization is turning into a crucial problem for the Internet of Things system as the number of connected things are growing rapidly. Authorization can be enforced at the basic IoT layers such as perception, networking and application. Practically, it references to the security service in charge of deciding user privileges and rights such as read, write, or delete. It also lists the access control guidelines for granting or denying authorization to IoT devices. As a result, stop users with restricted access from obtaining illegal access to devices and their data (Garcia-Morchon et al., 2019).
5. **Integrity:** It refers to the fact that no unauthorized party alters the message during transmission. Moreover, it ensures that the entire recipient has received the full message from the source. The basic goal is to prevent an unauthorized person from illegally modifying an object. The system must ensure data integrity and in order to maintain the security of smart devices in IoT networks no user should be allowed to access the unauthorised objects without appropriate authentication and authorization. Integrity can be enforced at the basic IoT layers such as perception, networking, and application.

6. CONCLUSION

The internet of things (IoT) has a big part in the recent rapid growth of technology. These technologies have facilitated data interchange. This study investigated the use of IoT in marketing research. With their creative abilities, IoT solutions have developed to assist marketers in changing conventional marketing research activities and replacing them with more thorough and precise data analysis forms. The usage of IoT solutions has been shown to improve the role and capabilities of information exchange in marketing research. Professionals in digital marketing are now able to improve their research and add new dimensions to marketing by utilizing a variety of IoT technologies and tactics. All parties involved in this process should therefore contribute to its safer, lawful, and advantageous operation. Marketers must create a transparent, in-depth policy outlining how and for what particular goals consumer data will be used. Additionally, they should develop marketing strategies tailored specifically for IoT because customer communication will differ from typical Internet marketing in terms of ways and approaches. It will enable businesses to appropriately develop their goods and services. Furthermore, businesses must reassure their customers that their personal data is stored safely and is safeguarded from outsiders in order to win the customers' trust, which is very crucial in businesses. All the customers need to be fully informed about the specifics of how and why marketers use their personal data. All the personal data that the digital marketing agencies are using should be highly confidential and authenticated.

REFERENCES

Al Hogail, A. (2018). Improving IoT technology adoption through improving consumer trust. *Technologies*, *6*(3), 64–80. doi:10.3390/technologies6030064

Arkhipova, N. & Gurieva, M. (2018). Internet of Things in Digital Marketing and Data Security. *3rd International Conference on Judicial, Administrative and Humanitarian Problems of State Structures and Economic Subjects (JAHP 2018).* Advances in Social Science, Education and Humanities Research (ASSEHR).

Atlam, H. F., Walters, R. J., & Wills, G. B. (2018). Internet of things: State-of-the-art, challenges, applications, and open issues. *International Journal of Intelligent Computing Research*, *9*(3), 928–938. doi:10.20533/ijicr.2042.4655.2018.0112

Bala, M., & Verma, D. (n.d.). A Critical review of Digital Marketing. *IJMRS.* www.ijmrs.us

Bhagowati, & Dutta, D. M. (2018). A study on literature review for identifying the factors impacting digital marketing. *International Journal of Sales & Marketing Management Research and Development*, *8*(3), 1-8.

Burhan, M., Rehman, R., Khan, B., & Kim, B.-S. (2018). IoT elements, layered architectures and security issues: a comprehensive survey. Sensors, 18(9).

Desai, V. (2019). Digital Marketing: A Review. *International Journal of Trend in Scientific Research and Development*, 196–200. doi:10.31142/ijtsrd23100

Murali, A. & Rao, M. (2020). *IoT: Security Issues and Challenges.* ICIDSSD, New Delhi, India. doi:10.4108/eai.27-2-2020.2303127

Desai, V. (2019). Digital Marketing: A Review. *International Journal of Trend in Scientific Research and Development (IJTSRD),* 196-200, www.ijtsrd.com

Garcia-Morchon, O., Kumar, S., & Sethi, M. (2019). Internet of things (IoT) security: state of the art and challenges. RFC.

Hasan, H. C., Yusof, F. N., & Daud, M. (2018). Comparison of authentication methods in internet of things technology. *International Journal of Computer and Systems Engineering*, *12*(3), 231–234.

Hughes, J. (2020). The Evolution of Digital Marketing. *Velocitize*. https://velocitize.com/2020/08/31/the-evolution-of-digital-marketing

Irakli, A. & Marcin, D. (2016). Internet of things in marketing: Opportunities and security issues. *Management Systems in Production Engineering 4*(24). doi:10.12914/MSPE-01-04-2016

Javed, Y., Khan, A., Qahar, A., & Abdullah, J. (2017). Preventing DoS attacks in IoT using AES. *J. Telecommun. Electron.Comput. Eng. JTEC, 9*, 3–11.

Kumar, S., Tiwari, P., & Zymbler, M. (2019). Internet of things is a revolutionary approach for future technology enhancement: a review. *Journal of Big Data*, *6*(1).

Lo, F. Y., & Campos, N. (2018). Blending Internet-of-Things (IoT) solutions into relationship marketing strategies. *Technological Forecasting and Social Change*, *137*, 10–18. doi:10.1016/j.techfore.2018.09.029

Moradi, M. (2021). Importance of Internet of Things (IoT) in Marketing Research and Its Ethical and Data Privacy Challenges. *Business Ethics and Leadership*, *5*(1), 22–30. doi:10.21272/bel.5(1).22-30.2021

Lavanya, A., & Radhikamani, M. (2021). Study on Digital Marketing and its Impact. *International Journal of Creative Research Thoughts, 9*. www.ijcrt.org

Orme, D. (2019). Can biometrics secure the Internet of Things? *Biometric Technology Today*, *5*(5), 5–7. doi:10.1016/S0969-4765(19)30068-2

Panchiwala, S., & Shah, M. (2020). A comprehensive study on critical security issues and challenges of the IoT world. *Journal of Digital Information Management*, *2*(4), 257–278.

Perera, C., Ranjan, R., & Wang, L. (2015). *Privacy of Big Data in the Internet of Things Era*. http://arxiv.org/ftp/arxiv papers/1412/1412.8339.pdf

Prabhakar, S. (2017). Network security in digitalization: Attacks and defence. *International Journal of Research in Computer Applications and Robotics*, *5*(5), 46–52.

Ray, P. P. (2018). A survey on Internet of Things architectures. *Journal of King Saud University-Computer and Information Sciences*, *30*(3), 291–319. doi:10.1016/j.jksuci.2016.10.003

Sharma, G., & Kalra, S. (2018). Identity based secure authentication scheme based on quantum key distribution for cloud computing. *Peer-to-Peer Networking and Applications*, *11*(2), 220–234. doi:10.100712083-016-0528-2

Sharma, G., & Kalra, S. (2018). A lightweight multi-factor secure smart card based remote user authentication scheme for cloud-IoT applications. *Journal of Information Security and Applications*, *42*, 95–106. doi:10.1016/j.jisa.2018.08.003

Somasundaram, K., & Selvam, K. (2018). Iot - attacks and challenges. *International Journal of Engineering and Technical, Research*, *8*(9), 9–12.

Cisco. (2015). *The Internet of Things. Reduce Security Risks with Automated Policies*. Cisco. https://www.cisco.com/c/dam/en_us/solutions/trends/iot/docs/security-risks.pdf

Vermesan, O., & Friess, P. (2014). Internet of Things – from research and innovation to market deployment. *Internet of Things Search*. http://www.internet-of-thingsresearch. eu/pdf/IoT-From%20Research%20and%20Innovation%20to%20Market%20Deployment_IERC_Cluster_eBook_978-87-93102-95-8_P.pdf

Vermesan, O., & Friess, P. (2014). *Internet of Things applications: From research and innovation to market deployment*. River Publishers. https://www.riverpublishers.com/pdf/ebook/RP_E9788793102958.pdf

Weinberg, B., Milne, G., Andonova, Y., & Hajjat, F. (2015). Internet of Things: Convenience vs. privacy and security. *Business Horizons*, *58*(6), 615–624. doi:10.1016/j.bushor.2015.06.005

Yasmin, STasneem, SFatema, K. (2015, April). Effectiveness of digital marketing in the challenging age: An empirical study. *Journal of International Business Research and Marketing*, *1*(5), 69–80.

Chapter 4
Exploring Dependence of Human Resource Management (HRM) on Internet of Things (IoT) and Digital Marketing in the Digital Era

Shafaq Zareen
Vivekananda College, India

Shad Ahmad Khan
https://orcid.org/0000-0001-7593-3487
University of Buraimi, Oman

ABSTRACT

The field of human resource management (HRM) has been impacted by the rise of the internet of things (IoT) in recent years. IoT technology allows for the collection and analysis of data on employee behaviour, performance, and engagement. This data can be used to improve HRM processes such as recruitment, training, and retention. Additionally, IoT technology can be used to improve communication and collaboration between employees and managers. However, there are also concerns about privacy and security when using IoT technology in the workplace. Overall, HRM is becoming increasingly dependent on IoT technology to gather important data and improve processes, but it is important to consider the potential negative impacts and take steps to mitigate them. This chapter has an implication on the organisations of all sizes that may utilise the IoT and digital marketing in strengthening their HRM practices, that shall help them to attract good talent and lead to satisfaction and loyalty among employees.

DOI: 10.4018/978-1-6684-8166-0.ch004

1. INTRODUCTION

In recent time, inquisitiveness and advancement in the field of technology have improved many folds. In such a circumstance, it can be correct to say that technology is the future of the human race. Out of all the advances in the technology, one such development is Internet of Things (IoT) which has penetrated in various sectors like businesses, human resource management, marketing, manufacturing, healthcare, education, sustainability, entertainment and the list is never-ending. Connecting IoT and Digital Marketing in the context of HRM is essentially a good idea (Venkatesh, 2017; Abdussamad et al., 2022; Mohanty & Mishra, 2020).

The current chapter will include the discussion on how the IoT in digital marketing is impacting Human Resource Management (HRM) both positively and negatively in daily working of organizations. Emphasis will also be made on problems faced by Human Resources of various organizations in tracking customers data for the improvement in the products manufactured and in keeping record of employees by these organizations. The second aspect which will be focused in this chapter will be a discussion on Employment opportunities created and modernized with the introduction of Internet of things (IoT). The benefit of matching job seekers with job providers, with the right type of requirements of both and creating an environment which helps in placing the right person on the right job to make them more employable and taking the benefit of right placement of employees to produce more satisfied customers will be discussed in this chapter (Venkatesh, 2017; Abdussamad et al., 2022; Mohanty & Mishra, 2020). The inferences drawn in this chapter are taken from the secondary source, which was collected from various websites, journals and online resources (Khan & Magd,2021; Kamal et al., 2022).

Thus, the objectives of the chapter are set as follows:

- To identify the impact of Internet of things (IoT) on Human Resource Management (HRM) in managing the functioning of the organisation
- To study the role of digital marketing in Human Resource Management (HRM) in the digital era
- To explore any other benefits and challenges revolving around the Internet of things (IoT) and Digital Marketing (DM)

1.1. Significance of the Study

The IoT has revolutionized many industries by connecting devices and machines, allowing for real-time data collection and analysis. In recent years, the HR industry has also begun to explore the potential benefits of IoT for workforce management and employee engagement. However, in order to fully understand the impact of IoT on HR, it is necessary to conduct a thorough study. The first step in conducting a study on IoT and HR is to identify the research question and objectives. For example, the study may aim to determine the effectiveness of using IoT devices for employee engagement and productivity, or to explore the impact of IoT on the recruitment and retention of employees.

Once the research question and objectives have been established, the next step is to design the study. This includes determining the sample size, selecting the appropriate research methods and tools, and establishing a data collection and analysis plan (Khan et al., 2022). One of the key considerations when designing a study on IoT and HR is the type of data that will be collected. This may include data on employee engagement, productivity, and turnover, as well as data on the use of IoT devices and their impact on these metrics.

Overall, conducting a study on IoT and HR can provide valuable insights into the impact of IoT on workforce management and employee engagement. By carefully designing the study, collecting and analysing the data, and interpreting the results, researchers can gain a better understanding of the potential benefits of IoT for the HR industry.

The phrase "Customer is the King" as used in marketing is now can be seeing in this digital era as new phrase "Data is King". With huge data anyone can manipulate the market as per his desire. Availability of Data is normally connected with the marketing process of the organisation but the use of data can be a boon for human resource managers also who can now focus more on their external customers along with internal employees. This chapter is an attempt to understand the impact of the IoT on various functions of HRM. The prime objective of this chapter is to determine the relationship between the IoT and HRM in digital marketing.

2. BACKGROUND OF THE STUDY

2.1. Internet of Things (IoT)

IoT refers to the network of physical devices, vehicles, buildings, and other objects that are connected to the internet and can collect and share data. These devices can range from simple sensors to complex machines and systems. The IoT has the ability to gather as well as perform large amount of data. This data can be used to improve efficiency, reduce costs, and make better decisions (Coetzee & Eksteen, 2011; Schoder, 2018). . For example, a smart thermostat can collect data on temperature and usage patterns to optimize energy consumption in a building. Similarly, a connected car can gather data on driving patterns and vehicle performance to optimize fuel efficiency and reduce maintenance costs (Weber & Weber, 2010). IoT also has the ability to automate the tasks and processes that in turn leads to reduction in time and cost. For example, a connected manufacturing facility can use IoT sensors to monitor and control the production process, reducing the need for human intervention. Similarly, a connected home can use IoT devices to control lighting, temperature, and security, allowing for greater convenience and comfort (Coetzee & Eksteen, 2011; Schoder, 2018; Weber & Weber, 2010)

The IoT also has the potential to improve safety and security. For example, a connected city can use IoT sensors to monitor traffic patterns and reduce congestion, making the roads safer for drivers and pedestrians. Similarly, a connected factory can use IoT sensors to monitor machinery and detect potential safety hazards.

However, the rapid growth of the IoT also raises concerns about privacy and security. As more devices are connected to the internet, there is an increased risk of cyber-attacks and data breaches (Alwarafy et al., 2020). This is especially true for devices that collect and share sensitive information such as personal health data or financial information. To address these concerns, it is important for businesses and individuals to implement strong security measures and to stay informed about the latest threats and vulnerabilities (Alwarafy et al., 2020).

2.2. Human Resource Management (HRM)

HRM is the process of managing people in organizations. In modern times, the role of HR has evolved to become more strategic and focused on the overall success of the company (Macke & Genari, 2019; Stone et al., 2020). One of the key responsibilities of HR in modern times is talent acquisition and management (Aziz et al., 2019). This includes recruiting and hiring employees, as well as developing and implementing training programs to ensure that employees are equipped with the skills and knowledge necessary to perform their jobs effectively. Additionally, HR is responsible for managing employee performance and providing feedback to help employees improve and reach their full potential (Pak et al., 2019).

Another key responsibility of HR in modern times is employee engagement and retention (Ratna & Chawla, 2012. This includes creating a positive and inclusive work environment, fostering employee development, and providing opportunities for employee involvement and feedback. By keeping employees engaged and satisfied, HR can help to reduce turnover and increase productivity (Macke & Genari, 2019).

In addition, HR plays an important role in managing employee relations (Ratna & Kaur, 2016). This includes ensuring that employees are treated fairly and equitably, addressing and resolving any conflicts that may arise, and communicating effectively with employees. HR also plays a key role in compliance with labor laws and regulations, such as the fair labour practices and relevant labour laws.

Modern HR departments are also increasingly focused on data and analytics to improve decision-making and drive business results . This includes using data to identify trends and patterns in employee behavior, as well as using analytics to predict future workforce needs (Pak et al., 2019; Ratna & Kaur, 2016))

Overall, the role of HR in modern times is to be a strategic business partner, working closely with other departments and the senior leadership team to drive the success of the organization. Through effective talent acquisition and management, employee engagement and retention, employee relations, and data-driven decision-making, HR can help to create a high-performing, engaged workforce that drives the overall success of the company (Strohmeier, 2020).

In short, HRM has undergone a significant shift in modern times, moving from a more administrative function to a more strategic one. HR departments are now more focused on the overall success of the company, and are responsible for key areas such as talent acquisition and management, employee engagement and retention, employee relations, and data-driven decision-making (Aziz et al., 2019). It is vital for organizations to have an effective HRM strategy in place to achieve their goals and stay competitive in today's business environment. In today's digital world, businesses are directed and working with the aim and requirements suited to the international business, transfer of goods are not only taking place within the borders but also takes place from one part of country to country in other parts of world, services are provided across borders without any barriers, managerial knowledge and technology is available between companies residing in different countries. The communication with different companies for different matters was made so easy in different parts of world due to Globalization.

2.3. Digital Marketing and HRM

HRM is an essential function of any organization, and its success depends on many factors. One of the key factors that have a significant impact on HRM is digital marketing. In today's digital age, digital marketing has become an integral part of HRM, and it is essential for organizations to understand and leverage its power (Sotnikova et al., 2020; Ratna & Kaur, 2016). Digital marketing is the process of promoting products or services through various digital channels, such as search engines, social media, and websites (Saleem et al., 2022). It is a cost-effective and efficient way to reach a large number of potential customers and employees. Digital marketing can help organizations to attract, engage, and retain top talent by reaching out to them through various digital channels.

One of the most important ways that digital marketing can impact HRM is through the use of social media. Social media platforms such as LinkedIn, Twitter, and Facebook have become powerful tools for recruiting and retaining top talent. Organizations can use these platforms to create a strong employer brand, post job openings, and connect with potential candidates. Social media can also be used to communicate with current employees and keep them engaged with the organization (Saleem et al., 2022; Rodrigues & Martinez, 2020; Strohmeier, 2020) .

Another way that digital marketing can impact HRM is through the use of search engine optimization (SEO). SEO is the process of optimizing a website to rank higher in search engine results pages (SERPs). This can help organizations to attract more potential candidates and customers to their website, which can lead to increased recruitment and sales (Rodrigues & Martinez, 2020; Strohmeier, 2020).

Digital marketing can also help organizations to increase employee engagement and retention. By using digital channels, such as email and messaging apps, organizations can communicate with employees more effectively and keep them engaged with the organization. This can lead to increased job satisfaction, higher productivity, and lower turnover rates (Ratna & Chawla, 2012).

In conclusion, digital marketing has become an essential part of HRM. By leveraging the power of digital marketing, organizations can attract and retain top talent, increase employee engagement and retention, and improve their overall performance. It is crucial for organizations to understand and use digital marketing effectively to stay competitive in today's digital age.

3. IMPACT AND APPLICATION OF IOT AND DIGITAL MARKETING ON HRM

The IoT refers to the millions of devices around us in the world that are connected via the internet to make our work easy. All these devices are collecting and sharing data thanks to the computer chips and wireless networks that can turn small things into big and big ones into small. Connecting all these information and adding sensors to them provides them artificial intelligence, which allows them to send and receive real time data without the involvement of humans. In this manner organizations can apply IoT in HRM. Human resources (HR) teams across several industries are taking the advantage of IoT to improve the health, safety, productivity, and comfort of every single employee (Strohmeier, 2020; Abdussamad et al.,2022).

HRM is a discipline where HR managers are responsible for monitoring and enhancing relationships among employees and with the organization right from hiring to retiring. It is the responsibility of HR managers to hire suitable talent for their organizations so that the gap in skills, safety of employees can be enhanced, and necessary services and benefits can also be taken care of (Ratna & Chawla, 2012). To excel in these responsibilities, HR managers need to work constantly and track all the employees' work, behaviour, activities, and comfort (Pak et al., 2019). Traditionally, HR manager used to monitor employees by observing them, using feedback forms, or by integrating various monitoring software in computers. But such methods are not useful these days and can't provide an accurate and objective assessment, which can lead to miscommunication and reduced employee engagement (Macke & Genari, 2019; Magd & Khan,2022b). Such limitations can be avoided by shifting towards the use of IoT in HRM, which can provide better usage of data and more precise monitoring of employees' growth, health, productivity, and comfort in an organization (Strohmeier, 2020; Abdussamad et al.,2022). Some of the application of IoT on HRM through digital marketing are:

- ***Recruitment***

Since IoT's main advantage is that it automates the traditional manual functions, it can be a robust and productive tool in the Human Resource toolset for automating the process of recruitment. Since the candidates are already researching potential companies and openings on their mobile devices, the companies can parse through their social media profiles and their online resumes and build a talent pool automatically with the help of IoT and AI, which helps in faster and cost-effective recruitment (Rodrigues & Martinez, 2020).

- ***Automating Payroll***

Since employee payroll is based on their attendance and work-time, Internet of Things will be able to provide accurate data for the same with the use of physical sensors (Strohmeier, 2020). For instance, with the combination of security cameras, smartphone GPS and RFID (Radio Frequency Identification) tags, the Internet of Things system would be able to detect when the employee comes and leaves the office as well as how much of their productive time is spent on casual breaks. This helps in collecting accurate productive hours and evaluating their efficiency which will be decisive for their appraisal and bonuses (Mahajan et al., 2015; Khan, 2014). For instance, employees have RFID tags with sensors attached to their identity cards. These cards are loaded with all the necessary details of the employee and supports the monitoring of issues like absenteeism, working hours etc. In certain cases, the amount of time the employee spent on their workstation can also be monitored along with the idle time (Gaur et al., 2019).

- ***Improving the Wellbeing of Employees***

Employee wellbeing is of utmost importance for any company as they would be more productive and efficient if they remain at the peak of their physical health (Ratna & Kaur, 2016). IoT systems can collect the data from company-provided fitness trackers to monitor employee health as well as take precautionary measures to combat office air pollution with the help of smart air purifiers. Similarly, IoT can also mitigate the risks in hazardous working environments by shutting down operations in case any malfunctions are detected. Employee health and well-being is a major concern for employers as a healthy employee can provide more productivity that leads to more revenue (Ratna & Kaur, 2016). HR managers can use IoT devices to keep track of employee health. Wearables can gather data about food intake, walking distance, vital readings of the employees which can help employees to monitor their health. IoT can also help in dealing with sick building syndrome, which refers to medical conditions caused by polluted indoor air, by using such devices that can facilitate air ventilation. Employee health and wellbeing should be a part of major concern for employers as it leads to increased productivity and revenue (Gaur et al., 2019). Based on the information gathered, HR personnel can figure out issues that are causing certain health problems and take appropriate measures to control them.

- ***Analytics***

Human Resource Management System (HRMS) software has inbuilt analytics and reporting capabilities, which can be further improved with the help of IoT (Gaur et al., 2019). A Human Resource Management System (HRMS) would be able to collect the data accurately with the help of sensors and the embedded AI in modern HRMS would be able to infer meaningful deductions as well as provide improvement suggestions (Strohmeier, 2020; Rodrigues & Martinez, 2020; Gaur et al., 2019)

- ***Measuring the Performance and productivity***

Since an IoT-enabled HRMS software is capable of monitoring employee performance constantly, it can provide an overview of the current collective employee productivity and suggest employee motivation techniques to improve it (Gaur et al., 2019). HRs would also be able to track the employee whereabouts easily with the help of IoT, which would reduce their slacking behaviour. Finding ways to increase productivity is one of human resource functions. One way that they can use IoT to improve productivity is by making sure the employee is alert all through the time he or she is at the office (Gaur et al., 2019; Mahajan et al., 2015). For that they can make use of eye tracking technology that uses sensors to detect eye movement. Through eye tracking technology HR personnel can find out specific hours where an employee feels sleepy and the background noises that distract the employee. To address this issue HR can organize time management and stress management sessions (Gaur et al., 2019).

Organizations can also provide career assistance and succession planning for their employees based on the productive tasks with the help of sensors using IoT. So, employees placed on some jobs on which they are not productive, can be shifted to those profiles on which they can prove themselves productive and can be utilised in much better way.

- ***Enhancing the Comfort of Employees***

For enhancing the comfort of employees and making them more productive, many organizations have the provision of open-plan seating arrangements, in this employee have the freedom to select and sit anywhere on any seat. This arrangement is to enhance collaboration, interaction, energy levels, and productivity (Zhang et al., 2022). But this system has many loopholes like this open-plan seating arrangement will lead to wastage of time as employees will be wasting time in finding their seats (Gaur et al., 2019). A well-organized system with IoT can help HR Manager in displaying real-time seat vacancy and can reduce wastage and enhance comfort of employees (Zhang et al., 2022, Gaur et al., 2019). IoT sensors implemented on working tables can easily detect the presence of a person, and can send signals to a connected display. Based on these signals, the connected devices display vacant seats and seats that are already taken by employees.

- ***Getting the real and meaningful Feedback***

Another option of including Internet of Things in HRMS is for gathering honest feedback. Studies have proven that non-verbal and anonymous feedback systems tend to be more impactful than face-to-face interactions (Tambe, et al., 2019). IoT systems can monitor employee facial expressions while they are providing feedback and detect whether they are being truthful about their opinions and hence, validate their feedback even before the HR has gone through it to save their valuable time (Zhang et al., 2022). Cameras can take images of an employee right after meetings. These images can be sent over the Internet and then analysed to find out if the employee is feeling happy or not with the way things are going. And further sessions can be organized accordingly (Gaur et al., 2019).

- ***Ideal Employee Profiling***

In today's fast-paced business world, companies are constantly looking for ways to improve their operations and attract the best talent. One way to do this is through employee profiling using IoT (Internet of Things) technology and digital marketing. IoT technology can be used to gather data on potential employees and create a detailed profile of their skills, experience, and qualifications (Rodrigues & Martinez, 2020; Strohmeier, 2020). This information can then be used to identify the best candidates for a particular job and attract them to the company. For example, a company may use IoT technology to track the performance of potential employees during a trial period or to monitor their progress during a training program. This data can be analysed to determine the candidate's strengths and weaknesses and to assess their suitability for a particular role.

Once a company has identified the ideal candidates for a job, they can then use digital marketing techniques to attract these individuals to the company. This could include creating personalized job ads or targeted social media campaigns that reach out to specific candidates. The use of digital marketing can also help companies to build a strong online presence and create a positive image of the company. This can be particularly important in attracting top talent, as many job seekers are now using online platforms to research potential employers. In addition to using IoT and digital marketing to attract the best talent, companies can also use these technologies to improve their operations and increase productivity. For example, IoT-enabled devices can be used to monitor employee performance and to identify areas where improvements can be made. Overall, the use of IoT and digital marketing can provide companies with a powerful tool to attract the best talent and improve their operations. By gathering data on potential employees and using digital marketing techniques to reach out to these individuals, companies can identify the best candidates for a job and build a strong online presence that attracts top talent (Khan & Magd,2021).

4. CHALLENGES OF INTERNET OF THINGS (IOT) FOR HR

The IoT has revolutionized the way businesses operate, providing new opportunities for growth and efficiency. However, it also poses significant challenges for human resources (HR) departments as they navigate the integration of these new technologies into their operations (Alwarafy et al., 2020; Abdussamad et al.,2022).

One of the biggest challenges for HR departments is managing the privacy and security of employee data. As IoT devices collect and transmit data about employees, it is crucial that this data is kept secure and protected from unauthorized access. This can be a complex task, as it requires a deep understanding of the different types of data being collected, as well as the various ways in which it can be transmitted and stored. Additionally, HR departments must ensure that they are compliant with all relevant laws and regulations related to data privacy and security (Alwarafy et al., 2020).

Another challenge for HR departments is the management of IoT-enabled devices. As more and more devices are introduced into the workplace, HR departments must ensure that they are properly configured and maintained, and that employees are trained on how to use them safely and efficiently. This can be a significant undertaking, as it requires HR departments to keep up with the latest trends and technologies in IoT, as well as to work closely with other departments and teams to ensure that the devices are integrated seamlessly into the workplace (Gaur et al., 2019; Alwarafy et al., 2020).

Another challenge for HR departments is the management of employee expectations. As IoT devices are introduced into the workplace, employees may have different expectations about how they will be used and what benefits they will provide. HR departments must be able to effectively communicate the benefits of these devices to employees, as well as to provide training and support to help them make the most of the new technologies (Magd & Khan, 2022a; Gaur et al., 2019; Alwarafy et al., 2020).

Finally, HR departments must also consider the impact of IoT on the workforce itself. As IoT devices automate many tasks and processes, there may be a need for employees to be retrained or reassigned to new roles. Additionally, there may be concerns about job loss or displacement as a result of the increased use of automation. HR departments must be prepared to address these concerns and work with employees to ensure that they are able to adapt to the changing workplace (Zhang et al., 2022; Alwarafy et al., 2020)

In conclusion, the Internet of Things poses significant challenges for human resources departments as they navigate the integration of these new technologies into their operations. These challenges include managing the privacy and security of employee data, managing IoT-enabled devices, managing employee expectations, and addressing the impact of IoT on the workforce. By being aware of these challenges and developing a comprehensive strategy to address them, HR departments can ensure that they are able to fully leverage the benefits of IoT while minimizing its potential negative impact on the workforce.

5. FUTURE OF IOT AND DIGITAL MARKETING IN HRM

The future of IoT and digital marketing in HRM is promising. As these technologies continue to evolve, companies will be able to use them to create more personalized and effective HR strategies. For example, companies will be able to use IoT devices to monitor employee wellbeing, which can help to improve employee engagement and reduce turnover. Additionally, companies will be able to use digital marketing to create more personalized recruitment campaigns, which can help to improve candidate engagement and retention (Sharma et al., 2019; Gaur et al., 2019; Pak et al., 2019). The future of IoT and digital marketing in HRM is likely to be shaped by several key trends, including:

1. Automation of HR processes: IoT devices and digital marketing tools can be used to automate a wide range of HR processes, such as recruitment, onboarding, performance management, and employee engagement. For example, IoT sensors can be used to track employee attendance, while digital marketing tools can be used to create personalized recruitment campaigns that target specific candidates.
2. Personalization of HR experiences: IoT and digital marketing technologies can be used to create personalized HR experiences for employees. For example, IoT devices can be used to monitor employee health and wellness, while digital marketing tools can be used to create personalized training and development programs.
3. Improved data analytics: IoT and digital marketing technologies can be used to collect and analyse large amounts of data about employees, including their skills, preferences, and performance. This data can be used to improve decision-making and optimize HR processes.
4. Remote working: IoT and digital marketing technologies can facilitate remote working, allowing employees to work from anywhere. This can improve employee engagement and reduce costs for companies (Bocar et al., 2022).

5. Increased use of AI: IoT and digital marketing technologies can be used to create AI-powered HR systems that can automate and optimize HR processes. For example, AI-powered chatbots can be used to answer employee queries and provide personalized recommendations.

Overall, the future of IoT and digital marketing in HRM is likely to be shaped by the growing use of automation, personalization, data analytics, remote working, and AI. These technologies have the potential to improve the employee experience, reduce costs, and increase efficiency in HRM. However, companies will need to navigate the potential privacy and security risks associated with these technologies.

6. DISCUSSION

IoT made life more comfortable and made companies capable of connecting, monitoring, tracking, analysing and evaluating performance of humans and collecting data through machines in a digital economy. IoT helps companies to deal with both types of data- personal and organizational and benefit organizations to find right type of data and to connect the job seekers through driven applications. The benefits provided by the IoT to the companies these days are effective in dealing with various Human Resource functions like Human resource planning, recruitment of employees, taking interviews, managing vast data, payroll mechanism etc.

HR department can also use IoT in different ways to improve employee's safety and health. Like monitoring machines, equipment etc. to increase the safety of employees. IoT with the help of Artificial Intelligence (AI), also has the power to detect patterns indicative of depression in employees. The sensors can easily extract behavioural information from employees and from those patterns it can be find out employees who are not looking normal in behaviour (Magd et al., 2022). Like one can easily identify depressed employees from normal employees and can send this data to HR department for further actions like counselling to improve their performance.

The IoT technology is being used in a variety of industries, including HRM. In this chapter we explored the way IoT is being used in HRM practices and the potential benefits and challenges of this technology. One of the main ways IoT is being used in HRM is through the use of wearables. Wearable devices, such as fitness trackers and smartwatches, are becoming increasingly popular among employees. These devices can track an employee's physical activity, sleep patterns, and other health data. This data can be used by HR managers to monitor the health and wellbeing of employees, identify potential health risks, and develop wellness programs to improve employee health.

Another way IoT is being used in HRM is through the use of location tracking technology. This technology can be used to track the location of employees in real-time, allowing managers to monitor attendance, productivity, and safety. For example, a construction company could use IoT-enabled hard hats to track the location of workers on a construction site, ensuring that they are working in safe areas and identifying potential hazards.

IoT can also be used to automate HR processes, such as onboarding, performance evaluations, and time tracking. For example, an IoT-enabled time clock can automatically track employee attendance, eliminating the need for manual timekeeping. This can save HR managers time and reduce the risk of errors. Additionally, IoT-enabled performance evaluations can use data collected from wearables and other devices to provide managers with more accurate and objective performance evaluations.

The use of IoT in HRM can also lead to improved employee engagement and communication. For example, an IoT-enabled employee portal can provide employees with real-time access to important information and resources, such as their pay stubs, benefits information, and company news. This can improve employee engagement and communication, making it easier for employees to stay connected with their employer.

However, there are also potential challenges associated with the use of IoT in HRM. One of the main challenges is the privacy and security of employee data. IoT devices collect a large amount of personal data, and it is important that this data is protected from unauthorized access or misuse. Additionally, employees may be concerned about the use of their personal data by their employer, and HR managers must ensure that they are transparent about how the data will be used and that employees have the right to opt-out of data collection.

Another challenge is the cost of IoT devices and the infrastructure required to support them. IoT devices can be expensive, and it can be difficult for small and medium-sized businesses to afford them. Additionally, HR managers must ensure that they have the necessary infrastructure, such as internet connectivity and data storage, to support the use of IoT devices. The relevance of IoT in HRM can be useful at the microlevel of businesses and industries including Self Help Group (SHGs) (Singh et al., 2020; Gangwar & Khan,2022). This includes the social entrepreneurship as well (Khan et al., 2019; Khatri et al., 2022; Khan et al., 2022; Magd et al., 2022b). This is expected to improve the level of satisfaction and loyalty in a long run (Khan et al., 2020; Ligori et al., 2022).

In conclusion, IoT is changing the way HR managers work, providing a range of benefits, such as improved employee engagement, increased productivity and safety, and more accurate performance evaluations. However, HR managers must also be aware of the potential challenges associated with the use of IoT, such as the privacy and security of employee data and the cost of devices and infrastructure. As the technology continues to evolve, HR managers will need to stay informed about the latest developments in IoT and be proactive in implementing IoT-enabled HR practices.

7. CONCLUSION

Human Resource Management (HRM) has undergone a significant shift in recent years with the rise of the Internet of Things (IoT) and digital marketing. These technological advancements have allowed HR professionals to streamline their processes, improve employee engagement, and increase productivity. In this chapter, we have explored the ways in which IoT and digital marketing are transforming HRM and the benefits they bring to organizations.

One of the most significant ways in which IoT is impacting HRM is through the use of smart devices and sensors. These devices can be used to track employee attendance, monitor their performance, and even measure their stress levels. This data can then be used to improve employee engagement and productivity by identifying areas of improvement and providing feedback. Additionally, IoT-enabled devices can also be used to improve communication and collaboration among employees, allowing teams to work more efficiently and effectively.

Another area where IoT is making an impact on HRM is in the recruitment process. IoT-enabled devices can be used to create virtual reality experiences that allow job candidates to experience a day in the life of an employee at the organization. This can provide valuable insight into the company culture and give candidates a better understanding of the role they are applying for. Additionally, IoT-enabled devices can also be used to conduct online interviews, making the recruitment process more efficient and cost-effective (Khan et al., 2021; Khan & Magd,2021; Bocar et al., 2022).

Digital marketing is also playing a significant role in transforming HRM. Social media platforms, such as LinkedIn and Twitter, are being used to create a strong online presence for organizations and to attract top talent. Additionally, digital marketing techniques such as search engine optimization (SEO) and pay-per-click (PPC) advertising can be used to increase the visibility of job postings and reach a wider audience of potential candidates.

One of the biggest benefits of incorporating IoT and digital marketing into HRM is the ability to gather and analyse data. With the vast amount of data generated by IoT-enabled devices and digital marketing campaigns, organizations can gain valuable insights into employee behaviour, performance, and satisfaction. This data can then be used to make informed decisions about employee engagement and recruitment strategies.

In conclusion, IoT and digital marketing are revolutionizing the way in which HR professionals approach their work. By incorporating these technologies into their processes, organizations can improve employee engagement, increase productivity, and streamline their recruitment efforts. Furthermore, the ability to gather and analyse data provides organizations with valuable insights that can be used to make informed decisions. As these technologies continue to evolve, the future of HRM looks bright, and organizations that embrace these changes are likely to reap the rewards.

8. MANAGERIAL IMPLICATIONS

The use of IoT data to make HR decisions is now a movement worldwide. Digital transformation in organisations doesn't just develop someone it is the need of hour. Most CEOs view digitalization as a positive change in their businesses, a way to increase their client base and profits. It is impossible to survive in this digital era without digitalization in every department and every field. Forward-thinking leaders have recognised this, and they are personally taking charge of the digital transformations occurring in their organisations. It is worth noting that there is no need to wait for advancements in IoT, it is already implemented and happening around us. It is up to the organisation and HR department to be conscious about it and start taking advantage of its presence by getting connected to it.

The IoT will provide fully integrated system that will allow for sharing of real-time data and help organisations realise smarter workforce planning. HR managers will be able to use this real-time data to make instant decisions on recruiting and hiring based on the future needs of their organisation and its upcoming projects.

REFERENCES

Abdussamad, Z., Agyei, I. T., Döngül, E. S., Abdussamad, J., Raj, R., & Effendy, F. (2022). Impact of internet of things (IOT) on human resource management: A review. *Materials Today: Proceedings*, *56*, 3534–3543. doi:10.1016/j.matpr.2021.11.247

Alwarafy, A., Al-Thelaya, K. A., Abdallah, M., Schneider, J., & Hamdi, M. (2020). A survey on security and privacy issues in edge-computing-assisted internet of things. *IEEE Internet of Things Journal*, *8*(6), 4004–4022. doi:10.1109/JIOT.2020.3015432

Aziz, M., Adnan, A., Afthanorhan, A., Foziah, H., Ishak, S., & Rashid, N. (2019). The influence of employer value proposition in talent demand towards talent shortage in the Malaysian Islamic banking institutions: A SEM approach. *Management Science Letters*, *9*(6), 843–850. doi:10.5267/j.msl.2019.3.004

Bocar, A. C., Khan, S. A., & Epoc, F. (2022). COVID-19 Work from Home Stressors and the Degree of its Impact: Employers and Employees Actions. *International Journal of Technology Transfer and Commercialisation. Inderscience*, *19*(2), 270–291.

Coetzee, L., & Eksteen, J. (2011, May). The Internet of Things-promise for the future? An introduction. In *2011 IST-Africa Conference Proceedings* (pp. 1-9). IEEE.

Gangwar, V., & Khan, S. (2022).Analyzing the Role of Micro-Entrepreneurship and Self-Help Groups (SHGs) in Women Empowerment and Development: A Bottom-of-Pyramid Perspective. Driving Factors for Venture Creation and Success in Agricultural Entrepreneurship. M. Arafat, I. Ali, A. Khan, & H. Hussain Balhareth (Eds.). Driving Factors for Venture Creation and Success in Agricultural Entrepreneurship; October 2021, IGI-Global Doi:10.4018/978-1-6684-2349-3.ch011

Gaur, B., Shukla, V. K., & Verma, A. (2019, April). Strengthening people analytics through wearable IOT device for real-time data collection. In 2019 international conference on automation, computational and technology management (ICACTM) (pp. 555-560). IEEE. doi:10.1109/ICACTM.2019.8776776

Kamal, S., Naim, A., Magd, H., Khan, S. A., & Khan, F. M. (2022). The Relationship Between E-Service Quality, Ease of Use, and E-CRM Performance Referred by Brand Image. In *Building a Brand Image Through Electronic Customer Relationship Management* (pp. 84–108). IGI Global. doi:10.4018/978-1-6684-5386-5.ch005

Khan, S. A. (2014). Comparison and Analysis of Leave System of Royal University Bhutan and Aligarh Muslim University with Respect to Improve the Leave Rules of Royal University of Bhutan. *Integral Review. Journal of Management*, *7*(1).

Khan, S. A., Devi, T. P., Ligori, T. A. A., & Saleem, M. (2020). Customer Satisfaction and Customer Loyalty in Online Shopping: A Study On University Students of Bhutan. *Delhi Business Review*, *21*(2), 11–22. doi:10.51768/dbr.v21i2.212202002

Khan, S.A, Epoc, F., Gangwar,V.P., Ligori T.A.A, Ansari, Z.A. (2021). Will Online banking sustain in Bhutan post Covid – 19? A quantitative analysis of the customer e-satisfaction and e-loyalty in the Kingdom of Bhutan, *Transnational Marketing Journal*, *9*(3), 607-624. doi:10.33182/tmj.v9i3.1288

Khan, S. A., & Magd, H. (2021). Empirical Examination of MS Teams in Conducting Webinar: Evidence from International Online Program conducted in Oman. *Journal of Content. Community and Communication*, *14*(8), 159–175. doi:10.31620/JCCC.12.21/13

Khan, S. A., Magd, H., Al Shamsi, I. R., & Masoom, K. (2022). Social Entrepreneurship Through Innovations in Agriculture. In Magd. H., Syed, R.T., Spicer, D. (Eds). International Perspectives on Value Creation and Sustainability Through Social Entrepreneurship (pp. 209-222). IGI Global. doi:10.4018/978-1-6684-4666-9.ch010

Khan, S. A., Magd, H., & Epoc, F. (2022a). Application of Data Management System in Business to Business Electronic Commerce. In A. Naim & P. K. Malik (Eds.), *Competitive Trends and Technologies in Business Management* (pp. 109–124).

Khan, S. A., Sharma, P.P., & Thoudam, P. (2019). Role of Attitude and Entrepreneurship Education towards Entrepreneurial Orientation among Business Students of Bhutan. *International Journal of Recent Technology and Engineering (IJRTE), 10*(10), 335-342.

Khatri, B., Arora, S., Magd, H., & Khan, S. A. K. (2022). Bibliometric Analysis of Social Entrepreneurship. In Magd. H., Syed, R.T., Spicer, D. (Eds). International Perspectives on Value Creation and Sustainability Through Social Entrepreneurship (pp. 46-60). IGI Global. doi:10.4018/978-1-6684-4666-9.ch003

Ligori, T. A. A., Suresh, N., Khan, S. A., Rabgay, T., & Yezer, K. (2022). The mediating effect of university image on the relationship between curriculum and student satisfaction: An empirical study of the Royal University of Bhutan. *International Journal of Pluralism and Economics Education. Inderscience, 13*(2), 192–208.

Macke, J., & Genari, D. (2019). Systematic literature review on sustainable human resource management. *Journal of Cleaner Production, 208*, 806–815. doi:10.1016/j.jclepro.2018.10.091

Magd, H., Jonathan, H., Khan, S. A., & El Geddawy, M. (2022). Artificial Intelligence—The Driving Force of Industry 4.0. A Roadmap for Enabling Industry 4.0 by Artificial Intelligence. Wiley.

Magd, H., & Khan, S. A. (2022a). Strategic Framework for Entrepreneurship Education in Promoting Social Entrepreneurship in GCC Countries During and Post COVID-19. In Magd. H., Syed, R.T., Spicer, D. (Eds). International Perspectives on Value Creation and Sustainability Through Social Entrepreneurship (pp. 61-75). IGI Global.

Magd. H., & Khan. S.A. (2022b). Effectiveness of using online teaching platforms as communication tools in higher education institutions in Oman: Stakeholders perspectives. *Journal of Content, Community and Communication, 16,* 148- 160. doi:10.31620/JCCC.12.22/13

Magd, H., Khan, S. A. K., & Bhuyan, U. (2022b). Social Entrepreneurship Intentions Among Business Students in Oman. In Magd. H., Syed, R.T., Spicer, D. (Eds). International Perspectives on Value Creation and Sustainability Through Social Entrepreneurship (pp. 76-93). IGI Global. doi:10.4018/978-1-6684-4666-9.ch005

Mahajan, K., Shukla, S., & Soni, N. (2015). A Review of Computerized Payroll System. *International Journal of Advanced Research in Computer and Communication Engineering, 4*(1), 67–70. doi:10.17148/IJARCCE.2015.4113

Mohanty, S., & Mishra, P. C. (2020). Framework for understanding Internet of Things in human resource management. *Revista ESPACIOS, 41*(12).

Pak, K., Kooij, D. T., De Lange, A. H., & Van Veldhoven, M. J. (2019). Human Resource Management and the ability, motivation and opportunity to continue working: A review of quantitative studies. *Human Resource Management Review*, *29*(3), 336–352. doi:10.1016/j.hrmr.2018.07.002

Ratna, R., & Chawla, S. (2012). Key factors of retention and retention strategies in telecom sector. *Global Management Review, 6*(3).

Ratna, R., & Kaur, T. (2016). The impact of information technology on job related factors like health and safety, job satisfaction, performance, productivity and work life balance. *Journal of Business & Financial Affairs*, *5*(1), 2–9.

Rodrigues, D., & Martinez, L. F. (2020). The influence of digital marketing on recruitment effectiveness: a qualitative study. *European Journal of Management Studies*.

Saleem, M., Khan, S. A., & Magd, H. (2022). Content Marketing Framework for Building Brand Image: A Case Study of Sohar International School, Oman. In Building a Brand Image Through Electronic Customer Relationship Management (pp. 64-83). IGI Global.

Schoder, D. (2018). Introduction to the Internet of Things. *Internet of things A to Z: technologies and applications*, 1-50.

Sharma, N., Shamkuwar, M., & Singh, I. (2019). The history, present and future with IoT. In *Internet of Things and Big Data Analytics for Smart Generation* (pp. 27–51). Springer. doi:10.1007/978-3-030-04203-5_3

Singh, E. H., Wangda, S., Khan, S., & Khan, S. A. (2020). Exploring the Obstacles for Start-ups in Bhutan: From a Prevented Entrepreneur Perspective. *International Journal of Innovation. Creativity and Change.*, *11*(04), 70–87.

Sotnikova, Y., Nazarova, G., Nazarov, N., & Bilokonenko, H. (2020). Digital technologies in HR management. *Management Theory and Studies for Rural Business and Infrastructure Development*, *42*(4), 527–535. doi:10.15544/mts.2020.54

Stone, R. J., Cox, A., & Gavin, M. (2020). *Human resource management*. John Wiley & Sons.

Strohmeier, S. (2020). Smart HRM–a Delphi study on the application and consequences of the Internet of Things in Human Resource Management. *International Journal of Human Resource Management*, *31*(18), 2289–2318. doi:10.1080/09585192.2018.1443963

Tambe, P., Cappelli, P., & Yakubovich, V. (2019). Artificial intelligence in human resources management: Challenges and a path forward. *California Management Review*, *61*(4), 15–42. doi:10.1177/0008125619867910

Venkatesh, D. A. N. (2017). Connecting the dots: Internet of Things and human resource management. *American International Journal of Research in Humanities, Arts and Social Sciences, ISSN (Print)*, 2328-3734.

Weber, R. H., & Weber, R. (2010). *Internet of things* (Vol. 12). Springer. doi:10.1007/978-3-642-11710-7

Zhang, W., Wu, Y., & Calautit, J. K. (2022). A review on occupancy prediction through machine learning for enhancing energy efficiency, air quality and thermal comfort in the built environment. *Renewable & Sustainable Energy Reviews*, *167*, 112704. doi:10.1016/j.rser.2022.112704

Chapter 5
Role of IoT in Industrial Transformation and Marketing Management

Arshi Naim
https://orcid.org/0000-0003-1325-6964
King Khalid University, Saudi Arabia

Hamed Alqahtani
King Khalid University, Saudi Arabia

ABSTRACT

This is an extended research article discussing the role and the applications of the internet of things (IoT) in industrial transformation (ITN) in general and in marketing management (MMgnt) under five research proposals. IoT has already reached its threshold of success in all the disciplines and MMgnt has also been applying it in many of its areas for optimum growth, development, and safe working. This chapter is a case-based qualitative analysis which involves the role of IoT in three fields of MMgnt, namely customer relationship management (CRM), business process models (BPM), and product life cycle (PLC). For study, many instances from the real retail firms are compared before and after the application of IoT and presented the distinguished achievement of classification of IoT. This study proposes five IoT plans for measuring the effectiveness of IoT for the above-mentioned three sections of MMgnt that depend on the collection and sharing of data from external and internal environments.

INTRODUCTION

World's industrial companies are stressed by the competitive and divided markets, continuing economic uncertainties, and growing operational costs (OC) (Thoma et al., 2012). All these issues have to be solved by reducing the OC, increasing productivity along with the achievement of competitive advantage. The solution is not easy to implement because that also requires some investment like increasing the cost of technology. Cost in Operation Technology (OT) may help in reducing OC

DOI: 10.4018/978-1-6684-8166-0.ch005

but increasing other technological-related expenditures. Traditional industries have focused on OT for competitive advantages but with the introduction of Information Systems (IS) better decision-making options came into existence. IS gave rise to new digital technological developments in ITN and offered solutions that could integrate OT and Information Technology (IT). This was the time of application of IoT in ITN. This combination could mean exploring more options for business processes and adding value to the products (Weinberg et al., 2015). IoT creates a liaison between business and all the human resources and other tangible assets and resources that give rise to obtaining valuable business vision for industrial competitors (Iwasaki et al., 2019).

Generally, ITN is the ratio of the variety of imitation- to innovation-based intermediate goods. To develop chronological changes and changes in operation in IoT, ITN have been applied in the context of industrial structure. IoT creates an integration of digital technology into all areas of an ITN and aids in the methods of operations, CRM, BPM, and other areas needed for transformations in industries. Apart from these changes IoT also brings changes in organizational culture (Porter & Heppelmann, 2015).

Industrial internet of things (IIoT) is an evolution of a distributed control system (DCS), and an interrelated connection of sensors, instruments or devices networked together with computerized manufacturing and energy management applications etc. in industry. According to (Glova et al., 2014), improvements in productivity and economies of scale can be achieved with IIoT. DCS has three essential components of a digital transformation, namely the repair of processes, the repair of operations, and the rebuilding of relationships with customers.

IoT has helped to all the users such as companies, suppliers, and consumers (Khan & Salah, 2018) in creating new and innovative products. Researchers of (Thoma et al., 2012) defined IoT products (IoTP) as a new category of data collecting and sharing products and they have extended the basic functionalities of regular products by offering the ability to collect and share data via the Internet. Smart products (SP) can make decisions that would require human learning and critical decision making to evaluate customer behavior, preferences, and complaints, provide recommendations or rating and reviews for further considering the achievement of customer satisfaction. Figure 1 shows the development stages from traditional products (TP) to (IoTP) to (SP) where TP has only basic functionalities, IotP includes the function of autonomous data collection and product analysis through virtual interfaces and finally, SP encompasses data analysis, Artificial applications, machine learning DSS applications for decision-making processes (Naim, 2022).

Figure 1. Transformation from TP to SP
Source: Naim (2022)

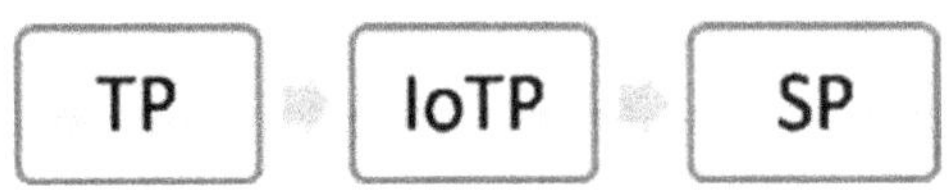

Developing SP involves many features and applications such as in, medical sector, education, automobile, retailing, traffic control automation, smart cities and home automation as IoT with CRM and BPM.

The chapter has six sections, Introduction part covers the conceptual framework and overview of the research, second part discusses the advancement of IoT in ITN, discusses the historical aspects of the concepts used in this chapter in the literature review. Third part gives the outline on the research methodology applied; Fourth part discusses the results for the research proposals for IoT for three M.Mgnt concepts; CRM, PLC, and BPM, and the fifth part give the brief discussion on the results. In the sixth part the final conclusion is explained for the research.

LITERATURE REVIEW

This section highlights the concepts of IoT techniques and its applications in Industrial Transformation (ITN) and MMgnt.. According to Porter and Heppelmann (2014), IoT is an infrastructure of networked physical objects that can auto-organize, share information, data, and resources, enabling anytime, anyplace connectivity for anything.

The economic historian from the UK in 1852 defined ITN as a way to UK's economic development (Lee & Lee, 2015). One of the most famous examples of ITN is the Textile industry which was the first to use modern production methods. IoT has brought major ITN by decreasing unpredicted economic depressions and increasing productivity by integrating IoT devices to energy-consuming devices of firms to balance power generation and energy usage which will help in ITN eventually (Naim et al., 2022).

Sensors (SN), Data Storage Application(DSA), Network Connectivity are elements of IoT.

Figure 2. IoT system
Source: Naim et al. (2022)

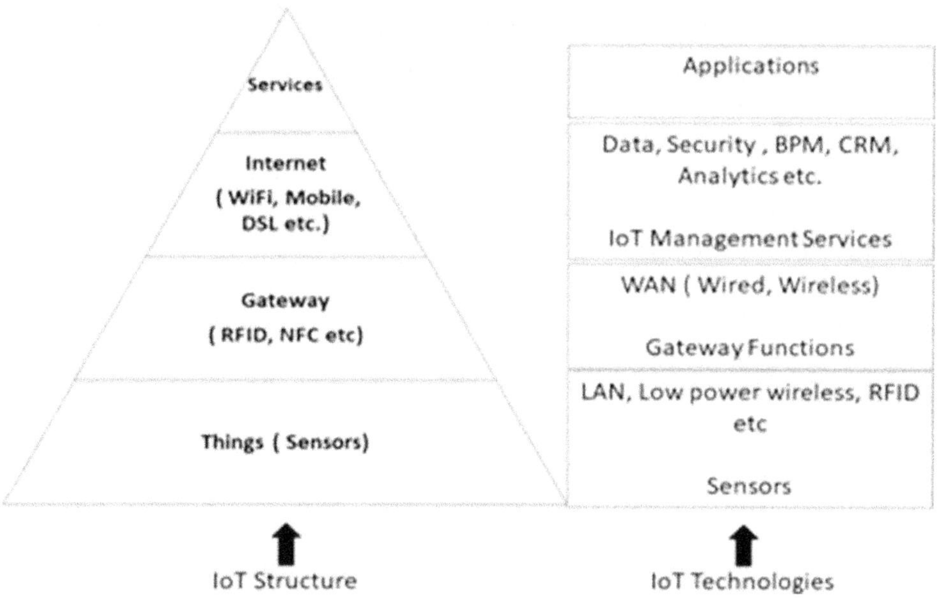

IoT is a global network that allows the communication between human-to-human, human-to-things, and things- to-things, which is anything in the world by providing a unique identity to every object and anything can be connected and communicates intelligently than ever before. It supports the coding and networking of everyday objects and things to render them individually machine-readable and traceable on the Internet, like the content created through coded RFID tags and IP addresses linked into an EPC (Electronic Product Code) network (Alqahtani & Naim, 2022). The IoT services help the enterprise for the following:

- Event processing: analyze data in real-time.
- Integration services: act on machine-to-machine (M2M) data and events.
- Analytics services: provide historical, real-time, and predictive analytics.
- User Interface (UI) services: visualize operational and analytical data through mobile/desktop
- Security and identity management service: Manage data security and identity of devices/apps.
- Driving innovation enables new revenue streams, and improves operational efficiencies.
- Build applications using IoT services, development kits, software tools, and services, which support the platform to a range of applications and use-cases.

The world changes day by day, with IoT along with it. Now it goes beyond M2M interaction. IoT services can collect requested data from different sources and transfer it to other devices and systems automatically. Thus, it became possible to solve daily personal issues and business tasks with ease and flexibility (Naim & Hassan, 2022).

Customer Relationship Management

Customer Relationship Management (CRM) (Naim & Khan, 2022) refers to all strategies, techniques, tools, and technologies used by enterprises for developing, retaining, and acquiring customers. It is a comprehensive strategy and process of acquiring, retaining, and partnering with selective customers to create superior value for the company and the customer. The scope of CRM is shown in Figure 3.

CRM software available in the market ensures that every step of the interaction with consumers goes smoothly and efficiently to increase the overall profits. The software gathers customer data from multiple channels. Hence, CRM stores detailed information on overall purchase history, personal info, and even purchasing behavior patterns. It involves the integration of marketing, sales, customer service, and the supply-chain functions of the organization to achieve greater efficiencies and effectiveness in delivering customer value (Naim, 2022) Importance of CRM for any organization (Naim, 2022) are given below:

- Enhance communication at internal and external organizational levels.
- Keep track of customer journey map.
- Helps in resolving customer cases.
- Improves sales force efficiency.
- Improves customer relationships leading to customer loyalty.

Figure 3. Scope of CRM
Source: Naim and Khan (2022)

Product Life Cycle (PLC)

PLC is the historical study of (sales of) the product (Naim, 2022). PLC covers the product life cycle as: When the product was introduced (Introduction Phase), when the product was getting rapid acceptance (Growth Phase), when the product was on the peak of its position (Between Growth and Maturity Phase), when the product started falling from the peak (Maturity Phase), when the product disappeared (Decline Phase).

Business Process Management (BPM)

Business Process Management (BPM) is a discipline involving any combination of modeling, automation, execution, control, measurement, and optimization of business activity flows, in support of enterprise goals, spanning systems, employees, customers, and partners within and beyond the enterprise boundaries (Naim, 2022)

It involves 5 steps namely, design, modeling, execution, monitoring, and optimization.

- Design: Identify current processes and design of proposed change.
- Modeling: What-if analysis to model change proposed on multiple variables.
- Execution: Use of software to track and manage.
- Monitoring: Keep track of competition level of changes and effectiveness.
- Optimization: Identify problems opportunities and apply changes for greater cost savings and efficiency.

Figure 4. Stages of PLC
Source: Naim (2022)

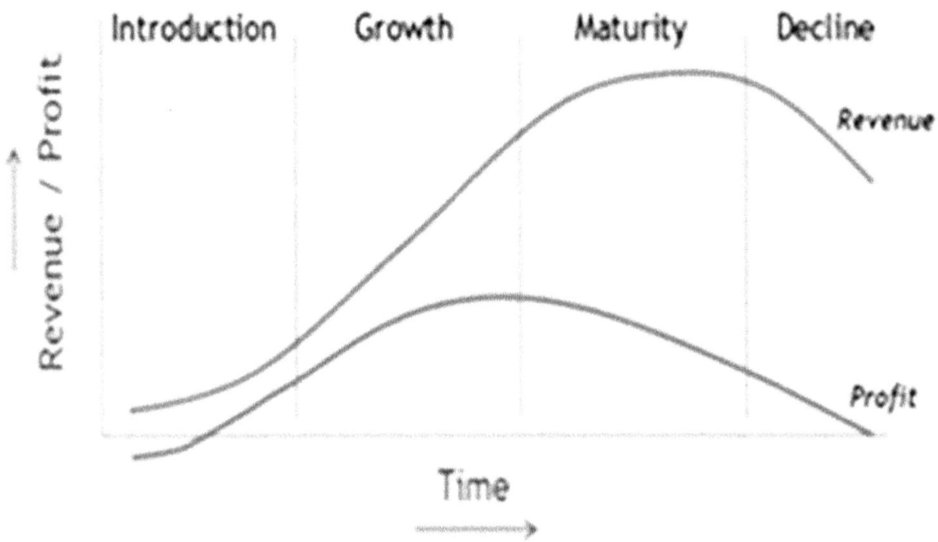

Figure 5. Business process management (BPM)
Source: Naim (2022)

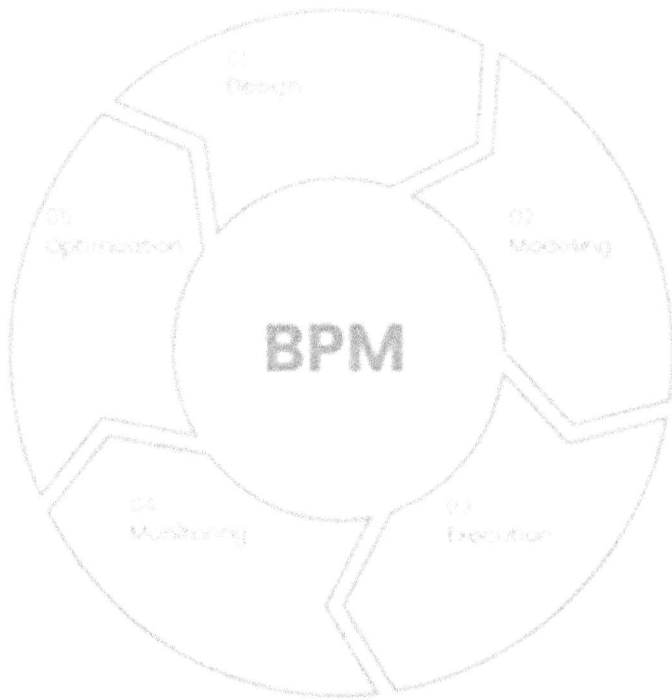

Ambient Intelligence (AmI)

AmI supports the environments that are integrated with sensors and intelligent systems. AmI needs to be driven by humanistic concerns, not technologically determined once" and should be "controllable by ordinary people. It is able to deliver personalized services automatically in anticipation of the needs of the inhabitants and visitors (Naim & Alqahtani, n.d.). The environments have the properties given in Figure 6 showing the role of AmI at various levels.

Figure 6. AmI for environment

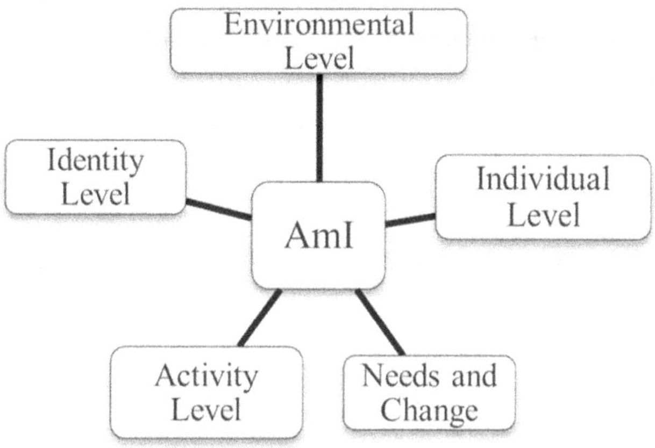

Figure 7. Ambient intelligence
Source: Naim and Kautish (2022)

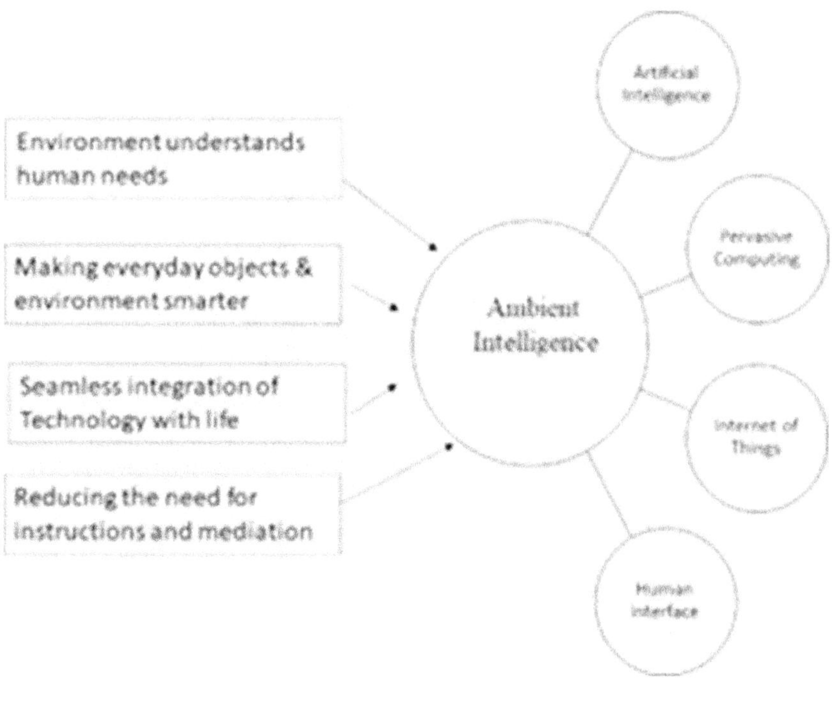

The “Ambient” side of the system includes sensors, processors, communications, and adaptive software. The smartphone, wearable, and IoT markets will continue to drive miniaturization and cost reduction (Nguyen & Simkin, 2017). The “Intelligence” side of the system will determine the success or failure of an AmI deployment. AmI applies to most IoT applications as well.

IoT and CRM Integration

CRM will be at the heart of digital initiatives in the coming years as enterprises look to create more targeted interactions in a multi-channel environment. CRM systems are increasingly leveraging IoT technology to improve front-end processes (Naim & Alqahtani, n.d.). With advancements in IoT, CRM is all set to change the business landscape. By connecting devices, products, and equipment to the internet, IoT drives insights throughout departments, including sales, marketing, and customer service. The combined powers of IoT and CRM enhance efficiency and visibility to help businesses respond quickly and effectively to customers. Impact of IoT and CRM on enterprise performance (See Figure 8).

Figure 8. Impact of IoT and CRM on enterprise performance
Source: Simões (2019)

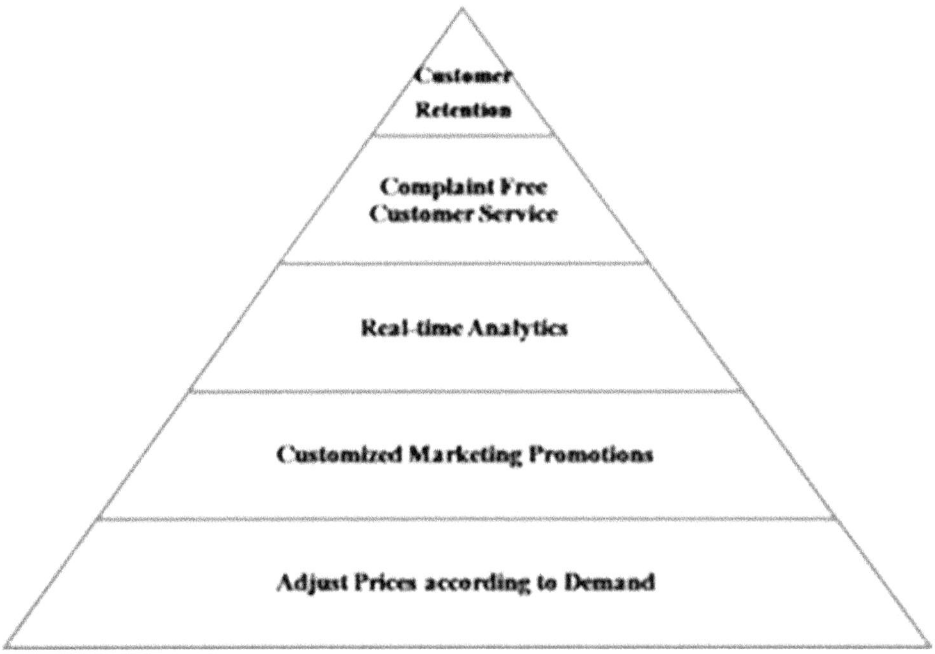

Adjust Prices according to demand:

- Get real-time data about the availability of products.
- Adjust prices, lower or increase based on the demands. Accordingly, the supply will be based on real-time updates of the system.

Customized Marketing Promotions

- Learn customer's interest towards products.
- Design the marketing campaigns and promotions accordingly which will improve targeting customers.

Real-time Analytics

- IoT can deliver real-time results regarding marketing campaigns, competitor prices, and promotions.
- Marketing and sales teams take quick action for the prevailing market trends.

Complaint Free Customer Service

- Solve customers' problems before they even know them.
- IoT devices can automatically detect malfunctions and take the necessary action on it.

Improve Customer Retention

- With notifications from IoT devices the customer support team should reach out to customer to know any dissatisfaction from their side. Customers will be encouraged to get discounts or special offers in order stay loyal to the brand.

IoT and BPM Integration

Businesses need to overcome several business and service challenges to be able to realize the smooth orchestration and manageability of disparate systems (Simões, 2019).

The IoT is changing the way we live our lives and that all businesses need to adapt to. The benefits of adopting IoT in business are as follow (Kotabe & Helsen, 2020).

Data: IoT devices records consumer's data continuously, and businesses utilize this data for marketing and product development purposes. BPM can automate this process, analyze and report on this data, to keep pace with technological changes.

New Ways of Buying: IoT supports consumer's buying process quickly and faster deliveries. BPM will be used to develop and manage this kind of process development to meet the customer's demand.

Innovation: IoT offers opportunities about new product development or upgrading existing products in businesses to deliver new benefits to their customers.

Customer Service: Products can fixed online when something goes wrong with the help of IoT. BPM will ensure customer service processes are effective and resilient to meet the consumers' expectations or not.

Centralized BPM: IoT data can be analyzed from a central location by Integrating BPM software into those devices.

IoT and Product Life Cycle

In PLM software, the customer feedback about the product only comes after the purchase, so it is almost impossible to collect real-time feedback as the customer is using the product that does not help much once the product has been sold and used by the end customer. Therefore, this feedback is not as actionable as product developers would like (Naim & Kautish, 2022). This is where IoT can be applied for the improvement of the PLC process.

IoT can enhance PLM software because (Rizvi, 2017) of the following reasons:

It uses smart devices and sensors that are both interconnected and connected to the internet. They can collect important information and relay it to interested parties. These gadgets can be embedded in any product, from vehicles to clothing.

It can inform product developers and manufacturers in real-time how a certain product is performing out in the world. This can be valuable to engineers and designers thinking about the next iteration of the product.

Companies can spot problems with the products on the field and fix them before they escalate, and the product breaks down. Such a preventive measure will help customers avoid unnecessary downtimes and increase their bottom line.

Companies can use both IoT and AI to predict future problems with a product and address them before they create inconvenience for the customer.

However, companies will become more customer-centric and the manufacturers will have mountains of data on how customers are using their products so that they can build new products in line with the customer's behaviors and usage patterns (Ploder et al., 2021).

IoT in MMgnt

The existing economic literatures, which are investigating IoT and smart products, focus on research questions in new business model (Haaker et al., 2021), supply chain management, the fields of management, transportation, market competition, smart home, and ambient assisted living, the organizational structure of companies, consumers' attitudes toward autonomously acting products, production planning and control, privacy and secrecy, wearable devices (Abdel-Basset et al., 2019).

According to Ghazaleh and Zabadi (2020) product analytics" and "remote access" are the two functionalities of IoT products in the view of marketing management, which provides new opportunities for marketing management.

Impacts of AmI on Marketing Paradigms

The AmI scheme predicts that ICT will progress more and become part of peoples' activities, communication on social media, and applications that may uplift the standard of living. AmI concepts establish integrated and group oriented working conditions, where online units will communicate with each other. These units include the humans, artificial agents, web/grid services, and able to interact with each other in an AmI environment to control the full potentiality of network-centric environments for productivity gains, boosting innovation, and creativity improvement (Janiesch et al., 2017).

The implementation of AmI concepts support the PLM business paradigm that can bring break though changes in the PLM systems. Functions from various sources can be combined in both online as well as physical structures. The mechanism of AmI will be units of humans, IT systems (as ERP), intelligent software, or mechanical agents (Naim, 2022). These units will interact in a P-2-P method and build up product-oriented dynamic networks. These networks are dynamic because on different steps of the PLC diversed units participate in the product-oriented network (Song et al., 2018).

RESEARCH METHODOLOGY

In the first part of the paper we discussed the general role of IoT in ITN and presented the major success of IoT in ITN, also we discussed some of the limitations created due to IoT applications in the working of ITN. The second part of the study shows the application of IoT and its realization in MMgnt under three areas; CRM, BPM, and PLC, where many research questions are answered showing the relationship between IoT and MMgnt concepts and how well they have been implemented by various firms in the real scenario. We developed some proposals and recommendations for MMgnt concepts with an application of IoT. This is a qualitative analysis and various firms are studied for the application of IoT and its classification in above mentioned MMgnt sectors. Real examples will justify the usefulness of IoT and comparative analysis will prove the success of IoT.

For the purpose of the study, five proposals are given to show the impact of IoT in different fields of MMgnt. Following are the framework of proposals on which the research chapter will confer its analysis and results.

First Proposal: Customers can easily be communicated for product specification and awareness can be created through IoT, in technical terms said as creating touch lines via IoT, additionally data collection can be transformed to data handling leading to resolving CRM issues along with developing multiple interactive platforms and media between Customers and firms.

Second Proposal: IoT helps to develop customized pricing strategies focusing on individual customers that can result in a greater return on investment and in developing smart Products for building CRM.

Third Proposal: IoT products will provide new kinds of customer switching costs as a new indicator of a company's performance. Switching costs is meant as "onetime costs that customers associate with the process of switching from one provider to another".

Fourth Proposal: IoT products may come without product generations. Available PLC models usually focus on the initial purchase of a product. Generation substitution models have been used to emphasize on repeat purchase. So, there is a need of improvisation in PLC model for the gradual adoption of IoT products.

Fifth Proposal: IoT supports the application of physical products with Internet-based business model. A transaction-dependent revenue model is commonly used with traditional products.

RESULTS AND DISCUSSION OF CONCEPTUAL FRAMEWORK

IoT plays a major role in ITN where asset-intensive industries, such as manufacturing, where the combination of OT and IT aids in improving new product developments, improving the existing product, and changing the mindset of old methods of performing business practices. IoT gives rise to the opening of new channels, developing new customers, identifying new products' usages, in simple terms a complete change over in industry's way of processing. IoT gave rise to ITN, where firms are able to enhance their value BPM by using various IT-based business models and developing the products as per the customers' requirement to meet customer satisfaction and good return on investment. Application of IoT-based solutions at any part of the firm, from the operation level to strategic or production level, the objective is to cut OC and use better OT and IT so that the firm can reach its breakeven point in less time and can increase profit. This is the most important reason for ITN to implement IoT in most of the industrial processes (Janiesch et al., 2020). In the current scenario, many companies use IoT solutions for receiving benefits from their investments and decreasing OC and other related expenditures. This is evident that IoT provides real-time vision and advantages to the BPM for any companies from collecting the data to analyzing and using it for decision-making processes for different levels of management. Apart from these monetary gains, IoT also aids ITN in effective SCM, building relationships between customers and firms, discovering new channels for the flow of products, encouraging firms to apply personalization approaches. IoT advances internal performances at industrial levels by empowering human resources and improving their performance, enhancing skills, and encouraging better results. As mentioned before, IoT is used for ITN for the purpose of resolving users-based problems such as problems related to services, usages, quality, durability, availability, etc. Considering the importance of IoT in ITN, there could be two major roles of IoT; firstly focusing on overall industrial improvement and specifically targeting at the internal level of related firms and secondly aiming to facilitate external factors such as creating needs, achieving CRM, contributing in economy of the nation and development of new as well as improved business models. When IoT has several advantages, there are also noticeable threats that the industry, in general, has to face. Some of the threats of application of IoT in ITN are given in Table 1.

Table 1. Threats of IoT in ITN

Data security and privacy concerns are seen as the most challenging issues in IoT initiatives and Strategies
Cultural change in the plants caused by implementing IoT solutions and smart machines
Data security and privacy concerns
Cost of purchase of IoT solutions
Lack of data scientists and analytics
Slow internet connections
Cost of implementation and management of IoT solutions
Employees Lack of technical development
Employee's internal organization challenges
Building the business case for IoT Investment

Source: Liu et al. (2020)

Table 2. Development of sectors with IoT applications

Internet of Things
Sensor Technologies
Wireless Communication , As Well As Supply
Layered Architectures Of Digital Technology
Energy Consumption
Harvesting
Strategic Management
Transportation
Supply Chain Management (SCM)
Market Competition And New Business Models
Customer Relationship Management (CRM)
Privacy And Security Applications
Wearable Devices

Source: Xin and Ojanen (2017)

IoT development has affected many areas and some of these areas are shown as examples in Table 2.

There are many examples and one example that can be witnessed extensively in the application of Smartphones. This device is the real example of the growing application and usefulness of IoT in communication and Information Technology. Another example is the automation of traffic management with the help of IoT applications. Homes are also not left behind with the successful implementation of IoT, smart homes are protected, secured, and prevented from accidents with the help of IoT. It has a potential impact on industries, markets, companies, products, services, and consumers, and if we refer to MMgnt; IoT has introduced more and better functionalities in the products which are not only beneficial to the customers but also the company's owners for data analysis. Therefore, IoT in MMgnt for product development is also called Product analytics (PAs) that allows remote access and virtual use. These examples evidently show the positive impact of IoT in M.Mgnt under three areas namely; CRM, PLC, and BPM. Our research discussion mainly involves the recommendations in the fields of CRM, PLC, and BPM (Eder et al., 2006).

CRM has developed into market-based learning, target connecting and making both organization worth and client esteem along with the value chain. Comparing learning connections have been recognized as the key achievement factor in CRM that improves an organization's capacity to increase selling potentially, diminish costs, give informal promotions, and eventually increment exchanging expenses. This field of exploration initially rose up out of the relationship of strategic management and high-profile executives, but in the current situation, it manages the mix of client-related connections and the utilization of frameworks that gather and dissect information across the organizations (Allmendinger & Lombreglia, 2006). Research work on CRM underscored the pertinence of business sectors and the managed market direction and market concentration.

A decade ago many prestigious journals in marketing research witnessed a drastic growth in CRM by the application of IoT that explained the concept of dual creation of value. The two ways communications have increased between all users in the process of marketing are with the help of the internet and precisely with the help of social media and emails. Some of the good examples of social media platforms are Facebook, Twitter, online discussion forums, Instagram, Youtube, WhatsApp, etc. These platforms have immensely affected the sale and product awareness for all the firms which are using E-commerce or IoT-based CRM solutions. So CRM has to understand the client's experience and his ventures. For example, while considering the services and information, the firms are required to know and comprehend the customer involvement in the process. To meet this need, IoT has played a major role and even today the importance of IoT is aggravating because it has aided in increasing return on investment (ROI) or to the limit of reaching breakeven in less time. Apart from benefits in sales, IoT has also affected the overall psychological behavior and understanding of the customers. IoT helped in evaluating the positive and negative customer influences and reactions for the products and particularly SP. These happenings of the association are generally indicated to as client touchpoints (TPs) (Korling, 2012).

Research Proposition 1: When multiple channels, called touchlines (TL), are involved, IoTP helps customers to use multiple TLs for interacting with a firm for various TPs. The purchase behavior throughout the life of a customer as a customer's journey (CJ) explains the set of TPs that are experienced by the customers for a firm and its different products. Current developments in

Internet and the www along with the availability of web-based and mobile applications suggest that the IoT will move forward this development process and turn customer TP into customer TL. IoTP regularly collects product data, its usage, and dissemination to the company in addition to enhancing the interaction with customers at different TP. PAs offer the option for the firms to check the CJ in real situations and provide connection, management, and control remotely. IoTP works in coordination with Pas for one to one customer's needs and preferences.

Figure 9. Changes in medium of communication
Source: Kowatsch et al. (2008)

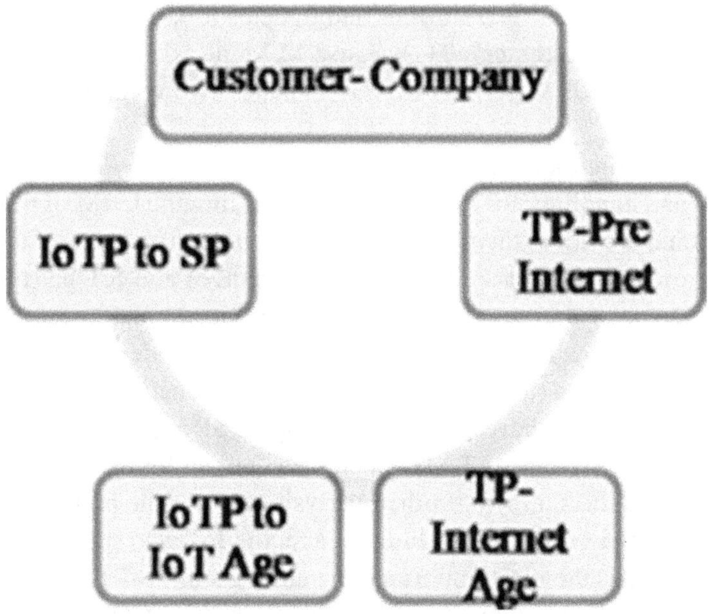

This theoretical situation of CJ starts with a TP can be illustrated to explain the scenario. For instance, Failure of many products in the post-purchase stage due to the serious rejection and dissatisfaction for the benefits of products which results in developing the negative behavior that will count for negative retrospective behavior. This example if it substituted during TP when internet or IoT did not have any importance of application, the number of customer TPs will be negligible or even least, simply because the firms are unable to receive authentic information and reasons for the failure and cannot even control negative word of mouth and therefore the product may decline and the customer may not use in future. This will result not in product failure but also affect the firms' image for future products. Some examples during the web era where IoT has great existence and presence TP can be increased easily because firms are able to do research and collect data on reasons and information on customers' preferences, disliking or complaints and eventually work on the improvement on the issues to achieve customer's satisfaction. A firm may have to bear a temporary loss or interruption in product development but in the long run, the product will not decline and the firm will be able to get ROI and develop good CRM. This can happen with help of IoTP that can give the firm true and authentic information on product usage. This resulted in the regular development of virtual customer's TL. Besides, PAs also contribute positively in this by allowing the firms to find or even forecast the reasons for product's failure, sometimes this process can be successful before the knowledge of a customer and therefore firms can solve the issues with the help of IoT remotely or virtually. Many firms have taken the advantage of IoT but automobile firms are the pioneers in this, they used Customer's TL and repaired the issues with help of IoT. Smartphones are also good examples of using IoT for achieving CRM. Nokia and Samsung are regularly exchanging data with their customers and solving detected software problems remotely (Mayer, 2010). In the current scenario, all smartphone firms are following the same customer's TLs and offering services remotely for the solutions and updates too.

IoTPs are affected by the customer's TL because M.Mgnt assumes that the category of CRM is present in all sectors, also CRM permits IoTP to enhance two ways of communication between customers and companies.

Earlier the CRM was more focused on the collection of data but IoTP made a change over from collection to analysis and handling. IoT is facilitated in building the CRM of the firms by analyzing the data of customers and providing them with what they expect from the products' services and also firms show annual growth and increase in firms' performances and IoT has also increased TP for CRM like now firms can use video conferencing or another virtual platform for communications. In the current scenario, many such tools have come such as online sales chat, social media interface, or even webinars on applications such as Zoom or other private networks that have enhanced CRM functionalities. These interactions have helped in developing SP as per the preferences of customer's choices. Although in the earlier times CRM concepts just aimed for data collection for the users of the firms' product through the survey but other analysis was not the pa rather limitation in CRM. As explained earlier with the growth of the Internet age, the IoT also started to function for several fields and the MMgnt field is the most important one amongst all. IoT has given many benefits and one integral benefit is in the production and collection of customer data in the post-purchase stage because this provides important information for further research and development in production with reference to positive and negative feedback directly through the users remotely. Apart from this, IoTP usually has more functionalities and benefits for the customers such as product usage, resale value, price comparison, etc. Based on their need and capacity to pay customers can choose their products and all this could happen with the inclusion of IoT in CRM. Marketing analytics (MktgA) supports the CRM systems from data collection to efficient data analysis (Resatsch, 2010).

Research Proposition 2: IoTP accelerates the application of price discrimination strategies (PDS). Companies have been applied the one-to-one pricing strategies (o2oPS) to maximize prices which an individual customer is ready to pay. PDS are made available online shops and online marketplaces. During 2000 many retail firms condemned the idea of PDS and suggested the net neutrality and equality should be the aim of online retail marketing and all customers should pay the same price for the same unit of products but the vision changed with more application on IoT, and the same firms introduced dynamic pricing strategies based on the frequency of purchase, being the active user, using a particular web service, affiliation to online membership, online payment methods, etc. The companies that are using PDS extensively are Noon.sa, Amazon.com, eBay, Alibaba, etc. Most

Figure 10. Criteria for IoTP for PDS
Source: Meyer et al. (2014)

of these online retail and online auction firms criticize the concept of PDS. IoTP currently follows PDS that is based on all the reasons mentioned above and a few more are presented in Figure 10.

While there are several reasons and advantages for PDS, there are many concerns also for applying o2oPS for IoTP, because PDS confers the idea of inequality amongst customers which may lead to customer turnover for the firms' products and services due to this reason. This may continue for CJ and customers may choose to opt-out. However, the growth of the Internet has enhanced the concept of personalization and therefore PDS works the best in this situation and customers also do not feel inequality and unimportant for the firms. Customers are usually choosing differentiated products and IoT has made it easier by providing remote access but at the same time, customers find difficulty in making price comparisons for other customers because of personalization as well as customization. Firms now have a complete edge on PDS from customers and customers also do not deny accepting the prices asked for. The most common examples are in the online purchase of software and other programs, where software firms ask for PDS based on the individual requirements and version they are willing to buy. PAs help firms to collect data for the functionalities of their products and customers too, which can aid in deciding on a range of dynamic pricing strategies.

Research Proposition 3: Generally cost is associated as an expenditure made by the firms for the CRM & M.Mgnt functions, and supply chain management. But switching costs (SCo) are associated and understood in terms of customers' expenditure as considered as one-time purchase (Zhou et al., 2015). Customers make SCo in the process of searching for the best available deal for them and the value of money therefore they compare and decide on changing or switching from one firm to another. It has been seen that most of the time customers do SCo for durable or high-value products. IoTP has facilitated customers in the effective decision-making process for SCo also other applications such as machine learning, data analytics can be used for SCo. IoTP aids customers in

Table 3. IoT favoring Sco for costs and risk

IoT facilitate in SCo for cost and Risk Analysis
1. Search Costs (SC)
2. Transaction Costs (TC)
3. Learning Costs (LC)
4. Loyalty Discounts/offers (LDo)
5. Customer style and culture (CSC)
6. Emotional Cost/ Sense of belongingness (ECB)
7. Cognitive Effort/Skills/Attitude Risks
8. Financial Risks (Short term and Long term)
9. Social Risks (Demographic and Custom)
10. Psychological Risk (Esteem and Self Awareness)

Source: Glova et al. (2014)

CSo and firms too for measuring customer retention, competition, enterprise profitability, satisfaction, and other important aspects of MMgnt. There are various reasons for customers to SCo and IoT offers comprehension for this analysis. Customers can have the following knowledge of various types of costs and risks through IoT applications that contribute to SCo and IoT helps in comparing the following costs and risks from one firm to another (Glova et al., 2014).

When IoT facilitates for customers, it is helpful for firms also as IoTP can achieve mass sale and profit too by creating awareness through digital technologies for personalization and customization and customers will acquire positive behavior and trust for SCo. IoTP provides data for R and D for firms and CRM and also helps customers to know their previous purchases, complaints, and satisfaction too. For example, many IoTP help customers to know their success in using particular services like services pertaining to health, security, education or even recreation. Online fitness and health clubs provide customers to know their health benefits, track their progress, requirements needed to reach a particular milestone, etc. In the education sector, for example, online learning helps users to learn remotely and can be easily accessed and eventually receive a credential for their education. Such sectors are also a part of IoTP (Porter & Heppelmann, 2015).

Every product, TP or SP has a life cycle commonly known as the Product Life Cycle (PLC). PLC has stages and phases from introduction to decline but product may have different duration for each phase depending on various factors but mostly PLC has bell shape showing the movement of product from one stage to another. PLC has stages such as introduction, growth, maturity and decline (Iwasaki et al., 2019). Apart from bell shape there are other shapes also associated with

Figure 11. Shapes of PLC in IoT environment
Source: Weinberg et al. (2015)

Table 4. Factors affecting the shape and length of PLC

Sales of Products
Changes in market and customers' needs
Changes in micro and macro economics
Level of Competition for the product category
Technological changes or advancements
Existing products and threats from new entrants

Source: Robson et al. (2016)

PLC and TP or SP may have either of these shapes for the phases too, some of these shapes are shown in Figure 11.

If we check the historical perspectives, PLC mostly concentrated on verification of functionalities of MMgnt and methods of product's introduction; also, the factors for the shape and length of the PLC. These factors and criteria are listed in Table 4.

In this chapter we have tried to focus on changes introduced by IoT for the phases, shapes, and length of the PLC, also we discussed how TP products had shorter PLC in comparison to SP.

Research Proposition 4: As discussed above, PLC has various stages but with the implication of IoT it may not have regular phases or lack proper generation of products. This is not because the product becomes obsolete or not usable for customers or any other complications, rather it's due to the role of technological advancement that makes good products ineffective. IoTP or SP are technology-driven products and the introduction of any new version of updated features can make existing products old although performance wise the products have no issues or complaints from customers, which is the main reason for IoTP for undefined PLC or generations. The main purpose of IoTP generated for CRM reduces the IT maturing because PAs allows the company to continuously monitor and update the software of IoTP. For example, some online assistants such as siri or alexa

Table 5. Types of internet-based model BPM

Internet-Based Business Models (IBBM)
Software-As-A-Service (Saas)
Product-As-A-Service (Paas)
In-Product Purchases (IPP)
The Network Business Model (NBM)

Source: Rocker (2013)

have overcome the issues of product generations and have automatic updates in their applications and hardware too. They are excellent examples of IoTP having greater PLC. We can conclude that IoTP focuses on utilization and has wider options of scalability for their hardware and software, PLC will have a longer generation and more linear shape. IoTP will also have repurchase behavior and customers will in general feel value for their money and also be willing to adopt the new IoTP.

Research Proposition 5: The IoT supports Internet-based business processes (IBBM) applications along with the TP. It is marketed with a transaction-dependent revenue mode (TDRM). In previous times or during the pre-internet age this BPM were facilitating the firms and customers positively because the use of BPM was more restricted to movement of products and maintain SPM and logistics but with the introduction of Internet and IoT, new BPM came into the significance and start to execute many functions successfully in a virtual environment. Life in the cloud is a good example of IoT for BPM. Also, examples of Alphabet (Google), Amazon, Instagram, snapchat, Linkedin, WhatsApp are other examples of IoT in BPM. IoT has given rise to many BPM; some of them are listed in Table 5.

IBBM is the most cost-effective BPM because of least OPC, having hardware and software scalability, and of performing analysis remotely for data for M.Mgnt. There are other BPM for IoTP models such as IBBM, SaaS, PaaS, IPP and NBM. These models can be used from service industries to durable goods such as for vehicles such as use of location tracking technologies for security and other purposes (Heinze et al., 2018). Often we mention such SP as smart cars, Chevrolet and General Motors have been using IoTP by applying IBBM. Another good example is if from online purchases for retail products, where NBM works successfully for BPM using recommendation methods for defining purchase behavior and decisions (Buttle & Maklan, 2019). Currently, all E-Commerce in retail use this method for effective BPM as well to achieve CRM. Also, IBBM facilitates customers to make SCo comparisons and decide for the best option and best value for their money. For firms, this IoTP helps in knowing customer demand, their profile and the trend of the economic cycle. Also, with IoTP, firms can know the various products' usage, the right customer, the right method of accessing data and making the availability of the products or services to the end-users. The feasibility does not restrict to a single firm. IBBM helps in providing learning and decision-making strategies for different related firms and know how customers relate to joining benefits from products (Kumar, 2010).

DISCUSSION

Innovation has become an imperative for the entire world's industrial companies. Dealing with cost pressure is the most crucial issue for most of companies. IoT has provided solutions to such critical issues and resolved OC and IT-related problems at internal as well as external levels. IoT has provided major advantages such as increasing productivity, reducing OC, improving operational efficiency by introducing new and advanced business models, effective data analysis, and achieving CRM. The majorities of companies are already using IoT applications in different phases of production, investment decisions, and analyzing customers' data and reached to beneficial solutions. Although there are many limitations and threats of IoT applications pertaining to privacy and security but industries for its transformation will continue using IoT because advantages are much more and limitations can be solved and prevented by the applications of other IS and IT tools.

The Internet has made fundamental changes in all the functions of M.Mgnt and with the IoT online environment has expanded to a greater extent. All major branches of M.Mgnt got affected and CRM, PLC and BPM also received a complete changeover for customers and firms. The notion of joining the TP to IoTP, growth of new product mix for collecting, analyzing the data remotely and automatically that eventually aids CRM. PAs are done by the IoTP for product usage and its value for the customers and sharing this information with other customers, firms and their competitors.

This proccss constitutes enhancing the PLC and solving SP- related issues more efficiently and achieving CRM more easily. With IoT products, customers are always checked by many sensors and TP giving rise to the TL for. Also, IoTP challenges the traditional CRM systems and introduces a change from only data collection to data analysis remotely. IoTPs have also witnessed the increase of strategic relevance for CRM. IoTP has also facilitated the application of PDS and SCo and developed new performance indicators for CRM.

PLC is adopting IoTP at a slower pace because IoTP usually does not have a product's age. The IoT facilitates the application of IBBM with SP as well as joint value creation for competitors.

The growth of the IoT era gave a new direction to MMgnt where customers use more IoTP or a SP. The CJ in an environment with distributed network of many related firms instead of single firm. The practical aspect of IoT can be seen in CRM and increase in strategic customer behavior. Further, the impact of SP is immense and significant on given MMgnt such as CRM, PLC, and BPM by connecting the SP in process of decision making for purchase behavior and product usage. Finally, IoT has not only affected the B2C but also in the B2B or C2C categories of MMgnt.

CONCLUSION

The industries will increase their IoT spending in the future for ITN and currently most of the firms are already investing in IoT applications for ITN because of high productivity and low OC. Also IoT has major relevance in CRM, PLC and BPM, like for CRM; IoT has given smart nature to existing products and customers are facilitated in having multiple channels for completing purchase behavior, building customer relationships with the firms, and developing strategies to enhance awareness and brand loyalty. IoT can develop a price discrimination policy focusing of the individual customer resulting in achieving profit maximization. For the development of smart products, IoT for PLC will provide high growth and longer maturity before decline stage; IoT can promote the new product development to retain its PLC. The IoT in BPM simplifies the application of Internet-based business models with physical products. IoT products accelerate the development of automatic options and joint value creation for business environments.

REFERENCES

Abdel-Basset, M., Mohamed, M., Chang, V., & Smarandache, F. (2019). IoT and its impact on the electronics market: A powerful decision support system for helping customers in choosing the best product. *Symmetry, 11*(5), 611. doi:10.3390ym11050611

Allmendinger, G., & Lombreglia, R. (2006). Four Strategies for the Age of Smart Services. *Harvard Business Review*. PMID:16250631

Alqahtani, H., & Naim, A. (2022). Critical Success Factors for Transforming CRM to SCRM for building E-CRM. In A. Naim, & S. Kautish (Ed.), Building a Brand Image Through Electronic Customer Relationship Management (pp. 139-168). IGI Global. doi:10.4018/978-1-6684-5386-5.ch007

Buttle, F., & Maklan, S. (2019). *Customer relationship management: concepts and technologies*. Routledge. doi:10.4324/9781351016551

Chatterjee, S., Chaudhuri, R., Vrontis, D., Thrassou, A., Ghosh, S. K., & Chaudhuri, S. (2020). Social customer relationship management factors and business benefits. *The International Journal of Organizational Analysis*. doi:10.1108/IJOA-11-2019-1933

Decker, R., & Stummer, C. (2017). Marketing management for consumer products in the era of the internet of things. *Advances in Internet of Things, 7*(3), 47–70. doi:10.4236/ait.2017.73004

Fatima, S., Alqahtani, H., Naim, A., & Alma'alwi, F. (2022). E-CRM Through Social Media Marketing Activities for Brand Awareness, Brand Image, and Brand Loyalty. In A. Naim & S. Kautish (Eds.), *Building a Brand Image Through Electronic Customer Relationship Management* (pp. 109–138). IGI Global. doi:10.4018/978-1-6684-5386-5.ch006

Ghazaleh, M. A., & Zabadi, A. M. (2020). Promoting a revamped CRM through Internet of Things and Big Data: An AHP-based evaluation. *The International Journal of Organizational Analysis, 28*(1), 66–91. doi:10.1108/IJOA-12-2018-1602

Glova, J., Sabol, T., & Vajda, V. (2014). Business Models for the Internet of Things Environment. *Procedia Economics and Finance, 15*, 1122–1129. doi:10.1016/S2212-5671(14)00566-8

Guo, Y., Liu, H., & Chai, Y. (2014). *The embedding convergence of smart cities and tourism internet of things in China: An advance perspective. Advances in Hospitality and Tourism Research*. AHTR.

Haaker, T., Ly, P. T. M., Nguyen-Thanh, N., & Nguyen, H. T. H. (2021). Business model innovation through the application of the Internet-of-Things: A comparative analysis. *Journal of Business Research, 126*, 126–136. doi:10.1016/j.jbusres.2020.12.034

Heinze, T. S., Amme, W., & Moser, S. (2018). Static analysis and process model transformation for an advanced business process to Petri net mapping. *Software, Practice & Experience*, *48*(1), 161–195. doi:10.1002pe.2523

Iwasaki, W., Morita, N., & Nagata, M. P. B. (2019). Iot sensors for smart livestock management. In Chemical, Gas, and Biosensors for Internet of Things and Related Applications (pp. 207-221). Elsevier. doi:10.1016/B978-0-12-815409-0.00015-2

Janiesch, C., Koschmider, A., Mecella, M., Weber, B., Burattin, A., Di Ciccio, C., & Zhang, L. (2020). The Internet of Things Meets Business Process Management: A Manifesto. *IEEE Systems, Man, and Cybernetics Magazine*, *6*(4), 34–44. doi:10.1109/MSMC.2020.3003135

Khan, M. A., & Salah, K. (2018). IoT security: Review, blockchain solutions, and open challenges. *Future Generation Computer Systems*, *82*, 395–411. doi:10.1016/j.future.2017.11.022

Khan, N., Naim, A., Hussain, M. R., Naveed, Q. N., Ahmad, N., & Qamar, S. (2019). The 51 v's of big data: survey, technologies, characteristics, opportunities, issues and challenges. In *Proceedings of the international conference on omni-layer intelligent systems* (pp. 19-24). ACM. 10.1145/3312614.3312623

Korling, M. (2012). *Smart Products: Why Adding a Digital Side to a Toothbrush Could Make a Lot of Sense*. Ericsson Business Review.

Kotabe, M. M., & Helsen, K. (2020). *Global marketing management*. John Wiley & Sons.

Kowatsch, T., Maass, W., Filler, A., & Janzen, S. (2008) Knowledge-Based Bundling of Smart Products on a Mobile Recommendation Agent. *Proceedings of the 7th International Conference on Mobile Business (ICMB 08)*. 10.1109/ICMB.2008.34

Kumar, V. (2010). *Customer relationship management*. Wiley international encyclopedia of marketing.

Lee, I., & Lee, K. (2015). The Internet of Things (IoT): Applications, investments, and challenges for enterprises. *Business Horizons*, *58*(4), 431–440. doi:10.1016/j.bushor.2015.03.008

Liu, Y., Zhang, Y., Ren, S., Yang, M., Wang, Y., & Huisingh, D. (2020). How can smart technologies contribute to sustainable product lifecycle management? *Journal of Cleaner Production*, *249*, 119423. doi:10.1016/j.jclepro.2019.119423

Ma, X. (2017). Influence research on the industrial transformation and upgrading based on internet plus strategy. *Journal of Computational and Theoretical Nanoscience*, *14*(9), 4384–4390. doi:10.1166/jctn.2017.6747

Marolt, M., Zimmermann, H. D., Žnidaršič, A., & Pucihar, A. (2020). Exploring social customer relationship management adoption in micro, small and medium-sized enterprises. *Journal of Theoretical and Applied Electronic Commerce Research, 15*(2), 38–58. doi:10.4067/S0718-18762020000200104

Mayer, P. (2010). *Economic Aspects of Smart Products* [White Paper]. Institute of Technology Management, University of St. Gallen, St. Gallen.

Mendling, J., & Simon, C. (2006). Business Process Design by View Integration. In J. Eder & S. Dustdar (Eds.), Lecture Notes in Computer Science: Vol. 4103. *Business Process Management Workshops. BPM 2006*. Springer. doi:10.1007/11837862_7

Meyer, G. G., Buijs, P., Szirbik, N. B., & Wortmann, J. C. (2014). Intelligent Products for Enhancing the Utilization of Tracking Technology in Transportation. *International Journal of Operations & Production Management, 34*, 422–446. doi:10.1108/IJOPM-11-2012-0530

Naim, A. (2020). Realization of diverse Electronic tools in learning and teaching for students with diverse skills. *Global Journal of Enterprise Information System.*

Naim, A. (2022a). Applications of E-Learning Tools for Achieving Students Learning Outcomes for Business Programs. *Competitive Trends and Technologies in Business Management*, 125. https:// doi:10.52305/VIXO9830

Naim, A. (2022b). Applications of Green Information Technologies in Business Process Management, Business Issues. *Competition and Entrepreneurship, 31*. doi:10.52305/VIXO9830

Naim, A. (2022c). Virtual Learning in Business Information Systems: A Case Study on Quality Matters Applications, Business Issues. *Competition and Entrepreneurship, 93*. doi:10.52305/VIXO9830

Naim, A. (2022d). Successful E-CRM by the Application of Management Information Systems, Business Issues. *Competition and Entrepreneurship, 19*. doi:10.52305/VIXO9830

Naim, A., & Alahmari, F. (2020). Reference model of e-learning and quality to establish interoperability in higher education systems. *International Journal of Emerging Technologies in learning.*

Naim, A., Alahmari, F., & Rahim, A. (2021). Role of Artificial Intelligence in Market Development and Vehicular Communication. *Smart Antennas: Recent Trends in Design and Applications.*

Naim, A., Alqahtani, H., Muniasamy, A., Bilfaqih, S. M., Mahveen, R., & Mahjabeen, R. (2023). Applications of Information Systems and Data Security in Marketing Management. In A. Naim, P. Malik, & F. Zaidi (Eds.), *Fraud Prevention, Confidentiality, and Data Security for Modern Businesses* (pp. 57–83). IGI Global. doi:10.4018/978-1-6684-6581-3.ch003

Naim &Alqahtani. (n.d.). Applications of Decision Support Systems in CRM. *Business Issues, Competition and Entrepreneurship, 1*. doi:10.52305/VIXO9830

Naim, A., & Bashir, A. (2016). *Application of Quality Matters Standards on Supportive and Online Module in Higher Education Program*. Research Revolution.

Naim, A., & Hassan, S. Z. (2022). Economies of Scale for Security Applications in Business, Business Issues. *Competition and Entrepreneurship*, *73*. doi:10.52305/VIXO9830

Naim, A., & Kautish, S. K. (Eds.). (2022). *Building a Brand Image Through Electronic Customer Relationship Management*. IGI Global. doi:10.4018/978-1-6684-5386-5

Naim, A., & Khan, M. F. (2021). Consumer Behavior for Health Services: A Psychological Approach. *Science Progress and Research 1*(4)

Naim & Khan. (2022). Consumer Behavior Appraisal for Health and Fitness Services Business Issues. *Competition and Entrepreneurship, 53*. https:// doi:10.52305/VIXO9830

Naim, A., Khan, M. F., Hussain, M. R., & Khan, N. (2019). "Virtual Doctor" Management Technique in the Diagnosis of ENT Diseases. *JOE, 15*(9), 88. doi:10.3991/ijoe.v15i09.10665

Naim, A. & Malik, P. (2022). *Competitive Trends and Technologies in Business Management*. Nova Science Publisher. doi:10.52305/VIXO9830

Naim, A., Malik, P. K., & Zaidi, F. A. (Eds.). (2023). *Fraud Prevention, Confidentiality, and Data Security for Modern Businesses*. IGI Global. doi:10.4018/978-1-6684-6581-3

Nguyen, B., & Simkin, L. (2017). *The Internet of Things (IoT) and marketing: the state of play, future trends and the implications for marketing*. Taylor and Francis. doi:10.1080/0267257X.2016.1257542

Piper, L. (2010). *The industrial transformation of subarctic Canada*. UBC Press.

Ploder, C., Bernsteiner, R., Dilger, T., & Huber, S. (2021). *Customer Relationship Management Improvement using IoT Data*. Academic Press.

Porter, M. E., & Heppelmann, J. E. (2014). How Smart, Connected Products Are Transforming Competition. *Harvard Business Review*.

Resatsch, F. (2010). *Ubiquitous Computing: Developing and Evaluating Near Field Communication Applications*. Springer. doi:10.1007/978-3-8349-8683-2

Rizvi, M. (2017). *Implications of internet of things (IoT) for CRM*. Academic Press.

Robson, K., Pitt, L. F., & Kietzmann, J. (2016) APC Forum: Extending Business Values through Wearables. *MIS Quarterly Executive*.

Rocker, C. (2013). Intelligent Environments as a Promising Solution for Addressing Current Demographic Changes. *International Journal of Innovation, Management and Technology*, *4*, 76–79. doi:10.1509/jmkg.2005.69.4.155

Simões, D., Filipe, S., & Barbosa, B. (2019). An Overview on IoT and Its Impact on Marketing. *Smart Marketing With the Internet of Things*, 1-20. doi:10.4018/978-1-5225-5763-0.ch001

Song, R., Wang, Y., Cui, W., Vanthienen, J., & Huang, L. (2018). Towards improving context interpretation in the iot paradigm: a solution to integrate context information in process models. In *Proceedings 2nd International Conference on Management Engineering, Software Engineering and Service Sciences* (pp. 223-228). ACM. 10.1145/3180374.3181341

Suri, K., Gaaloul, W., Cuccuru, A., & Gerard, S. (2017). Semantic framework for internet of things-aware business process development. *26th International Conference on Enabling Technologies: Infrastructure for Collaborative Enterprises (WETICE),* (pp. 214-219). IEEE. 10.1109/WETICE.2017.54

Thoma, M., Meyer, S., Sperner, K., Meissner, S., & Braun, T. (2012). On IoT-services: Survey, classification and enterprise integration. *IEEE International* Conference on Green Computing and Communications, (pp. 257-260). IEEE. 10.1109/GreenCom.2012.47

Weinberg, B.D., Milne, G.R., Andonova, Y.G., & Hajjat, F.M. (2015). *Internet of Things: Convenience vs. Privacy and Secrecy.* Business Horizons.

Weske, M. (2007). *Business process management architectures.* Springer Berlin Heidelberg.

Xin, Y., & Ojanen, V. (2017). The impact of digitalization on product lifecycle management: How to deal with it? *IEEE International Conference on Industrial Engineering and Engineering Management (IEEM),* (pp. 1098-1102). IEEE. 10.1109/IEEM.2017.8290062

Zhironkin, S., Gasanov, M., Barysheva, G., Gasanov, E., Zhironkina, O., & Kayachev, G. (2017) *Sustainable development vs. post-industrial transformation: Possibilities for Russia.* E3C. doi:10.1051/e3sconf/20184104021

Zhou, L., Chong, A. Y. L., & Ngai, E. W. T. (2015). Supply Chain Management in the Era of the Internet of Things. *International Journal of Production Economics*, *195*, 1–3. doi:10.1016/j.ijpe.2014.11.014

Chapter 6
Understanding Digital Marketing:
An Exemplary Approach

Arshi Naim
https://orcid.org/0000-0003-1325-6964
King Khalid University, Saudi Arabia

Kholoud Al Ghamdi
King Khalid University, Saudi Arabia

ABSTRACT

This chapter provides a practical sketch of the fundamentals of digital marketing. The framework comprises an overview of digital marketing development. This research is based on secondary data collected from social networking sites and e-commerce (E-com) sites for various firms to explain how they are using E-com business models. The research explicates the (E-com) different business models and the techniques used for the development of web presence, web search marketing that focuses on search engine optimization (SEO) and search engine marketing (SEM), e-mail marketing which offers interesting content to develop a successful newsletter, as well as social media marketing that addresses planning and the most important tools used to maximize communication through social media. The chapter presents a synopsis of digital marketing concepts and examples of some successful as well as an effective Web presence of some online firms.

INTRODUCTION

Digital marketing, also called online marketing, is the promotion of brands to connect with potential customers using the internet and other forms of digital communication (Filson, 2004). This includes not only email, social media, and web-based advertising, but also text and multimedia messages as a marketing channel. In the current scenario we are in the third wave which is about building trust and

DOI: 10.4018/978-1-6684-8166-0.ch006

respect through more creative digital experiences tailored to individuals. Digital marketing can be broadly divided into eight core classifications which are shown in Figure 1.

Figure 1. Classification of digital marketing
Source: Bandara et al. (2019)

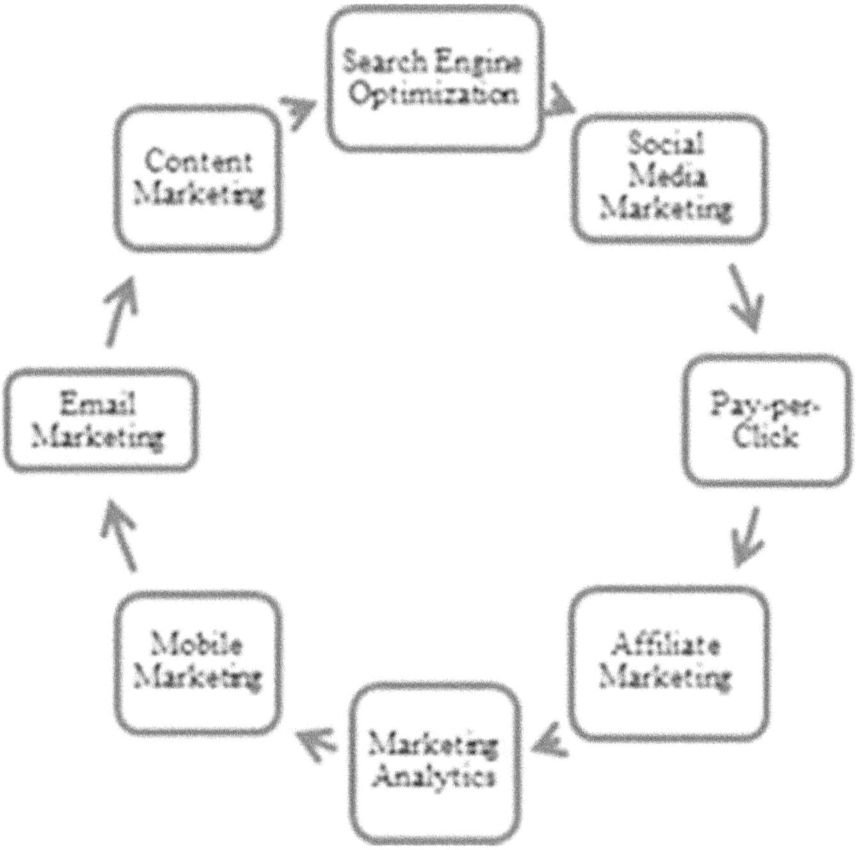

There are three main parts of digital marketing which are shown in Figure 2, and an entire digital marketing has three layered design as shown in Figure 3.

The data layer is necessary to digitize data sources by using technologies for easy-management. A business will implement transformative strategies for operational processes based on transformed data in the process and model layer (Castaneda et al., 2009).

The 2 pillars of digital marketing are Search Engine Optimization (SEO) which is a driving traffic to the company's website through free listings and organic, online visibility and Second pillar is Search Engine Marketing (SEM) which is a purchasing website traffic via paid search listings and ad words (Cetina et al., 2012; Choshin & Ghaffari, 2017; Naim, Alahmari, & Rahim, 2021).

Digital marketing is a career that combines traditional marketing, web design, SEO, social media marketing, content writing, and much more, so the traits required to succeed are many and varied.

For any strong inbound marketing plan to be effective, it must address the 3 stages of the buyer's journey as shown in Figure 4.

Figure 2. Parts of digital marketing
Source: Broome (2016)

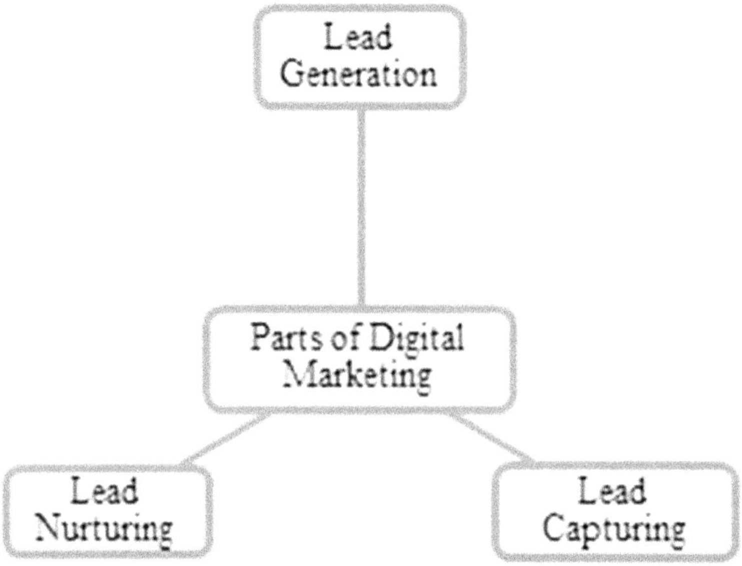

Figure 3. Three-layered design for digital marketing
Source: Naim and Alahmari (2020)

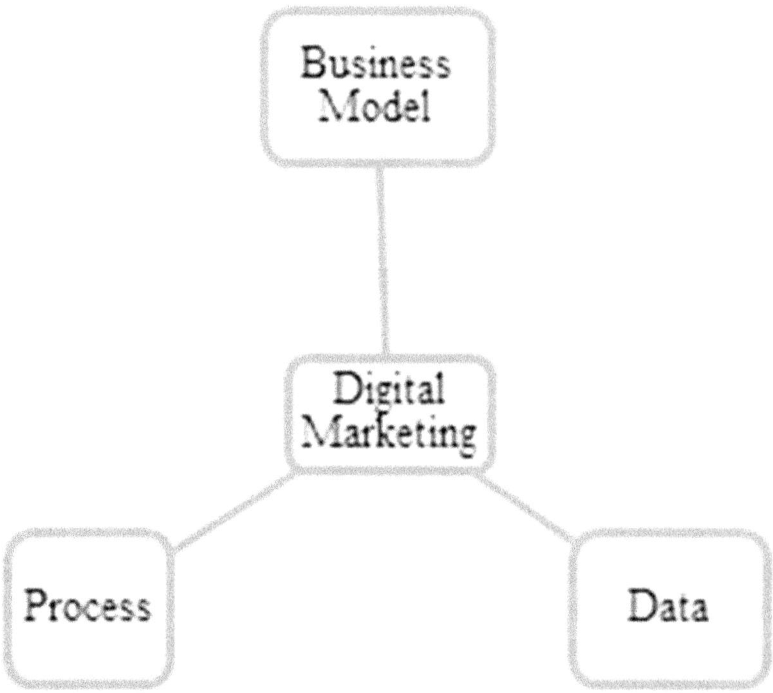

Figure 4. Three stages of inbound marketing
Source: Naim et al. (2021)

Many firms especially post Covid: 19, opted for Digital marketing for the global reach along with the local coverage. Also the Digital marketing has provided low entry cost in the market, identify target customers, and develop multiple strategies and content and increase engagements (Chouhan, 2017; Forman, 2005; Naim, Hussain, Naveed et al, 2019; Naim, Khan, Hussain et al, 2019).

The Digital marketing focuses on Content, Community & Commerce for social media marketing depending on 5 Ds of digital marketing. Figure 5 shows the 3 Cs of Digital marketing along with the 5 D of digital marketing (Dai, 2012).

Figure 5. Three Cs parallel with 5 Ds of digital marketing
Source: Doern and Fey (2006)

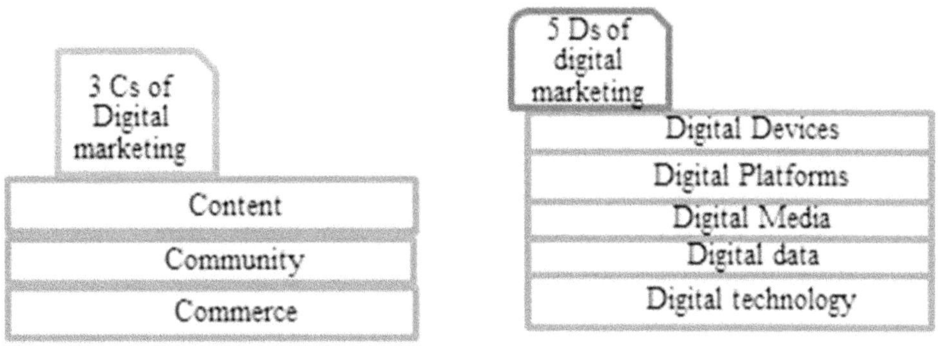

LITERATURE REVIEW

The evolution of marketing includes several eras including the simple trade era, the production era, the sales era, the marketing department era, the marketing company era, and the relationship marketing era (Naim, 2020).

Some argue that Gugliemo Marconi who invented the radio in 1896 (Darsono et al., 2019), was the world's first digital marketer. Others will say that computer engineer Ray Tomlinson should be credited with the birth of digital marketing because he sent the first-ever email in 1971 (Naim, 2022).

The development of digital marketing is inseparable from technology development (Naim & Khan,, 2022). One of the first key events happened in 1971, when Ray Tomlinson sent the first email, and his technology set the platform to allow people to send and receive files through different machines (Naim, Kautish, Doe et al, 2022; Naim, 2022). However, the more recognizable period as being the start of Digital Marketing is 1990 as this was where the Archie search engine was created as an index for FTP sites (Naim, 2022). In the 1980s, the storage capacity of computers was already big enough to store huge volumes of customer information. Companies started choosing online techniques, such as database marketing, rather than limited list broker (Agag & El-Masry, 2016; Ballestar et al., 2018; Naim, 2022). These kinds of databases allowed companies to track customers' information more effectively, thus transforming the relationship between buyer and seller. However, the manual process was not as efficient (Naim, 2022).

In the 1990s, the term Digital Marketing was first coined (Hallikainen & Laukkanen, 2018). With the debut of server/client architecture and the popularity of personal computers, the Customer Relationship Management (CRM) (Naim, 2021) applications became a significant factor in marketing technology. Fierce competition forced vendors to include more service into their software, for example, marketing, sales and service applications.

Figure 6. Growth of digital marketing from 1990 to 1998
Source: Changchit et al. (2018)

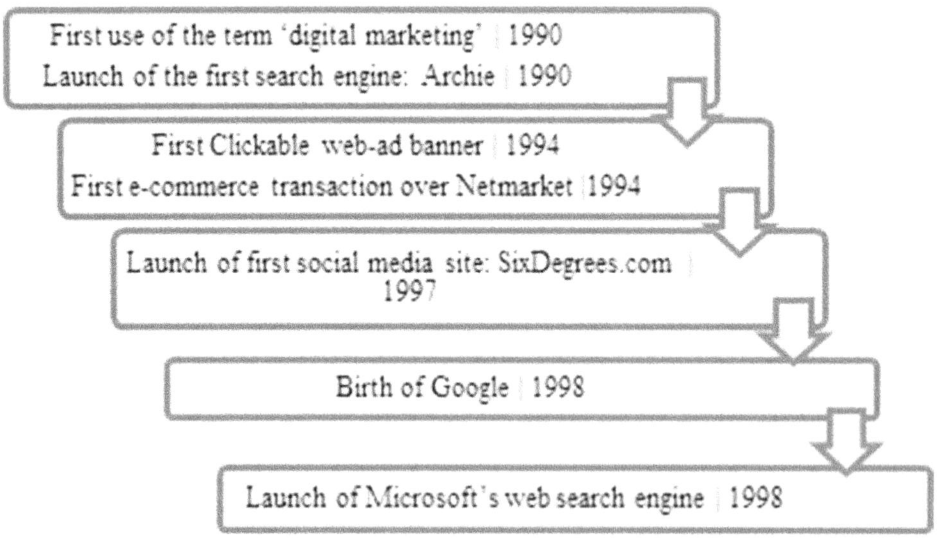

The 2000s saw a switch in customer behaviors. Through the prominence of search engines like Google and Yahoo, many customers began researching products online before making a purchase. This left a lot of marketers confused as they couldn't quite understand the buying behavior of consumers (Elseidi, 2018; Naim, 2022). This hurdle was solved by companies like Marketo, Act and Pardot when they introduced marketing automation platforms. This form of technology allowed marketing professionals to segment the market and attempt multi-channel campaigns as well as deliver personalized content especially for inbound marketing. It also had tools to schedule and track the performance of different mediums of marketing to get analytics for better understanding of consumers' buying behavior (Agag, 2019; Ayilyath, 2020; Naim, 2021; Naim & Hassan, 2022).

The 2000s also saw a boom in social media platforms, creating a new platform for marketing (Naim, 2021). It was also the decade where smart phones were popularized, giving consumers easier access to the internet, their social platforms and thus online marketing. Figure 7 shows the growth of digital marketing until 2009 (Belanche et al., 2020).

Figure 7. Growth of digital marketing until 2009
Source: Belwal et al. (2020)

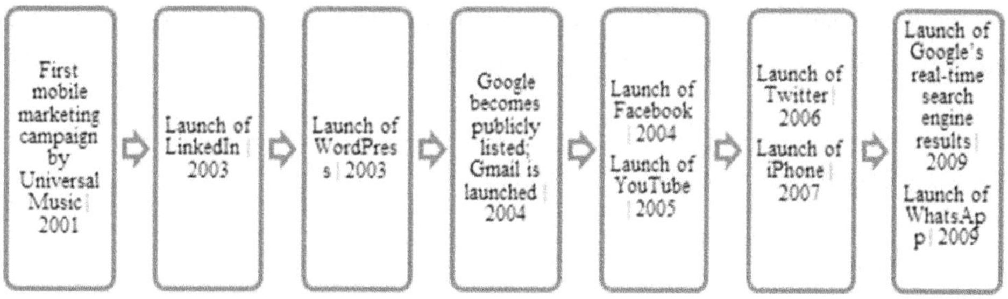

Digital marketing became more sophisticated in the 2000s and the 2010s, when the proliferation of devices' capable of accessing digital media led to sudden growth (Naim & Khan, 2021). Statistics produced in 2012 and 2013 showed that digital marketing was still growing (Brian et al., 2019). With the development of social media in the 2000s, such as LinkedIn, Facebook, YouTube and Twitter, consumers became highly dependent on digital electronics in daily lives (Edgar & Manz, 2017).

Digital marketing is also referred to as 'online marketing', 'internet marketing' or 'web marketing' (Naim, 2021). The term digital marketing has grown in popularity over time. In the USA online marketing is still a popular term. In Italy, digital marketing is referred to as web marketing. Worldwide digital marketing has become the most common term, especially after the year 2013 (Emma et al., 2017).

Digital marketing is now at its peak. Businesses need to make sure they have a good foot in with current practices to be able to gain the benefits of the advancements that are to come. From artificial intelligence in marketing to using social media for customer service, insight and data-driven marketing, as well as multilingual search engine optimization (SEO) (Harrigan et al., 2021; Harrisson et al., 2017; Naim, 2021).

DISCUSSION

The first approaches to digital marketing defined it as a projection of conventional marketing, its tools and strategies, on Internet. However, the particularities of the digital world and its appropriation for marketing have fostered the development of channels, formats and languages that have led to tools and strategies that are unthinkable offline.

Digital Marketing Plan

A digital marketing plan is a strategic document that takes the current situation of a particular organization to set some midterm goals and to determine the strategy and means to accomplish them. This document also describes the responsibilities, the time frame and control tools for monitoring (Elbeltagi & Agag, 2016; Naim, 2021; Naim & Alqahtani, 2021).

The aims of a digital marketing plan include discussing organizations and their environment. Likewise, it needs to be a roadmap of how to manage the organization's marketing strategy, so that resources are properly allocated. The plan also helps control and evaluate output and tackle any potential deviation from the organization's expected outcomes. In this line, a marketing plan becomes a flexible document that must be adapted to the situation of the company and that must feed into the results obtained by each of the actions developed, especially in the digital arena (Bashir & Naim, 2020; Durovic, 2020; Haupt, 2003; Naim, 2022).

The development of an online marketing plan is similar to a conventional one in its structure, but it also includes some variations at an operational level.

Social Media Marketing

Social media is a great opportunity to establish significant relationships and create ways of social interaction defined through dynamic exchanges between their members. Social media is booming in terms of the number and variety of platforms and users. Figure 8 shows the social media marketing plan.

Social Media Plan

A Social Media Plan (SMP) is the master document that guides an organization's presence on social media, and it covers all aspects to be considered when setting up, maintaining and integrating social networks in the organization's digital marketing strategies (UNCTAD, 2019). Therefore, any Social Media Plan must be in line with the marketing plan. A Social Media Plan is a living document that needs close control due to the liveliness of the virtual world in which it is implemented (Naim, 2021).

Social Media Advertisement

Most social networks show business models based on advertising. If we take for granted that a social network manager is a massive database, with large amounts of qualitative data from its users, using them allows brands for micro segmentation of their advertising actions (Khandelwal, 2018).

Figure 8. Social media marketing plan
Source: Naim (2022)

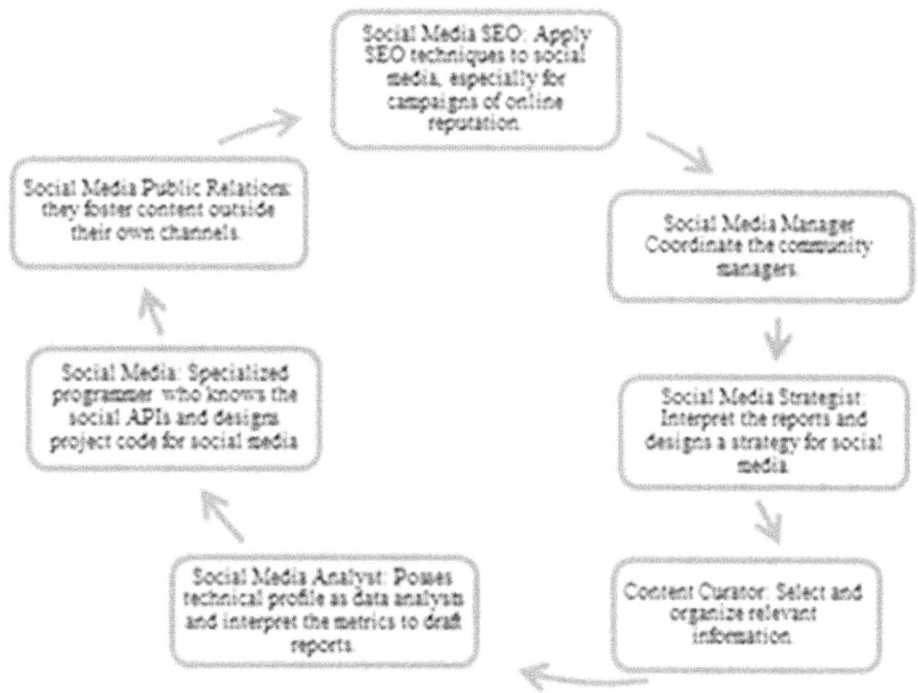

Figure 9. Basic metrics to assess the efficiency of e-mail marketing
Source: Miyazaki and Fernandez (2001)

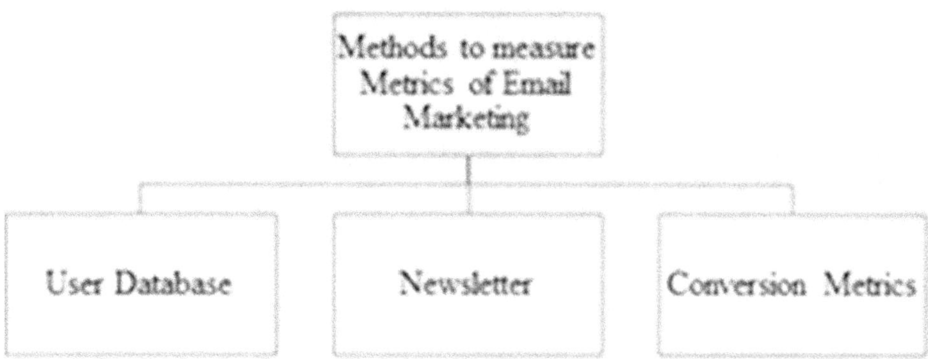

Facebook is the king of segmentation. Its advertising platform, Facebook Ads, allows for a delimitation of the target audience of each ad depending on location, age, sex, languages and even interests and behaviors. Facebook is the social network with more data on its users (Lahby et al., 2022). The basic data ðlled in by the user alone in the process of registration on Facebook includes name, e-mail, sex and age of the new user (Lăzăroiu et al., 2020).

Facebook advertising formats are inserted either on the sidebar on the right-hand side of the platform itself or on the users own timeline (Web and mobile), as well as on the logout page (Naim, 2022). These adverts must to be identiðed as such, while their goal is to foster as much interaction with users as possible.

Twitter, on the other hand, has less information on users; therefore, its segmentation capacity is lower (Kerick, 2019). However, through its advertisement platform, Twitter Ads, they have launched some highly efðcient publicity formats.

E-Mail Marketing

E-mail marketing is an online marketing technique that uses e-mail to send advertisements or commercial information (Naim, 2022). This is a communication tool used to attract new customers or make those that one already has loyal to the brand. Figure 9 shows the basic metrics to measure the efficiency of email marketing.

Figure 10. E-commerce categories
Source: Naim (2022)

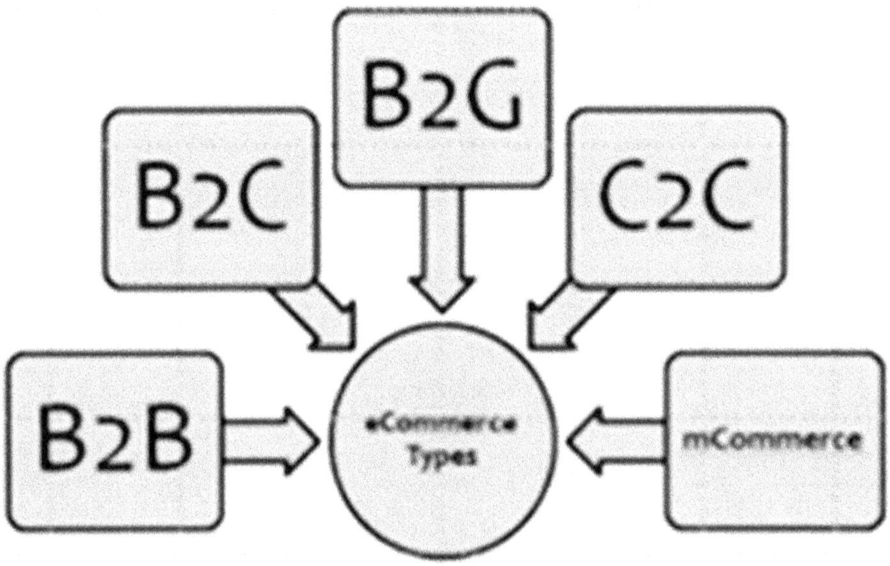

E-Commerce

E-commerce means the development of transactions between companies and/or individuals on Internet, mainly for buying and selling products and services, using applications such as e-mail, instant messages, shopping carts or Web services, to name a few (Shirazi et al., 2020).

The boom of mobile devices, smartphones in particular, has opened the doors to mobile commerce (m-commerce), i.e., electronic commerce using a mobile device. Figure 10 shows the categories of E-commerce.

E-Commerce Techniques

In order to purchase or sell on Internet, an online shop is not a must, but it becomes a useful Web tool for efðcient e-commerce (Mangiaracina & Perego, 2009). Some of the most common sections in any online shops shown in Figure 11.

Figure 11. Sections for online shopping
Source: Naim (2022)

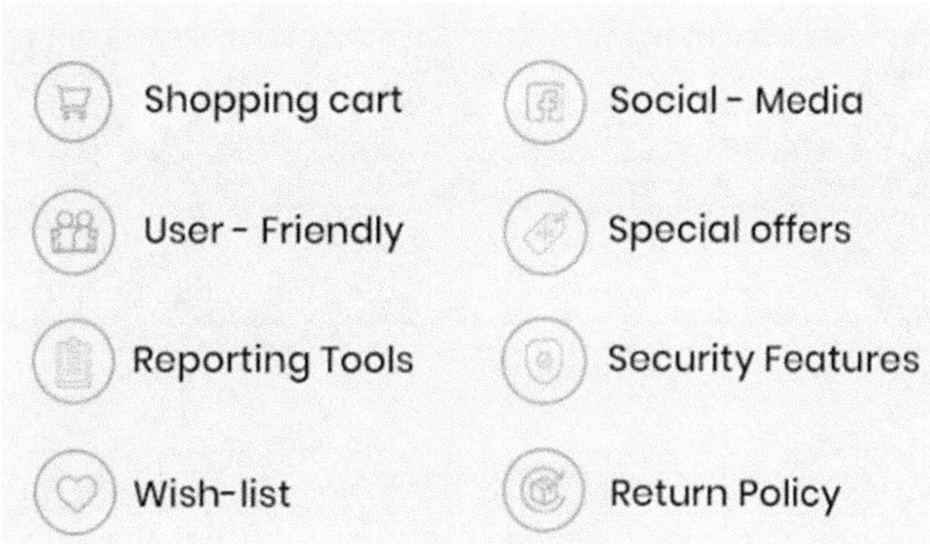

Properly structured product catalogue with sections, images displaying the product alone, as well as accurate and honest product descriptions. Shopping cart, always visible so that the customer can check, with just one click, the products added, shipping costs, taxes and discounts and the total purchase price (Naim, 2022). An internal search engine, which will be more important as the product catalogue and sections develop. Explanation of payment methods allowed and contact/customer support area. As there is no physical contact, companies must offer communication pathways for their online shops so that users can share their concerns and increase their trust in the company. The availability of several payment options is recommended. Some of the most common payment methods are credit card, which needs a safe payment gate- way, bank transfer or other e-services of great penetration and reliability such as PayPal (Milan et al., 2020).

This simple process is currently the most important pathway to access online content, while it becomes the marketing base for browsers: SEO and SEM (Naim, 2022).

SEO stands for search engine optimization, and it refers to a set of techniques applied on a website—structure, code, content and links—to improve positioning in the organic results of a concrete browser (Xiaodong & Min, 2020).

SEM stands for search engine marketing, and this refers to a publicity system of a browser offering users ads that are related to their search terms. Unlike SEO, SEM offers induced results (payment), even if they are presented to the Web surfer as the best result of their search (Naim, 2022).

Both types of positioning are opposing, even if they are both based on two key aspects: search engines and keywords. Figure 12 shows the distinction between SEO and SEM

Figure 12. Difference between SEO and SEM
Source: Siciliani et al. (2019)

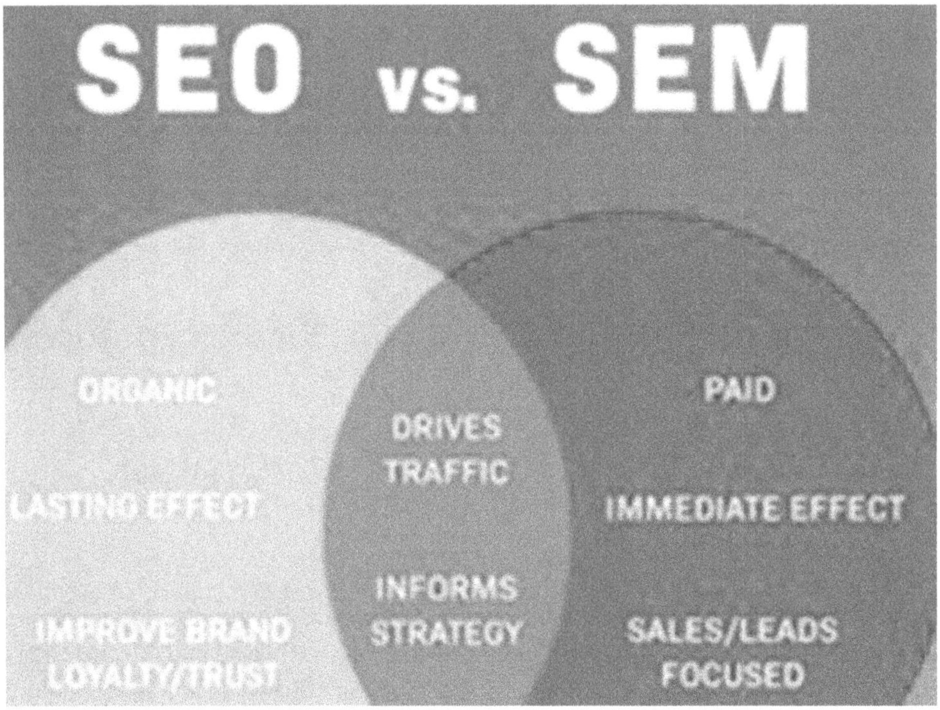

Table 1 shows the description on the difference between SEO and SEM.

Each search engine uses tracing software for websites for their indexing. The software used is known as Internet bot, Web crawler or Web spider, and periodically tracks the Web looking for new content or modiðcations on sites (Orendorff, 2019).

The search engine processes Web tracking, while it uses its own algorithm to classify websites and offer its results, as well as their order, depending on the search terms used.

In order to optimize resources for positioning, organizations need to adapt to the search engine's algorithm most widely used when speaking about positioning in browsers, usually meaning SEO and SEM action in Google (Naim, 2022).

Table 1. SEO vs. SEM

SEO	SEM
Mid- and long-term results	Quick and instant results
Results are sustained for longer	After the operations, results are removed
Live results	Paid results
Results are always shown at the center of the screen	Results appear mainly on the screen top or sides

Source: Naim (2022)

Keywords are the terms or phases that users use to search something on Internet. Likewise, keywords are search criteria matching a specific website.

How to Use SEO Techniques

SEO positioning is improved by working on two aspects: internally or externally, depending on the control level that the Webmaster has over the website (World Economic Forum, 2019). Figure 13 shows the working and use of SEO.

Figure 13. Use of SEO
Source: Yang et al. (2019)

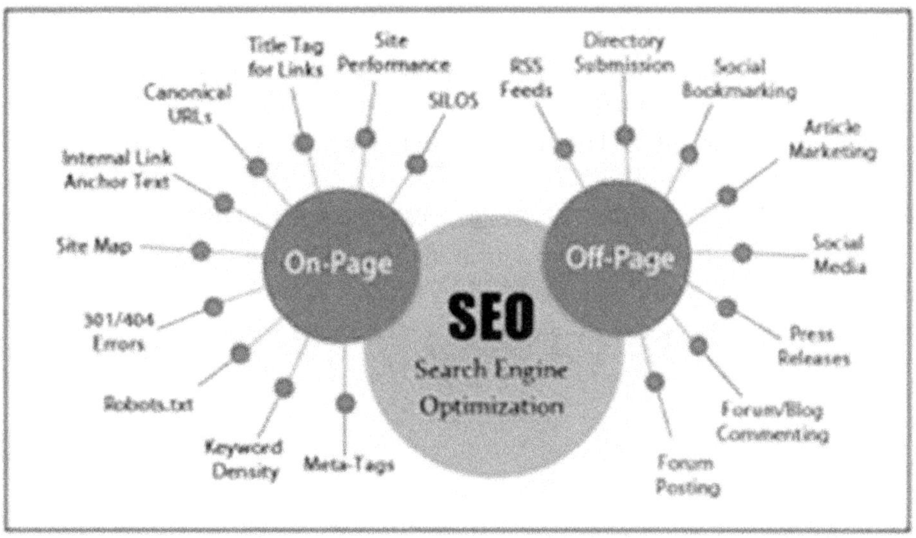

Internal SEO means undertaking actions to improve content, code and/or accessibility, aspects related to the website to be controlled by the Webmaster or company (Naim, 2022). Figure 14 shows the inclusions of keywords.

Figure 14. Inclusions of keywords with the description
Source: UNESAP and ADB (2019)

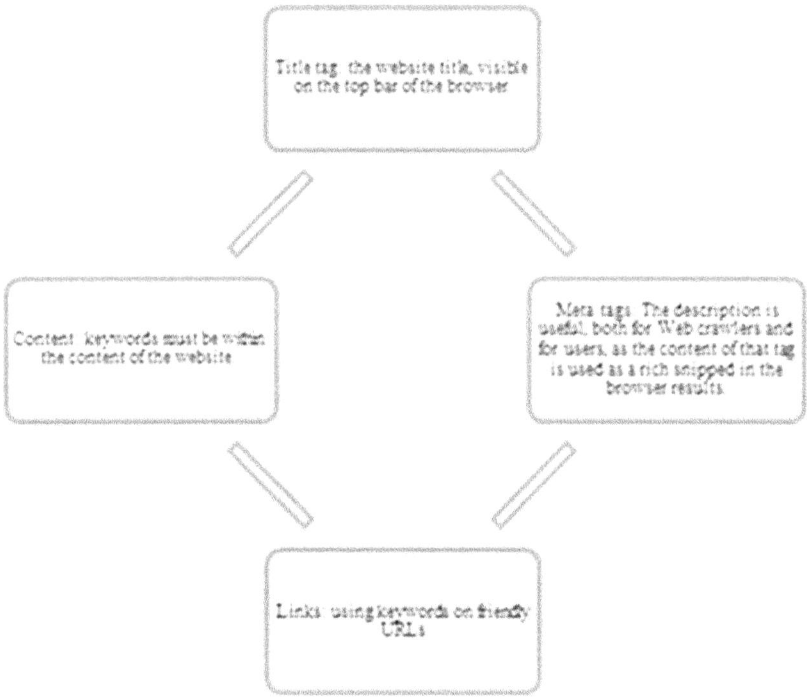

External SEO focuses on aspects that are less controllable for the company, for example incoming links coming from other websites, with the goal of gaining popularity and higher quality of the links. Figure 15 shows the process of SEO.

A link is perceived as a quality link when it is created by a site or reference platform from the sector the company is in and/or that works on the same topic. Links from social networking sites such as forums or social networks, adding the link and the signature to the message or the content shared (Wajeeha et al., 2019).

Link baiting: publishing content that encourages visitors to create links from their websites to that content. The key to success lies in their viral or mimetic nature, and though it is a technique that is difðcult to master, the results are outstanding (Naim, 2022).

Quality external links could also be improved by registering a website on general or theme-based directories.

Figure 15. SEO process
Source: Naim (2022)

How to Use SEM Techniques

SEM campaigns require being familiar with the keywords that are related to the business one tries to promote. Each click of a user who is not part of the target is lost money (Wang et al., 2019).

In order to optimize a marketing campaign using browsers, one has to know the structure of an ad. An ad usually has a title of less than 25 characters linked to the destination site: a visible URL, which need not be the destination site URL, and two lines of text, around 35 characters per line. The content of those texts must be carefully decided as it must create interest in users, especially in the body of the message as the ad will be placed on locations where only a single line will be visible (Zuhal, 2019). Figure 16 shows the inclusive and general scenario of SEM.

In order to successfully develop a SEM campaign, some questions should be addressed. These questions are discussed in Table 2.

Figure 16. General SEM scenario
Source: Naim (2022)

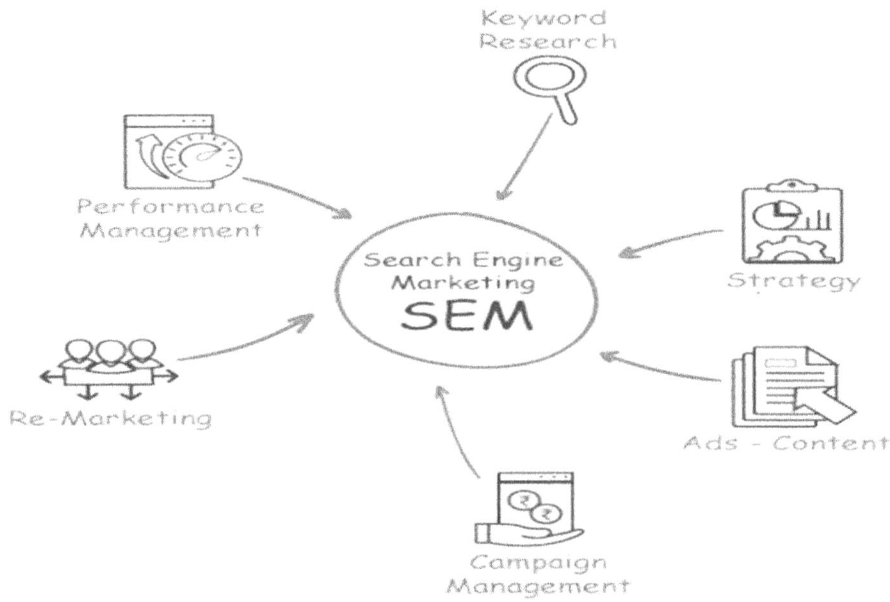

Table 2. Questions to develop successful SEM campaign

Are keywords different from the content?	If keywords that are different from the content of the website are bought to raise interest in users, many hits will be registered, but they will lack any value and shall only waste resources. Ad must have the keywords of the destination site
Does the value of keywords correlates with demand?	Ads ready to pay more per word will be placed at a better spot
Are Ads with more clicks are located in a better position?	Ads with more clicks should be located in a better position.
How can click ratio be optimized?	When designing a text, the most important aspect is that it matches the searches of users, in order to optimize the click ratio: concordance can be wide, of a sentence, exact or negative

Source: Naim (2022)

RESULTS

The study explains the benefits of digital marketing by presenting the examples of firms and how they gain recognition as well as profit by the application of digital marketing assets. Social Media Profiles, Website. Images and Video Content, Blog Posts and eBooks, Reviews and Customer Testimonials, Branded Logos, Images, or Icons (Naim, 2022). The four main types of digital advertising are social media, paid search, native, and display advertising. Using one or more of these ad channels can help the firms to establish an online presence and convert prospects into real customers. Direct marketing involves a more personalized message to build a good relationship between the customer and brands (Naim, 2022). Online ads, emails, promotional merchandise, newsletters, outdoor advertising are some direct marketing examples. Figure 17 shows how successfully Nike implemented direct marketing. Nike Stadium Shoebox is a classic example of direct marketing.

Figure 17. Nike Stadium Shoebox: Example of digital marketing
Source: Malik et al. (2022)

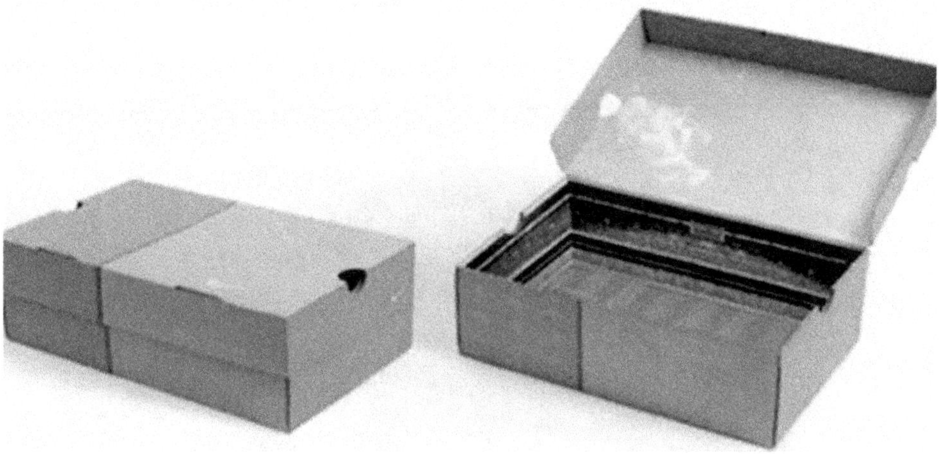

To promote sports amongst children, Nike sent targeted customers with a box. The box had a stadium designed within it and also played music when you opened it. This grabbed a lot of attention and made the user feel special.

Another example is about Inbound marketing is when the firms drive potential customers or prospects to their page or business instead of out rightly marketing the brand (Naim, 2022; Naim, 2022; Naim, 2022). The brand can be promoted through a blog, webinar, e-book, podcast, etc. Figure 18 shows the creative side of digital marketing where an example Weetabix UK recently stirred a multi-brand conversation featuring Heinz on their page. It was received with hilarious comments with other brands joining in the conversation as well (Naim, 2022).

Integrated Digital marketing is also another successful example where imagine that a content writer in a company write a blog that has gone live on the website (Naim & Alqahtani, n.d.). The YouTube team made a video on that blog and the social media team added a swipe up on Instagram for that blog.

Further, the firm can pay media team used that blog to run advertisements on Google. This is how integrated digital marketing is currently working where many departments and online media come together to promote or sell products and services (Naim, Kautish, Fatima et al, 2022; Jaipuriar et al., 2020; Naim, Kautish, Kamal et al, 2022; Naim & Kautish, 2022).

There are many examples of successful digital marketing some are discussed as cases in this study.

Figure 18. Example of creativity through digital marketing
Source: Naim (2022)

Apple #SHOTONIPHONE: Organic Social Media Marketing

Social media marketing refers to the use of social media platforms to engage a large digital audience. The end goals are to grow your brand by increasing brand awareness and loyalty, increasing sales and revenue, and driving website traffic (Naim, Kautish, Alqahtani et al, 2022; Naim, 2022). The Campaign objective was to create a viral campaign to demonstrate the clarity and unmatched quality of Apple's new camera. Apple executed the campaign by making 77 photo entries from 75 iPhone 6 users across 25 countries were compiled to create a campaign. iPhone 6 users from all over the world were asked to share their best shots from their phones with the hashtag #shotoniPhone. Once the campaign went live, it went viral. Apple leverages this by selecting images from different age groups and social demographics and displaying these images on 10,000 billboards all over the world. It was now a 360-degree campaign with ads in magazines, newspapers, TV ads, and paid media ads. The campaign had a tremendous impact worldwide (Išoraitė & Miniotienė, 2018). Figure 19 shows the results of successful digital marketing for Apple #SHOTONIPHONE.

Figure 19. Success factors for digital marketing for Apple #SHOTONIPHONE

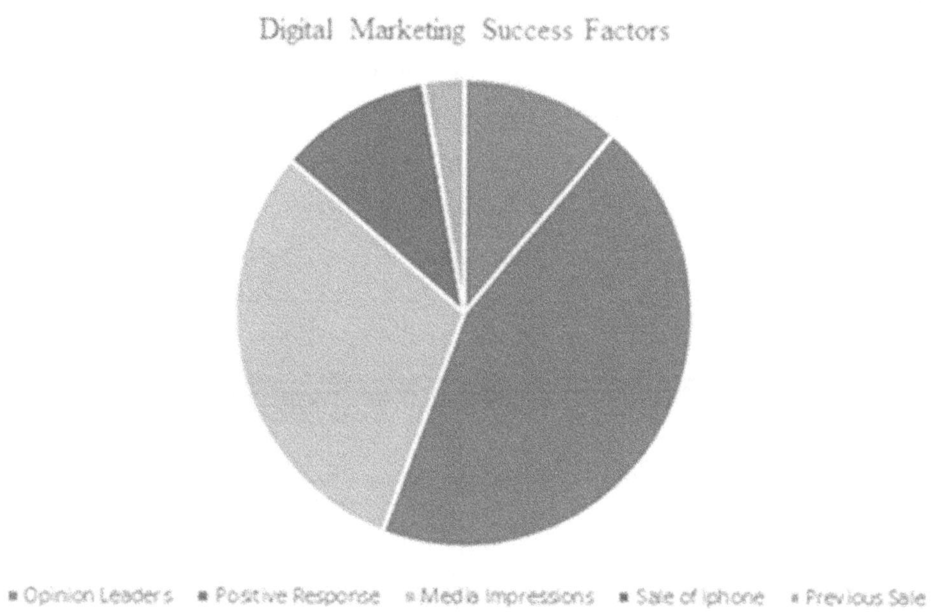

Existing users felt part of a worldwide community with the hashtag #shotoniphone and a trend of non-users also using the hashtag or converting to new users. This is a great example of how social media helped create hype around the iPhone technology and also user-generated content adds to the credibility of the brand. This differentiates them from other brands as consumers trust digital marketing more than traditional methods of marketing.

ABTA Travel With Confidence: Paid Social Media Marketing Example

Social media advertising is targeted advertising using social media as a channel (Naim, Malik, & Zaidi, 2023). They include paid social media, dynamic ads, Facebook ads, Twitter ads, Instagram ads, Reddit ads, LinkedIn ads, Quora ads, and more. ABTA is the U.K.'s largest travel association, previously known as the Association of British Travel Agents consisting of tour operators and travel agents (Liyang, 2019). The campaign objective was to increase awareness and sales of their offering for young travelers between the age groups of 18-35. They also wanted to increase bookings with their existing client base. The first step was to create video content for Facebook, Instagram, Twitter, and Youtube to appeal to the target audience. The campaign messages were divided into 3 broad categories – pre-holiday, holiday, and post-holiday. Figure 20 shows the main deliverables of ABTA after the application of digital marketing.

ABTA worked with good budget and could reallocate their set budgets on the basis of the best-performing channel. Reviewing and reallocating were key for better performance.

By targeting the right audiences and age groups, results show that ABTA has 738,218 unique users on Facebook alone. The Youtube view rates doubled from 20% to 40%. Facebook impressions increased from 128,519 to 4,260,668 (Naim, Malik, Zaidi et al., 2023).

Figure 20. Main deliverables of ABTA
Source: Naim, Malik, Zaidi et al. (2023)

Monster India: Search Engine Optimization (SEO)

SEO or search engine optimization is the method of improving the quality and quantity of traffic to your website (Helge et al., 2020). The main goal is to improve your brand's visibility when you search for a product or service. Monster India Google Search Campaign had an objective to improve the quality and expand their existing applicant and resume database. Monster Inc. India started using structured data with the goal to improve its database (Helge et al., 2020). The team added structured data to job postings. This makes the job posting eligible to appear in a special user experience in search results. Figure 21 shows the results of Monster India after the application of SEO.

Figure 21. Application of SEO for monster India

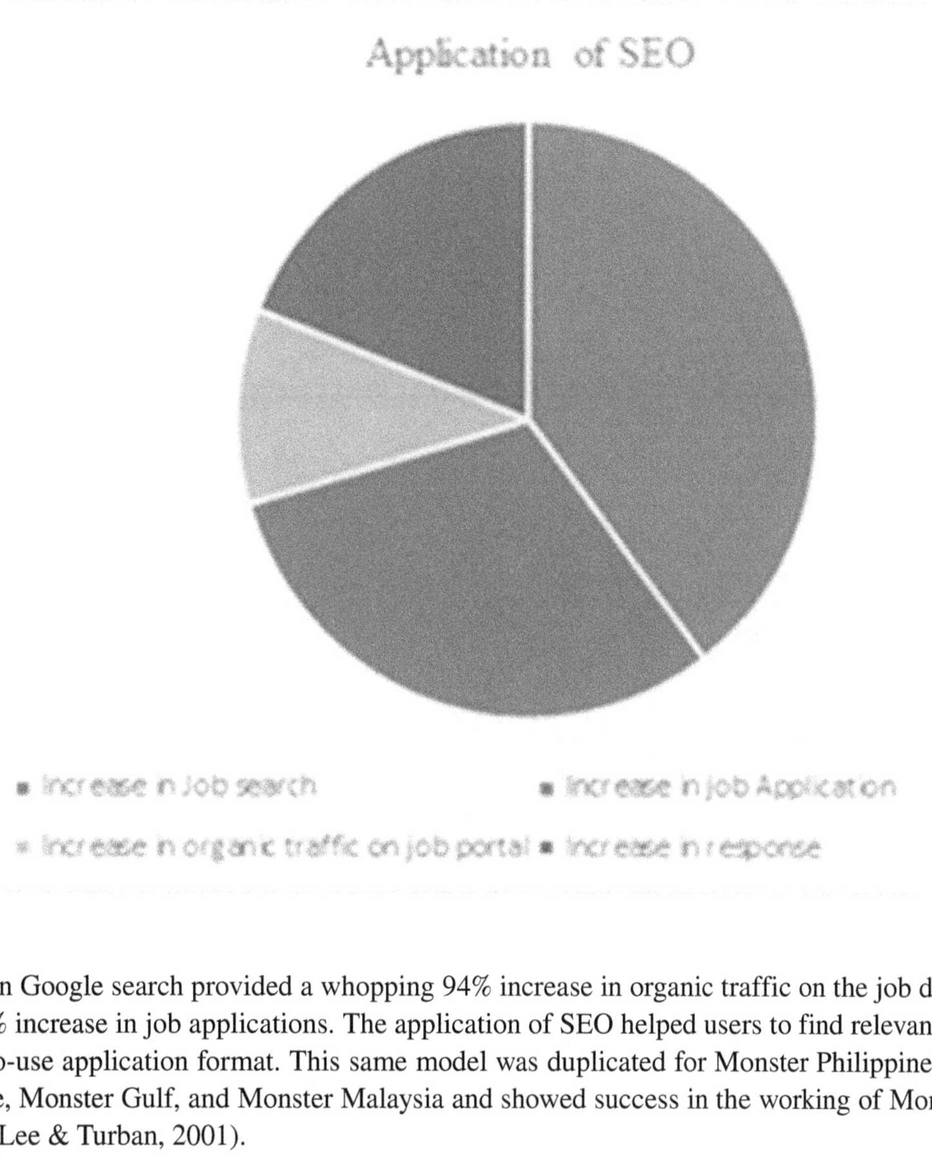

Jobs on Google search provided a whopping 94% increase in organic traffic on the job details page and a 10% increase in job applications. The application of SEO helped users to find relevant jobs with its easy-to-use application format. This same model was duplicated for Monster Philippines, Monster Singapore, Monster Gulf, and Monster Malaysia and showed success in the working of Monster International (Lee & Turban, 2001).

Zappos: Search Engine Marketing (SEM) Example

A search engine marketing (SEM) marketing is a campaign strategy that uses paid ads within search engines (Majithia, 2019). These target potential customers as they show up on SERPs or search engine result pages. The Campaign conducted by Zappos Summer shoe campaign was to increase sales for Zappos summer shoe variant. Zappos is one of the world's largest online shoe selling brands (Majithia, 2019). Figure 22 shows the results of Zappos after the application of SEM.

Figure 22. Increase in sale for Zappos after the application of SEM

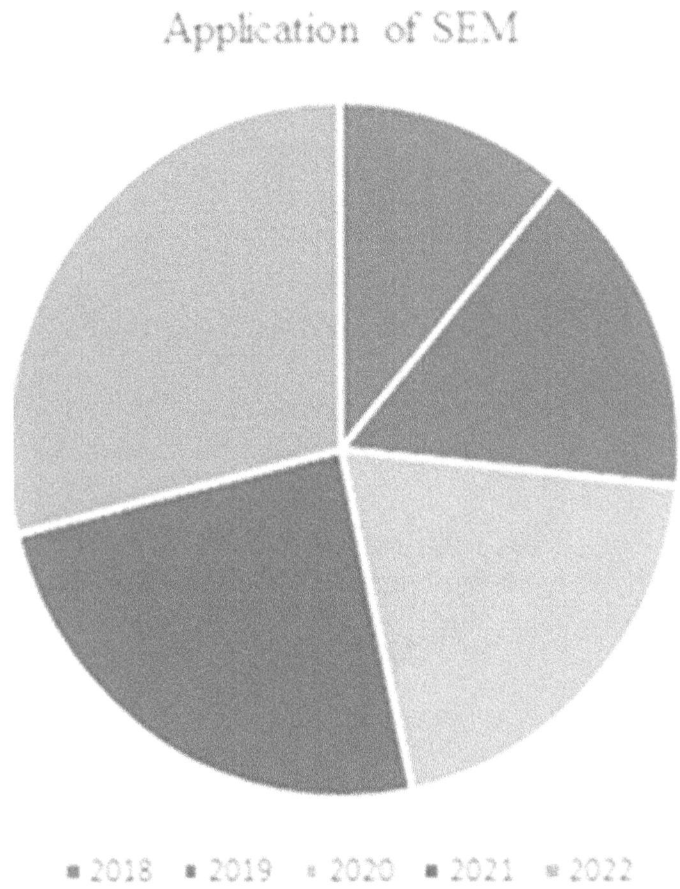

The results show that from 2018 to 2020, 10% increase in sale is witnessed by Zappos after the application of SEM. Most of the company's sales are through search engine marketing and word-of-mouth.

CONCLUSION

These digital marketing examples stimulate the firms to apply some of these techniques to their marketing mix. In the current context, no company, regardless of its size, can live without the application of digital marketing or having a presence on social media. In this chapter, we have presented some of the most extensively used and most operative digital marketing strategies. We have discussed some techniques to attract users and the right audiences, to create attractive and interesting content so that customers remain loyal to organizations and brands. In this chapter we have given examples from big and small companies and how they have implemented the digital marketing and receive over whelming response from consumers, created brand image, brand loyalty and became leader in their product mix.

REFERENCES

Agag, G. (2019). E-commerce ethics and its impact on buyer repurchase intentions and loyalty: An empirical study of small and medium Egyptian businesses. *Journal of Business Ethics*, *154*(2), 389–410. doi:10.100710551-017-3452-3

Agag, G., & El-Masry, A. A. (2016). Understanding consumer intention to participate in online travel community and effects on consumer intention to purchase travel online and WOM: An integration of innovation diffusion theory and TAM with trust. *Computers in Human Behavior*, *60*, 97–111. doi:10.1016/j.chb.2016.02.038

Alqahtani, H., & Naim, A. (2022). Critical Success Factors for Transforming CRM to SCRM for building E-CRM. In A. Naim & S. Kautish (Eds.), *Building a Brand Image Through Electronic Customer Relationship Management* (pp. 139–168). IGI Global. doi:10.4018/978-1-6684-5386-5.ch007

AyilyathM. (2020). Consumer protection in E-commerce transactions in India—need for reforms, SSRN. doi:10.2139/ssrn.3571069

Ballestar, M., Grau-Carles, P., & Sainz, J. (2018). Customer segmentation in e-commerce: Application to the cashback business model. *Journal of Business Research*, *88*, 407–414. doi:10.1016/j.jbusres.2017.11.047

Bandara, R., Fernando, M., & Akter, S. (2019). Explicating the privacy paradox: A qualitative inquiry of online shopping consumers. *Journal of Retailing and Consumer Services*, *52*, 220–233. doi:10.1016/j.jretconser.2019.101947

Bashir, M. A., & Naim, A. (2020). *ICT Adoption Analysis for Innovation in Higher Education Sector*. Academic Press.

Belanche, D., Flavián, M., & Pérez-Rueda, A. (2020). Mobile apps use and WOM in the food delivery sector: The role of planned behavior, perceived security and customer lifestyle compatibility. *Sustainability*, *12*(10), 4275. doi:10.3390u12104275

Belwal, R., Al Shibli, R., & Belwal, S. (2020). *Consumer protection and electronic commerce in the Sultanate of Oman. Journal of Information*. Communication and Ethics in Society. doi:10.1108/JICES-09-2019-0110

Brian, I. S., O'Neill, B. S., & Terence, T. O. (2019). The upside of showrooming: How online information creates positive spill-over for the brick-and-mortar retailer. *Journal of Organizational Computing and Electronic Commerce*, *29*(4), 294–315. doi:10.1080/10919392.2019.1671738

Broome, P. A. (2016). Conceptualizing the foundations of a regional e-commerce strategy: Open networks or closed regimes? The case of CARICOM. *Cogent Business &Management*, *3*(1), 1139–1441. doi:10.1080/23311975.2016.1139441

Castaneda, J. A., Rodriguez-Molina, M. A., & Martínez, T. L. (2009). Attitude's hierarchy of effects in online user behavior. *Online Information Review*, *33*(11), 7–21. doi:10.1108/14684520910944364

Cetina, I., Munthiu, M.-C., & Radulescu, V. (2012). Psychological and Social Factors that Influence Online Consumer Behavior. *Procedia: Social and Behavioral Sciences*, *62*, 184–188. doi:10.1016/j.sbspro.2012.09.029

Changchit, C., Cutshall, R., Lonkani, R., Pholwan, K., & Pongwiritthon, R. (2018). Determinants of online shopping influencing Thai consumer's buying choices. *Journal of Internet Commerce*, *18*(1), 1–23. doi:10.1080/15332861.2018.1496391

Choshin, M., & Ghaffari, A. (2017). An investigation of the impact of effective factors on the success of e-commerce in small- and medium-sized companies. *Computers in Human Behavior*, *66*(1), 67–74. doi:10.1016/j.chb.2016.09.026

Chouhan, R. (2017). E-Business and E-Commerce Management (Strategy, Implementation and Practice). *Pacific Business Review International*, *9*(10), 135–136.

Dai, Z. (2012). The Study on the Influence about Trust to Online Shopping Behavior. In: *Eleventh Wuhan International Conference on e-Business*. Association for Information Systems.

Darsono, J. T., Prihantono, E. Y., & Kasim, E. S. (2019). Strategic Policies for Small and Medium Businesses in marketing through E-commerce. *Entrepreneurship and Sustainability Issues*, *7*(2), 1230–1245. doi:10.9770/jesi.2019.7.2(30)

Doe, J. K., & Asamoah, G. K. (2022). CRM as Antecedent of Electronic Retailing and Online Customer Satisfaction. In A. Naim & S. Kautish (Eds.), *Building a Brand Image Through Electronic Customer Relationship Management* (pp. 169–200). IGI Global. doi:10.4018/978-1-6684-5386-5.ch008

Doern, R. R., & Fey, C. F. (2006). E-commerce developments and strategies for value creation: The case of Russia. *Journal of World Business*, *41*(4), 315–327. doi:10.1016/j.jwb.2006.08.001

Durovic, M. (2020). International consumer law: What is it all about? *Journal of Consumer Policy*, *43*(1), 125–143. doi:10.100710603-019-09438-9

Edgar, T. W., & Manz, D. O. (2017). *Research Methods for Cyber Security*. Elsevier.

Elbeltagi, I., & Agag, G. (2016). E-retailing ethics and its impact on customer satisfaction and repurchase intention: A cultural and commitment-trust theory perspective. *Internet Research*, *26*(1), 288–310. doi:10.1108/IntR-10-2014-0244

Elseidi, R. I. (2018). Understanding Egyptian consumers' intentions in online shopping. *International Journal of Online Marketing*, *8*(3), 1–18. doi:10.4018/IJOM.2018070101

Emma, P., Sara, F., Marta, S., & Ana, G. (2017). *Exploratory study of consumer issues in online peer-to-peer platform markets*. European Commission. file:///C:/Users/BASANT~1/AppData/Local/Temp/Annex5_Task5_Report May2017pdf

Fatima, S., Alqahtani, H., Naim, A., & Alma'alwi, F. (2022). E-CRM Through Social Media Marketing Activities for Brand Awareness, Brand Image, and Brand Loyalty. In A. Naim & S. Kautish (Eds.), *Building a Brand Image Through Electronic Customer Relationship Management* (pp. 109–138). IGI Global. doi:10.4018/978-1-6684-5386-5.ch006

Filson, D. (2004). The Impact of E-Commerce Strategies on Firm Value: Lessons from Amazon.com and Its Early Competitors. *The Journal of Business*, *77*(2), 135–154. doi:10.1086/381640

Forman, C. (2005). The corporate digital divide: Determinants of Internet adoption. *Management Science*, *51*(4), 641–654. doi:10.1287/mnsc.1040.0343

Hallikainen, H., & Laukkanen, T. (2018). National culture and consumer trust in ecommerce. *International Journal of Information Management*, *38*(1), 97–106. doi:10.1016/j.ijinfomgt.2017.07.002

Harrigan, M., Feddema, K., Wang, S., Harrigan, P., & Diot, E. (2021). How trust leads to online purchase intention founded in perceived usefulness and peer communication. *Journal of Consumer Behaviour: An International Research Review,* 1-16. . doi:10.1002/cb.1936

Harrisson, B., Jean, P., & Dahl, B. (2017). 10 ecommerce trends for 2018. *Project: Growth Strategies in an Omnichannel Retail Context*. . doi:10.13140/RG.2.2.34264.19205

Haupt, S. (2003). An economic analysis of consumer protection in Con-trAct law. *German Law Review,* *4*(11), 1137–1164.

Helge, S., Anne, H., & Guido, M. (2020). The function of ability, benevolence, and integrity-based trust in innovation networks. *Industry and Innovation*, *27*(6), 585–604. doi:10.1080/13662716.2019.1632695

Išoraitė, M., & Miniotienė, N. (2018). *Electronic commerce: Theory and practice.* Integrated Journal of Business and Economics. doi:10.33019/ijbe.v2i2.78

Jaipuriar, A., Khera, A., & Ganguly, S. (2020). *Consumer protection (e-commerce) rules, 2020: A compliance framework in the digital market.* https://www.mondaq.com/india/dodd-frank-consumer-protection-act/977768/consumer-protection-e-commerce-rules-2020-a-compl iance-framework-in-the-digital-market

Kamal, S., Naim, A., Magd, H., Khan, S. A., & Khan, F. M. (2022). The Relationship Between E-Service Quality, Ease of Use, and E-CRM Performance Referred by Brand Image. In A. Naim & S. Kautish (Eds.), *Building a Brand Image Through Electronic Customer Relationship Management* (pp. 84–108). IGI Global. doi:10.4018/978-1-6684-5386-5.ch005

Kerick, F. (2019). The growth of ecommerce. *Medium.* https://medium.com/swlh/the-growth-of-ecommerce-2220cf2851f3

Khandelwal, P. (2018). Ease of doing E-commerce business in India: The FDI policy relating to Ecommerce and its impact on the Indian economy. *RGNUL Financial and Mercantile Law Review*, 20–37. https://cf9d2836-9a17-4889-b084-bc78a1bb74ee.filesusr.com/ug d/0fa0b3_d7453802d99a4dd7a20ff4b3886b1d04.pdf

Lăzăroiu, G., Neguriţă, O., Grecu, I., Grecu, G., & Mitran, P. C. (2020). Consumers' decision-making process on social commerce platforms: Online trust, perceived risk, and purchase intentions. *Frontiers in Psychology*, *11*, 890. doi:10.3389/fpsyg.2020.00890 PMID:32499740

Lee, O. M. K., & Turban, E. (2001). A trust model for consumer internet shopping. *International Journal of Electronic Commerce*, *6*(1), 75–91. doi:10.1080/10864415.2001.11044227

Liyang, H. (2019). Superior bargaining power: The good, the bad and the ugly. *Asia Pacific Law Review*, *27*(1), 39–61. doi:10.1080/10192557.2019.1661589

Loannis, L., Despoina, M., Gracia, M. D., Amber, D., & d'Azza R. (2019). *The global governance of online consumer protection and E-commerce-building trust*. WeForum. https://www3.weforum.org/docs/WEF_consumer_protection.pdf

Majithia, V. (2019). The changing landscape of intermediary liability for E-commerce platforms : Emergence of a new regime. *International Journal of Law and Technology*, *15*, 470–493.

Malik, P. K., Naim, A., & Singh, R. (Eds.). (2022). *Printed Antennas: Design and Challenges*. CRC Press. doi:10.1201/9781003347057

Mangiaracina, R., & Perego, A. (2009). Payment systems in the B2C eCommerce: Are they a barrier for the online customer? *Journal of Internet Banking and Commerce*, *14*(3), 1–16.

Milan, J., Antonio, G., & Niklas, A. (2020). Exploring the growth challenge of mobile payment platforms: A business model perspective. *Electronic Commerce Research and Applications*, *40*, 100908. doi:10.1016/j.elerap.2019.100908

Miyazaki, A., & Fernandez, A. N. A. (2001). Consumer perceptions of privacy and security risks for online shopping. *The Journal of Consumer Affairs*, *35*(1), 27–44. doi:10.1111/j.1745-6606.2001.tb00101.x

Naim, A. (2020). Realization of diverse Electronic tools in learning and teaching for students with diverse skills. *Global Journal of Enterprise Information System*, *12*(1), 72–78.

Naim, A. (2021a). Green Information Technologies in Business Operations. Periodica Journal of Modern Philosophy. *Social Sciences and Humanities*, *1*, 36–49.

Naim, A. (2021b). Applications of MIS in building Electronic Relationship with customers: A case-based study. Periodica Journal of Modern Philosophy. *Social Sciences and Humanities*, *1*, 1–8.

Naim, A. (2021c). New Trends in Business Process Management: Applications of Green Information Technologies. *British Journal of Environmental Studies*, *1*(1), 12–23.

Naim, A. (2021d). Applications of Marketing Framework in Business Practices. *Journal of Marketing and Emerging Economics*, *1*(6), 55–70.

Naim, A. (2021e). Green Business Process Management. *International Journal of Innovative Analyses and Emerging Technology*, *1*(6), 125–134. https://openaccessjournals.eu/index.php/ijiaet/article/view/651

Naim, A. (2021f). Applications of E-Learning tools for Achieving Students Learning Outcomes. *Journal of Pedagogical Inventions and Practices*, *2*(2), 75–82. https://zienjournals.com/index.php/jpip/article/view/320

Naim, A. (2022a). Benefits of Artificial Intelligence (AI) in Financial Practices. *International Journal of Studies in Business Management, Economics and Strategies*, *1*, 1–12. https://scholarsdigest.org/index.php/bmes/article/view/7

Naim, A. (2022b). Applications of Green Information Technologies in Business Process Management, Business Issues. *Competition and Entrepreneurship, 31.* doi:10.52305/VIXO9830

Naim, A. (2022c). Neuromarketing as a Tool for Measuring Consumer Emotions for Games. *International Journal of Scientific Trends, 1*(1), 55–65. https://scientifictrends.org/index.php/ijst/article/view/6

Naim. (2022d). Emerging Technologies in Finance and Market: Applications of AI Business Issues. *Competition and Entrepreneurship, 137.* https:// doi:10.52305/VIXO9830

Naim, A. (2022e). Measurement of Electronic Commerce Effectiveness. *Neo Science Peer Reviewed Journal, 1,* 1–10. https://neojournals.com/index.php/nsprj/article/view/6

Naim. (2022f). Applications of E-Learning Tools for Achieving Students Learning Outcomes for Business Programs. *Competitive Trends and Technologies in Business Management*, 125. https:// doi:10.52305/ VIXO9830

Naim, A. (2022g). Neuro- Marketing Techniques for Proposing Information Driven Framework for Decision Making. *International Journal of Innovative Analyses and Emerging Technology*, 2(2), 87–94. https://openaccessjournals.eu/index.php/ijiaet/article/view/ 1060

Naim, A. (2022h). Economies of Scale for Antenna's Applications in Interior Regions. *International Journal of Innovative Analyses and Emerging Technology*, 2(2), 77–82. https://openaccessjournals.eu/index.php/ijiaet/article/view/ 1058

Naim, A. (2022i). Mapping of Social Customer Relationship Management With Electronic Customer Relationship Management. *European Journal of Interdisciplinary Research and Development*, *2*, 14–25. https://ejird.journalspark.org/index.php/ejird/article/view/ 10

Naim, A. (2022j). E-Learning Engagement through Convolution Neural Networks in Business Education. *European Journal of Innovation in Nonformal Education*, 2(2), 497–501.

Naim, A. (2022k). Measurement Consumer Mood and Emotions for Fast Moving Consumer Goods. *International Journal of Innovative Analyses and Emerging Technology*, 2(2), 83–86.

Naim, A. (2022l). Economies of Scale for Antenna's Applications in Interior Regions. *International Journal of Innovative Analyses and Emerging Technology*, 2(2), 77–82.

Naim, A. (2022m). Public Enterprises: Their Role, Importance And Need In Economic Development. *American Journal of Business Management, Economics and Banking, 1,* 1–11. https://americanjournal.org/index.php/ajbmeb/article/view/7

Naim, A. (2022n) Role Of Accounting And Finance In Performance Appraisal. *American Journal of Sociology, Economics and Tourism,* 1-17 https://americanjournal.org/index.php/ajset/issue/view/4

Naim, A. (2022o). Islamic Philosophy Based Business Model. *American Journal of Research in Humanities and Social Sciences,* 1-5. https://americanjournal.org/index.php/ajrhss/issue/view/2

Naim, A. (2022p). Mapping Of Social Customer Relationship Management With Electronic Customer Relationship Management. *European Journal of Interdisciplinary Research and Development, 2*, 14–25. https://ejird.journalspark.org/index.php/ejird/article/view/10

Naim, A. (2022q). Factors of Consumer Behaviour of youth from middle-east when purchasing Organic Food. *Global Scientific Review, 3*, 1–7. http://www.scienticreview.com/index.php/gsr/article/view/13

Naim, A. (2022r). Understanding The Customer Centric Approach To Add Value To Social Ecrm (Secrm). *British Journal of Global Ecology and Sustainable Development, 4*, 1–17. https://journalzone.org/index.php/bjgesd/article/view/45

Naim, A. (2022s). Cost Trend: Meaning and Importance of Cost Trend In Public Enterprises. *American Journal of Technology and Applied Sciences, 1*, 37–46. https://americanjournal.org/index.php/ajtas/article/view/11

Naim, A. (2022t). Role of Artificial Intelligence In Business Risk Management. American Journal of Business Management. *Economics and Banking, 1*, 55–66.

Naim, A. (2022u). Relevance of Online Learning In Higher Education. *American Journal of Pedagogical and Educational Research, 1*, 21–34.

Naim, A. (2022v). Factors of Consumer Behaviour of youth from middle-east when purchasing Organic Food. *Global Scientific Review, 3*, 1–7.

Naim, A. (2022w). Measurement of Electronic Commerce Effectiveness. *Neo Science Peer Reviewed Journal, 1*, 1–10. https://neojournals.com/index.php/nsprj/article/view/6

Naim, A. (2022x). Consumer Behavior for The Consumption and Buying Of Medical Services. *Intent Research Scientific Journal, 1*(1), 46–64.

Naim, A. (2022y). Developing Business Models as per Islamic Practices. *International Journal of Studies in Business Management, Economics and Strategies, 2*(2), 15–22. https://scholarsdigest.org/index.php/bmes/article/view/25

Naim, A. (2022z). Empathetic Approach to Customer Orientation for Social CRM and ECRM. *International Journal of Studies in Business Management, Economics and Strategies, 2*(2), 1–14. https://scholarsdigest.org/index.php/bmes/article/view/24

Naim, A. (2022aa). Virtual Learning in Business Information Systems: A Case Study on Quality Matters Applications, Business Issues. *Competition and Entrepreneurship, 93*. doi:10.52305/VIXO9830

Naim, A. (2022bb). Successful E-CRM by the Application of Management Information Systems, Business Issues. *Competition and Entrepreneurship, 19*. doi:10.52305/VIXO9830

Naim, A., & Alahmari, F. (2020). Reference model of e-learning and quality to establish interoperability in higher education systems. *International Journal of Emerging Technologies in Learning, 15*(2), 15–28. doi:10.3991/ijet.v15i02.11605

Naim, A., Alahmari, F., & Rahim, A. (2021). Role of Artificial Intelligence in Market Development and Vehicular Communication. Smart Antennas. *Recent Trends in Design and Applications*, *2*, 28–39. doi: 10.2174/9781681088594121020006

Naim, A., Alqahtani, H., Muniasamy, A., Bilfaqih, S. M., Mahveen, R., & Mahjabeen, R. (2023). Applications of Information Systems and Data Security in Marketing Management. In A. Naim, P. Malik, & F. Zaidi (Eds.), *Fraud Prevention, Confidentiality, and Data Security for Modern Businesses* (pp. 57–83). IGI Global., doi:10.4018/978-1-6684-6581-3.ch003

Naim, A., & Alqahtani, K. (2021). Role of Information Systems in Customer Relationship Management. *Pulse*, *2*(2).

Naim, A. & Alqahtani, K. (2020). Applications of Decision Support Systems in CRM. *Business Issues, Competition and Entrepreneurship 1*. doi:10.52305/VIXO9830

Naim, A., & Hassan, S. Z. (2022). Economies of Scale for Security Applications in Business, Business Issues. *Competition and Entrepreneurship*, *73*. doi:10.52305/VIXO9830

Naim, A., Hussain, M. R., Naveed, Q. N., Ahmad, N., Qamar, S., Khan, N., & Hweij, T. A. (2019, April). Ensuring interoperability of e-learning and quality development in education. In *2019 IEEE Jordan International Joint Conference on Electrical Engineering and Information Technology (JEEIT)* (pp. 736-741). IEEE. 10.1109/JEEIT.2019.8717431

Naim, A., & Kautish, S. K. (Eds.). (2022). *Building a Brand Image Through Electronic Customer Relationship Management*. IGI Global. doi:10.4018/978-1-6684-5386-5

Naim, A., & Khan, M. F. (2021). Measuring the Psychological Behavior of Consumers for Medical Services. *Zien Journal of Social Sciences and Humanities, 2,* 119–131. https://zienjournals.com/index.php/zjssh/article/view/316

Naim, A., & Khan, M.F. (2022) Consumer Behavior Appraisal for Health and Fitness Services. *Business Issues, Competition and Entrepreneurship 53*. https:// doi:10.52305/VIXO9830

Naim, A., Khan, M. F., Hussain, M. R., & Khan, N. (2019). "Virtual Doctor" Management Technique in the Diagnosis of ENT Diseases. *JOE*, *15*(9), 88. doi:10.3991/ijoe.v15i09.10665

Naim, A. & Malik, P. (2022). *Competitive Trends and Technologies in Business Management*. Nova Science Publisher. doi:10.52305/VIXO9830

Naim, A., Malik, P. K., & Zaidi, F. A. (Eds.). (2023). *Fraud Prevention, Confidentiality, and Data Security for Modern Businesses*. IGI Global. doi:10.4018/978-1-6684-6581-3

Naim, A., Muniasamy, A., Clementking, A., & Rajkumar, R. (2022). Relevance of Green Manufacturing and IoT in Industrial Transformation and Marketing Management. In M. Lahby, A. Al-Fuqaha, & Y. Maleh (Eds.), *Computational Intelligence Techniques for Green Smart Cities. Green Energy and Technology*. Springer. doi:10.1007/978-3-030-96429-0_19

Naim, A., Sattar, R. A., Al Ahmary, N., & Razwi, M. T. (2021) Implementation of Quality Matters Standards on Blended Courses: A Case Study. Indian Institute of Finance 35(3), 873 – 890.

Orendorff, A. (2019). *Global ecommerce statistics and trends to launch your business beyond borders.* Shopify. https://www.shopify.com/enterprise/global-ecommerce-statistics#8

Shirazi, F., Adam, N. A., Shanmugam, M., & Schultz, C. D. (2020). The importance of trust for electronic commerce satisfaction: An entrepreneurial perspective. *British Food Journal, 123*(2), 789–802. doi:10.1108/BFJ-07-2020-0626

Siciliani, P., Riefa, C., & Gamper, H. (2019). *Consumer theories of harm: An economic approach to consumer law enforcement and policy making*. Hart Publishing. doi:10.5040/9781509916887

UNCTAD. (2019). *Measuring E-commerce and the digital economy*. UNCTAD. https://unctad.org/topic/ecommerce-and-digital-economy/measuring-ecommerce-digital-economy

UNESAP & ADB. (2019). *Embracing the E-commerce revolution in Asia and the Pacific*. ADB. https://www.adb.org/sites/default/files/publication/430401/embracing-e-commerce-revolution.pdf

Wajeeha, A., Annas, H., & Kashif, F. (2019). Underlying factors influencing consumers' trust and loyalty in E-commerce. *Business Perspectives and Research, 8*(2), 186–204. doi:10.1177/2278533719887451

Wang, X., Tajvidi, M., Lin, X., & Hajli, N. (2019). Towards an ethical and trustworthy social commerce community for brand value Co-creation: A trust-commitment perspective. *Journal of Business Ethics, 167*(1), 137–152. doi:10.100710551-019-04182-z

World Economic Forum. (2019). The global governance of online consumer protection and e-commerce building trust. WEF. https://www3.weforum.org/docs/WEF_consumer_protection.pdf

Xiaodong, Q., & Min, L. (2020). E-commerce user type recognition based on access sequence similarity. *Journal of Organizational Computing and Electronic Commerce, 30*(3), 209–223. doi:10.1080/10919392.2020.1742552

Yang, Z., Van Ngo, Q., Chen, Y., Nguyen, C. X.-T., & Hoang, H. T. (2019). Does ethics perception foster consumer repurchase intention? Role of trust, perceived uncertainty, and shopping habit. *SAGE Open, 9*(2). doi:10.1177/2158244019848844

Zuhal, H. (2019). The gamut of E-commerce: Between online fraud and trust towards technology among generation Y. *International Journal of Mechanical Engineering and Technology, 10*(01), 830–836. http://www.iaeme.com/IJMET/issues.asp?JType=IJMET&VType=10&Type=01

Chapter 7
Understanding the Relationship Between IoT and Digital Marketing:
A Bibliometric Analysis

Hesham Magd
Modern College of Business and Science, Oman

Shad Ahmad Khan
https://orcid.org/0000-0001-7593-3487
University of Buraimi, Oman

Bhanupriya Khatri
Chandigarh University, India

Nidhi Sharma
https://orcid.org/0000-0002-3014-2312
Chandigarh University, India

Shaina Arora
Chandigarh University, India

ABSTRACT

This study aims to understand the relationship between the internet of things (IoT) and digital marketing (DM) by conducting a bibliometric analysis of existing literature. The analysis includes mainly the co-occurrence analysis to explore the major terms and keywords in the arena of IoT and DM. Results indicate a growing interest in the IoT and DM, with a significant increase in publications in the recent years. However, the findings reveal that very limited studies have been conducted in the intersection of IoT and digital marketing. This study thus looks at IoT and DM minutely, and attempts to identify the trends, works, and future possibilities. Thus, this study can serve as a valuable resource for researchers and practitioners in the field.

DOI: 10.4018/978-1-6684-8166-0.ch007

1. INTRODUCTION

Internet of things (IoT) is changing the way things are done in the modern time. IoT is the interconnection of computing devices via the internet where the everyday objects are interconnected in a way that they can send and receive the data among themselves without any human intervention. It would not be wrong if the IoT is defined as the way one device interacts with another. Digital marketing (DM) on the other hand has been transforming the shape and size of the marketing concepts. Digital marketing utilizes the digital platforms including internet and has given an exposure to the new level of possibilities to the marketing world. The linkage of IoT with digital marketing is expected t help the marketers in identifying the right market, the right buyer and will help them to create the right products. Many researchers and authors believe that this combination of IOT and digital marketing needs to be explored further to create ways for the newer opportunities and developments. As an attempt to make this vision a reality, a track of what already has happened in the body of knowledge, and the ways of creating better interpretation of the proposed concept, a bibliometric analysis is proposed by way of this chapter. This chapter will extract the bibliometric data from the Scopus database, the largest database of the scientific publications, and will analyze the data to arrive at a meaningful conclusion. The results and analysis of this study is expected to underpin many new dimensions to the IoT and DM relationship. This chapter will have an implication on all the budding digital marketers, businesses and other stakeholders who are interested in the field of IoT and DM.

1.1. Digital Marketing

DM is the process of promoting products, services, or brands using digital channels such as social media, search engines, and mobile apps (Langan et al., 2019; Saleem et al., 2022). It has received a hype due to the rise in the internet and digital technology in the recent years. Today DM has become an integral part of the marketing activities that offers variety of benefits to the business in reaching their target audience (Chaffey & Ellis-Chadwick, 2019). The tools like search engine optimization (SEO); social media; content marketing; email marketing etc are an important element of the DM today (Matta et al., 2020). SEO is a tool to optimize a website so that it appears at the top of the search engine results. It utilises the proper and relevant keywords to assist the businesses reach their target audience (Chaffey & Ellis-Chadwick, 2019; Hollebeek & Macky,2019). Through SEO business can improve their visibility and reach larger section of the audience.

Social media marketing is used in context of promoting products, services, or brands on social media platforms such as Facebook, Instagram, and Twitter (Langan et al., 2019; Hollebeek & Macky,2019). This involves content creation that is engaging for the target audience. The businesses can use this tool to create awareness, notify their clients and seek feedback on their products and services. Content marketing is another key element of digital marketing. It is a tool to create and distribute relevant content to attract, engage and retain the target audience (Al-Abdallah et al., 2021). Content marketing is the process of creating and distributing valuable and relevant content to attract, engage, and retain a clearly defined audience (Saleem et al., 2022). By creating valuable content, businesses can establish themselves as an authority in their industry and increase their visibility on search engines. Additionally, content marketing can help businesses generate leads and increase sales. Similarly, Email marketing can be used to promote products, services, or events, as well as to keep customers informed about new developments or promotions. By sending targeted and personalized emails, businesses can increase customer engagement and drive more sales.

Digital marketing offers a number of benefits for businesses. For example, digital marketing is cost-effective and can be targeted to a specific audience. Additionally, digital marketing allows businesses to reach a larger audience and generate more leads and sales. Furthermore, digital marketing provides valuable insights and data about customer behavior and preferences, which can be used to improve marketing strategies and increase ROI. To get started with digital marketing, businesses should first identify their target audience and their marketing goals. Next, they should create a content strategy and a social media plan. Additionally, businesses should optimize their website for search engines and use analytics to track the success of their campaigns (Hollebeek & Macky,2019. Thus, it can be inferred that, digital marketing is the process of promoting products, services, or brands using digital channels such as social media, search engines, and mobile apps. These channels are mainly dependent on the use of internet and digital devices that has seen a significant improvement in terms of acceptance of technology since the pandemic covid 19 (Magd & Khan,2022; Bocar et al., 2022; Khan et al., 2021; Khan & Magd,2021). By using different elements of digital marketing such as SEO, social media marketing, content marketing, and email marketing, businesses can reach a larger audience, increase their brand awareness, and drive more sales. With the rise of the internet and digital technology, digital marketing has become an essential part of any business's marketing strategy. The new concepts like Electronic Customer relationship management (E-CRM); Electronic service quality (E-Service Quality); Electronic satisfaction (E-Satisfaction) etc are often related with the digital marketing as it helps to improve the band image of the organisation (Ligori et al., 2022; Kamal et al., 2022; Khan et al., 2020). Machine Learning and Artificial Intelligence are also expected to play a key role in the industry 4.0 (Magd et al., 2022).

According to Kamal (2016), it is worth noting the way DM had evolved during the years, In the early days of the internet, digital marketing was relatively simple. Businesses would create a website and use basic SEO techniques to improve their search engine rankings. They would also use email marketing to reach out to their customers and promote their products and services. However, these early digital marketing efforts were limited in scope and were not as effective as they could have been. As the internet continued to evolve, so did digital marketing. The introduction of social media platforms such as Facebook, Twitter, and Instagram provided businesses with new opportunities to connect with their customers and promote their products and services. Social media marketing quickly became an essential part of any digital marketing strategy. Businesses could now create engaging content, build relationships with their customers, and drive website traffic through social media (Kamal, 2016). With the advent of mobile devices, digital marketing has become even more sophisticated. Mobile marketing has allowed businesses to reach their customers wherever they are, and at any time. From SMS and push notifications to mobile apps and mobile-optimized websites, businesses can now engage with their customers in new and innovative ways (Tong et al., 2020).

The rise of big data and analytics has also played a major role in the evolution of digital marketing. Businesses can now use data and analytics to track and measure the effectiveness of their digital marketing campaigns. This allows them to identify which strategies are working and which are not, and make adjustments accordingly (Sestino et al., 2020). The evolution of digital marketing has been rapid and ongoing. From the early days of the internet to the sophisticated digital marketing strategies of today, the industry has undergone a significant transformation. With the continued advancements in technology, the future of digital marketing looks bright and businesses will have more opportunities to connect with their customers and promote their products and services in new and innovative ways.

1.2. Internet of Things (IoT)

The Internet of Things (IoT) is a rapidly growing field that involves the connection of physical objects to the internet, allowing them to collect and share data (Schoder,2018; Weber & Weber,2010). This interconnected network of devices, which can include everything from home appliances to industrial equipment, has the potential to revolutionize various industries and improve our daily lives (Sharma et al., 2018). The concept of the IoT has been around for several decades, but it is only in recent years that advancements in technology have made it a reality. The key enablers for IoT are the miniaturization of sensors, the availability of low-cost computing power, and the widespread adoption of wireless communication technologies such as Wi-Fi, Bluetooth, and cellular networks (Sharma et al., 2018).

One of the most significant benefits of the IoT is the ability to collect and analyze large amounts of data from various sources (Abdussamad et al., 2022; Astill et al., 2020; Sestino et al., 2020). This data can be used to gain new insights and make better-informed decisions in a wide range of applications. For example, in the industrial sector, IoT-enabled machines and equipment can provide real-time data on their performance and usage, allowing companies to optimize their operations and reduce downtime (Astill et al., 2020; Sestino et al., 2020).

IoT also has the potential to improve our daily lives through the development of smart homes, where various appliances and devices can be controlled and monitored remotely (Shabber et al., 2021). For example, a smart thermostat can learn a person's habits and adjust the temperature accordingly, and a smart fridge can keep track of its contents and automatically order groceries when it detects that certain items are running low (Sayed et al.,2022; Shabber et al., 2021).

While the IoT has many potential benefits, there are also concerns about its security and privacy (Alwarafy et al, 2020). Because IoT devices collect and share large amounts of personal data, it's important to ensure that this data is protected from unauthorized access and misuse. Additionally, as the number of IoT devices continues to grow, it's important to ensure that they can work together seamlessly and that there are standards in place to govern their usage (Coetzee & Eksteen, 2011).

As per Sharma et al. (2019), the IoT has evolved in an interesting fashion, The early beginnings of IoT can be traced back to the 1980s, when the first attempts were made to connect devices to the internet. At this time, the focus was mainly on connecting computers to other computers and networks, rather than physical devices. However, this laid the foundation for the development of IoT technology. In the 1990s, the first IoT devices began to emerge. These early devices were primarily used in industrial settings, such as factories and warehouses. They were used to monitor and control industrial equipment, such as conveyor belts and assembly lines. This was a significant step forward in the evolution of IoT, as it demonstrated the potential of connecting physical devices to the internet. In the early 2000s, the focus of IoT shifted towards consumer applications. Companies began to develop and market IoT devices for use in homes and businesses. This included smart thermostats, security systems, and even refrigerators that could be controlled remotely. The introduction of these consumer devices marked a major turning point in the evolution of IoT, as it demonstrated the potential for the technology to improve our daily lives. In the 2010s, IoT technology began to mature and became more widely adopted. The number of connected devices increased dramatically, and a wide range of new applications were developed. This included the use of IoT in healthcare, transportation, and agriculture. Additionally, the development of low-power, low-cost sensors and wireless technologies made it possible to connect a wide range of devices to the internet, including those that were previously not considered "smart" (Sharma et al., 2019).

Today, IoT is considered a key technology for the future. The number of connected devices is expected to continue to grow at an unprecedented rate, and the potential applications for IoT are endless. From smart cities to autonomous vehicles, IoT is expected to play a major role in shaping the future of our world (Shabber et al., 2022; Sayed et al., 2022). The IoT is a rapidly growing field with the potential to revolutionize various industries and improve our daily lives. However, it's important to consider the security and privacy implications and ensure that standards are in place to govern their usage. As the number of digital devices (mostly enabled through IoT) continues to grow, their relevance for the digital marketing is expected to be high.

2. BIBLIOMETRIC ANALYSIS

Bibliometric analysis is a powerful tool for understanding the impact and influence of research publications in a specific field. It is a method of quantitatively analysing scientific literature to identify patterns and trends in research output, such as the most cited articles or authors, the most active research areas, and the most productive institutions (Pritchard, 1969; Donthu et al.,2021; Khatri et al., 2022). To conduct a bibliometric analysis, there are several key steps that need to be taken. The first step is to identify the research field of interest and gather relevant publications. This can be done by searching for articles in databases such as Scopus, Web of Science, or Google Scholar, using keywords related to the research field. It is important to ensure that the search is as comprehensive as possible, to capture all relevant publications in the field (Pritchard, 1969; Donthu et al.,2021).

The next step is to extract data from the publications, such as the authors, institutions, publication year, and number of citations. This can be done manually or using software such as VOSviewer or Sci2. The software programs also help in visualization of the data in different forms such as graphs and charts, making it easy to understand the results (Donthu et al.,2021)). Upon the cleaning and organising of the data, the next step is to analyse the data using various bibliometric techniques such as co-citation analysis, co-word analysis, and social network analysis. These techniques allow researchers to identify patterns and trends in the data, such as the most cited articles or authors, the most active research areas, and the most productive institutions.

Finally, it is important to interpret the results of the bibliometric analysis and draw meaningful conclusions. The results should be presented in a clear and concise manner, and the conclusions should be supported by the data. It's also important to keep in mind that bibliometric analysis is not a standalone method, therefore, it's important to validate the results with other methods such as literature review and expert interviews.

2.1. Importance of Bibliometric Analysis in the Field of Digital Marketing and IoT

Bibliometric analysis is a method of analyzing and quantifying the scientific literature in a specific field of study. This method is used to identify patterns and trends in the literature, such as the most frequently cited authors and journals, the most common keywords and themes, and the evolution of research over time. In the field of digital marketing and the Internet of Things (IoT), bibliometric analysis can be a valuable tool for understanding the current state of the field and identifying areas for future research (Faruk et al., 2021).

One of the main advantages of bibliometric analysis in the field of digital marketing and IoT is that it provides a quantitative overview of the literature. This can be useful for identifying the most important research in the field and understanding the areas that have been studied the most. Bibliometric analysis can also be used to identify gaps in the literature, which can help researchers identify areas where further research is needed (Faruk et al., 2021).

Another advantage of bibliometric analysis in digital marketing and IoT is that it can help identify the most influential authors and journals in the field. This can be useful for researchers who are looking for relevant literature to cite in their own research and for identifying experts in the field who may be able to provide guidance and feedback on their research. Additionally, bibliometric analysis can help identify the most commonly used keywords and themes in the literature, which can be useful for identifying the key concepts and ideas that are central to the field.

Bibliometric analysis is also useful for understanding the evolution of research in the field of digital marketing and IoT. By analysing the literature over time, researchers can identify trends and patterns in the field and understand how research has evolved. This can be useful for identifying areas of the field that are growing in importance and for understanding the trajectory of research in the field.

3. RESEARCH METHODOLOGY

Bibliometric analysis to explore the relationship between IoT and digital marketing involved the several steps. The first step was to search for the bibliometric data for which the Scopus database was selected as it is the largest scientific database of researches (Khatri et al.,2022; Pritchard,1969; Donthu et al., 2021). The key words used to extract the data were: "Internet of things" OR "IoT"; "Digital Marketing"; and "Internet of things" AND "Digital Marketing". A total of 2051 documents were extracted for IoT from the period 2022 onwards; 2023 documents were extracted for Digital marketing from 2018 onwards; and a total of 41 documents were extracted for Digital marketing and IoT from 2012 onwards. This speaks volume about the IoT being very popular among the researchers in the recent years at the same time it highlights the research gap in the area of IoT and Digital marketing. The collected data was analysed through Vos viewer, mainly the co-occurrence analysis was done to understand the prominent terms (key words) in the arena of IoT and Digital Marketing. Necessary bibliometric graphs were also generated to give a meaningful result to this chapter. This methodology will allow for a comprehensive and systematic analysis of the literature on IoT and digital marketing, providing insights into the current state of research in this area, identifying key trends and gaps, and informing future research directions. To put in terms of objectives this chapter deals with:

RO1 To check the number of documents in the domain of IoT and Digital marketing.
RO2 To identify the prominent terms in the arena of IoT and Digital Marketing
RO3 To identify the cluster of prominent keywords utilized in the studies.

4. ANALYSIS AND INTERPRETATIONS

4.1. Internet of Things (IoT)

It was an important consideration to identify the key word IoT itself in the beginning. The recommendations of the researchers (Khatri et al.,2022; Pritchard,1969; Donthu et al., 2021), was to run a co-occurrence analysis to check the major keywords in the field of IoT. The data extracted from Scopus database was huge for the analysis on IoT, by putting the selection period as 2022 onwards a total of 2051 studies were extracted and a co-occurrence analysis was run by keeping the minimum occurrences threshold as 80. A total of 15 prominent key words were extracted in the field of IoT as presented in table 1. In order to understand this extraction better cluster analysis was also done and all these key words were divided into three clusters as presented in table 2.

Table 1. Co-Occurrence analysis of IoT

S. No	Items	Occurrences	Total link strength
1.	internet of things (iot)	1855	3222
2.	block-chain	270	915
3.	machine learning	274	802
4.	network security	170	550
5.	deep learning	170	401
6.	energy utilization	147	378
7.	security	126	364
8.	learning systems	100	316
9.	energy efficiency	128	298
10.	edge computing	99	264
11.	digital storage	84	261
12.	authentication	81	245
13.	fog computing	84	226
14.	industrial internet of thing	82	213
15.	artificial intelligence	92	183

Source: Extracted from scopus.com via Vos Viewer (authors calculation)

Table 2. Cluster analysis of IoT

Cluster 1 (6 items)		
digital storage	**Cluster 2 (5 items)**	
edge computing	authentication	**Cluster 3 (4 items)**
energy efficiency	block-chain	artificial intelligence
energy utilization	industrial internet of things	deep learning
fog computing	network security	learning systems
internet of things	security	machine learning

Source: Extracted from scopus.com via Vos Viewer (authors calculation)

As visible from table 1 and table 2, the prominent terms extracted are block-chain, machine learning; network security; deep learning; energy utilization; security; learning systems etc. These terms are found to be very logical and relatable for the Digital marketing as well. In order to understand the relationship between all these keywords, a bibliometric graph is generated as given in Figure 1.

Figure 1. A bibliometric graph is generated

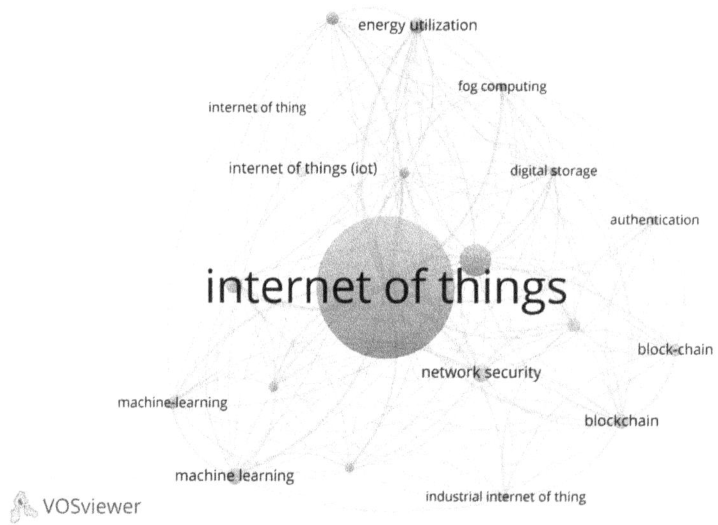

4.2. Digital Marketing

The next important consideration was to decode the term Digital Marketing, for this again the co-occurrence analysis was performed (Khan et al.,2022a). The data extraction was done in the timeline from 2018 onwards in which a total of 2023 documents were extracted. To perform co-occurrence analysis the minimum occurrence threshold was kept as 49, through which 20 key words were extracted as presented in table 3. Further the cluster analysis was performed here as well to understand the key words behaving in similar fashion or have high internal relation, a total of 4 cluster was identified as presented in 4.

Table 3. Co-Occurrence analysis of IoT

S. No	Items	Occurrences	Total link strength
1.	digital marketing	1109	1677
2.	marketing	476	1144
3.	commerce	350	1013
4.	social media	322	701
5.	social networking (online)	143	481
6.	sales	141	387
7.	electronic commerce	97	255
8.	marketing strategy	67	212
9.	artificial intelligence	79	211
10.	human	73	207
11.	machine learning	71	191
12.	big data	66	185
13.	consumer behavior	66	179
14.	e-commerce	74	159
15.	internet	54	141
16.	advertising	53	137
17.	covid-19	66	126
18.	digital transformation	55	120
19.	tourism	53	114
20.	social media marketing	66	110

Source: Extracted from scopus.com via Vos Viewer (authors calculation)

Table 4. Cluster analysis of digital marketing

Cluster 1 (8 items)			
Consumer Bebaviour	**Cluster 2 (5 items)**		
Covid-19	advertising	**Cluster 3 (5 items)**	
digital Marketing	human	artificial intelligence	**Cluster 4 (2 items)**
digital transformation	internet	big data	social media marketing
e-commerce	marketing	commerce	social networking (online)
electronic commerce	social media	machine learning	
sales		marketing strategy	
tourism			

Source: Extracted from scopus.com via Vos Viewer (authors calculation)

As visible from table 3 and table 4, it can be seen that the terms that IoT itself is not part of the top 20 keywords in the field of digital marketing, however, the terms like social media, social networking, electronic commerce, artificial intelligence, machine learning, internet, digital transformation etc, are important part of IoT. Thus, the inter-relationship of IoT and Digital marketing cannot be ignored. The cluster analysis suggests that certain cluster such as cluster 3 is comprised of, artificial intelligence; big data; commerce; machine learning; and marketing strategy, are very much dependent on what IoT look like as presented in table 1 and table 2. In order to understand the relationship between all these keywords, a bibliometric graph is generated as given in Figure 2.

Figure 2. A bibliometric graph

4.3. IoT and Digital Marketing

In order to understand the relationship between IoT and Digital marketing was explored. For this, the key words- "Internet of Things" AND "Digital Marketing," were checked. A data representing a total of 41 documents only were extracted from the year 2012 onwards. This signifies the limited studies conducted in the field of IoT and Digital marketing combined. Being the main part of this chapter, it was important to extract as many key words as possible, however, due to lack to studies in this field the occurrence threshold was kept as 3 that gave a total of 18 key words that can be interpreted in a better way. The same is presented in table 5. Also, the cluster analysis has been done for these extracted key words as presented in the table 6.

Table 5. IoT and digital marketing

S. No	Items	Occurrences	Total link strength
1.	internet of things (iot)	32	168
2.	digital marketing	22	109
3.	commerce	17	91
4.	marketing	14	66
5.	big data	10	52
6.	marketing strategy	7	43
7.	artificial intelligence	9	39
8.	digital technologies	5	29
9.	sales	6	28
10.	data analytics	3	22
11.	machine learning	3	22
12.	digital transformation	4	20
13.	customer experience	3	19
14.	digital devices	3	16
15.	augmented reality	3	15
16.	internet	4	15
17.	social media	3	14
18.	tourism	3	12

Source: Extracted from scopus.com via Vos Viewer (authors calculation)

Table 6. Cluster analysis of IoT and digital marketing

Cluster 1 (6 items)		
augmented reality	**Cluster 2 (6 items)**	
commerce	artificial intelligence	**Cluster 3 (5 items)**
digital marketing	big data	digital devices
digital transformation	customer experience	digital technology
internet of things (iot)	data analytics	marketing
sales	internet	marketing strategy
	machine learning	tourism
	social media	

Source: Extracted from scopus.com via Vos Viewer (authors calculation)

The cluster 1 suggest that the areas like augmented reality, digital transformation and IoT would be crucial for the area of sales, commerce and digital marketing. However, the terms like artificial intelligence, big data, data analytics, machine learning etc would be a consideration for the analytics part in which social media is going to play an important role (Cluster 2). Further digital devices, digital technology, tourism, marketing strategy etc are forming a cluster, that signifies a kind of role IoT and digital technology playing in mobility and tourism sector. In order to understand the relationship between all these keywords, a bibliometric graph is generated as given in Figure 3.

Figure 3. A bibliometric graph

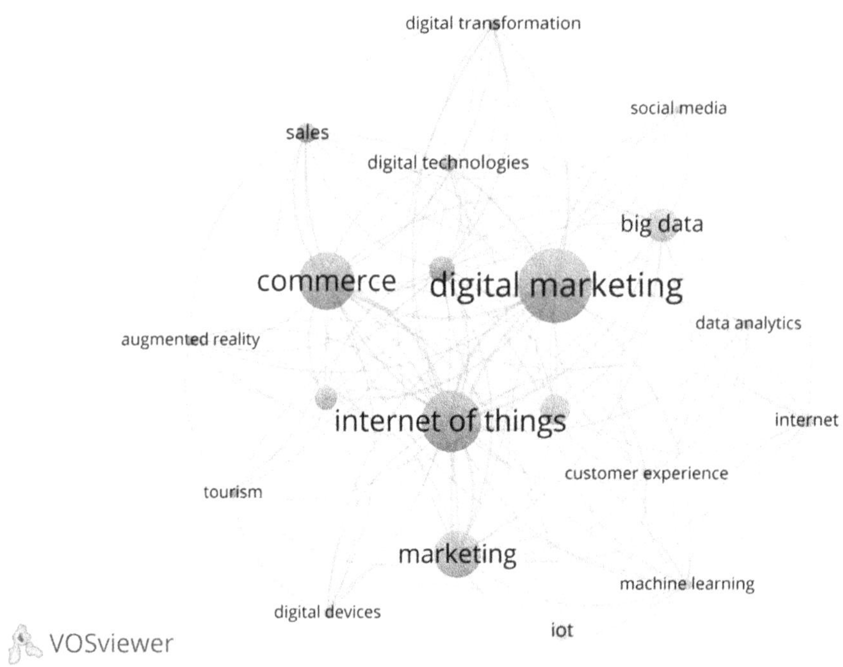

Since the number of studies conducted in the field of IoT and digital marketing is less, this study also checked the researcher countries that are contributing in this field. Researchers representing a total of 19 countries were explored as given in table 7. In which the researchers from, India, United States, United Arab Emirates, Romania, Russian Federation, Greece, and Turkey were found to be contributing more than 1 document to the scopus database. The other countries have only contributed 1 document, whereas, the rest part of the world including Oman, Saudi Arabia, African nations etc, is yet to open their account in this field.

Table 7. Country wise contribution analysis in the field of IoT and digital marketing

S.No	Country	Documents	Citations	Total Link Strength
1	India	9	9	4
2	United States	5	51	1
3	United Arab Emirates	4	5	4
4	Romania	3	14	1
5	Russian Federation	3	10	0
6	Greece	2	0	0
7	Turkey	2	0	1
8	Australia	1	0	2
9	Azerbaijan	1	0	1
10	Canada	1	0	1
11	China	1	1	0
12	Germany	1	0	1
13	Ghana	1	0	1
14	Indonesia	1	1	0
15	Jordan	1	0	2
16	Norway	1	36	1
17	Portugal	1	0	1
18	Ukraine	1	6	0
19	United Kingdom	1	0	0

5. DISCUSSION ON THE RESEARCH IN THE FIELD OF IOT AND DIGITAL MARKETING

DM and IoT are two rapidly growing areas of technology that have the potential to revolutionize the way businesses operate. As such, research in these areas is essential to understand the implications of these technologies and how they can be leveraged for the benefit of companies and consumers alike.

One key area of research in digital marketing is the use of artificial intelligence and machine learning. These technologies have the potential to help companies personalize their marketing efforts and target specific segments of their customer base. For example, researchers are exploring the use of machine learning algorithms to analyze customer data and predict which products and services they are most likely to be interested in.

Another area of research in digital marketing is the use of social media and influencer marketing. Social media platforms have become an important tool for businesses to reach and engage with customers. Research in this area aims to understand how businesses can effectively use social media to promote their products and services, and how they can leverage influencers to reach a larger audience.

The IoT is the network of devices, sensors, and other connected devices that can collect and share data. Research in this area aims to understand the implications of the IoT for businesses and consumers. This includes studying the security and privacy implications of having so many connected devices, as well as the potential benefits of having access to large amounts of data from these devices. This is of a great help to the market analysts and product developers. The use of sensor-based technology is another area worth considering in the field of digital marketing that can be useful in the arena of manufacturing, transportation, and healthcare. For example, researchers are studying the use of sensors to track the location of goods in a supply chain, and how this data can be used to improve logistics and reduce costs. The emerging concepts like smart devices and home automation also needs to be considered in the times to come as it has a direct impact on the customer experience.

6. FUTURE TRENDS IN DM AND IOT

One emerging area in digital marketing is the use of artificial intelligence (AI) and machine learning (ML). These technologies are being used to analyse data and provide insights that can help businesses better understand their customers and target their marketing efforts. For example, AI can be used to predict customer behaviour and provide personalized recommendations to customers, while ML can be used to analyse large amounts of data and identify patterns that can be used to improve marketing strategies.

Another emerging area in digital marketing is the use of virtual and augmented reality (VR/AR). These technologies are being used to create immersive experiences for customers, such as virtual tours of products or virtual try-on of clothes. This technology can also be used in the field of e-commerce to create virtual stores where customers can interact with products in a more realistic way.

The IoT, on the other hand, is an emerging technology that connects devices to the internet and allows them to communicate with each other. This technology is being used in a variety of industries, from healthcare to retail, to improve efficiency and provide new services to customers. For example, IoT-enabled devices can be used to track inventory in retail stores and automatically reorder products when stock runs low. In the healthcare industry, IoT devices can be used to monitor patients' vital signs remotely and alert healthcare providers if there are any changes.

Further, the Blockchain technology is going to be the foundation of many technologies in the future. It is a digital ledger that can be used to record transactions across a network of computers. This technology is being used to create secure, decentralized systems that can be used to manage data and transactions. For example, blockchain technology can be used to create a secure, decentralized system for tracking inventory in a supply chain, or for managing financial transactions.

Finally, another emerging area in the field of IoT is the use of edge computing. Edge computing is a technology that allows data to be processed at the edge of a network, rather than in a centralized location. This technology can be used to reduce latency and improve the performance of IoT devices. For example, edge computing can be used to process sensor data in real-time, allowing for faster and more accurate decision making.

7. CONCLUSION

In conclusion, digital marketing and IoT are two rapidly growing areas in the field of technology. As technology continues to advance, new opportunities are emerging for businesses to connect with customers in new and innovative ways. One of the most significant areas of research in digital marketing is the use of artificial intelligence (AI) and machine learning (ML) to personalize marketing efforts. AI and ML allow businesses to analyze large amounts of data to identify patterns and make predictions about customer behavior. This information can then be used to create customized marketing campaigns that are tailored to the specific needs and preferences of individual customers.

Another area of research in digital marketing is the use of social media to engage with customers and build brand loyalty. Social media platforms, such as Facebook, Twitter, and Instagram, have become an essential part of the digital marketing mix, and businesses are constantly looking for ways to use these platforms to connect with customers and build relationships. Research in this area is focused on understanding how businesses can use social media to create engaging content, build brand loyalty, and increase customer engagement.

In the area of IoT, research is focused on developing new technologies and applications that take advantage of the interconnectedness of devices. One of the most significant areas of research is in the development of smart homes and smart cities. These technologies allow for the integration of various devices, such as thermostats, lights, and security systems, to create a more efficient and convenient living environment. Research in this area is also focused on understanding how these technologies can be used to improve the efficiency of cities, reduce energy consumption, and improve the overall quality of life for citizens.

Another area of research in IoT is in the development of connected cars and smart transportation systems. These technologies allow for the integration of cars and other vehicles with the internet, making it possible for cars to communicate with each other and with other devices on the road. Research in this area is focused on understanding how these technologies can be used to improve traffic flow, reduce accidents, and make transportation more efficient.

Thus, research in the area of digital marketing and IoT is focused on developing new technologies and applications that take advantage of the interconnectedness of devices. These technologies and applications are having a significant impact on the way businesses operate, and they are creating new opportunities for businesses to connect with customers and improve their operations. As these areas continue to evolve, research will play an essential role in understanding how businesses can take advantage of these new technologies to increase efficiency, reduce costs, and improve customer engagement.

8. FUTURE DIRECTIONS

The IoT and DM, have the potential to revolutionize the way businesses operate. As technology continues to evolve, there are a number of exciting opportunities for future studies in these areas that will help businesses to better understand and utilize the potential of these technologies. One of the key areas for future studies in IoT is the development of new applications and services. The IoT is a network of devices and sensors that are connected to the internet, and this network is constantly growing. As more devices and sensors are connected, there will be an increasing number of opportunities for businesses to create new applications and services that take advantage of this connectivity. For example, businesses may develop new tools to monitor and control devices remotely, or create new services that allow customers to access and control their devices through the internet.

Another area for future studies in IoT is the development of new security and privacy measures. As more devices and sensors are connected to the internet, there is an increasing risk of cyber-attacks and data breaches. Future studies in IoT will need to focus on developing new security measures to protect against these threats and ensure that customer data is kept safe and secure.

In the field of digital marketing, one of the key areas for future studies is the use of artificial intelligence AI and ML. As technology continues to evolve, businesses are increasingly using these technologies to analyze customer data and make more accurate predictions about customer behavior. Future studies in digital marketing will need to focus on understanding how these technologies can be used to improve marketing campaigns and increase customer engagement.

Another area for future studies in digital marketing is the use of virtual reality and augmented reality. These technologies have the potential to revolutionize the way businesses interact with customers, and future studies will need to focus on understanding how these technologies can be used to create more immersive and engaging customer experiences.

Finally, another area for future studies in digital marketing is the use of blockchain technology. Blockchain technology is a decentralized system that allows for secure and transparent data sharing, and it has the potential to revolutionize the way businesses operate. Future studies in digital marketing will need to focus on understanding how blockchain technology can be used to improve marketing campaigns and increase customer engagement.

REFERENCES

Abdussamad, Z., Agyei, I. T., Döngül, E. S., Abdussamad, J., Raj, R., & Effendy, F. (2022). Impact of internet of things (IOT) on human resource management: A review. *Materials Today: Proceedings*, *56*, 3534–3543. doi:10.1016/j.matpr.2021.11.247

Al-Abdallah, G., Khair, N., & Elmarakby, R. (2021). The impact of social networking sites on luxury vehicles purchase decision process in Gulf Cooperation Council countries. *Journal of International Consumer Marketing*, *33*(5), 559–577. doi:10.1080/08961530.2020.1867023

Alwarafy, A., Al-Thelaya, K. A., Abdallah, M., Schneider, J., & Hamdi, M. (2020). A survey on security and privacy issues in edge-computing-assisted internet of things. *IEEE Internet of Things Journal*, *8*(6), 4004–4022. doi:10.1109/JIOT.2020.3015432

Astill, J., Dara, R. A., Fraser, E. D., Roberts, B., & Sharif, S. (2020). Smart poultry management: Smart sensors, big data, and the internet of things. *Computers and Electronics in Agriculture*, *170*, 105291. doi:10.1016/j.compag.2020.105291

Bocar, A. C., Khan, S. A., & Epoc, F. (2022). COVID-19 Work from Home Stressors and the Degree of its Impact: Employers and Employees Actions. *International Journal of Technology Transfer and Commercialisation. Inderscience*, *19*(2), 270–291.

Chaffey, D., & Ellis-Chadwick, F. (2019). *Digital marketing*.

Coetzee, L., & Eksteen, J. (2011, May). The Internet of Things-promise for the future? An introduction. In *2011 IST-Africa Conference Proceedings* (pp. 1-9). IEEE.

Donthu, N., Kumar, S., Mukherjee, D., Pandey, N., & Lim, W. M. (2021). How to conduct a bibliometric analysis: An overview and guidelines. *Journal of Business Research*, *133*, 285–296. doi:10.1016/j.jbusres.2021.04.070

Faruk, M., Rahman, M., & Hasan, S. (2021). How digital marketing evolved over time: A bibliometric analysis on scopus database. *Heliyon*, *7*(12), 08603. doi:10.1016/j.heliyon.2021.e08603 PMID:34988311

Hollebeek, L. D., & Macky, K. (2019). Digital content marketing's role in fostering consumer engagement, trust, and value: Framework, fundamental propositions, and implications. *Journal of Interactive Marketing*, *45*(1), 27–41. doi:10.1016/j.intmar.2018.07.003

Kamal, S., Naim, A., Magd, H., Khan, S. A., & Khan, F. M. (2022). The Relationship Between E-Service Quality, Ease of Use, and E-CRM Performance Referred by Brand Image. In *Building a Brand Image Through Electronic Customer Relationship Management* (pp. 84–108). IGI Global. doi:10.4018/978-1-6684-5386-5.ch005

Kamal, Y. (2016). Study of trend in digital marketing and evolution of digital marketing strategies. *International Journal of Engineering Science*, *6*(5), 5300–5302.

Khan, S. A., Devi, T. P., Ligori, T. A. A., & Saleem, M. (2020). Customer Satisfaction and Customer Loyalty in Online Shopping: A Study On University Students of Bhutan. *Delhi Business Review*, *21*(2), 11–22. doi:10.51768/dbr.v21i2.212202002

Khan, S.A, Epoc, F., Gangwar,V.P., Ligori T.A.A, Ansari, Z.A. (2021). Will Online banking sustain in Bhutan post Covid – 19? A quantitative analysis of the customer e-satisfaction and e-loyalty in the Kingdom of Bhutan, *Transnational Marketing Journal*, *9* (3), 607-624. doi:10.33182/tmj.v9i3.1288

Khan. S.A. & Magd. H. (2021). Empirical Examination of MS Teams in Conducting Webinar: Evidence from International Online Program conducted in Oman. *Journal of Content, Community and Communication, 14*(7). doi:10.31620/JCCC.12.21/13

Khan, S. A., Magd, H., & Epoc, F. (2022a). Application of Data Management System in Business to Business Electronic Commerce. In A. Naim & P. K. Malik (Eds.), *Competitive Trends and Technologies in Business Management* (pp. 109–124). Nova Science Publishers.

Khatri, B., Arora, S., Magd, H., & Khan, S. A. K. (2022). Bibliometric Analysis of Social Entrepreneurship. In Magd. H., Syed, R.T., Spicer, D. (Eds). International Perspectives on Value Creation and Sustainability Through Social Entrepreneurship (pp. 46-60). IGI Global. doi:10.4018/978-1-6684-4666-9.ch003

Langan, R., Cowley, S., & Nguyen, C. (2019). The state of digital marketing in academia: An examination of marketing curriculum's response to digital disruption. *Journal of Marketing Education*, *41*(1), 32–46. doi:10.1177/0273475318823849

Ligori, T. A. A., Suresh, N., Khan, S. A., Rabgay, T., & Yezer, K. (2022). The mediating effect of university image on the relationship between curriculum and student satisfaction: An empirical study of the Royal University of Bhutan. *International Journal of Pluralism and Economics Education. Inderscience*, *13*(2), 192–208.

Magd, H., Jonathan, H., Khan, S. A., & El Geddawy, M. (2022). *Artificial Intelligence—The Driving Force of Industry 4.0. A Roadmap for Enabling Industry 4.0 by Artificial Intelligence*. Wiley.

Magd, H., & Khan, S. A. (2022). Strategic Framework for Entrepreneurship Education in Promoting Social Entrepreneurship in GCC Countries During and Post COVID-19. In Magd. H., Syed, R.T., Spicer, D. (Eds). International Perspectives on Value Creation and Sustainability Through Social Entrepreneurship (pp. 61-75). IGI Global.

Matta, H., Gupta, R., & Agarwal, S. (2020, June). Search Engine optimization in digital marketing: present scenario and future scope. In *2020 International Conference on Intelligent Engineering and Management (ICIEM)* (pp. 530-534). IEEE. 10.1109/ICIEM48762.2020.9160016

Pritchard, A. (1969). Statistical bibliography or bibliometrics. *The Journal of Documentation*, *25*(4), 348–349.

Saleem, M., Khan, S. A., & Magd, H. (2022). Content Marketing Framework for Building Brand Image: A Case Study of Sohar International School, Oman. In Building a Brand Image Through Electronic Customer Relationship Management (pp. 64-83). IGI Global.

Sayed, A., Himeur, Y., Bensaali, F., & Amira, A. (2022). Artificial intelligence with IoT for energy efficiency in buildings. In *Emerging Real-World Applications of Internet of Things* (pp. 233–252). CRC Press. doi:10.1201/9781003304203-12

Schoder, D. (2018). Introduction to the Internet of Things. *Internet of things A to Z: technologies and applications*, 1-50.

Sestino, A., Prete, M. I., Piper, L., & Guido, G. (2020). Internet of Things and Big Data as enablers for business digitalization strategies. *Technovation*, *98*, 102173. doi:10.1016/j.technovation.2020.102173

Shabber, S. M., Bansal, M., Devi, P. M., & Jain, P. (2021, December). iHAS: An Intelligent Home Automation Based System for Smart City. In *2021 IEEE International Symposium on Smart Electronic Systems (iSES)(Formerly iNiS)* (pp. 48-52). IEEE. 10.1109/iSES52644.2021.00023

Sharma, N., Shamkuwar, M., & Singh, I. (2019). The history, present and future with IoT. In *Internet of Things and Big Data Analytics for Smart Generation* (pp. 27–51). Springer. doi:10.1007/978-3-030-04203-5_3

Tong, S., Luo, X., & Xu, B. (2020). Personalized mobile marketing strategies. *Journal of the Academy of Marketing Science*, *48*(1), 64–78. doi:10.100711747-019-00693-3

Weber, R. H., & Weber, R. (2010). *Internet of things* (Vol. 12). Springer. doi:10.1007/978-3-642-11710-7

Chapter 8
Use of IoT in Evaluating Content Digital Marketing and Optimization and Web Development

Aysha Abdulla
Ibn Rushd College for Management Sciences, Saudi Arabia

Omer Bin Hussain
King Khalid University, Saudi Arabia

ABSTRACT

The internet of things (IoT) is a concept that connects objects via the internet. The extensive adoption of IoT technologies unleashes various capabilities of designing a broad range of high-quality consumer applications. Smart cities, smart buildings, and e-health are among various application domains which benefit from IoT technologies. However, the precise use of IoT in evaluating content digital marketing is ambiguous. This chapter identifies the content digital marketing aspect of the IoT applications as well as the technological aspects of web development through literature review. The focus in this chapter lies in how IoT can be taken as a content marketing tool in the IoT applications. IoT offers unlimited creativity for content creation as well as targeted delivery of content. This research finding further presents a design of a monitoring control system based on the IoT. These results demonstrate the significant shift in marketing strategies that need to take place as they adopt IoT and the development of web applications for effective remote monitoring in IoT devices.

DOI: 10.4018/978-1-6684-8166-0.ch008

INTRODUCTION

There has been a great advancement in technology since the inception of internet. The fields of Artificial Intelligence and virtual reality have grown tremendously. Similarly, IoT will witness inevitable development in the following years.

The internet of things, also known as ambient Technologies or Embedded Systems, is a global system of IP-connected computer networks, sensors, actuators, machines, and devices, integrating this physical world with the virtual world of the internet (Constantinides, 2016). The internet of things is a crucial part of the Future Internet. It unveils new opportunities not only for businesses and marketers, but also for society as a whole. (Haller et al., 2009) Cognitive IoT technologies will provide deep insights of what is happening in the world to the business leaders. IoT can also be described as a network of interconnected objects that not only leverage information from the environment and interact with the physical world, but also use existing Internet standards to provide services for information transfer, analytics, applications, and communications (Gubbi et al, 2013). Adding intelligence into systems and processes will enable businesses to not only do things more efficiently, but also improve customer satisfaction through content marketing strategies, discover new business opportunities, and anticipate risks and threats in order to better deal with them. (Green, 2015).

IoT is an interconnection of a variety of smart devices, that impact routine tasks like e-health, e-learning, remote monitoring, surveillance etc. Similarly, IoT plays a significant role in industries such as automation and intelligent industrial manufacturing, smart logistics, smart transportation etc. (Atzori et al., 2010). Besides the IoT, there is the internet of services, 3D internet, internet of content, and next generation networks and more. It is noteworthy that these terms should not be regarded as different Internets that will exist in parallel, but rather as different dimensions of a common Future Internet. (Haller e al., 2009). IoT is made up of two terms. The first part conveys a network-oriented meaning of IoT and the second part relates to generic objects which are integrated into a common framework (Atzori et al., 2010). In the rudimentary sense, it is either "Internet oriented" or "Things oriented". In fact, ''Internet of Things" semantically means ''a world-wide network of interconnected objects uniquely addressable, based on standard communication protocols". The enabling technologies of IOT are Sensor network, embedded systems, RFID, etc. The key is the seamless and ubiquitous integration of these Things (objects) into business processes.

The rest of this paper is organized as follows: First, it investigates the evolution of IoT and its role in today's society. Secondly, the key elements of IoT, cognitive technology and big data are explained. The reason for choosing these elements is because these are the main and essential topics in IoT. Thirdly, there is an extensive discussion of the content digital marketing implications of using increasingly advanced technology to collect data, the current state of IoT in marketing, the most important trends and the future scope of IoT in marketing. Fourthly, the development of remote monitoring application to have remote monitoring control in various situations is elaborated. Lastly, various IoT applications are elaborated. Based on these applications, it gives a more vivid picture of IoT in real life. In this part, five application directions are introduced. They are: E-health, manufacturing, personal and home, Automation and transportation and logistics. Finally, it throws light on some of the challenges this new technology presents to both marketers and consumers.

Thus, this literature review provides a relatively comprehensive overview of the most common topics of IoT. The readers could understand what is the purpose of IoT, how IoT technologies are leveraged in real life, and what are the current problems caused by IoT. Lastly, readers will learn what is the current trend of IoT in marketing and what the future trend of IoT in marketing will be, how IoT will easily reach the targeted customers, and how IoT will revolutionize the marketing landscape in the future.

EVOLUTION OF IOT

The internet of things was first introduced by the MIT Auto-ID Center (Haller et al). Then, it represented an idea where all physical objects are tagged with an RFID transponder with a global unique ID. Since then, the concept of the Internet of Things has expanded (Haller.et al). Currently, the IoT is a novel technology that has sourced itself in modern wireless telecommunications (Atzori.L, et al., 2009). The US National Intelligence Council has enumerated IoT as one of the six disruptive civil technologies that has potential impact on US national power. In order to gain a vivid understanding of the evolution of IoT, one must first understand the evolution of the Web. Much of today's society is influenced by the Internet spanning from smartphones, computers and other devices. However, the development of the Internet in the past two decades have been distinct. Scholars define the various stages of web development as Web 1.0 as a tool for cognition, 2.0 as a medium for human communication, and 3.0 as networked digital technology that supports human cooperation then web 4.0 as a web of integration (Fuchs et al., 2010). Parallel with Web 1.0, IoT found its inception as MachinetoMachine communication (M2M) around 1989. M2M is not a novel technology as Internet is not. For instance, airplane communication devices are constant M2M feeds that send information from ground towers to airborne planes.

M2M communication evolved to interconnect multiple devices symbiotically with the web evolution. as shown in Figure 1 below.

Figure 1. Relation between Web and IoT development

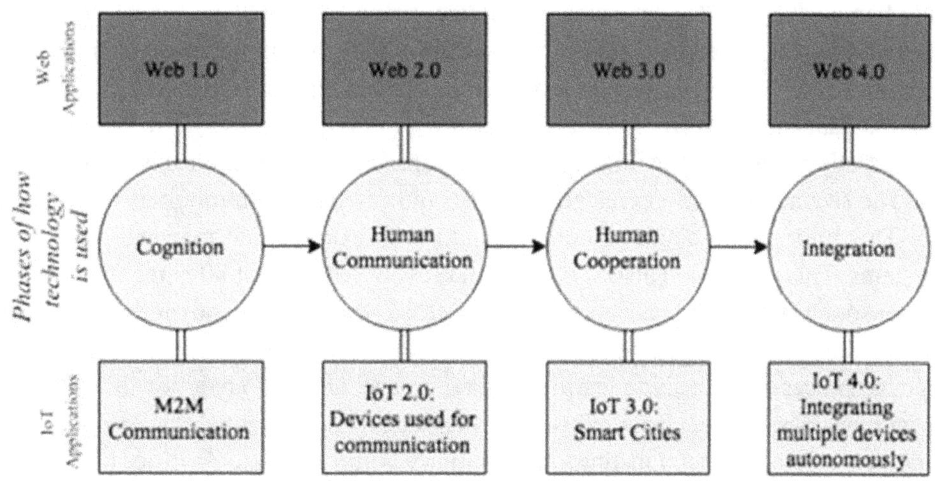

This gave rise to IoT 2.0 that evolved to facilitate human communication manifested in devices such as smartphones. Soon followed an IoT 3.0 of human cooperation with endeavors such as smart cities in Amsterdam, Barcelona, and New York. These cities leverage IoT technology to work seamlessly with daily chores while integrating the digital and real worlds. IoT devices offer services for regular issues such as resolving parking and traffic problems by redirecting traffic information sent to GPS and also by intimating government authorities when locality trash bins need to be emptied before overflowing (Henneke 2015) .

The latest definition of IoT refers to the ability of everyday objects to connect to the Internet and to send and receive data autonomously (Eaton et al., 2012) .An IoT 4.0 means every enabled device can be integrated. These devices constantly interact, communicating autonomously and working synchronously. These devices are integrated to support humans' daily needs by automating them and alleviating the completion of manual tasks. For instance, the morning routine could be automated, by programming the house to sense when a person wakes up and draw the curtains automatically and to start a smart coffee device to brew coffee according to the programmed timer. Automating these mundane tasks would allow people to save time and effectively use it for more significant tasks. Another example is a smart car that pulls the location of the first meeting of the day and connects to a GPS while playing a person's preferred music streaming application. This enables individuals to focus on other tasks such as driving rather than trivial tasks.

KEY ELEMENTS OF IOT

Here the concept of cognitive technology and big data are explained. These are the key concepts to understand the Internet of Things. The applications of IoT have become common, therefore it is time to capitalize on a second generation of internet of things technologies and capabilities. This is referred to as the cognitive internet of things by IBM (Green, 2015). According to the research conducted by IBM, it is said that Cognitive IoT technologies will make it possible for business leaders to draw deeper insights of what is happening in the world and it renders business operations more efficient and the business leaders could handle the business activities more effectively.

Sensor networks are a powerful technology. To achieve more, businesses need cognitive technologies that allow them to accumulate and integrate data from various types of sensors, to analyze that data, to capitalize on the data and learn from the interactions with it. (Green, 2015) The first generation of IoT technologies already brought us the information which made a huge difference in achieving operational efficiencies. The second generation created immense and extensive communities of devices that share information. This information could be comprehended contextually and managed by people who use cognitive systems. This generation also suffered great loss of data, about 90 percent of the data that was gathered by sensors was lost for a variety of reasons. It was due to the bandwidth limitations, security, and privacy constraints. (IBM). Therefore, it was imperative to add cognitive technologies to IoT like natural language processing, machine learning, video, image, and text analytics. It is also important to collaborate with business leaders from industries. As a starting point, it could be essential to collaborate with retailing, real estate, financial institutions, insurance companies, etc. In order to increase customer satisfaction, companies should be encouraged to store the data where the customers have easy access and can have timely utilization. For instance, the heating system of sensors at home could have temperature settings and power usage initially from a user. Soon, your home will be self-aware because of the cognitive technologies. These new technologies aid the managers understand the current state and the real needs of the customers. Another example is a situation in the shop, where several customers pick certain products but do not really buy it. This sends the information via cognitive assistants to the store manager through machine learning algorithms that notices this pattern. The manager can then conduct effective research to study why the products are dropped and thus facilitate its improvement.

Big data is defined by three main characteristics. They are: volume, variety and velocity. (Eaton, C., et al) as shown in figure 2 below. Volume refers to the size of the data such as terabytes (TB), petabytes (PB), zettabytes (ZB), etc. Variety defines the various type of data that is generated. Velocity means how frequently the data is generated. Big Data is ubiquitous. The significant amount of data generated allows us to make the right decision at the right time in both public and private sector. For example, in retail business, consumer behavior and preferences can be understood by analyzing the big data which includes, customer movement in the store or online website, transactions, product searches, etc. Big data allows decision making based on data Christopher J. Bucholtz (2012). In business perspective, big data has the potential to generate more revenue, reduce risk, and predict future outcomes with greater low-cost investment (Kevin Benedict, 2012). Some of the challenges which can be addressed by using big data have been identified by IBM (Yunan, 2012). For example, life-threatening situations at hospitals can be detected, weather conditions to plan optimal wind turbine usage can be predicted, and optimum capital expenditure on assets, identify criminals and threats from disparate video, audio, and data feeds and take decisions based on real-time transactional data (Zaslavsky et al., 2012).

Figure 2. Features of Big Data

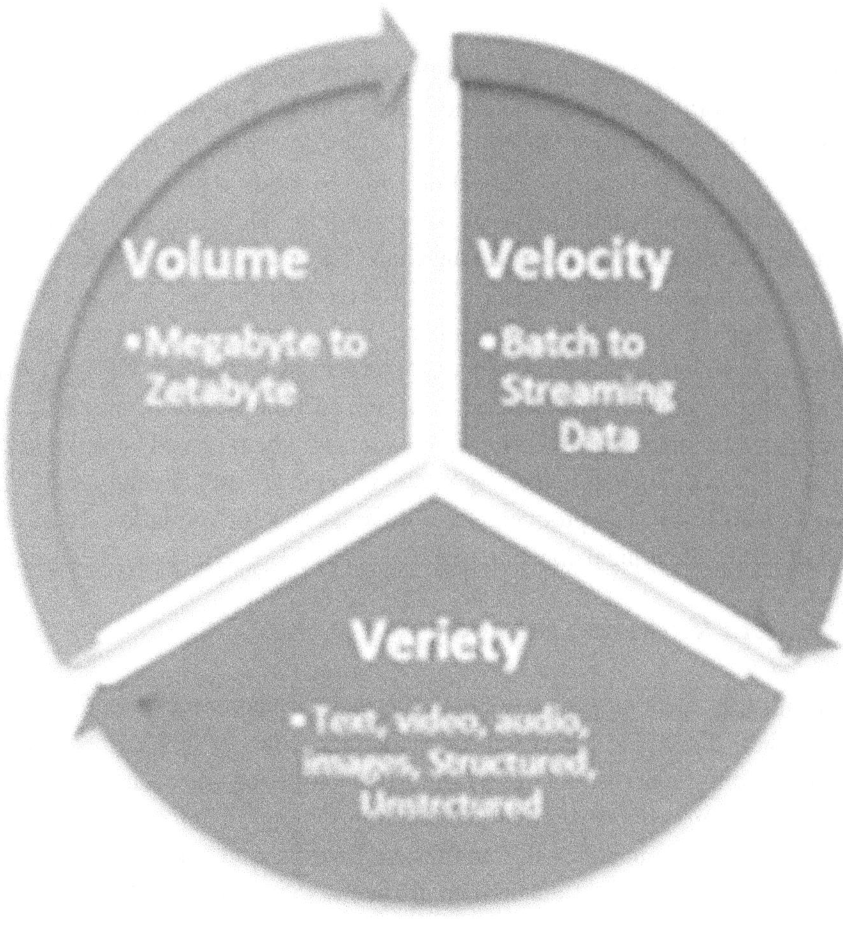

Content Digital Marketing

Marketers have diverted their attention from traditional marketing to content marketing. Content marketing deals with creating and distributing relevant and valuable content to attract, acquire, and engage a target audience in order to drive profit (Pulizzi, 2016).

Analytics can provide more specific content for marketers considering all of the data. Sensor driven analytics can assist human decision making through deep analysis and data visualization software. Contextualizing the data leads to unprecedented marketing automation and control, drastically relieving the marketers to categorize and find their audience. Thus, the marketing teams can create effective content for a few smaller segments rather than chasing a larger target customers for effective content.

According to Steve Reed, VP of Client Development at Elevation Marketing, the inherent value of IoT is in connecting devices to the cloud, regardless of an individual's physical location. The widespread use of smart devices, provides marketers several opportunities to market to potential buyers and to precisely target customers and gain immediate results (Adekoya & Olubukola, 2016). These devices provide detailed data on routine activities such as exercising, energy consumption, and workplace habits. Thus, businesses are enabled to develop more effective strategies and consequently, improve ROI on future marketing initiatives.

Also, IoT enhances user experiences. When smart devices do not perform as expected or begin to disintegrate, that information is provided to the supplier, providing an opportunity for immediate repair and maintenance. For instance, Tesla cars automatically receive software updates and alert drivers when maintenance is required.

Companies can outperform if they update smart devices with sophisticated customer relationship management (CRM) software, so that firms can do much more for the customers rather than just gather and organize customer data. CRM can be leveraged for advanced capabilities and better user experience. This software can do much more than data collection and into robust data analysis, allowing a business to take better decisions regarding marketing to its consumer base. This is valuable to marketers, because it overcomes information processing through a long chain, particularly IT departments (Olenski, 2015).

Better data collection fosters better targeting. With the rising influx of marketing messages, it is imperative to provide an appealing message to the audience in the most convincing way, IoT aids marketers build better customer experiences based on previous interactions with them (Olenski, 2015).

With respect to devices, added services and products will become even more prevalent. Thus, ordinary watches will be replaced by smart watches, kitchen blenders will be replaced by smart kitchen blenders, and this type of strategy will revamp marketing strategies and product development. The unique and distinctive features provided by such products gives them a competitive market share, and make them seem far more desirable to the typical consumer.

IoT and the Content Marketing Strategies

IoT widely permeates into marketing strategy both theoretically and practically. The core concept of marketing theory is the 4 P's. E. Jerome McCarthy marketing professor of Michigan State University is the primary scholar who has patented the development of marketing, specifically the concept of the 4 P's (product, place, price, promotion) within the marketing strategy (E Jerome McCarthy, 2011). When consumer customized messages includes all four of these fundamental features, it can result in effective marketing practices. Each of these fundamental areas successfully applies to IoT.

Products being offered to the consumers should be clearly defined in order to get a clear understanding of it. IoT allows highly customized products to reach the customers. A customized product offers a consumer thorough satisfaction and unique experience.

The placement of a product refers to its channel of distribution, such as whether the product can be purchased in physical stores or online marketplaces. Placement in a physical store can be further streamlined into the precise location such as the front aisle displays, end aisle displays, checkout line or the rear end of the store. Placement also refers to marketing messages, endorsed by advertisements on digital banners, billboards, television, and radio. IoT has revolutionized the way marketing messages reach consumers because the customers are permanently connected to the company via IoT devices. Thus, this enables ubiquitous placement of consumer from anywhere he is located.

The price of a product is a crucial driver and needs to be fixed meticulously as it mediates value to consumers. IoT has changed its meaning as it redefined placement. Items are dynamically priced based on customer preferences and their behavior through IoT connected devices contrary to the conventional segmentation of customers based on consumer demographics. For instance, Progressive Auto Insurance company has a device called the Snapshot that allows the company to collect actual driver information via constant connection to this device. Thus, the company can dynamically determine insurance based on driver behavior and preferences contrary to blanket rate offered to various demographics based on age or gender.

Finally, promotion is a key driver of marketing as it refers to the actual message content that companies deliver to customers. IoT fosters improved promotion schemes in a variety of ways. Since data collection practices have developed tremendously, marketers can effectively target individual consumers and hence customize content, thus creating highly individualized and personalized messages that are appealing and convincing to customers. Moreover, IoT allows marketers to create more effective content based on consumer data that is collected and analyzed. It also continuously tests and optimizes various messages.

Conclusively, IoT enables firms to effectively execute the four significant aspects of marketing: product, placement, pricing, and promotion. As consumers envisage IoT, this will broaden the opportunities of marketers to successfully market their items which could result in higher ROI.

IoT Applications

RFID (Radio-Frequency identification) and related technologies have been widely applied in the supply chain logistics applications in the retail industries and consumer products and transportations. It is quite likely that these technologies will saturate in the near future, however the potentials and capabilities of IoT technologies will extend wide and far. The most common IoT applications in various industries is discussed below.

Health and Fitness

Medical monitoring of remote patients and advanced medical diagnosis is possible using IoT. It is carried out by Identification and authentication of people, automatic data collection and sensing from various geographical locations. The staff, patients and objects can be easily tracked and kept under control. The Internet of Things can be effective in realizing the vision of ambient assisted living. (Haller,S. et al)

Health-conscious consumers could purchase an IoT connected cooking pan that calculates the nutritional value of the food they're cooking. It could be programmed to automatically send that data to a food app on their smart device such as MyFitnessPal powered by Under Armor. This would provide Under Armor with specific preferences and insights into key behaviors of their consumers. For example, based on dietary pattern, Under Armor could diistinguish which of their customers are serious athletes or purchase athleisure apparels. With that information, Under Armor could target more effectively with dynamic customized marketing messages created for different segments.

Similarly, sending that information to mobile apps developed for grocery stores would offer benefits from a different perspective. Grocers could avail this information to know what customers are actually cooking with their products. They could also send alerts based on expiration dates of the products to caution consumers when their food is about to decay. For this generation of health freaks, this application would be implemented soon. This would help to ensure that grocery stores' inventories are not depleted because they are aware beforehand what products are being consumed and when a customer is likely to make a repeat purchase. This will foster immediate replenishment of the inventories with the products that are being consumed.

Retail Shopping

The ambience of physical stores have a deep impact on emotional states, including mood enhancement and pleasure, which directly influences consumers' impulsive buying behaviors in the store (Xu and Yingjiao, 2007). Brick and mortar physical locations can significantly influence the psychology of consumers by the various aisle arrangement techniques and the contrasting combination of color hues involved . Additionally, implementing technology the stores could have added business benefits. A dressing room in a retail boutique could be implanted with an IoT enabled mirror so a consumer doesn't have to try on clothes directly rather it can scan a consumer's body and clad it with apparels of consumer's choice that is determined by previously collected data. Based on this data it could also recommend different outfits, and continue to market to the customer after he has evacuated the store. This will provide a unique user experience replete with satisfaction that could be customized to any segment, and could in turn augment ROI. The mirror could have an enhanced ability to advertise similar clothing or accessories. Moreover, if the consumer had an account from an online store, the mirror could recognize lost sales by tracking items left behind in a cart and advance marketing strategies to recover those sales, thus improving the online shopping experience of a customer.

Luxury Hotels

To provide a unique experience to each client would be an exciting avenue for businesses. Standard hotels who offer guests luxurious comfort as their service could substitute a customer's home environment to provide that customized experience. Hotels could fetch data from a customer's smart device to learn the temperature, lighting, alarms settings in their own home and offer similar settings in a hotel room that can provide a unique customer experience. Hilton hotel which is targeted towards customers can perfectly reflect these ideas through effective implementation (Trejos, 2016). This allows a more traditionally perceived brand such as the Hilton hotel to become iconic in the perception of its customers.

Manufacturing

As service-oriented architecture (SOA) concepts are going to be the standard to connect to enterprise applications, there is a trend of putting web services on the devices themselves and giving them the capability of providing their functionality as a service. Eventually, this will create cross layered web service, with services hosted at the enterprise, middleware and device level. (Moreira Sa de Souza, L, et al) Therefore device integration means service integration. Not only does this create a new dimension on the shop floor, but it would also encourage the development of new devices in the automation industry that would offer embedded web services (Haller et al.). But in the near future, intelligence will be embedded in each application and will be programmed individually. Thus, the factory will be programmed through artificial intelligence.

Personal and Home

A home can be designed with a smart environment by using IoT. The intelligent objects can make it conducive and comfortable. For instance, the heating systems can be modified according to our preferences and the weather. The lights can be set and adjusted according to the day and night time. Appropriate monitoring and supervisory control and alarm systems can alleviate the incidents of thefts and burglaries. Power consumption can be drastically reduced by automatically switching off the electrical devices when not in use.

Automation

Sensors and embedded systems have since long been a part of the automotive industry. It is predicted that the automotive industry will further proliferate when integrated with IoT. Every car will be connected to the internet and will be implanted with a sensor. When detecting the hazards, these "internet of vehicles" can generate and deliver accurate data containing a description to the car owners, insurance companies and people who need these data. This will in turn facilitate services like remote diagnosis of cars in case of break-downs, software version management and others.

Transportation and Logistics

The location and the status of an object can be easily tracked by Internet of Things, throughout the full product life-cycle and the supply chain. Through sensors it can be easily detected that the products were never exposed to a hazardous environment and that the products are in the suitable temperature settings. It is also able to track that the hazardous products will not be transported through polluted or sensitive environment. IoT technologies will be able to record all the emissions which were generated during the transportation and thus effectively realize green transportation. The companies can track all the processes and can alleviate certain governmental and legal issues in this area.

WEB DEVELOPMENT

With the rapid advancement of the internet in recent years, Internet-based applications such as remote monitoring systems have become increasingly popular. A remote monitoring system allows the user to have remote real-time control of the situation in an environment by using a smartphone or computer connected to the internet.

The fundamental technology of the IoT is wireless sensor networks (Xu et al., 2014; W. He and L. Xu, 2013) A WSN is a wireless network that deploys intelligent sensors for transmission and reception of data. The various industries that WSN finds applications in include health, environment, industrial, and traffic monitoring (Li et al., 2013; He and Xu, 2014). WSNs led to the development of devices and technologies that support the growth of the Internet, such as QR codes, intelligent phones, social networks, and cloud computing (Tao et al., 2013; Bandyopadhyay and Sen, 2011) besides contributing to the development of IoT (Wang et al., 2014).

The development of Internet of Vehicles, IoT, and cloud computing technologies have led to an increasing demand for intelligent power monitoring systems and remote supervisory control and data acquisition (SCADA) systems (Fachechi et al., 2015; Ding et al., 2015).

An IoT-based SCADA system allows for easy and efficient way of remotely monitoring industrial devices. A WSNs or wireless sensor and actuator networks can be effectively applied to a SCADA system and are beneficial because these networks are based on the well-developed TCP/IP and HTTP protocols for transferring data to a client from a server through a web application (Grilo et al., 2014).

The Microsoft SQL Server can be used for transferring data via open database connectivity (OBDC) method. The web server must be set up to offer services to the client. Microsoft Internet Information Services (IIS) is a service established on the web server in order to send data to the client in Extensible Markup Language (XML) format (Lipnickas et al., 2015). JSON being a lightweight data interchange format is easy for humans to read and write as well as easy for machines to parse and generate, therefore developers have replaced XML with JavaScript that is used for transferring data. JSON increases the decoding speed of a browser and improves the response rate of a website. Developers use a model–view–controller (MVC) architectural pattern to design a website because it divides a given application into three interconnected parts thus making development simple. The MVC design pattern segregates these parts, facilitating efficient code reuse and synchronous development. The cloud-based vehicle toll payment system adopts the aforementioned strategy for the development of a web application (Cvijic et al., 2016).

A monitoring system consists of the monitor tier, server tier, cloud tier, and client tier. Different tiers function differently in order to gain remote monitoring and data management by using devices and software (Kanagaraj et al., 2015).

Market research of browsers used in intelligent devices reveal that, majority of the people use browsers for browsing websites on devices such as smartphones, tablets, and laptops. Since the devices have different screen sizes, responsive web design (RWD) must be used to develop various websites to fit different devices with varying screen sizes (Peng and Zhou, 2015) .

Concept and Technologies Used in Web Development

The web application is developed using the ASP.NET framework in Visual Studio. The coding between the server and the client in the MVC structure is done using C#, SQL, JavaScript, HTML, and CSS languages. Razor and jQuery are some of the commonly used libraries and JSON, a popular format for transferring data were implemented in this project to achieve the function of asynchronous JavaScript and XML (AJAX).

ASP.NET MVC Architecture

A web application is designed for a remote monitoring system using an MVC architecture. As shown in figure 3 below, the developer must divide an application into three different parts.

(a) Data is stored in a model that is then extracted according to commands from the controllers. It consists of all data used in a project including the business logic .
(b) Based on the changes in the model, view presents the data from the controller.
(c) A controller discerns the data flow to and from the model and the view and sends commands accordingly.

Figure 3. MVC architecture

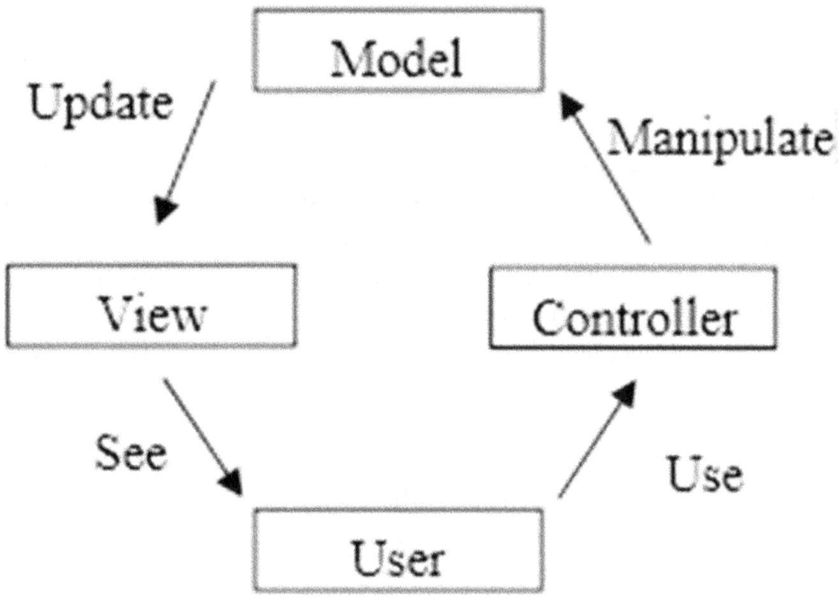

Figure 4. Life Cycle of an MVC

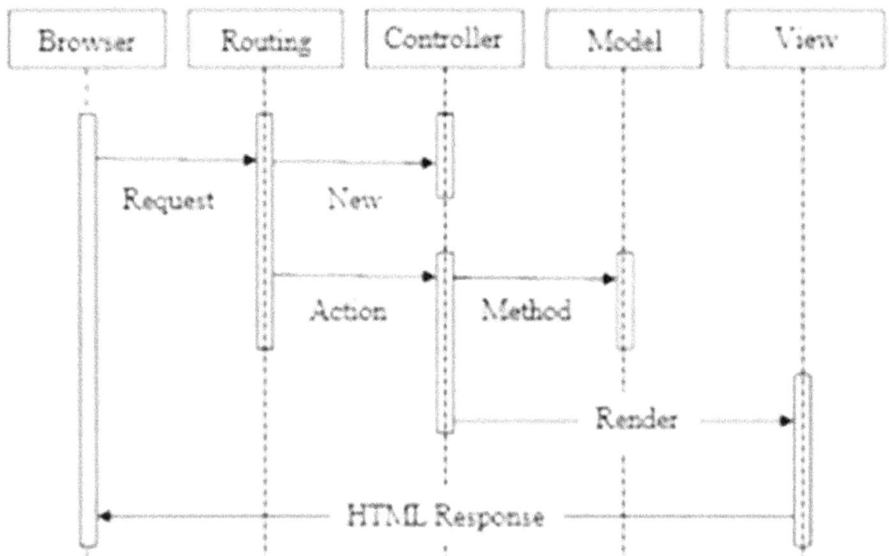

MVC frameworks that are used in web application development are common in programming languages like Java, C#, and PHP. Here, the ASP.NET MVC framework was applied to a remote monitoring and supervisory control system to evaluate digital marketing metrics.

The life cycle of an MVC architecture is presented in figure 4. The beginning for every MVC application is URL routing. When ASP.NET platform receives a request from a browser, a controller decides how it should be processed. The controller then discerns the view and presents the view through URL routing.

Relational Database

A relational database management system, namely Microsoft SQL Server is used to process four basic operations of a database, namely create, read, update, and delete. A common approach in industrial systems is to implement a database to store data acquired with an analog-to-digital converter and create relations among different types of data. Entity Framework is used to link the web application to an SQL Server. It allows a web designer link the object in their code with a table in the database. This database technique is called "Code First" since the developers first design the objects and write the related code, and then implement the database. This study includes a view that was created that provides the previous data acquired by the system to the users if required.

RWD

In order to develop a friendly user interface RWD was used in the IoT-based remote SCADA system. RWD is a feature of web designing that allows desktop webpages to be viewed in according to the size of the screen. For instance, a website with a wide original template will have a narrow display when the device screen pixels are less than 400 pixels. An RWD website in different devices displays different UI templates. A website developed with RWD adjusts the layout to the viewing environment by using fluid, proportion-based grids, and CSS3 media queries. The main advantage of a RWD website is reduced user scrolling and zooming. The data in a RWD website on smart devices makes supervision easier as it is more accurate than other websites without RWD. Also, it alleviates the problems of incorrect sensing of buttons and provides better user experiences.

AJAX

The more conventional websites should dynamically update by means of refreshing continuously. The users cannot browse a website effectively since it requires sometimes to wait for the blank page to refresh before the content of the page appears.

A new technology named AJAX allows a web application to send and receive data from a server asynchronously. AJAX, allows web page to change content dynamically without the need to reload the entire page. JSON replaces XML in most of the implementations since it is native to JavaScript.

AJAX is not a single rather a group of technologies. HTML, CSS, and JavaScript can be used parallelly in a project.

This study includes, the AJAX technique with the jQuery library in JavaScript to design the numerical and graphical interfaces for presenting the quantitative measurement data.

Communication

A system consisting of a server PC, an inverter, a WSN module, and a client device is designed. It is challenging to establish communication between these pieces of hardware. An electrical interface connects the server PC and inverter . The IEEE 802.11 standard is used to send data from a Wi-Fi data acquisition (DAQ) device to the server PC. A Wi-Fi router connects DAQ device and the server PC. Finally, the server PC communicates with the client devices using the TCP/IP protocol as the SCADA system is connected to the Internet.

IOT Challenges

IoT offers a myriad of opportunities in marketing applications, however it also presents various challenges that need to be addressed. Tracking big data, ensuring privacy and security of that data, and the ethics of collecting unnecessary data are among those challenges.

Technology Issues

IoT offers various opportunities and socio- economic benefits. Though, IoT is spreading rapidly at this stage, it also portrays several technical issues that need to be solved.

Capacity is of utmost concern and priority. As the number of devices connected to the internet are increasing (Lemoine) the Internet address space needs to expand widely. Not only the quantity but also the quality is of prominence. In various parts of the world, IPv6 is being used online in parallel with IPv4 system. (COM, 2008) It is imperative to develop the capacities of the computers, and also the new models and algorithms to aid the enterprise systems.

A unique ID needs to be attached to every object in the IoT in order to be able to identify the entities in the IoT.

The research challenges in IoT are listed by the ISTAG (Information Society Technologies Advisory Group) and the European Commission.

- Edge technologies, such as sensors and actuators, passive/active RFID tags, embedded systems, rendering devices that are attached to real-world objects smart enough to participate in Internet of Things application scenarios.
- Networking technologies, such as fixed, mobile, wired and wireless networks, allowing the highly available bi-directional communication at different levels;
- Middleware systems and service-oriented architectures putting real-world data into the context of various Internet of Things applications;
- Platform services ensuring scalability, high availability, and the safe and secure execution of the requested functionalities;
- Web service technologies making information and services available while reducing interoperability issues and enhancing extensibility, platform independence and standardized exchange of messages.

It is noteworthy that IoT employs the private network, public (open) network and hybrid network. In the supply chain, a need for the secure data sharing and transparency of business entities is imperative. It must be undermined that things in the world cannot be accessed at the speed of internet. Thus, interoperability will be a primary problem in the future in terms of IoT.

Bigger Than Big Data

Though it is important for companies to capture and collect big data, storing that data can become an issue. As data is growing continuously, its storage requirements and the costs is also increasing. Data storage must be scalable. If data is stored on servers or data warehouses, they could be saturated and get exhausted with data. Physical servers could be difficult to handle, expensive, and also difficult to maintain. Big data must be relatively easy to access, analyze, and organize. Thus, it enables easy retrieval and analysis of data.

Storage could also be an expensive affair. An alternative to conventional ways of storage such as servers or warehouses is cloud storage. For example, Yahoo would require to store 200 petabytes of data. Cloud services would typically charge around $1 million to support and store 200 petabytes of data, on the contrary conventional enterprise data warehouses could cost 100 times more (Bantleman, John, 2012).

Privacy

Pertaining to IoT, every object also has its virtual aspect which can create and avail services. This intricate and sophisticated connections will not only lead to comfort and economic benefits but will also need unprecedented approaches to deal with novel challenges like its safe and ethical use (Roman.R, et al).

It could be overwhelming for users as IoT can create huge amount of data in subtle ways. Moreover, the decision making process is also automated through devices and algorithms in decision support system. This might prove beneficial to certain people based on the application and would be in vain to the others

Users discussed the privacy issues involved in using IoT devices in a group discussion organized by the Federal Trade Commission (FTC). It was noted that the use of IoT presents a variety of potential risks and vulnerabilities that could be exploited to harm users. Unauthorized access, leaking of personal information due to lack of confidentiality create huge risks to personal safety. It was also noted that the collection of personal information, habits, locations, and physical conditions over time may lead to privacy risks (Internet of Things: Privacy and security in a connected world, 2015). Companies make use of this data to make credit, insurance, and employment decisions. Thus, it is worth considering that the "potential risks and harm to privacy and security, if not acknowledged, could shake the consumer confidence that can hinder these technologies to achieve their full potential, and might lead to less adoption.

Security

IoT has been in market while it is still a novel technology, its security standards are not full -fledged as that of smartphones. For example, a recent research finding by HP revealed that 70% of the IoT bestselling products were deficit of security constraints. (HPE Fortify and the Internet of Things, 2016)· The IoT supplier needs to automatically update IoT devices software in order to protect customers and improve security. It is of high risk if the companies do not have a scheduled security patch updated regularly (McElwee and Tim, 2016) . Hacking into IoT devices might not allow the hacker to harm directly, however the hacker can exploit the vulnerabilities in order to access other interconnected devices. IoT can serve as a pivot point to get into other devices with more significant and sensitive information.

Ethical Implications

Data collection and retention policies of companies give rise to several ethical questions to be considered. Data minimization is an important policy that companies should consider, which signifies that companies should limit the data they collect and retain, and dispose of it once they no longer need it. This can save the consumers from potential harm. Firstly, huge amount of data attracts more fraud through higher data theft. Secondly, if a company captures and stores large amounts of data, there is an increased risk that the data will be misused against the expectations of a customer.

Government Regulation

Verizon Wireless poses a good example of an internal security issue. This telecommunication company had been using hidden tracking technology known as "super cookies," which were used for tailored marketing and advertising towards a segment of customers without their permission (Kang, Ceclia , 2016) .Since the government licenses and regulations are feeble in the digital world, legal protection of businesses is of utmost prominence with respect to data collection and strorage digitally.

As a result, IoT poses several threats and challenges that need to be effectively dealt with. The widespread use of smart devices emphasizes secure measures of data collection and the use of data protection protocols. Furthermore, since there is inadequate government regulation in the digital world, the firms should work directly with consumers to set reasonable expectations of what data is required to be collected, how that data should be used, and when data should be permanently destroyed.

CONCLUSION

With the predicted growth of the IoT connected devices there is a substantial increase in the digital marketing landscape, particularly in the marketing messages tailored towards specific customer segments. It can be concluded from the literature review, that the scholars hold consensus that the IoT will greatly influence and revolutionize the future. But how wide and far reaching this impact would be is still unknown. The current research divulged the various concepts and aspects of IoT, its benefits to customers and the unique opportunities and challenges that it poses for marketers. Marketers will have to customize their marketing strategies and messages according to these consumer preferences so that it can generate significant ROI and secure a bigger market share. As consumers do not pay heed to conventional advertisements, companies should primarily send their messages to targeted customers through content marketing. Leveraging this technology allows brands to launch meaningful, innovative campaigns and employ favorable content to convince customers into buying and retaining relationship.

Moreover, brands can manufacture IoT enabled products and services that will foster a stronger bond between consumers and companies. It will improve the quality of life of the users by allowing them to carry out more sophisticated tasks rather than the mundane daily routines. The firms can capture and collect data that will aid them in future production decisions and generating marketing messages.

However, at the forefront of this technology lies several risks and concerns for data storage measures and consumer security and privacy. Firms will have to deploy special means in their infrastructure and analytical methods to capture and store large amounts of data. Also, customers need to be highly vigilant and aware of the security and privacy risks involved in voluntarily sharing their data. Lastly, firms and consumers should comply by the rules and regulations levied by the government in order to exercise safe usage of these devices through secure data exchanges.

With respect to all parties involved in the IoT technology, marketers, consumers, and firms the risks and challenges outweigh the benefits and opportunities. It is indeed of great interest to explore how this discovery will evolve and develop over the next decade and also the respective interaction between the consumers and the brands .

Finally, the remote monitoring and supervisory control system enables communication with intelligent devices. Users can remotely monitor a situation via a browser on their PC or intelligent device. This system monitors with basic functions. Although this system has limitations, it can incorporate more intricate functions in the future. This system can be applied in transportation vehicles such as intelligent yachts, autonomous cars, and personal rapid transit.

Recommendations for Future Research

The experts widely predict that IoT would bring a lot of business opportunities and revolutionize the marketing landscape. However, a business cannot readily embrace this novel technology of IoT due to various reasons that support it. This area of research presents several voids as mentioned above. There has been very narrow research conducted in this field with respect to business and digital marketing strategies. Also, the extent to which this new technology is envisaged is of concern due to its limitations in terms of security and privacy. Lastly it is imperative to use explicit government licenses and regulations in universal data exchange. For both the academia and industry, it is a challenge to bridge the gap present in the various shortcomings in IoT. There has to be a wider scope of research for the field of business models and content digital marketing in order to achieve improved content digital marketing strategies.

REFERENCES

Adekoya, O. (2016). Marketing and the Internet of Things. *Hot Sauce.*

Alqahtani, H., & Naim, A. (2022). Critical Success Factors for Transforming CRM to SCRM for building E-CRM. In A. Naim & S. Kautish (Eds.), *Building a Brand Image Through Electronic Customer Relationship Management* (pp. 139–168). IGI Global. doi:10.4018/978-1-6684-5386-5.ch007

Apple Inc. (2006, May) *Nike+iPod Sports Kit.* Apple. https://www.apple.com/ipod/nike/

Atzori, L., Iera, A., & Morabito, G. (2010). The Internet of Things: A Survey. *Computer Networks, 54*(15), 2787–2805. doi:10.1016/j.comnet.2010.05.010

Atzori, L., Iera, A., & Morabito, G. (2010). The internet of things: A survey. *Computer Networks, 54*(15), 2787–2805. doi:10.1016/j.comnet.2010.05.010

Bandyopadhyay, D., & Sen, J. (2011). Internet of things: Applications and challenges in technology and standardization. *Wireless Personal Communications, 58*(1), 49–69. doi:10.100711277-011-0288-5

Bantleman, J. (2012, April). The Big Cost Of Big Data. *Forbes, 16.*

Benedict, K. (2012). *Moneyball, Big Data, The Internet of Things and Enterprise Mobility.* Cloud Computing. http://cloudcomputing.sys-con.com/node/2181866

Eaton, C., Deroos, D., Deutsch, T., Lapis, G., & Zikopoulos, P. (2012). *Understanding Big Data.* McGraw-Hill Companies. http://public.dhe.ibm.com/common/ssi/ecm/en/iml14296usen/I M L14296USEN.pdf.

Christopher, J. Bucholtz. (2012, March) Customers, Big Data, and the Internet of Things. *Tech News World.* https://www.technewsworld.com/story/74692.html [Accessed on: 2012-06-08]

Chynal, P., & Sobecki, J. (2016). Eyetracking Evaluation of Different Chart Types Used for Web-Based System Data Visualization. *IEEE Conf. Network Intelligence Conference (ENIC),* IEEE. 10.1109/ENIC.2016.031

Cvijic, B., Bundalo, D., Pasalic, D., & Bundalo, Z. (2016). Cloud based web application supporting vehicle toll payment system. *5th Mediterranean Conference on Embedded Computing (MECO).* IEEE. 10.1109/MECO.2016.7525700

Ding, Z., Yang, B., Guting, R. H., & Li, Y. (2015, August). Network-Matched Trajectory-Based Moving-Object Database: Models and Applications. *IEEE Transactions on Intelligent Transportation Systems, 16*(4), 1918–1928. doi:10.1109/TITS.2014.2383494

Fachechi, A., Mainetti, L., Palano, L., Patrono, L., Stefanizzi, M. L., Vergallo, R., Chu, P., & Gadh, R. (2015). A new vehicle-to-grid system for battery charging exploiting IoT protocols. *IEEE Int. Conf. Industrial Technology (ICIT).* IEEE. 10.1109/ICIT.2015.7125414

Fuchs, C., Hofkirchner, W., Schafranek, M., Raffl, C., Sandoval, M., & Bichler, R. (2010). *Theoretical Foundations of the Web: Cognition, Communication, and CoOperation.* Multidisciplinary Digital Publishing Institute.

Green, H. (2015) *Cognitive IoT: Making the internet of Things Deliver for All of Us.*

Grilo, A. M., Chen, J., Diaz, M., Garrido, D., & Casaca, A. (2014, August). An Integrated WSAN and SCADA System for Monitoring a Critical Infrastructure. *IEEE Transactions on Industrial Informatics, 10*(3), 1755–1764. doi:10.1109/TII.2014.2322818

Gubbi, J., Buyya, R., Marusic, S., & Palaniswami. M. (2013). Internet of Things (IoT): A Vision, Architectural Elements, and Future Directions. Future Generation Computer Systems. *ScienceDirect.*

Haller, S., Karnouskos, S. and Schroth, C. (2009). *The Internet of Things in an Enterprise Context.*

He, W., & Xu, L. (2014, February). Integration of distributed enterprise applications: A survey. *IEEE Transactions on Industrial Informatics, 10*(1), 35–42. doi:10.1109/TII.2012.2189221

Henneke, S. (2016). Smart City Solution for Amsterdam: Intelligent Waste Disposal with M2M Telekom M2M Blog. *Telekom M2M Blog.*

Huo, Y., Tu, W., Sheng, Z., & Leung, C. M. (2015). A survey of in-vehicle communications: Requirements, solutions and opportunities in IoT. *IEEE Conf. 2nd World Forum on Internet of Things (WF-IoT)*, (pp.132–37). IEEE. 10.1109/WF-IoT.2015.7389040

IBM. (2015). *Redefining Boundaries: Insights from the Global C- suite Study*. IBM.

Federal Trade Commission. (2014). *Internet of Things: Privacy & Security in a Connected World.* FTC.

Kamal, S., Naim, A., Magd, H., Khan, S. A., & Khan, F. M. (2022). The Relationship Between E-Service Quality, Ease of Use, and E-CRM Performance Referred by Brand Image. In A. Naim & S. Kautish (Eds.), *Building a Brand Image Through Electronic Customer Relationship Management* (pp. 84–108). IGI Global. doi:10.4018/978-1-6684-5386-5.ch005

Kanagaraj, E., Kamarudin, M., Zakaria, A., Gunasagaran, R., & Shakaff, A. (2015). Cloud-based Remote Environmental Monitoring System with Distributed WSN Weather Stations. *IEEE Sensors.*

Kang, C. (2016). Verizon Settles With F.C.C. Over Hidden Tracking via 'Supercookies'. *The New York Times.*

Kao, K.-C. Jeng, S., & Chieng, W. (2018) *Design and development of an IoT-based web application for an intelligent remote SCADA system.* Semantic Scholar.

Li, S., Xu, L., & Wang, X. (2013). Compressed sensing signal and data acquisition in wireless sensor networks and internet of things. *IEEE Trans. Ind. Informat, 9*(4), 2177–86.

Lipnickas, A., Rutkauskas, R., & Cerkauskas, R. (2015). A resource oriented architecture for Web- integrated SCADA applications. *IEEE World Conference on Factory Communication Systems (WFCS)*. IEEE.

Liu, C., Guo, Z., Feng, Y., Hong, F., & Jing, W. (2017, March). CPCA: The Cloud Platform of Complex Virtual Instruments System Architecture. *IEEE Access : Practical Innovations, Open Solutions, 5*, 4350–4360. doi:10.1109/ACCESS.2017.2682258

Marques, R., Rocha, J., Rafael, S., & Martins, J. (2008). Design and Implementation of a Reconfigurable Remote Laboratory, Using Oscilloscope or PLC Network for WWW Access. *IEEE Transactions on Industrial Electronics, 55*(6).

McElwee, T. (2016). Expert Advice for Securing The Internet of Things. *Treeline Interactive Blog*.

Naim, A. & Malik, P. (2022). Competitive Trends and Technologies in Business Management. Nova Science Publisher. doi:10.52305/VIXO9830

Naim, A., Alqahtani, H., Muniasamy, A., Bilfaqih, S. M., Mahveen, R., & Mahjabeen, R. (2023). Applications of Information Systems and Data Security in Marketing Management. In A. Naim, P. Malik, & F. Zaidi (Eds.), *Fraud Prevention, Confidentiality, and Data Security for Modern Businesses* (pp. 57–83). IGI Global. doi:10.4018/978-1-6684-6581-3.ch003

Naim, A., & Kautish, S. K. (Eds.). (2022). *Building a Brand Image Through Electronic Customer Relationship Management*. IGI Global. doi:10.4018/978-1-6684-5386-5

Naim, A., Malik, P. K., & Zaidi, F. A. (Eds.). (2023). *Fraud Prevention, Confidentiality, and Data Security for Modern Businesses*. IGI Global. doi:10.4018/978-1-6684-6581-3

Olenski, S. (2015). How the Internet of Things Will Transform HighTech Marketing. Forbes. *Forbes Magazine*.

Oliveira, L. M. L., Reis, J., Rodrigues, J. J. P. C., & de Sousa, A. F. (2015). *IoT based solution for home power energy monitoring and actuating*. 13th Int. Conf. Industrial Informatics (INDIN. IEEE. 10.1109/INDIN.2015.7281869

Patidar, S., Rane, D., & Jain, P. (2022). *A Survey Paper on Cloud Computing*, 394-398.

Peng, W., & Zhou, Y. (2015). The Design and Research of Responsive Web Supporting Mobile Learning Devices. IEEE Conf. Educational Technology (ISET). IEEE. 10.1109/ISET.2015.40

Pogue, D. (November 30, 2011). A Thermostat That's Clever, Not Clunky. *New York Times*.

Pulizzi, J. (2012). *Content Marketing Definition*. Content Marketing Institute.

Radunovic, P., Vujicic, T., & Balota, A. (2017). Web application for lightning activity monitoring system (LAMS). IEEE Conf. Information System and Techologies (CISTI). IEEE. 10.23919/CISTI.2017.7975856

Cisco. (n.d.). *Smart+Connected Parking*. Cisco.

Tao, F., Laili, Y., Xu, L., & Zhang, L. (2013, November). FC-PACO-RM: A parallel method for service composition optimal-selection in cloud manufacturing system. *IEEE Transactions on Industrial Informatics, 9*(4), 2023–2033. doi:10.1109/TII.2012.2232936

Trejos, N. (2016). Hilton Announces New Affordable Hotel Brand, Tru. *USA Today*.

Wang, L., Xu, L., Bi, Z., & Xu, Y. (2014, February). Data filtering for RFID and WSN integration. *IEEE Transactions on Industrial Informatics, 10*(1), 408–418. doi:10.1109/TII.2013.2250510

Xu, L. D., He, W., & Li, S. (2014, November). Internet of Things in Industries: A Survey. *IEEE Transactions on Industrial Informatics, 10*(4), 2233–2243. doi:10.1109/TII.2014.2300753

Xu, Y. (2007). Impact of Store Environment on Adult Generation Y Consumers' Impulse Buying. *Journal of Shopping Center Research 14*(1).

Yunan, B. (2012). *What is Big Data's role in helping companies achieve competitive advantage through analytics.* IBM. https://www- 50.ibm.com/events/wwe/grp/grp004.nsf/v16_agenda?openform&seminar=9EBKW9ES&locale=en_US

Chapter 9
Applications and Impact of Internet of Things in Digital Marketing

Arshiya Mohammed
King Khalid University, Saudi Arabia

Asfia Sabahath Syed
King Khalid University, Saudi Arabia

ABSTRACT

Over the past few decades, curiosity and enthusiasm in science and technology have grown tremendously, to the extent that IoT is now being applied to a wide variety of sectors including business, marketing, manufacturing, sustainability, blockchain, and sports. Digital marketers are leveraging IoT technology in the current digital age to develop marketing strategies and adapt to changing industry trends. Marketers can implement new service-oriented strategies by combining IoT, Big Data, and data analytics. Among these technologies, IoT is crucial in assisting businesses in increasing utilization and manufacturing organizations. With the extensive exploration of IoT solutions, marketing practitioners and businesses can collect consumer data, store it in databases, increase sales, improve products and services, and develop revenue-boosting strategies. This chapter specifies how the consistent use of IoT technologies results in substantial organizational competitiveness and explains how IoT can be referred to as a new component of business analytics and digital marketing.

INTRODUCTION

Modern Information and Communication Technology (ICT) rapid development significantly impacts our daily activities, employment, way of life, and way of thinking. Household appliances could be controlled via our smartphones and exchange data using built-in sensors, while cars could choose the best route to avoid traffic and automatically order a new part to replace a broken one from the nearest workshop (Angelova et al., 2017). Technology makes life easier by providing convenience, accelerating access to

DOI: 10.4018/978-1-6684-8166-0.ch009

services, and automating management (Angelova et al., 2017). Among other technologies, the Internet of Things (IoT) plays a vital role in developing more intelligent manufacturing processes. The IoT includes services, machines, production modules, and products that can exchange information, trigger actions, and control each other, enabling an intelligent manufacturing environment (Weyer et al., 2015). These "smart" devices were part of science and fiction a few years ago, but technology has changed today's world. According to a McKinsey Global Institution report (& McKinsey & Company., 2018), IoT could have an annual economic impact of \$3.9 trillion to \$11.1 trillion by 2025 in various platforms such as factories, cities, retail environments, and the human body, as shown in figure 1.1.

Figure 1. Potential economic impact by segment

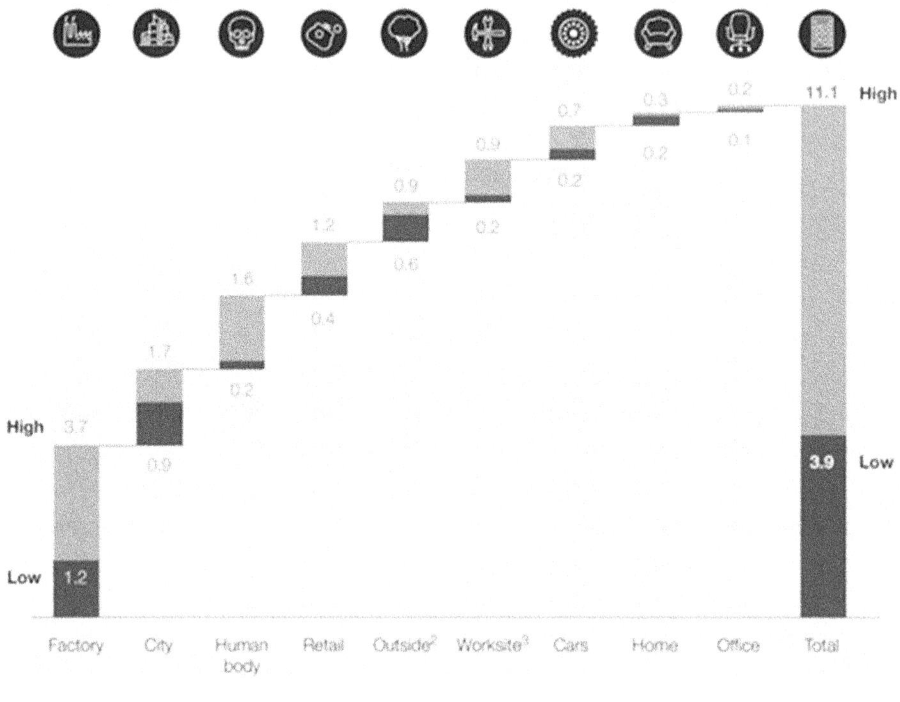

Because of the heterogeneity of the technology and hardware, there is no single unified definition of the term 'Thing' resulting in multiple interpretations of the concept of things and the IoT. Consequently, each stakeholder has defined the concept have a view of "Internet" and "Thing," which describe their features, ways of connecting, and ways of interacting. Niccolò Machiavelli- history's great futurist, might have predicted the Internet of Things (IoT) when he quotes, "There is nothing more difficult to take in hand, more perilous to conduct, or more uncertain in its success than to take the lead in the introduction of a new order of things" (Patel et al., 2018). The Internet of Things (IoT) refers to the emerging trend of augmenting physical objects and devices with sensing, computing, and communication capabilities, connecting them to form a network, and leveraging the collective effect of networked objects (Guo et al., 2013).

According to Adrin McEwen (McEwen & Cassimally, 2014) "The internet of things is formed by the combination of physical objects, controllers, sensors, and actuators, as well as the Internet, where actuators are the output into the world produced by the things". According to Forbes analyst Daniel Newman, "it is one of the most rapidly evolving trends today, in terms of the analytics arena, the development of edge computing, and the development of 5G networks" (Newman, 2017).

THEORETICAL FRAMEWORK

Definitions of IoT: One Concept, Many Definitions

The International Telecommunication Union (ITU) standardization section defines it as "a global infrastructure for the information society, enabling advanced services by interconnecting (Physical and Virtual) Things based on existing and evolving interoperable information and communication technologies" (International Telecommunication Union, 2018). In addition, the ITU recognizes three independent dimensions that characterize Things shown in figure (2.1.1). This demonstrates the IoT's adaptability in application domains with varying requirements and user needs (Guo et al., 2020).

Figure 2. Dimensions of the IoT
Source: Inspired by ITU-T (2012)

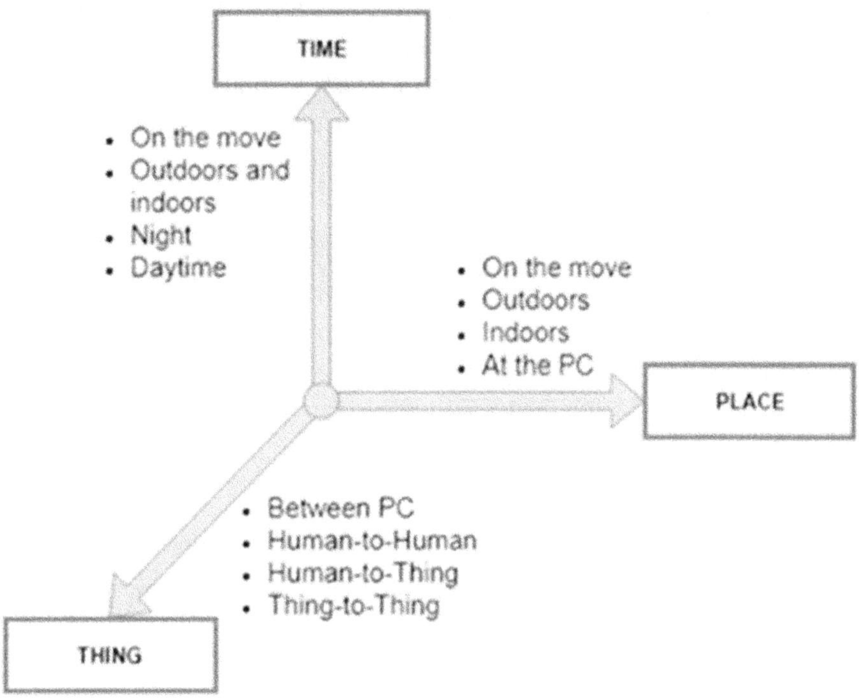

The Worldwide Consortium(W3C) has defined it as 'the abstraction of a physical or virtual entity that needs to be represented in IoT applications. This entity can be a device, a logical component of a device, a local hardware component, or even a logical entity such as location (e.g., room or building)'

(Kajimoto, ct al., 2017). The European Research Cluster on the Internet of Things (IERC) describes Things as "physical and virtual things with identities, physical attributes, and virtual personalities and smart user interfaces, and are seamlessly integrated into the information network" (Guo et al., 2020).

The Institute of Electrical and Electronics Engineers (IEEE) defines a "Thing" as a device with programmable capabilities and takes a more practical engineering view of Things, driven by two defining features: (i) Things can communicate technologically, and (ii) Things can connect to or integrate into an already connected into the environment (Guo et al., 2020).

The Internet Engineering Task Force (IETF), an international community of network designers, researchers, and operators, has considered the Things in the context of IoT, speculating on the possibility that "'things' are very varied such as computers, sensors, people, actuators, refrigerators, TVs, vehicles, mobile phones, clothes, food, medicines, books, etc. These things are classified into three scopes: people, machines (for example, sensors, actuators, etc.), and information (for example, clothes, food, medicine, books, etc.). These 'things' should be identified at least by one unique way to address and communicate with each other and verify their identities. In here, if the 'thing' is identified, we call it the 'object'" (Minerva et al., 2015).

Finally, the organization for the advancement of Structured Information Standards (OASIS), has described the IoT as a "System where the Internet is connected to the physical world via ubiquitous sensors" (Cosgrove-Sacks, 2014). OASIS emphasizes the pervasiveness of sensors, claiming that they can be found in "every mobile, every auto, every door, every room, every part, on every parts list, every sensor in every device in every bed, chair, or bracelet in every home, office, building, or hospital room in every city and village on Earth."(Guo et al., 2020).Figure 3 shows how these organizations and institutions view the Internet of Things (IoT) from physical and virtual connotations to the definition of 'Things.' Only the W3C has explicitly defined and acknowledged IoT as a location (Guo et al., 2020).

Figure 3. Classification of IoT definitions

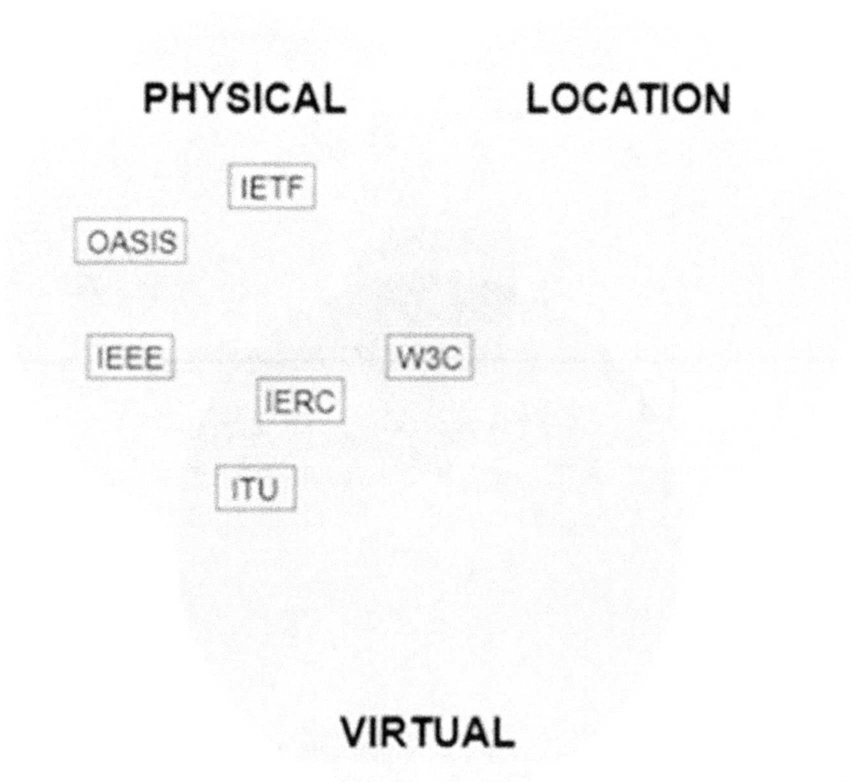

How IoT Changes our Lives

The Internet of Things, or IoT, is a collection of electronic devices connected to the Internet that can share and transfer data over a computer network. It can include almost anything, such as smartphones, heart monitors, livestock trackers, or even an airplane's jet engine. Through radio frequency identification (RFID), each device is assigned a unique digital identity, allowing components to communicate with one another and with the network as shown in Figure 4 (Crowley & Coutaz, 2015). IoT helps in improving the quality of human lives.

Figure 4. Role of IoT

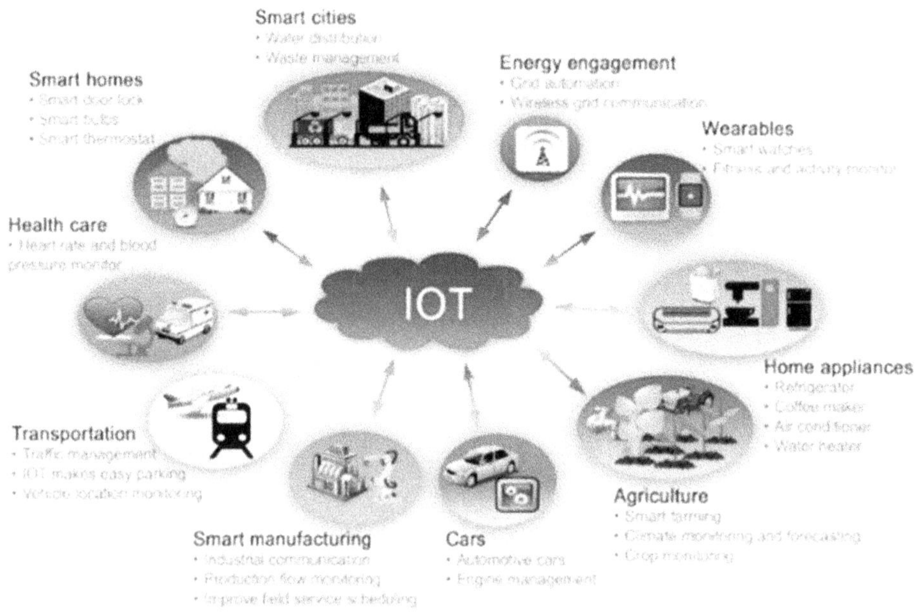

How IoT Works

Just as the Internet changed the way we live and communicate with one another by connecting through the WWW(Internet), IoT aims to connect to another level by connecting multiple devices to the internet at the same time, thereby facilitating man-to-machine and machine-to-machine interactions. There are four major components of the IoT:

1. **Sensors/Devices:** Sensors or devices aid in data collection from the surrounding environment. The data collected ranges in complexity from a simple temperature monitoring sensor to a complex video feed. Typical devices may contain multiple sensors that can do more than just detect things. The most fundamental step will always select and collect data from the surrounding environment, whether using a single sensor or multiple devices as shown in Figure 5. A sensor is able to measure physical phenomena like sound, heat, pressure, etc. and convert them into a digital representation.

Figure 5. IoT sensor/devices

2. **Connectivity:** The data is collected and sent to a cloud infrastructure as shown in Figure 6, but it requires a medium of transport. Sensors can communicate with the cloud via a variety of communication and transport mediums, including cellular networks, satellite networks, WiFi, Bluetooth, wide-area networks (WAN), low-power wide-area networks, and others. Each option has its own set of specifications and trade-offs in terms of power consumption, range, and bandwidth. As a result, selecting the best connectivity option for the IoT system is critical.

Figure 6. Cloud connectivity

3. **Data Processing:** The Internet of Things generates a massive amount of data. Storage and data analysis shown in Figure 7 takes place in the cloud infrastructure, which is referred to as the brain of IoT. Analyzing data entails interpreting raw data to determine which information is valuable to the end user and is used in the predictive analytics model.

Figure 7. Data processing

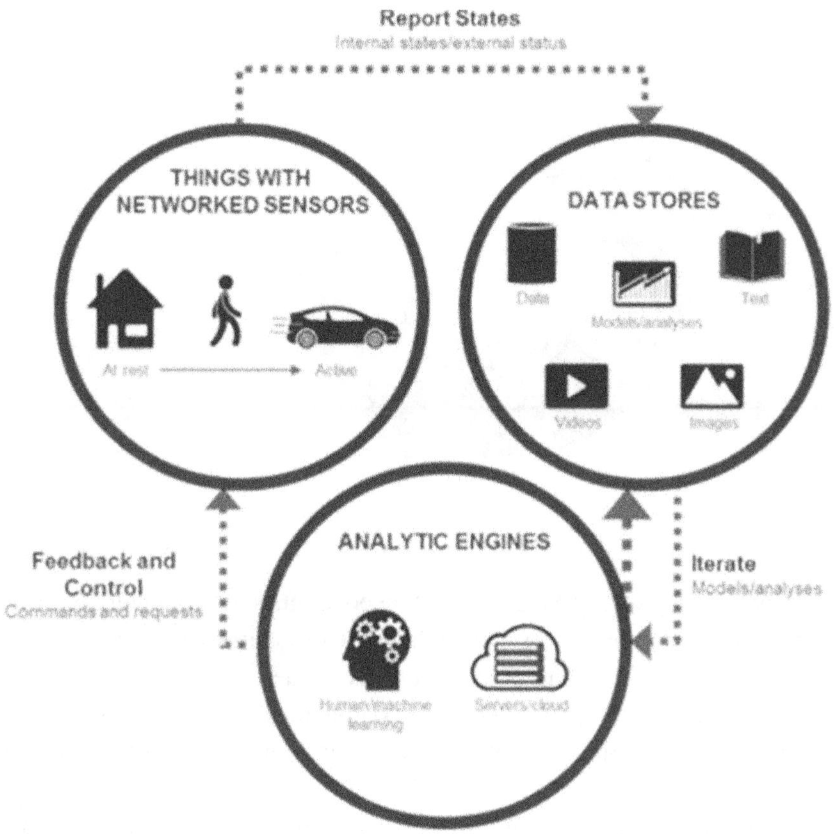

4. **User Interface:** The final component is the visible part of IoT, which is delivering useful information to the end-user. It transforms raw data into insights and displays charts, metrics, and indicators. Mobile apps serve as a user interface for controlling and monitoring smart devices.

Digital Transformation in Modern Business

IoT has become an overwhelming set of initiatives, technologies, and promises that are driving significant progress in businesses, but the value promised by IoT appears to be just beyond the horizon (McKinsey & Company, 2018). For businesses looking to capture value, a much more holistic approach to identifying opportunities across the entire business as part of a tech-enabled transformation that includes digital and analytics—from developing new products to improving operations is essentially shown in Figure 8 (McKinsey & Company., 2018).

Figure 8. Tech-enables transformations address all aspects of business

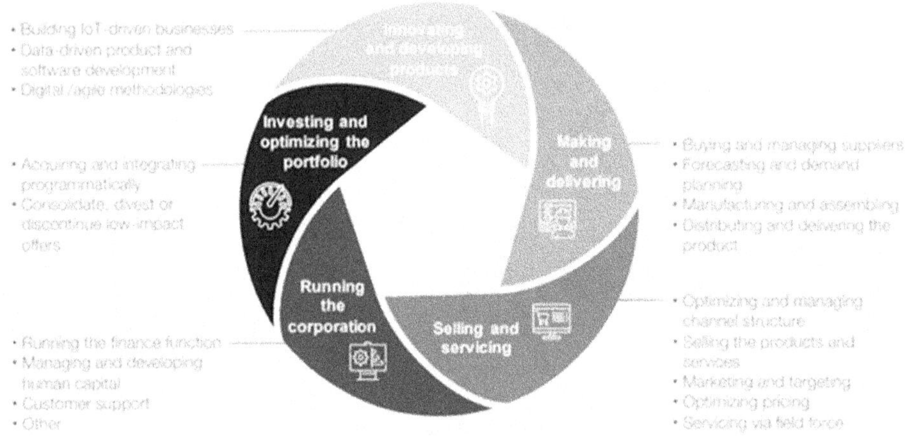

According to a recent McKinsey survey, 98 percent of respondents said that enterprise IoT initiatives are on the strategic roadmaps of companies in their industry. Companies will need an integrated program that builds value across the entire business to capture the value from those initiatives (McKinsey & Company, 2018). In the business sector, IoT has enabled companies to streamline business proposals, increase productivity, and develop cutting-edge products by combining sensor data and sophisticated analytical algorithms.

Enterprise IoT produces the greatest benefits in manufacturing and service operations where respondents believed that enterprise IoT would produce the most value in three areas: (i) diagnostics and prognostics, (ii) predictive maintenance, and (iii) monitoring and inspection. It enables manufacturers to use resources more efficiently, as well as optimize processes, asset utilization, and quality management shown in Figure 9 (McKinsey & Company, 2018).

Figure 9. IoT impact
Source: McKinsey analysis

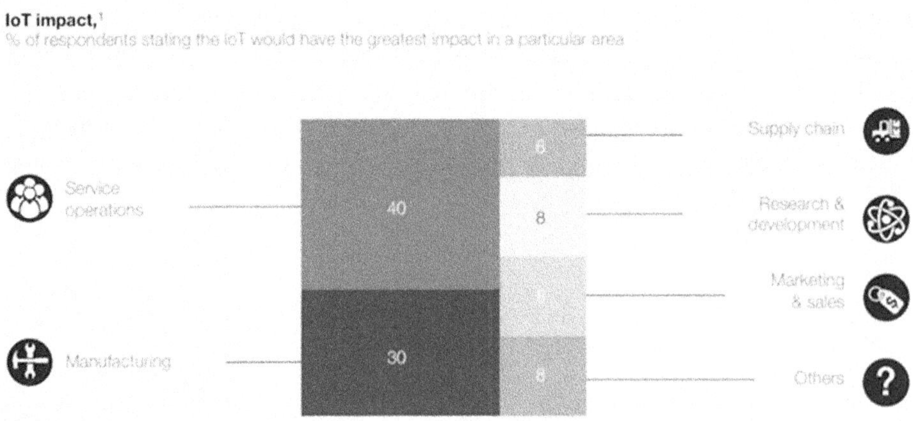

IoT in Digital Marketing

Smart appliances linked to IoT can track product supply in marketing, eventually providing recommendations to owners about new purchases, offers, and trends (Moradi, 2021). IoT devices are being used by businesses to promote their various products and services in the digital age. IoT is highly multidisciplinary because it incorporates a variety of technologies like artificial intelligence, machine learning, social media platforms, protocols, applications, scenarios, and disciplines (Atzori et al., 2010; Gubbi, Buyya, Marusic, & Palaniswami, 2013; Lo & Campos, 2018). IoT devices are primarily used to collect market data, assess marketing trends and performance indicators, and communicate with customers (Moradi, 2021).

The Internet of Things connects various types of devices that we use in our daily lives, and the amount of data generated by these devices allows marketers to use this data to generate actionable insights, identify patterns in customer interactions, and forecast customer behavior and lifestyle. This helps to visualize customer preferences and link them to purchase intent (Grover, 2021). IoT has an impact on digital marketing strategies as follows:

Personalization: Analyse Customer's Buying Behavior

IoT can unlock customer lifestyle by following the routine of the customer from alarm clock to coffee-making, booking cab, scheduling appointments, and fitness trackers, all these devices can provide data that helps marketers to extract valuable information to provide a rich customer experience. Example-A fitness enthusiast can be offered a discounted membership at a nearby gym.

Instant Service: Customer Satisfaction

Today, millions of devices are connected, allowing users to easily access products, services, and information whenever and wherever they want. Customers today expect service to be provided immediately, without any delays that result in a loss of opportunity.

Advertising Opportunities: Data Tracking

Connecting to the internet provides marketers with a plethora of advertising opportunities through data tracking, which allows marketers to predict when a customer requires a specific product or service. It is also used for sales timing and customer insights that help marketers increase sales (Rajanarthagi, 2020).

Analytics and Attribution

IoT generates massive amounts of data, which feeds machine learning algorithms, enhancing the capabilities of predictive analytics. IoT gathers a variety of information by tracking customers, allowing marketing analytics to identify the types of campaigns that customers are most responsive to, as well as what conditions and trends influence a customer's purchase decision. We can now combine attribution analytics with data from a customer's digital footprint, device usage, and interactions to better understand how a customer responds to various marketing engagements. IoT allows you to track the entire conversion path across all touchpoints and optimize outcomes in real-time (Grover, 2021).

Smart Platforms:

Advanced digital marketing platforms will be able to ingest, analyze, and act on massive amounts of data at scale, as well as process, interpret, and evaluate data sets in real-time. IoT will also have an impact on the development of IoT apps that integrate sensors, connected devices, networking, cloud, and analytics. IoT apps will become a standard feature of smartphones and may be used as a marketing and advertising platform (Rajanarthagi, 2020). Marketers have more responsibilities to design advertising campaigns without compromising the privacy of their customers. To prevent IoT devices from being compromised, customers will need to be informed about the selective use of their data, as well as device authentication, strong encryption, and other security mechanisms.

Product Development

With the help of IoT, digital marketers can understand what customers expect from their brand, allowing companies to improve the quality of their products. IoT not only improves product quality but also aids in forecasting demand and planning for new products. Accessing data from IoT devices will enable businesses to make better, faster decisions (Grover, 2021).

LITERATURE REVIEW

Digital marketing has been defined as "achieving marketing objectives through the use of digital technologies". The use of technologies to assist marketing activities to improve customer knowledge by matching their needs is known as digital marketing. Companies in the developed world have recognized the value of digital marketing. To be successful, businesses must combine online, and traditional methods of meeting customers' needs more precisely. Because of the rapid pace at which today's world is moving, the introduction of new technologies has created new business opportunities. As a result, marketers must adapt and improve with current technologies to manage their websites and achieve their business objectives

The IoT includes sensors/Devices that can be connected through the Internet (Crowley & Coutaz, 2015). The Internet of Things will open numerous business opportunities for manufacturers and service providers worldwide. This is because Internet connectivity imparts Internet intelligence to physical products, transforming them into smart products (Chuah et al., 2016; Nguyen & Simkin, 2017). IoT is going to create numerous opportunities for the manufacturers of Internet-based smart products.

According to (Dutton, 2014), As technology advances, household products are becoming a source of data and information. This in-depth knowledge of household products may provide an opportunity for manufacturers to discover new ways to improve existing products or design new ones (Porter & Heppelmann, 2014). Similarly, organizations will be able to introduce new customer-oriented services as a result of this massive data. These Internet-based sensors or tags have a low cost and low energy utility, which encourages manufacturers to embed them in products to take advantage of their benefits (Gubbi, Buyya, Marusic, & Palaniswami, 2013; Zanella et al., 2014).

The methodology for developing new products is critical in developing a sustainable competitive advantage for businesses using innovation (Oliana, 2016). This starts with the idea and ends with the product launch, which could be a physical product, digital product, or service.

Balaji and Roy (2021) has investigated the way in which IoT changes the customer's experience when shopping in a retailing context. Their study has proposed that customer interaction with IoT retail technology results in value co-creation, ease of use, superior functionality, aesthetic appearance, and presence are key determinants of value co-creation for IoT. The author has shown the value of co-creation influences customers' continuance intentions.

The author has demonstrated how current technological advances have aided in the conceptualization of customer adoptions and the long-term use of wearable technology for general health and fitness purposes. The Internet of Things has shifted the healthcare industry's focus to prevention programs that empower people to become active participants in their own healthcare. The research looked into how device, context, and user characteristics can help with the adoption and long-term use of health and fitness wearables. The discovery is advantageous to companies investing in the development and marketing of these devices, as well as to government initiatives aimed at combating rising levels of obesity and diabetes.

According to one study (Wu et al., 2017), a smart interaction on the Internet of Things IoT can improve consumers' perceptions and increase their emotional attachment to the brand. The results show that (i) produces a more positive brand than the engineer-like style, and (ii) improves brand competence. (iii) has a positive effect on user brand attachment, which (iv) is mediated by brand warmth and brand competence, and (v) the smart interaction and brand positioning style have a significant impact on brand warmth. The author has provided insights into how companies can improve their brand equity by utilizing IoT technologies.

The author (Woodside & Sood, n.d.) has offered vignettes on the introduction of IoT and its impact on revising the service-dominant logic paradigm in marketing. According to the study, most consumer households, except for smartphones, are not participating in the IoT revolution, but most product-service radical innovations include 20+ year low-growth start-ups. However, technological advances in smart devices are improving, and it is expected that the IoT revolution will significantly impact business-to-business applications before 2025.

According to Tudor et al. (2021), marketers aim to boost the sales and service of their product, which can be done by predicting customer needs. Thus, IoT can be used to optimize sales and offers to increase profit margins. However, it is important to remember that increasing sales must be done without sacrificing customer experience, which can be easily accomplished by personalizing their services and products. Personalization of products means that the product is designed to reach, connect, and engage with people from all walks of life.

According to Colella and Amatulli (2021), different communities and groups on social media can quickly become potential buyers of services and products, which is why data collection from social media and communication sites is also necessary. A digital marketer's job is to convert leads into potential customers. One issue with IoT in social media is that digital marketers can bombard customers with personalized messages and advertisements, which can be extremely annoying. Such issues should be addressed by agencies employing marketers as soon as possible. Traditional methods cannot keep up with the pace at which the world is moving today, so adaptation and improvement with current technologies are required.

An extraordinary example of social media Facebook has enabled businesses to communicate with millions of people about their products and services, as well as create new marketing opportunities in the market (Mangold & Faulds, 2009). This is only possible if managers are fully aware of how to use communication strategies to engage customers and improve their experience. Marketing professionals must truly understand online social marketing campaigns and programs and how to use performance measurement indicators to do so effectively. As market dynamics around the world change in relation to young audiences' access to and use of social media.

The Following Part is the Analysis of the Context of Specific Types of Digital Marketing

Consumer Electronics

The growing acceptance of online retailers such as Amazon and eBay, where identical products are frequently sold for less money, has had an impact on the sector. However, these online businesses have not had to manage physical storefronts or deal with the associated overhead. As online sales continue to rise, traditional businesses are looking for new ways to engage customers and entice them back into the store.

Consumers now recognize the benefits of internet purchasing; they like to compare prices, save money, and read online reviews from a variety of customers. Despite this, some customers prefer to interact with salespeople in order to save time while researching products, especially if they do so with a knowledgeable expert. Despite the decreasing need to physically inspect and test a product before purchasing it, people are increasingly using traditional stores as showrooms where they can inspect and test the goods before making an online purchase.

In addition, digital billboards can suggest relevant products that are currently on sale or direct customers to complementary items. Furthermore, to lure customers, there are other strategies. Understanding consumer behavior and placing an advertisement on their mobile phone's notification bar is an important marketing strategy. Retailers can also use this to assist customers while they are in the store. Furthermore, the store offers a chance to try out a product, see it in action, and hear how to use it from a sales associate.

The Internet of Things can be very helpful in this situation. For instance, the salesperson could check whether the item is in stock in-store using their smartwatch, which is linked to a database of all items with sensors. The assistant could simultaneously show the customer how the product works using a tablet. The salesperson could quickly complete the transaction using the same tablet and an mPOS system after that.

Supermarket and Foods

The customer experience has been revolutionized by a number of changes that have occurred in the retail industry over time. The most recent significant change was the emergence of supermarkets and then hypermarkets, which eliminated the consumer's need to visit a market or shop at a specialty store. Instead, shoppers could finish their entire shopping in a single location, all under one roof. The production process has also changed as a result of the growth of retail chains, many of which have their own factories.

Although the widespread use of supermarkets reduced the number of small local specialty businesses, it did not eliminate neighborhood delicatessens. When it came to food, online shopping had a mixed record when it first appeared in the 1990s. This one has taken much longer to perfect than other retail areas. Customers of supermarkets spend most of their money both online and offline.

Customers benefit most from online shopping (including mobile), just as they do from supermarkets. Customers can place orders from virtually anywhere in the world while remaining comfortable in their own homes, thanks to the widespread use of smartphones and mobile Internet. Furthermore, because the system has already chosen the customer's favorite items, subsequent purchases can be made much faster once the consumer has done so. This appeals to some customers, particularly those who don't have much time and regularly consume comparable goods.

It's debatable whether people will always buy their food from physical stores. There will always be food connoisseurs who prefer to touch, smell, and test products before purchasing them, and some will not feel comfortable letting someone else decide which products to buy. Some people see it as a fun experience and an opportunity to try something new, which often leads to impulsive purchases.

The Internet of Things may make traditional store shopping more enjoyable for some customers while discouraging others from doing so due to their online experiences. For example, modernizing businesses and equipping them with sensor technology may aid shoppers and sales representatives in locating specific products. Additionally, digital displays that can read sensors on goods can provide consumers with information on food descriptions or nutritional facts.

Retailers will also save money by not having to hire additional workers to relabel products. For example, the most recent price may be displayed on the digital display, along with recommendations for similar items or promotional offers. In the grocery industry, retailers recognize the value of omnichannel, which combines online and offline purchasing experiences. Deliveries, like other segments, present significant challenges. Most restaurants now provide one-hour delivery, and some go even further. With the passage of time, logistics have improved.

The Importance of Delivery for Online Businesses

Another important factor to consider when discussing the grocery industry is that many products have a limited shelf life and thus require special handling. IoT can be extremely beneficial in maintaining such things. A variety of technologies have already been implemented to ensure that the store delivers the appropriate goods to the consumer and maintains its condition from shipment to arrival. The Internet of Things can help to ensure that delivery deadlines are met.

In addition to providing the merchant with information about what is happening with the pre-packaged product, digitization can improve quality control. This will also help the shop with better resource planning for waste management, lowering overall waste. It will assist merchants in meeting standards on their own, as many countries health and safety laws require food sellers and caterers to report on their equipment.

This supports the claim that frozen foods have kept a consistent temperature to avoid freezer burn and other problems. Instead of manually recording this information and performing this operation with employees, an IoT-enabled device would do it automatically while recording any concerns. The cost of equipment servicing is reduced because the equipment can be managed using digital diagnostics to avoid business interruption. Because of the rising global cost of electricity, IoT products will also help organizations save money.

Fashion

The progress of fashion retail will not be based on a "one model fits all" approach. Because the customer landscape is so diverse, the Chief Experience Officer of a fashion store must deal with all the challenges that come with being an experience-based shop. Omnichannel initiatives, which should be supported and accepted, allow fashion businesses to reach everyone and everything. The community-centric method, on the other hand, which is highly targeted at consumer groups, is only available to small-scale and specialized fashion stylists. The goal becomes understanding and controlling ongoing, unstructured, and varied interactions between brands and consumers.

IOT'S CAPACITY FOR INNOVATION IN MARKETING RESEARCH

The Internet of Things has the potential to be a critical tool for improving various aspects of marketing research. Because of the technical capabilities of IoT, marketing managers can thoroughly plan and execute marketing research (Pauget & Dammak, 2019). (See Figure 10). Many factors must be considered to carry out this research effectively. Convenience, for example, has evolved into a strategic marketing strategy because it is a key component of both the consumer experience and the brand. Because of the approach and communication techniques, marketing managers can use IoT platforms for marketing research to build strong relationships with customers. Big data, automation, and Machine-to-Machine (M2M) communication are examples of Internet of Things (IoT) capabilities that can assist marketing managers in quickly identifying marketing opportunities and finely segmenting the market.

IoT can be viewed as a novel aspect of marketing and business analytics. Businesses may offer a new good or service based on consumer market segmentation (Vermesan & Friess, 2014). This characteristic can serve as a foundation for customer-centric marketing (Pauget & Dammak, 2019). IoT devices make the promotional process less stressful because they allow the target audience to learn about a product or brand based on their preferences and choices (Moradi & Badrinarayanan, 2021).

Figure 10. IoT in marketing research

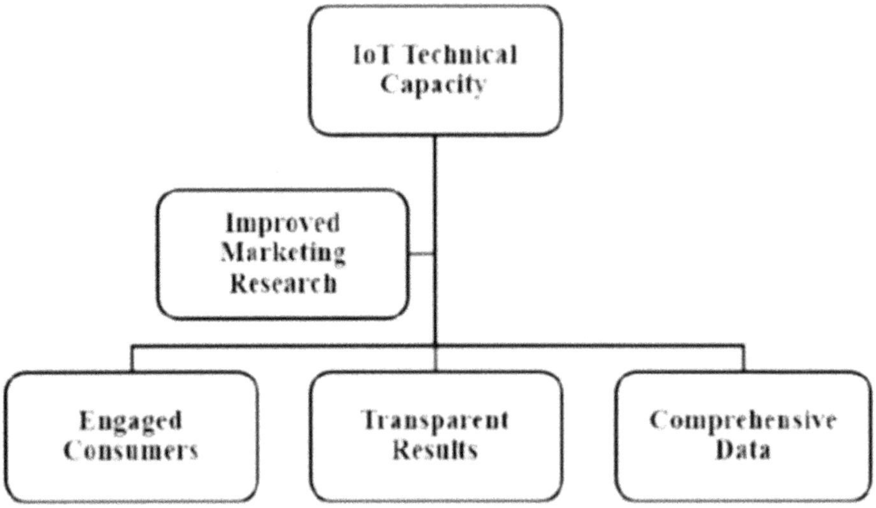

Marketing research is one of the primary goals of a marketing manager. Using IoT devices to collect big data for marketing research opens up a variety of possibilities, such as reaching the desired audience, increasing conversion rates, increasing brand awareness, and making quick business decisions (Vermesan & Friess, 2014). IoT platforms enable the collection of unrestricted volumes, rates, and types of consumer data. Age, gender, preferences, social position, income, interests, purchasing behavior, geography, and other types of behavior are frequently included (Moradi, 2021). Market segmentation now has more extensive and powerful prospects. Due to the adoption of IoT, marketing managers can quickly obtain detailed and varied consumer behavior features with the help of industrial automation tools because IoT has sped up the connection between interconnected computing devices. As a result, this procedure improves organizational performance and marketing research significantly. Consumers have already embraced modern technologies such as social networking, gadgets, and smartphones to assist them in making purchasing and payment decisions.

Enhancing Information Exchange in Marketing Research With the Use of IoT

When conducting marketing research, it is critical to consider the specific context in which customers use particular goods or services. The external environment and the circumstances surrounding the use of those goods or services influence customers' impressions (Caro & Sadr, 2019). According to this point of view, perceived data derived from client reactions is an important source of feedback for businesses. Typically, similar information is used to identify each person's unique demands and preferences. Marketers' primary goal is to provide a positive consumer experience. Tailoring the information that clients receive is one approach to satisfying them in today's competitive business world. Remembering that the information-sharing process should have significant value and meaning for individuals accessing the relevant data is critical.

Careful evaluation of human expectations and preferences is required to facilitate the overall breadth of marketing research and assist businesses in gaining more long-term competitive advantages (Ray, 2018). As a result, IoT technologies can be used to improve information sharing in marketing research. When used in marketing, IoT provides several benefits, including the ability to track and measure customers' emotional states as they use specific goods or services (Grzanka et al., 2017).

IoT technologies enable the transfer of data from users to businesses, thereby increasing communication among key players in each industry. Companies will then use the relevant data to develop new, more effective applications to meet the needs of their customers (Moradi, 2021). The use of IoT devices in marketing allows for more user and marketer interaction when accessing and evaluating information that can be strategically applied to help different demographic groups of people (Bockelmann et al., 2018). Companies' marketing departments are given pertinent information about client experiences with specific goods or services.

Such feedback indicates more opportunities for improvement and modification, which is consistent with businesses' top priority of providing the best customer experience possible. Customers want to be kept up to date on the latest IoT trends, so businesses must establish and maintain an open information exchange mechanism. People who value openness and transparency are more likely to make informed purchases or use of goods and services (Bockelmann et al., 2018). The multifaceted nature of IoT enables stakeholders to comprehend the consequences of the twenty-first century's continuously informed society. Stakeholders who are more knowledgeable about the organization's overall strategic direction and vision may suggest better solutions for business development.

IoT Technologies' Effects on Organizational Competitiveness

Organizations frequently maintain their focus on increasing organizational competitiveness because they consider the numerous consequences of personalizing the customer experience. It has been reported that information generated by smart, connected devices is important for competition (Moradi & Badrinarayanan, 2021). Organizations use the information they learn about user preferences and expectations to create new marketing tactics and methods that will engage customers even more. The investigation of sensing devices in the context of the IoT raises the question of how this process will affect organizational competitiveness. Using biosensors to gather relevant information about customer reactions is a sound strategy for gaining a competitive advantage.

Given the ability to recover information about people's intentions, activities, expressions, and even pulse rates, the possibilities represented by IoT technology are limitless (Gigli & Simon, 2011). When all these facts are combined, marketers can draw more thorough conclusions about current and future patterns in consumer behavior. The development and adaptation of IoT are appropriately considered because the emphasis is not only on satisfying customers but also on comprehending specific changes associated with the force of competition.

Development of IoT Tools and Challenges

The Creation of IoT Technologies Through Cooperation Between Academics and Practitioners

While effective IoT tools are associated with organizational success, it is critical to consider ongoing collaboration between academics and practitioners in developing the best possible methods that may lead to business excellence. In this context, referring to the collaborative IoT paradigm provides pertinent insights into the involvement of academics and marketing specialists, emphasizing the concept of collaboration in data collection and analysis. This ongoing collaboration also strengthens the concept of service sharing (Rahman & Taufiq, 2019). It is expected that academics will use their extensive knowledge to collect relevant data that can be used to develop comprehensive IoT technologies.

Using a holistic strategy to facilitate the evolution of such innovation distinguishes academic and practitioner collaboration in developing use of a holistic strategy to facilitate the evolution of such innovation distinguishes academic and practitioner collaboration in the development of IoT technologies. The advantage of this strategy is that academics can collect study data and analyze it from various perspectives. They can share knowledge that can provide marketing and IT professionals with relevant strategic recommendations. Academic researchers' experience can be used to create original and distinct concepts for the IoT market. To achieve the strategic goals of the collaboration between academics and practitioners, significant theoretical assumptions must be combined with real-world experience.

The most important takeaway from academic research on the use of IoT technologies is the concept of using technology to improve people's lives. Keeping this broad perspective in mind is a critical component of the collaboration between academics and practitioners in developing competitive IoT solutions. As a result of this ongoing collaboration, innovative solutions can be offered to various consumer groups. Academics, for example, may develop effective IoT solutions to assist people with speech problems after conducting extensive research on the limitless potential of IoT applications. Experts in a particular subject would confirm the findings after academics proposed their theories. High levels of trust, open communication, and flexibility in knowledge sharing are said to be characteristics of such teamwork.

Academics and practitioners have more clout when discussing the benefits of various IoT tools because they share similar goals. Both parties must pay close attention to using open communication channels to express their views as clearly as possible. Academics and practitioners value collaboration because it can move them in the right direction because they are motivated by the desired outcomes (Kiryakova et al., 2017). The top priority for academics and practitioners is to successfully complete specific projects using IoT tools, but they may require enough time to re-evaluate their strategic options in order to make a significant change. The process of academic and professional collaboration is depicted in Figure 11.

Figure 11. Academics and practitioners collaboration process

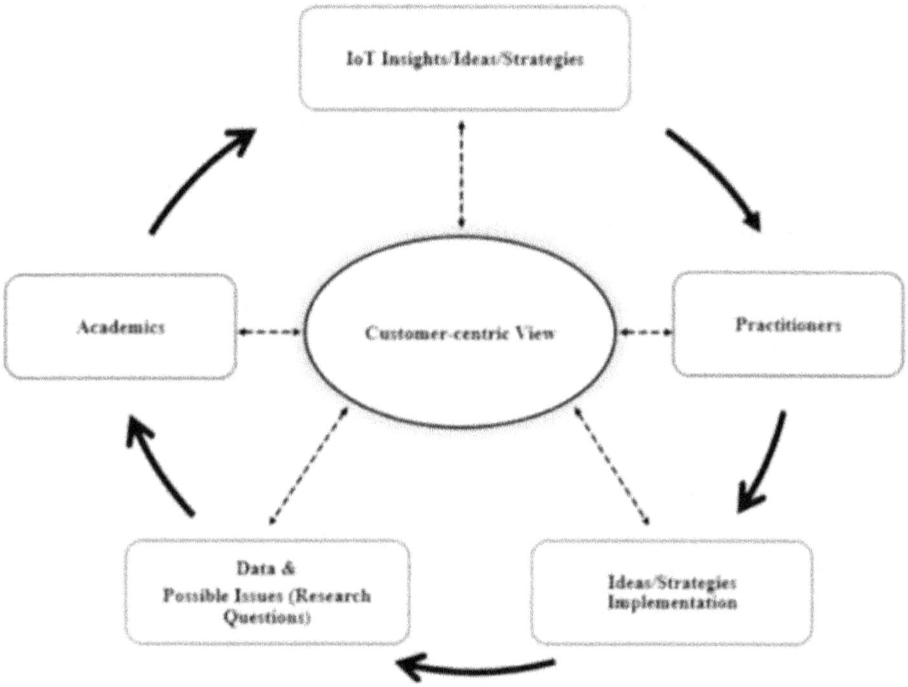

RESEARCH METHODOLOGY

The Effects of Digital Technologies on Consumption

Over the last thirty years, technological advancement has ushered in the information era for both people and societies. The Internet and the subsequent adoption of mobile technologies and devices have had an impact on all aspects of daily life. There are now many more ways to obtain knowledge thanks to the development of new channels such as websites, mobile applications, and social networks. On the plus side, this should help us make better decisions in theory. On the other hand, it has resulted in entropy, with an abundance of market options and little room for competition.

In this entropic state, decisions and actions are made using a vast amount of digitally produced knowledge by the human factors of feelings, logic, and values. Digital technologies, on the other hand, do not simply provide access to an infinite amount of knowledge. Furthermore, they bring tools to help us make decisions and progress and comprehend our knowledge (via data analytics tools). These technologies forecast new ideas or sentiments based on that knowledge. In the future, perhaps these digital technologies will make decisions for us (Artificial Intelligence). Shopping is a great example of how much has changed in recent years when we consider how digital technologies have affected our lives and the way we make decisions on a daily basis.

Prior to the Internet, almost every buyer had a similar experience when purchasing clothing. They may peruse fashion magazines, select an item they like, and then share their thoughts with their loved ones. They would then go to the store and, with the help of a store employee, try on various items. Customers may then decide whether to purchase the item or leave and visit another store. However, the growing use of the Internet and cell phones has provided consumers with access to new knowledge sources. Consumers now have access to a vast, comprehensive, and immediate flow of information on the clothing items they want to buy. This stream of knowledge follows them wherever they go. They can browse items on their smartphone, read reviews, leave comments, shop at various online stores, and purchase the item. And they are free to do so whenever and wherever they want.

Different Attitudes Toward Consumption

However, assuming that everyone embraces digital technologies uniformly is incorrect. The variety of new knowledge routes has two opposing effects: richness and entropy. As previously stated, each person reacts and uses digital technology differently depending on characteristics such as age, gender, culture, values, and feelings. As a result of these factors, the audience is very diverse, with a wide range of consumer attitudes.

As a result of digital technologies, consumers are becoming more aware of their options. As a result, they want to personalize their purchasing experience. They want to stand out from the crowd. They also hope to use the power and pervasiveness of technology to create more enjoyable and practical shopping experiences. To summarize, digital technologies empower customers rather than lord them over them. As a result, the consumption scenario has become highly complex.

Moving Toward Retailing Based on Experiences

Because of the complexity and adaptability of consumer behavior, a significant shift in retailing is required. As a result of the consumer-focused transformation, new retailers must be adaptable, agile, and eager to change. The new store should be experience-based, with the ability to redesign the experience as consumer behavior changes. This experience-based strategy should be implemented across all customer engagement channels.

These channels are as follows:

Actual Stores: The store is no longer always the point of sale. It now serves new functions, such as an entertainment venue. Pop-up shops, where businesses operate temporarily in designated areas, are also modern variations on physical stores.

Online Stores: This is the e-commerce platform where goods can be ordered and purchased. This platform is being further customized using data analytics technologies. Social media remains an important platform for brand-consumer interaction, as well as for increasing customer loyalty and brand exposure. Online marketplaces are also emerging from social media platforms.

Mobile Communications: Smartphones and tablets are used to interact with brands and as a source of information via mobile applications. Customers are increasingly using the same mobile apps to make direct purchases from online retailers.

Public Areas: Brands are using public spaces to interact with their customers. They achieve this, for example, by installing kiosks in shopping malls, QR barcodes, and NFC scanners at bus and rail stations.

IoT ANALYTICS

The growing number of sensors, actuators, and tags used in various sectors of daily life, commerce, and industry emphasizes the importance of the Internet of Things (IoT). In this regard, business analysts predict that the global IoT market will reach $800 billion USD (Statista, 2019) in 2023. Smart gadgets are already playing an important role in a variety of fields, including "Industry 4.0," "Smart Cities," "Smart Homes," and many others. These define intricate realms of application that not only present entirely new business and consumer application scenarios while also attempting to digitalize and optimize current industrial and commercial processes through the use of smart devices.

In this context, IoT data analytics are already critical in many IoT areas and will become even more important in the future (Statista, 2019). IoT analytics is the process of extracting insights and context from smart device data to support IoT applications (Siow et al., 2018). The ability to process, analyze, and comprehend IoT data (Simmhan & Perera, 2016), which comes from many heterogeneous smart devices and is released as data streams, is the foundation of IoT analytics. As a result, appropriate system architectures and analytics algorithms are required.

In this environment, IoT analytics architectures provide the means to effectively acquire, process, and integrate smart device data. They enable IoT analytics by providing tools for handling data using various data mining or machine learning methods. They also provide interfaces for data display and the use of the results by third-party applications. As a result, IoT analytics architectures are typically built with a variety of platforms, frameworks, and computing paradigms.

Although previous Big Data research has already provided a wide range of architectural solutions for data processing, analytics in IoT domains reveal novel or distinct problems, necessitating new strategies. IoT analytics, for example, contains situations that change rapidly in terms of requirements, data sources, desired insights, and so on. Furthermore, IoT data is frequently linked directly to human behaviour or the immediate environment and used to gain understanding and make decisions in critical sectors of daily life such as healthcare or transportation. Processing architectures must thus overcome a number of challenges, some of which are incompatible.

Today Consumers have transformed. They have abandoned the newspaper in favor of scanning TV commercials and unsolicited emails. Customers now have more options that fit their digital lifestyle. New school marketers (Michael Minelli et al., 2013) provide relevant interactive communication across the top digital power channels, including email, mobile, social, display, and the web. Big data and analytics have become integral components of marketing strategies, providing advantages for a variety of marketing activities. To understand this, we must first examine the marketing environment, Precision Targeting, and the role of big data in value creation, communication, and delivery (Arshiya & Sabahath, 2020).

According to a comparison of the number of references to difficulties in scientific literature and publications that address them, future research in all IoT sectors should focus on privacy and security, as well as personalization of analytics and energy efficiency of data processing. Because of the volume, variety, and dynamic nature of IoT data, privacy and security are not new concerns in information systems research, but they must be tailored to IoT environments. Another critical issue is the continuous transmission and processing of data. As a result, security guidelines, new security and privacy procedures, and security system design with an emphasis on the IoT's unique characteristics are required.

The difficulty of energy efficiency in IoT analytics systems is related to the enormous number of smart devices that could be used as sources for data processing and analytics. By utilizing previously existing computing capabilities at the network's edge, the amount of cloud computing resources required may be reduced, resulting in a reduction in energy consumption. Future research on IoT analytics architectures in all application domains must therefore incorporate fog and edge computing concepts and provide specific solutions to this problem.

Current IoT analytics architectures do not provide sufficient options for personalizing analytics. The two papers that address this topic build programmable, flow-based analytics pipelines that use both predefined and custom analytics operators. Given the growing number of IoT devices and the resulting complexity and dynamics of analytics scenario requirements, future research must look into how to develop and implement technical solutions to meet this challenge, particularly in user-centric application domains like Smart Homes.

DISCUSSION AND CONCLUSION

Businesses face both great opportunities and complex challenges as digital technologies evolve. Given the growing interest in IoT, the goal of this research was to outline the current state of the art in business digitalization and to supplement current theory. Over the last decade, the growing popularity of IoT and business intelligence has captured the e-commerce market (Begum, & , 2019), positioning them as critical components of business digitalization strategies. On the other hand, the transition from IT and technical domains to applied engineering, management, marketing, and social sciences has resulted in a mass of disorganized knowledge. Through a systematic literature review, this study examined IoT adoption in the field of business management to determine how these phenomena can positively affect the digitalization of business strategies. In particular, such massive data flows provide numerous untapped opportunities for human behavior studies, business process redesign, and service expansion.

To summarize, businesses that want to digitalize their operations must learn how to listen to and interpret massive amounts of data generated by IoT. If they pursue a simple technological adoption without considering a strategic framework, they may blunt – or even undermine – their effort to generate value. As part of a revitalization strategy, IoT and advanced analytical approaches have the potential to create intelligent environments capable of transforming structures, processes, and services. To summarize, businesses should consider IoT as a business opportunity rather than a technological one. To that end, they must not only arm themselves with the best technology available on the market but also devise strategies and practices for implementing it that will provide competitive advantages. Firms must simultaneously mitigate potential data security and privacy issues while balancing their desire for innovation and competitive advantage with consumer expectations and ethical norms (Sestino et al., 2020).

REFERENCES

Angelova, N., Kiryakova, G., & Yordanova, L. (2017). The great impact of internet of things on business. *Trakia Journal of Sciences*, *15*(Suppl. 1), 406–412. doi:10.15547/tjs.2017.s.01.068

Arshiya & Sabahath, A. (2020). *Implementation of Big Data in Modern Business: Fraud Detection and Prevention Techniques.* IGI Global. doi:10.4018/978-1-6684-6581-3

Atzori, L., Iera, A., & Morabito, G. (2010). The internet of things: A survey. *Computer Networks*, *54*(15), 2787–2805. doi:10.1016/j.comnet.2010.05.010

Balaji, M. & Roy, S. (2021). *Value co-creation with Internet of things technology in the retail industry.* Academic Press.

Begum, A. (2019). *Big Data and Advanced Analytics.* Springer. doi:10.1007/978-3-030-11890-7_57

Bockelmann, C., Pratas, N. K., Wunder, G., Saur, S., Navarro, M., Gregoratti, D., Vivier, G., De Carvalho, E., Ji, Y., Stefanovic, C., Popovski, P., Wang, Q., Schellmann, M., Kosmatos, E., Demestichas, P., Raceala-Motoc, M., Jung, P., Stanczak, S., & Dekorsy, A. (2018). Towards massive connectivity support for scalable mMTC communications in 5G networks. *IEEE Access : Practical Innovations, Open Solutions*, *6*, 28969–28992. doi:10.1109/ACCESS.2018.2837382

Canhoto, A. & Arp, S. (2016). *Exploring the factors that support adoption and sustained use of health and fitness wearables.* Taylor and Francis Online.

Caro, F., & Sadr, R. (2019). The Internet of Things (IoT) in retail: Bridging supply and demand. *Business Horizons*, *62*(1), 47–54. doi:10.1016/j.bushor.2018.08.002

Chuah, S. H.-W., Rauschnabel, P. A., Krey, N., Nguyen, B., Ramayah, T., & Lade, S. (2016). Wearable technologies: The role of usefulness and visibility in smartwatch adoption. *Computers in Human Behavior*, *65*, 276–284. doi:10.1016/j.chb.2016.07.047

Colella, G., & Amatulli, C. (2021). Digital Marketing and Digital Retail Strategies in the Luxury Sector: Critical Factors and Opportunities. In Handbook of Research on IoT, Digital Transformation, and the Future of Global Marketing, 112-129.

Cosgrove-Sacks, C. (2014). *Open Protocols for an Open, Interoperable Internet of Things.* Org. for Advancement of Structured Information Standards. www.oasis-open.org/presentations/open protocols-and-internet-of-things-oasis.ppt

Crowley, J. L., & Coutaz, J. (2015). An ecological view of smart home technologies. In *Proceedings of the European Conference on Ambient Intelligence.* Springer. 10.1007/978-3-319-26005-1_1

Dutton, W. H. (2014). Putting things to work: Social and policy challenges for the Internet of things. *Info*, *16*, 1–21. doi:10.1108/info-09-2013-0047

Gigli, M., & Simon, G. M. (2011). Internet of things: Services and applications categorization. *Adv. Internet Things*, *1*(2), 27–31. doi:10.4236/ait.2011.12004

Granell, C., Kamilaris, A., Kotsev, A., Ostermann, F. O., & Trilles, S. (2020). Internet of Things. In H. Guo, M. F. Goodchild, & A. Annoni (Eds.), *Manual of Digital Earth*. Springer. doi:10.1007/978-981-32-9915-3_11

Grover, V. (2021). *5 Way IoT is changing digital marketing*. Spiceworks. https://www.spiceworks.com/tech/iot/articles/5-ways-iot-is-changing-digital-marketing/#:~:text=IoT%20means%20having%20more%20touch,purchase%20decision%20of%20the%20customer

Grzanka, P., Santos, C., & Moradi, M. (2017). Intersectionality research in counseling psychology. *Journal of Counseling Psychology*.

Gubbi, J., Buyya, R., Marusic, S., & Palaniswami, M. (2013). Internet of Things (IoT): A vision, architectural elements, and future directions. *Future Generation Computer Systems*, *29*(7), 1645–1660. doi:10.1016/j.future.2013.01.010

Guo, B., Zhang, D., Wang, Z., Yu, Z., & Zhou, X. (2013). Opportunistic IoT: Exploring the harmonious interaction between human and the internet of things. *Journal of Network and Computer Applications*, *36*(6), 1531–1539. doi:10.1016/j.jnca.2012.12.028

International Telecommunication Union. (2018). *ITU internet reports 2005: the Internet of Things*. ITU. https://www.itu.int/pub/S-POL-IR.IT-2005/e

Kajimoto, K., Davuluru, U., Matsukura, R., Hund, J., Kovatsch, M., & Nimura, K. (2017). *Web of Things (WoT) architecture*. W3C.

Kiryakova, G, Yordanova, L., & Angelova. N. (2017). Can we make Schools and Universities smarter with the Internet of Things? *TEM Journal*, *6*.

Lo, F.-Y. &, & Campos, N. (2018). Blending Internet-of-Things (IoT) solutions into relationship marketing strategies. *Technological Forecasting and Social Change-Volume*, *137*, 10–18. doi:10.1016/j.techfore.2018.09.029

Mangold, G. W., & Faulds, D. J. (2009). Social Media: The New Hybrid Element of the Promotion Mix. *Business Horizons*, *52*(4), 357–365. doi:10.1016/j.bushor.2009.03.002

McEwen, A., & Cassimally, H. (2014). *Designing the Internet of Things*. Wiley.

McKinsey & Company. (2018). *The Internet of Things: How to capture the value of IoT.* Very Technology.

Minerva, R., Biru, A., & Rotondi, D. (2015). Towards a definition of the Internet of Things (IoT). *IEEE Internet Initiative*, *1*, 1–86.

Moradi, M. (2021). Importance of Internet of Things (IoT) in Marketing Research and Its Ethical and Data Privacy Challenges. *Business Ethics and Leadership*, *5*(1), 22–30. doi:10.21272/bel.5(1).22-30.2021

Moradi, M., & Badrinarayanan, V. (2021). The effects of brand prominence and narrative features on crowdfunding success for entrepreneurial aftermarket enterprises. *Journal of Business Research*, *124*, 286–298. doi:10.1016/j.jbusres.2020.12.002

Newman, D. (2017). The Top 8 IoT Trends For 2018. *Forbes*. https://www.forbes.com/sites/danielnewman/2017/12/19/the-top-8-iot-trends-for-2018/#1e35e7f467f7

Nguyen, B., & Simkin, L. (2017). The Internet of Things (IoT) and marketing: The state of play, future trends and the implications for marketing. *Journal of Marketing Management*, *33*(1-2), 1–6. doi:10.1080/0267257X.2016.1257542

Oliana, R. G. (2016). The Internet of Things: The next big thing for new product development? *J. Mark. Trends*, *5*, 159–176.

Patel, M., Shangkuan, J., & Thomas, C. (2018). *The Internet of Things: How to capture the value of IoT*. McKinsey.

Pauget, B., & Dammak, A. (2019). The Implementation of the Internet of Things: What Impact on Organizations? *Technological Forecasting and Social Change*, *140*, 140–146. doi:10.1016/j.techfore.2018.03.012

Porter, M. E., & Heppelmann, J. E. (2014). How smart, connected products are transforming competition. *Harvard Business Review*, *92*, 64–88.

Rahman, A. & Taufiq, A. (2019). The emergence of Internet of Things (IoT): Connecting anything, anywhere. *Computers* *8*(2), 40.

Rajanarthagi. (2020). *What is IoT? & Role of IoT in digital marketing*. GEC Designs. https://gecdesigns.com/blog/role-of-iot-in-digital-marketing

Sestino, A., Prete, M., Piper, L., & Guidob, G. (2020). Internet of Things and Big Data as enablers for business digitalization strategies. *Journal of Technovation.* doi:10.1016/j.technovation.2020.102173

Simmhan, Y., & Perera, S. (2016). Big data analytics platforms for real-time applications in IoT. In *Big data analytics* (pp. 115–135). Springer.

Siow, E., Tiropanis, T., & Hall, W. (2018). Analytics for the Internet of Things. *ACM Computing Surveys.*

Statista. (2017). *Size of the Internet of Things (IoT) market worldwide from 2017 to 2025.* Statista.

Statista. (2019a). Global IoT Market Size. *Statistia.* https://www.statista.com/statistics/976313/global-iot-market-size/

Statista. (2019b). *Size of the Internet of Things (IoT) market worldwide from 2017 to 2025.* Statista. https://www.statista.com/statistics/976313/global-iot-market-size/

Tudor, A. I. M., Chițu, I. B., Dovleac, L., & Brătucu, G. (2021). IoT Technologies as Instruments for SMEs' Innovation and Sustainable Growth. *Sustainability*, *13*(11), 6357. doi:10.3390u13116357

Vermesan, O., & Friess, P. (Eds.). (2014). *Internet of things-from research and innovation to market deployment* (Vol. 29). River publishers.

Weyer, S., Schmitt, M., Ohmer, M., & Gorecky, D. (2015). Towards Industry 4.0-Standardization as the crucial challenge for highly modular, multi-vendor production systems. *IFAC-PapersOnLine*, *2015*(48), 579–584. doi:10.1016/j.ifacol.2015.06.143

Woodside, A. & Sood, S. (2017). *Vignettes in the two-step arrival of the internet of things and its reshaping of marketing management's service-dominant logic*. Research Gate. doi: 1 doi:0.1080/0267257X.2016.1246748

Wu, J., Chen, J., & Dou, W. (2017). *The Internet of Things and interaction style: the effect of smart interaction on brand attachment.* doi:10.1080/0267257X.2016.1233132

Zanella, A., Bui, N., Castellani, A., Vangelista, L., & Zorzi, M. (2014). Internet of Things for Smart Cities. *IEEE Internet of Things Journal*, *1*(1), 22–32. doi:10.1109/JIOT.2014.2306328

Chapter 10
Abridging the Digital Marketing Gap:
Artificial Intelligence (AI) and Internet of Things (IoT) in Boosting Global Economic Growth

S. Uma
Hindusthan College of Engineering and Technology, India

ABSTRACT

The COVID-19 issue has, albeit at varied rates, pushed digital transformation in industry and services across the majority of nations. Achieving the objectives on the path to excellence depends on the delivery of customized goods or services and changing consumer needs. Digital marketing can aid in expanding customer reach internationally and strengthening client relationships. While data-driven decision-making reduces risk, technology can help marketers deliver customers more of what they want and need. Artificial intelligence (AI), the internet of things (IoT), remote collaboration, cloud computing, blockchain, and data analytics are among the technologies that are rapidly transforming the way that digital marketers do business and develop strategies leading to global economic growth. This book chapter explores the potential of AI and IoT in digital marketing. It also provides information on the impact of new technologies on digital marketing and the top trends in this field.

1.0 INTRODUCTION

Smart consumers have progressively higher standards for their online purchasing experiences. Many companies are concentrating their business expansion plans on expanding their online storefronts to accommodate the rising demand. Digital marketers will have access to more data and technologies in the future. The pandemic prompted a digital acceleration, as seen by the up to 60% spike in internet traffic that occurred in several countries shortly after the epidemic (OECD, 2020a). While these actions highlight the digital transformation's enormous promise, the pandemic has also highlighted the holes that

DOI: 10.4018/978-1-6684-8166-0.ch010

still need to be filled. Customers can participate in the discussion about a business thanks to the rise in online consumers, affordable digital marketing strategies, easily trackable campaigns, and more interactive experiences through digital marketing channels. Real-Time trends are simple to react to. Together with traditional print marketing, digital marketing strategies work well. In the current scenario, it is not a choice to use digital marketing. Many organizations are making investments in e-commerce options, cutting-edge technologies, and novel strategies to stay one step ahead of the competition.

New technology has had and will continue to have a significant impact on company marketing, from internet-of-things technologies and remote collaboration to AI and business data analytics. Impressive tracking and analytics capabilities are provided by AI and machine learning. As a result, it is feasible to ascertain which touchpoints are more successful in resulting in a conversion. IoT and digital visualization have already attracted investments from more than 50% of firms. With its monitoring capabilities, AI can improve Customer Experience (CX) for businesses in the insurance, healthcare, and manufacturing sectors. The latter might be useful for agent desktops to boost worker productivity.

Artificial intelligence has been incorporated into many aspects of our daily lives. Similarly, firms are implementing AI in digital marketing slowly but surely. It has already changed how brands interact with their audience and how marketing campaigns are created and run, from assisting companies in creating successful plans to impacting consumers' lives through chatbots. The marketing sector is being affected by artificial intelligence in terms of improved production, increased return on investment (ROI), and increased efficiency. AI has significantly changed the marketing environment and will give marketers more opportunities to change the dynamics of digital marketing in the future. This most recent technology reveals that there is still unrealized potential for brand marketing and advertising.

Future predictions are challenging because technology advances too quickly. But it is already widely acknowledged that artificial intelligence can dramatically advance and improve marketing in the future. AI is used by marketers to predict consumer demand for goods, create customer profiles, carry out programmatic ad buying, and other tasks. The other is the customer-facing aspect, in which marketers employ AI to enhance the customer experience, strengthening the brand and increasing sales. As a result, AI in digital marketing will keep developing and altering how companies promote their brands. These technological developments will be crucial in developing an immersive e-commerce experience, together with AI. As e-commerce sites mature digitally, they will offer a buying experience that goes above and beyond simply anticipating, satisfying, and exceeding the needs of their customers. Digital marketers will soon be able to create an e-commerce site that anticipates the wants of their customers, thanks to technology.

The use of AI-powered solutions will enable marketing teams to automate some cognitive work. Additionally, they will be able to identify current trends and forecast them for the future, which will help them make sure that their marketing strategies are successful. Additionally, it can make use of predictive analytics to generate useful recommendations for upcoming campaigns and enable real-time tailored marketing efforts at scale. Artificial intelligence (AI) and machine learning can help you finish jobs faster, more adaptable, and more affordable. They can decide how to allocate their money and who they should target after considering these factors. Brands can spend less money (and less time) on ineffective digital advertising and more time on high-value tasks. These AI applications have significant ramifications for customers and marketers alike.

From Amazon's personalized recommendations to Google's RankBrain and Voice search, AI has completely changed the digital landscape. AI is better at understanding and analyzing data and information. AI is becoming more adept than humans at identifying market trends.

IoT is one of the twenty-first-century technologies with disruptive potential, along with blockchain and machine learning, that are anticipated to have disruptive effects felt throughout the global economy. With sensors, devices, gateways, and platforms, IoT is all about improving business processes and solutions. Manufacturers may make wise decisions and create more effective operations by centralizing their data. IoT can be viewed from the perspective of digital marketing as the interconnectedness of digital devices, which offers businesses countless options to listen to and address the needs of their consumers with the appropriate message, at the appropriate time, on the appropriate device.

IoT provides the media and entertainment sector with a wealth of customer data, including demographics like age, location, and consumption-related activities. By better understanding their customers, businesses may use this data to improve the appeal and personalization of their offerings. IoT is anticipated to impact digital marketing by enabling marketers to better connect and coordinate the physical, social, and online worlds of consumers. The amount of data generated by the various types of connected gadgets in our daily lives will only increase. With the use of this data, marketers may develop insightful hypotheses, spot trends in customer interactions, and forecast consumer behavior and lifestyle.

IoT is a fantastic tool for connecting with target audiences. Consumer behavior and context can be revealed by tracking them across devices thanks to technology. Sensors can keep an eye on and record proximity, biometrics, sound, and light. Then, this information can be transmitted to mobile devices, wearables, smart TVs, or game consoles so that the inputs can be processed. Ad campaigns can be tailored with the use of the gathered data and developments in data analytics and machine learning. You could, for instance, make thorough consumer profiles. All of this increases advertising effectiveness while lowering expenses.

Furthermore, contextual marketing can benefit from proximity-aware digital signs. They may broadcast the proper advertisement to the proper audience at the proper time and location. GPS technology used in IoT devices makes it possible to locate individuals or items. Similar to the aforementioned Google search advertisements, this data can assist advertisers in delivering more pertinent advertisements. The technique might be used to display advertisements to those who are close to a physical store.

To personalize direct mail and track and target their marketing information, a variety of technical techniques are available. The secret to effective customer relations is more accurate information that has been gathered and structured in databases. Consumers can browse and research products using digital marketing tools from the comfort of their homes. As a result, technology boosts productivity, improves communication, offers simple access to information, aids in the establishment of new start-ups, saves time, brings people together, reduces costs, provides a competitive edge, and enables quicker decision-making.

The current trends in digital marketing for 2022 include influencer marketing, omnichannel marketing, artificial intelligence, video marketing, long-form content, social media shopping, and progressive web pages. With a compound annual growth rate (CAGR) of 16.7% from 2021 to 2026, the size of the IoT market is anticipated to increase from USD 300.3 billion in 2021 to USD 650.5 billion by 2026.

Access to low-cost, low-power sensor technologies, the availability of high-speed connectivity, the growing acceptance of the cloud, and the growing usage of data processing and analytics are the main drivers of the Internet of things market. Additionally, the expansion of smart city projects around the globe, an increase in connected devices that will fuel IoT growth, and the emergence of 5G technology that will facilitate IoT adoption globally will present attractive prospects for IoT manufacturers.

The IoT industry is expanding due to the increasing demand for automation and remote asset monitoring. The national government's notions for smart cities and the adoption of smart and connected concepts across sectors are predicted to propel the IoT market. In the coming years, the IoT market will be shaped by alliances, purchases, and new product development. A more sophisticated corporate strategy will be made possible by artificial intelligence. Here are some AI statistics from a study by true North that will astonish you (White, 2020).

- 61% of marketers feel artificial intelligence is the most crucial component of their data strategy.
- According to 80% of business and IT leaders, AI has already increased productivity.
- Up to 40% more corporate productivity can be achieved with current AI technologies.
- AI-powered voice assistants are used by 97% of mobile users.
- Eighty-three percent of early users of AI have already seen significant (30%) or modest (53%%) economic gains.

The constant emergence of new interconnected products serves as an example of the scope of this technological trend, which affects a wide range of industries, segments, and geographic areas worldwide. Modernizing business is a difficult and lengthy process that calls for perseverance, skill, and in-depth knowledge. The possibilities are unlimited now that almost everything may be given the ability for smart and remote communication. To gain the maximum benefits in our fast-paced world, it is crucial to keep up with the most recent fashions and adopt cutting-edge technology today.

To gain the maximum benefits in our fast-paced world, it is crucial to keep up with the most recent fashions and adopt cutting-edge technology today. The client is the company's internal mirror, thus businesses need to stay current on these advancements and rethink their value-creation processes around product marketing. However, the precise impact of AI on digital marketing roles over the coming years is still not well understood. The quantity of data that is accessible is increasing every day, and discovering methods to mine it, analyze it, and use it for marketing and advertising is making AI, IoT, and machine learning more and more alluring every year.

2.0 BACKGROUND

Technology development has led to the emergence of new marketing platforms. When digital marketing was created, traditional marketing for new-age enterprises was reduced to a secondary alternative. It made it possible for brands to more cost-effectively and effectively contact their target demographic. Later, all firms around the world used digital marketing to broaden their reach. All marketing initiatives that take place online are referred to as digital marketing, often known as "online marketing," "internet marketing," or "web marketing." To engage with present and potential customers, businesses use digital channels including search engines, social media, email, and other websites. This also involves messaging via text or other types of multimedia. Due to the global reach of digital media, clients can access information at any time.

When server/client architecture was introduced and personal computers became widely used in the 1990s, the term "digital marketing" was first used. As a result, Customer Relationship Management (CRM) programmes became an important component of marketing technology (2). Vendors were compelled by fierce competition to include more services, such as apps for marketing, sales, and service, into their software. After the first clickable banner went up in 1993, HotWired bought a number of them to use in their advertising. This signalled the start of the shift from traditional marketing to digital marketing (Avantika Monnappa, 2015). After the creation of the Internet, marketers were also able to own vast amounts of online customer data thanks to e CRM software. Companies might receive the priority of customer experience and update data on customer wants. This resulted in the "You Will" campaign by GE becoming the first clickable banner advertisement to go live in 1994.

Nearly, 44% of all viewers clicked on the advertisement over the first four months after it went online, according to AT&T (2). With an increasing number of Internet users and the with the introduction of the iPhone, customers began conducting product research and making decisions about their needs online before visiting a salesperson, which presented a new challenge for a company's marketing division. Additionally, a poll conducted in 2000 in the United Kingdom revealed that the majority of retailers had not set up their own domain name. These issues forced marketers to look for digital means of market expansion.

The growth of digital marketing since the 1990s and 2000s has altered how companies and brands use technology for marketing (Patel, 2019). Digital marketing efforts are becoming more common and effective as digital platforms are integrated into everyday life and marketing strategies and as individuals utilize digital gadgets rather than go to physical stores.

The idea of marketing automation was introduced in 2007 to address the aforementioned issue. Companies were able to conduct multichannel marketing campaigns, segment their consumer bases, and give customers personalized information thanks to marketing automation. But it took too long for it to become adaptable to consumer electronics.

In the 2000s and 2010s, when there was a significant increase in the number of devices that could access digital media, digital marketing grew more sophisticated. Customers developed a strong reliance on digital devices in daily life as a result of the rise of social media in the 2000s, including LinkedIn, Facebook, YouTube, and Twitter. They anticipated a seamless user experience when looking for product information through various media. The diversification of marketing technologies was improved by the shift in consumer behavior. Particularly since 2013, the term "digital marketing" has become the most used worldwide. Digital advertising spending increased by 48% in 2010, with an estimated 4.5 trillion internet ads served annually. Businesses that utilize Online Behavioral Advertising (OBA) to target advertising at internet users account for an increasing share of advertising, yet OBA creates issues with consumer privacy and data security.

Table 1. Important Milestones in the History of Digital Marketing (Avantika Monnappa, 2015)

Year	Milestones
1990	• The term "Digital Marketing" was first used. • Launch of "Archie", the first search engine
1993	• First clickable web-ad banner
1994	• First e-commerce transaction over Netmarket • Launch of Yahoo!
1996	• Launch of smaller search engines like Hotbot, Looksmart, and Alexa
1997	• Launch of first social media site, SixDegrees.com
1998	• Birth of Google • Microsoft launches MSN • Yahoo! launches Yahoo! Web search
2000	• Internet bubble bursts • Sixdegrees.com shutdown • Smaller search engines wiped out
2001	• First mobile marketing campaign (Universal Music)
2002	• Launch of LinkedIn
2003	• WordPress released • Launch of MySpace
2004	• Gmail launches • Google goes public • Facebook goes live
2005	• Launch of YouTube
2006	• Microsoft launches MS Live Search • Twitter launches • Amazon's e-commerce sales cross $10Billion • Split testing in marketing
2007	• Launch of Tumblr • Web-streaming service Hulu founded • iPhone launches
2008	• China overtakes US in number of internet-users • Spotify launches • Groupon goes live
2009	• Google launches instant for real-time search engine results • Google's Affiliate Network shutdown
2010	• Google Buzz launches • Whatsapp launches
2011	• Google Buzz shutdown • Launch of Google+ and Google Panda • Web-use overtakes figures for TV viewership among youth
2012	• Social Media budgets up 64%
2013	• Yahoo! acquires Tumblr
2014	• Mobile exceeds PC internet usage • Facebook Messenger app, tailored ads on LinkedIn, iWatch, and Facebook's Look Back launched • Facebook acquires Whatsapp
2015	• Snapchat launches 'Discover' feature • The rise of predictive analytics, wearable tech, and Content Marketing: Facebook launches 'Instant Articles'

The world continues to use the internet more and more, and digital benefits are becoming a significant source of income for both B2C and B2B marketing (Bhosale & Pralhad Raverkar, 2020). The huge prospects offered by digital marketing must receive a lot of attention, but the actual difficulties that businesses are having in becoming digital must receive less consideration.

Online marketing is the term used to describe the practice of promoting products or services through the use of web technologies, mostly the internet but also include mobile phones, exhibition promotion, and a few other digital standards. A medium for communication is the Internet. It allows for the discussion of money, but more importantly, it allows for the discussion of value. A firm on the Internet can gain more value from the customer's time, devotion, and support. Value can be added for the consumer in the forms of amusement, clarification, and utility; content marketing is one effective technique to generate importance.

Using the opportunities and difficulties presented by the digital standard, digital marketing policy builds on and adapts the values of traditional marketing. A strategy for online marketing should evolve and expand over time. Online marketers should constantly be optimizing and improving their online marketing activities because the Internet enables almost rapid feedback and data collection. There are internet users everywhere! We all utilize the internet throughout the day for everything from social media to google searches to our favorite apps. Digital marketing is expanding because so many people are participating online. It will rise even more in the future.

With the advent of powerful disruptive technologies such as Artificial Intelligence, machine learning, big data, Internet of Things, Data Science and Business Intelligence, Digital Marketing takes a new transformation.

3.0 IMPORTANCE OF DIGITAL MARKETING

Digital marketing encompasses all initiatives related to online marketing. A number of digital channels are available for connecting with current and potential clients, including search engines, email, websites, social media, etc. In contrast to conventional marketing, digital marketing allows an organization to reach a broader audience and target customers who are most likely to buy their products and services (Bhosale & Pralhad Raverkar, 2020). It is also far more affordable than conventional marketing. Furthermore, it allows an organization to evaluate results and adjust their marketing as necessary. Connecting with the target market at the right time and place has always been the key to effective marketing. Online is the ideal place to meet consumers today, since screen time is on the rise. Globally, businesses are embracing this reality. Digital marketing strategies ensure their marketing efforts reach customers more effectively and will, in turn, result in significant commercial benefits.

3.1 Global Reach

An international marketing campaign can be hard, expensive, and labor-intensive because traditional marketing is restricted by geography. Digital marketing, on the other hand, is done online, which gives it a wide reach (Simplilearn, 2021). Even a very modest local firm can use an internet store to connect with a global customer base. An organization can trade internationally and discover new markets on a website for very little money (NI Business info, 2019). With traditional marketing, this is either not possible or would be very expensive to achieve. This ease of access to the internet has provided businesses with numerous options for expansion (What Is Digital Marketing and Its Benefits?, 2022). Any firm has a lot to gain from having visibility and a worldwide reach.

3.2 Local Reach

Digital marketing offers a wide range of benefits, including increased local visibility, which is crucial if a company depends on neighboring clients (Simplilearn, 2021). Local SEO and ads that are tailored for local audiences might help businesses attract more customers to their doors (What Is Digital Marketing and Its Benefits?, 2022). Comparing one's ability to reach a neighborhood as a whole with digital marketing to one's ability to reach a community as a whole with printed flyers is illuminating.

3.3 Cost Effective

Digital marketing offers an organization, cost-effective methods for marketing the company both locally and globally (Benefits of Digital Marketing for Business in 2022, 2020). It enables the use of highly focused strategies by even the smallest businesses to compete with larger ones (What Is Digital Marketing and Its Benefits?, 2022). When done well, a digital marketing campaign can reach the right customers for a lot less money than a traditional marketing strategy (NI Business info, 2019). The majority of these tactics, including content marketing, social media, and SEO, won't even initially cost anything (Simplilearn, 2021). However, not all types of digital marketing are appropriate for all types of businesses, and some may even cost more than others. Based on its marketing objectives, a corporation can choose the best options (Storm, 2019).

3.4 Higher Conversion Rates

If an organization has a website, its clients are only a few clicks away from making a purchase. Unlike other forms of media that require users to stand up and dial a phone number or visit a store, internet marketing may be smooth and immediate (Storm, 2019).

3.5 Easy to Learn

Although there are a lot of components of digital marketing to grasp, getting started is pretty simple (What Is Digital Marketing and Its Benefits?, 2022). The nature of the objectives and the scope of the campaigns make it more complicated. Finding the best plan for a company, nevertheless, is all that is required.

3.6 Mobile Customers

Another of the several advantages of digital marketing is the ability to engage with customers.

People who use their mobile devices to browse, consume material. More than half of all online users access the internet via a mobile device. An organization may reach individuals through digital marketing on mobile devices, tablets, and desktop PCs.

3.7 Effective Targeting

Even if an organization doesn't have a clear idea of their target demographic, digital marketing gives the option to extract data to discover which demographics would perform best for the organization and optimize its campaign around them (What Is Digital Marketing and Its Benefits?, 2022). Using keywords for search engine optimization (SEO), pay-per-click advertising (PPC), or demographic information from social media are just a few ways to target an audience (Storm, 2019). An organization's access to such a vast array of targeting options ensures that every campaign is seen by the right people even at the beginning of the purchase experience (Storm, 2019). Additionally, it aids in the analysis of client behavior changes and the adaptation of campaigns to such changes (Benefits of Digital Marketing for Business in 2022, 2020). Any organization that can swiftly grasp the shifting needs of its clients will succeed (Sherman, 2018).

When done well, a digital marketing campaign can reach the right customers for a lot less money than a traditional marketing strategy (NI Business info, 2019). The majority of these tactics, including content marketing, social media, and SEO, won't even initially cost anything (Simplilearn, 2021). However, not all types of digital marketing are appropriate for all types of businesses, and some may even cost more than others. Based on its marketing objectives, a corporation can choose the best options (Storm, 2019).

3.8 Multiple Strategies

Different kinds of firms might utilize various digital marketing tactics. In comparison to a local business-to-consumer (B2C) clothing shop, a business-to-business (B2B) company interested in acquiring leads from abroad can employ a completely different approach (What Is Digital Marketing and Its Benefits?, 2022). Others can gain from conversion-based ad campaigns, while certain businesses can benefit more readily from content marketing and SEO. The secret is to continually assess the performance and, over time, improve the strategies and tactics. As the demands of the business change, a well-implemented digital marketing plan is one that adapts and changes rapidly.

Some of the most common types of digital marketing an organization can choose from is listed below:

- Social media marketing
- Email marketing
- Local search
- Remarketing
- Social paid ads
- Video marketing
- Influencer marketing
- SEO-based content creation
- Search engine marketing
- Forum engagement

3.9 Analytics and Optimization

Web analytics, which tracks the efficiency of digital marketing efforts in real-time, is another important advantage of digital marketing. This makes it easier to maximise future efforts and quickly fix mistakes.

Analyzing an organization's digital marketing strategies also allows it to pinpoint every source of traffic and get complete control over its sales funnels.

3.10 Measurable, Trackable Results

Monitoring an organization's internet marketing with web analytics and other online metric tools makes it easier to determine how effective its campaign was (NI Business info, 2019). It can get precise information about how customers interact with its website or react to its advertising.

3.11 Multiple Content Types

The variety of content kinds available to promote a company online is a vital benefit of digital marketing. It can choose from a variety of content kinds for many platforms to maintain the freshness of its brand and create successful online campaigns. In contrast to traditional marketing, it is simpler to copy one piece of content to fit as many platforms as an organization likes.

Some of the most common types of content that an organization can choose from is listed below.

- Infographics
- Blogs
- Social media posts
- Whitepapers
- Quizzes
- Webinars
- Podcasts
- Emailers
- Ebooks
- Visual content

3.12 Increased Engagement

Increased engagement is one of the most significant benefits of digital marketing. Digital marketing is supposed to be very engaging by default. Users can share a blog post, like a photo, bookmark a video, or interact with your website via a paid ad click. The nice aspect is that all of these acts are measurable. This allows an organization to make even more interesting posts to improve brand exposure or revenue. The more an organization interacts online, the more committed customers it can gain. Businesses that employ engaging formats effectively in their online initiatives have an easier time converting cold traffic to committed consumers.

3.13 Personalization

If an organization's client information is linked to its website, it can greet visitors with targeted offers whenever they visit (NI Business info, 2019). The more they buy from the organization, the more it can refine its consumer profile and promote effectively to them.

3.14 Openness

By utilising social media and carefully controlling it, an organization may increase customer loyalty and establish a reputation for being easy to engage with (NI Business info, 2019).

3.15 Social Currency

Using content marketing methods, digital marketing allows an organization to construct engaging campaigns (NI Business info, 2019). This content (pictures, movies, and articles) has the potential to generate social currency by being transferred from user to user and spreading virally.

3.16 Search Engine Optimization (SEO) and Local SEO

SEO is another effective digital marketing strategy that provides numerous advantages. It assists an organization in reaching out to more qualified buyers online by improving the web site content for search engines. Using relevant keywords that define an organization's product or service offering will assist in attracting more focused traffic to the site. This, in turn, increases conversions over time.

SEO isn't just for large corporations. Many people search online for local businesses, and these searches often lead to a purchase. In fact, Google reports that 28% of searches for anything nearby result in a purchase.

Local SEO can also be an effective digital marketing strategy for firms that operate in specific geographic areas, such as:

- physical stores
- restaurants, and
- other service-based enterprises

4.0 TRADITIONAL VS DIGITAL MARKETING STRATEGIES

An organization can quickly and easily adjust its plan and tactics to achieve the best results. Traditional marketing strategies, such as television or newspaper advertisements, requires to wait until the campaign is over to see the results. And, while an organization can use what it learns to tweak later campaign tactics. There isn't much it can do "in-the-moment" to optimise its plans.

Traditional marketing approaches may need weeks or even months of testing to understand which strategies are effective. While digital marketing allows an organization to see real-time campaign results and adjust its techniques to better results as it goes.

With website analytics, an organization can view:

- the amount of visitors to its site
- which pages they visit, and
- how long they stay on each page.

It can also examine the busiest days and hours for site visitors, as well as track conversion rates across the site. All of this data provides valuable insights that can help an organization better its campaigns over time. For example, Assume that an organization has created a series of blog entries as part of its content marketing plan. It needs to decide if it should continue writing blogs in this series or focus on other topics. It can easily check the blog stats to see how many people are reading the material. And how many individuals are converting or doing the desired step. Real-time tracking of success on this content marketing strategy allows it to decide the greatest use of its resources. Also, it can make the most of its campaign techniques (NI Business info, 2019).

5.0 CHALLENGES IN DIGITAL MARKETING

Though digital marketing has several advantages, yet a number of challenges are to be addressed. Some of them are listed below.

5.1 Skills and Training

An organization must guarantee that its employees have the necessary knowledge and competence to successfully carry out digital marketing. Tools, platforms, and trends evolve quickly, and it is critical that it stays current.

5.2 Time-Consuming

Duties like optimizing internet advertising campaigns and developing marketing content can be time-consuming. It is critical to track the progress of an organization in order to achieve a positive return on investment.

5.3 High Competition

While internet marketing allows you to access a global audience, it also exposes an organization to global competition. It might be difficult to stand out from the crowd and attract attention amid the various messages offered to consumers online.

5.4 Complaints and Feedback

Any bad feedback or criticism of an organization's brand might be seen by its target audience via social media and review websites. It might be difficult to provide excellent customer service online. Negative comments or a failure to respond appropriately might harm your brand's reputation.

5.6 Security and Privacy Concerns

There are several legal issues to consider when collecting and exploiting client data for digital marketing reasons. An organization should take care to follow privacy and data protection regulations.

6.0 TECHNOLOGIES ENABLING DIGITAL MARKETING

Social media and internet use have changed consumer behavior as well as how businesses run. Thanks to social and digital marketing, which reduces costs, increases brand awareness, and increases sales, businesses have a lot of opportunities (Dwivedi et al., 2021).

6.1 Artificial Intelligence

Because of its substantial contribution to altering enterprises and boosting sectors, artificial intelligence has attracted a lot of attention in recent years. New technologies are released on a regular basis in the digital marketing field, which is constantly growing (Lin, 2022). As a result, several of the technologies have the potential to drastically alter our perception of the online customer trip. Artificial intelligence has drastically altered the way organizations operate. It not only improves the efficiency of the organization, but it also greatly contributes by giving them more time to focus on innovation and creative ideas.

Artificial intelligence (AI) is also having a significant influence on the digital marketing business. Many companies are adopting AI into their digital marketing efforts. Artificial intelligence is being used in many firms' digital marketing efforts. AI allows for more precise targeting and tailored consumer engagements. Artificial intelligence technology enables businesses to develop more accurate and well-informed forecasts about client behavior, allowing them to implement more relevant marketing tactics. AI technology can also assist you in accelerating your marketing efforts. This improves your marketing success by offering high-quality content while also saving you substantial time and money.

Figure 1. Technologies enabling digital marketing

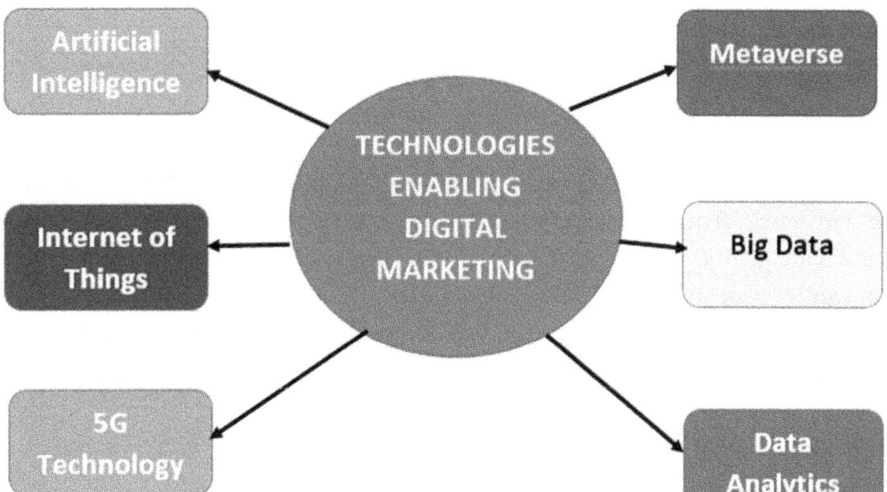

6.2 Internet of Things

IoT devices not only assist to communicate data, but also to collect and establish a client database, which is critical in this digital age. You've probably heard the expression "Data is King" (Trends, 2019). Digital marketers may gain better marketing insights and develop more accurate digital marketing plans with the support of a customer database.

6.3 Metaverse

The metaverse depicts the next level of digital shopping experiences, not just for physical items but also for virtual ones, in the new retail paradigm where consumer experience is king. The user base is predicted to grow across cohorts as the metaverse ecosystem evolves, as well as spend more time on it socializing, learning, working, and amusing themselves.

The concept of a metaverse is not new. It was initially envisioned in the 1992 science fiction novel Snow Crash, and it has since been connected to improvements in virtual reality technology as a result of the rapidly expanding desire for digital immersion (www.ETBrandEquity.com, 2022). Over the last two decades, online, multi-player, role-playing games have helped fuel the expansion of immersive technology, attracting millions of players and creating supporting ecosystems. This has naturally evolved into a common shared environment where people and entities may engage, work, be amused, and transact with one another - in some cases as virtual avatars - to create new experiences or replicate old ones.

A combination of developing ideas and technology has resulted in the Metaverse's tipping point. These include the growing availability of virtual reality (VR) headsets, the rise of blockchain-enabled digital currencies and Non-fungible Tokens (NFT) for transacting, the pandemic quickening life digitalization, and a tech-savvy, digitally expressive Gen Z customer base (www.ETBrandEquity.com, 2022).

6.4 5G Technology

5G basically implies faster surfing speeds, lower latency for customers, and more device density. However, the expansion creates a new creative landscape for businesses. Adopting 5G might allow up creatives to create interactive content and immersive experiences. It might also result in the complete customer journey being reinvented, from lead generation through transactions and follow-up care. While it will improve call and data quality, it will also offer up novel opportunities for organisations to revolutionise their advertising and consumer outreach. Downloads will be faster with 5G, buffering will be eliminated, and ideally, it will not matter how packed the place is because the network would be equally efficient (www.ETBrandEquity.com, 2022b).

6.5 Big Data

Big data is a vital component of modern marketing, whether done in-house or through a marketing agency. Customers want tailored messages and utmost comfort on their journey with the brand, so businesses must learn everything they can about them and how they act online. Big data assists enterprises with the following techniques.

- Identifying the target audience

- Improving engagement
- Forecasting the future
- Optimizing campaigns
- Pricing strategy

6.6 Data Analytics

On the internet, new information is being published at an exponential rate. Google and other search engines have had to consider how they would manage or filter internet material (Trends, 2019). As a result, search engines have begun to convert material into easily measurable and analyzable data. Search engines may now present users with appropriate links to their search queries, or even provide snippets that answer their enquiry, without the users having to click on a result. Many industries have taken advantage of this shift to improve their offerings. The degree of detail information provided by big data in conjunction with content analytics technologies driven by artificial intelligence is a game changer for marketing organizations in particular.

7.0 AI IN DIGITAL MARKETING

The ever-increasing impact and benefits of AI in digital marketing are continually being employed for new and inventive applications, and we can only conjecture on how marketing will look in a few years.

7.1 Content Marketing

Content Marketing's 5 Ps AI is based on actual conversations with entrepreneurs and engineers who are developing and utilising AI solutions. The framework is divided into five marketing categories, each with distinct use cases:

- Planning — Create smart tactics.
- Production – Create clever content.
- Personalization — Make intelligent consumer experiences more powerful.
- Promotion – Manage smart cross-channel promotions.
- Performance — Transform data into intelligence.

7.2 Chatbots with AI

The most visible illustration of how artificial intelligence technology is changing the face of digital marketing is chatbots. Chatbots are one of the most effective digital marketing tools, especially when used on social media and on your website. Using AI and chatbots together can help you provide an autonomously produced user experience that answers enquiries, actively assisting visitors to your website in understanding your company's offers. Chatbots powered by AI may enhance your customers' experiences and interactions by giving rapid answers to their questions 24 hours a day, seven days a week. An immediate response enables consumers to address difficulties quickly, resulting in a great customer experience (Jain, 2022). When utilised effectively, the chatbot will improve the image of your brand and boost the degree of trust connected with your company (Editorial, 2022).

Aside from offering instant replies to clients, including AI and chatbots into your digital marketing plan will help you collect vital data about your website's users and follow up with personalized offers on your behalf. This data may be used to improve your chatbot marketing approach as well as your overall marketing to achieve positive financial and communicative outcomes.

7.3 Increased Personalization

In the corporate sector, personalisation is a popular issue. People want their favourite companies to be personalised. They want to be heard, and the only way to do so is to personalise the commercials. Unfortunately, not all businesses recognise its relevance. A 2017 Accenture survey found that nearly 41% of customers moved to competitor companies due to a lack of trust and insufficient customization.

Integrating AI technology into your digital marketing plan may assist improve your visitors' experiences by providing intelligent customised service. It collects and analyses essential information about visitors to your website, such as their purchase history, preferences, location, and previous online activities.Using artificial intelligence, you can then personalise your website visitors' experiences by providing the best-fit items, information, and offers depending on their preferences. It also enables you to learn more about a customer's behaviour and deliver them a better tailored advertising message at the appropriate moment. This makes it easy to convert leads into sales at any moment (Editorial, 2022).

Figure 2. Artificial intelligence and digital marketing

7.4 Improve Shopping Experience

A good user experience may retain visitors on your website for longer periods of time, making it simpler to convert them into paying clients. Most marketers, however, are more focused with growing revenue and conversions than with improving the customer experience.

AI analyses relevant user data, such as consumer behaviour, to help you effectively identify and anticipate their needs. This allows you to tailor your website and client experience to each individual's needs, increasing customer happiness. Leveraging AI across all of your social media channels may help you provide the most relevant facts and impressions to your clients while also enhancing the website experience. By analysing relevant client data, you may deliver personalised adverts across all online media to target customers (Editorial, 2022).

7.5 Save Money and Time

Aside from customer service, AI has the ability to drastically improve things for marketers. Previously, a lot of marketing was done by guessing, testing, and adjusting to get things perfect. Even today, many organisations may test a variety of techniques to discover which one performs best. Many of these AI-powered systems will learn on their own and will not need human interaction. Based on past data, one should be able to determine which strategies are likely to be productive and which are not. As you may anticipate, this frees up a considerable number of personnel and opens new opportunities (Editorial, 2022).

7.6 Improve User and Consumer Experience

By analysing relevant client data, you may deliver personalised adverts across all online media to target customers (Editorial, 2022). Aside from customer service, AI has the ability to drastically improve things for marketers. Previously, a lot of marketing was done by guessing, testing, and adjusting to get things perfect **(Nowak, 2021)**. Even today, many organisations may test a variety of techniques to discover which one performs best. Many of these AI-powered systems will learn on their own and will not need human interaction. Based on past data, one should be able to determine which strategies are likely to be productive and which are not. As you may anticipate, this frees up a considerable number of personnel and opens new opportunities.

AI is a strong digital marketing technology that may assist you in improving your marketing game. By increasing the experiences and dialogues of your consumers, as well as optimising and speeding up different marketing operations. Incorporating AI into your digital advertising strategy will alter your business. This increases conversions and revenues (Editorial, 2022). Artificial intelligence may also be used to automate repetitive marketing operations, improving efficiency while saving money and time.

The importance of marketing materials and the desire for personalised customer experiences will rise in tandem. That is why I believe AI will be around for a long time. To stay one step ahead of their competition, marketing businesses should use AI as a tool that may provide them with a better group of consumers, reach higher levels of consumer engagement, and leverage video content techniques. All of these elements, as well as others, will eventually become key components of any marketer's toolset.

7.7 Big Data and AI Provide Better Insights

Understanding the target population is the major application of big data in marketing. Knowing client characteristics, interests, and habits in the digital environment enables organizations to design more efficient marketing efforts. This increases their chances of turning clicks into actual sales. Search engine optimization firms, such as BestSEOCompanies.com, employ big data to gain a better understanding of their clients' consumer base (Trends, 2019). SEO businesses may increase the effectiveness of their services by using specialized analytics solutions that leverage artificial intelligence to deliver rapid and meaningful information.

7.8 Increasing Shift Towards Targeted Marketing

Because analytics technologies are getting increasingly exact at sifting through thousands upon thousands of data points in a short period of time, there is a rising need for organizations to utilize customized marketing (Trends, 2019). Targeted marketing makes sense for businesses because, rather than spending millions of dollars attempting to appeal to a larger audience with no guarantee of a high conversion rate, custom analytics tools can use big data and AI to determine which specific web users are interested in products that businesses offer. Businesses are now interested in hiring big data professionals to supplement their marketing tactics and obtain a deeper knowledge of the volume of data available online (Future of Digital Marketing in India, 2022). This helps them to promote to those who are already interested in their products and yield higher conversion rates.

7.9 Programmatic Marketing

The technique of using AI to automate ad buying is known as programmatic advertising. By removing people from the ad-buying process, businesses gain a more trustworthy and cost-effective solution to their demands.

7.10 Multichannel Advertising

Omni-channel marketing was one of 2020's buzzwords. Despite the fact that the expression may now sound a little old, the strategy remains as practical and useful as ever. Marketing using several channels, such as social media, apps, email, and blog posts, to deliver a better consumer experience and a consistent brand message that promotes conversions and brand loyalty.

7.11 Marketing Based on Accounts (ABM)

Account-based marketing is a (often B2B) marketing strategy that focuses on specific accounts rather than a wide audience, allowing businesses to personalise their messaging and create connections with key decision-makers. This strategy allows firms to save time and money by focusing on the accounts that have the best potential of success. ABM also fosters strong customer connections, which may increase conversion rates and client loyalty.

7.12 Visual Content Marketing and Visual Search

Users may now enter photographs into searches using a new approach known as visual search. Two firms are adopting visual search, despite the fact that it is still in its early stages.

7.13 Google Lens

Google Lens is a visual search engine that identifies things and places using a camera app.

Pinterest jumped on the visual search bandwagon with the launching of Lens, a visual search tool that allows users to take a photo of an object to find out where to buy it online, search for comparable goods, or browse pinboards of related items (Mahender, 2022).

7.14 Predictive & Augmented Analytics

Data mining, predictive modelling, and machine learning are all techniques used in predictive analytics to identify trends and forecast the future. It has evolved and expanded throughout numerous sectors as a result of its potential (Mahender, 2022). In terms of digital marketing trends, we may expect an even higher number of predictive analytics tools and apps, such as enhanced lead scoring, customer segmentation, and personalisation.

7.15 Geo-Fencing

Although marketing clients based on their location is not a new concept, we do predict an increase in the use of geo-fencing, which is expected to reach $2.4 billion by 2023 (Mahender, 2022). Geo-fencing allows for real-time targeting depending on a user's location. When a user enters or exits a target zone, which is specified as being within a mile of a restaurant, they receive a push notification, text message, or other type of marketing contact.

7.16 Customer Relationship Management

Artificial Intelligence plays a significant role in Customer Relationship management (CRM). Through the many communication channels they employ, businesses may gain real-time data about how their consumers engage. Users can use statistical models to determine the best course of action after automatically assigning problems to the appropriate support group. In order to increase the client base, chatbots may be utilised to provide expertise via automated workflows. Following the analysis of customer data to identify the prospects most likely to convert to clients, support businesses in fostering these alliances (How Is AI Transforming the Future of Digital Marketing?, 2022).

8.0 IOT AND DIGITAL MARKETING

With the aid of IoT, digital marketers can better understand what their customers anticipate from their companies, allowing them to enhance product quality. The Internet of Things not only helps to improve product quality, but it also helps to estimate demand and prepare for new items. Accessing data from

IoT devices will enable organizations to make better and faster choices (Trends, 2019). IoT enables digital marketers to understand their consumers' purchasing behavior from beginning to end, providing a comprehensive picture of where the client is in their purchasing cycle (Trends, 2019).It also aids in the analysis of consumer demands, shopping patterns, what trends influence consumer purchase patterns, and geography, allowing marketers to tailor products accordingly.

8.1 Product Development

With the aid of IoT, digital marketers can better understand what customers anticipate from their companies, allowing them to enhance product quality. The Internet of Things not only helps to improve product quality, but it also assists in forecasting demand and planning for new items. Accessing data from IoT devices will enable firms to make better, faster decisions (Trends, 2019).

Figure 3. IOT and Digital Marketing

8.2 Analyze Customer's Buying Behavior

IoT enables digital marketers to understand their consumers' purchasing behaviour from beginning to end, and it provides a clear picture of where the client is in their purchasing journey (Trends, 2019). It also aids in the analysis of customer wants, purchasing patterns, how trends effect consumer purchase patterns, and geography, allowing marketers to tailor products accordingly. IoT can deliver more precise data on customer preferences.

8.3 Customer Analysis

An organization can read its customers' minds with smart gadgets. Smart devices generate massive amounts of data that may be used to gain deeper and more important insights on customers (Trends,

2019). Data from smart devices is utilized to better understand your customers' daily lives. It enables digital marketers to advertise items based on data obtained.

8.4 Data Tracking

Data tracking from IoT devices can assist marketers in predicting when a client will require a specific product or service. It is also utilized for sales scheduling, and real-time consumer data assist marketers in increasing sales (Trends, 2019). Smart gadgets enable marketers to collect a large amount of data about their customers, which can then be leveraged to create efficient marketing campaigns. IoT devices can deliver more data on customers via sensors than traditional research (Trends, 2019). Big data gives more precise insights, allowing marketers to decrease risk while increasing potential.

8.5 Better Personalization

Personalization is an effective method of reaching and engaging an organization's target audience. IoT enables marketers to communicate with their customers in real time. It allows for more precise audience targeting and increases the success of the marketing effort (Trends, 2019). IoT enables an organization to collect a range of information about its clients, which will assist in determining what sort of marketing should engage them.Marketers may provide the ideal message at the correct time to finish the purchase experience based on the data acquired. Marketers utilise it to create more relevant adverts as well.

IoT predictive analysis is a well-structured study that provides users with product or service suggestions. The Internet of Things analyses individual decisions and preferences based on user behavior patterns (Shah, 2022). Personalized analysis provides an organization's brand with a focused client base. As a result, it assists a company in swiftly determining the target demographic for their sponsored media campaign, influencing a user's purchasing behavior, and optimizing social media marketing. Companies now use IoT into their machines to better understand how their products and services operate. As a result, it will also assist marketers in creating content based on the tastes of their customers.

8.6 Marketing Automation

Normally, marketers spend a significant amount of time and effort gathering client data. However, IoT allows marketers to save time on data collection and analysis (Trends, 2019).

8.7 Customer Satisfaction

Everyone expects the fastest customer service in today's digital age, and it is critical for every marketer. Marketers can reply to their consumers more quickly with the support of real-time data (Trends, 2019).

8.8 Connectivity

Any smart gadget may be utilized as a channel to engage with your consumers via the Internet of Things. As a result, every smart product will assist marketers in connecting with their consumers, resulting in increased customer engagement (Trends, 2019).

8.9 Cost-Effective

Businesses benefit from the finest strategy provided by IoT. It assists businesses in increasing earnings by developing strategy and content plans, as well as establishing target audiences for paid advertisements on digital platforms. IoT-powered marketing approaches aid in increasing income and optimizing digital advertising. IoT also helps businesses run more efficiently. IoT may help organizations operate more intelligently by giving them with quick knowledge once they are connected with a variety of smart gadgets.

8.10 Revenue Acceleration

Data acquired from social media audiences may be used by AI to increase income by understanding which headlines, messages, and photos perform best to maximize interaction (Shah, 2022). Based on sentiment research, it may identify new audiences and trends, as well as anticipate who would buy more from social media communications.

8.11 Content Creation

We can now develop material not just for blogs but also for social media using efficient and smart AI tools. These softwares can also resize content for multiple social media networks, saving time (Shah, 2022). It can target audiences automatically and manage pace. Artificial intelligence technologies can write Facebook or Instagram advertising for specific audiences, proving to be quite useful.

8.12 Chatbots

Chatbots reply to messages via chat mediums such as Short Message Services (SMS), texts, and social media sites such as Instagram, Facebook, and Twitter. Natural Language Processing is used to train AI chatbots to conduct human-like conversations (NLP). NLP allows AI chatbots to read human language as it is written, allowing them to act more autonomously. On social media, a chatbot may be used for customer support, data and lead collection, and shopping collection.

9.0 FUTURE PROSPECTS IN GLOBAL ECONOMY

The advancement of artificial intelligence (AI) and the internet of things (IoT), as well as the widespread democratisation of access to their advantages, has focused attention on the changes they bring to our lives. The environment of digital marketing solutions develops so quickly that predicting its future is nearly impossible. It's gotten increasingly easier for entrepreneurs and enterprises to get a competitive advantage in the market (Pamintuan, 2022). The digital marketing environment is always changing and evolving, and the following characteristics are predicted to prevail in the future.

- Virtual Reality experiences
- Augmented Reality
- Personalized Content for Targeted Marketing
- Advanced Content Marketing

- In-vehicle apps and voice-activated assistants

Around 4.54 billion individuals, or 59% of the world's population, are active internet users, according to data from January 2020 (Statista, 2022).The use of social media has merged into many people's daily lives all across the world. There were 2.95 billion active social media users globally in 2019. By 2023, this is anticipated to rise to over 3.43 billion (Dixon, 2022). Companies may achieve their marketing goals at a cheap cost by using digital and social media marketing (Ajina, 2019). Over 50 million businesses have Facebook profiles, while more than 88% of companies utilize Twitter for marketing (Lister, 2018). All these avenues will definitely boost the global economy several folds from now. Four ideas to increase Customer Centric Energy innovations will strongly rely on the Digital Transformation roadmap's effective implementation.

a. Increase customer innovation by making data available to market participants.
b. Create enormous Energy Services as downloadable Apps via B2B, B2C, and C2C Energy Exchange Platforms.
c. Complete consumer engagement by making customer use as easy as a single click
d. Expand cross-border Energy Management to create a pan-European Energy Union of Customer Services.

It is anticipated that, with the enabling of IOT, Business Intelligence, Predictive Analytics, and Data Science, as well as established business models, 90% of Commercial and Industrial Customers and 70% of Residential Customers will embrace Smart Energy technologies by 2025. (Internet of Things (IOT), Big Data, Business Intelligence, Data Science, Digital Transformation: Hype or Reality? Facts and Figures – CIOCoverage- Driven for Technology Leaders, n.d.).

10.0 CONCLUSION

To achieve a competitive advantage in the market, it is critical to harness disruptive technologies such as artificial intelligence, the Internet of Things, machine learning, big data, 5G, and business intelligence. It may appear overwhelming and complex, but taking advantage of predictive insights, improved decision-making capabilities, and automation opportunities will enable businesses to stay ahead once big data and artificial intelligence become the new norm, which is expected to happen in the coming years. Early adopters of big data analytics, artificial intelligence, and IoT should expect more efficiency, reduced total costs, less risk, improved marketing effectiveness, increased sales, and, eventually, a higher Return on Investment (ROI).

The newest trend in marketing, known as experiential marketing, aims to go beyond the traditional methods that have lost their effectiveness for a variety of reasons, most notably the fact that the younger generation no longer believes in advertising and instead seeks out authentic, lasting interactions with brands. Businesses now have access to a variety of marketing tools, such as live shopping on social media platforms, 3D virtual shopping tours, and more (Dhawan, 2022). If these experiences are enhanced and expanded, users will continue to be interested in the current websites and online spaces. It will also open the door for future developments in the Web 3.0 era. Following new trends is essential if marketers are to be prepared for the new digital consumer environment they will be operating in.

REFERENCES

ETBrandEquity. (2022a, December 7). *5g Services: 5G and the new era of creativity in marketing, Marketing & Advertising News, ET BrandEquity*. ETBrandEquity.com. https://brandequity.economictimes.indiatimes.com/news/digital/5g-and-the-new-era-of-creativity-in-marketing/96038180

ETBrandEquity. (2022b, December 13). *The potential for retail in the metaverse, Marketing & Advertising News, ET BrandEquity*. ETBrandEquity.com. https://brandequity.economictimes.indiatimes.com/news/digital/the-potential-for-retail-in-the-metaverse/96180923

Ajina, A. S. (2019). The perceived value of social media marketing: An empirical study of online word-of-mouth in Saudi Arabian context. *Entrepreneurship and Sustainability Issues*, *6*(3), 1512–1527. doi:10.9770/jesi.2019.6.3(32)

Alexander, L. (2022, November 30). *The Who, What, Why, & How of Digital Marketing*. Blog.hubspot.com. https://blog.hubspot.com/marketing/what-is-digital-marketing#whatis

Monnappa, A. (2015, July 8). *The History and Evolution of Digital Marketing*. Simplilearn. https://www.simplilearn.com/history-and-evolution-of-digital-marketing-article

Benefits Of Digital Marketing For Business in 2022. (2020, September 28). Intellipaat Blog. https://intellipaat.com/blog/benefits-of-digital-marketing/

Bhosale, V., & Pralhad Raverkar, D. (2020, January). *(PDF) IMPORTANCE OF DIGITAL MARKETING IN THE NEW AGE*. ResearchGate. https://www.researchgate.net/publication/344851786_IMPORTANCE_OF_DIGITAL_MARKETING_IN_THE_NEW_AGE

Desai, V. (2019). *(PDF) Digital Marketing: A Review*. ResearchGate. https://www.researchgate.net/publication/333709419_Digital_Marketing_A_Review

Dhawan, M. K. (2022, December 14). *How are AI, web3 and other emerging technologies transforming the future of experiential Marketing?* CXOToday.com. https://www.cxotoday.com/cxo-bytes/how-are-ai-web3-and-other-emerging-technologies-transforming-the-future-of-experiential-marketing/

Dixon, S. (2022, September 16). *Number of Social Media Users Worldwide 2010-2021*. Statista. www.statista.com. https://www.statista.com/statistics/278414/number-of-worldwide-social-network-users/

Dwivedi, Y. K., Ismagilova, E., Hughes, D. L., Carlson, J., Filieri, R., Jacobson, J., Jain, V., Karjaluoto, H., Kefi, H., Krishen, A. S., Kumar, V., Rahman, M. M., Raman, R., Rauschnabel, P. A., Rowley, J., Salo, J., Tran, G. A., & Wang, Y. (2021). Setting the Future of Digital and Social Media Marketing research: Perspectives and Research Propositions. *International Journal of Information Management*, *59*(59), 102168. Science direct. doi:10.1016/j.ijinfomgt.2020.102168

Editorial. (2022, August 17). *Digital marketing leveraging artificial intelligence*. MediaNews4U. https://www.medianews4u.com/digital-marketing-leveraging-artificial-intelligence/

Future of Digital Marketing in India. (2022, March 14). Www.linkedin.com. https://www.linkedin.com/pulse/future-digital-marketing-india-madhu-kiran-g?trk=articles_directory

Gecdesigns. (2020, December 1). *What is IOT? & Role of IOT in digital marketing*. GEC Designs. https://gecdesigns.com/blog/role-of-iot-in-digital-marketing

How is AI Transforming the Future of Digital Marketing? (2022, February 28). Institute of Entrepreneurship Development. https://ied.eu/blog/how-ai-transforming-the-future-of-digital-marketing/#:~:text=AI%20assists%20businesses%20in%20analyzing

Internet Of Things (IOT), Big Data, Business Intelligence, Data Science, Digital Transformation: Hype Or Reality? Facts And Figures. (n.d.). CIOCoverage. https://www.ciocoverage.com/internet-of-things-iot-big-data-business-intelligence-data-science-digital-transformation-hype-or-reality-facts-and-figures/

Jain, A. K. (2022, December 13). Digital marketing tools that helping cos keep their promises to customers. *Bizz Buzz News*. https://www.bizzbuzz.news/markets/digital-marketing-tools-that-helping-cos-keep-their-promises-to-customers-1185244

Lin, P. (2022, October 7). *The Role of Big Data in AI-Powered Marketing*. Www.marketingaiinstitute.com. https://www.marketingaiinstitute.com/blog/big-data-ai-powered-marketing

Lister, M. (2018). 40 Essential Social Media Marketing Statistics for 2018. *Wordstream*. https://www.wordstream.com/blog/ws/2017/01/05/social-media-marketing-statistics

Mahender. (2022, December 19). Digital Marketing Trends 2023 by Dhananjay Yadav. *Newspatrolling*. https://newspatrolling.com/digital-marketing-trends-2023-by-dhananjay-yadav-seo-expert/

NI Business info. (2019, August 5). *Advantages and disadvantages of digital marketing*. NI Business. https://www.nibusinessinfo.co.uk/content/advantages-and-disadvantages-digital-marketing

Nowak, M. (2021, August 4). *The Internet of Things Helps Businesses across Industries*. Nomtek. https://www.nomtek.com/blog/how-iot-helps-business

Pamintuan, S. (2022, May 30). The future of digital marketing isn't what you think: 5 trends. *The Drum*. https://www.thedrum.com/opinion/2022/05/30/the-future-digital-marketing-isnt-what-you-think-5-trends

Patel, P. (2019, June 4). *Importance Of Digital Marketing In Today's Stage Of Affairs*. YourStory.com. https://yourstory.com/mystory/importance-of-digital-marketing-in-todays-stage-of

Shah, H. (2022, August 4). *How IoT and AI are giving a boost to digital marketing*. Afaqs! Marketplace; marketplace blog. https://marketplace.afaqs.com/blog/digital-marketing/how-iot-and-ai-are-giving-a-boost-to-digital-marketing

Sherman. (2018, September 13). *Digital Marketing Blog*. Digital Marketing Blog. https://www.lyfemarketing.com/blog/benefits-digital-marketing/

Simplilearn. (2021, June 29). *8 Benefits of Digital Marketing: All You Should Know*. Simplilearn. https://www.simplilearn.com/digital-marketing-benefits-article

Statista. (2022, April 26). *Global digital population 2022*. Statista. www.statista.com. https://www.statista.com/statistics/617136/digital-population-worldwide/

Storm, M. (2019, April 25). *6 Proven Benefits of Digital Marketing That You Can't Ignore*. WebFX Blog. https://www.webfx.com/blog/marketing/benefits-of-digital-marketing/

Trends, M. (2019, June 11). You are being redirected.... Analytical *Insidght*. https://www.analyticsinsight.net/how-big-data-and-ai-are-changing-digital-marketing/

What is Digital Marketing and Its benefits? (2022). Engaio Digital. https://engaiodigital.com/digital-marketing/

White, C. (2020, December 29). *How AI is Changing the Future of Digital Marketing*. Bramework. https://www.bramework.com/ai-marketing/

Chapter 11
Applications of the Internet of Things and Machine Learning Using Python in Digital Marketing

Arun Kumar Singh
Papua New Guinea University of Technology, Papua New Guinea

ABSTRACT

The internet of things (IoT) is a network of physical objects or "things" embedded with electronics, software, sensors, and network connectivity, which enables them to collect and exchange data. These objects can include everyday devices such as smart thermostats, home security systems, wearable fitness trackers, and even vehicles. However, IoT also raises concerns about privacy, security, and reliability, as the increasing number of connected devices creates new opportunities for cyber attacks and data breaches. As such, the development and deployment of IoT technology must be done in a responsible and secure manner. Through the use of sensors, it is now possible to collect, transmit, and transform data into knowledge. The marketing and sales sectors are capable of using data gathered through IoT to interact with customers on an individual basis. Python is an object oriented, scripted and interpreted language for both learning and real-world programming. Work in this chapter first introduces Python as a language, and gives summary about data science, machine learning, and IOT.

1 INTRODUCTION

1.1 Basic About Python in Digital Market

For general-purpose python is high-level programming language which became popular in the recent times. with this concern python allows programmer to write the code in fewer lines just like simple mathematical equation that is not possible with other languages. The main feature in Python programming is that it supports multiple programming prototypes. Python also provides a large set of extensive

DOI: 10.4018/978-1-6684-8166-0.ch011

standard library which is extensible. The main lineament of Python are unproblematic and easy to understand, Freeware and open source, High level programming language, Platform independent, Portability, Dynamically typed, Both procedure oriented and Object oriented, Interpreted, Extensible, Embedded, Extensive Library. (Holzinger et al., 2014)

Python is a popular programming language used in the digital market for a variety of applications. Its popularity is due to its ease of use, flexibility, and versatility. Some basic applications of Python in the digital market include:

- Web Development: Python can be used to create web applications using frameworks such as Django and Flask.
- Data Science: Python has several libraries for data science such as NumPy, Pandas, and SciPy, making it a popular language for data analysis and visualization.
- Machine Learning: Python's simplicity and flexibility make it a popular choice for machine learning applications, with libraries such as TensorFlow and Scikit-Learn.
- Automation: Python can be used to automate tasks, such as web scraping, data extraction, and file management.
- Game Development: Python can be used for game development with libraries like Pygame and PyOpenGL.

What we wants to include in our programs/ projects, a Python library is a reusable chunk of code. If you compare to languages like C++ or C, a Python libraries do not pertain to any specific context in Python. The python library contains built-in modules (written in C) and it provide access to system functionality such as file I/O that would otherwise be inaccessible to Python programmers, as well as modules written in Python that provide standardized solutions for many problems that occur in everyday programming.

In this article we are trying to give some basic idea about python in the field of Data science, IOT and Machine learning. Python is known to have acopiousness of libraries that aided with data analysis and scientific computing and informatics.

Overall, Python is a versatile and powerful programming language that is widely used in the digital market for a variety of applications, from web development and data science to automation and game development.

Figure 1. An accompanying w3school repository is provided to aid the tutorial. It contains a number of notebooks of python code for reference. It helps to go through number of examples related to different modules of Python
https://www.w3schools.com/python/default.asp

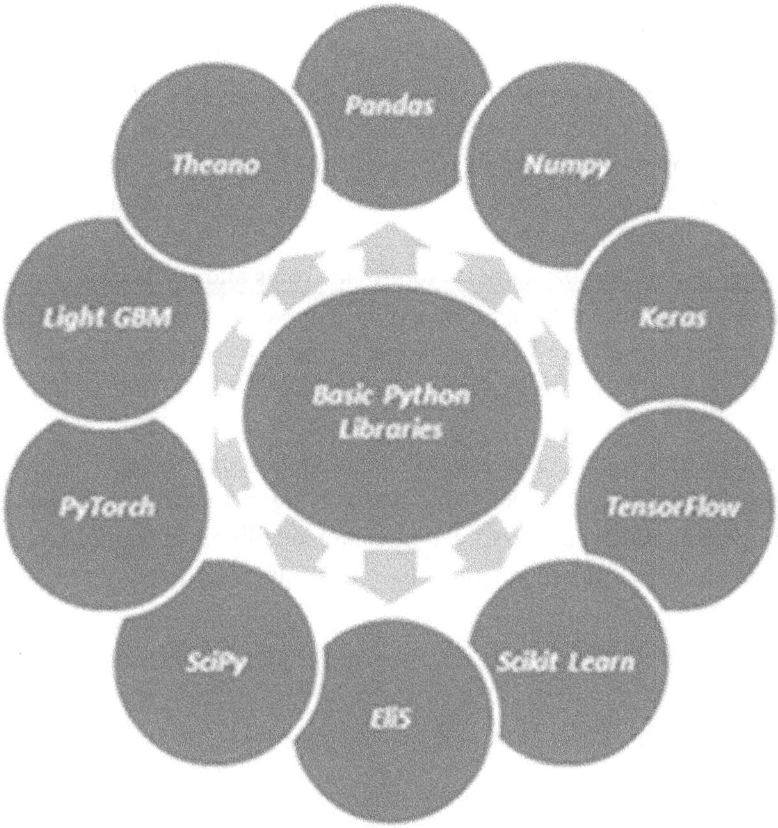

1.2 Data Science in Digital Market

Data science is a rapidly growing field in the digital market that involves extracting insights and knowledge from data using statistical and computational methods. In the digital market, data science is being used extensively for a variety of applications, including:

- Marketing: Companies are using data science to analyze consumer behavior and create personalized marketing campaigns that are more effective at reaching their target audience.
- Finance: Data science is being used in finance for fraud detection, risk management, and investment analysis.
- Healthcare: Data science is being used to improve patient outcomes, optimize treatments, and manage public health issues.
- E-commerce: Companies are using data science to optimize their supply chain and inventory management, as well as to create personalized product recommendations for their customers.

- Social Media: Social media platforms are using data science to analyze user behavior, detect trends, and create personalized content.

The demand for data scientists is rapidly growing in the digital market, as companies seek to gain insights from their data to improve their products and services, increase efficiency, and make more informed decisions. Data scientists use a variety of tools and techniques, including machine learning, data visualization, and statistical analysis, to extract insights from large datasets. Data science is related to data analytics, data mining and big data. It understands the phenomenon of the data. It employs techniques and theories drawn from many fields within the context of mathematics, statistics,computer science, and information scienceand applies knowledge and actionable insights from data across a broad range of application domains. (Jordan & Mitchell, 2015)

The most important disciplines of Statistics to provide tools and methods to find structure, to give deeper insight into data, and the most important discipline toanalyse and quantify uncertainty. Python provides various predefined modules to work on Data science projects. (Le et al, 2015)

The figure given below representing the five stage of the data science life cycle:

- Capture, (data acquisition, data entry, signal reception, data extraction)
- Maintain (data warehousing, data cleansing, data staging, data processing, data architecture)
- Process (data mining, clustering/classification, data modelling, data summarization)
- Analyse (exploratory/confirmatory, predictive analysis, regression, text mining, qualitative analysis)
- Communicate (data reporting, data visualization, business intelligence, decision making).

Figure 2. Representing the five stage of the data science life cycle

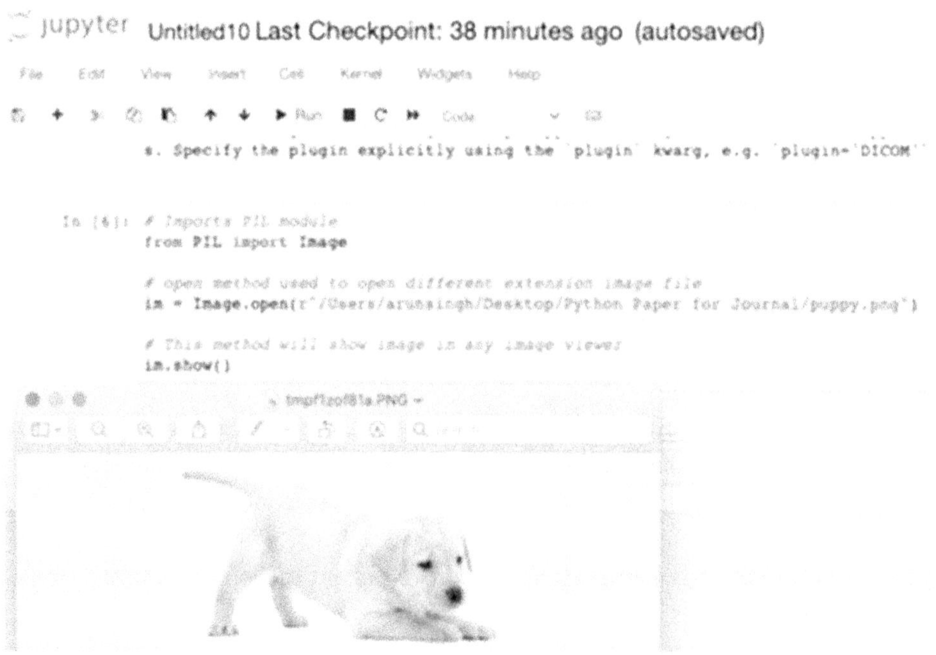

1.3 Machine Learning in Digital Market

Machine learning is a subset of artificial intelligence that involves training algorithms to learn from data and make predictions or decisions based on that data. In the digital market, machine learning is being used extensively for a variety of applications, including:

- Predictive Analytics: Machine learning algorithms are used to predict outcomes or trends based on historical data, such as predicting customer churn or forecasting sales.
- Natural Language Processing: Machine learning algorithms are used to process and analyze human language data, such as sentiment analysis, chatbots, and language translation.
- Image and Video Recognition: Machine learning algorithms are used to analyze and identify patterns in visual data, such as facial recognition, object detection, and image classification.
- Fraud Detection: Machine learning algorithms are used to detect anomalies in financial transactions, such as credit card fraud or money laundering.
- Autonomous Systems: Machine learning algorithms are used to control autonomous systems, such as self-driving cars or drones.

The demand for machine learning skills is rapidly growing in the digital market, as companies seek to automate and optimize their processes, improve customer experiences, and make more informed decisions. Machine learning requires expertise in programming, statistics, and data analysis, as well as knowledge of specialized tools and frameworks such as TensorFlow, PyTorch, and scikit-learn.(Naim&malik, 2022)

Figure 3. Machine learning algorithms

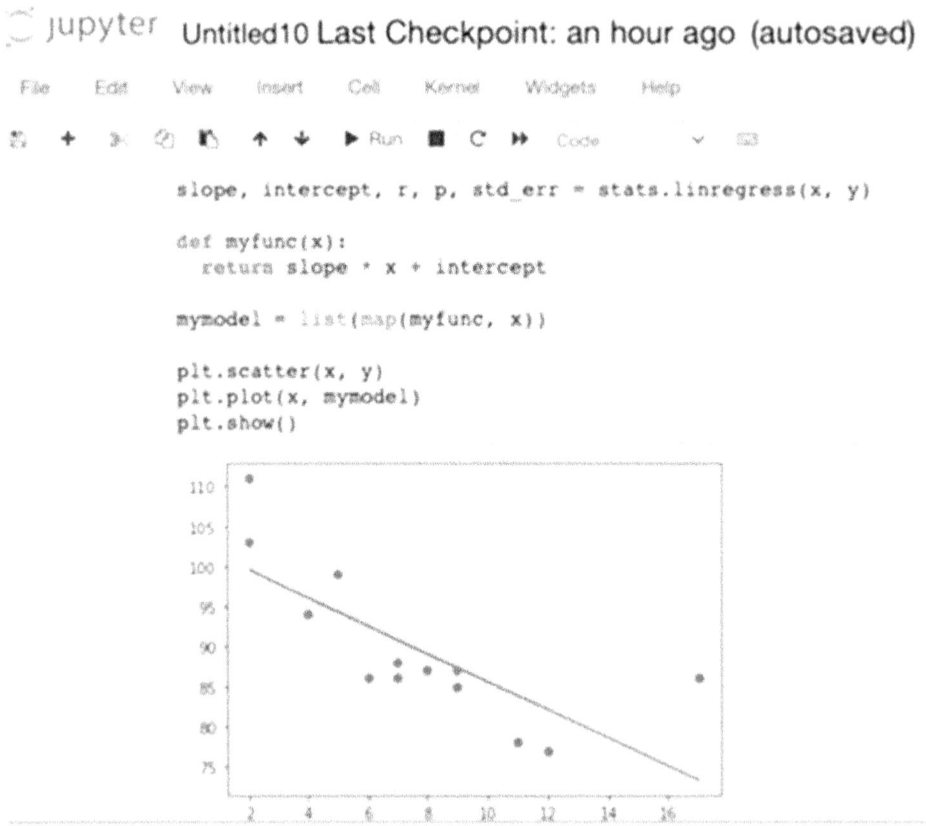

Python for beginner-friendly, and can do the same thing that other coding languages can, but in fewer lines of coding. (Naim&Kautish, 2022)

1.4 IOT in Digital Marketing

The Internet of Things (IOT) is a scenario in which objects, animals or people are provided with single identifiers and the capability to automatically transfer and the capability to automatically transfer data more to a network without requiring human-to-human or human-To-computer communication. The Internet of things describes physical objects with sensors, processing ability, software, and other technologies that connect and exchange data with other devices and systems over the Internet or other communications networks. (Singh &Pandey, 2021). IoT (Internet of Things) is a rapidly growing field in the digital market that involves connecting physical devices to the internet and collecting data from them. In the context of digital marketing, IoT can be used to collect data on consumer behavior and preferences, as well as to create personalized marketing campaigns. Some of the applications of IoT in digital marketing include:

- Smart Advertising: IoT devices can be used to collect data on consumer behavior, such as their location, interests, and purchasing habits, and use that data to create more targeted and personalized advertising campaigns.

- Personalized Customer Experiences: IoT devices can be used to collect data on customer behavior and preferences, such as their browsing history or product usage patterns, and use that data to create more personalized and customized experiences.
- Location-Based Marketing: IoT devices can be used to track the location of consumers and send them personalized offers and promotions based on their location.
- Product Optimization: IoT devices can be used to collect data on product usage patterns, such as how often a product is used and for how long, and use that data to optimize product design and improve customer satisfaction.
- Supply Chain Optimization: IoT devices can be used to track the movement of products through the supply chain and optimize inventory management and logistics.
- Customer Data Collection: IoT devices can collect customer data and usage patterns to personalize marketing efforts.
- Real-Time Analytics: IoT devices provide real-time data on customer behavior, enabling marketers to make informed decisions.
- Location-Based Marketing: IoT devices can send location-based advertisements and promotions to customers, increasing the chances of conversion.
- Predictive Maintenance: IoT devices can predict equipment failures, enabling marketers to prevent downtime and improve customer experience.
- Social Media Monitoring: IoT devices can monitor social media for brand mentions, providing marketers with valuable insights into customer sentiment.
- Augmented Reality Advertising: IoT devices can display augmented reality advertisements, enhancing the customer experience and increasing engagement.
- Inventory Management: IoT devices can track inventory levels, enabling marketers to make informed decisions about product stocking and pricing.

IOT has evolved from the meeting of wireless Technologies, micro-electromechanical systems (MEMS) and the internet. The demand for IoT skills is rapidly growing in the digital market, as companies seek to take advantage of the opportunities presented by connected devices and the data they generate. IoT requires expertise in hardware design, software development, data analysis, and security, as well as knowledge of specialized tools and platforms such as Arduino, Raspberry Pi, and AWS IoT.

Figure 4. IOT map

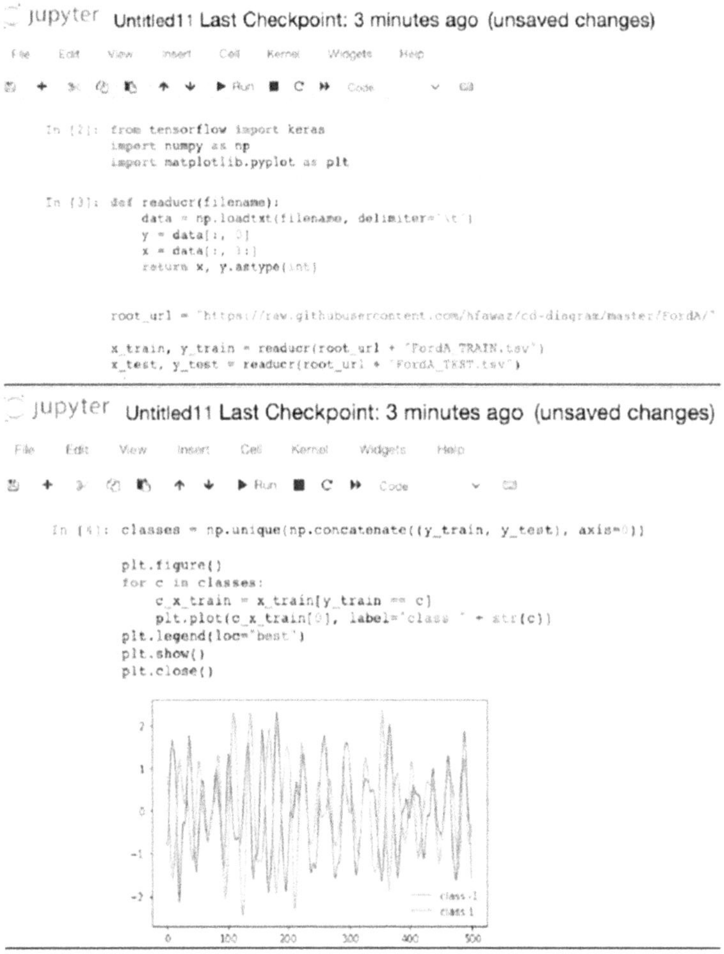

As per the TIOBE (The Importance Of Being Earnest)- TIOBE stands for The Importance of Being Earnest, the title of an 1895 comedy play by Oscar Wilde. The index is calculated from the number of search engine results for queries containing the name of the language. The index covers searches in Google, Google Blogs, MSN, Yahoo!, Baidu, Wikipedia and YouTube.

Index for python:

- Highest Position (since 2001): #1 in Apr 2022
- Lowest Position (since 2001): #13 in Feb 2003
- Language of the Year: 2007, 2010, 2018, 2020, 2021

Figure 5. TIOBE index for Python

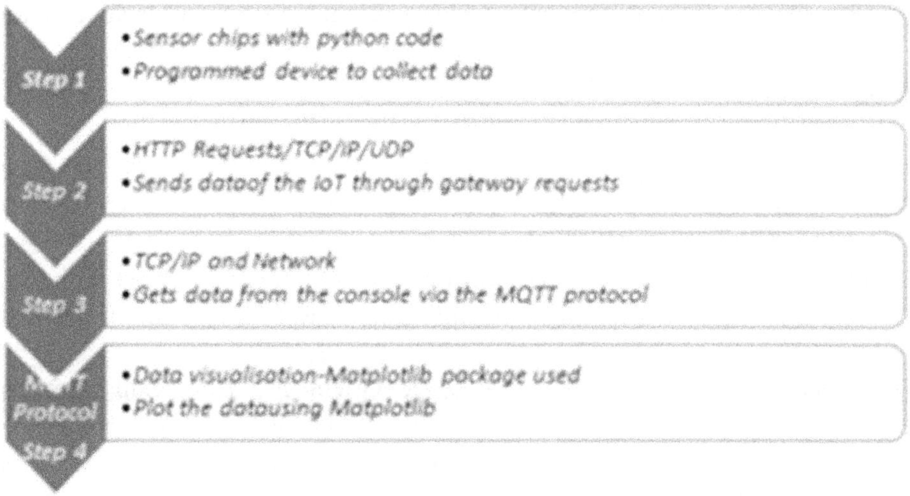

Python is mostly used for writing web applications, but it has gained popularity in the IOT system. It is an interpreted language that offers readability with syntax without compromising the size. This language has a large number of libraries; it can get more stuff done with fewer codes. Python's clean syntax is suitable for database arrangement. In case your app needs the data to be arranged in a database format or use tables. Python is the right choice available. Python is the right choice, for data analysis in IOT systems. The language is simple and can be easily deployed. Its large community helps in providing help and libraries as and when required. It is the ideal language for data-intensive applications. (Singh, 2021)

2 OBJECTIVES OF STUDY

1. To gestate the features of Python
2. To follow up python modules for Data Science like Numpy which is used for matrix and vectormanipulation,Scipy and 2D plotting library Matplotlib etc
3. To concern on python modules for Machine learning like Tensor flow numerical computations for machine learning, Keras for neural networks and deep learning

All points are discussed in this paper.

3. WORKS RELATED TO CONCERN TOPIC

3.1 Basic Working Features of python

Python is a much more powerful high-level language created by Guido van Rossum (First appeared in 20 February 1991; 31 years ago) and Its language constructs and object-oriented approach aim to help programmers write clear, logical code for small- and large-scale projects. Its design philosophy emphasizes code readability with the use of significant indentation. Python is an object oriented, scripted and interpreted language for both learning and real world programming. (Python Machine Learning, 2020)

Basic Working Features of Python

- Python is Interpreted – Python is processed at runtime by the interpreter. You do not need to compile your program before executing it. This is similar to PERL and PHP.Python can be used to handle big data and perform complex mathematics.
- Python is Interactive – you can actually sit at a Python prompt and interact with the interpreter directly to write your programs.Python can connect to database systems. It can also read and modify files.
- Python is Object-Oriented – Python supports Object-Oriented style or technique of programming that encapsulates code within objects.Python can be used alongside software to create workflows. Python can be used for rapid prototyping, or for production-ready software development.
- Python is a Beginner's Language – Python is a great language for the beginner-level programmers and supports the development of a wide range of applications from simple text processing to WWW browsers to games.Python can be used on a server to create web applications.

Figure 6. Basic working features of Python

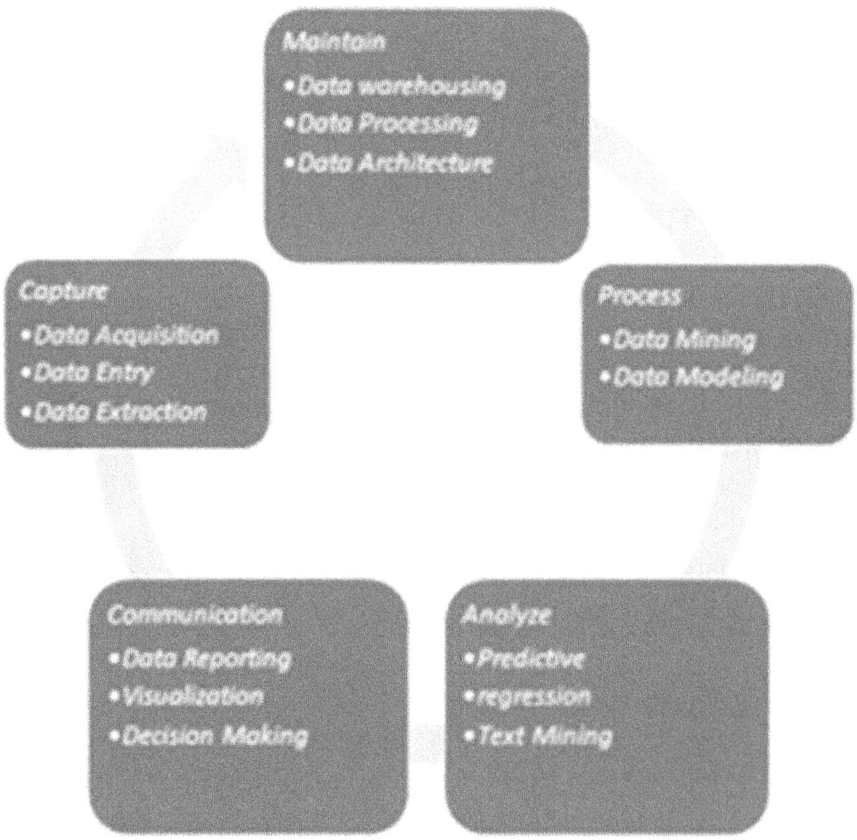

3.2 Python for Data Science

You have to know that there are the most essential Data Science libraries:

- Numpy
- Matplotlib
- Scipy

Numpy: Maybe it is difficult to do that directly, but since the concept is a crucial part of data science, many other libraries (well, almost all of them) are built on Numpy. Numpy will help us to manage multi-dimensional arrays very efficiently. Without Numpy it is difficult to use Pandas, Matplotlib, Scipy or Scikit-Learn.

Simple way we can say: NumPy is a Python library, NumPy is used for working with arrays and NumPy is short for "Numerical Python"

Figure 7. Numpy

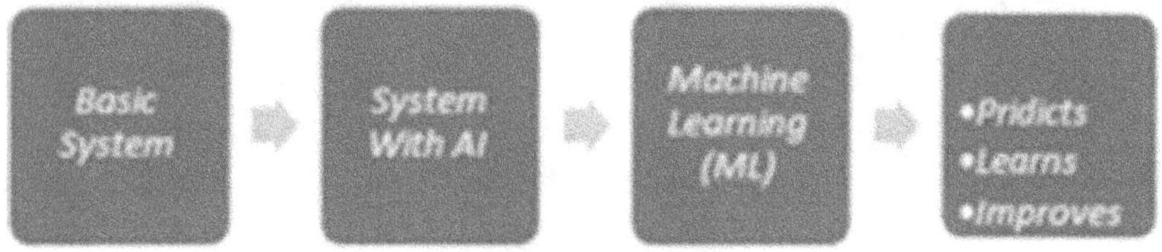

Figure 8. Numpy

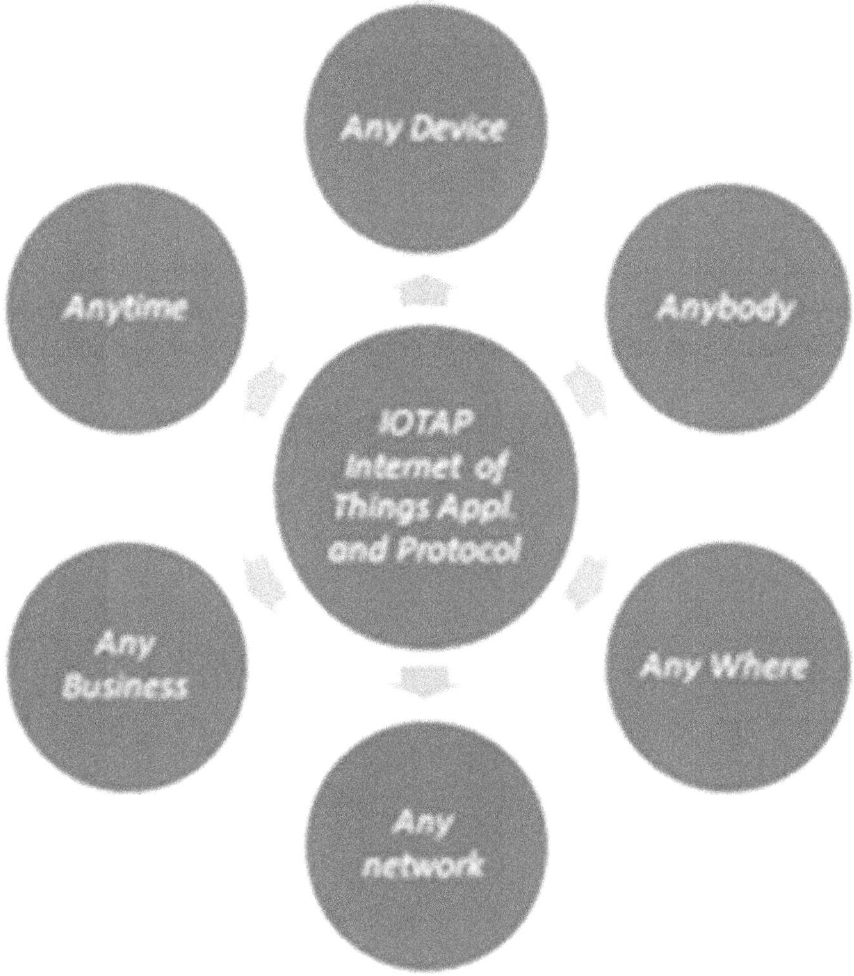

3-Dimensional NumpyArray:

But on the other hand 3-dimensional Numpy array, it also has a few well-implemented methods. It's quite to use Numpy random function, which is found slightly better than the random module of the standard library. And when it comes to simple predictive analytics tasks like linear or polynomial regression, Numpypolyfit function will be favourite (Engblom&Lukarski, 2016).

Figure 9. matplotlib

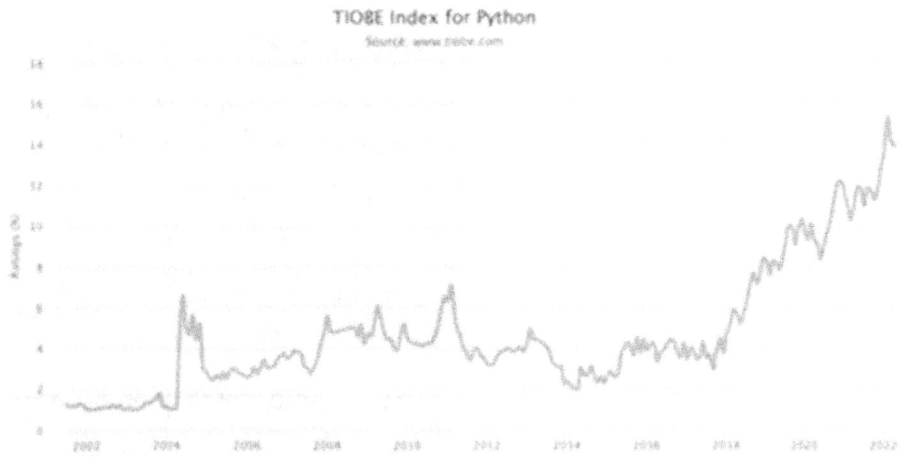

Matplotlib

For the Data lookout, Data visualization is very important and it's an easy process. Data visualization helps user to better understanding about the data, discover things that wouldn't discover in raw format and communicate findings more efficiently to others. The best and most well-known Python data visualization library is Matplotlib. (Singh, 2019)

Scipy

SciPy is a scientific computation library that uses NumPy underneath. SciPy stands for Scientific Python, It provides more utility functions for optimization, stats and signal processing like NumPy, SciPy is open source so we can use it freely. SciPy was created by NumPy's creator Travis Olliphant. If SciPy uses NumPy underneath, why can we not just use NumPy? SciPy has optimized and added functions that are frequently used in NumPy and Data Science. Mathematics deals with a huge number of concepts that are very important but at the same time, complex and time-consuming. However, Python provides the full-fledged scipy library that resolves this issue for us. In this scipy, we will be learning how to make use of this library along with a few functions and their examples.(Singh, 2017)

Figure 10. Open method

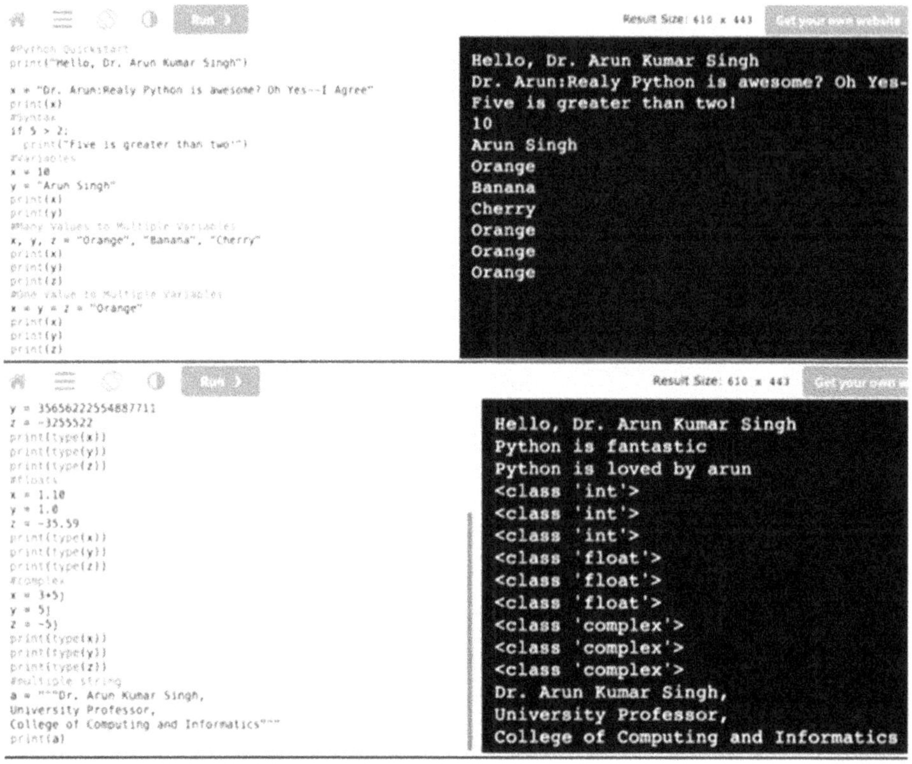

3.3 Python for Machine Learning

Tensor flow and keras libraries are general-purpose libraries for anything involving advanced data manipulation. This means they can all be used in implementing machine learning, and many of the higher level machine learning libraries makes use of some or all of these libraries. Getting acquainted with them is highly recommended if you plan on getting anywhere with scientific Python programming. (Singh, 2022)

This list is by no means exhaustive; it is meant to be a starting point for you as you explore machine learning through Python! Already we discussed Numpy, Matplotlib and Scipy which are used for machine learning too. But we are showing the work phenomenon of Tensor flow and keras libraries in machine learning. (Anand et al., 2022)

Figure 11. Return slope

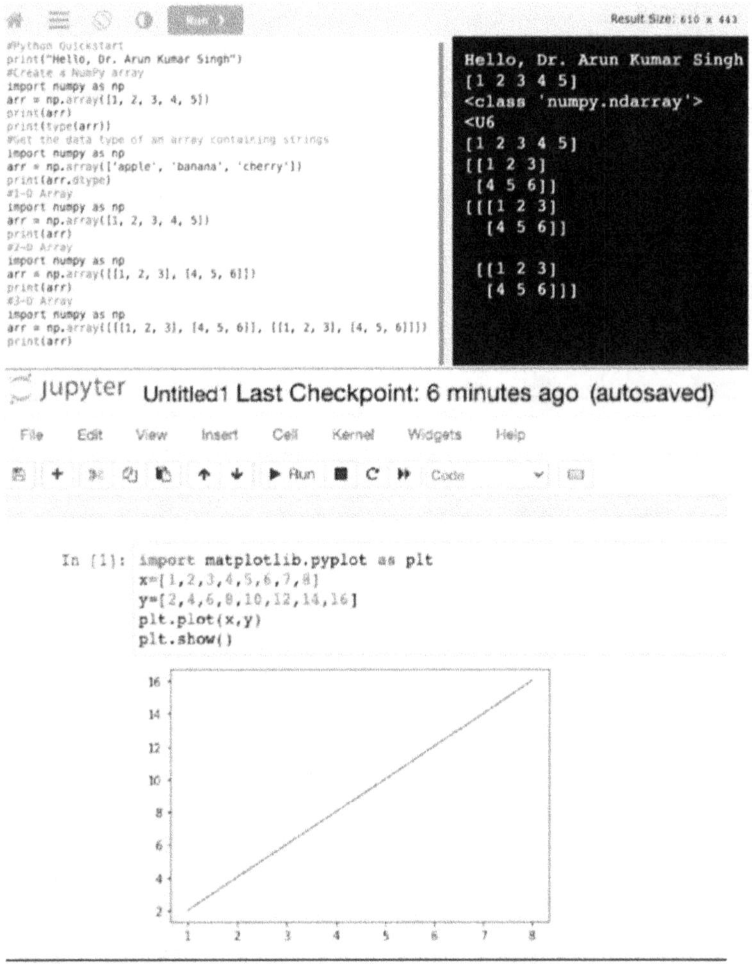

Tensor Flow

Tensor flow is the most well-known open source machine learning library available for Python. It was developed by Google, and is used in nearly every Google application that utilizes machine learning. If you've used Google Photos or voice search, then you've been using tensor flow. Tensor flow is extremely well documented and supported, and is optimized for speed. It is not easy to understand, however, because it is actually a Python front-end coded on top of C or C++, but as per your practice you can learn.

Keras

A high-level library for working with datasets and built on top of Theano and Tensor flow is Keras. Keras is best known for being one of the easiest machine learning libraries out there because it is coded entirely in Python, while using either Theano or Tensor flow as a back-end. It is easy and its beginner-friendly library for machine learning, includes functions for creating training datasets. Keras' neural networks API was developed for fast experimentation and is a good choice for any deep learning project that requires fast prototyping.

Figure 12. Keras

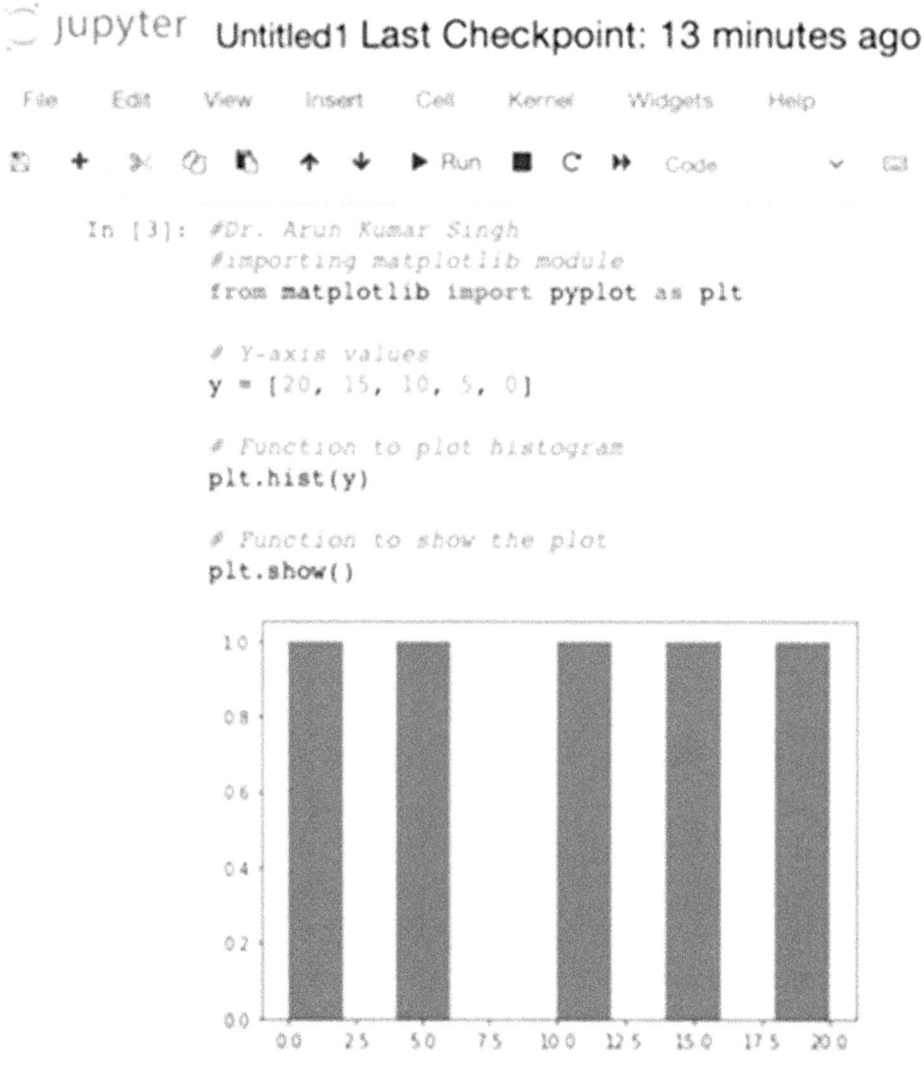

3.4 Python for IOT

A year back, python was only used for web applications; no one thought it would apply in IOT development also. Now developers are using python programming language for developing the IOT Applications and Protocols. With efficient programming and easy syntax, most of us looking towards python.

IoT applications function efficiently with the help of Python libraries/packages which include:

- Numpy.
- Sockets and MySQLdb.
- Matplotlib.
- Requests, Tkinter and Tensorflow.
- MQ Telemetry Transport (MQTT) sensor simulator.
- Azure IoT SDK in Python.
- CountlyIoT Raspberry Pi SDK.

MQ TELEMETRY TRANSPORT (MQTT) SENSOR SIMULATOR

MQTT protocol for the IoT in Python enables high-speed data exchange with low payloadcommunication between the devices. User-friendly requests of MQTT are made directly in Python. Data is collected in real-time and easily analysed in mathematical computation libraries like matplotlib. The diagram below shows the steps used for the data flow:

Figure 13. Steps used for data flow

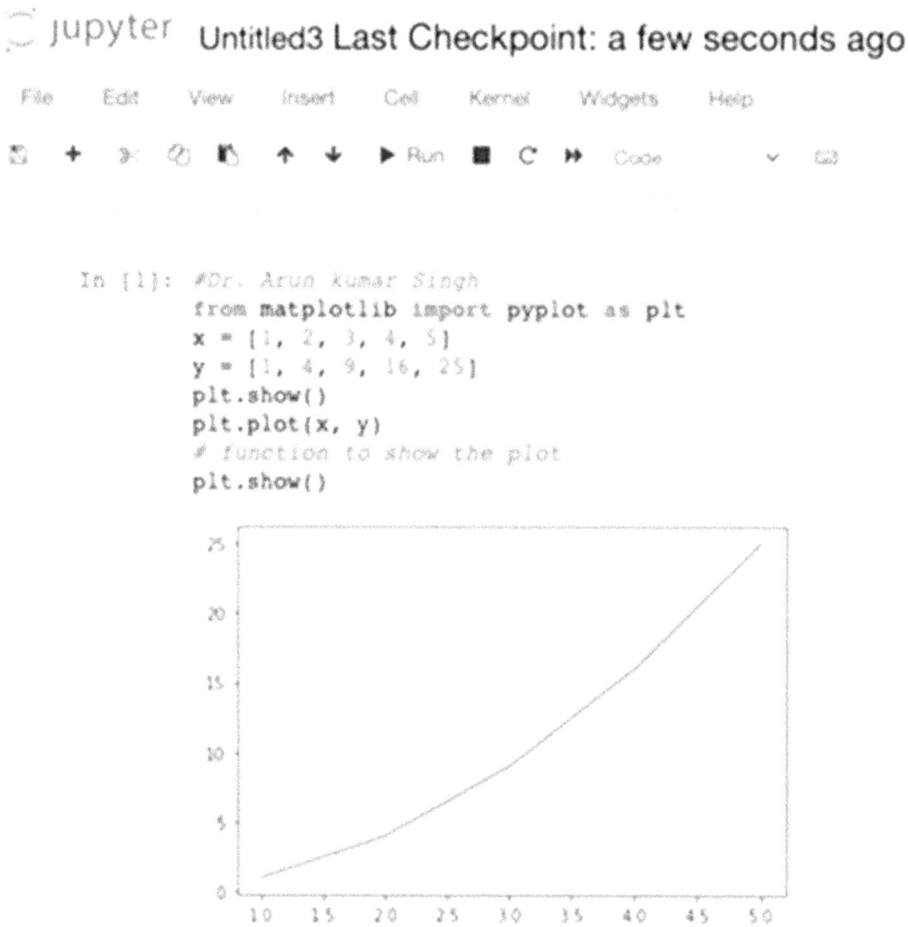

Developers have to create IOTAP devices to make life easy and comfort. small IOT devices use low computational power and memory, so developers choose python scripting language. Nowadays most popular microcontrollers also use python language like Micropython board and software package and other.Again, this is far from a comprehensive list of machine learning libraries. Python is a versatile language, and there is a library available for any preference. The highlighted libraries are a great place to begin your journey. (Wolfram, 1991)

CONCLUSION

Basic points what we have presented In this paper usage of python as a tool in various research areas like Data Science, Machine learning and IOT. Python design philosophy emphasizes code readability with the use of significant indentation. Python is an object oriented, scripted and interpreted language for both learning and real world programming.

Work in this paper first we introduce Python as a language, and give summary about Data science, Machine learning and IOT in digital market, and then details about the packages that are popular in the Data science and Machine learning communities, such as NumPy, SciPy, TensorFlow, Keras, Matplotlib etc. After that, we have shown the working criteria of python for building IOT applications. We used different code examples throughout. Along with Python, there are many other languages are used for Data Science, Machine Learning and for developing IOT devices like Java, C++ etc. But right now most of the developers use python scripting language than Java, C++. Because of its easy syntax, secure coding, and it's simplicity. When it comes to robust and performance, developers choose Python. IOTAP, when integrated with AI, will help developers to work with Python further.

With respect to the future work there is still huge space for this language to serve other upcoming research areas because of its features like simplicity, extensive library, Inbuilt and extensible modules. In future anyone can propose python as a powerful tool which is using by many research communities.

REFERENCES

Anandkumar, R., Dinesh, K., & Ahmed, J. Obaid, Malik, P., Sharma, R., Dumka, A., Singh, R., & Khatak, S. (2022). Securing e-Health application of cloud computing using hyperchaotic image encryption framework. *Computers and Electrical Engineering, 100.* doi:10.1016/j.compeleceng.2022.107860

Engblom, S., & Lukarski, D. (2016). Fast MATLAB compatible sparse assembly on multicore computers. *Parallel Computing*, *56*, 1–17. https://www.researchgate.net/publication/330513589_Internet_of_Things_IOT_Using_Raspberry_Pi. doi:10.1016/j.parco.2016.04.001

Holzinger, A., Dehmer, M., & Jurisica, I. (2014). Knowledge discovery and interactive data mining in bioinformatics - state-of-the-art, future challenges and research direc-tions. *BMC Bioinformatics*, *15*(S6), I1. doi:10.1186/1471-2105-15-S6-I1 PMID:25078282

Jordan, M. I., & Mitchell, T. M. (2015). Machine learning: Trends, perspectives, and prospects. *Science*, *349*(6245), 255–260. doi:10.1126cience.aaa8415 PMID:26185243

Le Cun, Y., Bengio, Y., & Hinton, G. (2015). Deep learning. *Nature*, *521*(7553), 436–444. doi:10.1038/nature14539 PMID:26017442

Naim, A., & Kautish, S. K. (Eds.). (2022). *Building a Brand Image Through Electronic Customer Relationship Management.* IGI Global., doi:10.4018/978-1-6684-5386-5

Naim, A., & Kautish, S. K. (2022). Competitive Trends and Technologies in Business Management. Nova Science Publisher. doi:10.52305/VIXO9830

Python Machine Learning (2020). A Guide To Getting Started. *Built In.*

Singh, A. K. (2017). The Active Impact Of Human Computer Interaction (Hci) On Economic, Cultural And Social Life. *IIOAB Journal, 8*(2), 141-146. https://www.iioab.org/vol8n2

Singh, A. K. (2017). PERSONA OF SOCIAL NETWORKING IN COMPUTING AND INFORMATICS ERA. *International Journal of Computer Science and Network Security (IJCSNS), 17*(4), 95-101. http://search.ijcsns.org/07_book/2017_04.h

Singh, A. K. (2019). A Wireless Networks Flexible Adoptive Modulation and Coding Technique in advanced 4G LTE. *International Journal of Information Technology*, *11*(1), 55-66 . https://link.springer.com/article/10.1007/s41870-018-0173-5 doi:10.1007/s41870-018-0173-5

Singh, A. K. (2020). Digital Era in the Kingdom of Saudi Arabia: Novel Strategies of the Telecom Service Providers Companies. *Webology, 17*(1). , http://www.webology.org/issue.php?volume=1&issue=1&page=2 doi:10.14704/WEB/V17I1/a219

Singh, A. K. (2021). Machine Learning in OpenFlow Network: Comparative Analysis of DDoS Detection Techniques. *The International Arab Journal of Information Technology, 18*(2), 221-226. https://iajit.org/PDF/Vol%2018,%20No.%202/19667.pdf doi:10.34028/iajit/18/2/11

Singh, D. K., Sobti, R., Jain, A., & Malik, P. K. (2022). LeD. (2022). N.: LoRa based intelligent soil and Irrigation Using Machine Learning", Security and Communication Networks, vol. weather condition monitoring with internet of things for precision agriculture in smart cities. *IET Communications*, *16*, 604–618. doi:10.1049/cmu2.12352

Kumar, S. (2017). Security and Management in Network: Security of Network Management versus Management of Network Security (SNM Vs MNS). *International Journal of Computer Science and Network Security (IJCSNS), Volume 17*(5), 166-173. http://search.ijcsns.org/07_book/2017_05.htm

Kumar, S. & Vikash, P. (2021). *IoT for Automation Clustering to Detect Power losses with Efficiency of Energy Consumption and survey of defense machinery against attacks*. CRC Press. https://www.routledge.com/Applied-Soft-Computing-and-Embedded-System-Applications-in-Solar-Energy/Pachauri-Pandey-Sharmu-Nautiyal-Ram/p/book/9780367625122

Kumar, S. (2019). An Intelligent Reallocation of Load for Cluster Cloud Environment. *International Journal of Innovative Technology and Exploring Engineering (IJITEE),* 8(8). https://www.ijitee.org/download/volume-8-issue-8/

Kumar, S. (2019). Texture-based Real-Time Character Extraction and Recognition in Natural Images. *International Journal of Innovative Technology and Exploring Engineering (IJITEE), 8*(8). https://www.ijitee.org/download/volume-8-issue-8/

Kumar, S., Sobti, R., Malik, P., Shrestha, S., Singh, P., & Ghafoor, K. (2022). IoT-Driven Model for Weather and Soil Conditions Based on Precision 2022. Hindawi. doi:10.1155/2022/7283975

Wolfram, S. (1991). *Mathematica: A System for Doing Mathematics by Computer*. Addi-son Wesley Longman Publishing Co., Inc.

Chapter 12
Critical Success Factors of Internet of Things and Digital Marketing

Shad Ahmad Khan
https://orcid.org/0000-0001-7593-3487
University of Buraimi, Oman

Hesham Magd
Modern College of Business and Science, Oman

Bhanupriya Khatri
Chandigarh University, India

Shaina Arora
Chandigarh University, India

Nidhi Sharma
https://orcid.org/0000-0002-3014-2312
Chandigarh University, India

ABSTRACT

The internet of things (IoT) and digital marketing are two rapidly growing fields that have the potential to revolutionize the way businesses operate. However, for businesses to truly take advantage of the opportunities these technologies provide, it is important to understand the critical success factors that must be in place. This paper explores the critical success factors of IoT and digital marketing, including the importance of data analytics, security, and integration with existing systems. For this purpose, bibliometric analysis has been utilized from the Scopus database. It was identified that not many studies have been conducted in this field, and hence a huge gap was explored and addressed. Through the inferences of literature and the practices in the arena of IoT and digital marketing, the critical success factors have been proposed. This chapter will provide valuable insights for organizations looking to implement IoT and digital marketing strategies, as well as for researchers studying the field.

DOI: 10.4018/978-1-6684-8166-0.ch012

1. INTRODUCTION

The world is transitioning to the digital era, where the acceptance of digital technology has become rampant to a level that was never anticipated before. Covid-19 pandemic has acted as a lubricant in the acceptance of the digital technology among people of all walks of life (Bocar et al., 2022; Khan & Magd, 2021; Magd & Khan, 2022). The availability of technology, internet penetration and the reliable digital platforms have further smoothened the acceptance of the digital technology. Electronic Marketing that used to have limitation in certain areas has re-evolved itself in the form of Digital Marketing, and has enabled the sellers across the globe to maximize their market space (Kamal et al., 2022; Fatima et al., 2022) . Further, the smart logistics companies have ensured a faster and reliable delivery network of goods and services across the globe. This enabled the marketers to defeat the limitation of demographic and geographic boundaries to a great extent. With this background, it must be clear that any technology doesn't get successful or gets accepted in isolation, there are many other direct and indirect factors that play a significant role. In short, the success of any activity depends on the critical success factors that is playing a vital role around that activity. In this study, a systematic literature will be undertaken to identify and endorse the critical success factors for Internet of Things and Digital Marketing. The chapter will employ the bibliometric analysis whereby the Scopus database relevant to this study will be utilized to perform bibliometric analysis using vos viewer. The study will also look into the aspects of the countries where the IoT and DM related studies are done to a significant level. Further, the study will try to identify the top contributing authors, whose studies can be utilized by the researchers in their future studies.

2. DECODING DIGITAL MARKETING (DM)

Digital marketing (DM) is a term used to describe the process of promoting a business, product or service through digital channels. These channels include search engines, social media, email marketing, display advertising, and mobile marketing. In today's digital age, businesses of all sizes and industries are using digital marketing to reach their target audience and promote their products and services (Langan et al., 2019; Saleem et al., 2022; Chaffey & Ellis-Chadwick, 2019).

One of the key components of digital marketing is search engine optimization (SEO). SEO is the process of optimizing a website for search engines so that it appears at the top of search engine results pages (SERPs). This can be done by using keywords in the website's content, meta tags, and URLs, as well as building backlinks from other websites. By improving a website's visibility in search results, businesses can increase the chances of attracting potential customers to their website (Matta et al., 2020, Chaffey & Ellis-Chadwick, 2019; Hollebeek & Macky,2019)

Social media marketing is another important aspect of digital marketing. Social media platforms like Facebook, Twitter, Instagram and LinkedIn are powerful tools for businesses to connect with their target audience and promote their products and services. Businesses can use social media to share news, updates and special promotions, as well as to engage with customers through comments and direct messages (Fatima et al., 2022; Langan et al., 2019; Saleem et al., 2022; Hollebeek & Macky,2019).

Email marketing is another effective digital marketing strategy. Businesses can use email marketing to send personalized messages to their target audience, promoting their products and services, and keeping customers informed about new developments. Email marketing can also be used to segment customers into different groups, allowing businesses to tailor their messages to specific audiences.

Display advertising is another digital marketing strategy that involves placing ads on websites and mobile apps. These ads can take many forms, including banner ads, video ads, and rich media ads. Display advertising allows businesses to reach a wide audience and can be targeted to specific demographics, such as age, gender, location, and interests (Hollebeek & Macky,2019; Al-Abdallah et al., 2021).

Lastly, mobile marketing is a digital marketing strategy that focuses on reaching customers through mobile devices. This can include SMS and MMS messaging, mobile apps, and mobile websites. With the rise of smartphones and tablets, mobile marketing has become an essential part of digital marketing, as more and more customers are accessing the internet and making purchases through their mobile devices (Tong et al., 2020; Varnali & Toker,2010).

Digital marketing is a complex and ever-evolving field that requires businesses to stay up-to-date with the latest trends and best practices. By understanding the different components of digital marketing, businesses can develop effective strategies that reach their target audience and promote their products and services in the most efficient way possible. Through SEO, social media marketing, email marketing, display advertising and mobile marketing, businesses can improve their online presence and increase their revenue.

2.1. Problems & Issues in Digital Marketing

Digital marketing has become an essential part of any business strategy in today's digital age. However, with the rapid evolution of digital technology, there are several problems that businesses must navigate to effectively market their products and services online. One of the biggest problems in digital marketing is the overwhelming amount of data and information that businesses must sift through to make informed decisions. With so much data available, it can be difficult for businesses to determine which metrics are the most important to track, and how to analyse and interpret the data effectively. This can lead to poor decision-making and wasted resources (Desai & Vidyapeeth, 2019; Hofacker et al., 2020). Another problem in digital marketing is the constant evolution of technology. As new digital platforms and tools are developed, businesses must continuously adapt their marketing strategies to keep up with the latest trends and best practices. This can be costly and time-consuming, and can make it difficult for businesses to stay ahead of the competition (Faruk et al., 2021).

Another problem that businesses face is the difficulty of reaching and engaging with their target audience. With the rise of ad-blockers and the increasing use of social media, it can be difficult for businesses to reach their target audience through traditional digital marketing channels. This can lead to a decrease in engagement and conversions, and a decrease in ROI (Visser et al., 2019). Additionally, the problem of fake reviews, fake social media followers and likes, and fake traffic to websites is also a major problem in digital marketing. Businesses are often tempted to buy fake reviews, followers, likes, and website traffic to boost their online presence. This practice is not only unethical, but it can also harm the reputation of the business in the long run (Kauffmann, 2020)

Another problem in digital marketing is the lack of personalization. With the rise of digital marketing, businesses are able to reach a large number of people at once, but this can also lead to a lack of personalization in the marketing message. Many businesses send the same message to all of their customers, regardless of their interests or needs, which can lead to a decrease in engagement and conversions (Bahera et al., 2020). Finally, the problem of fraud and scams in digital marketing is also a major concern. With the increasing use of digital platforms and tools, scammers have found new ways to defraud businesses and consumers. This can lead to a loss of trust in digital marketing and a decrease in the effectiveness of digital marketing campaigns (Neuhaus, 2021).

There are several problems that businesses must navigate when it comes to digital marketing. From the overwhelming amount of data and information, to the constant evolution of technology, to the difficulty of reaching and engaging with the target audience, digital marketing can be a complex and challenging field. However, by understanding and addressing these problems, businesses can effectively market their products and services online and stay ahead of the competition.

3. UNDERSTANDING INTERNET OF THINGS

The Internet of Things (IoT) is a rapidly growing technology that is changing the way we live, work, and interact with the world around us. At its core, IoT is the connection of everyday objects and devices to the internet, allowing them to communicate with each other and with us in ways that were previously impossible (Schoder, 2018; Weber & Weber, 2010).

One of the key features of IoT is the use of sensors and other technologies that allow devices to collect data and send it to the internet. These sensors can be used to track things like temperature, humidity, and even the movement of people and objects. This data can then be analysed and used to improve the performance of the device or to create new services and applications (Sestino et al.,, 2020).

One of the most important aspects of IoT is the ability to connect devices and objects that were not previously connected to the internet. This includes things like appliances, vehicles, and even buildings. By connecting these devices, we can create a more efficient and connected world, with devices that are able to communicate with each other and share data in real-time (Sharma et al., 2019; Shabber et al., 2021).

One of the most notable benefits of IoT is the ability to improve the efficiency and performance of systems and devices. By collecting data and analyzing it in real-time, devices can be optimized to work more efficiently, reducing costs and increasing productivity. For example, a factory can use IoT sensors to track the performance of its machines and improve the efficiency of its production process (Sharma et al., 2019; Shabber et al., 2021; Sestino et al.,, 2020).

Another important benefit of IoT is the ability to create new and innovative services and applications. By connecting devices and objects to the internet, we can create new ways for people to interact with their environment and with each other. For example, connected cars can communicate with traffic lights to optimize traffic flow, and smart homes can be controlled remotely through a smartphone app (Sayed et al., 2022; Sharma et al., 2019; Shabber et al., 2021; Astill et al., 2020).

However, with the rapid growth of IoT, there are also concerns about security and privacy. As more devices and objects are connected to the internet, there is an increased risk of cyberattacks and data breaches. It's important for businesses and individuals to take steps to protect their devices and personal information from potential threats (Alwarafy, 2020)

In conclusion, IoT is a rapidly growing technology that is changing the way we live, work, and interact with the world around us. By connecting everyday objects and devices to the internet, we can create a more efficient and connected world, with devices that are able to communicate with each other and share data in real-time. However, it's important to be aware of the potential security and privacy concerns that come with the growth of IoT.

4. CRITICAL SUCCESS FACTORS (CSFS)

Success factors are the key elements that contribute to the achievement of a specific goal or objective (Magd et al., 2022). These factors can vary depending on the type of business or organization, but there are some common success factors that apply to most organizations. In this chapter, in order to start with, we will discuss some of the most important success factors that organizations need to consider in order to achieve their goals (Shamshad et al., 2018; Ashworth et al., 2019; Magd et al., 2022; Alqahtani & Naim, 2022).

1. Clear Goals and Objectives: One of the most important success factors is having clear and measurable goals and objectives. Without a clear understanding of what you want to achieve, it is difficult to set a strategy and measure progress. Setting clear and measurable goals allows organizations to focus their efforts and resources on the most important tasks and activities, and to track progress towards achieving those goals.
2. Strong Leadership: Strong leadership is another critical success factor. A leader who can inspire and motivate employees, set a clear vision, and make difficult decisions is essential for any organization. Strong leaders are able to create a positive work culture, foster teamwork and collaboration, and make sure that employees are aligned with the organization's goals and objectives.
3. Adequate Resources: Having the right resources is another important success factor. This includes financial resources, human resources, and technological resources. Organizations need to have sufficient resources to achieve their goals and objectives. This means that they need to have the right people in the right roles, the right technology and equipment, and the financial resources to support their operations.
4. Strategic Planning: Strategic planning is also a critical success factor. Strategic planning is the process of developing a long-term plan for an organization, which includes identifying goals and objectives, analysing the organization's internal and external environment, and developing a plan to achieve those goals. Strategic planning allows organizations to identify potential opportunities and threats, and to develop a plan to take advantage of opportunities and mitigate risks.
5. Continuous Improvement: Continuous improvement is another important success factor. Organizations need to constantly look for ways to improve their operations, products, and services. This includes identifying areas of weakness and taking steps to improve them. Continuous improvement also involves staying up-to-date with the latest trends and best practices in the industry, and continuously learning and adapting to changes in the market.
6. Strong Communication: Strong communication is a key success factor. Effective communication ensures that everyone in the organization is informed, understands the goals, and knows what is expected of them. Strong communication also helps to build trust and create a positive work environment, which is essential for achieving goals and objectives.
7. Adaptability: Adaptability is another important success factor. Organizations need to be able to adapt to changes in the market and business environment. This means that they need to be able to respond quickly to new opportunities and challenges, and to make changes as needed.

The success factors are the key elements that contribute to the achievement of a specific goal or objective. These factors include clear goals and objectives, strong leadership, adequate resources, strategic planning, continuous improvement, strong communication, and adaptability. Organizations need to consider these factors in order to achieve their goals and objectives and be successful in today's competitive business environment.

4.1. Why Study CSFs

Studying critical success factors (CSFs) is crucial for understanding the key elements that drive business success. CSFs are specific, measurable, and actionable factors that organizations must achieve in order to achieve their goals and objectives. Identifying and understanding CSFs is essential for organizations to effectively manage and grow their business (Ashworth et al., 2019; Magd et al., 2022; Alqahtani & Naim, 2022).

One of the main reasons to study CSFs is to understand the drivers of business success. CSFs are the key elements that determine whether an organization will achieve its goals and objectives. By identifying and understanding these factors, organizations can develop strategies and tactics to achieve success. For example, if customer satisfaction is a critical success factor for a company, the company can focus on improving customer service and implementing customer feedback systems to improve overall satisfaction (Shamshad et al., 2018; Ligori et al., 2022; Khan et al., 2021; Khan et al., 2020).

Another reason to study CSFs is to identify potential risks and challenges. CSFs are not only important for achieving success, but also for identifying potential risks and challenges that may prevent an organization from achieving its goals. By understanding the CSFs, organizations can develop plans and strategies to mitigate these risks and challenges, and ensure that they are on track to achieve their goals (Shamshad et al., 2018; Ashworth et al., 2019).

Studying CSFs also helps organizations to measure their performance and progress. By identifying and understanding the CSFs, organizations can establish clear and measurable goals and objectives. This allows them to track their performance and progress, and make any necessary adjustments to their strategies and tactics to ensure they are on track to achieve their goals.

In addition, studying CSFs is essential for effective decision making. By identifying and understanding the CSFs, organizations can make informed decisions that align with their goals and objectives. This helps to ensure that resources are allocated in the most effective way, and that the organization is taking the right actions to achieve success.

Finally, studying CSFs is important for effective communication and alignment within the organization. By identifying and understanding the CSFs, organizations can communicate their goals and objectives more effectively to all stakeholders, and ensure that everyone is working towards the same objective. This helps to foster a culture of alignment and collaboration within the organization, which is essential for achieving success (Saleem et al., 2022; Ashworth et al., 2019; Neuhaus, 2021). It must be noted that in the modern times, the businesses needs to utilise the digital tools and AI in order to move towards the industry 4.0 (Magd et al., 2022a). Also, the smaller businesses like Self Helf Groups (SHGs), Entrepreneurs (including social entrepreneurs), start-ups etc need to harness the modern technologies (Gangwar & Khan, 2022; Khan et al., 2019; Khan et al., 2022a)

In conclusion, studying critical success factors is essential for understanding the key elements that drive business success. By identifying and understanding CSFs, organizations can develop strategies and tactics to achieve success, identify potential risks and challenges, measure their performance and progress, make informed decisions, and effectively communicate and align within the organization. Understanding CSFs is essential for effective management and growth of any business.

4.2. Challenges of CSFs

Critical success factors (CSFs) are the key areas of focus that organizations must address in order to achieve their goals and objectives. These factors can vary depending on the industry, organization, and goals, but they typically include areas such as customer satisfaction, financial performance, and operational efficiency. While CSFs are essential for organizational success, they also come with their own set of challenges that organizations must overcome (Shamshad et al., 2018; Ashworth et al., 2019).

One of the biggest challenges of CSFs is identifying the right ones. Organizations must be able to identify the key areas that are most critical to their success in order to effectively allocate resources and focus their efforts. This can be a difficult task, as different organizations have different priorities and goals. Additionally, CSFs can change over time, so organizations must be able to adapt and adjust their focus as needed (Fatima et al., 2022; Magd et al., 2022).

Another challenge of CSFs is measuring and tracking progress. Organizations must be able to measure and track their performance in the key areas identified as CSFs in order to determine if they are making progress towards their goals. This can be difficult, as different CSFs may require different metrics and data sources, and data may not always be easily accessible or reliable. Additionally, organizations may struggle to accurately interpret the data they collect and use it to make informed decisions (Fatima et al., 2022; Magd et al., 2022).

A third challenge of CSFs is aligning them with the overall strategic plan. Organizations must be able to align their CSFs with their overall strategic goals and objectives in order to ensure that they are working towards the same end goal. This can be difficult, as different departments and teams may have different priorities and goals, and it can be difficult to get everyone on the same page (Algahtani & Naim,2022; Magd et al., 2022).

Another challenge of CSFs is implementing them effectively. Organizations must be able to effectively allocate resources and implement plans to achieve their CSFs. This can be difficult, as different CSFs may require different resources and strategies, and organizations may struggle to coordinate efforts across departments and teams. Additionally, organizations may not have the necessary resources or expertise to effectively implement their CSFs (Shamshad et al., 2018).

Finally, one of the biggest challenges of CSFs is maintaining focus and commitment over time. Organizations must be able to maintain focus and commitment to their CSFs over time in order to achieve their goals. This can be difficult, as organizations may face unexpected challenges and distractions that can divert their attention away from their CSFs. Additionally, organizations may struggle to maintain the necessary level of commitment and engagement from employees and stakeholders over time (Shamshad et al., 2018; Ashworth et al., 2019; Magd et al., 2022.

In conclusion, critical success factors are essential for organizational success, but they also come with their own set of challenges. Organizations must be able to identify the right CSFs, measure and track progress, align them with the overall strategic plan, implement them effectively, and maintain focus and commitment over time. Overcoming these challenges requires strong leadership, clear communication, and effective collaboration across departments and teams. By addressing these challenges, organizations can ensure that they are focusing on the key areas that are most critical to their success and achieving their goals and objectives.

5. RESEARCH METHODOLOGY

Bibliometric analysis in this case was performed to understand the keywords in the field of CSFs, DM and IoT. For this purpose the relevant data was taken from the Scopus data base that has been recommended by the top bibliometric based researches (Donthu et al., 2021). The keywords used were "Critical Success Factors" OR "CSF", that gave us 2064 documents. The next keyword used was "Critical Success Factors OR CSF" AND " Internet of Things OR IOT", that gave 69 documents; Further the keyword, "Critical Success Factors OR CSF" AND "Digital Marketing" was used to extract 7 documents. Unfortunately, no documents were available on Scopus database on the area of "Critical Success Factors OR CSF" AND "Internet of Things OR IOT" AND "Digital Marketing". The collected data was analysed through voss viewer (Khan et al., 2022; Khatri etc al., 2022; Donthu et al., 2022). Considering the importance and relevance of bibliometric analysis (Pritchard,1969), the co-occurrence analysis, cluster analysis and bibliometric graph was found to be ideal for the purpose of this study. The objectives set were as follows:

1. To explore the number of documents in the domain of CSF, IoT and Digital marketing.
2. To analyse the prominent terms in the arena of CSF, IoT and Digital Marketing
3. To draw meaningful conclusions based on the bibliometric analysis in identification of the CSFs for the IoT and Digital Marketing for the real life businesses.

6. ANALYSIS AND FINDINGS ON BIBLIOMETRIC DATA

The main purpose of running this analysis was to check the prominent terms (keywords) in the field of CSFs, IoT and DM, thus the co-occurrence analysis, bibliometric graphs and cluster analysis is performed through vos viewer softaware ((Khatri et al.,2022; Khan et al., 2022; Pritchard,1969; Donthu et al., 2021).

6.1. Critical Success Factors (CSFs)

As a starting point it was felt necessary to check the prominent domains covered in the field of CSFs. The CSF data available on Scopus database was huge and thus the time period was kept as only one year i.e. 2022 for which a total of 2064 documents were extracted. Upon running the co-occurrence analysis on this data (as presented in table 1), 50 keywords were extracted setting the occurrence threshold as 127. As a matter of surprise, none of the key words extracted were found to be close to the business and marketing area. However, the keywords, like human, humans, review, follow up, article etc were found to have some level of relationship with the business management domain. This speaks volume about the research gaps with regards to CSFs in the field of modern business sciences and management. The reason of documenting 50 keywords was to document the fact that the business management related studies have very less representation in the body of literature of Scopus database.

Table 1. Co-Occurrence analysis of CSF and IoT

S. No	Items	Occurrences	Total link strength
1.	human	1360	12110
2.	article	1034	10978
3.	humans	973	9019
4.	male	798	8930
5.	female	760	8483
6.	controlled study	647	7425
7.	adult	629	6927
8.	cerebrospinal fluid	618	5882
9.	clinical article	391	4134
10.	aged	328	4003
11.	major clinical study	319	3785
12.	nonhuman	352	3667
13.	nuclear magnetic resonance imaging	337	3654
14.	biological marker	286	3285
15.	metabolism	294	2910
16.	biomarkers	266	2901
17.	cohort analysis	220	2794
18.	retrospective study	252	2726
19.	animal	272	2700
20.	animals	272	2700
21.	animal experiment	201	2388
22.	middle aged	209	2369
23.	alzheimer disease	197	2363
24.	mouse	211	2317
25.	unclassified drug	187	2117
26.	cerebrospinal fluid analysis	175	2052
27.	follow up	187	2049
28.	tau protein	156	1991
29.	genetics	200	1967
30.	animal model	156	1960
31.	human tissue	161	1952
32.	human cell	164	1888
33.	pathology	176	1869
34.	case report	211	1867
35.	mice	158	1784
36.	amyloid beta protein	139	1752
37.	diagnostic imaging	153	1738
38.	animal tissue	143	1729

Continued on following page

Table 1. Continued

S. No	Items	Occurrences	Total link strength
39.	complication	178	1717
40.	retrospective studies	157	1665
41.	neuroimaging	139	1588
42.	enzyme linked immunosorbent assay	139	1573
43.	child	161	1518
44.	interleukin 6	142	1450
45.	granulocyte macrophage colony stimulating factor	150	1447
46.	procedures	155	1428
47.	brain	136	1313
48.	cytokine	127	1212
49.	granulocyte colony stimulating factor	134	1131
50.	review	128	773

Source: Extracted from scopus.com via Vos Viewer (authors calculation)

6.2. Critical Success Factors & IoT

The next step was to check the intersecting terms between CSFs and IoT. The data extracted from Scopus database showed only 69 documents since 2013. Thus, in order to maximise the number of keywords extraction the occurrence threshold was kept as 4, that gave us only 17 keywords as presented in the table 2. The researchers also checked the bibliometric graph in order to have an understanding of the network of these keywords in a better way Figure 1.

Table 2. Co-Occurrence analysis of CSF and IoT

S. No	Items	Occurrences	Total link strength
1.	internet of things (iot)	60	165
2.	critical success factor	37	107
3.	industry 4.0	13	27
4.	information management	7	25
5.	big data	6	19
6.	success factors	6	16
7.	decision making	5	23
8.	digital transformation	5	15
9.	internet	5	12
10.	artificial intelligence	4	9
11.	cloud computing	4	13
12.	engineering education	4	6
13.	information systems	4	18
14.	machine learning	4	8
15.	smart devices	4	17
16.	surveys	4	16
17.	technology	4	18

Source: Extracted from scopus.com via Vos Viewer (authors calculation)

Figure 1. Bibliometric Graph- CSFs and IoT
Source: *Extracted from scopus.com via Vos Viewer (authors calculation)*

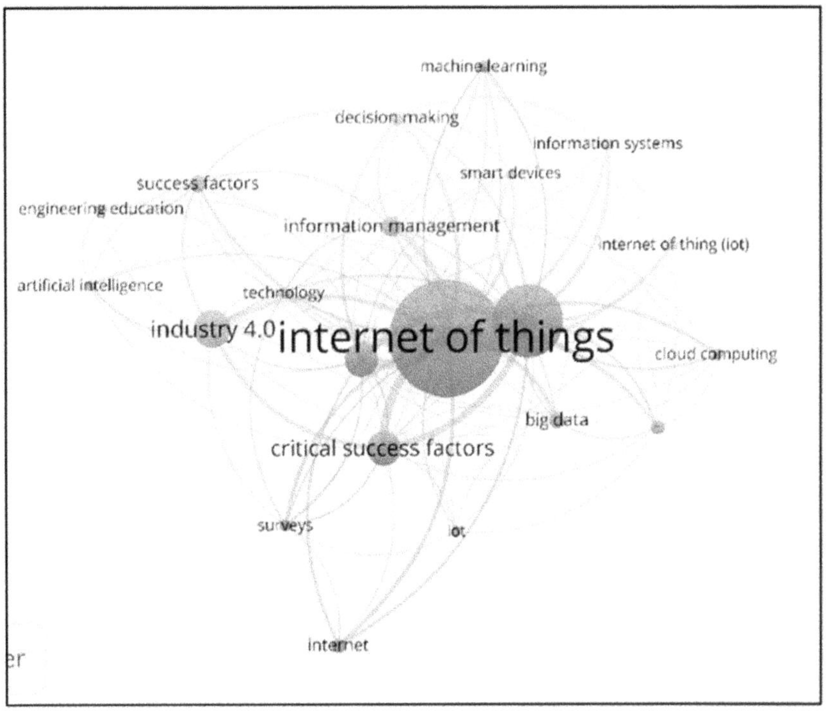

The IoT is related with the CSFs mainly through the keywords like surveys and internet. The application of IoT in the field of research has been dominated by these two areas. However, the components like AI, big data and cloud computing were also found to have a network with CSFs and IoT.

6.3. Critical Success Factors & DM

The relationship between CSFs and DM was also intended to be a major objective of this study, however, only 7 documents were extracted from the Scopus database, the oldest being published in the year 2017. As a matter of fact, no analysis could have given any good results. However, the researchers still made an attempt to understand the concept. There was total 50 keywords in the field of DM and CSFs. When Co-occurrence analysis was attempted, it was discovered that except one i.e., marketing, all the other items occurred only once. Thus, it was decided to document all the 50 items so as to understand the whole population of items covered in the studies in the field of CSFs and DM as presented in Table 3.

Table 3. Co-Occurrence analysis of CSF and DM

S. No	Items	Occurrences	Total link strength
1.	marketing	2	32
2.	adoption	1	22
3.	article	1	22
4.	awareness	1	22
5.	budget	1	22
6.	budgets	1	22
7.	cell phone	1	22
8.	commerce	1	22
9.	commercial phenomena	1	22
10.	expectancy	1	22
11.	functional status	1	22
12.	health care delivery	1	22
13.	human	1	22
14.	humans	1	22
15.	internet	1	22
16.	interview	1	22
17.	manager	1	22
18.	mobile phone	1	22
19.	negligence	1	22
20.	nigeria	1	22
21.	organization and management	1	22
22.	physician	1	22
23.	procedures	1	22
24.	contents	1	10
25.	customer engagement	1	10
26.	digital marketing	3	10
27.	digital storage	1	10
28.	digital strategies	1	10
29.	digital strategy	1	10
30.	experience	1	10
31.	omnichannel	1	10
32.	sales	1	10
33.	social media monitoring	1	10
34.	social networking (online)	1	10
35.	b2b	1	5
36.	business	1	5
37.	computer aided	1	5
38.	content analysis	1	5

Continued on following page

Table 3. Continued

S. No	Items	Occurrences	Total link strength
39.	content mining	1	5
40.	qda miner	1	5
41.	app user engagement	1	4
42.	b2b marketing	1	4
43.	germany	1	4
44.	insights	1	4
45.	linear regression	1	4
46.	literature review	1	4
47.	martech	1	4
48.	mobile crm	1	4
49.	higher education	1	2
50.	relationship marketing	1	2

Source: Extracted from scopus.com via Vos Viewer (authors calculation)

Further, the bibliometric graph was obtained for this data, that was able to give a meaningful conclusion to this analysis as presented in figure 2.

Figure 2. Bibliometric graph- CSFs and DM
Source: *Extracted from scopus.com via Vos Viewer (authors calculation)*

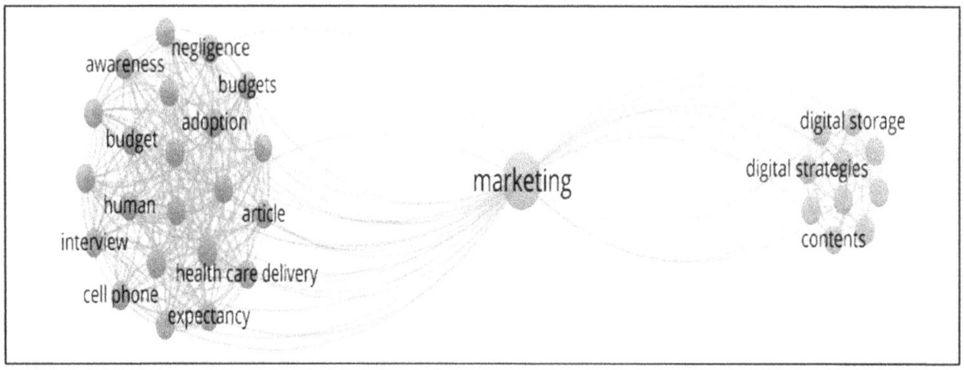

As visible from the figure 2, all the keywords are concentrated in two parts. The first part deals with the items like negligence, budget, delivery, interview, human etc., that can be termed as non-digital items. However, the second cluster deals with the items like contents, digital storage, digital strategies etc and thus, can be named as the digital cluster.

6.4. CSF, IoT, and Digital Marketing

No studies were found in the combined area of CSF and IoT and DM, thus, the data compilation was done for the two data sets extracted for CSF and IoT; and, CSF and DM. This compiled data however was dominated by the CSF-IoT documents. Thus, evolving on any conclusion would have resulted in a biasness on the part of the researchers and would have defeated the purpose. However, it was felt worthy to document the data as presented in table 4, to prove the dominance of IoT related data.

Table 4. Co-Occurrence analysis of CSF, IoT, and digital marketing

S. No	Items	Occurrences	Total link strength
1.	internet of things (iot)	60	168
2.	critical success factor	37	110
3.	industry 4.0	13	27
4.	information management	7	25
5.	big data	6	20
6.	internet	6	12
7.	success factors	6	16
8.	decision making	5	23
9.	digital transformation	5	15
10.	artificial intelligence	4	9
11.	cloud computing	4	14
12.	digital storage	4	8
13.	engineering education	4	6
14.	information systems	4	18
15.	machine learning	4	8
16.	smart devices	4	17
17.	surveys	4	16
18.	technology	4	18

Source: Extracted from scopus.com via Vos Viewer (authors calculation)

Further the cluster analysis was also performed on this data, and all the items were divided into five clusters as presented in table 5. The bibliometric graph (Figure 3) was generated, and based on the graph, arriving at certain level of conclusion was possible.

Table 5. Cluster analysis of CSF, IoT, and digital marketing

Cluster 1 (6 items)				
big data	**Cluster 2 (5 items)**			
cloud computing	Artificial Intelligence	**Cluster 3 (3 items)**		
critical success factor	Engineering education	internet	**Cluster 4 (3 items)**	
digital storage	industry 4.0	internet of things (iot)	decision making	**Cluster 5 (2 items)**
digital transformation	success factors	surveys	information management	information management
internet of things (iot)	technology		smart devices	machine learning

Source: Extracted from scopus.com via Vos Viewer (authors calculation

Figure 3. Bibliometric graph- CSFs, IoT and DM
Source: *Extracted from scopus.com via Vos Viewer (authors calculation)*

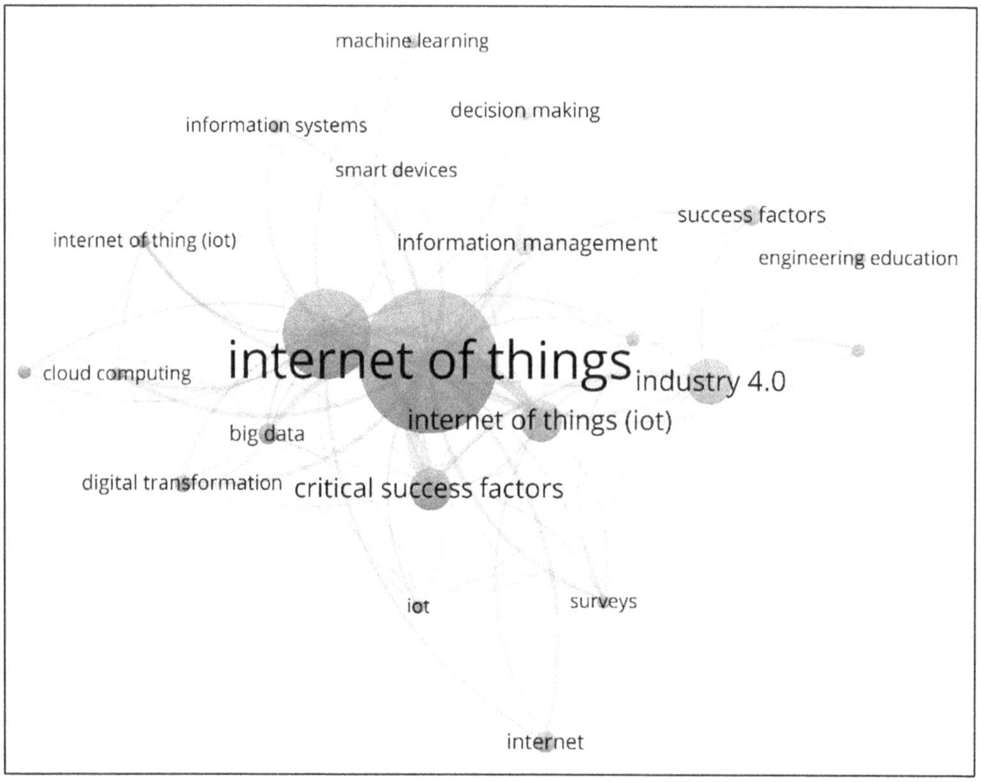

7. CONCLUSION: CRITICAL SUCCESS FACTORS OF DM AND IoT

Digital marketing and the Internet of Things (IoT) are two of the most important trends in today's digital landscape. Both have the potential to revolutionize the way businesses operate, but to take full advantage of these trends, companies must understand the critical success factors that are essential for achieving their goals. One of the most important critical success factors for digital marketing is the development of a clear and effective strategy. A digital marketing strategy should clearly define the target audience, goals, and key performance indicators (KPIs) that will be used to measure success. Additionally, companies must have a deep understanding of the digital channels and tools that will be used to reach and engage with their target audience, such as social media, search engine optimization (SEO), and email marketing.

Another critical success factor for digital marketing is the ability to collect and analyze data. Digital marketing generates a huge amount of data, and companies must have the ability to collect, store, and analyze this data to understand their target audience and optimize their campaigns. This requires a robust data management and analysis system, as well as a team of experts who are able to extract meaningful insights from the data. Another critical success factor for digital marketing and IoT is the ability to personalize the customer experience. With the explosion of data and new technologies, companies can now personalize their marketing messages and offers to the individual needs and preferences of their customers. This requires the ability to collect and analyze data on customer behavior and preferences, as well as the ability to use this data to tailor the customer experience.

For IoT, the critical success factors are security and privacy. As more and more devices are connected to the internet, security and privacy become increasingly important. Companies must ensure that their IoT devices and systems are secure and that customer data is protected from unauthorized access and breaches. Additionally, companies must have a clear and transparent privacy policy in place to ensure that customers understand how their data is being collected, stored, and used.

Finally, collaboration is a critical success factor for both digital marketing and IoT. Companies must work closely with their partners and customers to understand their needs and goals, and to develop solutions that meet those needs. This requires open communication, shared goals, and a willingness to work together to achieve success.

To put things into proper words the Critical Success Factors for the Digital Marketing through IoT would be:

1. **Developing a clear and well-defined digital marketing strategy:** A digital marketing strategy is a plan that outlines the goals, objectives, and tactics that a business will use to reach its target audience through digital channels. A well-defined strategy helps businesses to focus their efforts, set measurable goals, and allocate resources effectively.
2. **Understanding your target audience:** Understanding who your target audience is and what they are looking for is essential to creating a successful digital marketing campaign. By analyzing customer demographics, behavior, and interests, businesses can tailor their messaging and targeting to reach the right audience at the right time.
3. **Creating valuable and relevant content:** The quality of the content that a business produce is crucial to the success of its digital marketing efforts. Valuable and relevant content helps businesses to attract and engage their target audience, build trust and credibility, and ultimately convert leads into customers.
4. **Leveraging the power of social media:** Social media platforms like Facebook, Instagram, Twitter, and LinkedIn are powerful tools for reaching and engaging with customers. By building a strong presence on these platforms, businesses can increase brand awareness, drive website traffic, and generate leads.
5. **Utilizing search engine optimization (SEO) and pay-per-click (PPC) advertising:** SEO and PPC advertising are powerful tools for driving website traffic and generating leads. By optimizing website content and meta tags for search engines, businesses can improve their visibility in search

results and reach more customers. PPC advertising allows businesses to target specific keywords and demographics, and increase visibility on search engines.

6. **Measuring and analyzing campaign performance:** Measuring and analyzing the performance of a digital marketing campaign is critical to determining its success. By tracking key metrics such as website traffic, conversion rates, and return on investment (ROI), businesses can identify areas of improvement and adjust their strategy accordingly.

In conclusion, developing a clear and well-defined digital marketing strategy, understanding the target audience, creating valuable and relevant content, leveraging social media, utilizing SEO and PPC advertising, and measuring and analyzing campaign performance are the key success factors of digital marketing. By focusing on these factors, businesses can improve their online presence and reach more customers. Further it must be understood that, digital marketing is a powerful tool for businesses looking to reach a large audience and promote their products and services. However, the success of digital marketing efforts can be impacted by a variety of factors. Companies should focus on setting clear goals and objectives, understanding their target audience, creating valuable and engaging content, using SEO and social media effectively, measuring the success of campaigns using analytics, and being adaptable to the ever-changing digital landscape. By considering these critical success factors, companies can ensure that their digital marketing efforts are effective and drive results.

REFERENCES

Al-Abdallah, G., Khair, N., & Elmarakby, R. (2021). The impact of social networking sites on luxury vehicles purchase decision process in Gulf Cooperation Council countries. *Journal of International Consumer Marketing*, *33*(5), 559–577. doi:10.1080/08961530.2020.1867023

Alqahtani, H., & Naim, A. (2022). Critical Success Factors for Transforming CRM to SCRM for building E-CRM. In *Building a Brand Image Through Electronic Customer Relationship Management* (pp. 139–168). IGI Global. doi:10.4018/978-1-6684-5386-5.ch007

Alwarafy, A., Al-Thelaya, K. A., Abdallah, M., Schneider, J., & Hamdi, M. (2020). A survey on security and privacy issues in edge-computing-assisted internet of things. *IEEE Internet of Things Journal*, *8*(6), 4004–4022. doi:10.1109/JIOT.2020.3015432

Ashworth, S., Tucker, M., & Druhmann, C. K. (2019). Critical success factors for facility management employer's information requirements (EIR) for BIM. *Facilities*, *37*(1/2), 103–118. doi:10.1108/F-02-2018-0027

Astill, J., Dara, R. A., Fraser, E. D., Roberts, B., & Sharif, S. (2020). Smart poultry management: Smart sensors, big data, and the internet of things. *Computers and Electronics in Agriculture*, *170*, 105291. doi:10.1016/j.compag.2020.105291

Behera, R. K., Gunasekaran, A., Gupta, S., Kamboj, S., & Bala, P. K. (2020). Personalized digital marketing recommender engine. *Journal of Retailing and Consumer Services*, *53*, 101799. doi:10.1016/j.jretconser.2019.03.026

Bocar, A. C., Khan, S. A., & Epoc, F. (2022). COVID-19 Work from Home Stressors and the Degree of its Impact: Employers and Employees Actions. *International Journal of Technology Transfer and Commercialisation. Inderscience, 19*(2), 270–291.

Chaffey, D., & Ellis-Chadwick, F. (2019). *Digital marketing.*

Desai, V., & Vidyapeeth, B. (2019). Digital marketing: A review. *International Journal of Trend in Scientific Research and Development, 5*(5), 196–200. doi:10.31142/ijtsrd23100

Donthu, N., Kumar, S., Mukherjee, D., Pandey, N., & Lim, W. M. (2021). How to conduct a bibliometric analysis: An overview and guidelines. *Journal of Business Research, 133*, 285–296. doi:10.1016/j.jbusres.2021.04.070

Faruk, M., Rahman, M., & Hasan, S. (2021). How digital marketing evolved over time: A bibliometric analysis on scopus database. *Heliyon, 7*(12), 08603. doi:10.1016/j.heliyon.2021.e08603 PMID:34988311

Fatima, S., Alqahtani, H., Naim, A., & Alma'alwi, F. (2022). E-CRM Through Social Media Marketing Activities for Brand Awareness, Brand Image, and Brand Loyalty. In *Building a Brand Image Through Electronic Customer Relationship Management* (pp. 109–138). IGI Global. doi:10.4018/978-1-6684-5386-5.ch006

Gangwar, V., & Khan, S. (2022). Analyzing the Role of Micro-Entrepreneurship and Self-Help Groups (SHGs) in Women Empowerment and Development. In. M. Arafat, I. Ali, A. Khan, & H. Balhareth (Eds.). Driving Factors for Venture Creation and Success in Agricultural Entrepreneurship. IGI-Global. doi:10.4018/978-1-6684-2349-3.ch011

Hofacker, C., Golgeci, I., Pillai, K. G., & Gligor, D. M. (2020). Digital marketing and business-to-business relationships: A close look at the interface and a roadmap for the future. *European Journal of Marketing, 54*(6), 1161–1179. doi:10.1108/EJM-04-2020-0247

Hollebeek, L. D., & Macky, K. (2019). Digital content marketing's role in fostering consumer engagement, trust, and value: Framework, fundamental propositions, and implications. *Journal of Interactive Marketing, 45*(1), 27–41. doi:10.1016/j.intmar.2018.07.003

Kamal, S., Naim, A., Magd, H., Khan, S. A., & Khan, F. M. (2022). The Relationship Between E-Service Quality, Ease of Use, and E-CRM Performance Referred by Brand Image. In *Building a Brand Image Through Electronic Customer Relationship Management* (pp. 84–108). IGI Global. doi:10.4018/978-1-6684-5386-5.ch005

Kauffmann, E., Peral, J., Gil, D., Ferrández, A., Sellers, R., & Mora, H. (2020). A framework for big data analytics in commercial social networks: A case study on sentiment analysis and fake review detection for marketing decision-making. *Industrial Marketing Management, 90*, 523–537. doi:10.1016/j.indmarman.2019.08.003

Khan, S. A., Devi, T. P., Ligori, T. A. A., & Saleem, M. (2020). Customer Satisfaction and Customer Loyalty in Online Shopping: A Study On University Students of Bhutan. *Delhi Business Review, 21*(2), 11–22. doi:10.51768/dbr.v21i2.212202002

Khan, S.A, Epoc, F., Gangwar,V.P., Ligori T.A.A, Ansari, Z.A. (2021). Will Online banking sustain in Bhutan post Covid – 19? A quantitative analysis of the customer e-satisfaction and e-loyalty in the Kingdom of Bhutan, *Transnational Marketing Journal*, *9*(3), 607-624. doi:10.33182/tmj.v9i3.1288

Khan. S.A. & Magd. H. (2021). Empirical Examination of MS Teams in Conducting Webinar: Evidence from International Online Program conducted in Oman. *Journal of Content, Community and Communication, 14*(7). doi:10.31620/JCCC.12.21/13

Khan, S. A., Magd, H., Al Shamsi, I. R., & Masoom, K. (2022a). Social Entrepreneurship Through Innovations in Agriculture. In Magd. H., Syed, R.T., Spicer, D. (Eds). International Perspectives on Value Creation and Sustainability Through Social Entrepreneurship (pp. 209-222). IGI Global. doi:10.4018/978-1-6684-4666-9.ch010

Khan, S. A., Magd, H., & Epoc, F. (2022). Application of Data Management System in Business to Business Electronic Commerce. In A. Naim & P. K. Malik (Eds.), *Competitive Trends and Technologies in Business Management* (pp. 109–124). Nova Science Publishers.

Khan, S. A., Sharma, P.P., & Thoudam, P. (2019). Role of Attitude and Entrepreneurship Education towards Entrepreneurial Orientation among Business Students of Bhutan. *International Journal of Recent Technology and Engineering (IJRTE), 10*(10), 335-342.

Khatri, B., Arora, S., Magd, H., & Khan, S. A. K. (2022). Bibliometric Analysis of Social Entrepreneurship. In Magd. H., Syed, R.T., Spicer, D. (Eds). International Perspectives on Value Creation and Sustainability Through Social Entrepreneurship (pp. 46-60). IGI Global. doi:10.4018/978-1-6684-4666-9.ch003

Langan, R., Cowley, S., & Nguyen, C. (2019). The state of digital marketing in academia: An examination of marketing curriculum's response to digital disruption. *Journal of Marketing Education*, *41*(1), 32–46. doi:10.1177/0273475318823849

Ligori, T. A. A., Suresh, N., Khan, S. A., Rabgay, T., & Yezer, K. (2022). The mediating effect of university image on the relationship between curriculum and student satisfaction: An empirical study of the Royal University of Bhutan. *International Journal of Pluralism and Economics Education. Inderscience, 13*(2), 192–208.

Magd, H., Jonathan, H., Khan, S. A., & El Geddawy, M. (2022a). *Artificial Intelligence—The Driving Force of Industry 4.0. A Roadmap for Enabling Industry 4.0 by Artificial Intelligence*. Wiley.

Magd, H., Nzomkunda, A., Negi, S., & Ansari, M. (2022). Critical Success Factors of E-Learning Implementation in Higher Education Institutions: A Proposed Framework for Success. *Global Business and Management Research*, 14.

Matta, H., Gupta, R., & Agarwal, S. (2020, June). Search Engine optimization in digital marketing: present scenario and future scope. In *2020 International Conference on Intelligent Engineering and Management (ICIEM)* (pp. 530-534). IEEE. 10.1109/ICIEM48762.2020.9160016

Neuhaus, T. (2021). A nudge psychology perspective on digital marketing and communication: learning from the Nigerian scam. In *Innovative Perspectives on Corporate Communication in the Global World* (pp. 122–140). IGI Global. doi:10.4018/978-1-7998-6799-9.ch007

Pritchard, A. (1969). Statistical bibliography or bibliometrics. *The Journal of Documentation*, *25*(4), 348–349.

Saleem, M., Khan, S. A., & Magd, H. (2022). Content Marketing Framework for Building Brand Image: A Case Study of Sohar International School, Oman. In Building a Brand Image Through Electronic Customer Relationship Management (pp. 64-83). IGI Global.

Sayed, A., Himeur, Y., Bensaali, F., & Amira, A. (2022). Artificial intelligence with IoT for energy efficiency in buildings. In *Emerging Real-World Applications of Internet of Things* (pp. 233–252). CRC Press. doi:10.1201/9781003304203-12

Schoder, D. (2018). Introduction to the Internet of Things. *Internet of things A to Z: technologies and applications*, 1-50.

Sestino, A., Prete, M. I., Piper, L., & Guido, G. (2020). Internet of Things and Big Data as enablers for business digitalization strategies. *Technovation*, *98*, 102173. doi:10.1016/j.technovation.2020.102173

Shabber, S. M., Bansal, M., Devi, P. M., & Jain, P. (2021, December). iHAS: An Intelligent Home Automation Based System for Smart City. In *2021 IEEE International Symposium on Smart Electronic Systems (iSES)(Formerly iNiS)* (pp. 48-52). IEEE. 10.1109/iSES52644.2021.00023

Shamshad, M., Sarim, M., Akhtar, A., & Tabash, M. I. (2018). Identifying critical success factors for sustainable growth of Indian banking sector using interpretive structural modeling (ISM). *International Journal of Social Economics*, *45*(8), 1189–1204. doi:10.1108/IJSE-10-2017-0436

Sharma, N., Shamkuwar, M., & Singh, I. (2019). The history, present and future with IoT. In *Internet of Things and Big Data Analytics for Smart Generation* (pp. 27–51). Springer. doi:10.1007/978-3-030-04203-5_3

Singh, E. H., Wangda, S., Khan, S., & Khan, S. A. (2020). Exploring the obstacles for start-ups in Bhutan: From a prevented entrepreneurs perspective. *International Journal of Innovation. Creativity and Change*, *11*(04), 70–87.

Tong, S., Luo, X., & Xu, B. (2020). Personalized mobile marketing strategies. *Journal of the Academy of Marketing Science*, *48*(1), 64–78. doi:10.100711747-019-00693-3

Varnali, K., & Toker, A. (2010). Mobile marketing research: The-state-of-the-art. *International Journal of Information Management*, *30*(2), 144–151. doi:10.1016/j.ijinfomgt.2009.08.009

Visser, M., Sikkenga, B., & Berry, M. (2019). *Digital marketing fundamentals: From strategy to ROI.* Routledge. doi:10.4324/9781003021674

Weber, R. H., & Weber, R. (2010). *Internet of things* (Vol. 12). Springer. doi:10.1007/978-3-642-11710-7

Chapter 13
Explanatory Factors of the Behavior of Passage From Online Banking to Mobile Banking by Customers

Moez Ltifi
https://orcid.org/Orcid
Shaqra University, Saudi Arabia & Sfax University, Tunisia

ABSTRACT

This study is exploratory in nature and influences the behavioral change factors of online customers. This design was neglected in early studies. The main objective of this study is to empirically test the explanatory factors of the changeover behavior from online banking to mobile banking by customers, as well as to test their degree of importance. The data was collected from a sample of 430 Saudi customers. Participants were selected on the basis of convenience sampling. The results showed the advantage of using banking services, sources of enabling conditions, the influence of groups and the technology used. The financial advantage of the mobile bank is the most important factor in the influence of its influence on the attitude of the customers. Again, the conditions of the facilitating sources and the conditions of the technological sources are the two factors in the explanatory power of the perceived control of behavior.

INTRODUCTION

Today, the international banking sector is expanding in monetary and financial areas in line with exponential technological development. Relationships between banks and their customers have changed considerably (Danyali, 2018; Ltifi and Hichri, 2021). Online banking is transformed into an indispensable factor of e-commerce and plays a key role in its implementation.

The rapid growth of information technology has led to significant changes in the form of money as well as the transfer of resources in the banking sector. Then, he introduced new concepts and definitions such as electronic money and its ways of electronic transfer. These two concepts can install a new

DOI: 10.4018/978-1-6684-8166-0.ch013

bank model; nowadays it is the "electronic bank". Using the accessibility of the Internet for all and with its level of development, the ways of providing banking services have changed significantly in mobile banks and virtual banks (Taghavi Fard and Torabi, 2009; Zhu et al., 2022; Mittal and Agrawal, 2022).

Nowadays, banks provide virtual banking services to their customers over the Internet in many developed countries, and customers can easily do most of their banking business by connecting to banks home pages using their unique passwords without their actual presence in banks (Danyali, 2018).

The high level of competition between banks and even with non-bank institutes leads to the creation of a platform to facilitate commercial transactions with customers. For this, Motamedi, (2010), defines the electronic banking as the provision of certain facilities to customers who can access banking services without the need for their physical presence in a bank using secure interfaces. At this level, customers use a lot of electronic banking services such as access to accounts, transfer of money, payment of bills ... (Yu, 2014).

In this sector, mobile banking is considered one of the latest technological advances that offer many benefits to banks and their customers. This position allows the bank to stay in a competitive environment, reduce costs, further develop telecommunication activities, save the maximum possible time and money, easier access with greater speed in supply services can be listed as benefits that mobile banking has presented to customers. It is highly justified for bank managers to identify the factors and elements that can lead to the use of mobile services (Danyali, 2018; Mittal and Agrawal, 2022).

The question here is to determine the factors that affect the customer to accept and use this type of service. The mobile banking service will offer more appropriate planning in increasing the number of mobile banking users and the faster use of this modern phenomenon for both banks and users of this high-tech service (Mittal and Agrawal, 2022).

Comprehensive use of smart mobile phones with many consumers will offer banks the ability to absorb potential customers in a competitive environment and increase their profitability by introducing online electronic banking that is compatible with customer needs and eliminate the problems and limitations of the traditional banking system (Zhu et al., 2022).

Saudi Arabia is a young country in e-commerce and virtual banks, having a long way to go to reach an acceptable rank. The advent of modern technology has introduced new requirements for the processing and exchange of data, infrastructures, tools and appropriate solutions to introduce modern banking systems of service delivery.

To forecast the evolving needs of banking services in Saudi Arabia, we can draw on the experience of developed countries and the growth of e-commerce and online banking. Referring to the current traditional methods in the national banks and the inadequacy of these methods in the provision of new banking services. It is mandatory to put in place the necessary infrastructure in the banks, which fortunately begins to developed in the country. In addition, it is requested to promote electronic banking and other modern banking services (Vafaei, 2009).

REVIEW OF THE LITERATURE AND PROBLEMATIC

The rapid development of telecommunication technology and mobile applications has the effect of multiplying the progress of mobile commerce for organizations and customers. The most common example of mobile commerce is mobile banking, which allows customers to bank at various locations via their available smart devices. Although this service is a newly created service and represents a trend in the banking sector, but, it may encounter a significant problem in the development process due to the non-acceptance of its practical use by users (Mittal and Agrawal, 2022).

It is therefore necessary to conduct some studies to identify the influencing factors involved. This problem is likely to have a huge effect on the level of application and expansion of mobile banking, because we are facing a technology that is not widely welcomed by many public customers in the country. For the moment, despite the benefits offered and the substantial investments of the banks, the mobile bank has not received satisfactory acceptance and recognition by the public users

Therefore, it is decisive to determine the key compromised factors in the acceptance and use of this new technology (Amadeh and Jafarpour, 2009). The acceptance of technology by target groups has been one of the major research topics in the field of information technology in recent decades.

Planned behavior theory is considered to be one of the widely considered theories by researchers (Taylor and Todd, 1995). The results show that this theory provides a logical theoretical framework for understanding the reasons for accepting different types of information systems. The theory has advanced only three attitude factors (utility, accessibility, compatibility); subjective norm (peer and superior); and perceived behavioral control (resources, technology, self-efficacy) play an important role in changing the customer's behavior and decision and, ultimately, the practical use of the system by the customers.

In general, a more favorable attitude, a subjective norm and a higher attitude of behavioral control will reinforce the intention of the individuals to adopt the behavior (Elahi et al., 2012, Visentin et al, 2019; Zhu et al., 2022).

Today, all businesses are looking to captivate more customers and increase their satisfaction. It is especially fatal in the case of banks that are usually in contact with their customers. On the other hand, competition between banks and institutions for interest-free loans and other forms of financial resources is growing rapidly. Yet, it is useful to create competitiveness for the survival of banks. Modern bank with services deeply integrated with the information and telecommunications technologies that represent very important factors in the development of the competitiveness of the banks, by inducing the attraction of the customers and the increase of their satisfaction (Amiri, 2009; Mittal and Agrawal, 2022).

IMPORTANCE OF THE STUDY

The banking sector is evolving exponentially. Banks have undergone great changes with the development of the international economy and the competitiveness of the markets. Technology represents a great force that transcends geographical boundaries and industrial barriers and leads to the development of new services. According to available statistics and figures, the influence coefficient of the use of mobile telephony is higher than that of any other technology. All of this has led mobile commerce towards a universal revolution, which is progressing more and more rapidly in developing countries and in developed countries (Zhu et al., 2022).

In recent years, information technology has had a lot of impact on banking institutions. Banks have the ability to provide distinguished products and services to their customers. However, with the emergence of various types of technologies, the nature of providing financial services has changed a lot. Mobile banking has evolved into a wireless communications interface that enables customers to generate value in banking transactions (Mittal and Agrawal, 2022).

Smart phones (mobiles) represent the most modern technique of providing banking services is the provision of financial and banking services. Although the experience of using smart phones for banking and financial operations is not too long, we have noticed great progress in a short time, which indicates the important development of this modern technology of the electronic banking in the future (Wati et al, 2009; Zhu et al., 2022).

It should be mentioned that mobile banking technology has developed in recent years as a method of maintaining customer loyalty and increasing market share. In short, our study aims to study the factors influencing the behavioral change of online banking customers to mobile banking and have an effective role in increasing the number of customers using mobile banking (Mittal and Agrawal, 2022).

Mattila et al. (2003) have shown that household income and education play a major role in the adoption of Internet banking among Finnish customers, while the perceived difficulty of using a computer and the lack of personal services on the Internet are considered as the main obstacles to the use of Internet banking. Similarly, Danyali, (2018) has shown the importance of the explanatory factors and their importance for the use of mobile banking in the Iranian context (Alzaidi and Shehawy, 2022).

Research hypotheses:

H1. There is a significant relationship between the perceived benefit of using mobile banking and the attitude of customers towards the bank.

H2. There is a significant relationship between the complexity of using mobile banking and the attitude of customers towards the bank.

H3. There is a significant relationship between the compatibility of mobile phone use and the attitude of customers towards the bank.

H4. There is a significant relationship between peer groups and subjective norms.

H5. There is a significant relationship between higher groups and subjective norms.

H6. There is a significant relationship between personal effectiveness and perceived behavioral control.

H7. There is a significant relationship between the sources of enabling conditions and perceived behavioral control.

H8. There is a significant relationship between the sources of technological conditions and perceived behavioral control.

H9. There is a significant relationship between the attitude of bank customers and the tendency of their behavior to use mobile banking.

H10. There is a significant relationship between the subjective norms of the bank's customers and the tendency of their behavior to use mobile banking.

H11. There is a significant relationship between perceived behavioral control and the tendency of their behavior to use mobile banking.

H12. There is a significant relationship between the trend of using mobile banking and the actual behavior of customers with mobile banking.

Method

The main objective of this study is to empirically test the prediction of a theory with a quantitative method to provide a better and broader view of the situation and in a faster and more efficient way. This study was conducted in a real environment, objective and dynamic organization, based on concrete results.

The adopted population is made up of 430 customers of the "Al-Rajihi" bank of "Al-Riyadh" province who used Internet banking and mobile banking, of whom 390 were selected on the basis of sampling technique of convenience to explore the factors that influence the adoption of mobile banking. The size of our sample was determined based on the nature of the search, the number of search variables, the statistical analysis used, etc. (Malhotra et al., 2013).

The questionnaire is composed of closed questions in order to have a careful, precise and authentic look at the problem of research. A first part of the questionnaire on the theory of planned behavior comprising 39 questions, as well as a second part of the questionnaire including age, sex, level of education, monthly income were applied for the collection of data.

In order to ensure the reliability of the questionnaire, Cronbach α coefficient technique was used. Table I indicates the reliability of the variables included in the questionnaire.

In our sample, most respondents are men (58.3%); 72% are married. Regarding their level, 64% have higher levels of education. Finally, 67% have monthly incomes below 12000 Saudi Riyal.

Results

In order to identify the structure of the relationships between the items in our survey, we carried out a principal component analysis (PCA) with Varimax rotation, performed with the SPSS 20 software.

Based on the study of the different common points and the factorial weight of each item, we decided to keep all the items of the measures used, since all the points in common are less than 0.5 (Évrard et al., 2003) .

Similarly, we confirm the reliability of our measurements, since Cronbach α values are higher than the recommended value of 0.7 (Table 1). Also, the convergent validity of the model is also assured because the values of the average extracted variance (AVE) are higher than the recommended value of 0.05 (Hair et al., 2010).

Tests of hypotheses:

Table 1. Reliability and convergent validity of measures

Variables	α Cronbach	AVE
Perceived advantage	0.81	0.70
Complexity	0.92	0.81
Compatibility	0.78	0.69
Peer groups	0.82	0.76
Superior groups	0.76	0.66
Self-efficacy	0.72	0.63
Source facilitator conditions	0.73	0.65
Technology facilitator conditions	0.74	0.64
Attitude	0.88	0.77
Subjective norms	0.86	0.75
Perceived behavioral control	0.83	0.72
Behavioral tendency of using	0.87	0.76
Actual behavior of using	0.83	0.71

Table 2. Results of research hypotheses

Hypothesis	Standardized coefficient	t-value	p-value	Result
Perceived benefit of using mobile banking → Attitude	0.53	8.66	<0.01	Positive
Complexity of the use of mobile banking → Attitude	0.34	-5.53	<0.01	Positive
Compatibility of the use of mobile telephony → Attitude	0.16	2.85	<0.01	Positive
Peer Groups → Subjective norms	0.42	7.45	<0.01	Positive
Higher groups →Subjective norms	0.38	6.26	<0.01	Positive
Personal effectiveness →Perceived behavioral control.	0.08	1.26	<0.01	Negative
Conditions of the facilitating source →Perceived behavioral control.	0.47	6.16	<0.01	Positive
Technological facilitator conditions → Perceived behavioral control.	0.49	6.12	<0.01	Positive
Attitude of customers of the bank→Trend of their behavior to use mobile banking	0.62	09.85	<0.01	Positive
Subjective norms of bank customers → Trend of their behavior to use mobile banking	0.44	7.43	<0.01	Positive
Perceived behavioral control → Trend of their behavior to use mobile banking.	0.38	5.18	<0.01	Positive
Trend behavior to use mobile banking → Real behavior of customers with mobile banking.	0.68	11.71	<0.01	Positive

DISCUSSION OF THE RESULTS

Descriptive Results for the Main Variables of the Research

First, according to the results of our study we notice that the average value is equal to (3). The average value of all the variables are higher than the average level except the variable "complexity". The perceived benefit variable comes in first place with an average of (M = 5.23). Second place is for attitude with an average of (M = 4.82). The third place is for the perception of control behavior with an average of (M = 4.29). And the last place is for complexity with the lowest average that is (M = 2.36).

The Correlation of the Variables

After performing the Pearson correlation test, we found that the results showed a positive correlation between attitude, perceived benefit and compatibility (R = 0.81, 0.79, 0.77) with a significant level (p = 0.01). On the other hand, the correlation with the complexity is negative.

In addition, a positive and significant correlation was observed between subjective norms, peer groups (R = 0.70) and higher groups (R = 0.58). In addition, there is a positive and significant correlation between perceived behavioral control and self-efficacy (R = 0.64), with sources of enabling conditions (R = 0.66) and with technological facilitation conditions (R = 0.71).

Similarly, the correlation between attitude and behavioral tendency is (R = 0.61). The correlation between subjective norms and behavioral tendency is (R = 0.52). And the correlation between the perceived behavior of control and the behavioral tendency is (R = 0.56). Finally, there was a significant correlation between the behavioral trend and the current behavior of mobile banking use (R = 0.72).

Correlation Analysis of Research Elements

In short, the perception of the advantage of the use of the mobile bank is the element that has the greatest influence on the customer's attitude with a value of (R = 0.59). With respect to subjective norms, we observe that peer groups have the highest correlation with a value of (R = 0.48). Also, the conditions of the facilitating source and the technological enabler conditions have the highest correlation with perceived behavioral control with a value of (R = 0.45). Finally, the highest correlation was observed between the attitude of customers towards the bank and the behavioral tendency to use mobile banking with a value of (R = 062).

CONCLUSION AND THEORETICAL AND MANAGERIAL IMPLICATIONS

On the theoretical level, this work enriches the literature with a research model based on the model of the theory of planned behavior which is considered as one of the widely adopted theories by researchers (Taylor and Todd, 1995).

Our study leads to a better understanding of the role of the explanatory factors of real customer behaviors. This study refers to Taylor and Todd's (1995) model and demonstrates their validity in explaining the actual behavior of the change from one technology to another based on the model's history of customer attitude, perception of behavioral control, subjective norms...

In practical terms, this study proposes managerial solutions to explain customer behavior and to develop customer acquisition and retention strategies, particularly in the banking sector and to create a competitive advantage.

Following the results of our study, we can recommend several concrete recommendations to managers and managers of mobile banking institutions:

-They must adopt marketing strategies to further encourage customers to use mobile banking. As we have to provide diversified mobile banking services. Also to create new services compatible with technological advancement and which allows to create a competitive advantage for mobile banking.

- The convenience of using the technology adopted by the mobile bank is very important in the customer's decision. Simple and easy-to-use software and applications for mobile banking must be used to ensure that customers arrive at the accepted and used. It is necessary to take into consideration the intellectual levels of the customers. In other words, people with low literacy can easily use mobile banking services without complexity and inconvenience.
- We must check the compatibility of financial products marketed and mobile services offered with the needs, habits, experiences and values of customers ... .The environment of mobile banking with its different types changes rapidly. It is recommended to monitor this change with periodic field surveys and strategic intelligence to anticipate customer needs and demands, track their attitudes towards this new service and stimulate others.
- It is strongly suggested that staff and employees of the mobile bank should be well trained to properly promote this new service in the bank or in the environment of the bank (fair, living room...).

- The opening of the mobile bank on its environment is highly recommended as the organization of regular meetings with the heads of different organizations and explaining the benefits of using mobile banking. Signed preferred contracts with companies and boost their employees by offering special benefits and taking advantage of positive word of mouth among its employees.
- It is suggested that the mobile bank intervenes to improve the self-efficacy of individuals to use computers and banking systems over the Internet and this can be with the organization of workshops and training courses for the service of society. Mobile banking can also facilitate the conditions for using their services by providing qualified individuals or groups with strong communication skills and appropriate pedagogical skills, via the Internet and via telephone to guide and assist customers with service issues mobile banking.
- It is advisable that the mobile bank develops a kind of trust with its customers. The bank communicates and informs its customers about the technology infrastructure, systems, software, as well as the knowledge and skills needed to perform banking and mobile operations. The customer certainly uses mobile services with more confidence.
- It is suggested to those in charge of the mobile banks to make extensive use of the online service by offering brochures, homepages, websites, media, etc ... by providing guarantees to customers regarding the promise of the bank and respecting its commitments in mobile banking.
- It is also necessary to respect the bank's ethical rules and the regulations adopted by obliging bank executives and staff to act and behave according to these rules in order to fight against cybercrime and cyber violations. All this is to win the trust of customers and motivate them to use mobile banking.
- It is advisable for mobile bank managers to act on the perceptions and attitudes of families and groups of people by creating more tendency to use online banking through appropriate advertising via media and non-media marketing communication .
- It is suggested for mobile bank managers to respect the legal side and generally Internet security that can greatly influence customer confidence in the use of mobile banking. With this focus the bank can change the attitudes of customers in mobile banking by creating a favorable behavioral trend and interest among customers. A proper understanding of mobile banking and its values and benefits that are compatible with social and cultural norms and customer needs must be developed.
- According to the theory of planned behavior, the control of the perceived behavior reflects the perception of the internal and external limits of the behavior. So there are factors facilitating or preventing behavior are considered control beliefs. We can cite factors include internal control elements such as information, individual skills and capabilities and external control elements such as opportunities, resources and facilities to perform behavior. For this reason it is suggested to the managers of the mobile banks to satisfy the customers by offering a certain level of comfort of the mobile banking services on the basis of the complete knowledge of the external factors.
- Finally, in order to raise public awareness of the shift from online banking to mobile banking, it is recommended that all available means of communication be used to create a positive attitude among their customers using mobile banking. .

REFERENCES:

Alahmari, F., Naim, A., & Alqahtani, H. (). E-Learning Modeling Technique and Convolution Neural Networks in Online Education. In IoT-enabled Convolutional Neural Networks: Techniques and Applications (pp. 261-295). River Publishers.

Alqahtani, H., & Naim, A. (2022). Critical Success Factors for Transforming CRM to SCRM for building E-CRM. In A. Naim & S. Kautish (Eds.), *Building a Brand Image Through Electronic Customer Relationship Management* (pp. 139–168). IGI Global. doi:10.4018/978-1-6684-5386-5.ch007

Alzaidi, M. S., & Shehawy, Y. M. (2022). Cross-national differences in mobile learning adoption during COVID-19. *Education + Training*, *64*(3), 305–328. doi:10.1108/ET-05-2021-0179

Amadeh, H. & Jafarpour, M. (2009). Specification of obstacles and solutions of electronic banking development within the framework of Iran at 1404. Prospective. *Danesh va Tosee Journal, 26*(2), 2-43.

Amiri, Y. (2009). *Evaluation of the performance of electronic services provided in selected public banks of Fars province based on fuzzy BSC approach*. [MSc thesis, Yazd University].

Praveen K. Malik, Naim, A. & Malik, P. (2022). Competitive Trends and Technologies in Business Management. Nova Science Publisher. , doi:10.52305/VIXO9830

Danyali, A. (2018). Factors influencing customers' change of behaviors from online banking to mobile banking in Tejarat Bank, Iran. *Journal of Organizational Change Management, 31* (6), 1226-1233.

Elahi, S., Ghanbari, M. H., & Shayan, A. (2012). Determining the effective factors in implementing mobile banking technology by the customer. *Quarterly Journal of Commercial Law Research, 16*(63), 27–50.

Évrard, Y., Pras, B., & Roux, E. (2003). *Market: Etudes et Recherches en Marketing*. Dunod. B.

Fatima, S., Alqahtani, H., Naim, A., & Alma'alwi, F. (2022). E-CRM Through Social Media Marketing Activities for Brand Awareness, Brand Image, and Brand Loyalty. In A. Naim & S. Kautish (Eds.), *Building a Brand Image Through Electronic Customer Relationship Management* (pp. 109–138). IGI Global. doi:10.4018/978-1-6684-5386-5.ch006

Hair, J. F., Black, W. C., Babin, B. J., Anderson, R. E., & Tatham, R. L. (2010). *Multivariate Data Analysis, Upper Saddle River*. Pearson.

Kamal, S., Naim, A., Magd, H., Khan, S. A., & Khan, F. M. (2022). The Relationship Between E-Service Quality, Ease of Use, and E-CRM Performance Referred by Brand Image. In A. Naim & S. Kautish (Eds.), *Building a Brand Image Through Electronic Customer Relationship Management* (pp. 84–108). IGI Global., doi:10.4018/978-1-6684-5386-5.ch005

Ltifi, M., & Hichri, A. (2022). The effects of corporate governance on the customer's recommendations: A study of the banking sector at the time of COVID-19. *Journal of Knowledge Management*, *26*(1), 165–191. doi:10.1108/JKM-06-2020-0471

Malhotra, N. K., Birks, D. F., & Wills, P. (2013). *Essentials of Marketing Research*. Pearson Education.

Mattila, M., Karjaluoto, H., & Pento, T. (2003). Internet banking adoption among mature customer: Early majority or laggards? *Journal of Services Marketing*, *17*(5), 514–528. doi:10.1108/08876040310486294

Mittal, D., & Agrawal, S. R. (2022). Determining banking service attributes from online reviews: Text mining and sentiment analysis. *International Journal of Bank Marketing*, *40*(3), 558–577. doi:10.1108/IJBM-08-2021-0380

Motamedi, M. (2010). *Investigating the factors affecting the acceptance of the bank by the customers by using the models of technology acceptance and affiliated marketing*. [MSc Thesis, Shiraz University].

Naim, A., Alqahtani, H., Muniasamy, A., Bilfaqih, S. M., Mahveen, R., & Mahjabeen, R. (2023). Applications of Information Systems and Data Security in Marketing Management. In A. Naim, P. Malik, & F. Zaidi (Eds.), *Fraud Prevention, Confidentiality, and Data Security for Modern Businesses* (pp. 57–83). IGI Global. doi:10.4018/978-1-6684-6581-3.ch003

Naim, A., & Kautish, S. K. (Eds.). (2022). *Building a Brand Image Through Electronic Customer Relationship Management*. IGI Global. doi:10.4018/978-1-6684-5386-5

Naim, A., Malik, P. K., & Zaidi, F. A. (Eds.). (2023). *Fraud Prevention, Confidentiality, and Data Security for Modern Businesses*. IGI Global. doi:10.4018/978-1-6684-6581-3

Taghavi Fard, M. T., & Torabi, M. (2010). Factors affecting the use of mobile banking services by customersand rank them (Case Study: Commerce Bank branches in Tehran). *Journal of Excavation Business Management*, *3*, 136–162.

Taylor, S., & Todd, P. A. (1995). Understanding information technology usage: A test of competing models. *Information Systems Research*, *6*(2), 144–176. doi:10.1287/isre.6.2.144

Vafaei, N. (2009). *Identifying and explaining the factors influencing the adoption of banking with customers' perspectives: a case study in National Bank branches in Tehran* [MA Thesis in Economics, Faculty of Management and Economics, Tarbiat Modarres University].

Visentin, M., Pizzi, G., & Pichierri, M. (2019). Visentin. Marco; Pizzi. Gabriele & Pichierri Marco (2019), Fake News, Real Problems for Brands: The Impact of Content Truthfulness and Source Credibility on consumers' Behavioral Intentions toward the Advertised Brands. *Journal of Interactive Marketing*, *45*, 99–112. doi:10.1016/j.intmar.2018.09.001

Wati, Y., Koo, C., Jung, J. and Dahui, L. (2009). An empirical analysis of end-user satisfaction toward ebanking in Indonesia: a comparison model of ATMs, internet banking and mobile banking. *AMCIS 2009 Proceedings* (*1*, pp. 514-526). AMC.

Yu, C.-S. (2014). Consumers' switching behavior from online banking to mobile banking. *International Journal of Cyber Society and Education*, *7*(1), 1–28. doi:10.7903/ijcse.1108

Zhu, B., Charoennan, W., & Embalzado, H. (2022). The influence of perceived risks on millennials' intention to use m-payment for mobile shopping in Bangkok. *International Journal of Retail & Distribution Management*, *50*(4), 479–497. doi:10.1108/IJRDM-05-2020-0174

Chapter 14
Impact and Assessment of Electronic Commerce on Consumer Buying Behaviour

Arshi Naim
King Khalid University, Saudi Arabia

Shad Ahmad Khan
University of Buraimi, Oman

ABSTRACT

Electronic commerce (E-com) is now adopted by most of the firms, especially after the first phase of the COVID-19 pandemic. Consumers are conscious of increasing online purchases and demand sustainable consumption friendly actions. This study aims to analyze the intellectual, conceptual, and social knowledge of consumer buying behavior in E-com research to generate new understandings for online consumer behavior. A survey on LinkedIn was conducted to measure the impact of E-com on consumer behavior and results are shown on Likert's five scale. The survey questions were closed ended and not specific to any industry or firm rather general questions to measure the impact of E-com on consumer buying behavior. The questions were based on factors of customer satisfaction, security, information quality, payment methods, shipping, time, and delivery services. Analysis shows a variation in types, factors, and method of consumer buying behavior in an online environment.

INTRODUCTION

Electronic commerce (E-com) is growing as a means of doing business and shows every sign of continuing to expand at a rapid rate. The rise of this new medium is attracting increasing attention in policy circles (Bandara et al., 2019). Nevertheless, a lack of adequate data on the magnitude and relevance of electronic supply has made policy-making decisions all the more difficult. E-com can be divided into three stages: first, the pre-purchase stage including advertising and information-seeking; second, the purchase stage, including purchase and payment; and third, the delivery stage (Bandara et al., 2019). In

DOI: 10.4018/978-1-6684-8166-0.ch014

principle, all types of products can be advertised and purchased over electronic networks. The potential for electronic delivery, however, is more limited. It requires that a final product can be presented as digitalized information and transmitted electronically, typically over the Internet (Broome, 2016). Many services can be supplied as digitalized information, including financial transactions or legal advice. Some information and entertainment products typically characterized as goods, such as books, software, music and videos embody digitalized information that can also be supplied electronically over the Internet. Figure 1 shows the process of E-com working in the general scenario.

Figure 1. The process of e-commerce working
Source: Naim (2021)

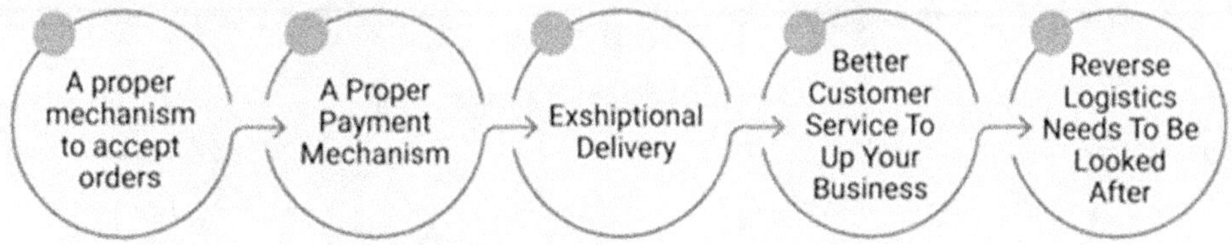

E-commerce will impinge upon some of the functions of wholesalers and retailers by connecting producers and consumers directly (Castaneda et al., 2009). Thus, they are likely to adopt new distribution methods to avoid being bypassed as a result of the information technology revolution. E-com is also likely to transform the way many financial and business services are provided, including accounting, computing and advertising. Figure 2 shows the E-Com development for any business.

Figure 2. E-commerce development cycle
Source: Cetina et al. (2012)

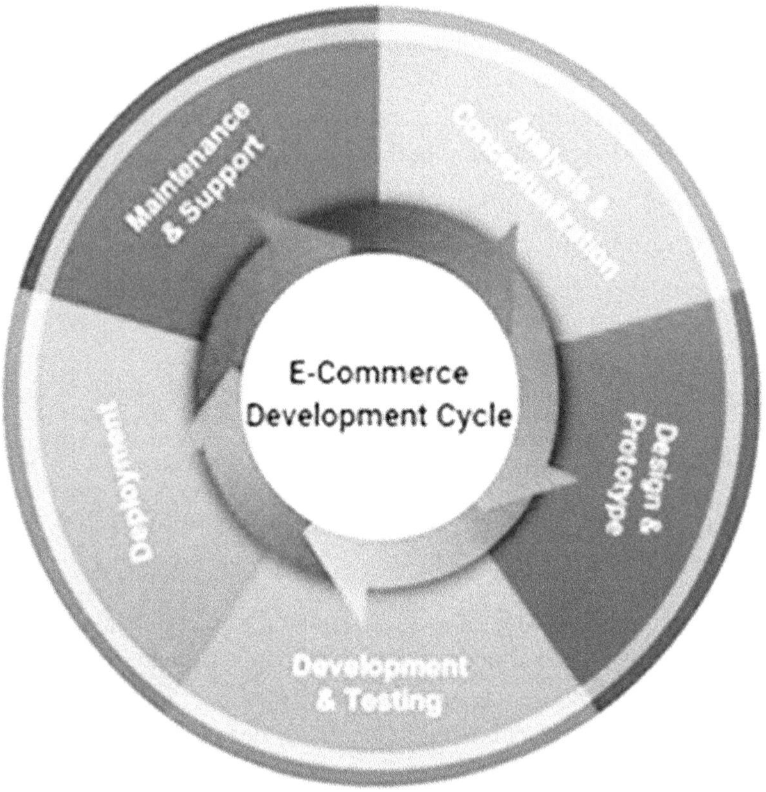

Considering that E-com will play an important role in transforming large shares of the economy, it is worthwhile discussing how trade is likely to be affected by E-com. E-com will probably have most impact on two types of products (Naim & Khan, 2021). First, a number of products which traditionally have been delivered as "goods" can now be sent across networks in digital form. Second, E-com will strongly affect trade in services. The former category of products is basically software and media products, and includes film and various types of printed material. Trade over networks reduces transportation and administration costs considerably, and many products including films and music, software and its upgrading are soon likely to be or are already downloadable over the Internet (Choshin & Ghaffari, 2017). Currently, retailing costs account for a large share of the price of such products when sold in a shop.

Electronic delivery plays an important economic and trade role in many services sectors. It has been crucial for the development of cross-border trade in services (Chouhan, 2017).

Consumer behaviour encompasses all the steps that lead the consumer to purchase a product or service. Online, it starts the moment the user turns on their computer or phone, and ends the moment they validate their payment. Sometimes, consumer behaviour also includes repeat business. Figure 3 presents factors that affect consumer behaviour for any product, services and information (Dai, 2012).

Figure 3. Factors influencing consumer behavior
Source: Dai (2012)

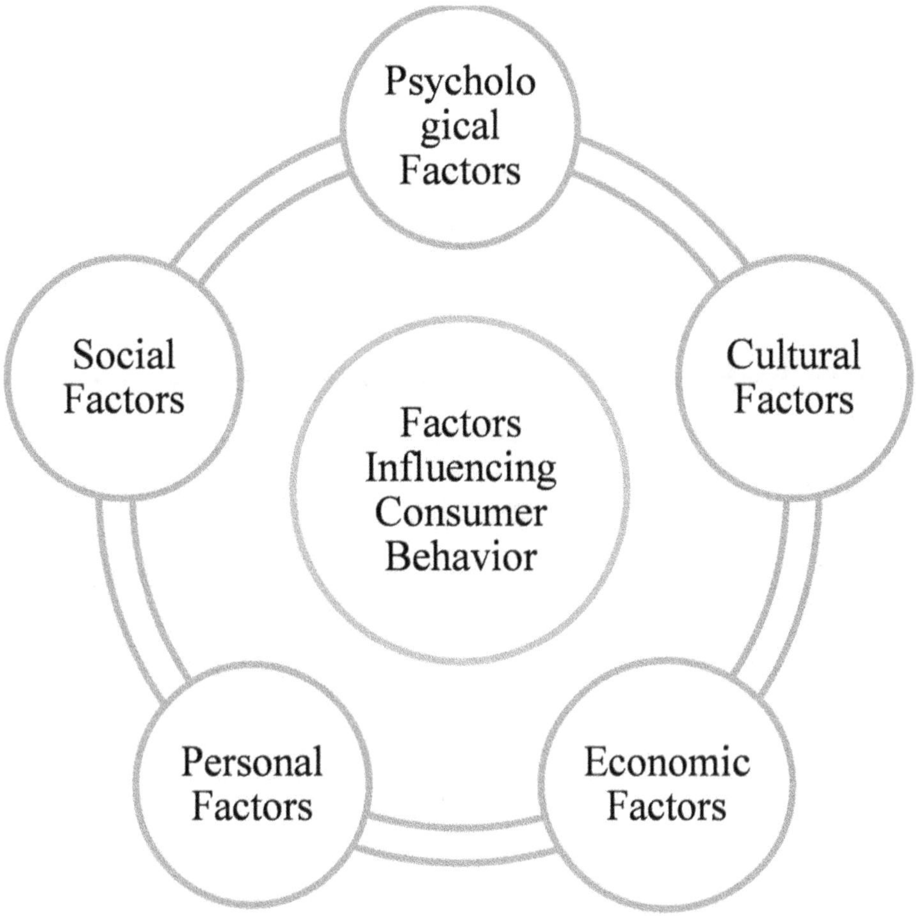

Consumer behavior is influenced by many factors such as situation, psychological, environmental and marketing factors, personal factors, family, and culture. Businesses try to collect data so that they can make decisions on how they can reach their target audience in the most efficient way (Darsono et al., 2019).

Experts agree that there are four main types of consumer behavior that are presented in Figure 4.

Figure 4. Types of consumer buying behavior
Source: Darsono et al. (2019)

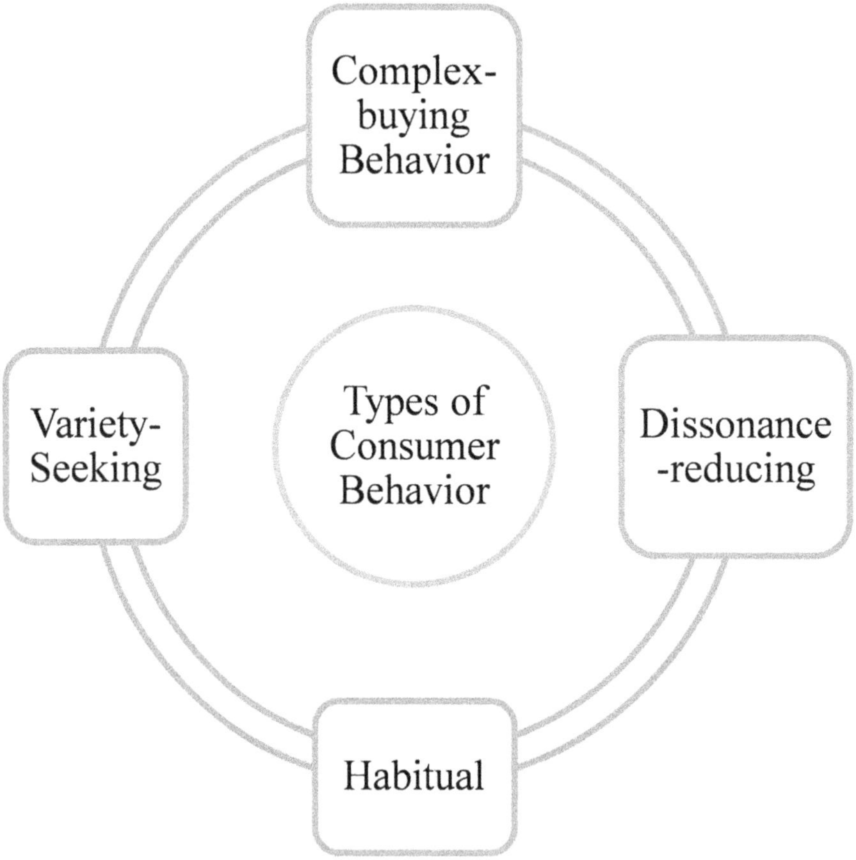

Consumer behaviour helps companies understand what their customers want and need, so they can offer products and services that appeal to their target audience (Doern & Fey, 2006). This is helpful for businesses who want to expand their reach into new markets or demographics. Consumer behaviour follows 5 steps for buying decisions. Figure 5 presents the decision making of consumer buying behaviour (Filson, 2004).

Figure 5. Steps of buying decision in consumer behaviour
Source: Filson (2004)

Consumer behaviour refers to the acquisition, consumption, and disposal of products, services, time, and ideas by decision-making units. There is no single cause for challenging behavior, but environment, relationships, discomfort and frustration are all common reasons (Forman, 2005).

There's been a rapid evolution in online consumer behavior. This evolution is the byproduct of drastic changes in E-commerce as a result of the COVID-19 pandemic (Naim et al., 2021). Launching E-commerce in the future far beyond any reasonable or predictable expectations, COVID-19 triggered a new age of retail. This new age of retail is marked by the transition of the customer buying experience from brick-and-mortar shopping to online shopping. And it occurred much more quickly and on a much larger scale than ever anticipated (Naim, Kautish, Kamal et al, 2022).

To be successful, E-commerce companies need to understand new trends in consumer shopping behavior stimulated by the pandemic. Before examining new trends in E-com and how to meet consumer demand, it's important to understand online consumer behaviour.

Online consumer behavior is the process of how consumers make decisions to purchase products in E-commerce. The consumer behaviours themselves such as identifying a problem or deciding to make a purchase are based on ever-evolving expectations and needs. And while needs look different for every shopper, the new expectations that currently drive online consumer behavior are entrenched in commonality (Naim, Kautish, Fatima et al, 2022).

Expectations like product availability, delivery transparency, affordable shipping, and more recently, a convenient buying journey all affect how consumers make decisions to buy items online.

In the last decade, online shopping has experienced an explosive growth due to the fact that it represents a more economic and convenient approach to purchasing in comparison to traditional shopping (Naim, Kautish, Alqahtani et al, 2022). Nevertheless, in the beginning, the transition from one to another, more modern purchase method, created a sense of concern among customers with respect to the following: leak of personal information, online fraud, inconsistency between the ordered product quality and the desired quality, unsuccessful shipping, etc. Today, these concerns are at a much lower level, as people recognized the advantages offered by online shopping. There are a number of reasons why people purchase via the Internet; for example, consumers can buy anything at any time without actually going to the store; consumers can stumble on the same product at a lower price by comparing different websites simultaneously; consumers want to avoid pressure felt when communicating face-to-face with the retailer; consumers want to avoid traffic jams that can occur on the way to the store, and so on (Naim, Kautish, Doe et al, 2022). Online shopping provides consumers with more information and opportunities to compare products and prices, with greater product selection, with convenience and ease of finding desired products online. It has been argued that online commerce offers more satisfaction to modern consumers who seek convenience and speed In online communication, when a consumer sees a banner ad or online promotion, it can attract their attention and stimulate their interest for these specific products from advertisements. Before deciding for purchase, the customer may seek additional information for help. If there is not enough information, they will browse for them through online channels, e.g. using online catalogs, websites or search engines (Hallikainen & Laukkanen, 2018).

Retaining the online consumers has attracted a lot of attention, since it serves as a means of gaining competitive advantage (Agag & El-Masry, 2016). When the consumers are satisfied with a particular online retail shop, they will purchase there more. Hence, both concepts, retaining and satisfying the customer, are becoming increasingly important for both online and offline business. It is therefore important to understand the factors that drive customer satisfaction and their choice of online stores (Ballestar et al., 2018). Customer satisfaction is the result of consumer experience throughout the different stages of purchase (Naim, 2021). Since the experience of online consumers, due to the inability of physical contact with the product, is solely based on information offered by online stores, it is clear that the information provided can affect consumer satisfaction, both in the information search stage and during the purchase decision phase (Changchit et al., 2018).

Consumer satisfaction is the result of comparing the expectations and the experience; in other words, the consumer is pleased when the delivery meets or exceeds their expectations. Satisfaction and loyalty are the key elements determining the success of the market concept implementation. Satisfied customers are the ones that will repeat the purchase if the service provider reached or exceeded their expectations. It is significant to identify the variables of consumer satisfaction, since they present the business benchmark and serve as a guide to future improvements (Elseidi, 2018).

Security is defined as the ability of the website to protect consumers' personal data from any unauthorized disclosure of information during electronic transactions (Naim, 2021). Security is considered to be an important factor perceived seriously by online purchase consumers. It is due to the fact that the issues of security and privacy play a crucial role in creating trust during online transactions (Agag, 2019).

Shoppers expect online retailers to provide all relevant and accurate information about the product (Ayilyath, 2020). Since online shoppers rarely have the opportunity to touch and feel the products before making a decision on a purchase, online retailers have to provide information regarding that.

Shipping is a link in the supply chain that directly affects the consumer and triggers their satisfaction (Naim & Alqahtani, 2021). Shipping presents a key activity in every process, and especially in online shopping (Naim, 2022). The product delivery service is a prerequisite for customer's satisfaction. It implies that the customer will receive the ordered product, which is well packed, and whose amount, quality and specification are in accordance with the order, as well as the set delivery time and place (Belanche et al., 2020; Belwal et al., 2020; Lahby et al., 2022).

The quality of products and services in online commerce has a positive impact on customer satisfaction. The perceived product quality is defined as the consumer's judgment about a product's overall excellence or superiority (Brian et al., 2019; Durovic, 2020; Edgar & Manz, 2017; Naim, 2022).

Pricing as an important factor in customer satisfaction, because consumers like to refer to pricing while assessing the values of products and services. From the consumer's perspective, price is what is given up or scarified to obtain a product (Naim, 2022). A number of studies have determined that the pricing is significantly related to customer satisfaction. Pricing directly affects the perception on the transaction's delivered value and usability, and, consequently, customer satisfaction (Emma et al., 2017).

Due to better purchase conditions, consumers use the Internet to buy the same product at a lower price than in the store (Harrigan et al., 2021). Many customers expect online stores to offer their products and services at the lower price in comparison to traditional stores. Discounts while purchasing influence consumers to believe in prices, and ultimately they affect their satisfaction (Harrisson et al., 2017). While shopping online, customers cannot see or test the product; hence, they are not certain that the delivered product is identical to the one on the website. Consequently, price perception has a more significant role (Naim, 2022).

Saving time is one of the most influential factors in online shopping. Time is the main resource that consumers spend when they purchase online or in traditional stores (Haupt, 2003). Browsing the online catalog during online shopping saves time and reduces stress compared to traditional shopping. According to, one of the possible explanations why buying online saves time is eliminating the travel required to go to the store (Naim, 2022).

LITERATURE REVIEW

E-Commerce or online shopping was invented by Michael Aldrich 1979; he was an English inventor, innovator and entrepreneur (Helge et al., 2020; Naim & Alqahtani, 2022). He invented online shopping to enable online transaction processing between consumers and businesses, or between one business and another, a technique known later as E-com. In the mid-90s, there were major advancements in the commercial use of the Internet. One of the first ecommerce sites was Amazon, which started in 1995 as an online bookstore but grew to become the largest online retailer in the world (Išoraitė & Miniotienė, 2018; Jaipuriar et al., 2020; Naim, 2022).

It's commonly thought e-commerce's roots were planted in the 1990s, at the beginning of the internet era but the history of ecommerce started over 40 years ago, when the introduction of early technology like Electronic Data Interchange (EDI) (Naim & Khan, 2022) and teleshopping in the 1970s paved the way for the modern-day ecommerce (Kerick, 2019). The history of ecommerce is closely intertwined with the history of the internet. Online shopping became possible when the internet was opened to the public in 1991 (Khandelwal, 2018). Amazon was one of the first ecommerce sites in the US to start selling products online and thousands of businesses have followed since. The convenience, safety, and enjoyable user experience of ecommerce have improved exponentially since the inception of online shopping (Lăzăroiu et al., 2020; Lee & Turban, 2001; Liyang, 2019).

Book Stacks Unlimited, an online bookstore created by Charles M. Stack in 1992, was one of the earliest consumer shopping experiences. Stack's store began as a dial-up bulletin board three years before Amazon was founded. In 1994, Book Stacks Unlimited moved to the Internet as Books.com and was eventually acquired by Barnes & Noble (Loannis, et al., 2019; Majithia, 2019).

Consumer behaviour emerged (Mangiaracina & Perego, 2009) in the 1940–1950s as a distinct sub-discipline of marketing, but has become an interdisciplinary social science that blends elements from psychology, sociology, social anthropology, anthropology, ethnography, ethnology, marketing, and economics (Milan et al., 2020; Miyazaki & Fernandez, 2001).

Martin Fishbein and Icek Ajzen originally conceived the theory of reasoned action that explained the consumer behavior theory that focuses on the relationship between marketing and the preexisting attitudes consumers bring to their purchasing decisions (Orendorff, 2019; Shirazi et al., 2020; Siciliani et al., 2019; UNCTAD, 2019; Xiaodong & Min, 2020).

When the COVID-19 pandemic hit (Xiaodong & Min, 2020), a remarkable and unprecedented shift occurred in E-commerce. Many brick-and-mortar stores were forced to close, and consumers were placed under stay-at-home orders (Naim, 2021).

Subsequently, consumers placed exceptional and unpredictable demand on the E-commerce marketplace to provide the products they previously purchased in person (UNESAP & ADB, 2019). In 2020, 84% of consumers shopped online more than before. Initially, online stores struggled to meet this incredible demand (Xiaodong & Min, 2020). Products sold out at record pace, stock dwindled or disappeared altogether, and fast shipping and delivery lagged. Eventually, E-commerce stores began to fall into step with this new, heightened demand. But along with that heightened demand for products, there was also a transformation in consumer expectations for what the online shopping experience should include (Wajeeha et al., 2019). These new expectations created different trends in online consumer behaviors. Even as brick-and-mortar stores began to reopen their doors, a large majority of consumers continued to utilize E-commerce to make purchases (Wang et al., 2019). Consumers discovered positive components to online shopping that they enjoyed that weren't available in the traditional offline shopping experience. These positive online shopping experiences further encouraged new trends in consumer behaviors to take a steadfast hold. A recent research study by Linnworks identified five significant E-commerce trends that help drive online consumer behavior. And while these trends materialize at various points in the customer buying journey, they all have one constituent in common which is convenience (Naim, 2021; World Economic Forum, 2019; Yang et al., 2019; Zuhal, 2019).

The key to success in E-commerce is understanding these new trends and adopting business strategies to meet the current expectations of a convenient buying journey (Naim, 2021).

Convenience Is a Top Priority

According to Linnworks' study, 76% of consumers value convenience as one of their top priorities (Naim, 2022). 78% of consumers now value convenience more than they did before COVID restrictions (Xiaodong & Min, 2020).

Easy Access Across All Devices

81% of online shoppers seek a seamless transfer between devices throughout a buying journey. In fact, the expectation is now that consumers can begin a buying journey on one device, such as a desktop, and end on another, like their mobile device without interruption (Naim, 2022; Naim, 2022; Naim, 2022; Naim & Kautish, 2022).

This cross-device experience is also expected to include checkouts with personal details already completed on whichever device customers finalize their buying journey (Naim, Kautish, & Hoda, 2022).

Access to Omni-Channel Shopping

With access to multiple technology options, consumers are engaged in an 'always-on' shopping experience, 70% of consumers now shop while multitasking (Naim, Kautish, & Song, 2022).

Effortless Payment

The simplicity of payment options drives 89% of consumers to make purchasing decisions more quickly and 84% of consumers purchase larger ticket items with offered effortless and flexible payment options (Naim, Kautish, Alquhtani et al, 2022). Consumers seek convenience throughout the entire buying journey. As part of that end-to-end buying convenience, they look to discover E-commerce online shops that have easy-to-setup payment gateways that also accept popular payment method such as "buy now, pay later (Naim, Kautish, Saleem et al, 2022)."

Fast and Reliable Delivery

95% of consumers feel that fast delivery options are a must-have factor when shopping online (Naim, Kautish, Verma et al, 2022). That's why ShipBob offers fast 2-day shipping and has a dispersed network of logistics centers to split inventory across to help reduce shipping costs, speed up delivery times, and meet customer expectations. Shipping transparency is also highly expected of online retailers (Naim, 2022). In fact, 72% of consumers have abandoned their purchases over a lack of shipping transparency on E-commerce sites (Naim, Kautish, & Abdulla, 2022).

The key to success for retailing in E-commerce understands the evolving and complex using a system such as Linnworks Multichannel. Listing Software will connect, manage, and automate commerce operations. A system like this allows retailers to meet consumers wherever they shop, providing convenience and capitalizing on as many revenue opportunities as possible (Naim, Kautish, Najar et al, 2022).

This research fills the gap by identifying the best E-com feature for consumer buying behavior and also measure the impact of E-com for consumer buying behavior.

RESEARCH METHODOLOGY

The research is based on data collection through linkedin survey and circulating survey on personal network. The likert scale is applied to measure the responses. The questionnaire was close ended and questions were based on factors of customer satisfaction, security, information quality, payment methods, shipping, time and delivery services. Figure 6 shows the steps we followed for this research.

Figure 6. Research methodology applied

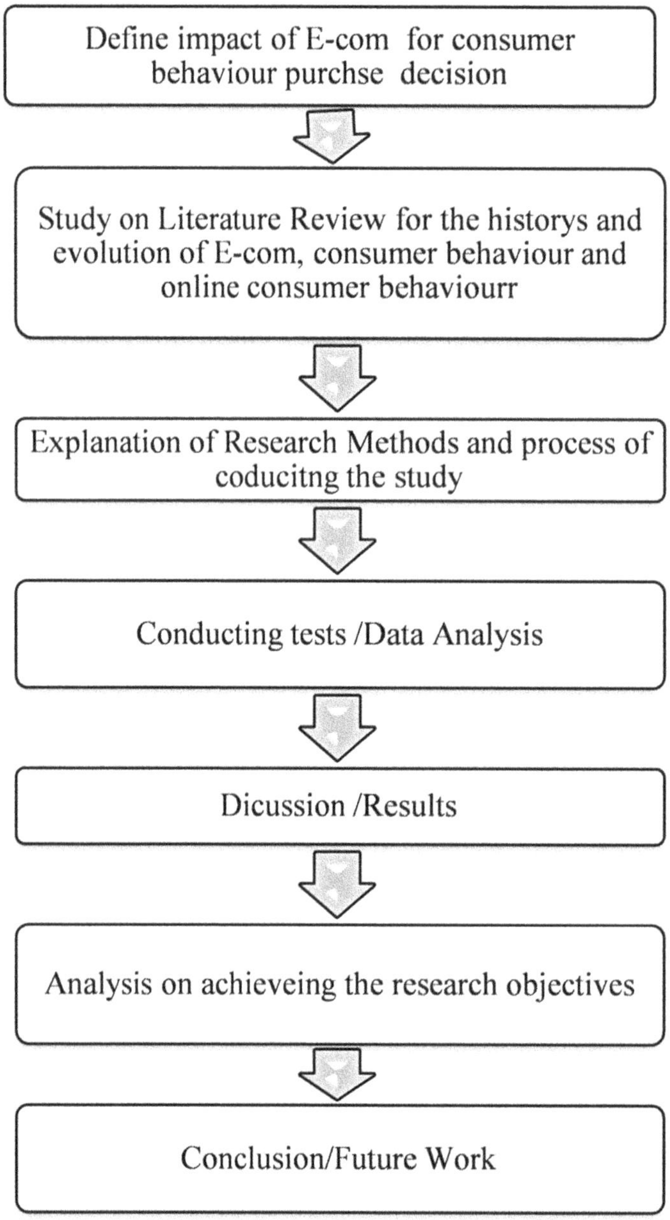

RESULT ANALYSES

The results presented in the research demonstrate that all examined determinants of online purchase and all items from the survey are suitable and related to customer satisfaction. All set hypotheses have been confirmed. However, the strength of the relationship varies for each dominant and hypothesis. Shipping, pricing and information availability have the greatest impact onto the e-customer satisfaction on the market. Considerably lower impact is attributed to quality, time and safety. We have also tried to identify what types of online shopper the respondents are? We categorized them into 5 groups such as Discount seekers, Wandering customers, Impulse buyers, Need-based shoppers and loyal customers.

Online Consumer means any natural person who is acting for purposes which are outside his or her business and who places an Order for the supply of Goods and/or Services on the Suppliers website. Digital consumer characteristics are more informed. The digital consumer searches before buying; they are more connected, less impulsive, more exigent and participative.

In this study we found that there are seven factors that affect consumer's online shopping buying behavior. These factors are perceived ease of use, perceived risk, perceived usefulness, effect of website design, Economic factor, availability of products, and customer satisfaction.

Convenience Is the Key for Online Buying

Major impact of E-com is found on the convenience in shopping, consumers find it easy, flexible and using their own devices to complete purchase decisions.

The consumers were asked about if they go for online shopping for convenience and their responses were listed from "strongly agree" to "strongly disagree." Figure 7 shows the results on the responses for the E-com for convenience.

Figure 7. Convenience is the key for online buying

Convenience is found to be an important impacting factor for E-commerce for consumer buying behavior because more than 80% strongly agree for the reason for online shopping and no one disagrees for this factor. This research therefore make an assumption that if the E-com focus on convenience while building their telecommunicating devices and interfaces, also promote only buying for convenience will bring successful results.

Online Buying Provides an Easy Access Across All Devices

E-com promotes the gold rush model which explains the use of sophisticated technology for the effective working of E-Com. The same theory is applied for the consumers also who are going online for accomplishing their purchases. The question was asked to measure the usage of different devices and easy access to E-com sites. Figure 8 shows the results on application of different devices for online buying and easy access to the online shopping.

Figure 8. Online Buying provides an easy access across all devices

The results show that 75% of the online consumers believe that easy access to the E-com sites help them to have positive buying experiences. Only 2% strongly disagree for the easy access to E-com site through various devices. The reason could be more personal on using the technology but majority of the consumers were found to have a positive feedback on easy access for various devices, therefore E-com sites are suggested to use easy medium of access for all type of devices.

Online Buying Provides Multichannel Technological Options

For the success of E-com, if options for access are not given to the consumers, then the chances of ineffective online buying are more witnessed. E-com sites giving multichannel options, browser compatibility and working on different devices and applications are found to have good impact on consumer buying behavior. Figure 9 shows the results on effective of E-com for multichannel options.

Figure 9. Online buying provides multichannel technological options

The results show mixed response and they do not much acknowledge the importance of multichannel access. But overall more than 70% of the online consumers gave positive feedback for the application of multichannel for E-com access point.

Online Buying Provides an Effortless Payment Options

Payment for the products and services with ease and security has always been vital features of E-com and all online firms take extra care for this feature. Same notion is with consumers also, they would like to have easy payment gateways and would like to have various payment options, like payment of delivery and online quick payment, payment through app, etc.

The Figure 10 shows the results on impact of payment system for purchase behavior for consumers.

Figure 10. Online buying provides an effortless payment options

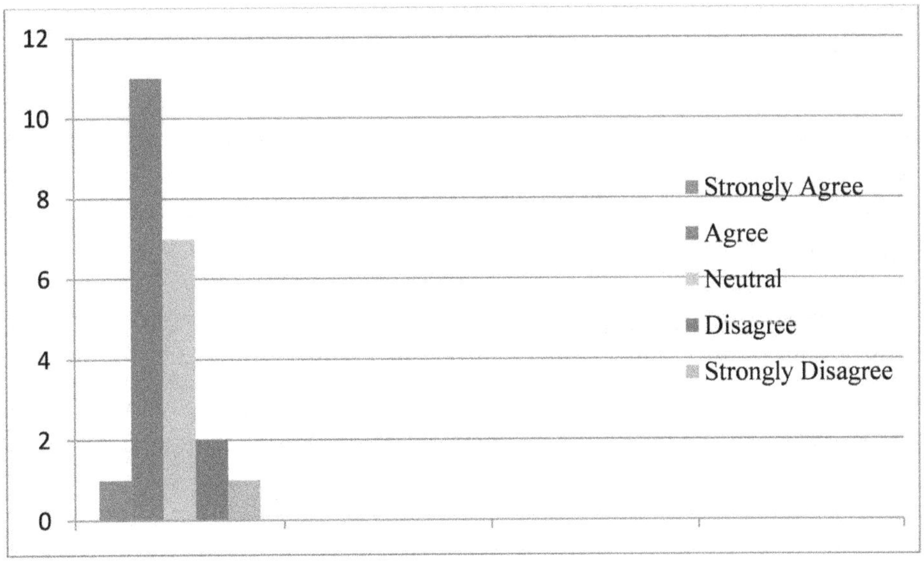

Most of the online consumers feel that online shopping have better options of payment and thc process is completed more easily and promptly. More than 85% of the consumers give importance to online easy payment systems for the success of E-commerce only few disagree for the feature. The research suggests, E-com sites to introduce more easy options for payment, payment on delivery should also be available without many conditions to facilitate online buying.

Online Buying Is Chosen for Fast and Reliable Delivery Services

In the current technological scenario, shipping and delivery of goods is another important E-com feature that encourages consumers to go for online buying. It reduces the pressure and efforts of bringing the products to home and the guarantee of products safely is also with the online firms.

Figure 11 shows the results on shipping and delivery services as success of E-com.

Figure 11. Online buying is chosen for fast and reliable delivery services

The results show mixed responses but mostly consumers were found either agreeing or being neutral for the feature of delivery as success of E-com. However no respondent strongly disagree for this feature therefore while taking care of E-com features, online firms have to give due attention on fast and secured delivery system because this also a key factor for online buying behavior.

Online Buying Offers Simple Return Processes/Policies

Sales promotions and return policies have always attracted the consumers so online consumers are also attracted with these features. Figure 12 shows the results on consumer's responses for discounts, offers and return policies for online shopping.

Figure 12. Online buying offers simple return processes/policies

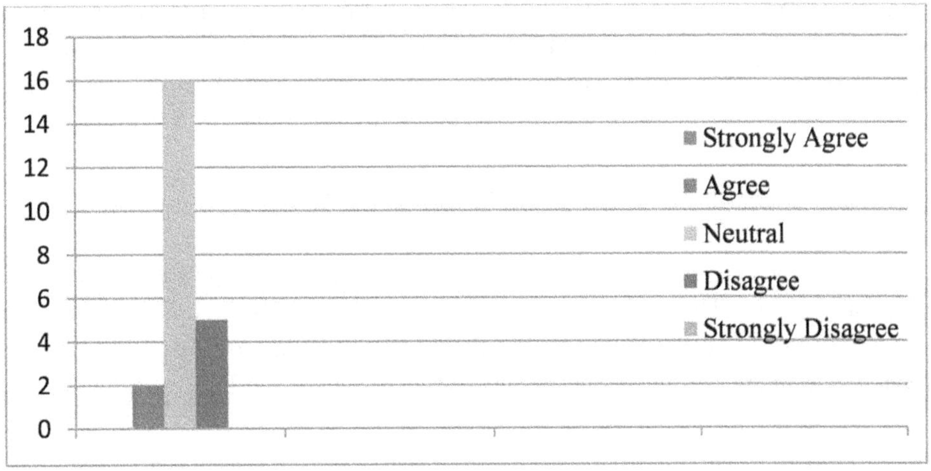

These two features were the only features where no responses were recorded for strongly agree or strongly disagree. Overall results show that consumers are neutral for this feature and do not give additional significance for online buying behavior.

Online Buying Creates Personalized Buying Experiences

One of the most significant features of E-com is to provide customized and personalized experience to the online consumers. Many firms promote their products for these features only but the study will show how much relevance, consumers give to these advantages. Figure 13 shows the results on personalized experience for online consumers.

Figure 13. Online buying creates personalized buying experiences

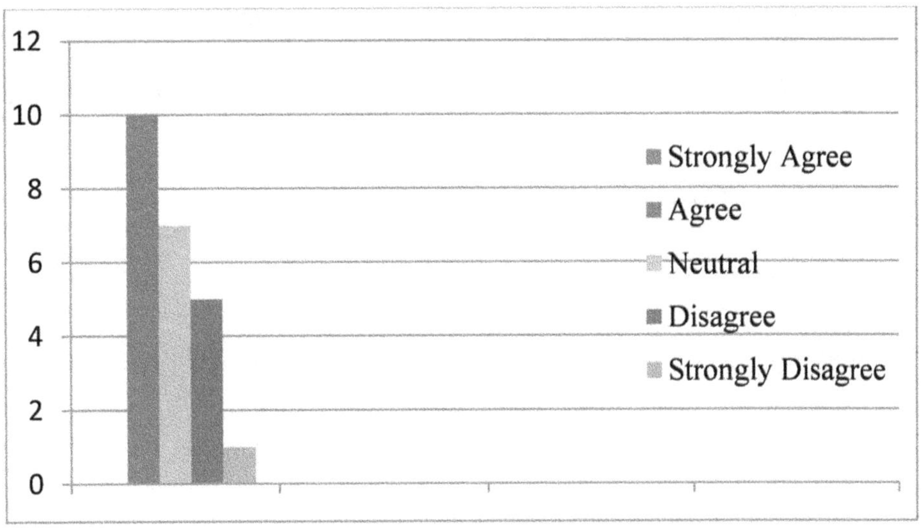

The results show more than 70% agree for the relevance of personalized shopping experience through E-com but many were found either neutral or disagree for this feature. The study suggests that if the products or services have options for customization and personalization, it should be well communicated to the online consumers so that they can know their needs and requirements to be communicated to the online firms.

Online Buying Provides Easy-to-Locate Product Reviews

There are many conscious consumers who like to know retrospective experience of consumers before actually making a purchase. This feature is important because it gives the opion of real users however these rating and reviews are easily manipulated with the current technological advancements. Figure 14 shows the results on reviews and rating for E-com.

Figure 14. Online buying creates personalized buying experiences

This feature of E-com is very specific for the conscious consumers, the results show that there were no responses for strongly agree or strongly disagree. 60% consumers agree for the adequacy of reviews and rating for E-com. This feature also shows significant percentage of disagree on the application of this feature for E-com impact and assessment.

What Type of Online Consumer Are You?

This question was to understand the consumers' characteristics for E-com. If consumers are going online purchase what are the driving forces to take them to E-com from traditional buying environment. Figure 15 shows the consumer characteristics and need for going for online shopping.

Figure 15. Characteristics of online consumer for e-com

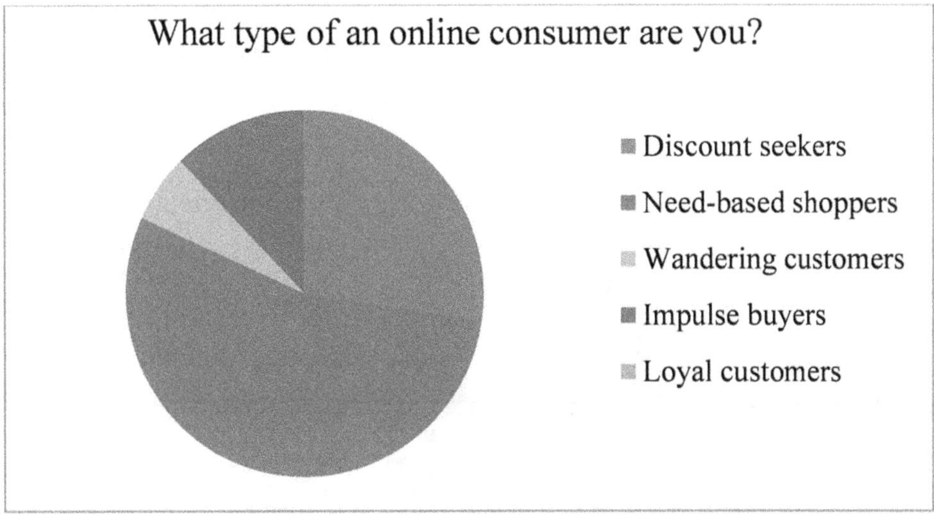

The results show, mostly need based consumers are opting for E-com and many were discount seekers too. There were fewer wandering consumers who were going for online window shopping.

What Is the Most Important Feature/Reason for Your Online Buying?

This question is a comprehensive enquiry where consumers were asked to identify the most important and powerful force for consumers for E-com. Figure 16 shows the results on most imperative feature for online buying.

Figure 16. Important features for online consumer buying

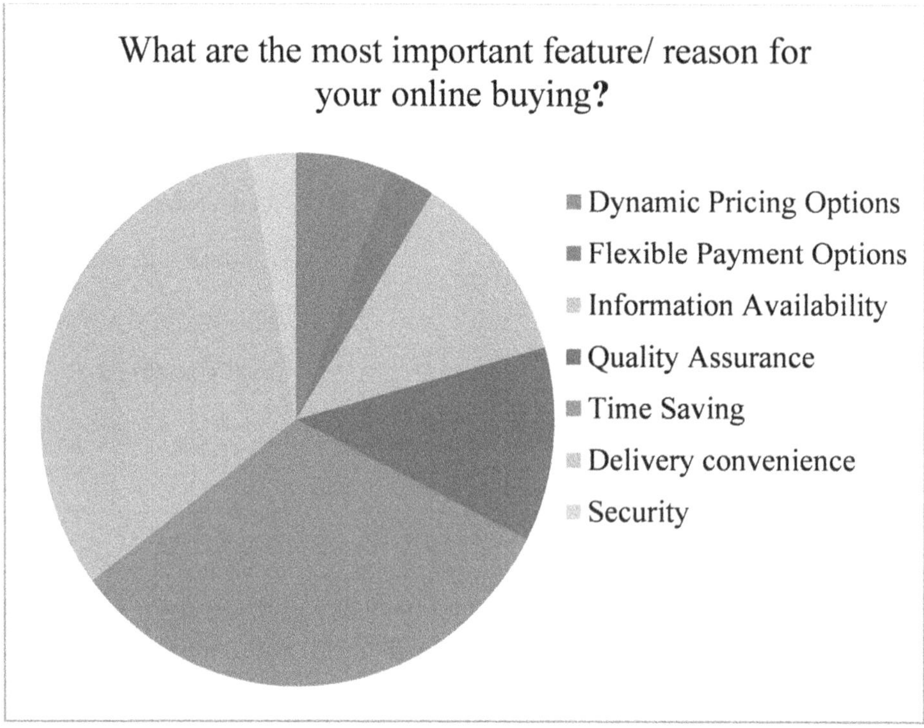

The results show that delivery and time saving are the most important features for online buying. Other features are also important like dynamic pricing, security and flexible payment options but Information availability and quality are the second most important features for online buying in E-com.

CONCLUSION

The study presents the features and factors that are important for understanding the impact of E-com for online buying behavior. Due to technological innovation, the traditional mode of purchase has become inadequate for some individuals. People now prefer simpler modes for acquiring brands and reaching stores, and it can be stated that the Internet has fundamentally changed the consumers' ideas on convenience, speed, price, and product and service information. As a result, vendors have found a new approach to create value for customers and build relationships with them. This study intended to reveal the scale in which the following variables - security, information availability, shipping, quality, pricing and time affect the dependent variable customer satisfaction. The results of this study confirmed that security, information availability, shipping, quality, pricing and time presented significant are features to measure the impact of E-com, however the level of significance varies. The study suggests the E-com to focus on all the features mentioned in the study but major features for decision making for online buying are shipping safety and convenience and time saving.

FUTURE STUDY

E-com is a general technological platform for online buying and selling of products, services and information but the strategies differ from firms to firms and types of products and services. Therefore it is suggested to conduct a quantitative as well as qualitative study based on type of firms and products at micro level and types of industries at macro level.

REFERENCES

Abdulla, A. (2022). Application of MIS in E-CRM: A Literature Review in FMCG Supply Chain. In A. Naim & S. Kautish (Eds.), *Building a Brand Image Through Electronic Customer Relationship Management* (pp. 237–264). IGI Global. doi:10.4018/978-1-6684-5386-5.ch010

Agag, G. (2019). E-commerce ethics and its impact on buyer repurchase intentions and loyalty: An empirical study of small and medium Egyptian businesses. *Journal of Business Ethics, 154*(2), 389–410. doi:10.100710551-017-3452-3

Agag, G., & El-Masry, A. A. (2016). Understanding consumer intention to participate in online travel community and effects on consumer intention to purchase travel online and WOM: An integration of innovation diffusion theory and TAM with trust. *Computers in Human Behavior, 60*, 97–111. doi:10.1016/j.chb.2016.02.038

Alqahtani, H., & Naim, A. (2022). Critical Success Factors for Transforming CRM to SCRM for building E-CRM. In A. Naim & S. Kautish (Eds.), *Building a Brand Image Through Electronic Customer Relationship Management* (pp. 139–168). IGI Global. doi:10.4018/978-1-6684-5386-5.ch007

Alquhtani, S. A., & Muniasamy, A. (2022). Development of Effective Electronic Customer Relationship Management (ECRM) Model by the Applications of Web Intelligence Analytics. In A. Naim & S. Kautish (Eds.), *Building a Brand Image Through Electronic Customer Relationship Management* (pp. 44–63). IGI Global. doi:10.4018/978-1-6684-5386-5.ch003

AyilyathM. (2020). Consumer protection in E-commerce transactions in India—need for reforms, SSRN. doi:10.2139/ssrn.3571069

Ballestar, M., Grau-Carles, P., & Sainz, J. (2018). Customer segmentation in e-commerce: Application to the cashback business model. *Journal of Business Research, 88*, 407–414. doi:10.1016/j.jbusres.2017.11.047

Bandara, R., Fernando, M., & Akter, S. (2019). Explicating the privacy paradox: A qualitative inquiry of online shopping consumers. *Journal of Retailing and Consumer Services, 52*, 220–233. doi:10.1016/j.jretconser.2019.101947

Belanche, D., Flavián, M., & Pérez-Rueda, A. (2020). Mobile apps use and WOM in the food delivery sector: The role of planned behavior, perceived security and customer lifestyle compatibility. *Sustainability, 12*(10), 4275. doi:10.3390u12104275

Belwal, R., Al Shibli, R., & Belwal, S. (2020). *Consumer protection and electronic commerce in the Sultanate of Oman. Journal of Information.* Communication and Ethics in Society. doi:10.1108/JICES-09-2019-0110

Brian, I. S., O'Neill, B. S., & Terence, T. O. (2019). The upside of showrooming: How online information creates positive spill-over for the brick-and-mortar retailer. *Journal of Organizational Computing and Electronic Commerce*, *29*(4), 294–315. doi:10.1080/10919392.2019.1671738

Broome, P. A. (2016). Conceptualizing the foundations of a regional e-commerce strategy: Open networks or closed regimes? The case of CARICOM. *Cogent Business &Management*, *3*(1), 1139–1441. doi:10.1080/23311975.2016.1139441

Castaneda, J. A., Rodriguez-Molina, M. A., & Martínez, T. L. (2009). Attitude's hierarchy of effects in online user behavior. *Online Information Review*, *33*(11), 7–21. doi:10.1108/14684520910944364

Cetina, I., Munthiu, M.-C., & Radulescu, V. (2012). Psychological and Social Factors that Influence Online Consumer Behavior. *Procedia: Social and Behavioral Sciences*, *62*, 184–188. doi:10.1016/j.sbspro.2012.09.029

Changchit, C., Cutshall, R., Lonkani, R., Pholwan, K., & Pongwiritthon, R. (2018). Determinants of online shopping influencing Thai consumer's buying choices. *Journal of Internet Commerce*, *18*(1), 1–23. doi:10.1080/15332861.2018.1496391

Choshin, M., & Ghaffari, A. (2017). An investigation of the impact of effective factors on the success of e-commerce in small- and medium-sized companies. *Computers in Human Behavior*, *66*(1), 67–74. doi:10.1016/j.chb.2016.09.026

Chouhan, R. (2017). E-Business and E-Commerce Management (Strategy, Implementation and Practice). *Pacific Business Review International*, *9*(10), 135–136.

Dai, Z. (2012). The Study on the Influence about Trust to Online Shopping Behavior. In: *Eleventh Wuhan International Conference on e-Business*, (pp. 24–29). Association for Information Systems.

Darsono, J. T., Prihantono, E. Y., & Kasim, E. S. (2019). Strategic Policies for Small and Medium Businesses in marketing through E-commerce. *Entrepreneurship and Sustainability Issues*, *7*(2), 1230–1245. doi:10.9770/jesi.2019.7.2(30)

Doe, J. K., & Asamoah, G. K. (2022). CRM as Antecedent of Electronic Retailing and Online Customer Satisfaction. In A. Naim & S. Kautish (Eds.), *Building a Brand Image Through Electronic Customer Relationship Management* (pp. 169–200). IGI Global. doi:10.4018/978-1-6684-5386-5.ch008

Doern, R. R., & Fey, C. F. (2006). E-commerce developments and strategies for value creation: The case of Russia. *Journal of World Business*, *41*(4), 315–327. doi:10.1016/j.jwb.2006.08.001

Durovic, M. (2020). International consumer law: What is it all about? *Journal of Consumer Policy*, *43*(1), 125–143. doi:10.100710603-019-09438-9

Edgar, T. W., & Manz, D. O. (2017). *Research Methods for Cyber Security*. Elsevier.

Elbeltagi, I., & Agag, G. (2016). E-retailing ethics and its impact on customer satisfaction and repurchase intention: A cultural and commitment-trust theory perspective. *Internet Research*, *26*(1), 288–310. doi:10.1108/IntR-10-2014-0244

Elseidi, R. I. (2018). Understanding Egyptian consumers' intentions in online shopping. *International Journal of Online Marketing*, *8*(3), 1–18. doi:10.4018/IJOM.2018070101

Emma, P., Sara, F., Marta, S., & Ana, G. (2017). *Exploratory study of consumer issues in online peer-to-peer platform markets.* European Commission. file:///C:/Users/BASANT~1/AppData/Local/Temp/Annex5_Task5_Report May2017pdf.

Fatima, S., Alqahtani, H., Naim, A., & Alma'alwi, F. (2022). E-CRM Through Social Media Marketing Activities for Brand Awareness, Brand Image, and Brand Loyalty. In A. Naim & S. Kautish (Eds.), *Building a Brand Image Through Electronic Customer Relationship Management* (pp. 109–138). IGI Global. doi:10.4018/978-1-6684-5386-5.ch006

Filson, D. (2004). The Impact of E-Commerce Strategies on Firm Value: Lessons from Amazon.com and Its Early Competitors. *The Journal of Business*, *77*(2), 135–154. doi:10.1086/381640

Forman, C. (2005). The corporate digital divide: Determinants of Internet adoption. *Management Science*, *51*(4), 641–654. doi:10.1287/mnsc.1040.0343

Hallikainen, H., & Laukkanen, T. (2018). National culture and consumer trust in ecommerce. *International Journal of Information Management*, *38*(1), 97–106. doi:10.1016/j.ijinfomgt.2017.07.002

Harrigan, M., Feddema, K., Wang, S., Harrigan, P., & Diot, E. (2021). How trust leads to online purchase intention founded in perceived usefulness and peer communication. *Journal of Consumer Behaviour: An International Research Review*, 1-16. . doi:10.1002/cb.1936

Harrisson, B., Jean, P., & Dahl, B. (2017). *10 ecommerce trends for 2018.* Project: Growth Strategies in an Omnichannel Retail Context. . doi:10.13140/RG.2.2.34264.19205

Haupt, S. (2003). An economic analysis of consumer protection in Con-trAct law. *German Law Review*, *4*(11), 1137–1164.

Helge, S., Anne, H., & Guido, M. (2020). The function of ability, benevolence, and integrity-based trust in innovation networks. *Industry and Innovation*, *27*(6), 585–604. doi:10.1080/13662716.2019.1632695

Hoda, N. (2022). E-CRM in Digital Payment Services: Its Role and Proposed Framework for Adoption. In A. Naim & S. Kautish (Eds.), *Building a Brand Image Through Electronic Customer Relationship Management* (pp. 1–18). IGI Global. doi:10.4018/978-1-6684-5386-5.ch001

Išoraitė, M., & Miniotienė, N. (2018). *Electronic commerce: Theory and practice.* Integrated Journal of Business and Economics. doi:10.33019/ijbe.v2i2.78

Jaipuriar, A., Khera, A., & Ganguly, S. (2020). *Consumer protection (e-commerce) rules, 2020: A compliance framework in the digital market.* https://www.mondaq.com/india/dodd-frank-consumer-protection-act/977768/consumer-protection-e-commerce-rules-2020-a-compl
iance-framework-in-the-digital-market

Kamal, S., Naim, A., Magd, H., Khan, S. A., & Khan, F. M. (2022). The Relationship Between E-Service Quality, Ease of Use, and E-CRM Performance Referred by Brand Image. In A. Naim & S. Kautish (Eds.), *Building a Brand Image Through Electronic Customer Relationship Management* (pp. 84–108). IGI Global., doi:10.4018/978-1-6684-5386-5.ch005

Kerick, F. (2019). The growth of ecommerce. *Medium.* https://medium.com/swlh/the-growth-of-ecommerce-2220cf2851f3

Khandelwal, P. (2018). Ease of doing E-commerce business in India: The FDI policy relating to Ecommerce and its impact on the Indian economy. *RGNUL Financial and Mercantile Law Review*, 20–37. https://cf9d2836-9a17-4889-b084-bc78a1bb74ee.filesusr.com/ugd/0fa0b3_d7453802d99a4dd7a20ff4b3886b1d04.pdf

Lăzăroiu, G., Neguriţă, O., Grecu, I., Grecu, G., & Mitran, P. C. (2020). Consumers' decision-making process on social commerce platforms: Online trust, perceived risk, and purchase intentions. *Frontiers in Psychology*, *11*, 890. doi:10.3389/fpsyg.2020.00890 PMID:32499740

Lee, O. M. K., & Turban, E. (2001). A trust model for consumer internet shopping. *International Journal of Electronic Commerce*, *6*(1), 75–91. doi:10.1080/10864415.2001.11044227

Liyang, H. (2019). Superior bargaining power: The good, the bad and the ugly. *Asia Pacific Law Review*, *27*(1), 39–61. doi:10.1080/10192557.2019.1661589

Loannis, L., Despoina, M., Gracia, M. D., Amber, D., & Azza R. (2019). *The global governance of online consumer protection and E-commerce-building trust.* We Forum. https://www3.weforum.org/docs/WEF_consumer_protection.pdf

Majithia, V. (2019). The changing landscape of intermediary liability for E-commerce platforms : Emergence of a new regime. *International Journal of Law and Technology*, *15*, 470–493.

Mangiaracina, R., & Perego, A. (2009). Payment systems in the B2C eCommerce: Are they a barrier for the online customer? *Journal of Internet Banking and Commerce*, *14*(3), 1–16.

Milan, J., Antonio, G., & Niklas, A. (2020). Exploring the growth challenge of mobile payment platforms: A business model perspective. *Electronic Commerce Research and Applications*, *40*, 100908. Advance online publication. doi:10.1016/j.elerap.2019.100908

Miyazaki, A., & Fernandez, A. N. A. (2001). Consumer perceptions of privacy and security risks for online shopping. *The Journal of Consumer Affairs*, *35*(1), 27–44. doi:10.1111/j.1745-6606.2001.tb00101.x

Naim, A. (2021a). New Trends in Business Process Management: Applications of Green Information Technologies. *British Journal of Environmental Studies*, *1*(1), 12–23.

Naim, A. (2021b). Green Business Process Management. *International Journal of Innovative Analyses and Emerging Technology*, *1*(6), 125–134. https://openaccessjournals.eu/index.php/ijiaet/article/view/651

Naim, A. (2021c). Applications of MIS in building Electronic Relationship with customers: A case-based study. Periodica Journal of Modern Philosophy. *Social Sciences and Humanities*, *1*, 1–8.

Naim, A. (2021d). Green Information Technologies in Business Operations. Periodica Journal of Modern Philosophy. *Social Sciences and Humanities, 1*, 36–49.

Naim, A. (2021e). Applications of MIS in building Electronic Relationship with customers: A case-based study. Periodica Journal of Modern Philosophy. *Social Sciences and Humanities, 1*, 1–8.

Naim, A. (2021f). Applications of Marketing Framework in Business Practices. *Journal of Marketing and Emerging Economics, 1*(6), 55–70.

Naim, A. (2022a). Neuro- Marketing Techniques for Proposing Information Driven Framework for Decision Making. *International Journal of Innovative Analyses and Emerging Technology, 2*(2), 87–94. https://openaccessjournals.eu/index.php/ijiaet/article/view/1060

Naim, A. (2022b). Measurement Consumer Mood and Emotions for Fast Moving Consumer Goods. *International Journal of Innovative Analyses and Emerging Technology, 2*(2), 83–86.

Naim, A. (2022c). Applications of Green Information Technologies in Business Process Management, Business Issues. *Competition and Entrepreneurship, 31*. doi:10.52305/VIXO9830

Naim, A. (2022d). Successful E-CRM by the Application of Management Information Systems, Business Issues. *Competition and Entrepreneurship, 19*. doi:10.52305/VIXO9830

Naim. (2022e). Emerging Technologies in Finance and Market: Applications of AI Business Issues. *Competition and Entrepreneurship, 137*. https:// doi:10.52305/VIXO9830

Naim, A. (2022f). Mapping of Social Customer Relationship Management with Electronic Customer Relationship Management. *European Journal of Interdisciplinary Research and Development, 2*, 14–25. https://ejird.journalspark.org/index.php/ejird/article/view/10

Naim, A. (2022g). Factors of Consumer Behaviour of youth from middle-east when purchasing Organic Food. *Global Scientific Review, 3*, 1–7.

Naim, A. (2022h). Understanding the Customer Centric Approach to Add Value to Social Ecrm (SE-CRM). *British Journal of Global Ecology and Sustainable Development, 4*, 1–17. https://journalzone.org/index.php/bjgesd/article/view/45

Naim, A., Alahmari, F., & Rahim, A. (2021). Role of Artificial Intelligence in Market Development and Vehicular Communication. Smart Antennas. *Recent Trends in Design and Applications, 2*, 28–39. doi:10.2174/9781681088594121020006

Naim, A., Alqahtani, H., Muniasamy, A., Bilfaqih, S. M., Mahveen, R., & Mahjabeen, R. (2023). Applications of Information Systems and Data Security in Marketing Management. In A. Naim, P. Malik, & F. Zaidi (Eds.), *Fraud Prevention, Confidentiality, and Data Security for Modern Businesses* (pp. 57–83). IGI Global., doi:10.4018/978-1-6684-6581-3.ch003

Naim, A., & Alqahtani, K. (2021). Role of Information Systems in Customer Relationship Management. *Pulse, 2*(2).

Naim, A., & Alqahtani, K. (2022). Applications of Decision Support Systems in CRM, Business Issues. *Competition and Entrepreneurship 1.* https://static1.squarespace.com/static/56330ad3e4b0733dcc0c8495/t/56b96e2f22482e110fab1f78/1454992944362/GLJ_Vol_04_No_11_Haupt.pdf doi:10.52305/VIXO9830

Naim, A., & Kautish, S. K. (Eds.). (2022). *Building a Brand Image Through Electronic Customer Relationship Management.* IGI Global., doi:10.4018/978-1-6684-5386-5

Naim, A., & Khan, M. F. (2021). Measuring the Psychological Behavior of Consumers for Medical Services. *Zien Journal of Social Sciences and Humanities, 2,* 119–131. https://zienjournals.com/index.php/zjssh/article/view/316

Naim, A. & Khan, M. F. (2022) Consumer Behavior Appraisal for Health and Fitness Services Business Issues. *Competition and Entrepreneurship 53.* https:// doi:10.52305/VIXO9830

Naim, A. & Malik, P. (2022). *Competitive Trends and Technologies in Business Management.* Nova Science Publisher. doi:10.52305/VIXO9830

Naim, A., Malik, P. K., & Zaidi, F. A. (Eds.). (2023). *Fraud Prevention, Confidentiality, and Data Security for Modern Businesses.* IGI Global. doi:10.4018/978-1-6684-6581-3

Naim, A., Muniasamy, A., Clementking, A., & Rajkumar, R. (2022). Relevance of Green Manufacturing and IoT in Industrial Transformation and Marketing Management. In M. Lahby, A. Al-Fuqaha, & Y. Maleh (Eds.), *Computational Intelligence Techniques for Green Smart Cities. Green Energy and Technology.* Springer. doi:10.1007/978-3-030-96429-0_19

Najar, M., Misbah, M., Yaqub, H., & Bilfagih, M. (2022). Entrepreneurial Marketing of E-CRM in SMEs. In A. Naim & S. Kautish (Eds.), *Building a Brand Image Through Electronic Customer Relationship Management* (pp. 265–285). IGI Global. doi:10.4018/978-1-6684-5386-5.ch011

Orendorff, A. (2019). *Global ecommerce statistics and trends to launch your business beyond borders.* Shopify. https://www.shopify.com/enterprise/global-ecommerce-statistics#8

Saleem, M., Khan, S. A., & Magd, H. (2022). Content Marketing Framework for Building Brand Image: A Case Study of Sohar International School, Oman. In A. Naim & S. Kautish (Eds.), *Building a Brand Image Through Electronic Customer Relationship Management* (pp. 64–83). IGI Global. doi:10.4018/978-1-6684-5386-5.ch004

Shirazi, F., Adam, N. A., Shanmugam, M., & Schultz, C. D. (2020). The importance of trust for electronic commerce satisfaction: An entrepreneurial perspective. *British Food Journal, 123*(2), 789–802. doi:10.1108/BFJ-07-2020-0626

Siciliani, P., Riefa, C., & Gamper, H. (2019). *Consumer theories of harm: An economic approach to consumer law enforcement and policy making.* Hart Publishing. doi:10.5040/9781509916887

Song, B. L. (2022). The Role of E-CRM in Building Customer Satisfaction and Repurchase Intention: Evidence From the FMCG Industry. In A. Naim & S. Kautish (Eds.), *Building a Brand Image Through Electronic Customer Relationship Management* (pp. 19–43). IGI Global. doi:10.4018/978-1-6684-5386-5.ch002

UNCTAD. (2019). *Measuring E-commerce and the digital economy*. UNCTAD. https://unctad.org/topic/ecommerce-and-digital-economy/measuring-ecommerce-digital-economy

UNESAP & ADB. (2019). *Embracing the E-commerce revolution in Asia and the Pacific*. UNCTAD. https://www.adb.org/sites/default/files/publication/430401/embracing-e-commerce-revolution.pdf

Verma, R., & Kumar, M. (2022). Brand Extension in FMCG Sector Through Social Media Enabled CRM and Investigating Its Impact on Brand Equity. In A. Naim & S. Kautish (Eds.), *Building a Brand Image Through Electronic Customer Relationship Management* (pp. 201–236). IGI Global. doi:10.4018/978-1-6684-5386-5.ch009

Wajeeha, A., Annas, H., & Kashif, F. (2019). Underlying factors influencing consumers' trust and loyalty in E-commerce. *Business Perspectives and Research*, *8*(2), 186–204. doi:10.1177/2278533719887451

Wang, X., Tajvidi, M., Lin, X., & Hajli, N. (2019). Towards an ethical and trustworthy social commerce community for brand value Co-creation: A trust-commitment perspective. *Journal of Business Ethics*, *167*(1), 137–152. doi:10.100710551-019-04182-z

World Economic Forum. (2019). The global governance of online consumer protection and e-commerce building trust. WEF. https://www3.weforum.org/docs/WEF_consumer_protection.pdf

Xiaodong, Q., & Min, L. (2020). E-commerce user type recognition based on access sequence similarity. *Journal of Organizational Computing and Electronic Commerce*, *30*(3), 209–223. doi:10.1080/10919392.2020.1742552

Yang, Z., Van Ngo, Q., Chen, Y., Nguyen, C. X.-T., & Hoang, H. T. (2019). Does ethics perception foster consumer repurchase intention? Role of trust, perceived uncertainty, and shopping habit. *SAGE Open*, *9*(2). doi:10.1177/2158244019848844

Zuhal, H. (2019). The gamut of E-commerce: Between online fraud and trust towards technology among generation Y. *International Journal of Mechanical Engineering and Technology*, *10*(01), 830–836. http://www.iaeme.com/IJMET/issues.asp?JType=IJMET&VType=10&Type=01

Chapter 15
Changing Trends of Media Ownership:
Marketing Through Community Engagement in Hindi Television News Channels

Nipunika Sarkar
Amity University, Noida, India

Ruhi Lal
Amity University, Noida, India

ABSTRACT

This research study is based on changing media ownership and its relationship with the audience, keeping ethics in context. Thematic review of literature was done to check the availability of information for the four objectives. The methodology adopted was case study of Network 18 and NDTV, taken over by business conglomerates Adani and Reliance. The study was also conducted by talking to senior journalists of NDTV, Network 18, Aajtak, ABP News, and News X. Ethics and connection with the audience in content by journalists was a major concern. The researcher has studied channels' ownership patterns, marketing strategies, and to established the role of ownership in media businesses.

INTRODUCTION

The media is critical in alerting the public about community engagement, public welfare, and environmental dangers. Amidst the fact that climate change is a worldwide issue, developing nations such as India are typically more sensitive to its consequences owing to poverty, illiteracy, and a lack of public knowledge (Thaker, Zhao, & Leiserowitz, 2017).

For the first time in nations "outside the West," such as the Middle East, Africa, and Asia, a new type of "entertaining news" received mostly through television has become a privileged sphere of politics. The

DOI: 10.4018/978-1-6684-8166-0.ch015

Indian media, by ensuring adequate and accurate coverage of community engagement issues from reliable sources, can help to increase public participation among a mainly uninformed populace (Roy, 2015).

Political media ownership and the creation of near monopolies in the markets for languages, states, and metros affect TV content distribution. Among the national cable providers, there are examples of cross-media ownership. Such information is either deeply buried or provided in an opaque manner. The companies are deploying marketing strategies to build community engagement as per the changing trends.

The political ramifications of this development How do media and politics intersect in these regions, and how does media ownership play an important role in it? These issues are discussed using a case study as a method of research. The world's biggest democracy, where two decades of media development and liberalisation have resulted in the world's largest number of commercial television news stations (Chakravartty & Roy, 2013), is the subject of this research.

Objectives

1. To assess the ownership patterns of Hindi TV news channels.
2. To explore the sources of revenue for Hindi TV news channels.
3. To find out about the ethical paradigm shift in Hindi, watch TV news channels.
4. to observe engagement with the community on Hindi TV news channels.

REVIEW OF LITERATURE

Sources of Revenue for Hindi TV News Channels

The media and communications industries have grown rapidly in India because of liberalisation and the opening up of the sky. When the researcher contemplates multiple cultural flows in the age of globalisation, capital privileges appear to be fading. This dissertation makes the case that a more accurate analysis would have to consider media ownership trends in order to identify who is in charge. This method does not have a single winner. New Indian enterprises that have profited from established Indian and worldwide commercial giants' political clout are challenging their interests and their big pockets. They are influencing our media landscape and history together (Sumanth, 2011). The Federation of Indian Chambers of Commerce and Business (FICCI) and KPMG (Klynveld Peat Marwick Goerdeler) jointly released a report in 2014 that stated, "Today, India's M&E industry reaches millions of people." These are all platforms with the capacity to effect change and act as catalysts for transformation. The year 2013 was turbulent for the sector. The industry encountered a number of difficulties during the economic downturn, both commercial and regulatory. The industry's basis, however, was strengthened in 2013 in order to position itself for expansion when the economy picked up. The study presents substantial proof that, in comparison to all other Indian industries, the media and entertainment sector in India has grown significantly (Thussu, 2007).

The sector is still expanding in many different ways, for a variety of reasons, and there is still room for greater growth, expansion, and penetration. India has a big, untapped media market. Thussu (2007) The majority of experts concur that this market will likely experience significant expansion, consolidation, and convergence during the next few years. The changes will be brought about by digitization, globalisation, and the proliferation of traditional media firms in markets like the internet and television, which they already have to some extent. But despite all of these expanding media facts, "media ownership and content" continues to be a major source of worry. Media ownership patterns and how they affect media content have always been contentious topics. The time when news values were primarily based on specific pre-set news values has long since passed. Instead, terminology like sensational news, paid news, advertorials, media biases, and media economics has taken their place. The goal of the article is to draw attention to a few key areas and problems related to the development of media ownership and its effect on media content (Mukherjee, 2015).

India is one of the top 15 international marketplaces for media and entertainment, with yearly revenues of roughly $17 billion in 2012. While India's rise as an emerging economy, its enormous promise as the largest democracy in the world, and its future growth trajectory have received a lot of attention recently, little is known about the role of India's developing media industry in this larger story. (Mehta, 2015). Due to the sizable and steadily rising urban middle class, global media mogul Rupert Murdoch has played a significant role in the exponential growth of the Indian television market. His Star network's success in India is a result of market-driven strategies, which include expert content localization (Thussu, 2007). As economic thought evolved, various theories were spread to explain money management and the actions that followed it to balance supply and demand (Jha, 2013). The study of the micro and macro features of each business broadens the economic vision. Today, the mass media has developed into a sector of the economy that offers consumers products and services. As mass media has grown, it has opened up opportunities for numerous important players to join this sector and play crucial roles like content providers, exhibitors, and distributors. Priorities and objectives in the media are always shifting to reflect the needs of the market. Every media industry is trying to figure out how to create content with little effort and make money off of it. The economic operation of the media sector may be impacted by any changes to regulatory laws and technological developments (Mehta, 2015).

Ethical Paradigm Shift in Hindi TV News Channels

In the past 15 years, the Indian media landscape has seen significant upheaval. Progressive privatisation and deregulation have led to more entertainment-focused news than news focused on public service. Various studies have examined the moral dilemmas Indian journalists encounter in today's highly internationalised media landscape. Interactive workshops were held in several Indian cities and served as the foundation for our research (Rao & Johal, 2006). The results of these workshops show that, despite the major ethical dilemmas that journalists face, media ethics is not a subject that is frequently discussed in Indian newsrooms and TV stations. Journalism ethics and problems, including accountability, independence, and conflict of interest, are being impacted by marketing demands, the tabloidization of news, managerial challenges, and economic pressures. Lack of professional training, particularly in the area of ethics, is harming journalists' comprehension of ideas like privacy and accuracy (Rao and Johal, 2006).

An important factor in figuring out how journalism is evolving is answering the question of who owns the media and why. There is a lack of openness in how news organisations are managed and financed, according to recent exposes of phoney transactions, dishonest business practises, and the use of black money to finance Indian news media. To demonstrate the point, an analysis of five incidents involving prominent Indian news organisations is presented. Additionally, the corporate takeover of news space by non-media entities foreshadows the emergence of a press that is no longer able to protect democracy (Saeed, 2015). The 1990s saw a media efflorescence in India, primarily in television, which has revolutionised the South Asian media landscape. Indian channels established their dominance, earned the highest viewership ratings, and compelled international channels to significantly increase their adoption of local programming as the novelty of foreign channels faded in the early 1990s. In localised markets and among India's enormous diaspora across continents, language- and region-specific channels replaced pan-Indian networks in the late 1990s. Furthermore, Indian media output is becoming seen as a form of cultural imperialism in South Asia, much as western output was throughout the 1960s and 1970s. The strength and vitality of Indian media seem to challenge the stereotype of media imperialism (Sonwalkar, 2001).

In order to recognise the speed of change in this era of globalisation, Sonwalkar (2001) contends that the Indian media situation has the makings of "small cultural/media imperialism" and advocates for a multi-centric perspective as opposed to a linear Western-centric one. India's media industry has undergone profound and transformative change over the past 20 years, which is reflected in the growth of both outlets and audiences. The nation has over 100 news channels that reach 161 million TV households, about 94,067 newspapers, and more than 200 million Internet users, according to recent estimates. These changes have given rise to an expanding body of discourse that highlights the expansion and vitality of the Indian media. This narrative is typically jubilant, but it doesn't pay attention to the more alarming structural patterns that are increasingly defining the nation's media environment. Commercialism, increased concentration, cross-media ownership, and increased governmental and corporate influence over the media are a few of these. Many studies have examined the development and operation of these structural changes from a political-economic perspective. It disputes the widely held belief that India's media environment is dynamic and pluralistic and makes the case that current developments in the Indian media environment have profoundly negative effects on news reporting and the nation's overall standard of journalism (Chadha, 2017).

Community Engagement in Hindi TV News Channels

Until 1991, Door Darshan, a public service broadcaster, was the only television station in India. Early in the 1990s, India's economy was opened up, allowing private broadcasters to set up shop there. There are now an enormous number of television channels. India had more than 200 digital channels by the year 2005. 800 television channels were available in 2012, up from 600 in 2010. More than 400 news and current affairs channels are included in this. Regional and specialised channels are expanding because of the severe rivalry created by technological advancements in news and entertainment channels. (Chadha, 2017)

Television continues to be the preferred medium for advertisers due to the expansion of cable, satellite, and direct-to-home television services. To boost their revenue, broadcasters are also utilising web and mobile media. As television is the most potent medium, this article aims to examine how the Government of India's media strategy has changed as a result of privatisation and how different institutional mechanisms have been developed to deal with the expansion of this medium. Despite linguistic and cultural limitations, television visuals are broadcast to a huge portion of the Indian population (Rani, 2013). In India, the relationship between the media, state, and market underwent a significant recasting in the 1990s with the start of economic reforms. The public broadcaster Doordarshan's long-standing monopoly in the television news media field has been challenged by the emergence of a plethora of competing private television news outlets. Private involvement in the television news industry was consistent with market capitalism (Sonwalkar, 2001).

The market-based news paradigm fundamentally changed how news is produced, represented, and consumed. The rise of views-opinion-based prime time programming in television news media in modern

India is one such prominent feature of news production that Devi investigates. Devi made an effort to understand the causes, nature, relevance, and anticipated impact of such programming on the nature of public discourse in India through a series of semi-structured interviews with journalists. (Devi, 2019). The main ethical issues raised by journalists and editors employed by media organisations in Hyderabad, India, are identified by Rao & Malik. The authors suggest using economist and Nobel laureate Amartya Sen's capabilities approach as a theoretical framework for the creation of future journalism ethics programmes in order to address these issues and difficulties (Malik and Rao, 2019).

Cross-media ownership, which promotes a political economy centred on revenue generation instead of journalism for the public good, problems with the publication of inaccurate information, which are now exacerbated by the ubiquitous nature of social media, and a culture of "democratic deficit," where journalists find it increasingly difficult to practise journalism safely and to report about poverty, corruption, and other social ills (Malik and Rao, 2019), These issues were the main challenges cited by the journalists and editors. Sen's capabilities approach suggests the integration of specific knowledge systems, including the study and reporting of injustices in democratic societies, the emphasis on whether people have flourishing lives that provide them with the opportunities, freedoms, and choices they require, and economic and political freedoms that enable journalists to comprehend and value reporting on inequality and bolstering democratic institutions (Malik and Rao, 2019).

The TV broadcasters prioritised celebrity campaigners and "ticket" distribution during the 2014 Lok Sabha elections over development-related initiatives. The media consistently gives sectarian politics and hate speech more attention than social sector issues. There was no mention of hunger, poverty, inequality, prejudice, or displacement in the discussion. Political organisations and figures, such as Narendra Modi of the Bharatiya Janata Party (BJP), who received more media attention than any of his rivals, similarly avoided providing a concrete definition of "progress," seemingly on purpose. It appears that the Modi brand has been used as a stand-in for progress and ethical leadership. On television, concerns like corruption and inflation seemed unimportant. (Chakrabarty & Roy, 2015). While elections today are "mediated" in the sense that they are influenced by the overt and covert actions of various media, the Indian national elections of 2014 highlight a particular logic of "mediated populism" that has recently gained prominence on a worldwide scale (Malik and Rao, 2019).

The researcher looked at the broader political-economic dynamics and circumstances that shape and entrench the Modi phenomenon to better understand the contexts and lineages of the current mediated populism. The study concentrated on how these specific political and historical factors have impacted and made possible the shifting relationships among privatised media across platforms, political elites, and conceptions and productions of "the people" (Malik and Rao, 2019). The political history of India has been strongly tied to the media since the country's independence movement, which got underway in the latter half of the nineteenth century. The media was crucial in organising and unifying the populace against the British. India became independent and, in keeping with its belief in democracy, held elections to choose its quasi-federal government every five years. At the regional or provincial level, there are now several influential, active players (Malik and Rao, 2019).

The fact that every political party either owns or runs a television channel to spread its ideas or honour its leaders demonstrates how closely media and politics are intertwined. Even those who are affiliated with enterprises have strong political party allegiances. Television has a much wider audience than any other form of communication in India, where there are currently more than 800 channels in operation (Mudgal, 2015). Gudipaty (2017) focuses on how 24-hour news television networks can influence most of the electorate and project exaggerated images of leaders that trump reality. Politicians use news channels creatively to develop a certain image despite allegations of nepotism and corruption. They also have the luxury of time and space on the channels to which they have access, which helps them win elections. Gudipaty examines the phenomenon of media influence in India through case studies of national, regional, and state leaders who used television to conceal their flaws and offer a theatrical experience to appeal to voters (Gudipaty, 2017).

Ownership Patterns of Hindi TV News Channels

In the past 15 years, the Indian media landscape has seen significant upheaval. Progressive privatisation and deregulation have led to more entertainment-focused news than news focused on public service. In such a globally connected media environment, Rao and Johal looked at the ethical challenges faced by Indian journalists (Johal & Rao, 2009). Interactive workshops were held in several Indian cities and served as the foundation for our research. The results of these workshops show that, despite the major ethical dilemmas that journalists face, media ethics is not a subject that is frequently discussed in Indian newsrooms and TV stations. Journalism ethics and problems, including accountability, independence, and conflict of interest, are being impacted by marketing demands, the tabloidization of news, managerial challenges, and economic pressures. Lack of professional training, particularly in the area of ethics, is harming journalists' comprehension of ideas like privacy and accuracy (Johal & Rao, 2009).

Media ownership structures in India are evolving very quickly lately. New cross-media corporations have been established by privately held family-owned newspapers and gone public. A few small, privately held television networks have also gone public on the stock market (e.g., New Delhi Television and TV Today). The government has permitted 26% FDI in print media in News1, even though significant control over editorial procedures, production, and distribution still rests in the hands of Indian owners (for instance, Mail Today is a partnership between Associated Newspapers of the UK and the India Today Group, and CNN-IBN has a CNN investment in Network 18, which runs the channel). Examples include the Oswal group's investment in New Delhi Television, Blackstone PE's investment in Jagran Media, which later led to the purchase of Mid-Day Multimedia, and Malaysia's Astro All Asia Networks' acquisition of interests in NDTV Lifestyle, Turmeric Vision, and Sun Direct TV. 2. Reliance Industries Limited (RIL), the largest private firm in India, has bought Network18 Group, the nation's largest news organisation. (Kumar, 2015) Through its subsidiary TV18 Broadcast Ltd., Network18 Group operates a variety of TV networks, including CNN-IBN, IBN7, CNBC-TV18, and CNBC Awaaz. Through another subsidiary, ETV News Network, the company also operates roughly a dozen regional-language TV networks. the growth of newspapers and news publications into television and radio broadcasting (for instance, Times of India has its own TV channel called Times Now and FM radio station Radio Mirchi; Living Media India Ltd., the publishers of India Today, has acquired interests in television and radio as well as the newspaper business); and the entry of television media into the newspaper business (Zed TV, for instance, is the owner of the DNA newspaper) have led to the formation of integrated media enterprises. (Jain, 2010). Along with vertical integration between cable distributors and television broadcasters, corporate investment in the media will also aid in its consolidation, lowering competition and options for newspaper and TV readers (Kumar, 2015). The Reliance-TV18 agreement is the most notable of these. The TV-18 agreement grants RIL priority access to material across all of its platforms, including websites and TV stations. Following this, Reliance Infratel and Mukesh Ambani's Reliance Infotel, which holds an all-India 4G telecom licence, signed a second agreement to share Reliance Infratel's 50,000 fibre-optic tower network. Most other mobile phone providers use microwave towers, which are less reliable for high-speed data transfer. (Jain, 2010).. The media content received from TV 18 can be provided through smart phones and tablets by Reliance Infotel once RIL introduces its 4G services, combined with free gadgets capable of delivering news and entertainment. It is foreseeable what will happen as a result of the massive corporate investment in the media: One is that the media industry will consolidate as vertical integration takes place between TV broadcasters and distributors, whether cable distributors or mobile service providers, diminishing competition and choice for news consumers. (Jain, 2010) .. Two, because the larger players tend to define the news agenda, pluralism and variety in the media will suffer. Three, news will be viewed more and more as a product that must be offered to people in formats that are pleasant and simple to consume. Four: as boardroom control over the newsroom grows, the already tenuous line separating the church and the state in media organisations is likely to be destroyed. The colour and flavour of new items will increasingly be determined by corporate economic and political agendas (Bhushan, 2015).

After the Bombay terrorist attacks in November 2008, the electronic media itself became the subject of a tale. While many people praised the comprehensive 60-hour coverage of the attacks, a discussion about the impact of the nonstop live broadcast on security operations and government actions soon emerged. Most significantly, more serious concerns about the evolving ethics and aesthetics of Indian electronic media have surfaced. Jain (2010) suggests examining how the Gujarat pogrom of 2002, the first significant Indian riots of the 24-hour television era, was represented in electronic media to comprehend this significant shift in media concerns, politics, and forms of representation. According to Jain, the comprehensive coverage of the Gujarat fire is what permanently altered how "crisis" is portrayed and its impact on the public sphere because of the 24-hour news phenomenon. (Jain, 2010).

Ownership Patterns of Hindi TV News Channels

In the past 15 years, the Indian media landscape has seen significant upheaval. Progressive privatisation and deregulation have led to more entertainment-focused news than news focused on public service. In such a globally connected media environment, Rao and Johal looked at the ethical challenges faced by Indian journalists (Johal & Rao, 2009). Interactive workshops were held in several Indian cities and served as the foundation for our research. The results of these workshops show that, despite the major ethical dilemmas that journalists face, media ethics is not a subject that is frequently discussed in Indian newsrooms and TV stations. Journalism ethics and problems, including accountability, independence, and conflict of interest, are being impacted by marketing demands, the tabloidization of news, managerial challenges, and economic pressures. Lack of professional training, particularly in the area of ethics, is harming journalists' comprehension of ideas like privacy and accuracy (Johal & Rao, 2009).

Media ownership structures in India are evolving very quickly lately. New cross-media corporations have been established by privately held family-owned newspapers and gone public. A few small, privately held television networks have also gone public on the stock market (e.g., New Delhi Television and TV Today). The government has permitted 26% FDI in print media in News1, even though significant control over editorial procedures, production, and distribution still rests in the hands of Indian owners (for instance, Mail Today is a partnership between Associated Newspapers of the UK and the India Today Group, and CNN-IBN has a CNN investment in Network 18, which runs the channel). Examples include the Oswal group's investment in New Delhi Television, Blackstone PE's investment in Jagran Media, which later led to the purchase of Mid-Day Multimedia, and Malaysia's Astro All Asia Networks' acquisition of interests in NDTV Lifestyle, Turmeric Vision, and Sun Direct TV. 2. Reliance Industries

Limited (RIL), the largest private firm in India, has bought Network18 Group, the nation's largest news organisation. (Kumar, 2015) Through its subsidiary TV18 Broadcast Ltd., Network18 Group operates a variety of TV networks, including CNN-IBN, IBN7, CNBC-TV18, and CNBC Awaaz. Through another subsidiary, ETV News Network, the company also operates roughly a dozen regional-language TV networks. the growth of newspapers and news publications into television and radio broadcasting (for instance, Times of India has its own TV channel called Times Now and FM radio station Radio Mirchi; Living Media India Ltd., the publishers of India Today, has acquired interests in television and radio as well as the newspaper business); and the entry of television media into the newspaper business (Zed TV, for instance, is the owner of the DNA newspaper) have led to the formation of integrated media enterprises. (Jain, 2010). Along with vertical integration between cable distributors and television broadcasters, corporate investment in the media will also aid in its consolidation, lowering competition and options for newspaper and TV readers (Kumar, 2015). The Reliance-TV18 agreement is the most notable of these. The TV-18 agreement grants RIL priority access to material across all of its platforms, including websites and TV stations. Following this, Reliance Infratel and Mukesh Ambani's Reliance Infotel, which holds an all-India 4G telecom licence, signed a second agreement to share Reliance Infratel's 50,000 fibre-optic tower network. Most other mobile phone providers use microwave towers, which are less reliable for high-speed data transfer. (Jain, 2010).. The media content received from TV 18 can be provided through smart phones and tablets by Reliance Infotel once RIL introduces its 4G services, combined with free gadgets capable of delivering news and entertainment. It is foreseeable what will happen as a result of the massive corporate investment in the media: One is that the media industry will consolidate as vertical integration takes place between TV broadcasters and distributors, whether cable distributors or mobile service providers, diminishing competition and choice for news consumers. (Jain, 2010). Two, because the larger players tend to define the news agenda, pluralism and variety in the media will suffer. Three, news will be viewed more and more as a product that must be offered to people in formats that are pleasant and simple to consume. Four: as boardroom control over the newsroom grows, the already tenuous line separating the church and the state in media organisations is likely to be destroyed. The colour and flavour of new items will increasingly be determined by corporate economic and political agendas (Bhushan, 2015).

After the Bombay terrorist attacks in November 2008, the electronic media itself became the subject of a tale. While many people praised the comprehensive 60-hour coverage of the attacks, a discussion about the impact of the nonstop live broadcast on security operations and government actions soon emerged. Most significantly, more serious concerns about the evolving ethics and aesthetics of Indian electronic media have surfaced. Jain (2010) suggests examining how the Gujarat pogrom of 2002, the first significant Indian riots of the 24-hour television era, was represented in electronic media to comprehend this significant shift in media concerns, politics, and forms of representation. According to Jain, the comprehensive coverage of the Gujarat fire is what permanently altered how "crisis" is portrayed and its impact on the public sphere because of the 24-hour news phenomenon. (Jain, 2010).

Digital Marketing Strategies for Community Engagement

The media companies are creating and sharing valuable content as an effective way to engage with the community by creating blog posts, videos, infographics, and other forms of content that will provide value to the audience. The brands share the content on social media and other platforms to reach a wider audience and connect (Oestreicher-Singer & Zalmanson, 2013). Online communities such as forums, groups, and message boards are commonly used as great places to engage with the community. Relevant communities participate in discussions to build relationships with the audience (Williamson & Ruming, 2020). Studies have investigated the environment of 24-hour private news channels in India today that involved interviews, observations, and content analysis on engaging communities (Rao & Malik, 2018). It provides interesting looks at how one of the largest news organisations in the world operates through marketing and how they create the reality that the viewers see daily. Studies based on fieldwork conducted in Mumbai and Kolkata not only provided a thorough description of the television newsroom, its rituals, and rhythms, but also went beyond it to look at how editorial and corporate strategies are converging more and more in a profit-driven sector of the media. Studies have investigated how news channels create a vision of nationhood and of a prosperous and vibrant economy that primarily serves the needs of the resurgent Indian middle class by analysing how TRPs work to produce a non-inclusive idea of the "audience" and looking at hundreds of hours of news content (Kumar, 2015).

Because of COVID-19, there is a global health problem. Marketers designed campaigns to use this as an opportunity to connect with the community and engage them. The search for a vaccine to stop the pandemic's spread is a top priority for all medical professionals, scientists, and government authorities. Since the globe is dealing with brand-new, terrifying diseases, television in particular has performed a very beneficial and responsible role in maintaining citizens' composure and motivation. With the use of television, the government and its representatives are able to reach the people and distribute urgent requests and directives for tackling the global problem (Ayedee & Manocha, 2020). The daily news and information broadcast by this antiquated medium makes people feel emotionally connected and protected. In this scenario, the nation might experience severe rioting, panic, and environmental disturbances, which could result in another big disaster and the spread of the fatal virus. Television and news media have been vital in dispelling rumours and fostering a positive and upbeat mood in the nation in order to keep this crisis under control and maintain the finest of tranquilly and peace. The most sombre box, as opposed to the funniest box, stupid box, or patriotic box, has emerged (Ayedee & Manocha, 2020). Rao (2018) looks at globalisation through a Ronald Robertson theoretical framework to understand the changes in Indian journalism practises and news content. When considered as a whole, the impact of globalisation on news in India may be seen as a series of actions taken by local media that have revitalised the local, absorbed the global, and provided audiences the chance to build democratic discourses. (Rao & Malik, 2018).

News content continues to be very locally focused in terms of its aim and breadth even as journalism techniques such as the integration of new information technology, enhanced audience feedback, and increased professional training of journalism students have become more widespread worldwide. (Rao, 2009). In his analysis of the tensions between journalistic standards and (imagined) audience expectations, Gluck (2021) finds three key characteristics of emotional engagement in news reporting. His study examines the connection between emotionally (dis)engaging aspects of television news coverage and the justification for their use by journalists. Gluck (2021) integrates two qualitative methodologies in order to address the production and content aspects of journalism. In addition to a detailed study of TV news, Gluck's research includes semi-structured interviews with about 50 journalists from each nation. The study is situated within a cross-national comparative framework of two very distinct television cultures—the United Kingdom and India—where discussions of emotional engagement contrast a rigidly regulated public service television market in the UK with fiercely competitive 24-hour commercial news programmes in India. The study illustrates how journalists currently envision news programmes. Gluck also aims to include a de-Westernising perspective within journalism studies by exposing journalistic practises outside of the normative model of Anglo-American journalism. (Gluck, 2021). The liberalisation of the Indian economy brought about a number of unforeseen changes, but none may have been as shocking or as far-reaching in their effects as the restructuring of the media sector, notably television. From its modest origins in 1959 as a state-sponsored educational project, the industry was estimated to be valued at more than 185 billion dollars by 2006 (about 230 million pounds) (Kohli, 2006). Gloss, glitz, and cash have taken the place of the old black-and-white days.

The state sponsored Doordarshan, the only channel on Indian airways until the early 1990s, has been surpassed, and private channels have experienced the most astonishing development over the past 20 years, increasing to a total of about 360 now (Batabyal, 2013). Nearly 160 more are awaiting official approval to broadcast. 1. Of all television viewers in the world today, Indians are the most spoiled for choice. In India, there are presently more than 100 million television-owning households (Batabyal, 2013). Seventy million of them have cable or satellite television connections. They have a wide range of choices at their disposal, including movie channels, music channels, television soap operas, and 24-hour newscasts. Cable News Network (CNN) and British Broadcasting Corporation (BBC), the Star TV channel bouquet owned by Rupert Murdoch, international sports networks, and the country's own Zed Television all compete for the Indian audience's attention (Batabyal, 2013). The revolution that brought about significant improvements in India's socioeconomic situation included the emergence of electronic media. (Singh,2015).

The purpose of the study is to examine trends in the presentation of primetime news material while also examining their historical development and perceived contributing elements. The specific goals are as follows: to examine the factors that have contributed to the evolution of primetime news formats; to analyse the content of primetime news programmes on Indian TV news channels in order to identify trends; to explore the evolution of primetime news formats in their historical context to gather and analyse public opinions about the changing primetime TV news formats; and to investigate the effects of these changing news formats on the news coverage in other media and public viewing habits. For this, the researcher largely used the content analysis approach, with the sociological survey method of study serving as an addition. To investigate the trends in news presentation, a content analysis of selected television channels' primetime newscasts was done.

RESEARCH METHODOLOGY

The research technique is case study analysis inside qualitative research with an interpretative approach targeted at in-depth examination. The case study research strategy is employed in this study as a method for data inquiry, and the goal is to support the integration of qualitative content analysis into data analysis in case study research. The study relied on secondary data from published sources to support theoretical arguments and discussions. The descriptive approach was used to investigate data acquired from many sources and draw conclusions based on the holistic and relevant qualities of real-life occurrences. The case study choose to rely on numerous sources of evidence, using data to converge in a triangulating method with theoretical hypotheses for data gathering and analysis.

The case stories were developed by taking information gleaned from formal interviews with ten journalists, two from each television channel, including NDTV, Network 18, ABP News, NEWS X, and AAJ TAK. The data collected through interviews was used to create a case study for analysis and findings.

In this research, a case study is taken as the research approach that is commonly used in the social and life sciences. A case study is an intense examination of a person, a group of persons, or a unit with the goal of generalising across numerous units. The study is an intense, systematic assessment of the community, in which the researcher examines detailed data on numerous factors.

Researchers explain how case studies investigate complicated events in their natural context to gain a better understanding of them.

Independent Variable: Ownership Pattern
Mediating: Marketing Strategies, Content
Dependent Variable: Ethical Paradigm Shift, Community Engagement

Sampling: In this research study purposive sampling, a non-probability sampling technique is used in which multiple case studies are selected because they have characteristics that are the need of the study. The case studies are selected to achieve the objectives of the research study.

Case Selection Procedure

The case selection is deliberate (non-random). In this research study, the case(s) chosen and identified for this comprehensive study is drawn from a specific population, and the grounds for this selection are determined by the field of research and relevance of the sample, as well as the sample's location within that community. A prior cross-case approach with qualitative evaluation analysis was used in the case study selection procedures. It was predicated on specific assumptions about the larger population, relevant data from the significant sample on essential factors for accuracy, and the conceptual validity of the variables. The qualitative case selection technique was used by the researcher.

Research Strategy

The research study strategy is a step-by-step methodical case study examination. Clarity, selection, and operationalization of qualitative data are all considered in this study. The research study was divided into four parts for analysis: I, the foundation phase; II, the pre-field phase; III, the field phase; and IV, the reporting phase. The research investigated all four phases of the case study by connecting them with learning from a review of literature and a theoretical foundation for in-depth multiple case studies with descriptions and theme analysis.

A multi-case study approach is chosen for parallel research. Two case studies are studied concurrently, which is noted in the records. This is the first and most important stage in carrying out the case study. The foundation phase is the initial step that focuses on considerations to eliminate ambiguity and establish the tone for each consideration. The philosophical paradigm arose from an acquaintance with notions and theories. Induction and deduction are two types of research logic that are often utilised in any study. In this study, deductive research logic is applied with theory to strengthen theoretical strength and test arguments. The research began with subjective descriptions of life, and theory is developed on the basis of these stories. The study looked at the philosophical issues and the link between language and concepts, as well as the phases of the research and the proper method for each step. Theoretical literature was read and analysed early on in order to identify the research goal. To comprehend the social phenomenon, the researcher contacted the participants. To extend the theory, the researcher tested it and the assumptions linked to it. The phenomenon's context and processes were thoroughly explored in order to evaluate particular events or actions in a constrained environment in order to find crucial factor processes and linkages, individual behaviour characteristics, actions, and interactions. Because there is minimal control over the incident in a real-life environment, case studies are used in studies.

The research study technique is a step-by-step, methodical case study examination. Coherence, selection, and operationalization of qualitative data are all considered in this study. The research study was divided into four parts for analysis: I, the foundation phase; II, the pre-field phase; III, the field phase; and IV, the reporting phase. The research investigated all four phases of the case study with learning from a literature review and a theoretical foundation for in-depth multi-case studies with narratives and themes analysis. A number of case studies are chosen for parallel research.

Case studies are studied concurrently, which is noted in records. This is the initial and most appropriate timeframe for carrying out the case study. The foundation phase is the initial step that focuses on considerations to eliminate ambiguity and establish the tone for each consideration. The philosophical paradigm arose from an acquaintance with notions and theories. Induction and deduction are two types of research logic that are often utilised in any study. In this study, deductive research logic is applied with theory to strengthen theoretical strength and test arguments. The research began with subjective descriptions of life, and theory is developed on the basis of these stories. The study looked at the philosophical issues and the link between language and concepts, as well as the phases of the research and the proper method for each step.

Theoretical literature was consulted and analysed early on in order to identify the research goal. To comprehend the social phenomenon, the researchers interviewed the participants. To extend the theory, the researcher tested it and the assumptions linked to it. The phenomenon's context and processes were thoroughly explored in order to evaluate particular events or actions in a constrained environment in order to find crucial factor processes and linkages, individual behaviour characteristics, actions, and interactions. Because there is minimal control over the incident in a real-life environment, case studies are used in studies.

Conceptual Framework

Figure 1. The conceptual framework of the ownership pattern of Hindi news channels

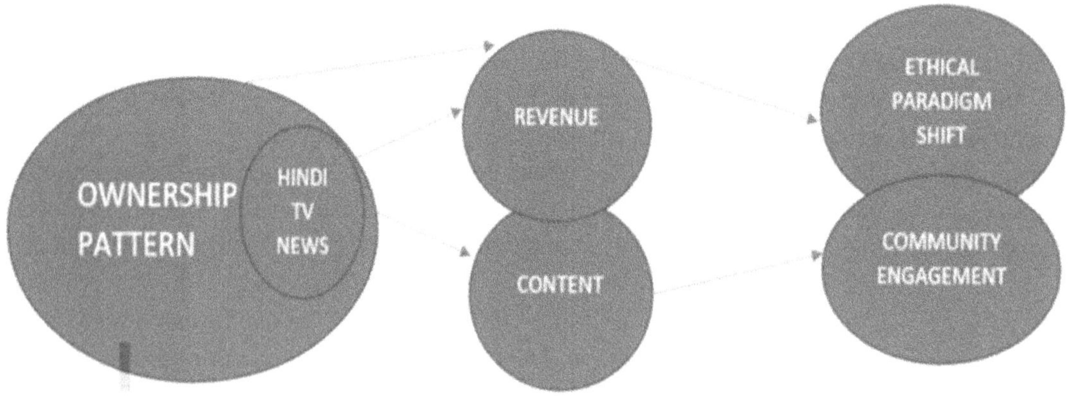

Ownership of the Hindi news networks causes a paradigm shift in ethics and community.

The Hindi TV news channel is part of the ownership, and a system is needed to attain the goals of a shift in ethics and community management. This process involves both content production and revenue generation. The ownership element, of which the Hindi TV news channel is only one component, generates this entire interrelated quadrilateral of revenue, content, ethical paradigm shift, and community management. Although money and content are closely related, as are the ethical paradigm and community management, all of these become intertwined when ownership is involved. Every ownership (in this case, a Hindi TV news channel) strives for an ethical paradigm shift and community management. The only ways to achieve the necessary objective, however, continue to be income and content. The conceptual framework connects the ownership patterns of Hindi TV news channels. The owners of different news channels generate revenue from different sources. The content of these channels, in relation to the revenue, leads to an ethical paradigm shift and community engagement of the viewers.

DATA ANALYSIS AND INTERPRETATION

Case Discussion

Based on the primary data collected from ten journalists of television news channels through formal interviews and the secondary data from published resources, two case studies were developed by the researchers for further analysis.

Case Story 1: Adani Group Overtook NDTV

NDTV had become one of the ultimate pinnacles of independent journalism. Gautam Adani, the richest billionaire in India and Asia, has taken over the independent news channel NDTV. In contrast to official news outlets, independent journalism is recognised for its neutrality and independence. However, now that Adanis owns NDTV, the channel, like other news channels, is expected to offer content beneficial to the Modi administration. Many academics and senior journalists consider the NDTV takeover a threat to media neutrality. In Reporters Without Borders' World Press Freedom Index, India was placed 150th out of 180 nations, its lowest rating ever. Such conclusions are rejected by the government, which cites a lack of openness and claims that a takeover is coming. The fact that Adani owns NDTV has triggered a catastrophic breakdown among NDTV personnel. The buyback might be part of the BJP's strategy to prepare for the general election in 2024, according to author Sandeep Bhushan. As industrialists and business magnates take control of private media networks, India's media is losing its diversity and independence. The objective of the media is no longer to create information but rather to sell their product. Until now, the risk presented by monopolies has been reduced by a media landscape composed of hundreds of news websites. However, there is rising worry among journalists about the consequences of corporate ownership. Aniruddha Bahal says: "Takeovers of media companies by huge industrial conglomerates are flooding the market." Previously, Indian media portrayed corruption and took a position in favour of truth-telling. We are becoming increasingly worried that the Indian media is participating in this deceptive strategy. We are all aware of the Modi administration's close association with the Adanis. They share a common ancestor, as well as the fact that Adani's prosperity resembles Modi's.

Case Story 2: RIL Has Taken Over Network 18

Ambani and Bahl are among the front-runners in the struggle for media control. It was not simple to combine Mukesh Ambani's Reliance Industries Ltd. (RIL) with Raghav Bahl's Network 18 and TV 18. Network18 Senior Professional Welfare Trust and Network Media and Investments own 51.95% of Network18 and 50% of TV18. Network18, which also owns CNN-IBN, IBN7, IBN-Lokmat, CVBC-TV18, and CNBC Awaaz, promotes TV18. Ambani spent Rs 3,800 crore on the debt-ridden Network18 and TV18 in exchange for privileged access to its programming. The arrangement centres on two future public rights offerings by Network 18 and TV 18, each totaling Rs 2,700 crore and set to take place in April. Bahl and his co-investors had raised significantly less than Rs 5,400 crore. Because Network18 holds a share in TV18, the rights issues will be worth Rs 4,000 crore in total. Ambani's Indian Media Trust has pledged Rs 1,700 crore to Bahl and his co-promoters under the terms of the deal. Bahl will use these monies to subscribe to the proposed rights issues, which he may use to pay off his obligation. The remaining Rs 1,900 crore would be used to wipe off the debts of Network 18 and TV 18. Bahl would save around Rs 250 crore in interest payments each year by retiring debt. When those savings are added to the Rs 430 crore from the rights offering, Bahl will have more than Rs 680 crore available following the deal. Ramoji Rao oversaw N.T. Rama Rao's dramatic climb to political prominence in Andhra Pradesh, when his Telugu Desam Party upended the Congress' fortunes. When Ramoji Rao's chit fund, Margadarsi Financiers, came into financial difficulties in 2008, Mukesh Ambani bailed it out. Rao had gotten close to NTR's son-in-law, N. Chandrababu Naidu, at this point

Table 1. Phases of case analysis

<table>
<tr><th colspan="4">Four Phases of Case Study Analysis</th></tr>
<tr><th>Foundation Phase</th><th>Pre-Field Phase</th><th>Field Phase</th><th>Reporting Phase</th></tr>
<tr><td>i. Philosophical & Sociological consideration</td><td>Decide</td><td>Contact</td><td rowspan="3">Case study Reporting</td></tr>
<tr><td>ii. Research Logic Consideration</td><td rowspan="2">Design and methodology for goal achievement
Case study protocol</td><td rowspan="2">Interact</td></tr>
<tr><td>iii. Ethical Consideration</td></tr>
</table>

In Table 1, the four phases of case study were analysed. In the foundation phase philosophical and sociological considerations are taken into account. The research logic consideration and ethical design is based on the goal achievement of the case study protocol. In the field phase "contact" and "Interact" are done. And the fourth phase, that is, the reporting phase is the "case study reporting".

Table 2. Process of data analysis from the case study

Sl. No.	Case Description	Participant Description	Relationship Description	Field Protocol
1.	Ownership pattern in Media	News Channels, Corporate	Takeover of Media ownership by business tycoon	Case analysis was done based on the interview conducted with the participants
2.	Independence and neutrality of the Journalism	Journalists	To maintain the balance and ethics in journalism under the work pressure of media owners as business conglomerate.	To develop clarity and justification before using each source of evidence. Case analysis was conducted to develop to understand the balance of the ethical concerns.

Table 2 stated the process of data analysis from the case studies. The case description contains "ownership pattern in media" and "Independence and neutrality of the Journalism". It is derived from News Channels, Corporates and Journalists. In the relationship description column, it is stated that there is "takeover of media ownership by business tycoon" and "to maintain the balance and ethics in journalism under the work pressure of media owners as business conglomerate". As per the field protocol "case analysis was done based on the interview conducted with the participants and also "case analysis was conducted to develop to understand the balance of the ethical concerns"

Table 3. Framework of case study consideration

Sl.No.	Philosophical Consideration	Research Logic Consideration	Ethical Consideration
1.	The interpretive paradigm was investigated.	Experiences were explored using semi-structured interviews and a deductive method.	The participants were completely aware of their duties. Confidentiality and secrecy were protected.
2.	The philosophical disparities in study fields were investigated. The social processes and phenomena were described to the participants in order to assess the impact of businessman's ownership of media on ethics and balance in journalism.	Deductive research logic, semi-structured interviews Emails were utilized as documents.	Consent was obtained prior to the interview procedure, and no deception occurred at any level of the study process.

Framework of Case Study Consideration is stated in Table 3. Under Philosophical Consideration, interpretive paradigm and philosophical disparities was investigated. The social processes and phenomena were described to the participants in order to assess the impact of businessman's ownership of media on ethics and balance in journalism. Experiences were explored and Deductive research logic was done through semi-structured interviews and a deductive method under Research Logic Consideration. The ethical considerations are participants were completely aware of their duties, confidentiality and secrecy were protected, consent was obtained prior to the interview procedure, and no deception occurred at any level of the study process.

CONCLUSION

The study concludes that many corporations have used media ownership to get favours for other organisations. The senior journalists are raising fears that journalistic independence must be safeguarded. Due to media ownership, television networks don't even come close in terms of independence. Not only is the government's point of view spread via them, but any counter-narrative, any information that challenges the government, is disregarded, and the researcher found that this tradition will continue. It jeopardises the credibility of the media.

A media environment comprised of hundreds of news sites operating in English, Hindi, and regional languages has hitherto mitigated the risk presented by conglomerates, but fear is growing about the implications of corporate ownership for journalism. Reliance acquired Network 18 Media and Investments, a media conglomerate that comprises CNBC TV18, CNN-IBN, and CNN Awaz, as well as online news portals.

In the research study, it was found out that the repercussions of huge corporations dominating media outlets in the absence of sufficient protections to protect editorial choices from tampering are a source of fear among senior journalists.

Advertising revenue is also one reason for compromising ethics in news channels. TV networks with the highest TRPs have the highest advertising charges. With a large fan base, TV channels are rapidly expanding, obtaining lucrative advertising agreements, and compromising their ethical behaviour.

Ethics in communication efforts by Indian news media, notably television, regarding its content on broadcast are now a source of contention in the nation. The news stations use "devious" methods to attract viewers. Political ownership of channels influences ethical behaviour. The performers on television make statements that disrupt societal order. The networks broadcast shows without first obtaining permission or copyright from the performers.

The audience's level of professionalism and credibility gets affected by biased screening of news content. This critical research looks at case studies of Indian television news channels, whether satellite or cable. This research focuses on the ethics of media and its influence on society, keeping in mind the relationship between media owners and journalists.

When people are denied access to instruments for self-expression and, as a result, the capacity to exercise their rights as citizens and as human beings, the organisations that allow this to happen are acting unethically. The current media monopoly environment is unethical because it interferes with the vast majority of people's right to free expression by eliminating viable alternative sites of communication, limiting direct access to media outlets as tools of communication, and preventing the creation of independent media outlets. The concept of media plurality serves as a pillar of a country's robust and healthy democracy. It contradicts the phenomenon of media ownership consolidation. A variety of issues have been highlighted because of media ownership concentration. The most serious of these is undoubtedly the threat it presents to free expression and democracy. There are significant problems concerning network capacity fees, multi-TV discounts, and income share sharing among various companies.

LIMITATION OF THE STUDY

The journalists from the news channels were not very comfortable talking about the ethics of content and the pressure of ownership. They were very limited in sharing their observations and experiences. The case studies chosen by the researcher had limited existence in the literature available.

FUTURE SCOPE OF STUDY

Media ownership is important in journalism studies because it is assumed that ownership has an influence on the contents and practises of journalism. News media ownership can take numerous forms, including governmental ownership, family ownership, political party ownership, trust ownership, and public or corporate ownership. In journalism studies, the fundamental issue with ownership is market concentration and monopolisation and the negative impact this may have on media diversity, public opinion formation, democracy, and journalistic autonomy. The possible financial and political benefits of owning journalistic media have been believed to constitute ownership reasons throughout the investigation. Benevolence is rarely assumed since the problematic characteristics of ownership are examined from both the management and critical political economics perspectives. News and journalism are often seen as public goods, the quality of which is frequently viewed as jeopardised by commercialism and market realities as a result of owners' economic goals. However, the many forms and shapes in which news media ownership takes have varying effects on rivalry among media outlets, editorial production organisations, journalistic and professional cultures, and the severity of corporate and profit-maximising ideologies that journalists labour under.

RECOMMENDATIONS

The Telecom Regulatory Authority of India (TRAI) is currently formulating recommendations on media ownership problems. The regulatory authority has recognised the difficulties that the television broadcasting industry is facing. Tariffs and rates that do not impose an unfair burden on consumers should be implemented by the industry. A timely resolution is critical for customers, broadcasters, and distributors. Ideally, a policy of tolerance, as used in the majority of established markets, should be embraced. The industry would like to see a complete national broadcast regulation encompassing the Cable Television Network Act as well as the continuation of a light-touch policy framework, particularly in content-related sectors. Not only must the regulatory and legal framework support the easy adoption of new technology, but it must also defend state and consumer interests. The major area on which the regulatory system must focus is content convergence. The same programming is now available on television, smart connected devices, and smartphones. These platforms present a regulatory difficulty because of the differences in their distribution mechanisms. As a result, in the new technological world of convergence, there is a need to consider possible regulatory regime alignment while keeping the scenario of multiple screens with the same content in mind. A light-touch framework that irons out discrepancies caused by technology interruptions is required. We cannot have a regulatory imbalance between traditional technologies and emerging ones. However, innovation and competition cannot be stifled at the same time.

REFERENCES

Ayedee, N., & Manocha, S. (2020). Role of media (television) in creating positive atmosphere in COVID 19 during lockdown in India. *Asian Journal of Management, 11*(4), 370–378. doi:10.5958/2321-5763.2020.00057.8

Batabyal, S. (2013). Editorial! Where art Thou? News Practices in Indian Television. In Indian Mass Media and the Politics of Change (pp. 58-83). Routledge India. doi:10.4324/9780203085226-10

Batabyal, S. (2014). *Making news in India: Star news and Star ananda*. Routledge India. doi:10.4324/9781315816135

Bhushan, B. (2015). The changing structure of media and ethics in India. In *Media ethics and justice in the age of globalization* (pp. 194–209). Palgrave Macmillan.

Chadha, K. (2017). The Indian news media industry: Structural trends and journalistic implications. *Global Media and Communication, 13*(2), 139–156. doi:10.1177/1742766517704674

Chakravartty, P., & Roy, S. (2013). Media pluralism redux: Towards new frameworks of comparative media studies "beyond the West". *Political Communication, 30*(3), 349-370.

Chakravartty, P., & Roy, S. (2015). Mr. Modi goes to Delhi: Mediated populism and the 2014 Indian elections. *Television & New Media, 16*(4), 311–322. doi:10.1177/1527476415573957

Devi, S. (2019). Making Sense of "Views" Culture in Television News Media in India. Journalism Practice, 13(9), 1075-1090. doi:10.1080/17512786.2019.1635041

Gudipaty, N. (2017). Television, Political Imagery, and Elections in India. In Citizenship, Democracies, and Media Engagement among Emerging Economies and Marginalized Communities (pp. 117-145). Palgrave Macmillan. doi:10.1080/17512786.2019.1635041

Jain, A. (2010). 'Beaming it live': 24-hour television news, the spectator and the spectacle of the 2002 Gujarat carnage. *South Asian Popular Culture*, *8*(2), 163–179. doi:10.1080/14746681003797989

Jha, S. (2013). Need of research related to Indian ownership patterns in media. Mass Communicator. *International Journal of Communication Studies*, *7*(3), 28–32.

Kumar, A. (2015). Ownership Patterns Affecting the Content of 24 x 7 News Channels in India: A Critical Analysis. *Amity Journal of Media & Communications Studies (AJMCS), 4.*

Mehta, N. (2015). India and its television: Ownership, democracy, and the media business. *Emerging Economy Studies*, *1*(1), 50–63. doi:10.1177/2394901514562304

Mudgal, V. (2015). Framing the 2014 elections: The curious absence of development. *Television & New Media*, *16*(4), 354–360. doi:10.1177/1527476415575907

Mukherjee, T. (2015). Media Ownership Patterns and Its Impact on Media Content: Issues & Implications. *Amity Journal of Media & Communications Studies (AJMCS), 4.*

Oestreicher-Singer, G., & Zalmanson, L. (2013). Content or community? A digital business strategy for content providers in the social age. *Management Information Systems Quarterly*, *37*(2), 591–616. doi:10.25300/MISQ/2013/37.2.12

Parthasarathi, V., & Srinivas, A. (2019). Problematic ownership patterns: The evolution of the television distribution networks in India. *Economic and Political Weekly*, *54*(12).

Rani, D. (2013). Privatisation, convergence and broadcast regulations: A Case study of the Indian Television Industry. In *The Asian Conference on Media and Mass Communication 2013-Official Conference Proceedings* (pp. 387-396). The International Academic Forum 2013 (IAFOR).

Rao, S. (2009). Glocalization of Indian journalism. *Journalism Studies, 10*(4), 474-488.

Rao, S., & Johal, N. S. (2006). Ethics and news making in the changing Indian mediascape. *Journal of Mass Media Ethics*, *21*(4), 286–303. doi:10.120715327728jmme2104_5

Rao, S., & Malik, K. K. (2019). Conversing Ethics in India's News Media: A capabilities approach to journalism ethics education and training. *Journalism Practice*, *13*(4), 509–523. doi:10.1080/17512786.2018.1491321

Roy, A. (2015). *ICTs as enablers of public participation for the hearing impaired: A case for television news closed captioning in India* [Doctoral dissertation]. University of Florida.

Shameer, S. M. (2015). Media Economics Study Prominence and Relevance in India. *Social Networking*, *4*(04), 112–118. doi:10.4236n.2015.44013

Singh, J. (2015). Trends in Primetime News: Study of Selected News Channels in India. Journal of Content. *Community & Communication*, *1*(1), 14–29.

Sonwalkar, P. (2001). India: Makings of little cultural/media imperialism? *Gazette (Leiden, Netherlands)*, *63*(6), 505–519. doi:10.1177/0016549201063006003

Sumanth, I. (2011). Contemporary Trends in National Media Ownership: Revisiting Political Economy Approach. *The IUP Journal of History and Culture*, *5*(1), 44–52.

Thaker, J., Zhao, X., & Leiserowitz, A. (2017). Media use and public perceptions of global warming in India. *Environmental Communication*, *11*(3), 353–369. doi:10.1080/17524032.2016.1269824

Thussu, D. K. (2007). TheMurdochization'of news? The case of Star TV in India. *Media Culture & Society*, *29*(4), 593–611. doi:10.1177/0163443707076191

Williamson, W., & Ruming, K. (2020). Can social media support large scale public participation in urban planning? The case of the# MySydney digital engagement campaign. *International Planning Studies*, *25*(4), 355–371. doi:10.1080/13563475.2019.1626221

Chapter 16
NFT Sports Collectibles:
Characteristics and Factors of Consumer Value

Sebastiano Mereu
Sports Business Research Academy, Switzerland

ABSTRACT

This chapter examines characteristics of non-fungible tokens (NFTs) and factors of perceived consumer value that influence the intention to purchase NFT sports collectibles. It further offers recommendations through which NFT experiences can be enhanced for collectors. The role of NFT sports collectibles is introduced in the context of the internet of things and internet of value before defining NFT characteristics and consumer value factors relevant to this study. The respective conceptual model is then analyzed and discussed. The main findings explain that NFT characteristics including scarcity, uniqueness, aesthetics, and functional utility have no direct effect on the purchase intention for NFT sports collectibles. However, they have a significant and positive influence on the purchase intention when mediated through consumer values like the enjoyment of collecting NFTs, the creativity stimulated from assembling a digital collection, and the social relationships that can be fostered with other collectors.

INTRODUCTION

The internet of things (IoT) has been revolutionary since the 2000s for companies and consumers, as it connects physical objects with each other through information and communication technology (ICT) systems (Balbi & Magaudda, 2018). The introduction of blockchain technology in the 2010s added new characteristics for digital items to the IoT, which allow the transfer of authenticated economic value through digital tokens (Zaucha & Agur, 2022). These tokens can now certify authenticity and represent ownership of digital and physical assets or asset types (Li & Chen, 2022). This was made possible by the internet's progression from a platform economy (i.e., Web 2.0) to a token economy (i.e., Web 3.0), hence, triggering the internet of value (IoV) (Treiblmaier, 2021).

DOI: 10.4018/978-1-6684-8166-0.ch016

Various types of assets can be digitized and exemplified as digital items of value on the IoV, and they can be securely traded without an intermediary because of blockchain technology (Truong et al., 2018). This also applies to non-fungible tokens, also known as NFTs. Li and Chen (2022) define an NFT as "a blockchain-based digital record representing a non-interchangeable digital or physical asset" that "has a unique identity with distinct qualities" and is "well-suited for representing unique digital identities and properties" (p. 4).

Sports organizations such as the National Basketball Association (NBA), National Football League (NFL), or Angel City FC offer specific NFTs that hold the above-mentioned unique digital properties. Their NFTs capture the value of sports moments in a digital item or represent other digital sports memorabilia. Such NFT sports collectibles can be defined as authenticated non-fungible digital items related to a sport or sports brand, e.g., sports moments and memories, digital sports trading cards, wearable sports NFTs, etc., created on the blockchain that unlock access to tangible or intangible items or experiences (Osivand, 2021; Baker et al., 2022). New technologies have been crucial for sports collectibles, especially trading cards, as they evolved from being a marketing gimmick to become a serious investment for fans (Spencer et al., 2003). The internet has enabled collectors to connect with like-minded others to discuss, buy, sell, and trade collectibles more efficiently and effectively across the world, while offering a more stimulating collector experience (cf. Balbi & Magaudda, 2018). Particularly, the advent of blockchain technology and NFTs has introduced new promotional and financial avenues for sports organizations and brands to create additional value for collectors and monetize it accordingly (Baker et al., 2022). Popular platforms through which such collectable NFTs can be purchased and sold include NBA Top Shot (see nbatopshot.com), Sorare (see sorare.com), and OpenSea (see opensea.io). The global market size for NFT sports collectibles reached USD 1.4 billion in 2021 (Market Decipher, 2021) and is estimated at USD 2 billion for 2022, with great potential for continued growth (Deloitte, 2021; PR Newswire, 2022).

This indicates a viable financial and promotional opportunity around NFT sports collectibles for sports brands and NFT creators. Yet, because the underlying technology and the offered services around digital collectibles represent a new phenomenon (see Dash, 2012), respective use cases, best practices, and empirical research are rather scarce. This means that, currently, marketing professionals have to conceptualize their strategies based upon a limited body of knowledge regarding the communication and marketing of NFTs. It becomes therefore necessary to examine collectors' expectations on NFT characteristics and their perceived consumer value, which may influence the purchase intention for such NFT sports collectibles (Baker et al., 2022).

NFT Sports Collectibles, the Internet of Value, and the Internet of Things

Human-beings are said to have been collecting physical objects for centuries; from artefacts to relics, from paintings to jewelry, and from travel souvenirs to trading cards, to name a few (Spencer et al., 2003). Although collectibles are generally assumed to be physical objects that can be traded, intangible experiences can be considered collectable memories; such collectibles hold a specific value to a collector, be it of financial, social, or psychological interest (Burton & Jacobsen, 1999). A noteworthy characteristic of collectibles is their high degree of uniqueness and limited substitutability, which applies to tangible as well as intangible collectibles (Ali & Bagui, 2021). Whereas the scarcity of physical items is given due to the tangible raw materials and production processes needed to create them, e.g., paper and cardboard to print trading cards, the scarcity of digital items has been much more difficult to achieve, since easily accessible technology, such as smartphones and computers, allows close to unlimited replicability and multiplication of digital items, like videos and photos, by its users (Balbi & Magaudda, 2018).

Nevertheless, blockchain technology introduced the possibility to turn digital items into non-fungible assets, e.g., NFTs. This enables producers to limit the number of digital items and add proof of ownership to enhance security and trust to the legitimacy of the item and increase its desirability (Li & Chen, 2022). It can therefore be argued that NFT sports collectibles are a viable component of the IoV, as they can contribute economic value through their rarity and popularity, social value offered by socializing with like-minded collectors through the act of collecting, and psychological value of owning a certain digital collectible important to its owners (Baker et al., 2022). NFT sports collectibles can also be considered a practical element of the IoT in a wider sense. They empower sports organizations to create contextual touchpoints through digital channels between their main product, i.e., the respective season-long tournament or championship in the physical world, and their fans, in order to provide a personalized brand and customer experience (Kotler et al., 2021). A possible offering could be for a sports organization to provide ownership of a specific moment in time from their main sports product through an NFT (Baker et al., 2022). This could bridge the physical and digital realm through the IoT, while registering a unique identification of the NFT on the blockchain and authenticating its legitimacy (Arcenegui et al., 2021).

With this in mind, the aim of this chapter is to examine and discuss characteristics of NFTs and factors of perceived consumer value that influence the intention to purchase NFT sports collectibles. Based upon that, the chapter shall further offer practical marketing and communications recommendations through which marketing professionals can enhance the NFT experience for their organizations' fans and customers and, ultimately, encourage consumers to start or expand their NFT collections.

THEORETICAL BACKGROUND

NFT Characteristics and Factors of Consumer Value

As a means to investigate the intention to purchase digital items, Kim et al. (2011) suggest the application of a conceptual model based upon the consumer value construct as proposed by Sweeney and Soutar (2001), which includes functional value (i.e., functional quality, price utility), emotional value (i.e., enjoyment, creativity), and social value (i.e., self-image expression, relationship support). Their model is adapted to the context of this study by including characteristics of NFTs (i.e., scarcity, uniqueness, aesthetics) as potential stimuli to consumer values (see Li & Chen, 2022). Given that functional quality and price utility can also be seen as characteristics that emphasize NFT utility (see Baker et al., 2022), this research applies them as both a stimulus and an organism variable. The following paragraphs define the characteristics of NFTs and factors of consumer value that influence the intention to purchase NFT sports collectibles examined in this research. Respective hypotheses are defined accordingly.

Scarcity

In economic terms, scarcity refers to the gap between availability of a product, i.e., goods or services, and consumers' level of desire for that product (Shi et al., 2020). As Cialdini (2001) points out, "People want more of what they can have less" and adds that business managers can "harness the scarcity principle with the organizational equivalents of limited-time, limited-supply, and one-of-a-kind offers" (p. 78).

The same is applicable to NFTs. NFT producers can decide how many unique pieces of a non-fungible collectible should be minted, i.e., securely recorded on the blockchain, and for how long they can be available for sale (Li & Chen, 2022). However, blockchain technology brings a significant change to the phenomenon of scarcity in regard to NFTs. Although the content of a unique NFT may be copied, e.g., an NFT representing a particular slam dunk by a popular NBA player, the value of the authenticated NFT can increase, if the content of the NFT itself reaches a wider audience through a variety of communication channels; this can happen when the NFT symbolizes a culturally significant piece of sports history (Baker et al., 2022). Furthermore, Zaucha and Agur (2022) note that NFT sports collectibles can provide "feelings of community and solidarity in an environment where people share stories and advice, talk about [sports], seek answers, and sometimes show off" (p. 6); this explains a possible positive relationship between scarcity and social value. Regarding the influence of scarcity on functional utility, Mekacher et al. (2022) find that scarcity and sale price of an NFT are positively correlated, whereas sale price and the number of sales of an NFT are negatively correlated. This implies that collectors are willing to pay higher prices for rare NFTs in a market where other collectors are more likely to horde their collectibles, as they probably increase in monetary value. This leads to the following hypothesis:

H1: Scarcity positively influences (a) functional utility, (b) enjoyment, (c) creativity, (d) social self-image expression, (e) social relationship support, and (f) the intention to purchase NFT sports collectibles.

Uniqueness

Uniqueness, in marketing, can be viewed from the perspective of a consumer's need for uniqueness and from the perspective of a product's characteristics that establish its perceived distinctiveness (Tian et al., 2001). In order to investigate the importance of the NFT's uniqueness for consumers, this research views uniqueness from the product perspective. In marketing terms, Franke and Schreier (2008) define the perceived uniqueness of a product as "the extent to which the customer regards the product as different from other products in the same category" (p. 95). Colicev (2022) assesses the value that NFTs bring to brands and explains, "While most physical products are seldom unique or rare, brands can offer symbolic benefits by designing unique features for each NFT and combining them with the physical product" (p. 3). With reference to the characteristics that constitute an NFT, it can be reasoned that an NFT's uniqueness and authenticity are essential features that can have an influence on their functional utility, as well as emotional and social value for consumers (Kim et al., 2011; Ha et al., 2021). NFTs can further offer ownership and access to specific tangible or intangible assets or experiences (Baker et al., 2022). They can also provide enjoyment through the process of collecting digital items; likewise, NFT collectibles can allow their owners to belong to a circle of like-minded collectors and, therefore, take advantage of benefits and augmented services they would otherwise not be able to enjoy (Li & Chen, 2022). These characteristics, coupled with communicative efforts and online interactions, can then influence the intention to purchase NFTs (Efendioglu, 2022). With the above in mind, the following hypothesis is defined:

H2: Uniqueness positively influences (a) functional utility, (b) enjoyment, (c) creativity, (d) social self-image expression, (e) social relationship support, and (f) the intention to purchase NFT sports collectibles.

Aesthetics

Aesthetics is often referred to as the "philosophical study of beauty and taste" (Britannica, 2022). With a growing number of commercial offerings and an increasing level of elaborate marketing efforts, aesthetic features that reflect the beauty of a tangible item or an intangible experience have been crucial elements for consumers in their decision-making process (Pine & Gilmore, 2020). Moreover, marketing tactics that emphasize a sensory experience "may be used to differentiate companies and products, to motivate customers, and to add value to products through, for example, aesthetics or excitement" (Schmitt, 1999, p. 64). This implies that aesthetics can affect functional utility and emotional value for consumers, which also applies to virtual environments (Schau & Gilly, 2003). Furthermore, Kim et al. (2011) find that aesthetics significantly influences the intention of users to purchase digital items. However, the concept of aesthetics can be multidimensional and not solely based upon beauty and taste. Santayana (1904) notes that aesthetics is "the science of expression; expression being itself so defined as to be identical with every form of apperception, intuition, or imaginative synthesis" and adds that "it has nothing in particular to do with art or with beauty" (p. 320). This traditional view is applicable to modern-day products and items such as NFTs, especially in the context of collectibles. Danet and Katriel (2012) explain that the act of collecting items can be considered an aesthetic experience, where collectors "strive towards completing a series or set" (p. 230). Completing a series or set would reflect a collector's interest in a specific body of work. In that regard, the motivation to keep collecting NFTs that are part of a specific collection may strengthen, given that various sports NFTs belong to a series or a respectively licensed platform such as NBA Top Shot or Sorare. Thus, the following hypothesis is offered:

H3: Aesthetics positively influences (a) functional utility, (b) enjoyment, (c) creativity, (d) social self-image expression, (e) social relationship support, and (f) the intention to purchase NFT sports collectibles.

Functional Utility

Functional value is occasionally referred to as functional utility and can indicate utility provided by a product or a brand (Vázquez et al., 2002). Sheth et al. (1991) view utility from a product's perspective and define it as, "The perceived utility acquired from an alternative's capacity for functional, utilitarian, or physical performance" (p. 160). According to Sweeney and Soutar (2001) functional value includes the sub-factors functional quality and price utility, where quality is "the utility derived from the perceived quality and expected performance of the product", and price utility is "the utility derived from the product due to the reduction of its perceived short term and longer term costs" (p. 211). Hence, functional quality indicates the degree to which a tangible or intangible product can be utilized to effectively, efficiently, and satisfactorily accomplish a specified task (Shen et al., 2021). In the case of NFT sports collectibles, functional quality can refer to the level of representation of their real-world counterpart or to the ease of access to a specific asset or experience, be it digital or physical. Furthermore, NFTs can provide functional value beyond an experience's perishability by "digitally storing" a specific moment from, for example, a sporting event such as a football game, and, therefore, create a collectable digital memory (Dwivedi et al., 2022). Such NFTs can hold more than just collectible value. Sports NFT platforms apply gamification elements to incite user interaction and reward NFT users for using their collectibles (Web3 Studios, 2022). This implies that NFTs hold price utility. Price is expected to reflect a product's quality and benefits, with higher-priced products suggesting a higher quality in contrast to lower-priced products and, therefore, being generally less vulnerable to similar products from competitors (Yoo et al., 2000). In regard to NFT sports collectibles, it can be argued that their characteristics can influence the emotional and social value over time (Baker et al., 2022). For example, an NFT on NBA Top Shot, that was minted in a comparably low and limited number (i.e., scarce), represents an outstanding athletic performance like a slam dunk (i.e., aesthetics), and belongs to a popular set or collection (i.e., unique), may be purchased for a set price and later sold for a multiple of that price as scarcity and uniqueness of the item may increase over time (cf. Mekacher et al., 2022). This can affect the intention for collectors to seek out NFTs with respective potential. Moreover, gathering information on NFTs that may increase in value in the future, while interacting with other collectors on community forums, can result in a playful environment that fosters enjoyment and creativity. Therefore, the following can be hypothesized:

H4: Functional utility positively influences (a) enjoyment, (b) creativity, (c) social self-image expression, (d) social relationship support, and (e) the intention to purchase NFT sports collectibles.

Playfulness: Enjoyment and Creativity

A traditional consumer perspective on goods and services may refer to apparent emotional value as "the utility derived from the feelings or affective states that a product generates" (Sweeney & Soutar, 2001, p. 211). However, Kim et al. (2011) offer a specific definition with regard to digital consumer items and state that emotional value is "*the perceived utility of a digital item based on the item's capacity to arouse feelings or affective states*" (p. 229, italics in original); they maintain that playfulness contributes emotional value to consumers and find a significant positive effect from playfulness on the intention to purchase digital items. This is supported by Aroean (2011), who highlights that a satisfactory consumer experience may result from a playful value co-creation between a company and its customers. Byun et al. (2017) delve further into the element of playfulness and find that it consists of two factors, enjoyment and creativity. Enjoyment can be seen as an element of fun, joy, or happiness that adds emotional value to a consumer's brand or customer experience, and it encourages the intention to purchase items (Ruangkanjanases & Wutthisith, 2018). Creativity, on the other hand, indicates the degree of a consumer's curiosity, open-mindedness, and appeal to imaginative situations (Byun et al., 2017). With regard to NFT sports collectibles, collecting digital items can provide emotional value to a collector, as it may be a fun pastime to search for a missing NFT, which can then turn into a strong sense of accomplishment and happiness when that NFT can be added to one's collection. Collecting NFTs can also offer emotional value through creativity in the form of seeking information about a specific NFT or different purchase opportunities, which could stimulate curiosity and arouse imagination in the process. It can further incite a more open-minded stance towards, for example, alternatives to unattainable digital collectibles. Based upon this, the following two hypotheses are proposed:

H5: Enjoyment positively influences the intention to purchase NFT sports collectibles.

H6: Creativity positively influences the intention to purchase NFT sports collectibles.

Social Value: Social Self-image Expression and Social Relationship Support

According to Kim et al. (2011), "People consume products to enhance their social image because the purchase, display, and use of goods can communicate one's symbolic meaning to others" (p. 230). Sweeney and Soutar (2001) offer a similar notion and explain that the benefit resulting from a product's capability to develop a social self-concept adds to a consumer's perception of product value and, therefore, creates social value. This also applies to NFTs, where the practicality of tokens can affect how their owners are seen by their peer-groups (Treiblmaier, 2021). For example, functional utility of scarce NFT sports collectibles can offer unique benefits to its owners, such as exclusive access to an asset or experience in a virtual space or in the real world. This could involve the possibility for a specific NFT wearable to allow a collector's avatar to wear a pair of limited-edition virtual sneakers or a virtual jersey and, respectively, to express a certain virtual image (see Hirschmiller, 2022). Support is found in research by Schau and Gilly (2003), who observe that, in general, online users' self-representation is inherently conscious and conspicuous and that they seek to express themselves more through virtual communication channels than in real-life. A further example could see a specific NFT providing its owners access to a virtual or physical stadium via a digital ticket or access pass in the form of an NFT with high functional utility (see PWC, 2022). Such functional utility can deliver augmented social value to respective NFT owners, as they will belong to an exclusive group of beneficiaries for the benefits offered by the digital item. Likewise, NFT owners may influence like-minded others by utilizing their NFTs for all other users to see (cf. Yocco, 2016). Ha et al. (2021) find that product characteristics can influence social value, and social value can have a significant effect on the purchase intention for these products.

In regard to social relationships, Schmitt (1999) investigates the associations between consumers and brands from an experiential marketing perspective and explains that active and relational communication activities enhance consumers' experiences in order to relate them to a wider social system. This implies that social relationships add a further perspective to consumers' perceived social value; it can be defined as "a digital item's perceived capability to help form, maintain, and enhance interpersonal relationships" (Kim et al., 2011, p. 230). In the context of NFTs, this means that owning certain digital collectibles could incite owners to form relational connections with other collectors, interact within a respective community, and, possibly, befriend some community members. With that in mind, Cialdini (2001) addresses social proof and maintains that "persuasion can be extremely effective when it comes from peers" (p. 75). Subsequently, social interaction can strengthen the love and commitment towards an online community or activity, such as a specific NFT collection or platform, which is mediated by consumers' perceived self-concept and their sense of belonging to a particular social group (Vernuccio et al., 2015). This means, if NFT collectors build relationships with like-minded others around NFT sports collectibles and interact with the community on a continuous basis, they reinforce their attachment and their commitment to the product and community (Yocco, 2016). A further consideration can be given to peer-to-peer (P2P) transaction, i.e., buying, selling, or trading a digital item directly with an individual, while bypassing a third-party vendor, which is considered an imperative feature of the decentralized Web 3.0 ecosystem. Social relationships in a community of NFT collectors can lead to cooperative pricing decisions, where buyers might be willing to purchase an NFT for a bit more and sellers could be willing to settle for a bit less, therefore, increasing the chances of a successful exchange (Huang & Savary, 2022). Consequently, the following hypotheses are defined:

H7: Social self-image expression positively influences the intention to purchase NFT sports collectibles.

H8: Social relationship support positively influences the intention to purchase NFT sports collectibles.

The Conceptual Model and Its Guiding Research Question

Based upon the theory presented above, the subsequent section analyzes how characteristics of NFT sports collectibles can affect perceived consumer value and the purchase intention for respective NFTs, as well as how perceived consumer value can impact the intention to buy NFT sports collectibles. The theoretical foundation in the previous section highlights how characteristics of an NFT offer stimuli to increase perceived consumer value to ultimately bolsters the intention to purchase the digital item. Consequently, the discourse leads to the following guiding research question for this chapter: "What are the NFT characteristics that influence perceived consumer value and the intention to purchase NFT sports collectibles, and what are the factors of perceived consumer value that influence the intention to purchase NFT sports collectibles?" Figure 1 offers a visualization of the conceptual model.

Figure 1. Conceptual model

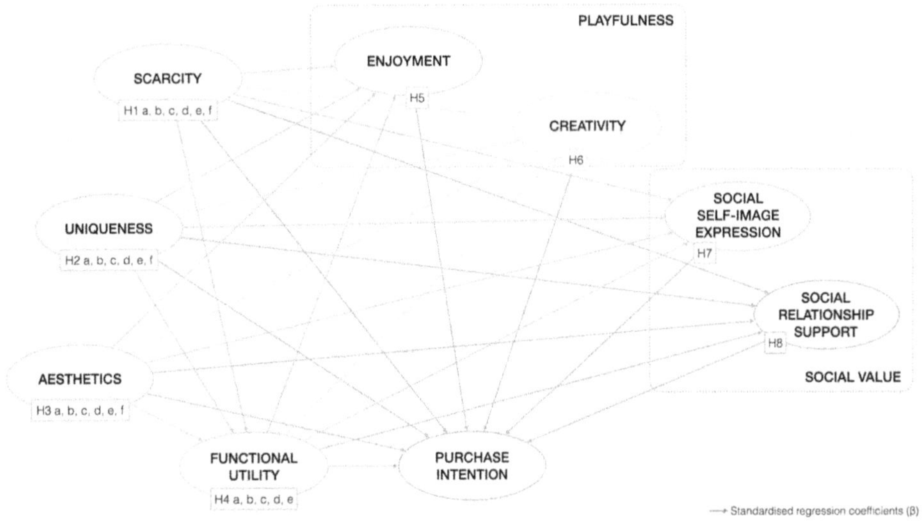

DATA ANALYSIS AND RESULTS

Respondents of the Study

The conceptual model portrayed in Figure 1 assesses causal relationships between characteristics of NFT sports collectibles, factors of perceived consumer value, and their influence on the intention to purchase NFTs. Primary data was gathered from a convenience sample of 300 sports NFT collectors in order to examine the hypotheses defined in the previous section. Collectors of sports NFTs were asked through various digital communication channels, i.e., social networking platforms, forums, and direct messages, to participate in the study by filling out a self-administered online questionnaire. All registered replies were considered valid and, thus, accepted. The sample consists of 115 female respondents (38.3%), 184 male respondents (61.3%), and 1 respondent (0.4%) that identifies as non-binary. Respondents in the age-bracket 25 to 34 are the largest age-group with 157 respondents (52.3%), followed by 72 respondents in the age-bracket 35 to 44 (24.0%). The youngest age-group of this sample, 18 to 24 years old, comprises 29 people (9.7%), closely followed by 24 respondents (8.0%) aged 45 to 54. Finally, 14 people are aged 55 to 64 and 4 people are 65 years of age or older. Most respondents live in the United States of America (USA), with 260 people making up 86.7% of the sample. The rest of the sample (40 respondents; 13.3%) is distributed across different countries and continents. One item of the questionnaire asked which NFT marketplace would the respondent use mostly, resulting in adequately distributed results. The marketplaces that are mentioned by more than 10% of the sample include AirNFTs (66 respondents; 22.0%), NBA Top Shot (41 respondents; 13.7%), Crypto.com (36 respondents; 12.0%), and NFL All Day (32 respondents; 10.7%). A respective overview is offered in Table 1.

In summary, this convenience sample suggests a reasonably gender-balanced view, somewhat inclined towards a male perspective with 25 to 44 years old consumers from the USA representing a great majority of the sample. An even distribution regarding NFT marketplace preference reflects a wider perspective on how NFT sports collectibles are purchased, sold, and traded. Hence, the sample can be considered suitable for assessing the conceptual model depicted in Figure 1.

Table 1. Characteristics of the sample

	N	%
Gender		
Female	115	38.3
Male	184	61.3
Non-binary	1	0.4
Age		
18-24	29	9.7
25-34	157	52.3
35-44	72	24.0
45-54	24	8.0
55-64	14	4.7
65+	4	1.3
Country		
USA	260	86.7
Rest of the world	40	13.3
Most used NFT marketplace		
AirNFTs	66	22.0
NBA Top Shot	41	13.7
Crypto.com	36	12.0
NFL All Day	32	10.7
Dibbs	26	8.7
OpenSea	21	7.0
Blockchain Brawlers	20	6.7
Candy	19	6.3
Fanzone Sports Club	14	4.7
Rest of the list	25	8.3

Note. N = 300.

Reliability, Validity, and Model Fit

Cronbach's Alpha (α) was computed to measure internal consistency of the scales applied in the questionnaire. Results present α values ranging from .591 to .860 (Saunders et al., 2007; Dunn et al., 2014). Moreover, construct reliability (CR) and average variance extracted (AVE) were computed in support (Saunders et al., 2007). Although some values measure slightly below the suggested thresholds, the constructs can be accepted, since this study tested this specific construct for the first time to the knowledge of the author. A correlations analysis between variables was also conducted, with results suggesting significant correlations at $p < 0.001$. Because of relatively high correlations among some of the observed variables, high collinearity needs to be considered (Field, 2018). Consequently, multicollinearity was tested by computing variance inflation factor (VIF) values amid the utilized scales (de Mesquita & Kostelijk, 2021), resulting in moderate VIF values between 1.748 and 2.857 (Daoud, 2017). A confirmatory factor analysis (CFA) was further applied in order to examine how well the data fit the conceptual model, which resulted in an overall acceptable model fit with $\chi2/df = 2.226$, RMSEA = .064, CFI = .902, NFI = .837, TLI = .885, and GFI = .838 (de Mesquita & Kostelijk, 2021). Lastly, coefficient of multiple determination (R^2) values were computed to examine the degree to which the undertaken multiple regression analyses fit the collected data (Saunders et al., 2007). All R^2 values show good fit with values ranging from .428 to .650 (Cohen, 1992; Sarstedt & Mooi, 2014). Table 2 offers a detailed overview of the above-mentioned metrics.

Table 2. Reliability, validity, and correlations

	α	CR	AVE	VIF	R^2	SCR	UNQ	AES	FNU	ENJ	CRE	SSI	SRS	PUI
SCR	.591	.570	.308	2.066	.516	1								
UNQ	.727	.687	.423	2.833	.647	.638	1							
AES	.719	.664	.332	2.525	.604	.567	.703	1						
FNU	.812	.785	.381	2.857	.650	.632	.740	.721	1					
ENJ	.672	.645	.379	1.748	.428	.535	.575	.579	.575	1				
CRE	.730	.715	.456	1.931	.482	.606	.594	.570	.618	.743	1			
SSI	.861	.820	.532	2.037	.509	.574	.609	.564	.680	.624	.691	1		
SRS	.844	.788	.482	1.802	.445	.552	.583	.528	.622	.581	.679	.838	1	
PUI	.800	.687	.423	2.532	.605	.530	.507	.516	.542	.703	.727	.601	.605	1
M	-	-	-	-	-	5.528	5.434	5.488	5.346	5.581	5.330	5.184	5.171	5.468
SD	-	-	-	-	-	.920	1.032	.906	.968	.980	1.093	1.212	1.224	1.116

Note 1. All correlations between variables are significant at $p < .001$.

Note 2. α: Cronbach's Alpha, CR: Construct reliability, AVE: Average variance extracted, SCR: Scarcity, UNQ: Uniqueness, AES: Aesthetics, FNU: Functional utility, ENJ: Enjoyment, CRE: Creativity, SSI: Social self-image expression, SRS: Social relationship support, PUI: Purchase intention, M: Mean, SD: Standard deviation.

Hypotheses Testing

As discussed above, acceptable reliability and validity of the collected primary data, as well as acceptable model fit, allowed to proceed with the testing of the hypotheses, defined in the theory section, through multiple regression analysis. With possible multicollinearity issues in mind, a ridge regression was undertaken in addition to the multiple regression analysis (see Hoerl & Kennard, 1970; Marquardt & Snee, 1975). Values computed through the ridge regression at zero penalty, did, however, not show any considerable deviation from the ordinary regression values. Hence, multicollinearity is hereafter disregarded and results from the ordinary regression analysis are further discussed. Table 3 summarizes all tested hypotheses and includes standardized regression weights (β), significance levels (p), and final regression results. A detailed discussion of the results is offered in the next section of this chapter.

Table 3. Hypotheses testing results

Hypotheses no.	IV	DV	β	p	*Result*
H1a	Scarcity	Functional utility	.209	***	supported
H1b		Enjoyment	.206	.002	supported
H1c		Creativity	.347	***	supported
H1d		Social self-image expression	.250	***	supported
H1e		Social relationship support	.274	***	supported
H1f		Purchase intention	.082	.203	not supported
H2a	Uniqueness	Functional utility	.345	***	supported
H2b		Enjoyment	.160	.022	supported
H2c		Creativity	.146	.049	supported
H2d		Social self-image expression	.165	.038	supported
H2e		Social relationship support	.206	.016	supported
H2f		Purchase intention	-.061	.364	not supported
H3a	Aesthetics	Functional utility	.374	***	supported
H3b		Enjoyment	.258	***	supported
H3c		Creativity	.172	.030	supported
H3d		Social self-image expression	.080	.350	not supported
H3e		Social relationship support	.077	.401	not supported
H3f		Purchase intention	.051	.479	not supported
H4a	Functional utility	Enjoyment	.158	.036	supported
H4b		Creativity	.259	.001	supported
H4c		Social self-image expression	.517	***	supported
H4d		Social relationship support	.407	***	supported
H4e		Purchase intention	.029	.703	not supported
H5	Enjoyment	Purchase intention	.370	***	supported
H6	Creativity	Purchase intention	.351	***	supported
H7	Social self-image expression	Purchase intention	-.007	.922	not supported
H8	Social relationship support	Purchase intention	.135	.037	supported

Note. $*p < .05$; $**p < .01$; $***p < .001$. IV: Independent variable, DV: Dependent variable.

DISCUSSION

A visualization of the applied conceptual model discussed earlier in this chapter is illustrated in Figure 2 and includes β, R^2, and p. The following discussion elaborates on the portrayed results by offering theoretical findings and practical recommendations.

Figure 2. Conceptual model with β, R^2, and p

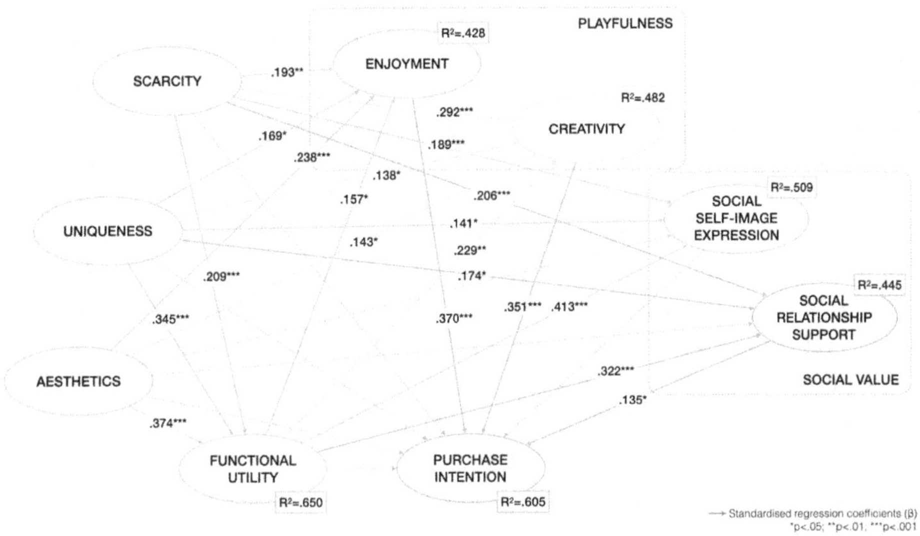

THEORETICAL FINDINGS

Scarcity of NFT sports collectibles has significant and positive influence on functional utility (H1a, $\beta = .209$, $p < .001$), enjoyment (H1b, $\beta = .193$, p $< .01$), creativity (H1c, $\beta = .292$, $p < .001$), social self-image expression (H1d, $\beta = .189$, $p < .001$), and social relationship support (H1e, $\beta = .206$, $p < .001$), but no direct influence on the intention to purchase respective NFTs (H1f, *not supported*). These results are supported in Mekacher et al. (2022), who find a positive relationship between the scarcity and functional utility of an NFT. For the case at hand, it means that NFT sports collectibles benefit from being scarce, as it increases their price utility. Moreover, Zaucha and Agur (2022) describe a positive association between scarcity and social value, as found in this study. Accordingly, NFTs offer collectors the opportunity for self-representation through digital communication avenues, as they consciously show off their NFT collections in dedicated online communities, while connecting with like-minded others. The non-significant impact of scarcity onto purchase intention parallels findings by Broeder and Wentink (2022) in the context of e-commerce. Thus, collectors of sports NFTs may not directly want to purchase an NFT because of its scarcity, but because of the perceived consumer value possibly intensified by scarcity.

Like scarcity, the uniqueness of NFT sports collectibles is found to significantly and positively affect functional utility (H2a, $\beta = .345$, $p < .001$), enjoyment (H2b, $\beta = .169$, p $< .05$), creativity (H2c, $\beta = .138$, $p < .05$), social self-image expression (H2d, $\beta = .141$, $p < .05$), and social relationship support (H2e,

$\beta = .174$, $p < .05$), but does not directly affect purchase intention (H2f, *not supported*). These findings parallel findings from Ha (2021), who found significant positive effect from a product's uniqueness on social value and price utility. Accordingly, if an NFT collectible is highly unique, its functional value will increase, as it may contribute exclusivity towards an NFT collection and, therefore, strengthen its functional quality and price utility (cf. Franke & Schreier, 2007). Regarding social value, sports NFTs may represent a culturally important event in sports history, for example, Michael Jordan's 1989 eponymous game-winning play 'The Shot' (see NBA.com, 2021). A respective NFT collectible may add considerable value to an NFT collection, because it can be admired by many, but, probably, only be owned by few; and it can be used as an object of sociality to connect with like-minded through discussions and, hence, increase its popularity and the desire to own it (Baker et a., 2022; Kietzmann et al., 2011). Uniqueness alone might not incite the intention to buy an NFT, but it can bolster functional, emotional, and social value to stimulate the purchase intention.

Aesthetics of NFT sports collectibles has significant and positive influence on functional utility (H3a, $\beta = .374$, $p < .001$), enjoyment (H3b, $\beta = .238$, p < .001), and creativity (H3c, $\beta = .143$, $p < .05$). It has, however, no significant influence on social self-image expression (H3d, *not supported*), social relationship support (H3e, *not supported*), and the intention to purchase NFTs (H3f, *not supported*). This contradicts research by Ho and Wu (2012) and Ruangkanjanases and Wutthisith (2018), who found a significant, direct influence from aesthetics onto the intention to purchase virtual items. Arguably, NFT aesthetics alone does not impact the intention to buy an NFT, but aesthetics can affect playfulness, i.e., enjoyment and creativity of collecting NFTs (Danet & Katriel, 2012), which might act as a mediator to purchase intention. Also, these findings differ from Kim et al. (2011), who note a positive influence from aesthetics on social self-image expression fostered by digital items in social networking communities. It can further be debated that NFT sports collectibles are not necessarily characterized by their beauty or aesthetic appeal, but rather by what their content represents. Therefore, aesthetics needs to be mediated by functional utility to influence social value and, eventually, the intention to buy an NFT.

Functional utility significantly and positively influences the playfulness of collecting sports NFTs, which includes enjoyment (H4a, $\beta = .157$, $p < .05$) and creativity (H4b, $\beta = .229$, $p < .01$); it has also positive influence on social self-image expression (H4c, $\beta = .413$, $p < .001$), and social relationship support (H4d, $\beta = .322$, $p < .001$), but has no impact on NFT purchase intention (H4e, *not supported*). These results parallel findings by Hsu et al. (2011), who explain that a digital service's functional quality affects users' perceived playfulness. It may therefore be contended that as long as a respective NFT can effectively, efficiently, and satisfactorily add consumer value to a collector's NFT experience, a high degree of functional utility can be considered (Shen et al., 2021). Moreover, Kim et al. (2011) find that functional value of digital items in social networking communities positively affects their social value. Respectively, collectors owning NFTs that perform as expected, may proudly present them to their social circles in order to connect over a common interest and present themselves in a certain way. Different from findings of this study, Gan and Wang (2017) found that functional value directly influences the purchase intention in social commerce. It is, however, debatable if collectors would purchase an NFT upon its functional quality without considering the specific consumer value resulting from it. Hence, functional utility may need to be mediated by either emotional or social value.

Enjoyment has a significant and positive effect on NFT purchase intention (H5, $\beta = .370$, $p < .001$). This is indirectly supported by findings from Cho and Lee (2022), who explain that there is a significant degree to which NFTs improve the experience of buying, selling, owning, and investing in digital assets and, therefore, can foster the gratification felt from collecting NFTs. The addition of gamification elements by NFT marketplaces to enhance the experience of collecting digital memorabilia (cf. Spencer et al., 2003; Baker et al., 2022), supports the argument that collecting NFT sports collectibles is based upon having fun hunting for particular pieces to complete one's collection (Danet & Katriel, 2012; Ruangkanjanases & Wutthisith, 2018). This, however, opposes Ho and Wu's (2012) research, which does not find a significant effect from playfulness onto the purchase intention for virtual items.

Creativity involved in collecting sports NFTs has significant and positive influence on the intention to purchase NFTs (H6, $\beta = .351, p < .001$). This is in line with Cho and Lee's (2022) findings, which describe that NFT owners' readiness to try new technologies and willingness to search for specific information positively affects their intention to use NFTs. A further explanation is found in Byun et al. (2017), who note that the relationship between creativity-based playfulness and a consumer's purchase intention is mediated by self-congruity. For the case at hand, it means that the more open-minded and adventurous NFT collectors are and the closer their association with the brand or organization issuing a certain set of NFTs is, the stronger their intention to purchase those NFTs will be.

This study does not find a significant effect from social self-image expression to the intention to buy NFT sports collectibles (H7, *not supported*), which parallels findings by Ho and Wu (2012) in regard to purchase intentions of virtual goods in online games. However, it contradicts research by Kim et al. (2017), who find that purchasing digital items in social networking communities allow their owners to express themselves in ways they may not be able to in real-life, i.e., through heightened representation and articulation. This seems to apply only partially to sports NFTs. Certain NFTs offer the possibility for their owners to decorate their avatars through digital garments or accessories and, consequently, enhance their digital self, e.g., with limited-edition digital sneakers (Hirschmiller, 2022). Other NFTs, such as collectible digital trading cards in their purest form, cannot be used to embellish a collector's digital appearance, unless a specific utility would come with the NFT. Hence, NFT sports collectibles as currently offered on marketplaces like NBA Top Shot or Sorare do seem to offer limited incentives to be purchased in order to strengthen a collector's self-image.

Lastly, social relationship support significantly and positively influences the intention to purchase NFT sports collectibles (H8, $\beta = .135, p < .05$). Ho and Wu (2012) report similar findings with social relationship support having a significant positive impact on the intention to purchase virtual items in online games. Likewise, research by Ruangkanjanases and Wutthisith (2018) supports this claim and suggests that social value significantly affects purchase intention of virtual items, when the respective items allow their users to foster social relationships. However, Kim et al. (2017) report different findings and note that users tend to place less importance on online social relationships when buying digital items on social networking communities. Arguably, social relationships may only be of interest or importance to collectors, if NFTs are conceptualized as a driver for interaction on a respective platform.

PRACTICAL RECOMMENDATIONS

The discourse above stresses the necessity for a sports organization to design and provide NFT sports collectibles for their fans, based upon NFT characteristics, i.e., scarcity, uniqueness, aesthetics, and functional utility, as well as perceived consumer values like playfulness, i.e., enjoyment and creativity, and social value, i.e., social self-image expression and social relationship support. Although some of these variables may not directly influence the intention to purchase NFTs in the provided context, marketers should consider all variables explored in this research when conceptualizing an NFT experience.

These variables may indirectly influence NFT purchase intention or simply contribute to the overall NFT experience for collectors. The following discourse uses the above-discussed NFT characteristics as a foundation for the recommended considerations. These characteristics offer stimuli for consumer values upon which high-level practical recommendations are offered on how a sports organization can design their NFT sports collectibles and respective marketing communications efforts. These recommendations seek to bridge the physical and virtual realm by offering digitized real-world moments that add value to their owner's experience.

In order for a collector to purchase an NFT sports collectible because of its scarcity, the NFT needs to offer functional utility, playfulness, and social relationship support. This can be partially achieved by limiting an NFT's availability and, therefore, creating exclusivity. Such rarity can considerably heighten the item's price utility (Spencer et al., 2003). Functional quality would have to be conceptualized into the NFT by adding, for example, exclusive access to a service related to the issuing brand or company (Baker et al., 2022). This could include VIP access to a sporting event or first-buyer access to a limited-edition jersey. Regarding playfulness, NFT scarcity could be used to gamify an NFT marketplace. For example, a marketplace could hold challenges for which collectors need to utilize their digital collectibles. Depending on an item's level of scarcity, its value in the game may increase and offer owners greater chances for winning. Consequently, collectors could become intrigued by the collectible's functional utility and invest more time and effort to find the item at an adequate price and add it to their collection. An NFT's scarcity can also amplify social relationships by creating opportunities where owners of a rare NFT mingle in communities with like-minded others to talk about their collectibles and related topics, ask questions, and give advice on collecting respective items (Zaucha & Agur, 2022). NFT providers should consider creating such community places, online or offline, that foster interactivity and relationship building between NFT collectors. An active and pleasant community, where members know each other, will ensure a sustainable environment beneficial to its members and the organization running the community (Vernuccio et al., 2015).

Uniqueness of an NFT needs to be mediated through the same variables as scarcity, thus, functional utility, playfulness, and social relationship support, in order to affect the purchase intention for NFT sports collectibles. For example, functional utility can be influenced while considering the degree by which an NFT can be differentiated from other NFTs in the same category (Franke & Schreier, 2008). This could include offering NFT collections that emphasize brand assets unique to a sports brand or organization, i.e., athletes, entities, products, or moments, and offer specific augmented services with them. Playfulness might result from such uniqueness, as it encourages collectors to search for additional information on an NFT and its augmented services and enjoy the respective process. Additionally, the process could lead collectors to online or offline communities, where they might develop the feeling of belonging to a group of like-minded people, hence, fostering social relationships (Baker et al., 2022; Cho & Lee, 2022). With that in mind, NFT-providing organizations should consider conceptualizing various NFTs with a different degree of uniqueness to them. This could create an overall diversified NFT experience within a marketplace, as some NFTs would artificially boost functional, emotional, and social value, whereas perceived consumer values for certain other NFTs would, correspondingly, be lower.

Aesthetics of an NFT indirectly influences NFT purchase intention through functional utility and playfulness. Sports organizations should approach NFT aesthetics less from the perspective of beauty and more as a way to express particular brand values or promote individual brand attributes (Santayana, 1904). For example, the NBA Top Shot platform focuses its NFT aesthetics on short videos called moments that represent specific plays from their athletes such as dunks, steals, 3-pointers, etc. Hence, the use of

NFT aesthetics should not be limited to the degree of visual beauty, but should be used to conceptualize an overall communicative expression of the providing organization. This would add playfulness, i.e., emotional value, to the NFT experience, as collectors might be intrigued by the expressive nature of the provided NFTs and find joy in browsing through their collection and playing their video collectibles (Byun et al., 2017). Similarly, an NFT's functional utility can be enhanced with expressive aesthetic communication design that adds visual value to the item and, possibly, economic value, because of its one-of-a-kind visual interpretation of the real-life moment.

Social self-image expression may not have an effect on the intention to buy NFT sports collectibles in the context of this study, but it can still contribute to the greater brand experience, thus, affecting the satisfaction and loyalty of NFT owners (see Brakus et al., 2009). Sports organizations should consider that consumers wish to express themselves more via online communication channels than in real-life. Hence, online users may want to show off their digital possessions to look good in front of their virtual audience (Schau & Gilly, 2003). Accordingly, NFT providers need to ensure that collectors can easily share their collectibles with others. This could be implemented by adding specific functional utility to an NFT, which, for example, would offer its owners exclusive access to a tangible or intangible item or experience (Baker et al., 2022). Being able to access such an exclusive item or experience for anyone in the community to see, allows owners of the NFT to improve the way they are perceived by others (Treiblmaier, 2021). Scarcity of the sports NFT can affect a collector's self-image expression by allowing them to make a certain impression on others with a rare and sought-after digital item, which they would not be able to achieve in the real world, because that item might not exist in real-life or because it would not be accessible to that collector (Kim et al., 2017). Moreover, sports organizations can enhance the uniqueness of their NFT sports collectibles by including culturally significant moments from the history of the company in certain NFTs in order to highlight their brand values and attributes (Baker et al., 2022). This would add a unique aspect to their NFT collectibles, to which invested fans might feel a stronger association because of their higher degree of identification, and would want to present their unique NFT in return for admiration from other community members (Franke & Schreier, 2008).

CONCLUSION

Collecting sports memorabilia can be an integral part of the sports fan experience. Jerseys, trading cards and other collectibles connect fans with their favorite teams and athletes, while creating emotional, functional, and social value. The internet has augmented the collector experience with wider and easier accessibility to collectibles and other collectors alike. Blockchain technology has now added another significant layer of value to a collector's experience by allowing digital collectibles to gain value with product characteristics that previously only applied to physical items, thus, providing the foundation for NFT collectibles. This chapter introduced the role of NFT sports collectibles in an IoT and IoV context, before elaborating on characteristics of NFTs and factors of perceived consumer value that influence the intention to purchase NFT sports collectibles. In order to answer the respective research question, literature on contemporary marketing, product characteristics, digital items, NFTs, and consumer values was reviewed and synthesized with data gathered specifically for this publication. The chapter's main findings show that NFT characteristics, i.e., scarcity, uniqueness, aesthetics, and functional utility, do not directly influence the intention to buy NFT sports collectibles, but significantly and positively affect purchase intention when mediated through consumer values such as the enjoyment of collecting NFTs, the creativity that is aroused from collecting these digital items, and the respective social relationships that can be built and maintained accordingly. The chapter further finds no significant impact from social self-image expression onto purchase intention for an NFT. A rather novel perspective to functional value in a consumer value context is offered and legitimized by the findings of this chapter. This study presents functional utility not only as a consumer value, but also as a characteristic of the examined digital item category, as the elements of functional quality and price utility can also be regarded as features of an NFT. It finds support in the corresponding statistical analysis, which indicates an acceptable overall fit for the proposed conceptual model. This chapter adds novel findings to the body of knowledge in the fields of marketing and communications of NFTs in the sports and entertainment industry, while supporting certain findings on perceived consumer value of digital items and contradicting certain other results.

LIMITATIONS AND FUTURE RESEARCH

Limitations of this chapter include, but are not limited to, a sample bias as respondents of the online questionnaire were recruited solely through digital communications channels and represent a mainly North American audience. Furthermore, the sample is considerably influenced by responses from Millennials. With this in mind, future research could examine the differences in consumption behavior amongst different generations of users. The research could also be expanded to test in other countries with a different penetration of NFT sports collectibles to the USA; a comparison between collectors in different countries would also add value to the body of knowledge. Another limitation of this study is the somewhat high degree of multicollinearity. Future research could examine the utilized scales in more depth and adapt them more specifically to the context of NFTs, as NFT characteristics can be considered different from characteristics of traditional digital or physical items. Lastly, NFT sports collectibles may not reflect the same characteristics and values of other digital tokens. Hence, research on other tokens might provide further insights to how digital tokens can be utilized.

REFERENCES

Ali, M., & Bagui, S. (2021). Introduction to NFTs: The future of digital collectibles. *International Journal of Advanced Computer Science and Applications*, *12*(10), 50–56. doi:10.14569/IJACSA.2021.0121007

Alqahtani, H., & Naim, A. (2022). Critical Success Factors for Transforming CRM to SCRM for building E-CRM. In A. Naim & S. Kautish (Eds.), *Building a Brand Image Through Electronic Customer Relationship Management* (pp. 139–168). IGI Global. doi:10.4018/978-1-6684-5386-5.ch007

Arcenegui, J., Arjona, R., Román, R., & Baturone, I. (2021). Secure combination of IoT and blockchain by physically binding IoT devices to smart non-fungible tokens using PUFs. *Sensors (Basel)*, *21*(9), 3119. Advance online publication. doi:10.339021093119 PMID:33946227

Aroean, L. (2012). Friend or foe: In enjoying playfulness, do innovative consumers tend to switch brand? *Journal of Consumer Behaviour*, *11*(1), 67–80. doi:10.1002/cb.370

Baker, B. J., Pizzo, A. D., & Su, Y. (2022). Non-fungible tokens: A research primer and implications for sport management. *Sports Innovation Journal*, *1*, 1–15. doi:10.18060/25636

Balbi, G., & Magaudda, P. (2018). *A history of digital media: An intermedia and global perspective*. Routledge. doi:10.4324/9781315209630

Britannica. (2022). *Aesthetics*. https://www.britannica.com/topic/aesthetics

Broeder, P., & Wentink, E. (2022). Limited-time scarcity and competitive arousal in e-commerce. *International Review of Retail, Distribution and Consumer Research, 32*(5), 549–567. doi:10.1080/09593969.2022.2098360

Burton, B. J., & Jacobsen, J. P. (1999). Measuring returns on investments in collectibles. *The Journal of Economic Perspectives, 13*(4), 193–212. doi:10.1257/jep.13.4.193

Byun, K. A., Dass, M., Kumar, P., & Kim, J. (2017). An examination of innovative consumers' playfulness on their pre-ordering behavior. *Journal of Consumer Marketing, 34*(3), 226–240. doi:10.1108/JCM-01-2016-1684

Cho, K. H., & Lee, W. B. (2022). A study on influencing factors on intention to adopt NFTs using UTAUT. *The Journal of the Korea Contents Association, 22*(3), 17–34. doi:10.5392/JKCA.2022.22.03.017

Cialdini, R. B. (2001). The science of persuasion. *Scientific American, 284*(2), 76–81. doi:10.1038scientificamerican0201-76

Cohen, J. (1992). Quantitative methods in psychology: A power primer. *Psychological Bulletin, 112*(1), 155–159. doi:10.1037/0033-2909.112.1.155 PMID:19565683

Colicev, A. (2022). How can non-fungible tokens bring value to brands. *International Journal of Research in Marketing*. Advance online publication. doi:10.1016/j.ijresmar.2022.07.003

Cram, T. (2008). Pricing. In M. J. Baker & S. J. Hart (Eds.), *The Marketing Book* (pp. 281–295). Elsevier. doi:10.1016/B978-0-7506-8566-5.50018-2

Danet, B., & Katriel, T. (2012). No two alike: play and aesthetics in collecting. In S. M. Pearce (Ed.), *Interpreting objects and collections* (pp. 220–239). Routledge.

Daoud, J. I. (2017). Multicollinearity and regression analysis. *Journal of Physics: Conference Series, 949*(1), 012009. Advance online publication. doi:10.1088/1742-6596/949/1/012009

Dash, A. (2021). NFTs weren't supposed to end like this. *The Atlantic*. https://www.theatlantic.com/ideas/archive/2021/04/nfts-werent-supposed-end-like/618488/

de Mesquita, J. M. C., & Kostelijk, E. (2021). *Marketing analytics: Statistical tools for marketing and consumer behavior using SPSS*. Routledge. doi:10.4324/9781003196617

Deloitte. (2021). *From trading cards to digital video: Sports NFTs kick sports memorabilia into the digital age*. https://www2.deloitte.com/content/dam/insights/articles/GLOB164584_Sports-NFT/DI_Sports-NFT.pdf

Dunn, T. J., Baguley, T., & Brunsden, V. (2014). From alpha to omega: A practical solution to the pervasive problem of internal consistency estimation. *British Journal of Psychology, 105*(3), 399–412. doi:10.1111/bjop.12046 PMID:24844115

Dwivedi, Y. K., Hughes, L., Wang, Y., Alalwan, A. A., Ahn, S. J., Balakrishnan, J., ... Wirtz, J. (2022). Metaverse marketing: How the metaverse will shape the future of consumer research and practice. *Psychology and Marketing*. Advance online publication. doi:10.1002/mar.21767

Efendioglu, I. H. (2022). The rise of the non-fungible token (NFT) market in Turkey: The effect of social media interaction and the need for uniqueness on NFT purchase pntention. *Review of Marketing Science*. doi:10.1515/roms-2022-0065

Fai, A. (2021). *Smart collectibles: Unlocking the value of non-fungible tokens (NFTs)*. EthinkWeb Co.

Fatima, S., Alqahtani, H., Naim, A., & Alma'alwi, F. (2022). E-CRM Through Social Media Marketing Activities for Brand Awareness, Brand Image, and Brand Loyalty. In A. Naim & S. Kautish (Eds.), *Building a Brand Image Through Electronic Customer Relationship Management* (pp. 109–138). IGI Global., doi:10.4018/978-1-6684-5386-5.ch006

Field, A. (2018). *Discovering statistics using IBM SPSS statistics* (5th ed.). Sage Publications.

Franke, N., & Schreier, M. (2008). Product uniqueness as a driver of customer utility in mass customization. *Marketing Letters*, *19*(2), 93–107. doi:10.100711002-007-9029-7

Gan, C., & Wang, W. (2017). The influence of perceived value on purchase intention in social commerce context. *Internet Research*, *27*(4), 772–785. doi:10.1108/IntR-06-2016-0164

Ha, T. M. (2021). The impact of product characteristics of limited-edition shoes on perceived value, brand trust and purchase intention. *Cogent Business & Management*, *8*(1), 1–19. doi:10.1080/23311975.2021.1953680

Hirschmiller, S. (2022). *Adidas first wearable NFT collection marks the first time you can dress AND undress your bored ape*. https://www.forbes.com/sites/stephaniehirschmiller/2022/11/16/adidas-launches-first-nft-wearables-collection/?sh=7a0da82337fe

Ho, C. H., & Wu, T. Y. (2012). Factors affecting intent to purchase virtual goods in online games. *International Journal of Electronic Business Management*, *10*(3), 204–212.

Hoerl, A. E., & Kennard, R. W. (1970). Ridge regression: Applications to nonorthogonal problems. *Technometrics*, *12*(1), 69–82. doi:10.1080/00401706.1970.10488635

Huang, L., & Savary, J. (2022). When payments go social: The use of person-to-person payment methods attenuates the endowment effect. *JMR, Journal of Marketing Research*. Advance online publication. doi:10.1177/00222437221128255

Kamal, S., Naim, A., Magd, H., Khan, S. A., & Khan, F. M. (2022). The Relationship Between E-Service Quality, Ease of Use, and E-CRM Performance Referred by Brand Image. In A. Naim & S. Kautish (Eds.), *Building a Brand Image Through Electronic Customer Relationship Management* (pp. 84–108). IGI Global. doi:10.4018/978-1-6684-5386-5.ch005

Kietzmann, J. H., Hermkens, K., McCarthy, I. P., & Silvestre, B. S. (2011). Social media? Get serious! Understanding the functional building blocks of social media. *Business Horizons*, *54*(3), 241–251. doi:10.1016/j.bushor.2011.01.005

Kim, H. W., Gupta, S., & Koh, J. (2011). Investigating the intention to purchase digital items in social networking communities: A customer value perspective. *Information & Management*, *48*(6), 228–234. doi:10.1016/j.im.2011.05.004

Li, S., & Chen, Y. (2022). How non-fungible tokens empower business model innovation. *Business Horizons*. Advance online publication. doi:10.1016/j.bushor.2022.10.006

Market Decipher. (2021). Sp*orts NFT Market Size, Statistics, Growth Trend Analysis and Forecast Report, 2022 - 2032*. https://www.marketdecipher.com/report/sports-nft-market

MarketResearch.com. (2022). *Global Sports Trading Card Market Size, Status and Forecast 2022-2028*. https://www.marketresearch.com/QYResearch-Group-v3531/Global-Sports-Trading-Card-Size-31719180/

Marquardt, D. W., & Snee, R. D. (1975). Ridge regression in practice. *The American Statistician*, *29*(1), 3–20.

Mekacher, A., Bracci, A., Nadini, M., Martino, M., Alessandretti, L., Aiello, L. M., & Baronchelli, A. (2022). Heterogeneous rarity patterns drive price dynamics in NFT collections. *Scientific Reports*, *12*(1), 1–9. doi:10.103841598-022-17922-5 PMID:34992227

Naim, A., Alqahtani, H., Muniasamy, A., Bilfaqih, S. M., Mahveen, R., & Mahjabeen, R. (2023). Applications of Information Systems and Data Security in Marketing Management. In A. Naim, P. Malik, & F. Zaidi (Eds.), *Fraud Prevention, Confidentiality, and Data Security for Modern Businesses* (pp. 57–83). IGI Global. doi:10.4018/978-1-6684-6581-3.ch003

Naim, A., & Kautish, S. K. (Eds.). (2022). *Building a Brand Image Through Electronic Customer Relationship Management*. IGI Global. doi:10.4018/978-1-6684-5386-5

Naim, A., Malik, P. K., & Zaidi, F. A. (Eds.). (2023). *Fraud Prevention, Confidentiality, and Data Security for Modern Businesses*. IGI Global. doi:10.4018/978-1-6684-6581-3

NBA.com. (2021). *Top Moments: Michael Jordan hits 'The Shot', breaks Cavs' hearts*. https://www.nba.com/news/history-top-moments-jordan-shot-cavaliers-1989

Newswire, P. R. (2022). *$1.3 billion sports NFT market doubles in 2022*. https://www.prnewswire.com/in/news-releases/-1-3-billion-sports-nft-market-doubles-in-2022-a-100-growth-10-years-cagr-36-3-says-market-decipher-850146589.html

Osivand, S. (2021). Smart collectibles; use case of NFT tokens. *Open Access Research Journal of Engineering and Technology*, *1*(2), 24–31. doi:10.53022/oarjet.2021.1.2.0113

Pine, B. J., & Gilmore, J. H. (2020). *The experience economy: Competing for customer time, attention, and money*. Harvard Business Review Press.

PWC. (2022). *NFTs: The future of digital assets in sports*. https://www.pwc.com/us/en/tech-effect/emerging-tech/nfts-the-future-of-digital-assets-in-sports.html

Ruangkanjanases, A., & Wutthisith, M. (2018). Predicting intention to purchase digital stickers in an application for instant communications on mobile devices: A comparative study. *Journal of Telecommunication, Electronic and Computer Engineering, 10*(1-10), 75-80.

Ruby, D. (2022). *33+ NFT Statistics 2022* [Facts, Trends & Data]. https://www.demandsage.com/nft-statistics/

Sarstedt, M., & Mooi, E. (2014). *A concise guide to market research: The process, data, and methods using IBM SPSS statistics* (2nd ed.). Springer-Verlag. doi:10.1007/978-3-642-53965-7

Saunders, M., Lewis, P., & Thornhill, A. (2007). *Research methods for business students* (4th ed.). FT Prentice Hall.

Schau, H. J., & Gilly, M. C. (2003). We are what we post? Self-presentation in personal web space. *The Journal of Consumer Research, 30*(3), 385–404. doi:10.1086/378616

Schmidt, M., & Banusch, B. (2022). *How do non-fungible tokens create tangible value in the metaverse?* https://www.ey.com/en_ch/technology/how-do-non-fungible-tokens-create-tangible-value-in-the-metaverse

Schmitt, B. (1999). *Experiential marketing: How to get customers to sense, feel, think, act, relate to your company and brands*. Free Press.

Shen, B., Tan, W., Guo, J., Zhao, L., & Qin, P. (2021). How to promote user purchase in metaverse? A systematic literature review on consumer behavior research and virtual commerce application design. *Applied Sciences (Basel, Switzerland), 11*(23), 1–29. doi:10.3390/app112311087

Sheth, J. N., Newman, B. I., & Gross, B. L. (1991). Why we buy what we buy: A theory of consumption values. *Journal of Business Research, 22*(2), 159–170. doi:10.1016/0148-2963(91)90050-8

Shi, X., Li, F., & Chumnumpan, P. (2020). The use of product scarcity in marketing. *European Journal of Marketing, 54*(2), 380–418. doi:10.1108/EJM-04-2018-0285

Spencer, N. E., Cuneen, J., & Schneider, R. (2003). Collecting celebrity: The meanings and process of collecting sports memorabilia. *Visions in Leisure and Business, 21*(1), 8–29.

Sweeney, J. C., & Soutar, G. N. (2001). Consumer perceived value: The development of a multiple item scale. *Journal of Retailing, 77*(2), 203–220. doi:10.1016/S0022-4359(01)00041-0

Tian, K. T., Bearden, W. O., & Hunter, G. L. (2001). Consumers' need for uniqueness: Scale development and validation. *The Journal of Consumer Research, 28*(1), 50–66. doi:10.1086/321947

Treiblmaier, H. (2021). Beyond blockchain: How tokens trigger the internet of value and what marketing researchers need to know about them. *Journal of Marketing Communications*, •••, 1–13. doi:10.1080/13527266.2021.2011375

Truong, N. B., Um, T. W., Zhou, B., & Lee, G. M. (2018). *Strengthening the blockchain-based internet of value with trust. In 2018 IEEE international conference on communications*. ICC. doi:10.1109/ICC.2018.8423014

Vázquez, R., Del Rio, A. B., & Iglesias, V. (2002). Consumer-based brand equity: Development and validation of a measurement instrument. *Journal of Marketing Management*, *18*(1-2), 27–48. doi:10.1362/0267257022775882

Vernuccio, M., Pagani, M., Barbarossa, C., & Pastore, A. (2015). Antecedents of brand love in online network-based communities. A social identity perspective. *Journal of Product and Brand Management*, *24*(7), 706–719. doi:10.1108/JPBM-12-2014-0772

Web3 Studios. (2022). *Market report: Sports in the metaverse*. https://www.web3-studios.com/research

Yocco, V. S. (2016). *Design for the mind: Seven psychological principles of persuasive design*. Manning Publications Co.

Yoo, B., Donthu, N., & Lee, S. (2000). An examination of selected marketing mix elements and brand equity. *Journal of the Academy of Marketing Science*, *28*(2), 195–211. doi:10.1177/0092070300282002

Zaucha, T., & Agur, C. (2022). Newly minted: Non-fungible tokens and the commodification of fandom. *New Media & Society*. Advance online publication. doi:10.1177/14614448221080481

KEY TERMS AND DEFINITIONS

NFT Characteristics: Potential stimuli to consumer values based on features of an NFT such as scarcity, uniqueness, aesthetics, and functional utility.

NFT Marketplace: A platform where users can buy, sell, and trade NFTs.

NFT Sports Collectible: A specific type of NFT that represents ownership of a digital collectible related to a particular sport or sports team; they can take many forms, such as digital trading cards, virtual tickets to games, or virtual versions of physical sports memorabilia.

Non-Fungible Token (NFT): An authenticated, non-fungible digital item created on the blockchain that unlocks access to specific value for tangible or intangible items or experiences.

Perceived Consumer Value: The subjective value that a consumer assigns to a product based on their perception of its worth, considering characteristics and benefits.

Chapter 17
E-Marketing, E-Commerce, E-Business, and Internet of Things:
An Overview of Terms in the Context of Small and Medium Enterprises (SMEs)

Shad Ahmad Khan
University of Buraimi, Oman

ABSTRACT

Small and medium enterprises (SMEs) are often considered an economic engine. The digital boom that has happened in the recent years offers a variety of tools to these SMEs to reach out to their target audience in a very cost-effective manner. Automation of marketing is often related with the digitization of marketing, internet of things, and related activities. This mainly harnesses the use of internet and other electronic sources to communicate with their stakeholders. Terms like e-marketing, e-commerce, e-business, and internet of things (IoT) have gained prominence in the arena of modern business management. In this chapter, an attempt has been made to connect e-marketing, e-commerce, e-business, and internet of things in context of SMEs and marketing automation by performing bibliometric analysis of Scopus database and review of literature. This will help in understanding the way concepts have evolved in recent times. This chapter also attempts to differentiate the four terms in light of literature and theories.

INTRODUCTION

E-Marketing, E-Commerce, E-Business, and Internet Marketing are closely related terms that are often used interchangeably in the context of Small and Medium Enterprises (SMEs). These terms refer to the use of digital technologies, such as the internet, mobile devices, and social media, to market and sell products and services, as well as to manage business operations. In this overview, we will explore these terms in more detail and consider their implications for SMEs in today's increasingly digital market-

DOI: 10.4018/978-1-6684-8166-0.ch017

place. This chapter deals with the concepts of E-marketing, important terms in the field of E-marketing, E-business, and E-commerce. As an attempt to understand and document the relationship between E-marketing, E-business, and E-commerce, diagrammatic representations have been made. Also, a brief bibliometric analysis of the E-marketing, E-business, and E-commerce and SMEs have been performed to check the status of researches in this field.

E-MARKETING

Electronic Marketing (E-Marketing) used to be the business practice and philosophy associated with buying and selling of goods, services, information and ideas via the internet and the other electronic means. As per Frost & Strauss (2016) E marketing is the use of electronic data and applications for planning and executing the conception, distribution and pricing of ideas, goods and services to create exchanges that satisfy individual and organizational objectives. In the modern times it is considered to be synonymous to digital marketing i.e., is the process of promoting a product or service through electronic channels, such as the internet, mobile devices, and social media (Wymbs, 2011). However, E-marketing was found to be more popular word outside the USA as compared to Digital marketing (Shaltoni,2016). It is a fast-growing and ever-evolving field that has become essential for businesses of all sizes to reach and engage with their target audiences. The rise of digital technology and the internet has transformed the way businesses communicate with their customers (Sawicki, 2016). Traditional marketing methods, such as print advertisements and billboards, are no longer as effective as they once were. Consumers today have access to an abundance of information at their fingertips, and they are not limited to a specific location or time.

E-marketing allows businesses to reach a global audience and target specific demographics with precision (Dickey & Lewis, 2012). One of the major advantages of e-marketing is the ability to track and measure the effectiveness of campaigns. With digital tools, businesses can track the number of website visitors, conversion rates, and customer engagement (Bag et al., 2022). This data allows businesses to make informed decisions about their marketing strategies, such as which channels are most effective and where to allocate their budget (Bughin et al., 2010).

Today E-Marketing harnesses various digital platforms to reach wider population of audience. Social media is growing as a prominent platform offering variety of benefits discussed in the later part of this chapter. Another popular e-marketing channel is email marketing. Email marketing allows businesses to reach their customers directly, providing them with personalized and relevant information. E-marketing also includes paid advertising, such as pay-per-click (PPC) and display advertising (Szymanski & Lininski, 2018). E-marketing has become an essential part of consideration for any business business strategy. With the rise of digital technology and the internet, it has become necessary for businesses to reach and engage with their target audiences through electronic channels (Bala & Verma,2018). E-marketing allows businesses to reach a global audience, track the effectiveness of their campaigns, and make informed decisions about their marketing strategies.

IMPORTANT TERMS IN THE FIELD OF E-MARKETING

In the modern times many new terms have emerged in the field of E-marketing (Frost & Strauss, 2016), as the technology is growing newer terms are expected to emerge as per the time and need. However, some of the prominent terms are discussed below:

Search Engine Optimization (SEO)

SEO is the process of optimizing a website or online content to improve its visibility and ranking in search engine results pages (SERPs) (Vyas, 2019; Lammenett, 2019). Search engines such as Google, Bing, and Yahoo use complex algorithms to determine the relevance and authority of a website. These algorithms take into account various factors, including the use of keywords, the quality of content, and the number and quality of links pointing to the site. SEO is the process of understanding and working within these algorithms to improve a website's visibility and ranking (Nabih, 2019; Lammenett, 2019). Keyword research is the first step in the SEO process that requires identification of the keywords that people use for searching products and services offered by a business (Vyas, 2019; Nabih, 2019; Lammenett, 2019). Businesses that want to succeed in the digital economy must understand the importance of SEO and how to effectively leverage it to reach and engage customers.

Search Engine Marketing (SEM)

Search Engine Marketing (SEM) is a form of digital marketing that involves the use of paid advertising to increase visibility and drive traffic to a website. SEM is an integral part of an overall online marketing strategy, and it is particularly useful for businesses that are looking to reach customers in a specific geographic location or industry (Nabih, 2019; Salmiah et al., 2020).The most common form of SEM is pay-per-click (PPC) advertising i.e., sponsored listing that appear in the top search list of a search engine results page (SERPs).

The most popular platforms for SEM are Google and Bing. Google Ads, formerly known as Google Adwords, is the largest and most popular platform for PPC advertising. Bing Ads is another popular platform that allows businesses to advertise on Bing and Yahoo search engines (Salmiah et al., 2020; Levy, 2021). SEM is a powerful tool for businesses looking to increase visibility and drive traffic to their website. It allows businesses to reach a highly targeted audience, control their ad spend, and measure the success of their campaigns. To make the most of SEM, businesses should conduct keyword research, create compelling ad copy, and use analytics to track the performance of their campaigns.

Social Media Marketing (SMM)

SMM is the process of using social media platforms to promote a product, service, or brand (Mason et al., 2021; Saleem et al., 2022; Lammenett, 2019). This powerful tool can be used by business of any size, offering any product. It is a cost effective solution to reach a wide and diverse range of audience (Mason et al., 2021; Saleem et al., 2022; Lammenett, 2019).

The most popular social media platforms for marketing include Facebook, Twitter, Instagram, LinkedIn, and YouTube (Saleem et al., 2022). Each platform offers unique features and benefits, and businesses should carefully consider which platforms are most appropriate for their target audience and marketing goals. Each social media platforms offer a variety of tools and metrics to track engagement and analyze the effectiveness of marketing campaigns (Saleem et al., 2022).Social media marketing also offers a number of opportunities to engage with customers and build relationships.

To be successful in social media marketing, businesses must have a clear strategy and plan in place. This includes identifying target audiences, setting marketing goals, creating content, and analysing performance. Businesses should also be prepared to be consistent and active on social media platforms, as well as being responsive to customer feedback and engagement.

Content Marketing (CM)

Content is the main element of any digital marketing practice; it decides on what information or content the business want to deliver to its audience. CM is a strategic approach to creating and distributing valuable, relevant, and consistent content to attract and engage a clearly defined audience (Müller & Christandl,2019; Saleem et al., 2022; Yaghtin et al., 2020; Lammenett, 2019).

The foundation of content marketing is the creation of high-quality content that is relevant and valuable to the target audience. This can include blog posts, videos, infographics, e-books, and more (Yaghtin et al., 2020; Lammenett, 2019). The key is to create content that is interesting, informative, and provides value to the audience. It should be tailored to their needs, interests, and pain points (Müller & Christandl,2019; Saleem et al., 2022).

Once the content is created, it must be distributed and promoted. This can be done through a variety of channels, such as social media, email marketing, and SEO (Müller & Christandl,2019; Saleem et al., 2022). The goal is to reach as many people as possible and to make it easy for them to find and share the content. Content marketing is not just about creating and distributing content, it's also about measuring and analyzing the results. By tracking metrics such as website traffic, engagement, and conversions, businesses can gain insight into what is working and what is not (Yaghtin et al., 2020; Lammenett, 2019). Content marketing is an effective way to establish trust and credibility with potential customers. It helps to build a relationship with them, to educate them about the products or services, and to demonstrate Business expertise.

Influencer Marketing

Influencer marketing is a form of social media marketing that leverages the power and influence of individuals who have built a following on social media platforms to promote a brand or product (Vrontis et al., 2021; Campbell et al., 2020; Lammenett, 2019). These individuals are called influencers. They have the ability to reach a large audience, and their recommendations and endorsements can be highly effective in driving engagement and sales. This is due in part to the rise of social media platforms such as Instagram, TikTok, and YouTube, which have made it easier for individuals to build a following and for businesses to connect with potential customers (Vrontis et al., 2021; Campbell et al., 2020).

There are a few different types of influencer marketing strategies that businesses can use, including:

- **Micro-Influencer Marketing:** This strategy involves working with individuals who have a relatively small following (typically between 1,000 and 100,000 followers) but a high level of engagement with their audience. Micro-influencers are often seen as more authentic and relatable than larger influencers, and their recommendations can carry a lot of weight with their followers.

- **Macro-Influencer Marketing:** This strategy involves working with individuals who have a large following (typically 100,000 or more followers) and a high level of visibility on social media. Macro-influencers are often celebrities or public figures, and their recommendations can be highly effective in reaching a large audience.
- **Nano-Influencer Marketing:** This strategy involves working with individuals who have a very small following (typically under 1,000 followers) but are considered experts in their niche or have a highly engaged audience.
- **Celebrity Influencer Marketing:** This strategy involves working with celebrities who have a large following and a high level of visibility on social media to promote a brand or product.

To succeed in influencer marketing, it is important to choose the right influencer for the brand or product. This means looking for individuals who have a following that is relevant to the target audience, and who align with the brand values and message of a company. It is also important to have clear goals for influencer marketing campaign, whether it's driving sales, increasing brand awareness, or building a community around the brand (Vrontis et al., 2021; Campbell et al., 2020).

Email Marketing (EM)

Email marketing allows businesses to target specific segments of their audience, personalize their messaging, and track the results of their campaigns. The key elements of email marketing and how businesses can use it to achieve their marketing goals are needed to be explored (Hartemo, 2016; Jenkins, 2008; Pavlov et al., 2008; Zhang et al., 2017). The main components include the email list, the email content, and the email delivery platform. The email list is a database of email addresses that businesses have collected from their customers or website visitors. The email content is the message that businesses want to send to their audience. And the email delivery platform is the software or service that businesses use to send their emails. Email Marketing offers personalization i.e., is the process of tailoring the content and messaging of an email to specific individuals (Jenkins, 2008; Hartemo, 2016). This can include things like using the recipient's name in the subject line or customizing the content based on their interests or purchase history. Personalization can increase the effectiveness of an email campaign by making the message more relevant and engaging to the recipient. This allows businesses to track the results of their campaigns. This can include things like open rates, click-through rates, and conversion rates. Tracking these metrics allows businesses to see which campaigns are most effective and make adjustments as needed (Zhang et al., 2017). Thus, by understanding the key elements of email marketing and how to effectively use them, businesses can create more targeted and personalized campaigns, increase their ROI and achieve their marketing goals. As technology and consumer behavior change, email marketing will continue to evolve and businesses will have to adapt and find new ways to make the most of it.

Mobile Marketing (MM)

Mobile marketing is a digital marketing strategy that targets customers through their mobile devices, such as smartphones and tablets (Leppäniemi et al., 2006; Shankar & Balasubramanian, 2009; Tong et al., 2020). This form of marketing has grown in popularity in recent years as more and more people use mobile devices to access the internet and make purchasing decisions. As a result, businesses have been looking for new and innovative ways to reach and engage their mobile customers (Tong et al., 2020).

One of the most popular forms of mobile marketing used to be SMS or text message marketing. This involves sending promotional messages to customers through SMS, which can include discounts, coupons, and special offers. SMS marketing is effective because it allows businesses to reach customers in real-time, and it has a high open and click-through rate (Leppäniemi et al., 2006; Shankar & Balasubramanian, 2009). Today more popular form of mobile marketing is mobile apps. Many businesses have developed mobile apps that allow customers to interact with their business and make purchases directly from their mobile device. Mobile apps can also be used to collect customer data, such as location and browsing history, which can be used to personalize marketing campaigns and improve the customer experience (Tong et al., 2020; Gao et al., 2020). Mobile advertising is also a popular form of mobile marketing. This includes advertising on mobile-specific platforms, such as mobile websites and mobile apps, as well as advertising on mobile search engines, such as Google and Bing. Mobile advertising allows businesses to target their ads to specific audiences, such as location and device type, which can improve the effectiveness of their marketing campaigns (Tong et al., 2020; Gao et al., 2020).

Affiliate Marketing (AM)

In affiliate marketing (AM), a business will typically recruit a group of affiliates to promote their products or services. These affiliates will then be provided with a unique link or code that they can use to promote the business on their own channels (usually social media channels on various platforms). When a customer clicks on the link or uses the code, the affiliate will be credited with the sale or conversion (Pradina & Poeradisastra, 2019; Lammenett, 2019). There are a variety of different ways that affiliates can be compensated for their efforts, including commissions on sales, pay-per-click, or a flat fee. The compensation model will typically be agreed upon by the business and the affiliate prior to the start of the partnership. One of the keys to successful affiliate marketing is selecting the right affiliates to promote the products or services. Businesses should look for affiliates who have a large and engaged audience and are likely to be a good fit for their products or services. Additionally, businesses should also ensure that their affiliates are transparent about their marketing efforts and are not using any deceptive or spammy tactics to drive traffic (Pradina & Poeradisastra, 2019).

Another important aspect of affiliate marketing is tracking and reporting on the performance of the partnership. Businesses should have a system in place to track the number of clicks and conversions generated by each affiliate, as well as any other relevant metrics such as revenue or customer lifetime value. This data can be used to optimize the partnership and ensure that the business is getting the most out of their affiliate marketing efforts (Pradina & Poeradisastra, 2019; Lammenett, 2019). Overall, affiliate marketing is a powerful tool that can help businesses to increase their revenue and exposure without having to invest heavily in advertising or marketing efforts. By selecting the right affiliates and tracking the performance of the partnership, businesses can maximize the return on their investment and achieve long-term success with this channel.

ELECTRONIC BUSINESS (E-BUSINESS)

Electronic business, also known as e-business, also uses the digital technologies to conduct transactions and manage business operations. This includes the use of the internet, mobile devices, and other digital tools to buy and sell goods and services, communicate with customers and partners, and manage internal operations. The rise of electronic business has had a profound impact on the way businesses operate and has opened up new opportunities for companies of all sizes and in all industries (Combe, 2012; Feng, 2007; Gordijn et al., 2000). The most common forms of electronic business include online retail, digital marketing, and e-commerce. Online retail refers to the sale of goods and services over the internet. This includes both B2C (business-to-consumer) and B2B (business-to-business) transactions (Khan et al., 2022).

One of the key advantages of electronic business is its ability to reach a global audience. With the internet and mobile devices, businesses can now reach customers and partners in every corner of the world. This has opened up new opportunities for companies, particularly in developing countries, to expand their customer base and increase their revenue. Additionally, electronic business has made it easier for businesses to conduct transactions and manage operations, which has led to increased efficiency and cost savings (Combe, 2012; Feng, 2007). E-Commerce and Electronic Marketing are believed to be the sub-units of E-Business (El-Gohary et al., 2008). This is the reason E-Business enjoys all the benefits of all the sub units falling under it along with the associated problems and issues.

ELECTRONIC COMMERCE

Electronic commerce, also known as e-commerce, refers to the buying and selling of goods and services through the internet. This has revolutionized the way businesses operate, allowing them to reach a global audience and providing consumers with more convenience and options (Vladimir, 1996; Laudon & Traver, 2013; Watson et al., 2013). E-commerce has grown exponentially over the past few decades, becoming a vital part of the global economy (Ilmudeen, 2021).

E-commerce allows business to reach a larger customer base and expand their market beyond geographical boundaries. This can lead to increased revenue and growth. Additionally, e-commerce allows businesses to reach customers 24/7, providing a competitive advantage. It offers convenience and accessibility to wider range to products for the consumers (Tokar et al., 2021). Online shopping allows customers to purchase goods from the comfort of their own homes, and with the help of search engines and comparison websites, customers can find the best deals and products. Moreover, e-commerce platforms also provide customers with reviews and ratings of products, which can aid in the purchasing decision.

The businesses today can take advantage of many new E-commerce business model, such as drop-shipping and subscription-based models (Shi et al., 2020). Drop-shipping allows businesses to sell products without holding inventory, while subscription-based models allow customers to receive regular deliveries of products (Shi et al., 2020).

E-commerce also has a significant impact on the economy. It has led to the creation of new jobs in areas such as web design, online marketing, and customer service. Additionally, it has also led to the growth of logistics and transportation companies, which are responsible for delivering goods to customers (Babenko et al., 2019).

However, e-commerce also has issues like Cybersecurity, data privacy etc (Khan & Shazia, 2019). It is important for businesses and governments to address these challenges in order to ensure a sustainable and equitable e-commerce industry.

RELATIONSHIP BETWEEN E-MARKETING, E-COMMERCE, E-BUSINESS

E-marketing, e-commerce, and e-business are all terms that are often used interchangeably, but they each refer to different aspects of doing business online. Understanding the relationship between these three concepts is essential for businesses looking to succeed in the digital economy.

E-marketing refers to the use of digital channels to promote and sell products or services. This can include activities such as search engine optimization (SEO), social media marketing, email marketing, and online advertising. E-marketing is focused on reaching and engaging customers through digital channels, and it is an essential component of any e-commerce or e-business strategy.

E-commerce, on the other hand, refers to the buying and selling of products or services online. This can include activities such as online shopping, online payments, and online customer service. E-commerce is focused on the transactions and logistics of buying and selling online, and it is a key component of any e-business strategy.

E-business, finally, refers to the use of digital technologies to conduct all aspects of a business. This can include activities such as digital marketing, e-commerce, supply chain management, and customer service. E-business is focused on using digital technologies to improve efficiency, reduce costs, and increase revenue, and it is the overarching concept that encompasses e-marketing and e-commerce.

In summary, e-marketing is the digital marketing component of e-business and e-commerce, e-commerce is the buying and selling component of e-business, and e-business is the overall concept that encompasses both e-marketing and e-commerce. This relationship can be understood through the Figure 1.

Figure 1. Relationship between e-business, e-commerce, and e-marketing

Businesses that want to succeed in the digital economy must understand the relationship between these three concepts and how to effectively leverage them to reach and engage customers, conduct transactions, and improve efficiency and revenue.

SMALL AND MEDIUM ENTERPRISES

Small business enterprises, also known as SMEs, have different meaning and connotations varying from country to country (Koirala, 2019). Usually, they are categorised as SMEs based on their capital invested and number of people employed (Koirala, 2019). This also means that their sales volume is also low as compared to the large enterprises. These types of businesses make up the majority of companies in the United States and around the world, and play a vital role in the economy by providing goods and services, creating jobs, and stimulating local and national economic growth (Južnik Rotar et al., 2019; Tambunan, 2019; Bakhtiari et al., 2019). SMEs come in all shapes and sizes, from retail shops and restaurants to technology start-ups and consulting firms. They can be found in urban, suburban, and rural areas, and can serve both local and global markets. Some common types of small businesses include sole proprietorships, partnerships, small to medium size companies, etc.

Despite the many benefits that small businesses provide, they also face a number of challenges. Access to capital, lack of resources, and competition from larger companies are just a few of the obstacles that small businesses must overcome in order to succeed. In addition, small businesses often struggle to comply with government regulations and find qualified employees (Bakhtiari et al., 2019). To help small businesses succeed, governments and other organizations around the world offer a variety of resources and support. Certain government agencies, provide SMEs access to capital, counselling, and training. In addition, many states and local governments offer small business development centres and other resources to help small businesses grow and succeed (Naradda Gamage et al., 2020). Few important areas that have developed in this field are entrepreneurship (Khan et al., 2019; Magd et al., 2022; Khan et al., 2022); Self Help Groups (Gangwar & Khan, 2022); Social Enterprises (Khan et al., 2022) etc.

In conclusion, small business enterprises are an important part of the global economy. They provide goods and services, create jobs, and stimulate local and national economic growth. Despite the challenges they face, small businesses are an important source of innovation and competition, and are well worth the support and resources provided by governments and other organizations.

METHODOLOGY AND INFERENCES ON THE WORK DONE IN THE FIELD OF E-MARKETING AND SMEs

In order to understand the areas where E-Marketing, E-Commerce and E-Business are playing an important role, Bibliometric analysis was performed to gain better insights of this concept (Khatri et al.,2022). The Keywords utilised were “E-Marketing” AND “E-Commerce” AND “E-Business”. The second set of key word utilised was “E-Marketing” OR “E-Commerce” OR “E-Business”, the extracted files were merged with basic filtration to avoid duplication of entries. A total of 2987 documents were found in this area, signifying the amount of work done. Keeping the occurrences threshold as 65, a total of 32 keywords were extracted as presented in Table 1.

Table 1. Co-occurrences of prominent keywords in e-marketing, e-commerce, and e-business

S.No	Keyword	Occurrences	Total Link Strength
1.	marketing	985	2742
2.	electronic commerce	822	2447
3.	internet	572	1876
4.	e-commerce	466	1038
5.	commerce	348	1134
6.	sales	328	1061
7.	human(s)	270	1056
8.	social media	169	457
9.	social networking (online)	130	433
10.	competition	120	461
11.	article	116	471
12.	customer satisfaction	112	386
13.	internet marketing	106	283
14.	consumer behavior	105	378
15.	e-business	104	363
16.	websites	102	357
17.	decision making	101	349
18.	information technology	100	367
19.	marketing strategy	99	323
20.	digital marketing	98	219
21.	e-marketing	96	257
22.	strategic planning	95	411
23.	big data	94	257
24.	e-learning	83	205
25.	information management	80	276
26.	data mining	77	255
27.	machine learning	77	220
28.	world wide web	74	297
29.	costs	73	284
30.	online systems	72	285
31.	information systems	66	227
32.	female	65	291

Source: Author's Calculation

Talking about the top 10 keywords: marketing; electronic commerce; internet; e-commerce; commerce; sales; human(s); social media; social networking (online); and competition were found to be prominent in the field of research.

Next, in order to specifically extract the information in context of SMEs, the keyword utilised was "Small Medium Enterprises" OR "SMEs" AND "E-Marketing" AND "E-Commerce" AND "E-Business", a total of 143 documents were identified. Upon processing them on vos viewer, 25 prominent key words were obtained in the co-occurrence analysis by keeping the occurrence threshold as 7. The researches in the context of SMEs were found to be less as compared to the amount of research happening globally in the field of E-Business, E-commerce and E-marketing. The results are presented in Table 2.

Table 2. Co-occurrences of prominent keywords in e-marketing, e-commerce, and e-business

S.No	Keyword	Occurrences	Total Link Strength
1.	electronic commerce	72	240
2.	marketing	54	182
3.	e-commerce	44	114
4.	commerce	25	109
5.	internet	23	93
6.	sales	19	85
7.	competition	17	83
8.	smes	24	81
9.	industry	15	71
10.	small and medium enterprise	14	58
11.	small and medium-sized enterprise	13	58
12.	information systems	10	48
13.	e-business	11	47
14.	e-marketing	11	45
15.	ebusiness	7	40
16.	enterprise resource planning	7	39
17.	sme	10	39
18.	social networking (online)	8	39
19.	information management	8	38
20.	world wide web	7	38
21.	internet marketing	10	37
22.	websites	8	37
23.	business to business	7	31
24.	industrial management	7	24
25.	small to medium-sized enterprises	7	12

Source: Author's Calculation

DISCUSSION AND INFERENCES

SMEs and E-Marketing

SMEs are a vital part of the global economy, accounting for a significant portion of economic growth and employment. However, despite their importance, SMEs often struggle to compete with larger, more established companies. One way for SMEs to level the playing field is through the use of digital marketing.

One of the biggest advantages of E- marketing for SMEs is its ability to reach a global audience. Social media platforms, such as Facebook and Instagram, have billions of users worldwide. This means that even a small business can reach a large audience with a minimal budget. Additionally, digital marketing allows for more precise targeting, so businesses can reach their desired audience with more accuracy.

Another benefit of digital marketing for SMEs is the ability to measure and track the success of a campaign. Digital marketing platforms, such as Google Analytics, provide detailed data on website traffic, conversion rates, and customer engagement. This allows businesses to see which campaigns are working and which are not, and make adjustments accordingly.

One of the most cost-effective digital marketing tools for SMEs is search engine optimization (SEO). SEO is the process of optimizing a website for search engines, such as Google, to improve its visibility in search engine results pages (SERPs). By improving a website's SEO, SMEs can increase their visibility in search results and reach more potential customers.

Another cost-effective digital marketing strategy for SMEs is email marketing. Email marketing allows businesses to send targeted messages to a specific audience, and is typically less expensive than other forms of advertising. Additionally, email marketing campaigns can be automated, so businesses can reach their audience without having to spend a lot of time or money on marketing efforts.

Social media marketing is also a powerful tool for SMEs. Social media platforms, such as Facebook and Twitter, have millions of users, making them ideal for reaching a large audience. Additionally, social media platforms allow businesses to engage with customers in real-time, which can help build brand loyalty and trust.

In conclusion, digital marketing is a cost-effective and powerful tool for SMEs looking to reach new customers and grow their business. By using digital marketing techniques such as search engine optimization, email marketing, and social media marketing, SMEs can compete with larger, more established companies and take their business to the next level.

SMEs and IoT

SMEs are the backbone of many economies around the world. They provide jobs, drive innovation, and contribute significantly to economic growth. In recent years, the internet of things (IoT) has emerged as a powerful technology that can help SMEs to improve their operations, reduce costs, and increase efficiency.

The IoT is a network of physical devices, vehicles, buildings, and other items embedded with sensors, software, and connectivity that enable them to collect and exchange data. This data can be used to improve decision-making, automate processes, and create new business models.

One of the key benefits of IoT for SMEs is the ability to collect and analyze data from a wide range of sources. This can help SMEs to identify patterns and trends that can be used to improve operations, reduce costs, and increase efficiency. For example, an SME that manufactures a product can use IoT sensors to collect data on the production process, including machine performance, energy usage, and worker productivity. This data can be analyzed to identify bottlenecks and inefficiencies, which can then be addressed to improve the overall efficiency of the production process.

Another key benefit of IoT for SMEs is the ability to automate processes. This can help SMEs to reduce the need for manual labor, increase productivity, and improve the accuracy and consistency of their operations. For example, an SME that operates a fleet of delivery vehicles can use IoT sensors to track the location of the vehicles, monitor fuel consumption, and ensure that the vehicles are being driven safely and efficiently. This data can be used to optimize routes and schedules, which can help to reduce fuel costs and improve delivery times.

IoT also can help SMEs to create new business models. For example, an SME that produces and sells a product can use IoT sensors to monitor usage and provide real-time feedback to customers. This can help the SME to identify new revenue streams, such as selling product usage data to third-party companies or developing new products or services based on customer feedback.

There are also some challenges in the adoption of IoT by SMEs. One of the main challenges is the cost of implementing IoT solutions. Many SMEs may not have the financial resources to invest in IoT technologies, and may not be able to afford the ongoing costs of data analysis and maintenance. Another challenge is the lack of technical expertise. Many SMEs may not have the technical skills or knowledge to implement and maintain IoT solutions, and may need to hire specialized personnel or outsource these tasks.

In conclusion, IoT can provide SMEs with a range of benefits, including improved efficiency, reduced costs, and new business models. However, the adoption of IoT by SMEs can also present challenges, including the cost of implementation and the lack of technical expertise. To overcome these challenges, SMEs may need to invest in training and education, seek funding and grants, or partner with larger companies or technology providers. With the right approach, IoT can help SMEs to improve their operations, reduce costs, and increase efficiency, and ultimately contribute to economic growth.

CONCLUSION

Small and medium-sized enterprises (SMEs) have always been the backbone of any economy. They are known for their flexibility, innovation, and adaptability. However, with the rapid advancement of technology, SMEs are facing a new set of challenges. The internet of things (IoT) and digital marketing are two such areas that are revolutionizing the way businesses operate. SMEs can leverage the benefits of IoT and digital marketing by implementing a comprehensive digital strategy. This strategy should include the following elements:

- **IoT Devices:** SMEs should invest in IoT devices that can automate and optimize business processes, reduce costs, and improve customer experiences.
- **Digital Marketing:** SMEs should use digital marketing channels to reach a wider audience, create targeted campaigns, and track the effectiveness of marketing efforts.
- **Analytics:** SMEs should use analytics tools to gather data on business performance and customer behavior. This data can be used to identify trends and to make better business decisions.
- **Security:** SMEs should ensure that IoT devices and digital marketing systems are secure to protect against cyber threats.

In conclusion, SMEs can leverage the benefits of IoT and digital marketing to stay ahead of the competition and grow their businesses. By implementing a comprehensive digital strategy, SMEs can automate and optimize business processes, reduce costs, improve customer experiences, and make better business decisions. Additionally, by utilizing digital marketing channels and analytics, SMEs can reach wider audiences, create targeted campaigns, and track the effectiveness of marketing efforts. With the right approach, SMEs can harness the power of IoT and digital marketing to achieve success in the digital age.

REFERENCES

Babenko, V., Kulczyk, Z., Perevosova, I., Syniavska, O., & Davydova, O. (2019). Factors of the development of international e-commerce under the conditions of globalization. In *SHS Web of Conferences* (Vol. 65, p. 04016). EDP Sciences. 10.1051hsconf/20196504016

Bag, S., Srivastava, G., Bashir, M. M. A., Kumari, S., Giannakis, M., & Chowdhury, A. H. (2022). Journey of customers in this digital era: Understanding the role of artificial intelligence technologies in user engagement and conversion. *Benchmarking*, *29*(7), 2074–2098. doi:10.1108/BIJ-07-2021-0415

Bakhtiari, S., Breunig, R., Magnani, L., & Zhang, J. (2020). Financial constraints and small and medium enterprises: A review. *The Economic Record*, *96*(315), 506–523. doi:10.1111/1475-4932.12560

Bala, M., & Verma, D. (2018). A critical review of digital marketing. *International Journal of Management, IT & Engineering*, *8*(10), 321–339.

Bughin, J., Chui, M., & Manyika, J. (2010). Clouds, big data, and smart assets: Ten tech-enabled business trends to watch. *The McKinsey Quarterly*, *56*(1), 75–86.

Campbell, C., & Farrell, J. R. (2020). More than meets the eye: The functional components underlying influencer marketing. *Business Horizons*, *63*(4), 469–479. doi:10.1016/j.bushor.2020.03.003

Combe, C. (2012). *Introduction to E-business*. Routledge. doi:10.4324/9780080492780

Dickey, I. J., & Lewis, W. F. (2012). An overview of digital media and advertising. *E-marketing: Concepts, methodologies, tools, and applications*, 31-61.

El-Gohary, H., Trueman, M., & Fukukawa, K. (2008). E-marketing and small business enterprises: A review of the methodologies. *Journal of Business and Public Policy*, *2*(2), 64–93.

Feng, L. (2007). *What is e-business*. Blackwell Publishing.

Frost, R., & Strauss, J. (2016). *E-marketing*. Routledge.

Gangwar, V. P., & Khan, S. A. (2022). Analyzing the Role of Micro-Entrepreneurship and Self-Help Groups (SHGs) in Women Empowerment and Development: A Bottom-of-Pyramid Perspective. In Driving Factors for Venture Creation and Success in Agricultural Entrepreneurship (pp. 213-226). IGI Global.

Gao, H., Kuang, L., Yin, Y., Guo, B., & Dou, K. (2020). Mining consuming behaviors with temporal evolution for personalized recommendation in mobile marketing apps. *Mobile Networks and Applications*, *25*(4), 1233–1248. doi:10.100711036-020-01535-1

Gordijn, J., Akkermans, H., & Van Vliet, H. (2000). What's in an electronic business model? In *Knowledge Engineering and Knowledge Management Methods, Models, and Tools: 12th International Conference, EKAW 2000 Juan-les-Pins, France, October 2–6, 2000 Proceedings 12* (pp. 257-273). Springer Berlin Heidelberg.

Hartemo, M. (2016). Email marketing in the era of the empowered consumer. *Journal of Research in Interactive Marketing*, *10*(3), 212–230. doi:10.1108/JRIM-06-2015-0040

Ilmudeen, A. (2021). Big data, artificial intelligence, and the internet of things in cross-border E-commerce. *Cross-border E-commerce marketing and management*, 257-272.

Jenkins, S. (2008). *The truth about email marketing*. FT Press.

Južnik Rotar, L., Kontošić Pamić, R., & Bojnec, Š. (2019). Contributions of small and medium enterprises to employment in the European Union countries. *Ekonomska Istrazivanja*, *32*(1), 3296–3308.

Khan, D., & Shazia, W. (2019). Cyber security issues and challenges in E-commerce. *Proceedings of 10th international conference on digital strategies for organizational success*. 10.2139srn.3323741

Khan, S. A., Magd, H., Al Shamsi, I. R., & Masoom, K. (2022). Social Entrepreneurship Through Innovations in Agriculture. In *International Perspectives on Value Creation and Sustainability Through Social Entrepreneurship* (pp. 209–222). IGI Global. doi:10.4018/978-1-6684-4666-9.ch010

Khan, S. A., Magd, H., & Epoc, F. J. (2022). Application of Data Management System in Business-to-Business Electronic Commerce. *Competitive Trends and Technologies in Business Management*, 109-124.

Khan, S. A., Sharma, P. P., & Thoudam, P. (2019). Role of attitude and entrepreneurship education towards entrepreneurial orientation among business students of Bhutan. *International Journal of Recent Technology and Engineering*, *8*, 335–345.

Khatri, B., Arora, S., Magd, H., & Khan, S. A. K. (2022). Bibliometric Analysis of Social Entrepreneurship. In *International Perspectives on Value Creation and Sustainability Through Social Entrepreneurship* (pp. 46–60). IGI Global. doi:10.4018/978-1-6684-4666-9.ch003

Koirala, S. (2019). *SMEs: Key drivers of green and inclusive growth*. Academic Press.

Lammenett, E. (2019). *Praxiswissen Online-Marketing: Affiliate-, Influencer-, Content-und E-Mail-Marketing, Google Ads, SEO, Social Media, Online-inklusive Facebook-Werbung*. Springer-Verlag. doi:10.1007/978-3-658-25135-2

Laudon, K. C., & Traver, C. G. (2013). *E-commerce*. Pearson.

Leppäniemi, M., Sinisalo, J., & Karjaluoto, H. (2006). A review of mobile marketing research. *International Journal of Mobile Marketing*, *1*(1), 30–40.

Levy, S. (2021). *In the plex: How Google thinks, works, and shapes our lives*. Simon & Schuster.

Magd, H., Khan, S. A. K., & Bhuyan, U. (2022). Social Entrepreneurship Intentions Among Business Students in Oman. In *International Perspectives on Value Creation and Sustainability Through Social Entrepreneurship* (pp. 76–93). IGI Global. doi:10.4018/978-1-6684-4666-9.ch005

Mason, A. N., Narcum, J., & Mason, K. (2021). Social media marketing gains importance after Covid-19. *Cogent Business & Management, 8*(1), 1870797. doi:10.1080/23311975.2020.1870797

Müller, J., & Christandl, F. (2019). Content is king–But who is the king of kings? The effect of content marketing, sponsored content & user-generated content on brand responses. *Computers in Human Behavior, 96*, 46–55. doi:10.1016/j.chb.2019.02.006

Nabih, K. (2019). *Digital Marketing: Search Engine Optimization and Search Engine Marketing in Germany and its possibilities for Reviews International* [Doctoral dissertation]. Universitas Gadjah Mada.

Naradda Gamage, S. K., Ekanayake, E. M. S., Abeyrathne, G. A. K. N. J., Prasanna, R. P. I. R., Jayasundara, J. M. S. B., & Rajapakshe, P. S. K. (2020). A review of global challenges and survival strategies of small and medium enterprises (SMEs). *Economies, 8*(4), 79. doi:10.3390/economies8040079

Pavlov, O. V., Melville, N., & Plice, R. K. (2008). Toward a sustainable email marketing infrastructure. *Journal of Business Research, 61*(11), 1191–1199. doi:10.1016/j.jbusres.2007.11.010

Pradina, Y. D., & Poeradisastra, T. (2019). The implementation of affiliate marketing on marketing communication strategy of travel tour agencies to build awareness in Jakarta. *American Journal of Humanities and Social Sciences Research, 3*(3), 94–103.

Saleem, M., Khan, S. A., & Magd, H. (2022). Content Marketing Framework for Building Brand Image: A Case Study of Sohar International School, Oman. In Building a Brand Image Through Electronic Customer Relationship Management (pp. 64-83). IGI Global.

Salmiah, S., Fajrillah, F., Sudirman, A., Siregar, M. N. H., Simarmata, J., Suleman, A. R., & Jamaludin, J. (2020). *Online Marketing*. Yayasan Kita Menulis.

Sawicki, A. (2016). Digital marketing. *World Scientific News*, (48), 82–88.

Shaltoni, A. M. (2016). E-marketing education in transition: An analysis of international courses and programs. *International Journal of Management Education, 14*(2), 212–218. doi:10.1016/j.ijme.2016.04.004

Shankar, V., & Balasubramanian, S. (2009). Mobile marketing: A synthesis and prognosis. *Journal of Interactive Marketing, 23*(2), 118–129. doi:10.1016/j.intmar.2009.02.002

Shi, S., Sun, J., & Cheng, T. C. E. (2020). Wholesale or drop-shipping: Contract choices of the online retailer and the manufacturer in a dual-channel supply chain. *International Journal of Production Economics, 226*, 107618. doi:10.1016/j.ijpe.2020.107618

Szymanski, G., & Lininski, P. (2018, September). Model of the effectiveness of Google Adwords advertising activities. In *2018 IEEE 13th International Scientific and Technical Conference on Computer Sciences and Information Technologies (CSIT)* (Vol. 2, pp. 98-101). IEEE. 10.1109/STC-CSIT.2018.8526633

Tambunan, T. (2019). Recent evidence of the development of micro, small and medium enterprises in Indonesia. *Journal of Global Entrepreneurship Research, 9*(1), 18. doi:10.118640497-018-0140-4

Tokar, T., Jensen, R., & Williams, B. D. (2021). A guide to the seen costs and unseen benefits of e-commerce. *Business Horizons, 64*(3), 323–332. doi:10.1016/j.bushor.2021.01.002

Tong, S., Luo, X., & Xu, B. (2020). Personalized mobile marketing strategies. *Journal of the Academy of Marketing Science*, *48*(1), 64–78. doi:10.100711747-019-00693-3

Vladimir, Z. (1996). Electronic commerce: Structures and issues. *International Journal of Electronic Commerce*, *1*(1), 3–23. doi:10.1080/10864415.1996.11518273

Vrontis, D., Makrides, A., Christofi, M., & Thrassou, A. (2021). Social media influencer marketing: A systematic review, integrative framework and future research agenda. *International Journal of Consumer Studies*, *45*(4), 617–644. doi:10.1111/ijcs.12647

Vyas, C. (2019). Evaluating state tourism websites using Search Engine Optimization tools. *Tourism Management*, *73*, 64–70. doi:10.1016/j.tourman.2019.01.019

Watson, R. T., Berthon, P., Pitt, L. F., & Zinkhan, G. M. (2013). *Electronic commerce: The strategic perspective*. Academic Press.

Wymbs, C. (2011). Digital marketing: The time for a new "academic major" has arrived. *Journal of Marketing Education*, *33*(1), 93–106. doi:10.1177/0273475310392544

Yaghtin, S., Safarzadeh, H., & Karimi Zand, M. (2020). Planning a goal-oriented B2B content marketing strategy. *Marketing Intelligence & Planning*, *38*(7), 1007–1020. doi:10.1108/MIP-11-2019-0559

Zhang, X., Kumar, V., & Cosguner, K. (2017). Dynamically managing a profitable email marketing program. *Journal of Marketing Research*, *54*(6), 851–866. doi:10.1509/jmr.16.0210

Chapter 18
Internet of Things in Marketing:
Applications and Concerns

Ratiba Riyaz
University of Kashmir, India

Mushtaq Ahmad Darzi
https://orcid.org/0000-0001-6345-821X
University of Kashmir, India

Romana Riyaz
Islamic University of Science and Technology, India

Yusra Showkat Bakshi
University of Kashmir, India

ABSTRACT

The internet of things (IoT) has emerged as one of the most significant 21st-century technologies in recent years. People can work and live more efficiently with the aid of the internet of things. Along with offering smart home automation gadgets, the internet of things is essential to businesses. IoT gives businesses a real-time glimpse into how their systems actually function, offering insights into everything from machine performance to supply chain and logistics operations. The expectations, attitudes, and needs of consumers are being altered by the technology that large businesses are attempting to incorporate into their marketing strategies. The chapter makes an effort to explore various elements of leveraging the internet of things for marketing, identify some of the key issues, and propose potential solutions. The marketers can make use of IoT's enormous potential in the future. However, there isn't a lot of literature out there yet that is geared toward marketing IoT. Thus, this chapter might provide a brief overview of the subject.

DOI: 10.4018/978-1-6684-8166-0.ch018

INTRODUCTION

The Internet of Things (IoT) gained popularity as a term when it was used by Ashton in a presentation about Procter & Gamble's use of radio frequency identification (RFID) in supply chain management (Ashton, 2009). IoT refers to the use of physical things to connect to and share data with other systems and devices using the Internet or other communications networks (Brown, 2016; Gillis, 2021). The term "device" can be used to refer to anything, including computers, smartphones, cars, household appliances, manufacturing equipment, medical implants, entire buildings, and much more. The Internet of things was developed as a result of the ability of technologies like radio-frequency identification (RFID) to connect each product to its unique identity in the world. The Internet of Things is a key component of the Internet, and it offers a wealth of new opportunities for businesses and society at large (Haller et al., 2009). Businesses will be able to operate more effectively, increase customer satisfaction, find new business possibilities, and foresee problems and threats so they can better deal with them by incorporating intelligence into systems and processes (Steve, 2015). The ubiquitous and seamless integration of IoT into business processes will continue to be the key to its success. Business managers will be able to thoroughly and deeply comprehend what is happening in the world with the aid of cognitive IoT technologies. These technologies will also improve the efficiency of things or businesses, allowing business managers to better manage activities that take place during business processes (Steve, 2015). Extensive networks of information-sharing devices can be used to interpret data in a wider perspective.

Healthcare, home automation, retail, and transportation are a few common industries where IoT technology is used. There are undoubtedly countless applications for IoT technology, including those in marketing, infrastructure management, media, environmental monitoring, and home automation. Governments and business organizations could both benefit from the applicabilities of IoT in their operations. The Internet of Things can also be viewed as a tool for promoting goods and services, interacting with customers, gathering marketing data, identifying target markets, and serving a number of other marketing objectives. Utilizing IoT in marketing makes it possible to communicate with customers in ways that are more personal than before. IoT has the potential to serve as the foundation for more effective personalized marketing. It can transform how businesses engage with their current or potential customers and become a crucial component of integrated marketing communications. Only businesses that can effectively leverage all available channels of communication, including IoT technology, will be able to maintain market share. Marketers need accurate and reliable consumer data in order to execute a variety of marketing strategies. IoT technology makes it possible to gather enormous and high-quality consumer data.

The integration of IoT in marketing has resulted in participative and contextual marketing. Participatory marketing relies on consumer contact with products through universal identification to enable consumers to share their knowledge and experiences as well as their opinions while contextual marketing depends on real time data of consumer location, context and behaviour to deliver relevant and timely marketing messages. The IoTs' ability to connect with items and gather data about them as well as customer experiences expands the traditional marketing elements. The Internet of Things has the potential to enhance all facets of marketing. Further, its technical skills will let marketers plan and carry out marketing initiatives in an entirely unique way. In this process, competition and the drive to win over customer loyalty reach their highest. The practical development of the Internet of Things and internet marketing is well ahead of its theoretical foundation in these fields. Consequently, there is a greater demand for scientific investigation due to the risks and hazards it may present. There has generally been very little research into the marketing side of the IoT, despite the fact that it can offer new opportunities for marketing operations and high quality data for market research (Nguyen & Simkin, 2017).

APPLICATIONS OF IoT IN MARKETING

Marketing managers are now able to gather extensive consumption data to identify emerging trends or new gaps in consumer behavior due to easy accessibility of new tools. IoT is an important technology that has a significant impact on marketing performance (Mehralian, 2022). The primary marketing benefit of IoT is the use of real-time data to assist decisions and campaigns (Hofacker et al., 2016). The Internet of Things has the potential to greatly broaden the scope of market research (Woodside & Sood, 2017). The potential utility of data from IoT-enabled devices for guiding marketing decisions and carrying out marketing campaigns is what drives its interest in the marketing sector (Hofacker et al., 2016). A manufacturer's Internet-enabled products can be used to collect data that can be analyzed to determine usage patterns, including when, how, and where the device is utilized. Additionally, by combining geolocation information from Internet-connected devices with socioeconomic data sets, it is possible to identify and analyze the socio economic status of device users. Apart from business organizations, government organizations and institutions can integrate IoT technology to promote various public services and benefit schemes. A significant amount of quantitative data about consumption and experience is available as a result of IoT technology. With information on consumption amount and depletion for specific contexts, interactions between objects and between people and objects, and environmental data, would add a dimension of visibility where none previously existed (Parry et al., 2016). IoT would make it possible to view how users connect and interact with anything and everyone, any network, and any service whenever they want, wherever they are (Vermesan et al., 2011). Due to availability of sensors, a new set of dispositional-situational parameters would emerge, together with other social and environmental factors like location, weather, temperature, and air quality, to operationalize and measure verb' parameters like 'waiting' for a bus or 'eating' a meal (Ng & Wakenshaw, 2017).

Maintaining relationships with consumers is possible due to IoT capabilities (Groopman, 2015). Marketing evolves from the campaign-driven start-and-stop activities of the previous century to embrace the idea that markets are truly continuous conversations with users via the newly emerging yet widely used voice control systems on everything from mobile phones to televisions (Levine et al., 2001). Products made with IoT technology provide a different approach as they can be extensively modified to meet the needs of every consumer (Körling, 2012; Porter & Heppelmann, 2015). The usage information gathered by one IoT product can then be used to enhance similar IoT products. Businesses can also take into account how other customers use the products to raise the value of the focal consumer (Decker & Stummer, 2017). The producer of the IoT home appliances may offer smartphone applications that may be used to monitor and operate the Internet-enabled gadget. By using these smartphone applications, the manufacturer can reach out to the customer via the Internet-enabled device and open up a new approach for customer relationship management. Smart connected devices offer companies fresh insights into how their products add value for customers by analyzing product usage data (Porter & Heppelmann, 2015). Service industries such as banks, hotels and hospitals may connect with consumers on an emotional level by extracting information using IoT and utilize it for maintaining better relationships with customers. For instance information regarding birthdays or religious festivals may be used to wish consumers which may influence their decisions to make purchases from the company.

The IoT offers the possibility of participatory marketing, which would evolve marketing through the capabilities of ubiquitous identification and interaction made possible by the IoT (Jara et al., 2013). Consumer experiences are also referred to as consumer 'Touchpoints' (Meyer & Schwager, 2007) that offer different ways for comprehending the data or information needed to manage customer interactions more effectively. As IoT products do not interact with customers at discrete touch points but rather continuously gather data on product usage and depending on the specific purpose of the data collection, transfer this data to the company. Internet of Things will transform customer touch points into what is known as customer touch lines (Decker & Stummer, 2017). A substantial amount of data is being generated in the immediate environment of the customer due to the evolution of customer touch lines (Kaur & Arora, 2015). Customers exhibit a growing willingness to use wearable and mobile devices while shopping. This fact is particularly intriguing for retailers as they can build statistical databases with information about every single purchase and consumer type, which will later assist a marketing team in improving the product, delivery method, advertising strategy, targeting strategy, and numerous other things (Gregory, 2015). The capacity of IoT technology to track customer locations should get special consideration. Knowledge of a consumer's activity during a specific time can aid marketers decide where to deliver a product (Abashidze & Dąbrowski, 2016). Although a lot of customers are naturally apprehensive about the possibility of someone tracking their activities, a sizable portion of consumers are willing to provide this information to businesses in exchange for a discount or benefit (Abashidze & Dąbrowski, 2016). IoT devices can provide a variety of information about the whereabouts, movements, and health of device users (Lee & Lee, 2015). All this information has a significant social component due to its potential for consumer welfare. While data on health and movements could provide information about physical fitness levels, wearable technology could be utilised to share information with family and friends.

IoT can improve marketing performance by enhancing a company's capacity to comprehend and gather data from clients and competitors (Yu et al., 2016). The IOT's capabilities include the integration of production systems with cloud computing, pervasive sensing, big data analytics, machine learning, deep learning and cognitive computing (Agarwal & Brem, 2015). For instance data can be retrieved from Cloud internet of things (CIOT) where smart data mining algorithms could be employed effectively to construct an efficient framework that can enhance marketing campaigns (Liu et al., 2023). Artificial intelligence technology called deep learning can process data by emulating the behaviour of the human brain. Deep learning can be employed as a forecasting tool to accurately predict ambiguous market factors (Mansouri et al., 2023). Also, the product analytics and remote access functions of IoT devices are of particular interest from a marketing management perspective (Decker & Stummer, 2017). Product analytics is dependent on the autonomous collection of usage data from the consumer's environment to provide businesses with information about the actual product consumption. Remote access provides options for remotely operating the IoT device, altering its parameters or adjusting its properties, activating and deactivating its functions, and handling data entering to the IoT product (Decker & Stummer, 2017). Product analytics and remote access can be used separately or in tandem to create a variety of new opportunities for marketing management (Decker & Stummer, 2017). With the use of product analytics, businesses may continuously track the customer experience in real-time and use remote access to monitor or even control it by altering the characteristics of the products or personalizing IoT solutions to meet different customers' demands. An increasing variety of products have the capability to sense their surroundings and transmit information to users, other devices, and/or businesses using IoT technology. The basic functionality of regular products is extended by enabling data collection and sharing via the Internet (Bauer & Mead, 1995; Porter & Heppelmann, 2015). IoT can have a huge influence on business models because connected things alter the flow of operational resources and information, which has an impact on the micro-interactions across business models (Langley et al., 2021). The development toward multichannel, multimodal, and omnichannel experiences will boost users' involvement, which may then increase customer retention and data accessibility. Additionally, smart products (those embedded with IoT) are proliferating in the retail industry and in the environment of shopping, which helps to create omnichannel experiences (Novak & Hoffman, 2019). Through an information exchange between the user and the object or object to object, IoT highlights not only the physical and local functionality of the "thing," but also the service digitally on a global scale (Fleisch et al., 2014). These transactions result in "thing-as-a-service" (TaaS), which includes offering a service that automatically anticipates consumer usage (Woodside & Sood, 2016). Price discrimination strategies have made their way into online stores and markets (Hannak et al., 2014). IoT devices will further ease the use of pricing discrimination strategies. Employing one-to-one pricing strategy enables businesses to maximize prices in consideration of the price a specific customer is willing to pay (Decker & Stummer, 2017).

CONCERNS RELATED TO IoT APPLICATION

One of the most frequently raised topics in IoT is security and privacy. Companies may risk harming their own credibility if they don't take steps to protect consumers from privacy or data loss (Guo et al., 2013; Lohachab & Jangra, 2019). Consumer profiling can be helpful for streamlining internal procedures or assessing consumers' preferences, however the collection of personal information and its comparison with other profiles raises a number of security issues (Ziegeldorf et al., 2014). Companies ought to put in place an ethical system that can meet these new requirements as the volume of data increases. Companies must operate in a way that generates the kind of trust that encourages loyalty as people are becoming more and more worried about how businesses use their personal data. Because of this, decision-makers must include users while creating digital ethics guidelines. Customers will attempt to keep their data private or to manipulate the data if they lose faith in the business and feel that their information is being used against them (Nguyen & Mutum, 2012). Once they are aware of the tracking and analytics procedures used by the IoT product, opportunistic customers may take advantage of premium benefits (Decker & Stummer, 2017).

A substantial amount of data is being generated in the immediate environment of the consumer (Kaur & Arora, 2015). Due to bandwidth limitations, security issues, and privacy concerns, a significant amount of the data collected by sensors is lost (IBM, 2015). In the case of the Internet of Things, the sources of personal information are likely numerous and include not only computers and mobile devices but also a variety of wearables, cars, home appliances, medical implants, and other items that could expose information to misuse in a number of ways (Abashidze & Dąbrowski, 2016). CRM systems face a new hurdle with IoT products i.e. difficulties in data analytics or marketing analytics in addition to data collection (Verhoef et al., 2015; Wedel & Kannan, 2016). Product analytics must be able to handle huge, frequently complicated streams of data with high accuracy and little lag in order to monitor and manage the customer journey in real-time which is not possible through manual human interactions. In this context, substantial advancements in the disciplines of machine learning, deep learning (Lecun et al., 2015), and cognitive computing (Modha et al., 2015) can aid marketers in the real-time analysis of enormous volumes of even unstructured marketing data (Wedel & Kannan., 2016). New business complexities brought on by the growth of smart connected devices necessitate the creation of new marketing techniques and skill sets (Porter & Heppelmann, 2015).

IoT devices run the danger of malfunction, which may have a detrimental impact on a user's personal life, financial situation, or even health (Abashidze & Dąbrowski, 2016). Users' private information may get leaked as a result of hacking, and the company could suffer significant financial loss, reputational harm, crisis in public relations and even bankruptcy (Abashidze & Dąbrowski, 2016). The use of IoT technologies in marketing raises further legal concerns. Customers may file a lawsuit against a firm and demand both moral and financial compensation if personal data is stolen or improperly shared to a third party (Abashidze & Dąbrowski, 2016). The adoption of one-to-one pricing techniques can raise questions about favoritism if customers feel they are being treated unfairly. Such worries could have a detrimental impact on the customer experience and possibly lead to customer attrition (Decker & Stummer, 2017). Customers switching costs for IoT products will take new forms. IoT solutions promote widespread customisation outside of the point of sale, which can increase the cost of customers switching to another brand (Cao & Folan, 2011; Körling, 2012; Mayer, 2010).

In terms of data protection legislation, it is necessary to take into account the confidentiality of data collected by IoT devices (Bi & Cochran, 2015). Since many people may not be aware of the possible privacy risk posed by the Internet of Things devices to which they are exposed, there is an increasing need for suitable regulation along with technical measures to ensure that people's rights are safeguarded (Michael et al., 2014; Weber, 2015) . IoT devices can offer a wealth of information on device users' whereabouts and movements, health, and shopping preferences, all of which raise serious privacy concerns (Lee & Lee, 2015). IoT gadgets sharing geolocation information raise significant concerns (Hofacker & Belanche, 2016). Data analytics for the Internet of Things must take customers' privacy and data security into account (Wedel & Kannan, 2016)

DISCUSSION

The use of IOT is advantageous to both consumers and enterprises (Perera et al., 2015). It is possible to highlight the benefits of integrating marketing and IoT, particularly when done well and within the framework of a strong foundation of trust regarding data utilization. The combination can provide new market opportunities and provide a platform for establishing competitive advantages. Direct relationship between producers and consumers indicates better information acquired, demonstrating congruence with the relationship marketing idea. Longer connections have demonstrated that more pertinent data may be gleaned, particularly in the environment where customers are eager to provide direct input to the businesses; producing quality data that better supports corporate plans. Regardless of touch points or phases in the total customer life cycle, marketers can develop innovative solutions and optimize communication with customers in a much broader manner as a result of IoT. Relationship marketing and IoT solutions work together strategically to help predict client demands, and the collection of large amounts of consumer data allows for more detailed consumer profiling. Through the development of specialized software, requesting people to contribute their data to the research, all forms of actual data, including emotions, pulse rates, and location, can be voluntarily collected.

An IoT world with open APIs (application programming interface) makes it possible for software to be made to pull data directly from willing data donors, whereas in the past such data would be stored by businesses and hence less available to researchers. IoT has made it feasible for marketing analysts to truly comprehend consumer behavior in a way that was not previously conceivable. Physical products can now be created with flexible design features, such as an application interface that enables customization during usage to respond to unexpected contextual situations or a sensor that can alter the physical product's functionality based on intelligence. A blend of IoT data and knowledge engineering algorithms could provide real-time understanding of when a need arises and how to satisfy it through recommendations (Ng & Wakenshaw, 2017). Additionally, IOT can lead to high customer satisfaction as it can be utilized by companies to proactively address customer concerns and contingencies (Nguyen & Simkin, 2017). Therefore, this technology has the potential to significantly reduce human error, save money and time when used properly.

The Internet of Things (IoT) phenomenon and its effects on well-known marketing theories and concepts are not isolated occurrences within the studied domains but rather are signs of a more fundamental and paradigm-shifting trend. Researchers expect that a new paradigm characterized by ecosystems will emerge as a result of the impending IoT era (Tiwana et al., 2010; Yoo et al., 2010). Most of the time, customers who use (and do not necessarily own) an IoT or smart product automatically choose to be connected to a specific ecosystem, which also entails a choice of specific suppliers. Internet of Things expands existing social media marketing and value-driven marketing into a more interactive relationship with customers through participation. Consumer experiences as a part of participatory marketing give products a new functional dimension that enables verification of the brand's values, product quality, and reputation on a global scale. The value of the customer's experience and their input serve as the basis for participative marketing since consumer feedback allows for continual value creation and enhancement.

The development of digital and communication technologies as a "corporate marketing internet revolution" necessitates a fundamental reevaluation of marketing practice (Balmer & Yen, 2016). The IOT era poses some prospects and difficulties for advertising (Aksu et al., 2018). Acquisition of new skills for the marketer is crucial for the growth and sustainability of IoT marketing. In addition to employing analytical insights from the IoT device to anticipate customer needs before they are made explicit, a new role known as the anticipatory marketer also emerges from the realization that regularity in human actions generates predictability (Scellato et al., 2011). There are some risks associated with the adoption of IoT in marketing or in enterprises as a whole, particularly when it comes to ensuring the security of information utilization, preventing leakage, and not misusing it. Data security is essential since any issues with consumer data will have an effect on the relationship between a company and its customers (Lo & Campos, 2018). However, data security problems vary across business sectors and relationship marketing elements like commitment, trust, and reliability may aid lessen ambiguity-related feelings (Lo & Campos, 2018). All IoT network stakeholders must respond appropriately to three key challenges: anonymity, freedom of choice, and consent on data transfer from users (Perera et al., 2015). Consumer data privacy and confidentiality with respect to data obtained from Internet-enabled devices must adhere to the data protection laws in the nations where the product is sold and utilized. Privacy concerns may fade as people become more accepting of sharing personal information and the benefits that come with it (Gutierrez et al., 2019). More suitable gadgets that better meet customer needs can be created with the right thought and consideration for the acquisition, analysis, and use of data from IoT devices. These devices also provide potential for more environmentally conscious design and operation (Taylor et al., 2018).

Future marketing strategies may benefit greatly from the IoT technology (Celik, 2016). A tentative 4-point framework for marketers is informed by existing marketing theory and practice that shifts the focus away from the traditional four Ps to a service-dominant marketing turn for things, design and complexity of things, products as brand relationships and conversations and marketing skills for IoT (Woodside & Sood, 2016). The Internet of Things-assisted E-marketing and Distribution Framework (IoT-EDF) can be used to enhance marketing tactics throughout the many stages of the distribution, procurement, and promotion processes in E-marketing (Joghee, 2021). When compared to other methods, IoT-EDF achieves the highest levels of efficiency, including improved production rate, enhanced distribution rate, increased satisfaction rate, adaptability rate, reduced computational cost, and performance metrics (Joghee, 2021). According to research, the firm's business model will fundamentally change in the IoT era to incorporate value creation (the experience will be more visible), value proposition (the offering will be flexible), and value "capture" or creating worth for exchanges (i.e. the economic model will have shifting boundaries) (Ng & Wakenshaw, 2017). More research is required in the field of IoT and marketing as IoT is still in an evolving phase and its applications in marketing are limitless. It is crucial to investigate how to adapt to the shift brought about by IoT and how to restructure business models and marketing tactics to increase customer satisfaction and compete with the market. Attention must also be paid to how IoT will affect data analytics capabilities.

CONCLUSION

Businesses have greatly benefited from the integration of IoT with marketing. They are able to connect with customers in a manner that was previously unthinkable. Effective marketing strategies may be devised as real data from consumer experiences can be retrieved with the help of IoT. The Internet of things can produce useful information when used in conjunction with other data analysis techniques. Integration of IoT and AI can open up a world of marketing opportunities. Although IoT has several benefits, businesses will need to modify their business models and skills in order to effectively utilize IoT. Inability to employ this technology by marketers may harm consumer confidence and their reputation in the marketplace. In extreme circumstances, they might have to deal with significant financial losses and possibly legal action. In addition to business organizations, government and society at large can reap the benefits of IoT due its countless applications in marketing and other activities.

REFERENCES

Abashidze, I., & Dąbrowski, M. (2016). Internet of Things in Marketing: Opportunities and Security Issues. *Management Systems in Production Engineering*, *24*(4), 217–221. doi:10.2478/mspe-01-04-2016

Agarwal, N., & Brem, A. (2015). Strategic business transformation through technology convergence: Implications from General Electric's industrial internet initiative. *International Journal of Technology Management*, *67*(2), 196–214. doi:10.1504/IJTM.2015.068224

Aksu, H., Babun, L., Conti, M., Tolomei, G., & Uluagac, A. S. (2018). Advertising in the IoT Era: Vision and Challenges. *IEEE Communications Magazine*, *56*(11), 138–144. doi:10.1109/MCOM.2017.1700871

Alqahtani, H., & Naim, A. (2022). Critical Success Factors for Transforming CRM to SCRM for building E-CRM. In A. Naim & S. Kautish (Eds.), *Building a Brand Image Through Electronic Customer Relationship Management* (pp. 139–168). IGI Global. doi:10.4018/978-1-6684-5386-5.ch007

Ashton, K. (2009). That "Internet of Things" Thing. *RFiD Journal*, *22*, 97–114.

Balmer, J. M. T., & Yen, D. A. (2016). The Internet of total corporate communications, quaternary corporate communications and the corporate marketing Internet revolution. *Journal of Marketing Management*, *33*(1-2), 131–144. doi:10.1080/0267257X.2016.1255440

Bauer, S. R., & Mead, P. (1995). After You Open the Box: Making Smart Products More Usable, Useful, and Desirable Through Interactive Technology. *Design Management Journal*, *6*(4), 21–26. doi:10.1111/j.1948-7169.1995.tb00453.x

Bi, Z., & Cochran, D. (2015). Big data analytics with applications. *Journal of Management Analytics*, *1*(4), 249–265. doi:10.1080/23270012.2014.992985

Brown, E. (2016). *21 Open Source Projects for IoT*. Linux.Com.

Cao, H., & Folan, P. (2011). Product life cycle: the evolution of a paradigm and literature review from 1950–2009. *Production Planning & Control: The Management of Operations,* 641–662. . doi:10.1080/09537287.2011.577460

Celik, F. (2016). *Internet of Things as a source of future marketing tools* [Bachelor's thesis]. University of Twente.

Decker, R., & Stummer, C. (2017). Marketing Management for Consumer Products in the Era of the Internet of Things. *Advances in Internet of Things*, *7*(3), 47–70. doi:10.4236/ait.2017.73004

Fatima, S., Alqahtani, H., Naim, A., & Alma'alwi, F. (2022). E-CRM Through Social Media Marketing Activities for Brand Awareness, Brand Image, and Brand Loyalty. In A. Naim & S. Kautish (Eds.), *Building a Brand Image Through Electronic Customer Relationship Management* (pp. 109–138). IGI Global. doi:10.4018/978-1-6684-5386-5.ch006

Fleisch, E., Weinberger, M., & Wortmann, F. (2014). *Business models for the internet of things*. Bosch Lab White Paper.

Gillis, A. (2021). *What is internet of things (IoT)?* IOT Agenda.

Gregory. J. (2015). *The Internet of Things: Revolutionizing the Retail Industry*. Available: accenture.com/_acnmedia/Accenture/ Conversion-Assets/DotCom/Documents/Global/PDF/Dualpub_14/Accenture-The-Internet-Of-Th
ings.pdf.

Groopman, J. (2015). *Customer experience in the internet of things: Five ways brands can use sensors to build better customer relationships*. Altimeter. http://pages. altimetergroup.com/customer-experience-in-the-internet-of-things-report.html

Guo, B., Zhang, D., Wang, Z., Yu, Z., & Zhou, X. (2013). Opportunistic IoT: Exploring the harmonious interaction between human and the internet of things. *Journal of Network and Computer Applications*, *36*(6), 1531–1539. doi:10.1016/j.jnca.2012.12.028

Gutierrez, A., O'Leary, S., Rana, N. P., Dwivedi, Y. K., & Calle, T. (2019). Using privacy calculus theory to explore entrepreneurial directions in mobile location-based advertising: Identifying intrusiveness as the critical risk factor. *Computers in Human Behavior, 95*, 295–306. doi:10.1016/j.chb.2018.09.015

Haller, S., Karnouskos, S., & Schroth, C. (2009). The Internet of things in an enterprise context. Lecture Notes in Computer Science, 5468, 14–28. 1 doi:0.1007/978-3-642-00985-3_2/COVER

Hannak, A., Soeller, G., Lazer, D., Mislove, A., & Wilson, C. (2014). Measuring price discrimination and steering on E-commerce web sites. *Proceedings of the ACM SIGCOMM Internet Measurement Conference, IMC*, 305–318. 10.1145/2663716.2663744

Hofacker, C. F., & Belanche, D. (2016). Eight social media challenges for marketing managers. *Spanish Journal of Marketing - ESIC, 20*(2), 73–80. . doi:10.1016/j.sjme.2016.07.003

Hofacker, C. F., Malthouse, E. C., & Sultan, F. (2016). Big Data and consumer behavior: Imminent opportunities. *Journal of Consumer Marketing, 33*(2), 89–97. doi:10.1108/JCM-04-2015-1399

IBM. (2015). *Redefining Boundaries: Insights from the Global C Suite Study*. IBM.

Jara, A. J., Skarmeta, A. F., & Parra, M. C. (2013). Enabling participative marketing through the internet of things. *Proceedings - 27th International Conference on Advanced Information Networking and Applications Workshops, WAINA 2013*, 1301–1306. 10.1109/WAINA.2013.270

Joghee, S. (2021). Internet of Things-assisted E-marketing and distribution framework. *Soft Computing, 25*(18), 12291–12303. doi:10.100700500-021-05920-0

Kamal, S., Naim, A., Magd, H., Khan, S. A., & Khan, F. M. (2022). The Relationship Between E-Service Quality, Ease of Use, and E-CRM Performance Referred by Brand Image. In A. Naim & S. Kautish (Eds.), *Building a Brand Image Through Electronic Customer Relationship Management* (pp. 84–108). IGI Global. doi:10.4018/978-1-6684-5386-5.ch005

Kaur, P., & Arora, S. (2015). Regression and Endogeneity Bias in Big Marketing Data. *Procedia Computer Science, 70*, 41–47. doi:10.1016/j.procs.2015.10.025

Körling, M. (2012). Smart Products: Why Adding a Digital Side to a Toothbrush Could Make a Lot of Sense. *Ericsson Business Review, 18*, 26–31.

Langley, D. J., van Doorn, J., Ng, I. C. L., Stieglitz, S., Lazovik, A., & Boonstra, A. (2021). The Internet of Everything: Smart things and their impact on business models. *Journal of Business Research, 122*, 853–863. doi:10.1016/j.jbusres.2019.12.035

Lecun, Y., Bengio, Y., & Hinton, G. (2015). Deep learning. *Nature, 521*(7553), 436–444. . doi:10.1038/nature14539

Lee, I., & Lee, K. (2015). The Internet of Things (IoT): Applications, investments, and challenges for enterprises. *Business Horizons, 58*(4), 431–440. doi:10.1016/j.bushor.2015.03.008

Levine, R., Locke, C., Searle, D., & Weinberger, D. (2001). *The cluetrain manifesto: The end of business as usual*. Academic Press.

Liu, Y., Alzahrani, I. R., Jaleel, R. A., & Sulaie, S. A. (2023). An efficient smart data mining framework based cloud internet of things for developing artificial intelligence of marketing information analysis. *Information Processing & Management, 60*(1). doi:10.1016/j.ipm.2022.103121

Lo, F. Y., & Campos, N. (2018). Blending Internet-of-Things (IoT) solutions into relationship marketing strategies. *Technological Forecasting and Social Change, 137*, 10–18. doi:10.1016/j.techfore.2018.09.029

Lohachab, A., & Jangra, A. (2019). Opportunistic Internet of Things (IoT): Demystifying the Effective Possibilities of Opportunistic Networks Towards IoT. *2019 6th International Conference on Signal Processing and Integrated Networks, SPIN 2019*, 1100–1105. 10.1109/SPIN.2019.8711621

Mansouri, S. A., Jordehi, A. R., Marzband, M., Tostado-Veliz, M., Jurado, F., & Aguado, J. A. (2023). An IoT-enabled hierarchical decentralized framework for multi-energy microgrids market management in the presence of smart prosumers using a deep learning-based forecaster. *Applied Energy, 333*. doi:10.1016/j.apenergy.2022.120560

Mayer, P. (2010). *Economic Aspects of Smart Products.* White Paper, Institute of Technology Management, University of St. Gallen.

Mehralian, M. M. (2022). Effect of Internet of Things on Marketing Performance: The Mediating Role of Entrepreneurship Orientation. *SSRN Electronic Journal*. doi:10.2139/SSRN.4195987

Meyer, C., & Schwager, A. (2007). Understanding customer experience. *Harvard Business Review, 85*(2), 116. PMID:17345685

Michael, M. G., Michael, K., & Perakslis, C. (2014). Uberveillance and the internet of things and people. *Faculty of Engineering and Information Sciences - Papers. Part A, 1381*, 1381–1386. Advance online publication. doi:10.1109/IC3I.2014.7019829

Modha, D. S., Ananthanarayanan, R., Esser, S. K., Ndirango, A., Sherbondy, A. J., & Singh, R. (2015). Cognitive Computing. *Communications of the ACM, 54*(8), 62–71. doi:10.1145/1978542.1978559

Naim, A., Alqahtani, H., Muniasamy, A., Bilfaqih, S. M., Mahveen, R., & Mahjabeen, R. (2023). Applications of Information Systems and Data Security in Marketing Management. In A. Naim, P. Malik, & F. Zaidi (Eds.), *Fraud Prevention, Confidentiality, and Data Security for Modern Businesses* (pp. 57–83). IGI Global. doi:10.4018/978-1-6684-6581-3.ch003

Ng, I. C. L., & Wakenshaw, S. Y. L. (2017). The Internet-of-Things: Review and research directions. *International Journal of Research in Marketing, 34*(1), 3–21. doi:10.1016/j.ijresmar.2016.11.003

Nguyen, B., & Mutum, D. S. (2012). A review of customer relationship management: Successes, advances, pitfalls and futures. *Business Process Management Journal, 18*(3), 400–419. doi:10.1108/14637151211232614

Nguyen, B., & Simkin, L. (2017). The Internet of Things (IoT) and marketing: The state of play, future trends and the implications for marketing. *Journal of Marketing Management, 33*(1–2), 1–6. doi:10.1080/0267257X.2016.1257542

Novak, T. P., & Hoffman, D. L. (2019). Relationship journeys in the internet of things: A new framework for understanding interactions between consumers and smart objects. *Journal of the Academy of Marketing Science*, *47*(2), 216–237. doi:10.100711747-018-0608-3

Parry, G. C., Brax, S. A., Maull, R. S., & Ng, I. C. L. (2016). Operationalising IoT for reverse supply: The development of use-visibility measures. *Supply Chain Management*, *21*(2), 228–244. doi:10.1108/SCM-10-2015-0386

Perera, C., Liu, C. H., & Jayawardena, S. (2015). The Emerging Internet of Things Marketplace from an Industrial Perspective: A Survey. *IEEE Transactions on Emerging Topics in Computing*, *3*(4), 585–598. doi:10.1109/TETC.2015.2390034

Porter, M. E., & Heppelmann, J. E. (2015). How smart, connected products are transforming companies. In *Harvard Business Review* (Vol. 2015, pp. 96–114). https://hbr.org/2015/10/how-smart-connected-products-are-transforming-companies

Scellato, S., Musolesi, M., Mascolo, C., Latora, V., & Campbell, A. T. (2011). NextPlace: A spatio-temporal prediction framework for pervasive systems. Lecture Notes in Computer Science, 6696, 152–169. doi:10.1007/978-3-642-21726-5_10

Steve, H. (2015). *Cognitive IoT: Making the internet of Things Deliver for All of Us*. Available: https://www.ibm.com/blogs/think/2015/12/cognitive-iot-making-the-internet-of-things-deliver-for-all-of-us/

Taylor, M., Reilly, D., & Wren, C. (2018). Internet of things support for marketing activities. *Journal of Strategic Marketing*, *28*(2), 149–160. doi:10.1080/0965254X.2018.1493523

Tiwana, A., Konsynski, B., & Bush, A. A. (2010). Research Commentary—Platform Evolution: Co-evolution of Platform Architecture, Governance, and Environmental Dynamics. *Information Systems Research*, *21*(4), 675–687. doi:10.1287/isre.1100.0323

Verhoef, P. C., Kannan, P. K., & Inman, J. J. (2015). From Multi-Channel Retailing to Omni-Channel Retailing. Introduction to the Special Issue on Multi-Channel Retailing. *Journal of Retailing*, *91*(2), 174–181. doi:10.1016/j.jretai.2015.02.005

Vermesan, O., Peter, F., Patrick, G., & Sergio, G. (2011). Internet of Things: Strategic Research Roadmap. In Internet of Things-Global Technological and Societal Trends (pp. 9–52). Academic Press.

Weber, R. H. (2015). Internet of things: Privacy issues revisited. *Computer Law & Security Review*, *31*(5), 618–627. doi:10.1016/j.clsr.2015.07.002

Wedel, M., & Kannan, P. K. (2016). Marketing analytics for data-rich environments. *Journal of Marketing*, *80*(6), 97–121. doi:10.1509/jm.15.0413

Woodside, A. G., & Sood, S. (2017). Vignettes in the two-step arrival of the internet of things and its reshaping of marketing management's service-dominant logic. Journal of Marketing Management, 33(1-2), 98–110. doi:10.1080/0267257X.2016.1246748

Yoo, Y., Henfridsson, O., & Lyytinen, K. (2010). The new organizing logic of digital innovation: An agenda for information systems research. *Information Systems Research*, *21*(4), 724–735. doi:10.1287/isre.1100.0322

Yu, X., Nguyen, B., & Chen, Y. (2016). Internet of things capability and alliance: Entrepreneurial orientation, market orientation and product and process innovation. *Internet Research*, *26*(2), 402–434. doi:10.1108/IntR-10-2014-0265

Ziegeldorf, J. H., Morchon, O. G., & Wehrle, K. (2014). Privacy in the Internet of Things: Threats and challenges. *Security and Communication Networks*, *7*(12), 2728–2742. doi:10.1002ec.795

Compilation of References

Abashidze, I., & Dąbrowski, M. (2016). Internet of Things in Marketing: Opportunities and Security Issues. *Management Systems in Production Engineering*, *24*(4), 217–221. doi:10.2478/mspe-01-04-2016

Abdel-Basset, M., Mohamed, M., Chang, V., & Smarandache, F. (2019). IoT and its impact on the electronics market: A powerful decision support system for helping customers in choosing the best product. *Symmetry*, *11*(5), 611. doi:10.3390ym11050611

Abdulla, A. (2022). Application of MIS in E-CRM: A Literature Review in FMCG Supply Chain. In A. Naim & S. Kautish (Eds.), *Building a Brand Image Through Electronic Customer Relationship Management* (pp. 237–264). IGI Global. doi:10.4018/978-1-6684-5386-5.ch010

Abdullah, M. H. T., Jing, H. F., Ridzuan, A. R., & Zainodin, W. H. W. (2019). Blog: A platform towards democratization of information in Malaysia. *International Journal of Academic Research in Business & Social Sciences*, *9*(3), 626–640. doi:10.6007/IJARBSS/v9-i3/5731

Abdussamad, Z., Agyei, I. T., Döngül, E. S., Abdussamad, J., Raj, R., & Effendy, F. (2022). Impact of internet of things (IOT) on human resource management: A review. *Materials Today: Proceedings*, *56*, 3534–3543. doi:10.1016/j.matpr.2021.11.247

Adam, M. G., Tran, P. T., & Balasubramanian, R. (2021). Air quality changes in cities during the COVID-19 lockdown: A critical review. *Atmospheric Research*, *264*, 105823. doi:10.1016/j.atmosres.2021.105823 PMID:34456403

Adekoya, O. (2016). Marketing and the Internet of Things. *Hot Sauce*.

Afum, E., Zhang, R., Agyabeng-Mensah, Y., & Sun, Z. (2021). Sustainability excellence: The interactions of lean production, internal green practices and green product innovation. *International Journal of Lean Six Sigma*, *12*(6), 1089–1114. doi:10.1108/IJLSS-07-2020-0109

Agag, G. (2019). E-commerce ethics and its impact on buyer repurchase intentions and loyalty: An empirical study of small and medium Egyptian businesses. *Journal of Business Ethics*, *154*(2), 389–410. doi:10.100710551-017-3452-3

Agag, G., & El-Masry, A. A. (2016). Understanding consumer intention to participate in online travel community and effects on consumer intention to purchase travel online and WOM: An integration of innovation diffusion theory and TAM with trust. *Computers in Human Behavior*, *60*, 97–111. doi:10.1016/j.chb.2016.02.038

Agarwal, N., & Brem, A. (2015). Strategic business transformation through technology convergence: Implications from General Electric's industrial internet initiative. *International Journal of Technology Management*, *67*(2), 196–214. doi:10.1504/IJTM.2015.068224

Ahuja, V., & Alavi, S. (2018). Using Facebook as a digital tool for developing trust amongst consumers using netnography and social media analytics: A study of Jet Airways. *Journal of Relationship Marketing*, *17*(3), 171–187. doi:10.1080/15332667.2018.1440145

Ajina, A. S. (2019). The perceived value of social media marketing: An empirical study of online word-of-mouth in Saudi Arabian context. *Entrepreneurship and Sustainability Issues*, *6*(3), 1512–1527. doi:10.9770/jesi.2019.6.3(32)

Aksu, H., Babun, L., Conti, M., Tolomei, G., & Uluagac, A. S. (2018). Advertising in the IoT Era: Vision and Challenges. *IEEE Communications Magazine*, *56*(11), 138–144. doi:10.1109/MCOM.2017.1700871

Al Hogail, A. (2018). Improving IoT technology adoption through improving consumer trust. *Technologies*, *6*(3), 64–80. doi:10.3390/technologies6030064

Al-Abdallah, G., Khair, N., & Elmarakby, R. (2021). The impact of social networking sites on luxury vehicles purchase decision process in Gulf Cooperation Council countries. *Journal of International Consumer Marketing*, *33*(5), 559–577. doi:10.1080/08961530.2020.1867023

Alahmari, F., Naim, A., & Alqahtani, H. (). E-Learning Modeling Technique and Convolution Neural Networks in Online Education. In IoT-enabled Convolutional Neural Networks: Techniques and Applications (pp. 261-295). River Publishers.

Alexa, E. L., Alexa, M., & Stoica, C. M. (2012). The use of online marketing and social media in higher education institutions in Romania. *Journal of Marketing Research & Case Studies*, *2012*, 1–9. doi:10.5171/2012.721221

Alexander, L. (2022, November 30). *The Who, What, Why, & How of Digital Marketing*. Blog.hubspot.com. https://blog.hubspot.com/marketing/what-is-digital-marketing#whatis

Ali, M., & Bagui, S. (2021). Introduction to NFTs: The future of digital collectibles. *International Journal of Advanced Computer Science and Applications*, *12*(10), 50–56. doi:10.14569/IJACSA.2021.0121007

Allmendinger, G., & Lombreglia, R. (2006). Four Strategies for the Age of Smart Services. *Harvard Business Review*. PMID:16250631

Alqahtani, H., & Naim, A. (2022). Critical Success Factors for Transforming CRM to SCRM for building E-CRM. In A. Naim, & S. Kautish (Ed.), Building a Brand Image Through Electronic Customer Relationship Management (pp. 139-168). IGI Global. doi:10.4018/978-1-6684-5386-5.ch007

Alquhtani, S. A., & Muniasamy, A. (2022). Development of Effective Electronic Customer Relationship Management (ECRM) Model by the Applications of Web Intelligence Analytics. In A. Naim & S. Kautish (Eds.), *Building a Brand Image Through Electronic Customer Relationship Management* (pp. 44–63). IGI Global. doi:10.4018/978-1-6684-5386-5.ch003

AlSadrah, S. A. (2021). Social media use for public health promotion in the Gulf Cooperation Council: An overview. *Saudi Medical Journal*, *42*(1), 9–20. doi:10.15537mj.2021.1.25470 PMID:33399166

Alwarafy, A., Al-Thelaya, K. A., Abdallah, M., Schneider, J., & Hamdi, M. (2020). A survey on security and privacy issues in edge-computing-assisted internet of things. *IEEE Internet of Things Journal*, *8*(6), 4004–4022. doi:10.1109/JIOT.2020.3015432

Alzaidi, M. S., & Shehawy, Y. M. (2022). Cross-national differences in mobile learning adoption during COVID-19. *Education + Training*, *64*(3), 305–328. doi:10.1108/ET-05-2021-0179

Amadeh, H. & Jafarpour, M. (2009). Specification of obstacles and solutions of electronic banking development within the framework of Iran at 1404. Prospective. *Danesh va Tosee Journal, 26*(2), 2-43.

Amiri, Y. (2009). *Evaluation of the performance of electronic services provided in selected public banks of Fars province based on fuzzy BSC approach.* [MSc thesis, Yazd University].

Anandkumar, R., Dinesh, K., & Ahmed, J. Obaid, Malik, P., Sharma, R., Dumka, A., Singh, R., & Khatak, S. (2022). Securing e-Health application of cloud computing using hyperchaotic image encryption framework. *Computers and Electrical Engineering, 100.* doi:10.1016/j.compeleceng.2022.107860

Angelova, N., Kiryakova, G., & Yordanova, L. (2017). The great impact of internet of things on business. *Trakia Journal of Sciences, 15*(Suppl. 1), 406–412. doi:10.15547/tjs.2017.s.01.068

Ansu-Mensah, P. (2021). Green product awareness effect on green purchase intentions of university students': An emerging market's perspective. *Future Business Journal, 7*(1), 1–13. doi:10.118643093-021-00094-5

Apple Inc. (2006, May) *Nike+iPod Sports Kit.* Apple. https://www.apple.com/ipod/nike/

Arcenegui, J., Arjona, R., Román, R., & Baturone, I. (2021). Secure combination of IoT and blockchain by physically binding IoT devices to smart non-fungible tokens using PUFs. *Sensors (Basel), 21*(9), 3119. Advance online publication. doi:10.339021093119 PMID:33946227

Arkhipova, N. & Gurieva, M. (2018). Internet of Things in Digital Marketing and Data Security. *3rd International Conference on Judicial, Administrative and Humanitarian Problems of State Structures and Economic Subjects (JAHP 2018).* Advances in Social Science, Education and Humanities Research (ASSEHR).

Aroean, L. (2012). Friend or foe: In enjoying playfulness, do innovative consumers tend to switch brand? *Journal of Consumer Behaviour, 11*(1), 67–80. doi:10.1002/cb.370

Ashton, K. (2009). That "Internet of Things" Thing. *RFiD Journal, 22*, 97–114.

Ashworth, S., Tucker, M., & Druhmann, C. K. (2019). Critical success factors for facility management employer's information requirements (EIR) for BIM. *Facilities, 37*(1/2), 103–118. doi:10.1108/F-02-2018-0027

Astill, J., Dara, R. A., Fraser, E. D., Roberts, B., & Sharif, S. (2020). Smart poultry management: Smart sensors, big data, and the internet of things. *Computers and Electronics in Agriculture, 170*, 105291. doi:10.1016/j.compag.2020.105291

Atlam, H. F., Walters, R. J., & Wills, G. B. (2018). Internet of things: State-of-the-art, challenges, applications, and open issues. *International Journal of Intelligent Computing Research, 9*(3), 928–938. doi:10.20533/ijicr.2042.4655.2018.0112

Atzori, L., Iera, A., & Morabito, G. (2010). The Internet of Things: A Survey. *Computer Networks, 54*(15), 2787–2805. doi:10.1016/j.comnet.2010.05.010

Ayedee, N., & Manocha, S. (2020). Role of media (television) in creating positive atmosphere in COVID 19 during lockdown in India. *Asian Journal of Management, 11*(4), 370–378. doi:10.5958/2321-5763.2020.00057.8

AyilyathM. (2020). Consumer protection in E-commerce transactions in India—need for reforms, SSRN. doi:10.2139/ssrn.3571069

Aziz, M., Adnan, A., Afthanorhan, A., Foziah, H., Ishak, S., & Rashid, N. (2019). The influence of employer value proposition in talent demand towards talent shortage in the Malaysian Islamic banking institutions: A SEM approach. *Management Science Letters, 9*(6), 843–850. doi:10.5267/j.msl.2019.3.004

Babenko, V., Kulczyk, Z., Perevosova, I., Syniavska, O., & Davydova, O. (2019). Factors of the development of international e-commerce under the conditions of globalization. In *SHS Web of Conferences* (Vol. 65, p. 04016). EDP Sciences. 10.1051hsconf/20196504016

Bag, S., Srivastava, G., Bashir, M. M. A., Kumari, S., Giannakis, M., & Chowdhury, A. H. (2022). Journey of customers in this digital era: Understanding the role of artificial intelligence technologies in user engagement and conversion. *Benchmarking, 29*(7), 2074–2098. doi:10.1108/BIJ-07-2021-0415

Baker, B. J., Pizzo, A. D., & Su, Y. (2022). Non-fungible tokens: A research primer and implications for sport management. *Sports Innovation Journal, 1*, 1–15. doi:10.18060/25636

Bakhtiari, S., Breunig, R., Magnani, L., & Zhang, J. (2020). Financial constraints and small and medium enterprises: A review. *The Economic Record, 96*(315), 506–523. doi:10.1111/1475-4932.12560

Bala, M., & Verma, D. (n.d.). A Critical review of Digital Marketing. *IJMRS.* www.ijmrs.us

Balaji, M. & Roy, S. (2021). *Value co-creation with Internet of things technology in the retail industry*. Academic Press.

Bala, M., & Verma, D. (2018). A critical review of digital marketing. *International Journal of Management, IT & Engineering, 8*(10), 321–339.

Balbi, G., & Magaudda, P. (2018). *A history of digital media: An intermedia and global perspective*. Routledge. doi:10.4324/9781315209630

Ballestar, M., Grau-Carles, P., & Sainz, J. (2018). Customer segmentation in e-commerce: Application to the cashback business model. *Journal of Business Research, 88*, 407–414. doi:10.1016/j.jbusres.2017.11.047

Balmer, J. M. T., & Yen, D. A. (2016). The Internet of total corporate communications, quaternary corporate communications and the corporate marketing Internet revolution. *Journal of Marketing Management, 33*(1-2), 131–144. doi:10.1080/0267257X.2016.1255440

Bandara, R., Fernando, M., & Akter, S. (2019). Explicating the privacy paradox: A qualitative inquiry of online shopping consumers. *Journal of Retailing and Consumer Services, 52*, 220–233. doi:10.1016/j.jretconser.2019.101947

Bandyopadhyay, D., & Sen, J. (2011). Internet of things: Applications and challenges in technology and standardization. *Wireless Personal Communications, 58*(1), 49–69. doi:10.100711277-011-0288-5

Bantleman, J. (2012, April). The Big Cost Of Big Data. *Forbes, 16.*

Bashir, M. A., & Naim, A. (2020). *ICT Adoption Analysis for Innovation in Higher Education Sector*. Academic Press.

Bashir, M. F., Ma, B., & Shahzad, L. (2020). A brief review of socio-economic and environmental impact of Covid-19. *Air Quality, Atmosphere & Health, 13*(12), 1403–1409. doi:10.100711869-020-00894-8 PMID:32837620

Batabyal, S. (2013). Editorial! Where art Thou? News Practices in Indian Television. In Indian Mass Media and the Politics of Change (pp. 58-83). Routledge India. doi:10.4324/9780203085226-10

Batabyal, S. (2014). *Making news in India: Star news and Star ananda*. Routledge India. doi:10.4324/9781315816135

Bauer, S. R., & Mead, P. (1995). After You Open the Box: Making Smart Products More Usable, Useful, and Desirable Through Interactive Technology. *Design Management Journal, 6*(4), 21–26. doi:10.1111/j.1948-7169.1995.tb00453.x

Baumann, S. (2022). Geopolitical Overview of Social Media Platforms: From Beijing to Berlin. The SAGE Handbook of Social Media Marketing, 183.

Begum, A. (2019). *Big Data and Advanced Analytics*. Springer. doi:10.1007/978-3-030-11890-7_57

Behera, R. K., Gunasekaran, A., Gupta, S., Kamboj, S., & Bala, P. K. (2020). Personalized digital marketing recommender engine. *Journal of Retailing and Consumer Services, 53*, 101799. doi:10.1016/j.jretconser.2019.03.026

Belanche, D., Flavián, M., & Pérez-Rueda, A. (2020). Mobile apps use and WOM in the food delivery sector: The role of planned behavior, perceived security and customer lifestyle compatibility. *Sustainability, 12*(10), 4275. doi:10.3390u12104275

Belwal, R., Al Shibli, R., & Belwal, S. (2020). *Consumer protection and electronic commerce in the Sultanate of Oman. Journal of Information*. Communication and Ethics in Society. doi:10.1108/JICES-09-2019-0110

Benedict, K. (2012). *Moneyball, Big Data, The Internet of Things and Enterprise Mobility.* Cloud Computing. http://cloudcomputing.sys-con.com/node/2181866

Benefits Of Digital Marketing For Business in 2022. (2020, September 28). Intellipaat Blog. https://intellipaat.com/blog/benefits-of-digital-marketing/

Bhagowati, & Dutta, D. M. (2018). A study on literature review for identifying the factors impacting digital marketing. *International Journal of Sales & Marketing Management Research and Development*, *8*(3), 1-8.

Bhosale, V., & Pralhad Raverkar, D. (2020, January). *(PDF) IMPORTANCE OF DIGITAL MARKETING IN THE NEW AGE.* ResearchGate. https://www.researchgate.net/publication/344851786_IMPORTANCE_OF_DIGITAL_MARKETING_IN_THE_NEW_AGE

Bhushan, B. (2015). The changing structure of media and ethics in India. In *Media ethics and justice in the age of globalization* (pp. 194–209). Palgrave Macmillan.

Bibri, S. E., Krogstie, J., & Kärrholm, M. (2020). Compact city planning and development: Emerging practices and strategies for achieving the goals of sustainability. *Developments in the built environment, 4*, 100021.

Bi, Z., & Cochran, D. (2015). Big data analytics with applications. *Journal of Management Analytics, 1*(4), 249–265. doi:10.1080/23270012.2014.992985

Bocar, A. C., Khan, S. A., & Epoc, F. (2022). COVID-19 Work from Home Stressors and the Degree of its Impact: Employers and Employees Actions. *International Journal of Technology Transfer and Commercialisation. Inderscience, 19*(2), 270–291.

Bocar, A. C., Khan, S. A., & Epoc, F. J. (2022). COVID-19 work from home stressors and the degree of its impact: Employers and employees actions. *International Journal of Technology Transfer and Commercialisation, 19*(2), 270–291. doi:10.1504/IJTTC.2022.124349

Bockelmann, C., Pratas, N. K., Wunder, G., Saur, S., Navarro, M., Gregoratti, D., Vivier, G., De Carvalho, E., Ji, Y., Stefanovic, C., Popovski, P., Wang, Q., Schellmann, M., Kosmatos, E., Demestichas, P., Raceala-Motoc, M., Jung, P., Stanczak, S., & Dekorsy, A. (2018). Towards massive connectivity support for scalable mMTC communications in 5G networks. *IEEE Access : Practical Innovations, Open Solutions, 6*, 28969–28992. doi:10.1109/ACCESS.2018.2837382

Brancaccio, E., & Fontana, G. (2011). The global economic crisis. *New perspectives on the Critique of Economic Theory and Policy.*

Brian, I. S., O'Neill, B. S., & Terence, T. O. (2019). The upside of showrooming: How online information creates positive spill-over for the brick-and-mortar retailer. *Journal of Organizational Computing and Electronic Commerce, 29*(4), 294–315. doi:10.1080/10919392.2019.1671738

Britannica. (2022). *Aesthetics.* https://www.britannica.com/topic/aesthetics

Broeder, P., & Wentink, E. (2022). Limited-time scarcity and competitive arousal in e-commerce. *International Review of Retail, Distribution and Consumer Research, 32*(5), 549–567. doi:10.1080/09593969.2022.2098360

Broome, P. A. (2016). Conceptualizing the foundations of a regional e-commerce strategy: Open networks or closed regimes? The case of CARICOM. *Cogent Business &Management*, *3*(1), 1139–1441. doi:10.1080/23311975.2016.1139441

Brown, E. (2016). *21 Open Source Projects for IoT*. Linux.Com.

Bughin, J., Chui, M., & Manyika, J. (2010). Clouds, big data, and smart assets: Ten tech-enabled business trends to watch. *The McKinsey Quarterly*, *56*(1), 75–86.

Burhan, M., Rehman, R., Khan, B., & Kim, B.-S. (2018). IoT elements, layered architectures and security issues: a comprehensive survey. Sensors, 18(9).

Burton, B. J., & Jacobsen, J. P. (1999). Measuring returns on investments in collectibles. *The Journal of Economic Perspectives*, *13*(4), 193–212. doi:10.1257/jep.13.4.193

Buttle, F., & Maklan, S. (2019). *Customer relationship management: concepts and technologies*. Routledge. doi:10.4324/9781351016551

Byun, K. A., Dass, M., Kumar, P., & Kim, J. (2017). An examination of innovative consumers' playfulness on their preordering behavior. *Journal of Consumer Marketing*, *34*(3), 226–240. doi:10.1108/JCM-01-2016-1684

Campbell, C., & Farrell, J. R. (2020). More than meets the eye: The functional components underlying influencer marketing. *Business Horizons*, *63*(4), 469–479. doi:10.1016/j.bushor.2020.03.003

Canhoto, A. & Arp, S. (2016). *Exploring the factors that support adoption and sustained use of health and fitness wearables*. Taylor and Francis Online.

Cao, H., & Folan, P. (2011). Product life cycle: the evolution of a paradigm and literature review from 1950–2009. *Production Planning & Control: The Management of Operations*, 641–662. . doi:10.1080/09537287.2011.577460

Carletti, E., Claessens, S., Fatás, A., & Vives, X. (2020). *Post-Covid-19 World*. Centre for Economic Policy Research.

Caro, F., & Sadr, R. (2019). The Internet of Things (IoT) in retail: Bridging supply and demand. *Business Horizons*, *62*(1), 47–54. doi:10.1016/j.bushor.2018.08.002

Castaneda, J. A., Rodriguez-Molina, M. A., & Martínez, T. L. (2009). Attitude's hierarchy of effects in online user behavior. *Online Information Review*, *33*(11), 7–21. doi:10.1108/14684520910944364

Celik, F. (2016). *Internet of Things as a source of future marketing tools* [Bachelor's thesis]. University of Twente.

Cetina, I., Munthiu, M.-C., & Radulescu, V. (2012). Psychological and Social Factors that Influence Online Consumer Behavior. *Procedia: Social and Behavioral Sciences*, *62*, 184–188. doi:10.1016/j.sbspro.2012.09.029

Chadha, K. (2017). The Indian news media industry: Structural trends and journalistic implications. *Global Media and Communication*, *13*(2), 139–156. doi:10.1177/1742766517704674

Chaffey, D., & Ellis-Chadwick, F. (2019). *Digital marketing*.

Chakravartty, P., & Roy, S. (2013). Media pluralism redux: Towards new frameworks of comparative media studies "beyond the West". *Political Communication, 30*(3), 349-370.

Chakravartty, P., & Roy, S. (2015). Mr. Modi goes to Delhi: Mediated populism and the 2014 Indian elections. *Television & New Media*, *16*(4), 311–322. doi:10.1177/1527476415573957

Changchit, C., Cutshall, R., Lonkani, R., Pholwan, K., & Pongwiritthon, R. (2018). Determinants of online shopping influencing Thai consumer's buying choices. *Journal of Internet Commerce*, *18*(1), 1–23. doi:10.1080/15332861.2018.1496391

Chang, S. S., Stuckler, D., Yip, P., & Gunnell, D. (2013). Impact of 2008 global economic crisis on suicide: Time trend study in 54 countries. *BMJ (Clinical Research Ed.)*, *347*(sep17 1), 347. doi:10.1136/bmj.f5239 PMID:24046155

Chatterjee, S., Chaudhuri, R., Vrontis, D., Thrassou, A., Ghosh, S. K., & Chaudhuri, S. (2020). Social customer relationship management factors and business benefits. *The International Journal of Organizational Analysis*. doi:10.1108/IJOA-11-2019-1933

Chen, T. L., Kim, H., Pan, S. Y., Tseng, P. C., Lin, Y. P., & Chiang, P. C. (2020). Implementation of green chemistry principles in circular economy system towards sustainable development goals: Challenges and perspectives. *The Science of the Total Environment*, *716*, 136998. doi:10.1016/j.scitotenv.2020.136998 PMID:32044483

Chen, Y., Kwilinski, A., Chygryn, O., Lyulyov, O., & Pimonenko, T. (2021). The green competitiveness of enterprises: Justifying the quality criteria of digital marketing communication channels. *Sustainability*, *13*(24), 13679. doi:10.3390u132413679

Cho, K. H., & Lee, W. B. (2022). A study on influencing factors on intention to adopt NFTs using UTAUT. *The Journal of the Korea Contents Association*, *22*(3), 17–34. doi:10.5392/JKCA.2022.22.03.017

Choshin, M., & Ghaffari, A. (2017). An investigation of the impact of effective factors on the success of e-commerce in small- and medium-sized companies. *Computers in Human Behavior*, *66*(1), 67–74. doi:10.1016/j.chb.2016.09.026

Chouhan, R. (2017). E-Business and E-Commerce Management (Strategy, Implementation and Practice). *Pacific Business Review International*, *9*(10), 135–136.

Christopher, J. Bucholtz. (2012, March) Customers, Big Data, and the Internet of Things. *Tech News World*. https://www.technewsworld.com/story/74692.html [Accessed on: 2012-06-08]

Chuah, S. H.-W., Rauschnabel, P. A., Krey, N., Nguyen, B., Ramayah, T., & Lade, S. (2016). Wearable technologies: The role of usefulness and visibility in smartwatch adoption. *Computers in Human Behavior*, *65*, 276–284. doi:10.1016/j.chb.2016.07.047

Chynal, P., & Sobecki, J. (2016). Eyetracking Evaluation of Different Chart Types Used for Web-Based System Data Visualization. *IEEE Conf. Network Intelligence Conference (ENIC)*, IEEE. 10.1109/ENIC.2016.031

Cialdini, R. B. (2001). The science of persuasion. *Scientific American*, *284*(2), 76–81. doi:10.1038cientificamerican0201-76

Cisco. (2015). *The Internet of Things. Reduce Security Risks with Automated Policies*. Cisco. https://www.cisco.com/c/dam/en_us/solutions/trends/iot/docs/security-risks.pdf

Cisco. (n.d.). *Smart+Connected Parking*. Cisco.

Coetzee, L., & Eksteen, J. (2011, May). The Internet of Things-promise for the future? An introduction. In *2011 IST-Africa Conference Proceedings* (pp. 1-9). IEEE.

Cohen, J. (1992). Quantitative methods in psychology: A power primer. *Psychological Bulletin*, *112*(1), 155–159. doi:10.1037/0033-2909.112.1.155 PMID:19565683

Colella, G., & Amatulli, C. (2021). Digital Marketing and Digital Retail Strategies in the Luxury Sector: Critical Factors and Opportunities. In Handbook of Research on IoT, Digital Transformation, and the Future of Global Marketing, 112-129.

Colicev, A. (2022). How can non-fungible tokens bring value to brands. *International Journal of Research in Marketing*. Advance online publication. doi:10.1016/j.ijresmar.2022.07.003

Combe, C. (2012). *Introduction to E-business*. Routledge. doi:10.4324/9780080492780

Cosgrove-Sacks, C. (2014). *Open Protocols for an Open, Interoperable Internet of Things.* Org. for Advancement of Structured Information Standards. www.oasis-open.org/presentations/open protocols-and-internet -of-things-oasis.ppt

Cram, T. (2008). Pricing. In M. J. Baker & S. J. Hart (Eds.), *The Marketing Book* (pp. 281–295). Elsevier. doi:10.1016/B978-0-7506-8566-5.50018-2

Crowley, J. L., & Coutaz, J. (2015). An ecological view of smart home technologies. In *Proceedings of the European Conference on Ambient Intelligence*. Springer. 10.1007/978-3-319-26005-1_1

Cvijic, B., Bundalo, D., Pasalic, D., & Bundalo, Z. (2016). Cloud based web application supporting vehicle toll payment system. *5th Mediterranean Conference on Embedded Computing (MECO).* IEEE. 10.1109/MECO.2016.7525700

Dai, Z. (2012). The Study on the Influence about Trust to Online Shopping Behavior. In: *Eleventh Wuhan International Conference on e-Business*, (pp. 24–29). Association for Information Systems.

Dai, Z. (2012). The Study on the Influence about Trust to Online Shopping Behavior. In: *Eleventh Wuhan International Conference on e-Business.* Association for Information Systems.

Danet, B., & Katriel, T. (2012). No two alike: play and aesthetics in collecting. In S. M. Pearce (Ed.), *Interpreting objects and collections* (pp. 220–239). Routledge.

Dantas, T. E. T., de-Souza, E. D., Destro, I. R., Hammes, G., Rodriguez, C. M. T., & Soares, S. R. (2021). How the combination of Circular Economy and Industry 4.0 can contribute towards achieving the Sustainable Development Goals. *Sustainable Production and Consumption*, *26*, 213–227. doi:10.1016/j.spc.2020.10.005

Danyali, A. (2018). Factors influencing customers' change of behaviors from online banking to mobile banking in Tejarat Bank, Iran. *Journal of Organizational Change Management, 31* (6), 1226-1233.

Daoud, J. I. (2017). Multicollinearity and regression analysis. *Journal of Physics: Conference Series*, *949*(1), 012009. Advance online publication. doi:10.1088/1742-6596/949/1/012009

Darsono, J. T., Prihantono, E. Y., & Kasim, E. S. (2019). Strategic Policies for Small and Medium Businesses in marketing through E-commerce. *Entrepreneurship and Sustainability Issues*, *7*(2), 1230–1245. doi:10.9770/jesi.2019.7.2(30)

Dash, A. (2021). NFTs weren't supposed to end like this. *The Atlantic*. https://www.theatlantic. com/ideas/archive/2021/04/nfts-werent-supposed-end-like/618488/

de Mesquita, J. M. C., & Kostelijk, E. (2021). *Marketing analytics: Statistical tools for marketing and consumer behavior using SPSS.* Routledge. doi:10.4324/9781003196617

Decker, R., & Stummer, C. (2017). Marketing management for consumer products in the era of the internet of things. *Advances in Internet of Things*, *7*(3), 47–70. doi:10.4236/ait.2017.73004

Deloitte. (2021). *From trading cards to digital video: Sports NFTs kick sports memorabilia into the digital age.* https://www2.deloitte.com/content/dam/insights/articles/GLOB164584_Sports-NFT/DI_Sports-NFT.pdf

Desai, V. (2019). *(PDF) Digital Marketing: A Review.* ResearchGate. https://www.researchgate.net/publication/333709419_Digital_Marketing_A_Review

Desai, V. (2019). Digital Marketing: A Review. *International Journal of Trend in Scientific Research and Development (IJTSRD),* 196-200, www.ijtsrd.com

Desai, V. (2019). Digital Marketing: A Review. *International Journal of Trend in Scientific Research and Development,* 196–200. doi:10.31142/ijtsrd23100

Devi, S. (2019). Making Sense of "Views" Culture in Television News Media in India. Journalism Practice, 13(9), 1075-1090. doi:10.1080/17512786.2019.1635041

Dhawan, M. K. (2022, December 14). *How are AI, web3 and other emerging technologies transforming the future of experiential Marketing?* CXOToday.com. https://www.cxotoday.com/cxo-bytes/how-are-ai-web3-and-other-emerging-technologies-transforming-the-future-of-experiential-marketing/

Dhingra, M., & Mudgal, R. K. (2019, March). Historical evolution of social media: an overview. In *International Conference on Advances in Engineering Science Management & Technology (ICAESMT),* Uttaranchal University. 10.2139srn.3395665

Dickey, I. J., & Lewis, W. F. (2012). An overview of digital media and advertising. *E-marketing: Concepts, methodologies, tools, and applications*, 31-61.

Ding, Z., Yang, B., Guting, R. H., & Li, Y. (2015, August). Network-Matched Trajectory-Based Moving-Object Database: Models and Applications. *IEEE Transactions on Intelligent Transportation Systems*, *16*(4), 1918–1928. doi:10.1109/TITS.2014.2383494

Dixon, S. (2022, September 16). *Number of Social Media Users Worldwide 2010-2021.* Statista. www.statista.com. https://www.statista.com/statistics/278414/number-of-worldwide-social-network-users/

Doe, J. K., & Asamoah, G. K. (2022). CRM as Antecedent of Electronic Retailing and Online Customer Satisfaction. In A. Naim & S. Kautish (Eds.), *Building a Brand Image Through Electronic Customer Relationship Management* (pp. 169–200). IGI Global. doi:10.4018/978-1-6684-5386-5.ch008

Doern, R. R., & Fey, C. F. (2006). E-commerce developments and strategies for value creation: The case of Russia. *Journal of World Business*, *41*(4), 315–327. doi:10.1016/j.jwb.2006.08.001

Donthu, N., Kumar, S., Mukherjee, D., Pandey, N., & Lim, W. M. (2021). How to conduct a bibliometric analysis: An overview and guidelines. *Journal of Business Research, 133*, 285–296. doi:10.1016/j.jbusres.2021.04.070

Dunn, T. J., Baguley, T., & Brunsden, V. (2014). From alpha to omega: A practical solution to the pervasive problem of internal consistency estimation. *British Journal of Psychology*, *105*(3), 399–412. doi:10.1111/bjop.12046 PMID:24844115

Durovic, M. (2020). International consumer law: What is it all about? *Journal of Consumer Policy*, *43*(1), 125–143. doi:10.100710603-019-09438-9

Dutton, W. H. (2014). Putting things to work: Social and policy challenges for the Internet of things. *Info*, *16*, 1–21. doi:10.1108/info-09-2013-0047

Dwivedi, Y. K., Ismagilova, E., Hughes, D. L., Carlson, J., Filieri, R., Jacobson, J., Jain, V., Karjaluoto, H., Kefi, H., Krishen, A. S., Kumar, V., Rahman, M. M., Raman, R., Rauschnabel, P. A., Rowley, J., Salo, J., Tran, G. A., & Wang, Y. (2021). Setting the Future of Digital and Social Media Marketing research: Perspectives and Research Propositions. *International Journal of Information Management, 59*(59), 102168. Science direct. doi:10.1016/j.ijinfomgt.2020.102168

Dwivedi, Y. K., Hughes, L., Wang, Y., Alalwan, A. A., Ahn, S. J., Balakrishnan, J., ... Wirtz, J. (2022). Metaverse marketing: How the metaverse will shape the future of consumer research and practice. *Psychology and Marketing*. Advance online publication. doi:10.1002/mar.21767

Eaton, C., Deroos, D., Deutsch, T., Lapis, G., & Zikopoulos, P. (2012). *Understanding Big Data*. McGraw-Hill Companies. http://public.dhe.ibm.com/common/ssi/ecm/en/iml14296usen/I M L14296USEN.pdf.

Ebekozien, A., Aigbavboa, C., Thwala, W. D., Amadi, G. C., Aigbedion, M., & Ogbaini, I. F. (2022). A systematic review of green building practices implementation in Africa. *Journal of Facilities Management.*

Edgar, T. W., & Manz, D. O. (2017). *Research Methods for Cyber Security*. Elsevier.

Editorial. (2022, August 17). *Digital marketing leveraging artificial intelligence*. MediaNews4U. https://www.medianews4u.com/digital-marketing-leveraging-artificial-intelligence/

Efendioglu, I. H. (2022). The rise of the non-fungible token (NFT) market in Turkey: The effect of social media interaction and the need for uniqueness on NFT purchase pntention. *Review of Marketing Science*. doi:10.1515/roms-2022-0065

Ekung, S., Odesola, I., & Opoku, A. (2022). Demystifying cost misperception as a challenge to green building adoption in Nigeria. *Journal of Engineering. Design and Technology*, *20*(6), 1716–1737. doi:10.1108/JEDT-01-2021-0049

Elahi, S., Ghanbari, M. H., & Shayan, A. (2012). Determining the effective factors in implementing mobile banking technology by the customer. *Quarterly Journal of Commercial Law Research*, *16*(63), 27–50.

Elbeltagi, I., & Agag, G. (2016). E-retailing ethics and its impact on customer satisfaction and repurchase intention: A cultural and commitment-trust theory perspective. *Internet Research*, *26*(1), 288–310. doi:10.1108/IntR-10-2014-0244

El-Gohary, H., Trueman, M., & Fukukawa, K. (2008). E-marketing and small business enterprises: A review of the methodologies. *Journal of Business and Public Policy*, *2*(2), 64–93.

Elseidi, R. I. (2018). Understanding Egyptian consumers' intentions in online shopping. *International Journal of Online Marketing*, *8*(3), 1–18. doi:10.4018/IJOM.2018070101

Emma, P., Sara, F., Marta, S., & Ana, G. (2017). *Exploratory study of consumer issues in online peer-to-peer platform markets*. European Commission. file:///C:/Users/BASANT~1/AppData/Local/Temp/Annex5_Task5_Report May2017pdf

Emma, P., Sara, F., Marta, S., & Ana, G. (2017). *Exploratory study of consumer issues in online peer-to-peer platform markets*. European Commission. file:///C:/Users/BASANT~1/AppData/Local/Temp/Annex5_Task5_Report May2017pdf.

Engblom, S., & Lukarski, D. (2016). Fast MATLAB compatible sparse assembly on multicore computers. *Parallel Computing*, *56*, 1–17. https://www.researchgate.net/publication/330513589_Internet_of_Things_IOT_Using_Raspberry_Pi. doi:10.1016/j.parco.2016.04.001

Erickson, L. E. (2017). Reducing greenhouse gas emissions and improving air quality: Two global challenges. *Environmental Progress & Sustainable Energy*, *36*(4), 982–988. doi:10.1002/ep.12665 PMID:29238442

ETBrandEquity. (2022a, December 7). *5g Services: 5G and the new era of creativity in marketing, Marketing & Advertising News, ET BrandEquity*. ETBrandEquity.com. https://brandequity.economictimes.indiatimes.com/news/digital/5g-and-the-new-era-of-creativity-in-marketing/96038180

ETBrandEquity. (2022b, December 13). *The potential for retail in the metaverse, Marketing & Advertising News, ET BrandEquity*. ETBrandEquity.com. https://brandequity.economictimes.indiatimes.com/news/digital/the-potential-for-retail-in-the-metaverse/96180923

Évrard, Y., Pras, B., & Roux, E. (2003). *Market: Etudes et Recherches en Marketing*. Dunod. B.

Fachechi, A., Mainetti, L., Palano, L., Patrono, L., Stefanizzi, M. L., Vergallo, R., Chu, P., & Gadh, R. (2015). A new vehicle-to-grid system for battery charging exploiting IoT protocols. *IEEE Int. Conf. Industrial Technology (ICIT)*. IEEE. 10.1109/ICIT.2015.7125414

Fai, A. (2021). *Smart collectibles: Unlocking the value of non-fungible tokens (NFTs)*. EthinkWeb Co.

Faruk, M., Rahman, M., & Hasan, S. (2021). How digital marketing evolved over time: A bibliometric analysis on scopus database. *Heliyon*, *7*(12), 08603. doi:10.1016/j.heliyon.2021.e08603 PMID:34988311

Fatima, S., Alqahtani, H., Naim, A., & Alma'alwi, F. (2022). E-CRM Through Social Media Marketing Activities for Brand Awareness, Brand Image, and Brand Loyalty. In A. Naim & S. Kautish (Eds.), *Building a Brand Image Through Electronic Customer Relationship Management* (pp. 109–138). IGI Global. doi:10.4018/978-1-6684-5386-5.ch006

Federal Trade Commission. (2014). *Internet of Things: Privacy & Security in a Connected World.* FTC.

Feng, L. (2007). *What is e-business*. Blackwell Publishing.

Ferrari, M. M., & Pagliari, M. S. (2021). No country is an island. International cooperation and climate change. *International Cooperation and Climate Change.(June 2021). Banque de France Working Paper*, (815).

Field, A. (2018). *Discovering statistics using IBM SPSS statistics* (5th ed.). Sage Publications.

Filson, D. (2004). The Impact of E-Commerce Strategies on Firm Value: Lessons from Amazon.com and Its Early Competitors. *The Journal of Business*, *77*(2), 135–154. doi:10.1086/381640

Fleisch, E., Weinberger, M., & Wortmann, F. (2014). *Business models for the internet of things*. Bosch Lab White Paper.

Forman, C. (2005). The corporate digital divide: Determinants of Internet adoption. *Management Science*, *51*(4), 641–654. doi:10.1287/mnsc.1040.0343

Franke, N., & Schreier, M. (2008). Product uniqueness as a driver of customer utility in mass customization. *Marketing Letters*, *19*(2), 93–107. doi:10.100711002-007-9029-7

Frost, R., & Strauss, J. (2016). *E-marketing*. Routledge.

Fuchs, C., Hofkirchner, W., Schafranek, M., Raffl, C., Sandoval, M., & Bichler, R. (2010). *Theoretical Foundations of the Web: Cognition, Communication, and CoOperation.* Multidisciplinary Digital Publishing Institute.

Future of Digital Marketing in India. (2022, March 14). Www.linkedin.com. https://www.linkedin.com/pulse/future-digital-marketing-india-madhu-kiran-g?trk=articles_directory

Gan, C., & Wang, W. (2017). The influence of perceived value on purchase intention in social commerce context. *Internet Research*, *27*(4), 772–785. doi:10.1108/IntR-06-2016-0164

Gangwar, V. P., & Khan, S. A. (2022). Analyzing the Role of Micro-Entrepreneurship and Self-Help Groups (SHGs) in Women Empowerment and Development: A Bottom-of-Pyramid Perspective. In Driving Factors for Venture Creation and Success in Agricultural Entrepreneurship (pp. 213-226). IGI Global.

Gangwar, V., & Khan, S. (2022).Analyzing the Role of Micro-Entrepreneurship and Self-Help Groups (SHGs) in Women Empowerment and Development: A Bottom-of-Pyramid Perspective. Driving Factors for Venture Creation and Success in Agricultural Entrepreneurship. M. Arafat, I. Ali, A. Khan, & H. Hussain Balhareth (Eds.). Driving Factors for Venture Creation and Success in Agricultural Entrepreneurship; October 2021, IGI-Global Doi:10.4018/978-1-6684-2349-3.ch011

Ganichev, N. A., & Koshovets, O. B. (2021). Forcing the digital economy: How will the structure of digital markets change as a result of the COVID-19 pandemic. *Studies on Russian Economic Development*, *32*(1), 11–22. doi:10.1134/S1075700721010056 PMID:33642845

Gao, H., Kuang, L., Yin, Y., Guo, B., & Dou, K. (2020). Mining consuming behaviors with temporal evolution for personalized recommendation in mobile marketing apps. *Mobile Networks and Applications*, *25*(4), 1233–1248. doi:10.100711036-020-01535-1

Garcia-Morchon, O., Kumar, S., & Sethi, M. (2019). Internet of things (IoT) security: state of the art and challenges. RFC.

Gaur, B., Shukla, V. K., & Verma, A. (2019, April). Strengthening people analytics through wearable IOT device for real-time data collection. In 2019 international conference on automation, computational and technology management (ICACTM) (pp. 555-560). IEEE. doi:10.1109/ICACTM.2019.8776776

Gecdesigns. (2020, December 1). *What is IOT? & Role of IOT in digital marketing*. GEC Designs. https://gecdesigns.com/blog/role-of-iot-in-digital-marketing

Ghazaleh, M. A., & Zabadi, A. M. (2020). Promoting a revamped CRM through Internet of Things and Big Data: An AHP-based evaluation. *The International Journal of Organizational Analysis*, *28*(1), 66–91. doi:10.1108/IJOA-12-2018-1602

Ghorfi, T., & Hatimi, I. E. (2020). Impact of Social Media Usage on MENA Countries Economy. *Business and Social Media in the Middle East: Strategies, Best Practices and Perspectives*, 77-99.

Gigli, M., & Simon, G. M. (2011). Internet of things: Services and applications categorization. *Adv. Internet Things*, *1*(2), 27–31. doi:10.4236/ait.2011.12004

Gillis, A. (2021). *What is internet of things (IoT)?* IOT Agenda.

Glova, J., Sabol, T., & Vajda, V. (2014). Business Models for the Internet of Things Environment. *Procedia Economics and Finance*, *15*, 1122–1129. doi:10.1016/S2212-5671(14)00566-8

Gordijn, J., Akkermans, H., & Van Vliet, H. (2000). What's in an electronic business model? In *Knowledge Engineering and Knowledge Management Methods, Models, and Tools: 12th International Conference, EKAW 2000 Juan-les-Pins, France, October 2–6, 2000 Proceedings 12* (pp. 257-273). Springer Berlin Heidelberg.

Granell, C., Kamilaris, A., Kotsev, A., Ostermann, F. O., & Trilles, S. (2020). Internet of Things. In H. Guo, M. F. Goodchild, & A. Annoni (Eds.), *Manual of Digital Earth*. Springer. doi:10.1007/978-981-32-9915-3_11

Green, H. (2015) *Cognitive IoT: Making the internet of Things Deliver for All of Us*.

Gregory. J. (2015). *The Internet of Things: Revolutionizing the Retail Industry*. Available: accenture.com/_acnmedia/Accenture/ Conversion-Assets/DotCom/Documents/Global/PDF/Dualpub_14/Accenture-The-Internet-Of-Th ings.pdf.

Grilo, A. M., Chen, J., Diaz, M., Garrido, D., & Casaca, A. (2014, August). An Integrated WSAN and SCADA System for Monitoring a Critical Infrastructure. *IEEE Transactions on Industrial Informatics*, *10*(3), 1755–1764. doi:10.1109/TII.2014.2322818

Groopman, J. (2015). *Customer experience in the internet of things: Five ways brands can use sensors to build better customer relationships.* Altimeter. http://pages. altimetergroup.com/customer-experience-in-the-internet-of-things-report.html

Grover, V. (2021). *5 Way IoT is changing digital marketing.* Spiceworks. https://www.spiceworks.com/tech/iot/articles/5-ways-iot-is-changing-digital-marketing/#:~:text=IoT%20means%20having%20more%20touch,purchase%20decision%20of%20the%20customer

Grzanka, P., Santos, C., & Moradi, M. (2017). Intersectionality research in counseling psychology. *Journal of Counseling Psychology.*

Gubbi, J., Buyya, R., Marusic, S., & Palaniswami. M. (2013). Internet of Things (IoT): A Vision, Architectural Elements, and Future Directions. Future Generation Computer Systems. *ScienceDirect.*

Gubbi, J., Buyya, R., Marusic, S., & Palaniswami, M. (2013). Internet of Things (IoT): A vision, architectural elements, and future directions. *Future Generation Computer Systems, 29*(7), 1645–1660. doi:10.1016/j.future.2013.01.010

Guo, B., Zhang, D., Wang, Z., Yu, Z., & Zhou, X. (2013). Opportunistic IoT: Exploring the harmonious interaction between human and the internet of things. *Journal of Network and Computer Applications, 36*(6), 1531–1539. doi:10.1016/j.jnca.2012.12.028

Guo, Y., Liu, H., & Chai, Y. (2014). *The embedding convergence of smart cities and tourism internet of things in China: An advance perspective. Advances in Hospitality and Tourism Research.* AHTR.

Gutierrez, A., O'Leary, S., Rana, N. P., Dwivedi, Y. K., & Calle, T. (2019). Using privacy calculus theory to explore entrepreneurial directions in mobile location-based advertising: Identifying intrusiveness as the critical risk factor. *Computers in Human Behavior, 95*, 295–306. doi:10.1016/j.chb.2018.09.015

Haaker, T., Ly, P. T. M., Nguyen-Thanh, N., & Nguyen, H. T. H. (2021). Business model innovation through the application of the Internet-of-Things: A comparative analysis. *Journal of Business Research, 126*, 126–136. doi:10.1016/j.jbusres.2020.12.034

Hair, J. F., Black, W. C., Babin, B. J., Anderson, R. E., & Tatham, R. L. (2010). *Multivariate Data Analysis, Upper Saddle River.* Pearson.

Haller, S., Karnouskos, S. and Schroth, C. (2009). *The Internet of Things in an Enterprise Context.*

Haller, S., Karnouskos, S., & Schroth, C. (2009). The Internet of things in an enterprise context. Lecture Notes in Computer Science, 5468, 14–28. 1 doi:0.1007/978-3-642-00985-3_2/COVER

Hallikainen, H., & Laukkanen, T. (2018). National culture and consumer trust in ecommerce. *International Journal of Information Management, 38*(1), 97–106. doi:10.1016/j.ijinfomgt.2017.07.002

Hanaysha, J. R., & Momani, A. M. (2021). An exploration of social media marketing features and brand loyalty in the fast food industry. *Journal of content community and communication, 14*(8), 81-92.

Hannak, A., Soeller, G., Lazer, D., Mislove, A., & Wilson, C. (2014). Measuring price discrimination and steering on E-commerce web sites. *Proceedings of the ACM SIGCOMM Internet Measurement Conference, IMC*, 305–318. 10.1145/2663716.2663744

Harrigan, M., Feddema, K., Wang, S., Harrigan, P., & Diot, E. (2021). How trust leads to online purchase intention founded in perceived usefulness and peer communication. *Journal of Consumer Behaviour: An International Research Review,* 1-16. . doi:10.1002/cb.1936

Harrisson, B., Jean, P., & Dahl, B. (2017). 10 ecommerce trends for 2018. *Project: Growth Strategies in an Omnichannel Retail Context.* . doi:10.13140/RG.2.2.34264.19205

Hartemo, M. (2016). Email marketing in the era of the empowered consumer. *Journal of Research in Interactive Marketing, 10*(3), 212–230. doi:10.1108/JRIM-06-2015-0040

Hasan, H. C., Yusof, F. N., & Daud, M. (2018). Comparison of authentication methods in internet of things technology. *International Journal of Computer and Systems Engineering, 12*(3), 231–234.

Hasan, M. M., Nekmahmud, M., Yajuan, L., & Patwary, M. A. (2019). Green business value chain: A systematic review. *Sustainable Production and Consumption, 20*, 326–339. doi:10.1016/j.spc.2019.08.003

Hassib, B., & Shires, J. (2022). Cybersecurity in the GCC: From Economic Development to Geopolitical Controversy. *Middle East Policy, 29*(1), 90–103. doi:10.1111/mepo.12616

Ha, T. M. (2021). The impact of product characteristics of limited-edition shoes on perceived value, brand trust and purchase intention. *Cogent Business & Management, 8*(1), 1–19. doi:10.1080/23311975.2021.1953680

Haupt, S. (2003). An economic analysis of consumer protection in Con-trAct law. *German Law Review, 4*(11), 1137–1164.

Heinze, T. S., Amme, W., & Moser, S. (2018). Static analysis and process model transformation for an advanced business process to Petri net mapping. *Software, Practice & Experience, 48*(1), 161–195. doi:10.1002pe.2523

Helge, S., Anne, H., & Guido, M. (2020). The function of ability, benevolence, and integrity-based trust in innovation networks. *Industry and Innovation, 27*(6), 585–604. doi:10.1080/13662716.2019.1632695

Henneke, S. (2016). Smart City Solution for Amsterdam: Intelligent Waste Disposal with M2M Telekom M2M Blog. *Telekom M2M Blog.*

Herman, J. D., Quinn, J. D., Steinschneider, S., Giuliani, M., & Fletcher, S. (2020). Climate adaptation as a control problem: Review and perspectives on dynamic water resources planning under uncertainty. *Water Resources Research, 56*(2), e24389. doi:10.1029/2019WR025502

Hertwich, E. G., Ali, S., Ciacci, L., Fishman, T., Heeren, N., Masanet, E., Asghari, F. N., Olivetti, E., Pauliuk, S., Tu, Q., & Wolfram, P. (2019). Material efficiency strategies to reducing greenhouse gas emissions associated with buildings, vehicles, and electronics—A review. *Environmental Research Letters, 14*(4), 043004. doi:10.1088/1748-9326/ab0fe3

He, W., & Xu, L. (2014, February). Integration of distributed enterprise applications: A survey. *IEEE Transactions on Industrial Informatics, 10*(1), 35–42. doi:10.1109/TII.2012.2189221

Heydemann, S. (2020). Rethinking social contracts in the MENA region: Economic governance, contingent citizenship, and state-society relations after the Arab uprisings. *World Development, 135*, 105019. doi:10.1016/j.worlddev.2020.105019

Himelein-Wachowiak, M., Giorgi, S., Devoto, A., Rahman, M., Ungar, L., Schwartz, H. A., Epstein, D. H., Leggio, L., & Curtis, B. (2021). Bots and misinformation spread on social media: Implications for COVID-19. *Journal of Medical Internet Research, 23*(5), e26933. doi:10.2196/26933 PMID:33882014

Hirschmiller, S. (2022). *Adidas first wearable NFT collection marks the first time you can dress AND undress your bored ape.* https://www.forbes.com/sites/stephaniehirschmiller/2022/11/16/adidas-launches-first-nft-wearables-collection/?sh=7a0da82
337fe

Ho, C. H., & Wu, T. Y. (2012). Factors affecting intent to purchase virtual goods in online games. *International Journal of Electronic Business Management, 10*(3), 204–212.

Hoda, N. (2022). E-CRM in Digital Payment Services: Its Role and Proposed Framework for Adoption. In A. Naim & S. Kautish (Eds.), *Building a Brand Image Through Electronic Customer Relationship Management* (pp. 1–18). IGI Global. doi:10.4018/978-1-6684-5386-5.ch001

Hoerl, A. E., & Kennard, R. W. (1970). Ridge regression: Applications to nonorthogonal problems. *Technometrics*, *12*(1), 69–82. doi:10.1080/00401706.1970.10488635

Hofacker, C. F., & Belanche, D. (2016). Eight social media challenges for marketing managers. *Spanish Journal of Marketing - ESIC, 20*(2), 73–80. . doi:10.1016/j.sjme.2016.07.003

Hofacker, C. F., Malthouse, E. C., & Sultan, F. (2016). Big Data and consumer behavior: Imminent opportunities. *Journal of Consumer Marketing*, *33*(2), 89–97. doi:10.1108/JCM-04-2015-1399

Hofacker, C., Golgeci, I., Pillai, K. G., & Gligor, D. M. (2020). Digital marketing and business-to-business relationships: A close look at the interface and a roadmap for the future. *European Journal of Marketing*, *54*(6), 1161–1179. doi:10.1108/EJM-04-2020-0247

Hollebeek, L. D., & Macky, K. (2019). Digital content marketing's role in fostering consumer engagement, trust, and value: Framework, fundamental propositions, and implications. *Journal of Interactive Marketing*, *45*(1), 27–41. doi:10.1016/j.intmar.2018.07.003

Holzinger, A., Dehmer, M., & Jurisica, I. (2014). Knowledge discovery and interactive data mining in bioinformatics - state-of-the-art, future challenges and research direc-tions. *BMC Bioinformatics*, *15*(S6), I1. doi:10.1186/1471-2105-15-S6-I1 PMID:25078282

How is AI Transforming the Future of Digital Marketing ? (2022, February 28). Institute of Entrepreneurship Development. https://ied.eu/blog/how-ai-transforming-the-future-of-digital-marketing/#:~:text=AI%20assists%20businesses%20in%20analyz
ing

Huang, L., & Savary, J. (2022). When payments go social: The use of person-to-person payment methods attenuates the endowment effect. *JMR, Journal of Marketing Research*. Advance online publication. doi:10.1177/00222437221128255

Hughes, J. (2020). The Evolution of Digital Marketing. *Velocitize*. https://velocitize.com/2020/08/31/the-evolution-of-digital-marketing

Huifeng, W., Kadry, S. N., & Raj, E. D. (2020). Continuous health monitoring of sportsperson using IoT devices based wearable technology. *Computer Communications*, *160*, 588–595. doi:10.1016/j.comcom.2020.04.025

Huo, Y., Tu, W., Sheng, Z., & Leung, C. M. (2015). A survey of in-vehicle communications: Requirements, solutions and opportunities in IoT. *IEEE Conf. 2nd World Forum on Internet of Things (WF-IoT)*, (pp.132–37). IEEE. 10.1109/WF-IoT.2015.7389040

IBM. (2015). *Redefining Boundaries: Insights from the Global C- suite Study*. IBM.

IBM. (2015). *Redefining Boundaries: Insights from the Global C Suite Study*. IBM.

Ilmudeen, A. (2021). Big data, artificial intelligence, and the internet of things in cross-border E-commerce. *Cross-border E-commerce marketing and management*, 257-272.

International Telecommunication Union. (2018). *ITU internet reports 2005: the Internet of Things*. ITU. https://www.itu.int/pub/S-POL-IR.IT-2005/e

Internet Of Things (IOT), Big Data, Business Intelligence, Data Science, Digital Transformation: Hype Or Reality? Facts And Figures. (n.d.). CIOCoverage. https://www.ciocoverage.com/internet-of-things-iot-big-data-business-intelligence-data-science-digital-transformation-hy pe-or-reality-facts-and-figures/

Irakli, A. & Marcin, D. (2016). Internet of things in marketing: Opportunities and security issues. *Management Systems in Production Engineering 4*(24). doi:10.12914/MSPE-01-04-2016

Išoraitė, M., & Miniotienė, N. (2018). *Electronic commerce: Theory and practice.* Integrated Journal of Business and Economics. doi:10.33019/ijbe.v2i2.78

Iwasaki, W., Morita, N., & Nagata, M. P. B. (2019). Iot sensors for smart livestock management. In Chemical, Gas, and Biosensors for Internet of Things and Related Applications (pp. 207-221). Elsevier. doi:10.1016/B978-0-12-815409-0.00015-2

Jain, A. K. (2022, December 13). Digital marketing tools that helping cos keep their promises to customers. *Bizz Buzz News.* https://www.bizzbuzz.news/markets/digital-marketing-tools-that-helping-cos-keep-their-promises-to-customers-1185244

Jain, A. (2010). 'Beaming it live': 24-hour television news, the spectator and the spectacle of the 2002 Gujarat carnage. *South Asian Popular Culture*, *8*(2), 163–179. doi:10.1080/14746681003797989

Jaipuriar, A., Khera, A., & Ganguly, S. (2020). *Consumer protection (e-commerce) rules, 2020: A compliance framework in the digital market.* https://www.mondaq.com/india/dodd-frank-consumer-protection-act/977768/consumer-protection-e-commerce-rules-2020-a-compl iance-framework-in-the-digital-market

Janiesch, C., Koschmider, A., Mecella, M., Weber, B., Burattin, A., Di Ciccio, C., & Zhang, L. (2020). The Internet of Things Meets Business Process Management: A Manifesto. *IEEE Systems, Man, and Cybernetics Magazine*, *6*(4), 34–44. doi:10.1109/MSMC.2020.3003135

Jara, A. J., Skarmeta, A. F., & Parra, M. C. (2013). Enabling participative marketing through the internet of things. *Proceedings - 27th International Conference on Advanced Information Networking and Applications Workshops, WAINA 2013*, 1301–1306. 10.1109/WAINA.2013.270

Javed, Y., Khan, A., Qahar, A., & Abdullah, J. (2017). Preventing DoS attacks in IoT using AES. *J. Telecommun. Electron.Comput. Eng. JTEC, 9*, 3–11.

Jenkins, S. (2008). *The truth about email marketing.* FT Press.

Jha, S. (2013). Need of research related to Indian ownership patterns in media. Mass Communicator. *International Journal of Communication Studies*, *7*(3), 28–32.

Joghee, S. (2021). Internet of Things-assisted E-marketing and distribution framework. *Soft Computing*, *25*(18), 12291–12303. doi:10.100700500-021-05920-0

Jones, M. O. (2022). *Digital authoritarianism in the Middle East: Deception, disinformation and social media.* Hurst Publishers.

Jordan, M. I., & Mitchell, T. M. (2015). Machine learning: Trends, perspectives, and prospects. *Science*, *349*(6245), 255–260. doi:10.1126cience.aaa8415 PMID:26185243

Južnik Rotar, L., Kontošić Pamić, R., & Bojnec, Š. (2019). Contributions of small and medium enterprises to employment in the European Union countries. *Ekonomska Istrazivanja*, *32*(1), 3296–3308.

Kajimoto, K., Davuluru, U., Matsukura, R., Hund, J., Kovatsch, M., & Nimura, K. (2017). *Web of Things (WoT) architecture*. W3C.

Kamal, S., Naim, A., Magd, H., Khan, S. A., & Khan, F. M. (2022). The Relationship Between E-Service Quality, Ease of Use, and E-CRM Performance Referred by Brand Image. In *Building a Brand Image Through Electronic Customer Relationship Management* (pp. 84–108). IGI Global. doi:10.4018/978-1-6684-5386-5.ch005

Kamal, Y. (2016). Study of trend in digital marketing and evolution of digital marketing strategies. *International Journal of Engineering Science*, *6*(5), 5300–5302.

Kanagaraj, E., Kamarudin, M., Zakaria, A., Gunasagaran, R., & Shakaff, A. (2015). Cloud-based Remote Environmental Monitoring System with Distributed WSN Weather Stations. *IEEE Sensors.*

Kang, C. (2016). Verizon Settles With F.C.C. Over Hidden Tracking via 'Supercookies'. *The New York Times.*

Kao, K.-C. Jeng, S., & Chieng, W. (2018) *Design and development of an IoT-based web application for an intelligent remote SCADA system.* Semantic Scholar.

Kauffmann, E., Peral, J., Gil, D., Ferrández, A., Sellers, R., & Mora, H. (2020). A framework for big data analytics in commercial social networks: A case study on sentiment analysis and fake review detection for marketing decision-making. *Industrial Marketing Management*, *90*, 523–537. doi:10.1016/j.indmarman.2019.08.003

Kaur, P., & Arora, S. (2015). Regression and Endogeneity Bias in Big Marketing Data. *Procedia Computer Science*, *70*, 41–47. doi:10.1016/j.procs.2015.10.025

Kerick, F. (2019). The growth of ecommerce. *Medium.* https://medium.com/swlh/the-growth-of-ecommerce-2220cf2851f3

Khan, S. A., & Magd, H. (2021). Empirical examination of ms teams in conducting webinar: Evidence from international online program conducted in oman. *Journal of Content, Community and Communication*, 159-175.

Khan, S. A., Magd, H., & Epoc, F. J. (2022). Application of Data Management System in Business-to-Business Electronic Commerce. *Competitive Trends and Technologies in Business Management*, 109-124.

Khan, S. A., Sharma, P.P., & Thoudam, P. (2019). Role of Attitude and Entrepreneurship Education towards Entrepreneurial Orientation among Business Students of Bhutan. *International Journal of Recent Technology and Engineering (IJRTE), 10*(10), 335-342.

Khan. S.A. & Magd. H. (2021). Empirical Examination of MS Teams in Conducting Webinar: Evidence from International Online Program conducted in Oman. *Journal of Content, Community and Communication, 14.* doi:10.31620/JCCC.12.21/13

Khan, D., & Shazia, W. (2019). Cyber security issues and challenges in E-commerce. *Proceedings of 10th international conference on digital strategies for organizational success.* 10.2139srn.3323741

Khandelwal, P. (2018). Ease of doing E-commerce business in India: The FDI policy relating to Ecommerce and its impact on the Indian economy. *RGNUL Financial and Mercantile Law Review*, 20–37. https://cf9d2836-9a17-4889-b084-bc78a1bb74ee.filesusr.com/ugd/0fa0b3_d7453802d99a4dd7a20ff4b3886b1d04.pdf

Khan, M. A., & Salah, K. (2018). IoT security: Review, blockchain solutions, and open challenges. *Future Generation Computer Systems*, *82*, 395–411. doi:10.1016/j.future.2017.11.022

Khan, N., Naim, A., Hussain, M. R., Naveed, Q. N., Ahmad, N., & Qamar, S. (2019). The 51 v's of big data: survey, technologies, characteristics, opportunities, issues and challenges. In *Proceedings of the international conference on omni-layer intelligent systems* (pp. 19-24). ACM. 10.1145/3312614.3312623

Khan, S. A. (2014). Comparison and Analysis of Leave System of Royal University Bhutan and Aligarh Muslim University with Respect to Improve the Leave Rules of Royal University of Bhutan. *Integral Review. Journal of Management*, *7*(1).

Khan, S. A., Devi, T. P., Ligori, T. A. A., & Saleem, M. (2020). Customer Satisfaction and Customer Loyalty in Online Shopping: A Study On University Students of Bhutan. *Delhi Business Review*, *21*(2), 11–22. doi:10.51768/dbr.v21i2.212202002

Khan, S. A., Devi, T. P., & Sharma, P. P. (2020). Vertical farming: Why it matters for Bhutan. *Stud. Indian Place Names*, *40*(1), 1323–1329.

Khan, S. A., Epoc, F., Al Shamsi, I. R., & Shamim, A. (2022). How Far Modern Vertical Farming is Appropriate for Developing Countries Like Oman?: A Review Based Analysis. *Delhi Business Review*, *23*(2), 9–15. doi:10.51768/dbr.v23i2.232202202

Khan, S. A., Epoc, F., Gangwar, V., Ligori, T. A. A., & Ansari, Z. A. (2021). Will Online Banking Sustain in Bhutan Post COVID-19? A Quantitative Analysis of The Customer E-Satisfaction and E-Loyalty in The Kingdom of Bhutan. *Transnational Marketing Journal*, *9*(3), 607–624. doi:10.33182/tmj.v9i3.1288

Khan, S. A., & Gurung, M. (2019). Green public procurement through lens of practicality and policies a study on royal university of Bhutan. *Delhi Business Review*, *20*(1), 23–32. doi:10.51768/dbr.v20i1.201201913

Khan, S. A., Magd, H., Al Shamsi, I. R., & Masoom, K. (2022b). Social Entrepreneurship Through Innovations in Agriculture. In *International Perspectives on Value Creation and Sustainability Through Social Entrepreneurship* (pp. 209–222). IGI Global. doi:10.4018/978-1-6684-4666-9.ch010

Khan, S. A., Magd, H., & Epoc, F. (2022a). Application of Data Management System in Business to Business Electronic Commerce. In A. Naim & P. K. Malik (Eds.), *Competitive Trends and Technologies in Business Management* (pp. 109–124).

Khan, S. A., Sharma, P. P., & Thoudam, P. (2019). Role of attitude and entrepreneurship education towards entrepreneurial orientation among business students of Bhutan. *International Journal of Recent Technology and Engineering*, *8*, 335–345.

Kharroubi, S., Naja, F., Diab-El-Harake, M., & Jomaa, L. (2021). Food insecurity pre-and post the COVID-19 pandemic and economic crisis in Lebanon: Prevalence and projections. *Nutrients*, *13*(9), 2976. doi:10.3390/nu13092976 PMID:34578854

Khatri, B., Arora, S., Magd, H., & Khan, S. A. K. (2022). Bibliometric Analysis of Social Entrepreneurship. In *International Perspectives on Value Creation and Sustainability Through Social Entrepreneurship* (pp. 46–60). IGI Global. doi:10.4018/978-1-6684-4666-9.ch003

Kietzmann, J. H., Hermkens, K., McCarthy, I. P., & Silvestre, B. S. (2011). Social media? Get serious! Understanding the functional building blocks of social media. *Business Horizons*, *54*(3), 241–251. doi:10.1016/j.bushor.2011.01.005

Kim, H. W., Gupta, S., & Koh, J. (2011). Investigating the intention to purchase digital items in social networking communities: A customer value perspective. *Information & Management*, *48*(6), 228–234. doi:10.1016/j.im.2011.05.004

Kiryakova, G, Yordanova, L., & Angelova. N. (2017). Can we make Schools and Universities smarter with the Internet of Things? *TEM Journal*, *6*.

Koirala, S. (2019). *SMEs: Key drivers of green and inclusive growth*. Academic Press.

Körling, M. (2012). Smart Products: Why Adding a Digital Side to a Toothbrush Could Make a Lot of Sense. *Ericsson Business Review*, *18*, 26–31.

Korling, M. (2012). *Smart Products: Why Adding a Digital Side to a Toothbrush Could Make a Lot of Sense*. Ericsson Business Review.

Kotabe, M. M., & Helsen, K. (2020). *Global marketing management*. John Wiley & Sons.

Kowatsch, T., Maass, W., Filler, A., & Janzen, S. (2008) Knowledge-Based Bundling of Smart Products on a Mobile Recommendation Agent. *Proceedings of the 7th International Conference on Mobile Business (ICMB 08)*. 10.1109/ICMB.2008.34

Kramp, T., Van Kranenburg, R., & Lange, S. (2013). Introduction to the Internet of Things. *Enabling things to talk: Designing IoT solutions with the IoT architectural reference model*, 1-10

Kumar, A. (2015). Ownership Patterns Affecting the Content of 24 x 7 News Channels in India: A Critical Analysis. *Amity Journal of Media & Communications Studies (AJMCS), 4.*

Kumar, S. & Vikash, P. (2021). *IoT for Automation Clustering to Detect Power losses with Efficiency of Energy Consumption and survey of defense machinery against attacks*. CRC Press. https://www.routledge.com/Applied-Soft-Computing-and-Embedded-System-Applications-in-Solar-Energy/Pachauri-Pandey-Sharmu-Nautiyal-Ram/p/book/9780367625122

Kumar, S. (2017). Security and Management in Network: Security of Network Management versus Management of Network Security (SNM Vs MNS). *International Journal of Computer Science and Network Security (IJCSNS), Volume 17*(5), 166-173. http://search.ijcsns.org/07_book/2017_05.htm

Kumar, S. (2019). An Intelligent Reallocation of Load for Cluster Cloud Environment. *International Journal of Innovative Technology and Exploring Engineering (IJITEE),* 8(8). https://www.ijitee.org/download/volume-8-issue-8/

Kumar, S. (2019). Texture-based Real-Time Character Extraction and Recognition in Natural Images. *International Journal of Innovative Technology and Exploring Engineering (IJITEE), 8*(8). https://www.ijitee.org/download/volume-8-issue-8/

Kumar, S., Sobti, R., Malik, P., Shrestha, S., Singh, P., & Ghafoor, K. (2022). IoT-Driven Model for Weather and Soil Conditions Based on Precision 2022. Hindawi. doi:10.1155/2022/7283975

Kumar, S., Tiwari, P., & Zymbler, M. (2019). Internet of things is a revolutionary approach for future technology enhancement: a review. *Journal of Big Data*, *6*(1).

Kumar, V. (2010). *Customer relationship management.* Wiley international encyclopedia of marketing.

Kumar, M., & Rodrigues, V. S. (2020). Synergetic effect of lean and green on innovation: A resource-based perspective. *International Journal of Production Economics*, *219*, 469–479. doi:10.1016/j.ijpe.2018.04.007

Kushwaha, B. P., Singh, R. K., Varghese, N., & Singh, V. N. (2020). Integrating social media and digital media as new elements of integrated marketing communication for creating brand equity. *Journal of Content. Community & Communication*, *11*(6), 52–64.

Kuzemko, C., Bradshaw, M., Bridge, G., Goldthau, A., Jewell, J., Overland, I., Scholten, D., Van de Graaf, T., & Westphal, K. (2020). Covid-19 and the politics of sustainable energy transitions. *Energy Research & Social Science*, *68*, 101685. doi:10.1016/j.erss.2020.101685 PMID:32839704

Lammenett, E. (2019). *Praxiswissen Online-Marketing: Affiliate-, Influencer-, Content-und E-Mail-Marketing, Google Ads, SEO, Social Media, Online-inklusive Facebook-Werbung*. Springer-Verlag. doi:10.1007/978-3-658-25135-2

Langan, R., Cowley, S., & Nguyen, C. (2019). The state of digital marketing in academia: An examination of marketing curriculum's response to digital disruption. *Journal of Marketing Education*, *41*(1), 32–46. doi:10.1177/0273475318823849

Langley, D. J., van Doorn, J., Ng, I. C. L., Stieglitz, S., Lazovik, A., & Boonstra, A. (2021). The Internet of Everything: Smart things and their impact on business models. *Journal of Business Research*, *122*, 853–863. doi:10.1016/j.jbusres.2019.12.035

Laudon, K. C., & Traver, C. G. (2013). *E-commerce*. Pearson.

Lavanya, A., & Radhikamani, M. (2021). Study on Digital Marketing and its Impact. *International Journal of Creative Research Thoughts, 9*. www.ijcrt.org

Lăzăroiu, G., Neguriţă, O., Grecu, I., Grecu, G., & Mitran, P. C. (2020). Consumers' decision-making process on social commerce platforms: Online trust, perceived risk, and purchase intentions. *Frontiers in Psychology*, *11*, 890. doi:10.3389/fpsyg.2020.00890 PMID:32499740

Le Cun, Y., Bengio, Y., & Hinton, G. (2015). Deep learning. *Nature*, *521*(7553), 436–444. doi:10.1038/nature14539 PMID:26017442

Lee, I., & Lee, K. (2015). The Internet of Things (IoT): Applications, investments, and challenges for enterprises. *Business Horizons*, *58*(4), 431–440. doi:10.1016/j.bushor.2015.03.008

Lee, O. M. K., & Turban, E. (2001). A trust model for consumer internet shopping. *International Journal of Electronic Commerce*, *6*(1), 75–91. doi:10.1080/10864415.2001.11044227

Leppäniemi, M., Sinisalo, J., & Karjaluoto, H. (2006). A review of mobile marketing research. *International Journal of Mobile Marketing*, *1*(1), 30–40.

Levine, R., Locke, C., Searle, D., & Weinberger, D. (2001). *The cluetrain manifesto: The end of business as usual.* Academic Press.

Levy, S. (2021). *In the plex: How Google thinks, works, and shapes our lives.* Simon & Schuster.

Li, S., Xu, L., & Wang, X. (2013). Compressed sensing signal and data acquisition in wireless sensor networks and internet of things. *IEEE Trans. Ind. Informat, 9*(4), 2177–86.

Ligori, T. A. A., Suresh, N., Khan, S. A., Rabgay, T., & Yezer, K. (2022). The mediating effect of university image on the relationship between curriculum and student satisfaction: An empirical study of the Royal University of Bhutan. *International Journal of Pluralism and Economics Education. Inderscience*, *13*(2), 192–208.

Li, K., Kim, D. J., Lang, K. R., Kauffman, R. J., & Naldi, M. (2020). How should we understand the digital economy in Asia? Critical assessment and research agenda. *Electronic Commerce Research and Applications*, *44*, 101004. doi:10.1016/j.elerap.2020.101004 PMID:32922241

Lin, P. (2022, October 7). *The Role of Big Data in AI-Powered Marketing*. Www.marketingaiinstitute.com. https://www.marketingaiinstitute.com/blog/big-data-ai-powered-marketing

Lindsey, R., & Dahlman, L. (2020). Climate change: Global temperature. *Climate. gov, 16*.

Lipnickas, A., Rutkauskas, R., & Cerkauskas, R. (2015). A resource oriented architecture for Web- integrated SCADA applications. *IEEE World Conference on Factory Communication Systems (WFCS)*. IEEE.

Li, S., & Chen, Y. (2022). How non-fungible tokens empower business model innovation. *Business Horizons*. Advance online publication. doi:10.1016/j.bushor.2022.10.006

Lister, M. (2018). 40 Essential Social Media Marketing Statistics for 2018. *Wordstream.* https://www.wordstream.com/blog/ws/2017/01/05/social-media-marketing-statistics

Liu, Y., Alzahrani, I. R., Jaleel, R. A., & Sulaie, S. A. (2023). An efficient smart data mining framework based cloud internet of things for developing artificial intelligence of marketing information analysis. *Information Processing & Management, 60*(1). doi:10.1016/j.ipm.2022.103121

Liu, C., Guo, Z., Feng, Y., Hong, F., & Jing, W. (2017, March). CPCA: The Cloud Platform of Complex Virtual Instruments System Architecture. *IEEE Access : Practical Innovations, Open Solutions, 5*, 4350–4360. doi:10.1109/ACCESS.2017.2682258

Liu, Y., Zhang, Y., Ren, S., Yang, M., Wang, Y., & Huisingh, D. (2020). How can smart technologies contribute to sustainable product lifecycle management? *Journal of Cleaner Production, 249*, 119423. doi:10.1016/j.jclepro.2019.119423

Liyang, H. (2019). Superior bargaining power: The good, the bad and the ugly. *Asia Pacific Law Review, 27*(1), 39–61. doi:10.1080/10192557.2019.1661589

Loannis, L., Despoina, M., Gracia, M. D., Amber, D., & Azza R. (2019). *The global governance of online consumer protection and E-commerce-building trust.* We Forum. https://www3.weforum.org/docs/WEF_consumer_protection.pdf

Loannis, L., Despoina, M., Gracia, M. D., Amber, D., & d'Azza R. (2019). *The global governance of online consumer protection and E-commerce-building trust.* WeForum. https://www3.weforum.org/docs/WEF_consumer_protection.pdf

Lo, F. Y., & Campos, N. (2018). Blending Internet-of-Things (IoT) solutions into relationship marketing strategies. *Technological Forecasting and Social Change, 137*, 10–18. doi:10.1016/j.techfore.2018.09.029

Lohachab, A., & Jangra, A. (2019). Opportunistic Internet of Things (IoT): Demystifying the Effective Possibilities of Opportunistic Networks Towards IoT. *2019 6th International Conference on Signal Processing and Integrated Networks, SPIN 2019*, 1100–1105. 10.1109/SPIN.2019.8711621

Ltifi, M., & Hichri, A. (2022). The effects of corporate governance on the customer's recommendations: A study of the banking sector at the time of COVID-19. *Journal of Knowledge Management, 26*(1), 165–191. doi:10.1108/JKM-06-2020-0471

Lustig, N., & Mariscal, J. (2020). 20 How COVID-19 could be like the Global Financial Crisis (or worse). *Mitigating the COVID economic crisis: Act fast and do whatever*, 185.

Lu, Y., Xu, X., & Wang, L. (2020). Smart manufacturing process and system automation–a critical review of the standards and envisioned scenarios. *Journal of Manufacturing Systems, 56*, 312–325. doi:10.1016/j.jmsy.2020.06.010

Mach, Ł. (2019). Measuring and assessing the impact of the global economic crisis on European real property market. *Journal of Business Economics and Management, 20*(6), 1189–1209. doi:10.3846/jbem.2019.11234

Macke, J., & Genari, D. (2019). Systematic literature review on sustainable human resource management. *Journal of Cleaner Production, 208*, 806–815. doi:10.1016/j.jclepro.2018.10.091

Magd, H., & Khan, S. A. (2022). Strategic Framework for Entrepreneurship Education in Promoting Social Entrepreneurship in GCC Countries During and Post COVID-19. In International Perspectives on Value Creation and Sustainability Through Social Entrepreneurship (pp. 61-75). IGI Global. doi:10.4018/978-1-6684-4666-9.ch004

Magd, H., & Khan, S. A. (2022). Strategic Framework for Entrepreneurship Education in Promoting Social Entrepreneurship in GCC Countries During and Post COVID-19. In Magd. H., Syed, R.T., Spicer, D. (Eds). International Perspectives on Value Creation and Sustainability Through Social Entrepreneurship (pp. 61-75). IGI Global.

Magd, H., & Khan, S. A. (2022a). Strategic Framework for Entrepreneurship Education in Promoting Social Entrepreneurship in GCC Countries During and Post COVID-19. In Magd. H., Syed, R.T., Spicer, D. (Eds). International Perspectives on Value Creation and Sustainability Through Social Entrepreneurship (pp. 61-75). IGI Global.

Magd, H., Jonathan, H., Khan, S. A., & El Geddawy, M. (2022). Artificial Intelligence—The Driving Force of Industry 4.0. A Roadmap for Enabling Industry 4.0 by Artificial Intelligence. Wiley.

Magd. H., & Khan. S.A. (2022b). Effectiveness of using online teaching platforms as communication tools in higher education institutions in Oman: Stakeholders perspectives. *Journal of Content, Community and Communication, 16.* doi:10.31620/JCCC.12.22/13

Magd, H., Jonathan, H., Khan, S. A., & El Geddawy, M. (2022). *Artificial Intelligence—The Driving Force of Industry 4.0. A Roadmap for Enabling Industry 4.0 by Artificial Intelligence.* Wiley.

Magd, H., Khan, S. A. K., & Bhuyan, U. (2022). Social Entrepreneurship Intentions Among Business Students in Oman. In *International Perspectives on Value Creation and Sustainability Through Social Entrepreneurship* (pp. 76–93). IGI Global. doi:10.4018/978-1-6684-4666-9.ch005

Magd, H., Nzomkunda, A., Negi, S., & Ansari, M. (2022). Critical Success Factors of E-Learning Implementation in Higher Education Institutions: A Proposed Framework for Success. *Global Business and Management Research,* 14.

Mahajan, K., Shukla, S., & Soni, N. (2015). A Review of Computerized Payroll System. *International Journal of Advanced Research in Computer and Communication Engineering, 4*(1), 67–70. doi:10.17148/IJARCCE.2015.4113

Mahender. (2022, December 19). Digital Marketing Trends 2023 by Dhananjay Yadav. *Newspatrolling.* https://newspatrolling.com/digital-marketing-trends-2023-by-dhananjay-yadav-seo-expert/

Majithia, V. (2019). The changing landscape of intermediary liability for E-commerce platforms : Emergence of a new regime. *International Journal of Law and Technology, 15,* 470–493.

Malhotra, N. K., Birks, D. F., & Wills, P. (2013). *Essentials of Marketing Research.* Pearson Education.

Malik, P. K., Naim, A., & Singh, R. (Eds.). (2022). *Printed Antennas: Design and Challenges.* CRC Press. doi:10.1201/9781003347057

Mangiaracina, R., & Perego, A. (2009). Payment systems in the B2C eCommerce: Are they a barrier for the online customer? *Journal of Internet Banking and Commerce, 14*(3), 1–16.

Mangold, G. W., & Faulds, D. J. (2009). Social Media: The New Hybrid Element of the Promotion Mix. *Business Horizons, 52*(4), 357–365. doi:10.1016/j.bushor.2009.03.002

Mansouri, S. A., Jordehi, A. R., Marzband, M., Tostado-Veliz, M., Jurado, F., & Aguado, J. A. (2023). An IoT-enabled hierarchical decentralized framework for multi-energy microgrids market management in the presence of smart prosumers using a deep learning-based forecaster. *Applied Energy, 333.* doi:10.1016/j.apenergy.2022.120560

Maritz, A., Perenyi, A., De Waal, G., & Buck, C. (2020). Entrepreneurship as the unsung hero during the current COVID-19 economic crisis: Australian perspectives. *Sustainability, 12*(11), 4612. doi:10.3390u12114612

Market Decipher. (2021). Sp*orts NFT Market Size, Statistics, Growth Trend Analysis and Forecast Report, 2022 - 2032.* https://www.marketdecipher.com/report/sports-nft-market

MarketResearch.com. (2022). *Global Sports Trading Card Market Size, Status and Forecast 2022-2028*. https://www.marketresearch.com/QYResearch-Group-v3531/Global-Sports-Trading-Card-Size-31719180/

Marolt, M., Zimmermann, H. D., Žnidaršič, A., & Pucihar, A. (2020). Exploring social customer relationship management adoption in micro, small and medium-sized enterprises. *Journal of Theoretical and Applied Electronic Commerce Research*, *15*(2), 38–58. doi:10.4067/S0718-18762020000200104

Marquardt, D. W., & Snee, R. D. (1975). Ridge regression in practice. *The American Statistician*, *29*(1), 3–20.

Marques, R., Rocha, J., Rafael, S., & Martins, J. (2008). Design and Implementation of a Reconfigurable Remote Laboratory, Using Oscilloscope or PLC Network for WWW Access. *IEEE Transactions on Industrial Electronics, 55*(6).

Mason, A. N., Narcum, J., & Mason, K. (2021). Social media marketing gains importance after Covid-19. *Cogent Business & Management*, *8*(1), 1870797. doi:10.1080/23311975.2020.1870797

Matta, H., Gupta, R., & Agarwal, S. (2020, June). Search Engine optimization in digital marketing: present scenario and future scope. In *2020 International Conference on Intelligent Engineering and Management (ICIEM)* (pp. 530-534). IEEE. 10.1109/ICIEM48762.2020.9160016

Mattila, M., Karjaluoto, H., & Pento, T. (2003). Internet banking adoption among mature customer: Early majority or laggards? *Journal of Services Marketing*, *17*(5), 514–528. doi:10.1108/08876040310486294

Ma, X. (2017). Influence research on the industrial transformation and upgrading based on internet plus strategy. *Journal of Computational and Theoretical Nanoscience*, *14*(9), 4384–4390. doi:10.1166/jctn.2017.6747

Mayer, P. (2010). *Economic Aspects of Smart Products* [White Paper]. Institute of Technology Management, University of St. Gallen, St. Gallen.

Mayer, P. (2010). *Economic Aspects of Smart Products.* White Paper, Institute of Technology Management, University of St. Gallen.

McElwee, T. (2016). Expert Advice for Securing The Internet of Things. *Treeline Interactive Blog*.

McEwen, A., & Cassimally, H. (2014). *Designing the Internet of Things*. Wiley.

McKinsey & Company. (2018). *The Internet of Things: How to capture the value of IoT.* Very Technology.

Mehralian, M. M. (2022). Effect of Internet of Things on Marketing Performance: The Mediating Role of Entrepreneurship Orientation. *SSRN Electronic Journal*. doi:10.2139/SSRN.4195987

Mehta, N. (2015). India and its television: Ownership, democracy, and the media business. *Emerging Economy Studies*, *1*(1), 50–63. doi:10.1177/2394901514562304

Meier, A., & Reinecke, L. (2021). Computer-mediated communication, social media, and mental health: A conceptual and empirical meta-review. *Communication Research*, *48*(8), 1182–1209. doi:10.1177/0093650220958224

Mekacher, A., Bracci, A., Nadini, M., Martino, M., Alessandretti, L., Aiello, L. M., & Baronchelli, A. (2022). Heterogeneous rarity patterns drive price dynamics in NFT collections. *Scientific Reports*, *12*(1), 1–9. doi:10.103841598-022-17922-5 PMID:34992227

Mendling, J., & Simon, C. (2006). Business Process Design by View Integration. In J. Eder & S. Dustdar (Eds.), Lecture Notes in Computer Science: Vol. 4103. *Business Process Management Workshops. BPM 2006*. Springer. doi:10.1007/11837862_7

Meyer, C., & Schwager, A. (2007). Understanding customer experience. *Harvard Business Review*, *85*(2), 116. PMID:17345685

Meyer, G. G., Buijs, P., Szirbik, N. B., & Wortmann, J. C. (2014). Intelligent Products for Enhancing the Utilization of Tracking Technology in Transportation. *International Journal of Operations & Production Management*, *34*, 422–446. doi:10.1108/IJOPM-11-2012-0530

Michael, M. G., Michael, K., & Perakslis, C. (2014). Uberveillance and the internet of things and people. *Faculty of Engineering and Information Sciences - Papers. Part A*, *1381*, 1381–1386. Advance online publication. doi:10.1109/IC3I.2014.7019829

Milan, J., Antonio, G., & Niklas, A. (2020). Exploring the growth challenge of mobile payment platforms: A business model perspective. *Electronic Commerce Research and Applications*, *40*, 100908. doi:10.1016/j.elerap.2019.100908

Minerva, R., Biru, A., & Rotondi, D. (2015). Towards a definition of the Internet of Things (IoT). *IEEE Internet Initiative*, *1*, 1–86.

Mittal, D., & Agrawal, S. R. (2022). Determining banking service attributes from online reviews: Text mining and sentiment analysis. *International Journal of Bank Marketing*, *40*(3), 558–577. doi:10.1108/IJBM-08-2021-0380

Miyazaki, A., & Fernandez, A. N. A. (2001). Consumer perceptions of privacy and security risks for online shopping. *The Journal of Consumer Affairs*, *35*(1), 27–44. doi:10.1111/j.1745-6606.2001.tb00101.x

Modha, D. S., Ananthanarayanan, R., Esser, S. K., Ndirango, A., Sherbondy, A. J., & Singh, R. (2015). Cognitive Computing. *Communications of the ACM*, *54*(8), 62–71. doi:10.1145/1978542.1978559

Mohan, R. (2009). Global financial crisis: Causes, impact, policy responses and lessons. *Reserve Bank of India Bulletin*, 879-904.

Mohanty, S., & Mishra, P. C. (2020). Framework for understanding Internet of Things in human resource management. *Revista ESPACIOS, 41*(12).

Monnappa, A. (2015, July 8). *The History and Evolution of Digital Marketing*. Simplilearn. https://www.simplilearn.com/history-and-evolution-of-digital-marketing-article

Moradi, M. (2021). Importance of Internet of Things (IoT) in Marketing Research and Its Ethical and Data Privacy Challenges. *Business Ethics and Leadership*, *5*(1), 22–30. doi:10.21272/bel.5(1).22-30.2021

Moradi, M., & Badrinarayanan, V. (2021). The effects of brand prominence and narrative features on crowdfunding success for entrepreneurial aftermarket enterprises. *Journal of Business Research*, *124*, 286–298. doi:10.1016/j.jbusres.2020.12.002

Motamedi, M. (2010). *Investigating the factors affecting the acceptance of the bank by the customers by using the models of technology acceptance and affiliated marketing*. [MSc Thesis, Shiraz University].

Mudgal, V. (2015). Framing the 2014 elections: The curious absence of development. *Television & New Media*, *16*(4), 354–360. doi:10.1177/1527476415575907

Mukherjee, T. (2015). Media Ownership Patterns and Its Impact on Media Content: Issues & Implications. *Amity Journal of Media & Communications Studies (AJMCS), 4*.

Müller, J., & Christandl, F. (2019). Content is king–But who is the king of kings? The effect of content marketing, sponsored content & user-generated content on brand responses. *Computers in Human Behavior*, *96*, 46–55. doi:10.1016/j.chb.2019.02.006

Murali, A. & Rao, M. (2020). *IoT: Security Issues and Challenges.* ICIDSSD, New Delhi, India. doi:10.4108/eai.27-2-2020.2303127

Nabih, K. (2019). *Digital Marketing: Search Engine Optimization and Search Engine Marketing in Germany and its possibilities for Reviews International* [Doctoral dissertation]. Universitas Gadjah Mada.

Naim, A. (2020). Realization of diverse Electronic tools in learning and teaching for students with diverse skills. *Global Journal of Enterprise Information System.*

Naim, A. (2022a). Applications of E-Learning Tools for Achieving Students Learning Outcomes for Business Programs. *Competitive Trends and Technologies in Business Management*, 125. https:// doi:10.52305/VIXO9830

Naim, A. (2022a). Benefits of Artificial Intelligence (AI) in Financial Practices. *International Journal of Studies in Business Management, Economics and Strategies, 1*, 1–12. https://scholarsdigest.org/index.php/bmes/article/view/7

Naim, A. (2022e). Measurement of Electronic Commerce Effectiveness. *Neo Science Peer Reviewed Journal, 1*, 1–10. https://neojournals.com/index.php/nsprj/article/view/6

Naim, A. (2022m). Public Enterprises: Their Role, Importance And Need In Economic Development. *American Journal of Business Management, Economics and Banking, 1*, 1–11. https://americanjournal.org/index.php/ajbmeb/article/view/7

Naim, A. (2022n) Role Of Accounting And Finance In Performance Appraisal. *American Journal of Sociology, Economics and Tourism,* 1-17 https://americanjournal.org/index.php/ajset/issue/view/4

Naim, A. (2022o). Islamic Philosophy Based Business Model. *American Journal of Research in Humanities and Social Sciences,* 1-5. https://americanjournal.org/index.php/ajrhss/issue/view/2

Naim, A. (2022q). Factors of Consumer Behaviour of youth from middle-east when purchasing Organic Food. *Global Scientific Review, 3*, 1–7. http://www.scienticreview.com/index.php/gsr/article/view/13

Naim, A. (2022w). Measurement of Electronic Commerce Effectiveness. *Neo Science Peer Reviewed Journal, 1*, 1–10. https://neojournals.com/index.php/nsprj/article/view/6

Naim, A. (2022y). Developing Business Models as per Islamic Practices. *International Journal of Studies in Business Management, Economics and Strategies, 2*(2), 15–22. https://scholarsdigest.org/index.php/bmes/article/view/25

Naim, A. (2022z). Empathetic Approach to Customer Orientation for Social CRM and ECRM. *International Journal of Studies in Business Management, Economics and Strategies, 2*(2), 1–14. https://scholarsdigest.org/index.php/bmes/article/view/24

Naim, A., & Alahmari, F. (2020). Reference model of e-learning and quality to establish interoperability in higher education systems. *International Journal of Emerging Technologies in learning.*

Naim, A., & Khan, M. F. (2021). Consumer Behavior for Health Services: A Psychological Approach. *Science Progress and Research 1*(4)

Naim, A., & Khan, M. F. (2021). Measuring the Psychological Behavior of Consumers for Medical Services. *Zien Journal of Social Sciences and Humanities, 2,* 119–131. https://zienjournals.com/index.php/zjssh/article/view/316

Naim, A., Alahmari, F., & Rahim, A. (2021). Role of Artificial Intelligence in Market Development and Vehicular Communication. *Smart Antennas: Recent Trends in Design and Applications.*

Naim, A., Khan, M. F., Hussain, M. R., & Khan, N. (2019). "Virtual Doctor" Management Technique in the Diagnosis of ENT Diseases. *JOE, 15*(9), 88. doi:10.3991/ijoe.v15i09.10665

Naim, A., Sattar, R. A., Al Ahmary, N., & Razwi, M. T. (2021) Implementation of Quality Matters Standards on Blended Courses: A Case Study. Indian Institute of Finance 35(3), 873 – 890.

Naim, A. (2020). Realization of diverse Electronic tools in learning and teaching for students with diverse skills. *Global Journal of Enterprise Information System*, *12*(1), 72–78.

Naim, A. (2021a). Green Information Technologies in Business Operations. Periodica Journal of Modern Philosophy. *Social Sciences and Humanities*, *1*, 36–49.

Naim, A. (2021b). Applications of MIS in building Electronic Relationship with customers: A case-based study. Periodica Journal of Modern Philosophy. *Social Sciences and Humanities*, *1*, 1–8.

Naim, A. (2021c). New Trends in Business Process Management: Applications of Green Information Technologies. *British Journal of Environmental Studies*, *1*(1), 12–23.

Naim, A. (2021d). Applications of Marketing Framework in Business Practices. *Journal of Marketing and Emerging Economics*, *1*(6), 55–70.

Naim, A. (2021e). Green Business Process Management. *International Journal of Innovative Analyses and Emerging Technology*, *1*(6), 125–134. https://openaccessjournals.eu/index.php/ijiaet/article/view/651

Naim, A. (2021f). Applications of E-Learning tools for Achieving Students Learning Outcomes. *Journal of Pedagogical Inventions and Practices*, *2*(2), 75–82. https://zienjournals.com/index.php/jpip/article/view/320

Naim, A. (2022c). Neuromarketing as a Tool for Measuring Consumer Emotions for Games. *International Journal of Scientific Trends*, *1*(1), 55–65. https://scientifictrends.org/index.php/ijst/article/view/6

Naim, A. (2022f). Mapping of Social Customer Relationship Management with Electronic Customer Relationship Management. *European Journal of Interdisciplinary Research and Development*, *2*, 14–25. https://ejird.journalspark.org/index.php/ejird/article/view/10

Naim, A. (2022g). Neuro- Marketing Techniques for Proposing Information Driven Framework for Decision Making. *International Journal of Innovative Analyses and Emerging Technology*, *2*(2), 87–94. https://openaccessjournals.eu/index.php/ijiaet/article/view/1060

Naim, A. (2022h). Economies of Scale for Antenna's Applications in Interior Regions. *International Journal of Innovative Analyses and Emerging Technology*, *2*(2), 77–82. https://openaccessjournals.eu/index.php/ijiaet/article/view/1058

Naim, A. (2022h). Understanding the Customer Centric Approach to Add Value to Social Ecrm (SECRM). *British Journal of Global Ecology and Sustainable Development*, *4*, 1–17. https://journalzone.org/index.php/bjgesd/article/view/45

Naim, A. (2022i). Mapping of Social Customer Relationship Management With Electronic Customer Relationship Management. *European Journal of Interdisciplinary Research and Development*, *2*, 14–25. https://ejird.journalspark.org/index.php/ejird/article/view/10

Naim, A. (2022j). E-Learning Engagement through Convolution Neural Networks in Business Education. *European Journal of Innovation in Nonformal Education*, *2*(2), 497–501.

Naim, A. (2022k). Measurement Consumer Mood and Emotions for Fast Moving Consumer Goods. *International Journal of Innovative Analyses and Emerging Technology*, *2*(2), 83–86.

Naim, A. (2022p). Mapping Of Social Customer Relationship Management With Electronic Customer Relationship Management. *European Journal of Interdisciplinary Research and Development*, *2*, 14–25. https://ejird.journalspark.org/index.php/ejird/article/view/10

Naim, A. (2022r). Understanding The Customer Centric Approach To Add Value To Social Ecrm (Secrm). *British Journal of Global Ecology and Sustainable Development*, *4*, 1–17. https://journalzone.org/index.php/bjgesd/article/view/45

Naim, A. (2022s). Cost Trend: Meaning and Importance of Cost Trend In Public Enterprises. *American Journal of Technology and Applied Sciences*, *1*, 37–46. https://americanjournal.org/index.php/ajtas/article/view/11

Naim, A. (2022t). Role of Artificial Intelligence In Business Risk Management. American Journal of Business Management. *Economics and Banking*, *1*, 55–66.

Naim, A. (2022u). Relevance of Online Learning In Higher Education. *American Journal of Pedagogical and Educational Research*, *1*, 21–34.

Naim, A. (2022v). Factors of Consumer Behaviour of youth from middle-east when purchasing Organic Food. *Global Scientific Review*, *3*, 1–7.

Naim, A. (2022x). Consumer Behavior for The Consumption and Buying Of Medical Services. *Intent Research Scientific Journal*, *1*(1), 46–64.

Naim, A., & Alahmari, F. (2020). Reference model of e-learning and quality to establish interoperability in higher education systems. *International Journal of Emerging Technologies in Learning*, *15*(2), 15–28. doi:10.3991/ijet.v15i02.11605

Naim, A., Alahmari, F., & Rahim, A. (2021). Role of Artificial Intelligence in Market Development and Vehicular Communication. Smart Antennas. *Recent Trends in Design and Applications*, *2*, 28–39. doi:10.2174/9781681088594121020006

Naim, A., Alqahtani, H., Muniasamy, A., Bilfaqih, S. M., Mahveen, R., & Mahjabeen, R. (2023). Applications of Information Systems and Data Security in Marketing Management. In A. Naim, P. Malik, & F. Zaidi (Eds.), *Fraud Prevention, Confidentiality, and Data Security for Modern Businesses* (pp. 57–83). IGI Global. doi:10.4018/978-1-6684-6581-3.ch003

Naim, A., & Alqahtani, K. (2021). Role of Information Systems in Customer Relationship Management. *Pulse*, *2*(2).

Naim, A., & Bashir, A. (2016). *Application of Quality Matters Standards on Supportive and Online Module in Higher Education Program*. Research Revolution.

Naim, A., Hussain, M. R., Naveed, Q. N., Ahmad, N., Qamar, S., Khan, N., & Hweij, T. A. (2019, April). Ensuring interoperability of e-learning and quality development in education. In *2019 IEEE Jordan International Joint Conference on Electrical Engineering and Information Technology (JEEIT)* (pp. 736-741). IEEE. 10.1109/JEEIT.2019.8717431

Naim, A., & Kautish, S. K. (Eds.). (2022). *Building a Brand Image Through Electronic Customer Relationship Management*. IGI Global. doi:10.4018/978-1-6684-5386-5

Naim, A., Malik, P. K., & Zaidi, F. A. (Eds.). (2023). *Fraud Prevention, Confidentiality, and Data Security for Modern Businesses*. IGI Global. doi:10.4018/978-1-6684-6581-3

Naim, A., Muniasamy, A., Clementking, A., & Rajkumar, R. (2022). Relevance of Green Manufacturing and IoT in Industrial Transformation and Marketing Management. In M. Lahby, A. Al-Fuqaha, & Y. Maleh (Eds.), *Computational Intelligence Techniques for Green Smart Cities. Green Energy and Technology*. Springer. doi:10.1007/978-3-030-96429-0_19

Najar, M., Misbah, M., Yaqub, H., & Bilfagih, M. (2022). Entrepreneurial Marketing of E-CRM in SMEs. In A. Naim & S. Kautish (Eds.), *Building a Brand Image Through Electronic Customer Relationship Management* (pp. 265–285). IGI Global. doi:10.4018/978-1-6684-5386-5.ch011

Naradda Gamage, S. K., Ekanayake, E. M. S., Abeyrathne, G. A. K. N. J., Prasanna, R. P. I. R., Jayasundara, J. M. S. B., & Rajapakshe, P. S. K. (2020). A review of global challenges and survival strategies of small and medium enterprises (SMEs). *Economies*, *8*(4), 79. doi:10.3390/economies8040079

NBA.com. (2021). *Top Moments: Michael Jordan hits 'The Shot', breaks Cavs' hearts.* https://www.nba.com/news/history-top-moments-jordan-shot-cavaliers-1989

Neuhaus, T. (2021). A nudge psychology perspective on digital marketing and communication: learning from the Nigerian scam. In *Innovative Perspectives on Corporate Communication in the Global World* (pp. 122–140). IGI Global. doi:10.4018/978-1-7998-6799-9.ch007

Newman, D. (2017). The Top 8 IoT Trends For 2018. *Forbes*. https://www.forbes.com/sites/danielnewman/2017/12/19/the-top-8-iot-trends-for-2018/#1e35e7f467f7

Newswire, P. R. (2022). *$1.3 billion sports NFT market doubles in 2022.* https://www.prnewswire.com/in/news-releases/-1-3-billion-sports-nft-market-doubles-in-2022-a-100-growth-10-years-cagr-36-3-says-market-decipher-850146589.html

Ng, I. C. L., & Wakenshaw, S. Y. L. (2017). The Internet-of-Things: Review and research directions. *International Journal of Research in Marketing*, *34*(1), 3–21. doi:10.1016/j.ijresmar.2016.11.003

Nguyen, B., & Simkin, L. (2017). *The Internet of Things (IoT) and marketing: the state of play, future trends and the implications for marketing.* Taylor and Francis. doi:10.1080/0267257X.2016.1257542

Nguyen, B., & Mutum, D. S. (2012). A review of customer relationship management: Successes, advances, pitfalls and futures. *Business Process Management Journal*, *18*(3), 400–419. doi:10.1108/14637151211232614

NI Business info. (2019, August 5). *Advantages and disadvantages of digital marketing.* NI Business. https://www.nibusinessinfo.co.uk/content/advantages-and-disadvantages-digital-marketing

Novak, T. P., & Hoffman, D. L. (2019). Relationship journeys in the internet of things: A new framework for understanding interactions between consumers and smart objects. *Journal of the Academy of Marketing Science*, *47*(2), 216–237. doi:10.100711747-018-0608-3

Nowak, M. (2021, August 4). *The Internet of Things Helps Businesses across Industries.* Nomtek. https://www.nomtek.com/blog/how-iot-helps-business

Oestreicher-Singer, G., & Zalmanson, L. (2013). Content or community? A digital business strategy for content providers in the social age. *Management Information Systems Quarterly*, *37*(2), 591–616. doi:10.25300/MISQ/2013/37.2.12

Olenski, S. (2015). How the Internet of Things Will Transform HighTech Marketing. Forbes. *Forbes Magazine.*

Oliana, R. G. (2016). The Internet of Things: The next big thing for new product development? *J. Mark. Trends*, *5*, 159–176.

Oliveira, L. M. L., Reis, J., Rodrigues, J. J. P. C., & de Sousa, A. F. (2015). *IoT based solution for home power energy monitoring and actuating.* 13th Int. Conf. Industrial Informatics (INDIN. IEEE. 10.1109/INDIN.2015.7281869

Orendorff, A. (2019). *Global ecommerce statistics and trends to launch your business beyond borders.* Shopify. https://www.shopify.com/enterprise/global-ecommerce-statistics#8

Orme, D. (2019). Can biometrics secure the Internet of Things? *Biometric Technology Today*, *5*(5), 5–7. doi:10.1016/S0969-4765(19)30068-2

Osivand, S. (2021). Smart collectibles; use case of NFT tokens. *Open Access Research Journal of Engineering and Technology*, *1*(2), 24–31. doi:10.53022/oarjet.2021.1.2.0113

Pak, K., Kooij, D. T., De Lange, A. H., & Van Veldhoven, M. J. (2019). Human Resource Management and the ability, motivation and opportunity to continue working: A review of quantitative studies. *Human Resource Management Review*, *29*(3), 336–352. doi:10.1016/j.hrmr.2018.07.002

Pamintuan, S. (2022, May 30). The future of digital marketing isn't what you think: 5 trends. *The Drum.* https://www.thedrum.com/opinion/2022/05/30/the-future-digital-marketing-isnt-what-you-think-5-trends

Panchal, A., Shah, A., & Kansara, K. (2021). Digital marketing-search engine optimization (SEO) and search engine marketing (SEM). *International Research Journal of Innovations in Engineering and Technology*, *5*(12), 17.

Panchiwala, S., & Shah, M. (2020). A comprehensive study on critical security issues and challenges of the IoT world. *Journal of Digital Information Management*, *2*(4), 257–278.

Paris Agreement. (2015, December). Paris agreement. In *Report of the Conference of the Parties to the United Nations Framework Convention on Climate Change (21st Session, 2015: Paris).* HeinOnline.

Parry, G. C., Brax, S. A., Maull, R. S., & Ng, I. C. L. (2016). Operationalising IoT for reverse supply: The development of use-visibility measures. *Supply Chain Management*, *21*(2), 228–244. doi:10.1108/SCM-10-2015-0386

Parthasarathi, V., & Srinivas, A. (2019). Problematic ownership patterns: The evolution of the television distribution networks in India. *Economic and Political Weekly*, *54*(12).

Patel, M., Shangkuan, J., & Thomas, C. (2018). *The Internet of Things: How to capture the value of IoT.* McKinsey.

Patel, P. (2019, June 4). *Importance Of Digital Marketing In Today's Stage Of Affairs.* YourStory.com. https://yourstory.com/mystory/importance-of-digital-marketing-in-todays-stage-of

Patidar, S., Rane, D., & Jain, P. (2022). *A Survey Paper on Cloud Computing*, 394-398.

Pauget, B., & Dammak, A. (2019). The Implementation of the Internet of Things: What Impact on Organizations? *Technological Forecasting and Social Change*, *140*, 140–146. doi:10.1016/j.techfore.2018.03.012

Pavlov, O. V., Melville, N., & Plice, R. K. (2008). Toward a sustainable email marketing infrastructure. *Journal of Business Research*, *61*(11), 1191–1199. doi:10.1016/j.jbusres.2007.11.010

Peng, W., & Zhou, Y. (2015). The Design and Research of Responsive Web Supporting Mobile Learning Devices. IEEE Conf. Educational Technology (ISET). IEEE. 10.1109/ISET.2015.40

Perera, C., Ranjan, R., & Wang, L. (2015). *Privacy of Big Data in the Internet of Things Era.* http://arxiv.org/ftp/arxiv papers/1412/1412.8339.pdf

Perera, C., Liu, C. H., & Jayawardena, S. (2015). The Emerging Internet of Things Marketplace from an Industrial Perspective: A Survey. *IEEE Transactions on Emerging Topics in Computing*, *3*(4), 585–598. doi:10.1109/TETC.2015.2390034

Pimonenko, T., Liuliov, O., & Us, Y. (2019). Marketing strategies of green investments: Basic concepts and specific features. *Herald of Economics*, (1 (91)), 177–185.

Pine, B. J., & Gilmore, J. H. (2020). *The experience economy: Competing for customer time, attention, and money.* Harvard Business Review Press.

Piper, L. (2010). *The industrial transformation of subarctic Canada.* UBC Press.

Ploder, C., Bernsteiner, R., Dilger, T., & Huber, S. (2021). *Customer Relationship Management Improvement using IoT Data.* Academic Press.

Pogue, D. (November 30, 2011). A Thermostat That's Clever, Not Clunky. *New York Times.*

Porter, M. E., & Heppelmann, J. E. (2014). How smart, connected products are transforming competition. *Harvard Business Review*, *92*, 64–88.

Porter, M. E., & Heppelmann, J. E. (2014). How Smart, Connected Products Are Transforming Competition. *Harvard Business Review.*

Porter, M. E., & Heppelmann, J. E. (2015). How smart, connected products are transforming companies. In *Harvard Business Review* (Vol. 2015, pp. 96–114). https://hbr.org/2015/10/how-smart-connected-products-are-transforming-companies

Prabhakar, S. (2017). Network security in digitalization: Attacks and defence. *International Journal of Research in Computer Applications and Robotics*, *5*(5), 46–52.

Pradina, Y. D., & Poeradisastra, T. (2019). The implementation of affiliate marketing on marketing communication strategy of travel tour agencies to build awareness in Jakarta. *American Journal of Humanities and Social Sciences Research*, *3*(3), 94–103.

Prideaux, B., Thompson, M., & Pabel, A. (2020). Lessons from COVID-19 can prepare global tourism for the economic transformation needed to combat climate change. *Tourism Geographies*, *22*(3), 667–678. doi:10.1080/14616688.2020.1762117

Pritchard, A. (1969). Statistical bibliography or bibliometrics. *The Journal of Documentation*, *25*(4), 348–349.

Pulizzi, J. (2012). *Content Marketing Definition.* Content Marketing Institute.

PWC. (2022). *NFTs: The future of digital assets in sports.* https://www.pwc.com/us/en/tech-effect/emerging-tech/nfts-the-future-of-digital-assets-in-sports.html

Python Machine Learning (2020). A Guide To Getting Started. *Built In.*

Radunovic, P., Vujicic, T., & Balota, A. (2017). Web application for lightning activity monitoring system (LAMS). IEEE Conf. Information System and Techologies (CISTI). IEEE. 10.23919/CISTI.2017.7975856

Rahman, A. & Taufiq, A. (2019). The emergence of Internet of Things (IoT): Connecting anything, anywhere. *Computers 8*(2), 40.

Rajanarthagi. (2020). *What is IoT? & Role of IoT in digital marketing.* GEC Designs. https://gecdesigns.com/blog/role-of-iot-in-digital-marketing

Rani, D. (2013). Privatisation, convergence and broadcast regulations: A Case study of the Indian Television Industry. In *The Asian Conference on Media and Mass Communication 2013-Official Conference Proceedings* (pp. 387-396). The International Academic Forum 2013 (IAFOR).

Rao, S. (2009). Glocalization of Indian journalism. *Journalism Studies, 10*(4), 474-488.

Rao, S., & Johal, N. S. (2006). Ethics and news making in the changing Indian mediascape. *Journal of Mass Media Ethics*, *21*(4), 286–303. doi:10.120715327728jmme2104_5

Rao, S., & Malik, K. K. (2019). Conversing Ethics in India's News Media: A capabilities approach to journalism ethics education and training. *Journalism Practice*, *13*(4), 509–523. doi:10.1080/17512786.2018.1491321

Ratna, R., & Chawla, S. (2012). Key factors of retention and retention strategies in telecom sector. *Global Management Review, 6*(3).

Ratna, R., & Kaur, T. (2016). The impact of information technology on job related factors like health and safety, job satisfaction, performance, productivity and work life balance. *Journal of Business & Financial Affairs*, *5*(1), 2–9.

Ray, P. P. (2018). A survey on Internet of Things architectures. *Journal of King Saud University-Computer and Information Sciences*, *30*(3), 291–319. doi:10.1016/j.jksuci.2016.10.003

Reid, A. (2019). Climate change education and research: Possibilities and potentials versus problems and perils? *Environmental Education Research*, *25*(6), 767–790. doi:10.1080/13504622.2019.1664075

Rena, R. (2010). The Impact of Global Economic Crisis on the Namibian Economy: Issues and Challenges. [RBTR]. *Review of Business & Technology Research*, *3*(1), 475.

Rena, R., & Msoni, M. (2014). Global financial crises and its impact on the South African economy: A further update. *Journal of Economics*, *5*(1), 17–25. doi:10.1080/09765239.2014.11884980

Resatsch, F. (2010). *Ubiquitous Computing: Developing and Evaluating Near Field Communication Applications*. Springer. doi:10.1007/978-3-8349-8683-2

Rizvi, M. (2017). *Implications of internet of things (IoT) for CRM*. Academic Press.

Roberts, B. W. (2009). The macroeconomic impacts of the 9/11 attack: Evidence from real-time forecasting. *Peace Economics, Peace. Science & Public Policy*, *15*(2), 341–367.

Robson, K., Pitt, L. F., & Kietzmann, J. (2016) APC Forum: Extending Business Values through Wearables. *MIS Quarterly Executive*.

Rocker, C. (2013). Intelligent Environments as a Promising Solution for Addressing Current Demographic Changes. *International Journal of Innovation, Management and Technology*, *4*, 76–79. doi:10.1509/jmkg.2005.69.4.155

Rodrigues, D., & Martinez, L. F. (2020). The influence of digital marketing on recruitment effectiveness: a qualitative study. *European Journal of Management Studies*.

Roscoe, S., Subramanian, N., Jabbour, C. J., & Chong, T. (2019). Green human resource management and the enablers of green organisational culture: Enhancing a firm's environmental performance for sustainable development. *Business Strategy and the Environment*, *28*(5), 737–749. doi:10.1002/bse.2277

Roy, A. (2015). *ICTs as enablers of public participation for the hearing impaired: A case for television news closed captioning in India* [Doctoral dissertation]. University of Florida.

Ruangkanjanases, A., & Wutthisith, M. (2018). Predicting intention to purchase digital stickers in an application for instant communications on mobile devices: A comparative study. *Journal of Telecommunication, Electronic and Computer Engineering, 10*(1-10), 75-80.

Ruby, D. (2022). *33+ NFT Statistics 2022* [Facts, Trends & Data]. https://www.demandsage.com/nft-statistics/

Saleem, M., Khan, S. A., & Magd, H. (2022). Content Marketing Framework for Building Brand Image: A Case Study of Sohar International School, Oman. In Building a Brand Image Through Electronic Customer Relationship Management (pp. 64-83). IGI Global.

Saleem, M., Khan, S. A., & Magd, H. (2022). Content Marketing Framework for Building Brand Image: A Case Study of Sohar International School, Oman. In A. Naim & S. Kautish (Eds.), *Building a Brand Image Through Electronic Customer Relationship Management* (pp. 64–83). IGI Global. doi:10.4018/978-1-6684-5386-5.ch004

Salmiah, S., Fajrillah, F., Sudirman, A., Siregar, M. N. H., Simarmata, J., Suleman, A. R., & Jamaludin, J. (2020). *Online Marketing*. Yayasan Kita Menulis.

Sanson, A. V., Van Hoorn, J., & Burke, S. E. (2019). Responding to the impacts of the climate crisis on children and youth. *Child Development Perspectives*, *13*(4), 201–207. doi:10.1111/cdep.12342

Sarstedt, M., & Mooi, E. (2014). *A concise guide to market research: The process, data, and methods using IBM SPSS statistics* (2nd ed.). Springer-Verlag. doi:10.1007/978-3-642-53965-7

Saunders, M., Lewis, P., & Thornhill, A. (2007). *Research methods for business students* (4th ed.). FT Prentice Hall.

Sawicki, A. (2016). Digital marketing. *World Scientific News*, (48), 82–88.

Sayed, A., Himeur, Y., Bensaali, F., & Amira, A. (2022). Artificial intelligence with IoT for energy efficiency in buildings. In *Emerging Real-World Applications of Internet of Things* (pp. 233–252). CRC Press. doi:10.1201/9781003304203-12

Scellato, S., Musolesi, M., Mascolo, C., Latora, V., & Campbell, A. T. (2011). NextPlace: A spatio-temporal prediction framework for pervasive systems. Lecture Notes in Computer Science, 6696, 152–169. doi:10.1007/978-3-642-21726-5_10

Schau, H. J., & Gilly, M. C. (2003). We are what we post? Self-presentation in personal web space. *The Journal of Consumer Research*, *30*(3), 385–404. doi:10.1086/378616

Schmidt, M., & Banusch, B. (2022). *How do non-fungible tokens create tangible value in the metaverse?* https://www.ey.com/en_ch/technology/how-do-non-fungible-tokens-create-tangible-value-in-the-metaverse

Schmitt, B. (1999). *Experiential marketing: How to get customers to sense, feel, think, act, relate to your company and brands*. Free Press.

Schoder, D. (2018). Introduction to the Internet of Things. *Internet of things A to Z: technologies and applications*, 1-50.

Seegebarth, B., Peyer, M., Balderjahn, I., & Wiedmann, K. P. (2016). The sustainability roots of anticonsumption lifestyles and initial insights regarding their effects on consumers' well-being. *The Journal of Consumer Affairs*, *50*(1), 68–99. doi:10.1111/joca.12077

Sestino, A., Prete, M. I., Piper, L., & Guido, G. (2020). Internet of Things and Big Data as enablers for business digitalization strategies. *Technovation*, *98*, 102173. doi:10.1016/j.technovation.2020.102173

Shabber, S. M., Bansal, M., Devi, P. M., & Jain, P. (2021, December). iHAS: An Intelligent Home Automation Based System for Smart City. In *2021 IEEE International Symposium on Smart Electronic Systems (iSES)(Formerly iNiS)* (pp. 48-52). IEEE. 10.1109/iSES52644.2021.00023

Shah, H. (2022, August 4). *How IoT and AI are giving a boost to digital marketing*. Afaqs! Marketplace; marketplace blog. https://marketplace.afaqs.com/blog/digital-marketing/how-iot-and-ai-are-giving-a-boost-to-digital-marketing

Shaltoni, A. M. (2016). E-marketing education in transition: An analysis of international courses and programs. *International Journal of Management Education, 14*(2), 212–218. doi:10.1016/j.ijme.2016.04.004

Shameer, S. M. (2015). Media Economics Study Prominence and Relevance in India. *Social Networking, 4*(04), 112–118. doi:10.4236n.2015.44013

Shamshad, M., Sarim, M., Akhtar, A., & Tabash, M. I. (2018). Identifying critical success factors for sustainable growth of Indian banking sector using interpretive structural modeling (ISM). *International Journal of Social Economics, 45*(8), 1189–1204. doi:10.1108/IJSE-10-2017-0436

Shankar, V., & Balasubramanian, S. (2009). Mobile marketing: A synthesis and prognosis. *Journal of Interactive Marketing, 23*(2), 118–129. doi:10.1016/j.intmar.2009.02.002

Sharma, G., & Kalra, S. (2018). A lightweight multi-factor secure smart card based remote user authentication scheme for cloud-IoT applications. *Journal of Information Security and Applications, 42*, 95–106. doi:10.1016/j.jisa.2018.08.003

Sharma, G., & Kalra, S. (2018). Identity based secure authentication scheme based on quantum key distribution for cloud computing. *Peer-to-Peer Networking and Applications, 11*(2), 220–234. doi:10.100712083-016-0528-2

Sharma, N., Shamkuwar, M., & Singh, I. (2019). The history, present and future with IoT. In *Internet of Things and Big Data Analytics for Smart Generation* (pp. 27–51). Springer. doi:10.1007/978-3-030-04203-5_3

Shen, B., Tan, W., Guo, J., Zhao, L., & Qin, P. (2021). How to promote user purchase in metaverse? A systematic literature review on consumer behavior research and virtual commerce application design. *Applied Sciences (Basel, Switzerland), 11*(23), 1–29. doi:10.3390/app112311087

Sherman. (2018, September 13). *Digital Marketing Blog*. Digital Marketing Blog. https://www.lyfemarketing.com/blog/benefits-digital-marketing/

Sheth, J. N., Newman, B. I., & Gross, B. L. (1991). Why we buy what we buy: A theory of consumption values. *Journal of Business Research, 22*(2), 159–170. doi:10.1016/0148-2963(91)90050-8

Shirazi, F., Adam, N. A., Shanmugam, M., & Schultz, C. D. (2020). The importance of trust for electronic commerce satisfaction: An entrepreneurial perspective. *British Food Journal, 123*(2), 789–802. doi:10.1108/BFJ-07-2020-0626

Shi, S., Sun, J., & Cheng, T. C. E. (2020). Wholesale or drop-shipping: Contract choices of the online retailer and the manufacturer in a dual-channel supply chain. *International Journal of Production Economics, 226*, 107618. doi:10.1016/j.ijpe.2020.107618

Shittu, O. (2020). Emerging sustainability concerns and policy implications of urban household consumption: A systematic literature review. *Journal of Cleaner Production, 246*, 119034. doi:10.1016/j.jclepro.2019.119034

Shi, X., Li, F., & Chumnumpan, P. (2020). The use of product scarcity in marketing. *European Journal of Marketing, 54*(2), 380–418. doi:10.1108/EJM-04-2018-0285

Siciliani, P., Riefa, C., & Gamper, H. (2019). *Consumer theories of harm: An economic approach to consumer law enforcement and policy making*. Hart Publishing. doi:10.5040/9781509916887

Simmhan, Y., & Perera, S. (2016). Big data analytics platforms for real-time applications in IoT. In *Big data analytics* (pp. 115–135). Springer.

Simões, D., Filipe, S., & Barbosa, B. (2019). An Overview on IoT and Its Impact on Marketing. *Smart Marketing With the Internet of Things*, 1-20. doi:10.4018/978-1-5225-5763-0.ch001

Simplilearn. (2021, June 29). *8 Benefits of Digital Marketing: All You Should Know*. Simplilearn. https://www.simplilearn.com/digital-marketing-benefits-article

Singh, A. K. (2017). PERSONA OF SOCIAL NETWORKING IN COMPUTING AND INFORMATICS ERA. *International Journal of Computer Science and Network Security (IJCSNS), 17*(4), 95-101. http://search.ijcsns.org/07_book/2017_04.h

Singh, A. K. (2017). The Active Impact Of Human Computer Interaction (Hci) On Economic, Cultural And Social Life. *IIOAB Journal, 8*(2), 141-146. https://www.iioab.org/vol8n2

Singh, A. K. (2019). A Wireless Networks Flexible Adoptive Modulation and Coding Technique in advanced 4G LTE. *International Journal of Information Technology, 11*(1), 55-66 . https://link.springer.com/article/10.1007/s41870-018-0173-5 doi:10.1007/s41870-018-0173-5

Singh, A. K. (2020). Digital Era in the Kingdom of Saudi Arabia: Novel Strategies of the Telecom Service Providers Companies. *Webology, 17*(1). , http://www.webology.org/issue.php?volume=1&issue=1&page=2 doi:10.14704/WEB/V17I1/a219

Singh, A. K. (2021). Machine Learning in OpenFlow Network: Comparative Analysis of DDoS Detection Techniques. *The International Arab Journal of Information Technology, 18*(2), 221-226. https://iajit.org/PDF/Vol%2018,%20No.%202/19667.pdf doi:10.34028/iajit/18/2/11

Singh, D. K., Sobti, R., Jain, A., & Malik, P. K. (2022). LeD. (2022). N.: LoRa based intelligent soil and Irrigation Using Machine Learning", Security and Communication Networks, vol. weather condition monitoring with internet of things for precision agriculture in smart cities. *IET Communications, 16*, 604–618. doi:10.1049/cmu2.12352

Singh, E. H., Wangda, S., Khan, S., & Khan, S. A. (2020). Exploring the Obstacles for Start-ups in Bhutan: From a Prevented Entrepreneur Perspective. *International Journal of Innovation. Creativity and Change., 11*(04), 70–87.

Singh, E. H., Wangda, S., Khan, S., & Khan, S. A. (2020). Exploring the obstacles for start-ups in Bhutan: From a prevented entrepreneurs perspective. *International Journal of Innovation. Creativity and Change, 11*(4), 70–87.

Singh, J. (2015). Trends in Primetime News: Study of Selected News Channels in India. Journal of Content. *Community & Communication, 1*(1), 14–29.

Singh, R. P., & Chauhan, A. (2020). Impact of lockdown on air quality in India during COVID-19 pandemic. *Air Quality, Atmosphere & Health, 13*(8), 921–928. doi:10.100711869-020-00863-1 PMID:32837613

Siow, E., Tiropanis, T., & Hall, W. (2018). Analytics for the Internet of Things. *ACM Computing Surveys.*

Siripraphanukul, P., & Wasi, N. (2009). Fighting Unemployment during Recessions: A Review of Fiscal Policies in Theory and Practice. *TDRI Quarterly Review, 24*(4), 14–24.

Somasundaram, K., & Selvam, K. (2018). Iot - attacks and challenges. *International Journal of Engineering and Technical, Research, 8*(9), 9–12.

Song, B. L. (2022). The Role of E-CRM in Building Customer Satisfaction and Repurchase Intention: Evidence From the FMCG Industry. In A. Naim & S. Kautish (Eds.), *Building a Brand Image Through Electronic Customer Relationship Management* (pp. 19–43). IGI Global. doi:10.4018/978-1-6684-5386-5.ch002

Song, R., Wang, Y., Cui, W., Vanthienen, J., & Huang, L. (2018). Towards improving context interpretation in the iot paradigm: a solution to integrate context information in process models. In *Proceedings 2nd International Conference on Management Engineering, Software Engineering and Service Sciences* (pp. 223-228). ACM. 10.1145/3180374.3181341

Sonwalkar, P. (2001). India: Makings of little cultural/media imperialism? *Gazette (Leiden, Netherlands)*, *63*(6), 505–519. doi:10.1177/0016549201063006003

Sotnikova, Y., Nazarova, G., Nazarov, N., & Bilokonenko, H. (2020). Digital technologies in HR management. *Management Theory and Studies for Rural Business and Infrastructure Development*, *42*(4), 527–535. doi:10.15544/mts.2020.54

Spencer, N. E., Cuneen, J., & Schneider, R. (2003). Collecting celebrity: The meanings and process of collecting sports memorabilia. *Visions in Leisure and Business*, *21*(1), 8–29.

Statista. (2017). *Size of the Internet of Things (IoT) market worldwide from 2017 to 2025.* Statista.

Statista. (2019a). Global IoT Market Size. *Statistia*. https://www.statista.com/statistics/976313/global-iot-market-size/

Statista. (2019b). *Size of the Internet of Things (IoT) market worldwide from 2017 to 2025.* Statista. https://www.statista.com/statistics/976313/global-iot-market-size/

Statista. (2022, April 26). *Global digital population 2022.* Statista. www.statista.com. https://www.statista.com/statistics/617136/digital-population-worldwide/

Steve, H. (2015). *Cognitive IoT: Making the internet of Things Deliver for All of Us.* Available: https://www.ibm.com/blogs/think/2015/12/cognitive-iot-making-the-internet-of-things-deliver-for-all-of-us/

Stone, R. J., Cox, A., & Gavin, M. (2020). *Human resource management.* John Wiley & Sons.

Storm, M. (2019, April 25). *6 Proven Benefits of Digital Marketing That You Can't Ignore.* WebFX Blog. https://www.webfx.com/blog/marketing/benefits-of-digital-marketing/

Strohmeier, S. (2020). Smart HRM–a Delphi study on the application and consequences of the Internet of Things in Human Resource Management. *International Journal of Human Resource Management*, *31*(18), 2289–2318. doi:10.1080/09585192.2018.1443963

Sumanth, I. (2011). Contemporary Trends in National Media Ownership: Revisiting Political Economy Approach. *The IUP Journal of History and Culture*, *5*(1), 44–52.

Suri, K., Gaaloul, W., Cuccuru, A., & Gerard, S. (2017). Semantic framework for internet of things-aware business process development. *26th International Conference on Enabling Technologies: Infrastructure for Collaborative Enterprises (WETICE),* (pp. 214-219). IEEE. 10.1109/WETICE.2017.54

Surn, A., & Khatiwada, I. (2010). The Nation's Underemployed in the Great Recession of 2007-09. *Monthly Labor Review*, *133*, 3.

Sweeney, J. C., & Soutar, G. N. (2001). Consumer perceived value: The development of a multiple item scale. *Journal of Retailing*, *77*(2), 203–220. doi:10.1016/S0022-4359(01)00041-0

Szymanski, G., & Lininski, P. (2018, September). Model of the effectiveness of Google Adwords advertising activities. In *2018 IEEE 13th International Scientific and Technical Conference on Computer Sciences and Information Technologies (CSIT)* (Vol. 2, pp. 98-101). IEEE. 10.1109/STC-CSIT.2018.8526633

Taghavi Fard, M. T., & Torabi, M. (2010). Factors affecting the use of mobile banking services by customersand rank them (Case Study: Commerce Bank branches in Tehran). *Journal of Excavation Business Management*, *3*, 136–162.

Talwar, S., Dhir, A., Kaur, P., Zafar, N., & Alrasheedy, M. (2019). Why do people share fake news? Associations between the dark side of social media use and fake news sharing behavior. *Journal of Retailing and Consumer Services*, *51*, 72–82. doi:10.1016/j.jretconser.2019.05.026

Tambe, P., Cappelli, P., & Yakubovich, V. (2019). Artificial intelligence in human resources management: Challenges and a path forward. *California Management Review*, *61*(4), 15–42. doi:10.1177/0008125619867910

Tambunan, T. (2019). Recent evidence of the development of micro, small and medium enterprises in Indonesia. *Journal of Global Entrepreneurship Research*, *9*(1), 18. doi:10.118640497-018-0140-4

Tao, F., Laili, Y., Xu, L., & Zhang, L. (2013, November). FC-PACO-RM: A parallel method for service composition optimal-selection in cloud manufacturing system. *IEEE Transactions on Industrial Informatics*, *9*(4), 2023–2033. doi:10.1109/TII.2012.2232936

Tariq, E., Alshurideh, M., Akour, I., Al-Hawary, S., & Kurdi, B. (2022). The role of digital marketing, CSR policy and green marketing in brand development. *International Journal of Data and Network Science*, *6*(3), 995–1004. doi:10.5267/j.ijdns.2022.1.012

Taylor, M., Reilly, D., & Wren, C. (2018). Internet of things support for marketing activities. *Journal of Strategic Marketing*, *28*(2), 149–160. doi:10.1080/0965254X.2018.1493523

Taylor, S., & Todd, P. A. (1995). Understanding information technology usage: A test of competing models. *Information Systems Research*, *6*(2), 144–176. doi:10.1287/isre.6.2.144

Thaker, J., Zhao, X., & Leiserowitz, A. (2017). Media use and public perceptions of global warming in India. *Environmental Communication*, *11*(3), 353–369. doi:10.1080/17524032.2016.1269824

Thoma, M., Meyer, S., Sperner, K., Meissner, S., & Braun, T. (2012). On IoT-services: Survey, classification and enterprise integration. *IEEE International* Conference on Green Computing and Communications, (pp. 257-260). IEEE. 10.1109/GreenCom.2012.47

Thussu, D. K. (2007). TheMurdochization'of news? The case of Star TV in India. *Media Culture & Society*, *29*(4), 593–611. doi:10.1177/0163443707076191

Tian, K. T., Bearden, W. O., & Hunter, G. L. (2001). Consumers' need for uniqueness: Scale development and validation. *The Journal of Consumer Research*, *28*(1), 50–66. doi:10.1086/321947

Tiwana, A., Konsynski, B., & Bush, A. A. (2010). Research Commentary—Platform Evolution: Coevolution of Platform Architecture, Governance, and Environmental Dynamics. *Information Systems Research*, *21*(4), 675–687. doi:10.1287/isre.1100.0323

Tokar, T., Jensen, R., & Williams, B. D. (2021). A guide to the seen costs and unseen benefits of e-commerce. *Business Horizons*, *64*(3), 323–332. doi:10.1016/j.bushor.2021.01.002

Tong, S., Luo, X., & Xu, B. (2020). Personalized mobile marketing strategies. *Journal of the Academy of Marketing Science*, *48*(1), 64–78. doi:10.100711747-019-00693-3

Treiblmaier, H. (2021). Beyond blockchain: How tokens trigger the internet of value and what marketing researchers need to know about them. *Journal of Marketing Communications*, •••, 1–13. doi:10.1080/13527266.2021.2011375

Trejos, N. (2016). Hilton Announces New Affordable Hotel Brand, Tru. *USA Today*.

Trends, M. (2019, June 11). You are being redirected.... Analytical *Insidght*. https://www.analyticsinsight.net/how-big-data-and-ai-are-changing-digital-marketing/

Truong, N. B., Um, T. W., Zhou, B., & Lee, G. M. (2018). *Strengthening the blockchain-based internet of value with trust. In 2018 IEEE international conference on communications.* ICC. doi:10.1109/ICC.2018.8423014

Tudor, A. I. M., Chițu, I. B., Dovleac, L., & Brătucu, G. (2021). IoT Technologies as Instruments for SMEs' Innovation and Sustainable Growth. *Sustainability, 13*(11), 6357. doi:10.3390u13116357

Umair, M., Cheema, M. A., Cheema, O., Li, H., & Lu, H. (2021). Impact of COVID-19 on IoT adoption in healthcare, smart homes, smart buildings, smart cities, transportation and industrial IoT. *Sensors (Basel), 21*(11), 3838. doi:10.339021113838 PMID:34206120

UNCTAD. (2019). *Measuring E-commerce and the digital economy*. UNCTAD. https://unctad.org/topic/ecommerce-and-digital-economy/measuring-ecommerce-digital-economy

UNCTAD. (2019). *Measuring E-commerce and the digital economy*. UNCTAD. https://unctad.org/topic/ecommerce-and-digital-economy/measuring-ecommerce-digital-economy

UNESAP & ADB. (2019). *Embracing the E-commerce revolution in Asia and the Pacific*. ADB. https://www.adb.org/sites/default/files/publication/430401/embracing-e-commerce-revolution.pdf

UNESAP & ADB. (2019). *Embracing the E-commerce revolution in Asia and the Pacific*. UNCTAD. https://www.adb.org/sites/default/files/publication/430401/embracing-e-commerce-revolution.pdf

Vafaei, N. (2009). *Identifying and explaining the factors influencing the adoption of banking with customers' perspectives: a case study in National Bank branches in Tehran* [MA Thesis in Economics, Faculty of Management and Economics, Tarbiat Modarres University].

Vanham, D., Leip, A., Galli, A., Kastner, T., Bruckner, M., Uwizeye, A., van Dijk, K., Ercin, E., Dalin, C., Brandão, M., Bastianoni, S., Fang, K., Leach, A., Chapagain, A., Van der Velde, M., Sala, S., Pant, R., Mancini, L., Monforti-Ferrario, F., ... Hoekstra, A. Y. (2019). Environmental footprint family to address local to planetary sustainability and deliver on the SDGs. *The Science of the Total Environment, 693*, 133642. doi:10.1016/j.scitotenv.2019.133642 PMID:31635013

Varnali, K., & Toker, A. (2010). Mobile marketing research: The-state-of-the-art. *International Journal of Information Management, 30*(2), 144–151. doi:10.1016/j.ijinfomgt.2009.08.009

Vásquez, G. A. N., & Escamilla, E. M. (2014). Best practice in the use of social networks marketing strategy as in SMEs. *Procedia: Social and Behavioral Sciences, 148*, 533–542. doi:10.1016/j.sbspro.2014.07.076

Vázquez, R., Del Rio, A. B., & Iglesias, V. (2002). Consumer-based brand equity: Development and validation of a measurement instrument. *Journal of Marketing Management, 18*(1-2), 27–48. doi:10.1362/0267257022775882

Venkatesh, D. A. N. (2017). Connecting the dots: Internet of Things and human resource management. *American International Journal of Research in Humanities, Arts and Social Sciences, ISSN (Print)*, 2328-3734.

Verhoef, P. C., Kannan, P. K., & Inman, J. J. (2015). From Multi-Channel Retailing to Omni-Channel Retailing. Introduction to the Special Issue on Multi-Channel Retailing. *Journal of Retailing, 91*(2), 174–181. doi:10.1016/j.jretai.2015.02.005

Verma, R., & Kumar, M. (2022). Brand Extension in FMCG Sector Through Social Media Enabled CRM and Investigating Its Impact on Brand Equity. In A. Naim & S. Kautish (Eds.), *Building a Brand Image Through Electronic Customer Relationship Management* (pp. 201–236). IGI Global. doi:10.4018/978-1-6684-5386-5.ch009

Vermesan, O., & Friess, P. (2014). Internet of Things – from research and innovation to market deployment. *Internet of Things Search.* http://www.internet-of-thingsresearch. eu/pdf/IoT-From%20Research%20and%20Innovation%20to%20Market%20Deployment_IERC_Cluster_eBook_978-87-93102-95-8_P.pdf

Vermesan, O., Peter, F., Patrick, G., & Sergio, G. (2011). Internet of Things: Strategic Research Roadmap. In Internet of Things-Global Technological and Societal Trends (pp. 9–52). Academic Press.

Vermesan, O., & Friess, P. (2014). *Internet of Things applications: From research and innovation to market deployment.* River Publishers. https://www.riverpublishers.com/pdf/ebook/RP_E9788793102958.pdf

Vermesan, O., & Friess, P. (Eds.). (2014). *Internet of things-from research and innovation to market deployment* (Vol. 29). River publishers.

Vernuccio, M., Pagani, M., Barbarossa, C., & Pastore, A. (2015). Antecedents of brand love in online network-based communities. A social identity perspective. *Journal of Product and Brand Management, 24*(7), 706–719. doi:10.1108/JPBM-12-2014-0772

Visentin, M., Pizzi, G., & Pichierri, M. (2019). Visentin. Marco; Pizzi. Gabriele & Pichierri Marco (2019), Fake News, Real Problems for Brands: The Impact of Content Truthfulness and Source Credibility on consumers' Behavioral Intentions toward the Advertised Brands. *Journal of Interactive Marketing, 45*, 99–112. doi:10.1016/j.intmar.2018.09.001

Visser, M., Sikkenga, B., & Berry, M. (2019). *Digital marketing fundamentals: From strategy to ROI.* Routledge. doi:10.4324/9781003021674

Vladimir, Z. (1996). Electronic commerce: Structures and issues. *International Journal of Electronic Commerce, 1*(1), 3–23. doi:10.1080/10864415.1996.11518273

Vrontis, D., Makrides, A., Christofi, M., & Thrassou, A. (2021). Social media influencer marketing: A systematic review, integrative framework and future research agenda. *International Journal of Consumer Studies, 45*(4), 617–644. doi:10.1111/ijcs.12647

Vyas, C. (2019). Evaluating state tourism websites using Search Engine Optimization tools. *Tourism Management, 73*, 64–70. doi:10.1016/j.tourman.2019.01.019

Wajeeha, A., Annas, H., & Kashif, F. (2019). Underlying factors influencing consumers' trust and loyalty in E-commerce. *Business Perspectives and Research, 8*(2), 186–204. doi:10.1177/2278533719887451

Wang, L., Xu, L., Bi, Z., & Xu, Y. (2014, February). Data filtering for RFID and WSN integration. *IEEE Transactions on Industrial Informatics, 10*(1), 408–418. doi:10.1109/TII.2013.2250510

Wang, X., Tajvidi, M., Lin, X., & Hajli, N. (2019). Towards an ethical and trustworthy social commerce community for brand value Co-creation: A trust-commitment perspective. *Journal of Business Ethics, 167*(1), 137–152. doi:10.100710551-019-04182-z

Wati, Y., Koo, C., Jung, J. and Dahui, L. (2009). An empirical analysis of end-user satisfaction toward ebanking in Indonesia: a comparison model of ATMs, internet banking and mobile banking. *AMCIS 2009 Proceedings* (*1*, pp. 514-526). AMC.

Watson, R. T., Berthon, P., Pitt, L. F., & Zinkhan, G. M. (2013). *Electronic commerce: The strategic perspective.* Academic Press.

Web3 Studios. (2022). *Market report: Sports in the metaverse.* https://www.web3-studios.com/research

Weber, R. H. (2015). Internet of things: Privacy issues revisited. *Computer Law & Security Review*, *31*(5), 618–627. doi:10.1016/j.clsr.2015.07.002

Weber, R. H., & Weber, R. (2010). *Internet of things* (Vol. 12). Springer. doi:10.1007/978-3-642-11710-7

Wedel, M., & Kannan, P. K. (2016). Marketing analytics for data-rich environments. *Journal of Marketing*, *80*(6), 97–121. doi:10.1509/jm.15.0413

Weinberg, B.D., Milne, G.R., Andonova, Y.G., & Hajjat, F.M. (2015). *Internet of Things: Convenience vs. Privacy and Secrecy.* Business Horizons.

Weinberg, B., Milne, G., Andonova, Y., & Hajjat, F. (2015). Internet of Things: Convenience vs. privacy and security. *Business Horizons*, *58*(6), 615–624. doi:10.1016/j.bushor.2015.06.005

Weske, M. (2007). *Business process management architectures*. Springer Berlin Heidelberg.

Weyer, S., Schmitt, M., Ohmer, M., & Gorecky, D. (2015). Towards Industry 4.0-Standardization as the crucial challenge for highly modular, multi-vendor production systems. *IFAC-PapersOnLine*, *2015*(48), 579–584. doi:10.1016/j.ifacol.2015.06.143

What is Digital Marketing and Its benefits ? (2022). Engaio Digital. https://engaiodigital.com/digital-marketing/

White, C. (2020, December 29). *How AI is Changing the Future of Digital Marketing.* Bramework. https://www.bramework.com/ai-marketing/

Williamson, W., & Ruming, K. (2020). Can social media support large scale public participation in urban planning? The case of the# MySydney digital engagement campaign. *International Planning Studies*, *25*(4), 355–371. doi:10.1080/13563475.2019.1626221

Wolfram, S. (1991). *Mathematica: A System for Doing Mathematics by Computer*. Addi-son Wesley Longman Publishing Co., Inc.

Woodside, A. & Sood, S. (2017). *Vignettes in the two-step arrival of the internet of things and its reshaping of marketing management's service-dominant logic*. Research Gate. doi: 1 doi:0.1080/0267257X.2016.1246748

Woodside, A. G., & Sood, S. (2017). Vignettes in the two-step arrival of the internet of things and its reshaping of marketing management's service-dominant logic. Journal of Marketing Management, 33(1-2), 98–110. doi:10.1080/0267257X.2016.1246748

World Economic Forum. (2019). The global governance of online consumer protection and e-commerce building trust. WEF. https://www3.weforum.org/docs/WEF_consumer_protection.pdf

Wu, J., Chen, J., & Dou, W. (2017). *The Internet of Things and interaction style: the effect of smart interaction on brand attachment.* doi:10.1080/0267257X.2016.1233132

Wymbs, C. (2011). Digital marketing: The time for a new "academic major" has arrived. *Journal of Marketing Education*, *33*(1), 93–106. doi:10.1177/0273475310392544

Xiaodong, Q., & Min, L. (2020). E-commerce user type recognition based on access sequence similarity. *Journal of Organizational Computing and Electronic Commerce*, *30*(3), 209–223. doi:10.1080/10919392.2020.1742552

Xin, Y., & Ojanen, V. (2017). The impact of digitalization on product lifecycle management: How to deal with it? *IEEE International Conference on Industrial Engineering and Engineering Management (IEEM)*, (pp. 1098-1102). IEEE. 10.1109/IEEM.2017.8290062

Xu, Y. (2007). Impact of Store Environment on Adult Generation Y Consumers' Impulse Buying. *Journal of Shopping Center Research 14*(1).

Xu, L. D., He, W., & Li, S. (2014, November). Internet of Things in Industries: A Survey. *IEEE Transactions on Industrial Informatics, 10*(4), 2233–2243. doi:10.1109/TII.2014.2300753

Yaghtin, S., Safarzadeh, H., & Karimi Zand, M. (2020). Planning a goal-oriented B2B content marketing strategy. *Marketing Intelligence & Planning, 38*(7), 1007–1020. doi:10.1108/MIP-11-2019-0559

Yang, Z., Van Ngo, Q., Chen, Y., Nguyen, C. X.-T., & Hoang, H. T. (2019). Does ethics perception foster consumer repurchase intention? Role of trust, perceived uncertainty, and shopping habit. *SAGE Open, 9*(2). doi:10.1177/2158244019848844

Yasmin, STasneem, SFatema, K. (2015, April). Effectiveness of digital marketing in the challenging age: An empirical study. *Journal of International Business Research and Marketing, 1*(5), 69–80.

Yocco, V. S. (2016). *Design for the mind: Seven psychological principles of persuasive design*. Manning Publications Co.

Yoo, B., Donthu, N., & Lee, S. (2000). An examination of selected marketing mix elements and brand equity. *Journal of the Academy of Marketing Science, 28*(2), 195–211. doi:10.1177/0092070300282002

Yoo, Y., Henfridsson, O., & Lyytinen, K. (2010). The new organizing logic of digital innovation: An agenda for information systems research. *Information Systems Research, 21*(4), 724–735. doi:10.1287/isre.1100.0322

Younies, H., & Na, T. (2020). Effect of cybercrime laws on protecting citizens and businesses in the United Arab Emirates (UAE). *Journal of Financial Crime, 27*(4), 1089–1105. doi:10.1108/JFC-04-2020-0055

Yu, C.-S. (2014). Consumers' switching behavior from online banking to mobile banking. *International Journal of Cyber Society and Education, 7*(1), 1–28. doi:10.7903/ijcse.1108

Yunan, B. (2012). *What is Big Data's role in helping companies achieve competitive advantage through analytics.* IBM. https://www- 50.ibm.com/events/wwe/grp/grp004.nsf/v16_agenda?openfor m&seminar=9EBKW9ES&locale=en_US

Yu, X., Nguyen, B., & Chen, Y. (2016). Internet of things capability and alliance: Entrepreneurial orientation, market orientation and product and process innovation. *Internet Research, 26*(2), 402–434. doi:10.1108/IntR-10-2014-0265

Zanella, A., Bui, N., Castellani, A., Vangelista, L., & Zorzi, M. (2014). Internet of Things for Smart Cities. *IEEE Internet of Things Journal, 1*(1), 22–32. doi:10.1109/JIOT.2014.2306328

Zaucha, T., & Agur, C. (2022). Newly minted: Non-fungible tokens and the commodification of fandom. *New Media & Society*. Advance online publication. doi:10.1177/14614448221080481

Zhang, W., Wu, Y., & Calautit, J. K. (2022). A review on occupancy prediction through machine learning for enhancing energy efficiency, air quality and thermal comfort in the built environment. *Renewable & Sustainable Energy Reviews, 167*, 112704. doi:10.1016/j.rser.2022.112704

Zhang, X., Kumar, V., & Cosguner, K. (2017). Dynamically managing a profitable email marketing program. *Journal of Marketing Research, 54*(6), 851–866. doi:10.1509/jmr.16.0210

Zhironkin, S., Gasanov, M., Barysheva, G., Gasanov, E., Zhironkina, O., & Kayachev, G. (2017) *Sustainable development vs. post-industrial transformation: Possibilities for Russia*. E3C. doi:10.1051/e3sconf/20184104021

Zhou, L., Chong, A. Y. L., & Ngai, E. W. T. (2015). Supply Chain Management in the Era of the Internet of Things. *International Journal of Production Economics, 195*, 1–3. doi:10.1016/j.ijpe.2014.11.014

Zhu, B., Charoennan, W., & Embalzado, H. (2022). The influence of perceived risks on millennials' intention to use m-payment for mobile shopping in Bangkok. *International Journal of Retail & Distribution Management*, *50*(4), 479–497. doi:10.1108/IJRDM-05-2020-0174

Ziegeldorf, J. H., Morchon, O. G., & Wehrle, K. (2014). Privacy in the Internet of Things: Threats and challenges. *Security and Communication Networks*, *7*(12), 2728–2742. doi:10.1002ec.795

Zuhal, H. (2019). The gamut of E-commerce: Between online fraud and trust towards technology among generation Y. *International Journal of Mechanical Engineering and Technology*, *10*(01), 830–836. http://www.iaeme.com/IJMET/issues.asp?JType=IJMET&VType=10&Type=01

About the Contributors

Arshi Naim is an Associate Professor and Quality Programme head in Business Management, KSA She has completed her PHD in business management Singhania University Rajasthan, MBA in marketing management from HNB University and economics honours from AMU, Aligarh, India. Also, she has accomplished some certificates like QM peer reviewer and E-Learning expert from quality matters, US, ICDL from Australia and certificate on digital skills and digital marketing from UK. She is expert in curriculum and programme development, quality and accreditation process, E-learning and Quality Matters Peer Reviewer. She has research publications in Web of Sceince, IEEE, ACM, and Scopus Indexed Journals. She has also published books with Taylor and Francis, Nova Science Publications, IGI, and Springer. She is also closely associated with international and national universities for supervising PHD students.

V. Ajantha Devi is working as a Research Head in AP3 Solutions, Chennai. She conceived her PhD from University of Madras in 2015. She has worked as Project Fellow under UGC Major Research Project. She has been certified as "Microsoft Certified Application Developer" (MCAD) and "Microsoft Certified Technical Specialist" (MCTS) from Microsoft Corp. She had published more than 30 numbers of Papers in International level Journals and Conference Proceedings. Her work is based on Artificial intelligence, Machine learning and Deep learning techniques under Image Processing, Signal Processing, Pattern Matching and Natural Language Processing. She has received a good number of best paper presentation awards. She received few research oriented international awards.

* * *

Ibrahim Rashid Al Shamsi is working as an Associate Professor and Dean at College of Business, University of Buraimi, Oman.

Shaina Arora is working as an Assistant Professor, University Institute of Tourism and Hospitality Management, Chandigarh.

Iswarya B., MCA, M.Phil., Ph.D, is working as Assistant Professor in Department of Computer Applications, SNMV College of Arts and Science, Malumichampatti, Coimbatore.

Mushtaq Darzi is a professor, Department of Management Studies, & Director, UGC-HRDC, University of Kashmir.

Shad Ahmad Khan is serving as Assistant Professor in College of Business, University of Buraimi in Sultanate of Oman. He is an active researcher who has a professional strength in the area of Business Management and Marketing. He has a vast experience of organizing international events like conferences and seminars. His area of interest is Data Sciences, green practices, entrepreneurship, administration sciences and marketing.

Bhanupriya Khatri is working as Associate Professor in University School of Business at Chandigarh University, Mohali, India.

Ruhi Lal is Head (Student Support)/Associate Professor with Amity school Communication, Amity University, Noida. Dr. Lal is highly skilled Advertising professional, Academician, and Researcher. She is D.Litt. from Vinoba Bhave University, Hazaribagh, Jharkhand state University and holds Ph.D. degree in Mass Communication. She is recipient of Best Media Educator of the year 2021 in advertising Research by Media Federation of India. Received 5th Gyan Shree National award for promoting talents in Hindi Literature from Savitri Foundations. She received VISHIST SEWA SAMMAN from BJP Delhi for delivering services to especially abled people in Dec 2021. She has 22 years of work experience blend of 8 years of Industry (H.T. Media Ltd, Purple Focus Pvt Ltd, Noida Ad Agency) 14 years of Teaching and Research experience at Amity School of Communication. Dr. Lal has 104 Research contributions – 8 Books, 32 research papers (4 - Scopus, 2-Web of Science, 15- UGC Care Listed Journals, 18 other journals of repute) National, International Journals with high Impact factors, 30 case studies, 29 paper presentations (IIT Kharagpur, IIM Indore, MICA, AMU, JNU, DU and many more), 10 (chapters in books). The six funded Projects done by her are – MGNCRE-MHRD, SWAYAM -MHRD, AJK-MCRC -MHRD, Radio Amity, Amity MOOC Project. Dr. Lal chaired many technical sessions on National International conferences. She conducted workshops on 'Advertising Research methods', 'Qualitative research methods', 'Campaign planning', 'Storytelling' in Advertising. She served as IQAC head, Stream head for 'Advertising & Marketing Communication', Board of studies, AAB & PRC committee member, Academic advisory board, Outcome assessment head, Academic Planning and review committee member, external examiner, paper setter and guest speakers for many Universities. She chaired more than 50 admission boards for the selection of students.

Hesham Magd is working as an Associate Dean for Quality Assurance, Modern College of Business and Science, Oman.

Sebastiano Mereu is a Researcher for the Sports Business Research Academy, as well as Lecturer of Digital Marketing and Branding at BHMS Business & Hotel Management School and Kalaidos University of Applied Sciences in Switzerland. His main research interests include second-screening and spectator sports, uses and gratifications of watching unscripted shows, metaverse adoption, brand experience and experiential marketing, NFTs, social media engagement, intentions to watch women's sports, and more. He also works as a Digital Media and Marketing Specialist for the Swiss National Museum. Dr. Mereu holds a Doctor of Business Administration degree and a Master of Science in Marketing degree from Heriot-Watt University, UK, and a Bachelor of Science (Hons.) in International Management degree from FHNW University of Applied Sciences Northwestern Switzerland.

Moez Ltifi is a Ph.D in Business Administration. He is currently associate professor (HDR) in marketing at the University of Shaqra in Saudi Arabia and at the University of Sfax in Tunisia. Dr Ltifi is a reviewer in various international academic journals. His research work focuses on digital marketing, consumer attitudes, online shopping, customer satisfaction, customer trust, acceptance of new technologies, electronic loyalty, retailing, bank marketing, m.mobile, consumer behaviour, corporate governance, performance, branding. His most recent articles are published in refereed international ranked and impacted journals such as International Journal of Bank Marketing, Management and Organization Review, Management Decision, Journal of Management Science, Management 2000, Journal of Global Marketing, International Journal of Law and Management, Corporate Governance: The International Journal of Business in Society, Journal of Knowledge Management, Journal of Air Transport Management..

Ravinder Rena is a profound academician and distinguished scholar in economics with over 30 years of teaching and research experience. Prof Rena is a Professor of Economics at the DUT Business School, Faculty of Management Sciences, Durban University of Technology, South Africa. He also serves as an Adjunct Professor of Economics at Monarch Business School, Monarch University, Switzerland. He published widely in development economics, especially on African issues. He published over 150 peer-reviewed articles in reputed journals and 50 chapters in edited books across the globe. He is the founding Editor-in-Chief of the International Journal of Education, Economics and Development. He supervised over 60 PhDs, M.Phils and Masters' theses and dissertations across the globe. He served on many academic and professional committees as a chairman and panel member. He has also been an external examiner/moderator for Masters and PhD at different Universities in Africa, Europe, Asia, America, and Australia.

Ratiba Riyaz is a Ph.D. Scholar, Department of Management Studies, University of Kashmir.

Romana Riyaz is an Assistant Professor, Department of Computer Science, Islamic University of Science and Technology.

Muhammad Saleem is working as a Lecturer in the College of Business, University of Buraimi, Oman.

Nipunika Sarkar is a Broadcast Professional and an educator for Media studies, for the past 24 years. She is Assistant Professor, Amity School of Communication. She is an expert Voice Over artist and an English News Reader, with the Public Broadcaster All India Radio, reading National, International and Prime Time bulletins and Parliament News. She is coordinator for many educational projects of the Government of India, including SWAYAM of the MHRD. Her journey in leading news channels of India, has given her niche expertise to train media students at Amity. Nipunika's expertise is in Broadcast Journalism, Anchoring & Presentation. Her latest projects include Compering the 7th India Water Week, organized by the ministry of Jal Shakti, Government of India. The programme was Inauurated by President of India, Smt. Draupadi Murmu, along with Minister for Jal Shakti, Gajendra Singh Shekhawat, Mos Jalshakti Sr. Prahlad Singh Patel, Governor of Uttar Pradesh, Smt Anandi Ben Patel and Chief Minister of Uttar Pradesh, Sh . Yogi Adityanath. The programme valedictory was graced by Vice President of India, Sh. Jagdeep Dhankar. In July, 2022, she moderated session on Qualitative techniques in Research. She has been felicitated by many honours. DFRAC felicitated her for contributions to academics and media, in August 2022. Bharat Vikas Parishad has felicitated Nipunika with the title 'Iconic Woman of

North India 2019'. She was delegated to be part of the 3-Continent course of BA (J&MC) 3C at London, UK in 2019. She is Coordinator, Industry Interaction for ASCO. She is working on a book on media branding, for academic purpose. She is course coordinator for 'SWAYAM', an initiative by the MHRD. Earlier she has coordinated, designed & anchored E-content subjects for Jamia Millia Islamia & for UGC DD VYAS Channel. Her guest lectures and workshops on Broadcast Journalism includes at IIMC New Delhi, Galgotia University Noida, Sharda University Noida, Mangalayatan University Aligarh, IES University Bhopal & Prestige Institute of Management and Research Indore (PIMR). She is Member of Board of Studies (BoS), Mangalayatan University, Aligarh. She is part of 'Folkartopedia', an initiative to preserve and document Indian fork art culture. She has credit to be part of Social Media Campaigns of Centre for Social Research (CSR). She voiced film on cancer awareness with legendry DD Anchor Shammi Narang. She also voiced documentary on 'Girl Child Abuse'; which was premiered at Oslo, Norway. She has moderated multiple webinars with industry experts & eminent personalities. In her kit she has hundreds of articles and scripts for Print, Web & Electronic Media. Her interviews published and broadcasted at National channel of AIR and Interviewtimes.com. She was part of script writing & voicing for 'AIR Year Ender' Programme 2008, 2010, 2011, 2013, 2015. Her articles were published in Press Council Journals. Apart from teaching and news reading she is pursuing her PhD from Amity University. Her overall experience is 24 years in which more than 15 years in academic & 9 years in Electronic and Print Media.

Nidhi Sharma is working as a Ph.D. Scholar in University School of Business, Chandigarh University, Mohali, India.

Arun Kumar Singh is working as an Asso. Professor in the Department of Mathematics and Computer Science (PNG University of Technology, PNG). He received Ph.D. in CS/IT under the guidance of Dr. Neelam Srivastava (IET Lucknow) and Dr. R. P. Agarwal (IIT Roorkee), M.Tech. (IT-WCC) degree in 2005 from IIIT-Prayagraj under the guidance of Prof. M. Radha Krishnan and B.E. (ECE) degree in 2002 from Dr. B. R. Ambedkar University, Agra, India. His research interests are IoT, Machine Learning, Big Data, Network Management, Wireless networking, Social Networking and Mobile computing.

S. Uma is Professor in the Department of Computer Science and Engineering at Hindusthan College of Engineering and Technology, Coimbatore, Tamil Nadu, India. She received her B.E., degree in Computer Science and Engineering (CSE) in First Class with Distinction from P.S.G. College of Technology, M.S. (By Res.,)., degree from Anna University, Chennai, Tamil Nadu. She received her Ph.D., in the faculty of Information and Communication Engineering from Anna University, Chennai with High Commendation. She has 32 years of academic experience and organized many National and International seminars, workshops and conferences. She has published many research papers in National and International Conferences, Journals, Book Chapters, Patents and Books. She is a potential reviewer of Reputed Scopus Indexed and Web of Science International Journals such as Springer, IGI Global, Inderscience, IET, etc., and Member of Professional Bodies like ISTE, CSI, IEEE, IAENG, etc., She has received received several grants from Government Agencies. She is a recipient of "Bharath Jyoti", "Certificate of Excellence" and "Best Citizen of India" Awards. Her research interests are Programming, Pattern Recognition and Analysis Of Nonlinear Time Series Data, Artificial Intelligence, and Digital Analytics.

Shafaq Zareen is working as an Assistant Professor and Member of IQAC at Vivekananda College, University of Delhi.

Index

D

E

F

G

H

I

J

L

M

N

O

P

R

S

T

W

www.ingramcontent.com/pod-product-compliance
Lightning Source LLC
LaVergne TN
LVHW062112300926
849161LV00010B/2447
9781668481660